Lecture Notes in Computer Science 8348

Commenced Publication in 1973
Founding and Former Series Editors:
Gerhard Goos, Juris Hartmanis, and Jan van Leeuwen

For further volumes:
http://www.springer.com/series/7408

José Luiz Fiadeiro · Zhiming Liu
Jinyun Xue (Eds.)

Formal Aspects of Component Software

10th International Symposium, FACS 2013
Nanchang, China, October 27–29, 2013
Revised Selected Papers

 Springer

Editors
José Luiz Fiadeiro
Royal Holloway University of London
Egham
UK

Zhiming Liu
Birmingham City University
Birmingham
UK

Jinyun Xue
Laboratory of High-Performance
    Computing
Jiangxi Normal University
Nanchang
China

ISSN 0302-9743   ISSN 1611-3349   (electronic)
ISBN 978-3-319-07601-0   ISBN 978-3-319-07602-7   (eBook)
DOI 10.1007/978-3-319-07602-7
Springer Cham Heidelberg New York Dordrecht London

Library of Congress Control Number: 2014941590

LNCS Sublibrary: SL2 – Programming and Software Engineering

Printed on acid-free paper

Springer is part of Springer Science+Business Media (www.springer.com)

Preface

This volume contains the papers presented at FACS 2013, the International Symposium on Formal Aspects of Component Software, held during October 27–29, 2013, in Nanchang, China. This was the 10th edition of FACS, a series of events that address component-based software development, a paradigm that has been offering novel solutions for addressing the complexity of present-day software systems by bringing together sound engineering principles and formal methods into software engineering.

A total of 51 submissions were received, each of which was reviewed by an average of three Program Committee members. The committee accepted 19 papers for presentation at the conference. The authors were then invited to take into account feedback received at the conference to submit an extended and revised version of their accepted submission, which was again reviewed. These are the versions that are published in this volume, together with the three invited talks.

We are particularly thankful to the Organizing Committee for their work, in particular the organization of satellite workshops and tutorials, and Jiangxi Normal University for hosting the event and offering participants the chance of interacting with so many young researchers and visiting the city of Nanchang.

We would also like to thank Springer for their continued support in publishing the proceedings of FACS, and EasyChair for providing the environment in which papers were reviewed and this volume was put together.

Finally, our thanks to all authors, Program Committee members, and invited speakers for helping us uphold the quality of FACS.

January 2014

José Luiz Fiadeiro
Zhiming Liu
Jinyun Xue

Organization

Program Committee

Farhad Arbab	CWI and Leiden University, The Netherlands
Christian Attiogbe	University of Nantes, France
Luis Barbosa	Universidade do Minho, Portugal
Roberto Bruni	Università di Pisa, Italy
Tevfik Bultan	University of California at Santa Barbara, USA
Carlos Canal	University of Málaga, Spain
Chunqing Chen	HP Labs Singapore
Xin Chen	Nanjing University, China
Zhenbang Chen	National University of Defense Technology, China
Van Hung Dang	Vietnam National University, Vietnam
Zhenhua Duan	Xidian University, China
José Luiz Fiadeiro	Royal Holloway University of London, UK
Marcelo Frias	Instituto Tecnologico Buenos Aires, Argentina
Lindsay Groves	Victoria University of Wellington, New Zealand
Rolf Hennicker	Ludwig-Maximilians-Universität München, Germany
Axel Legay	IRISA/Inria, Rennes, France
Jing Liu	East China Normal University
Shaoying Liu	Hosei University, Japan
Zhiming Liu	Birmingham City University, UK
Antónia Lopes	University of Lisbon, Portugal
Markus Lumpe	Swinburne University of Technology, Australia
Eric Madelaine	Inria, Sophia Antipolis, France
Tom Maibaum	McMaster University, Canada
Dominique Mery	Université de Lorraine, LORIA, France
Peter Olveczky	University of Oslo, Norway
Corina Pasareanu	CMU/NASA Ames Research Center, USA
Frantisek Plasil	Charles University, Prague, Czech Republic
Pascal Poizat	Université Paris Ouest Nanterre, France
Shaz Qadeer	Microsoft Research, USA
Markus Roggenbach	Swansea University, UK
Gwen Salaün	Grenoble INP - Inria - LIG, France
Bernhard Schaetz	TU München, Germany
Marjan Sirjani	Reykjavik University, Iceland
Meng Sun	Peking University, China

Neil Walkinshaw	University of Leicester, UK
Farn Wang	National Taiwan University, Taiwan
Gianluigi Zavattaro	University of Bologna, Italy
Naijun Zhan	Chinese Academy of Sciences, China
Jianjun Zhao	Shanghai Jiao Tong University, China

Additional Reviewers

Aminof, Benjamin	Nyman, Ulrik
Astefanoaei, Lacramioara	O'Reilly, Liam
Betarte, Gustavo	Piterman, Nir
Bozga, Marius	Regis, German
Bucchiarone, Antonio	Schlingloff, Holger
Böhm, Thomas	Tiezzi, Francesco
Fijalkow, Nathanael	Truong, Hoang
Gerostathopoulos, Ilias	Viroli, Mirko
Hauzar, David	Wang, Guobin
Igna, Georgeta	Wang, Shuling
Jackson, Ethan	Welner, Yaron
Jaghoori, Mohammad Mahdi	Wolovick, Nicolas
Keznikl, Jaroslav	Yan, Rongjie
Khalil, Maged	Yang, Shaofa
Khosravi, Ramtin	Ye, Lina
Knapp, Alexander	Yin, Ling
Komuravelli, Anvesh	Yuan, Zhenheng
Lanese, Ivan	Zhao, Hengjun
Liu, Jie	Zhu, Jiaqi
Moscato, Mariano	

Contents

Probabilistic Modal Specifications
(Invited Extended Abstract)

Kim G. Larsen[1] and Axel Legay[2]([✉])

[1] Aalborg University, Aalborg, Denmark
kgl@cs.aau.dk
[2] INRIA/IRISA, Rennes, France
axel.legay@inria.fr

Abstract. This extended abstract offers a brief survey presentation of the specification formalism of modal transition systems and its recent extensions to the stochastic setting.

1 Modal Transition Systems: The Origines

Modal transition systems [18] provids a behavioural compositional specification formalism for reactive systems. They grew out of the notion of relativized bisimulation, which allows for simple specifications of components by allowing the notion of bisimulation to take the restricted use that a given context may have in its.

A modal transition system is essentially a (labelled) transition system, but with two types of transitions: so-called *may* transitions, that any implementation may (or may not) have, and *must* transitions, that any implementation must have. In fact, ordinary labelled transition systems (or implementations) are modal transition systems where the set of may- and must-transitions coincide. Modal transition systems come equipped with a bisimulation-like notion of (modal) refinement, reflecting that the more must-transitions and the fewer may-transitions a modal specification has the more refined and closer to a final implementation it is.

Example 1. Consider the modal transition system shown in Fig. 1 which models the requirements of a simple email system in which emails are first received and then delivered – must and may transitions are represented by solid and dashed arrows, respectively. Before delivering the email, the system may check or process the email, e.g. for en- or decryption, filtering of spam emails, or generating automatic answers using as an auto-reply feature. Any implementation of this email system specification must be able to receive and deliver email, and it may also be able to check arriving email before delivering it. No other behavior is allowed. Such an implementation is given in Fig. 2.

Modal transition systems play a major role in various areas. However, the model is best known by its application in compositional reasoning, which has

J.L. Fiadeiro et al. (Eds.): FACS 2013, LNCS 8348, pp. 1–4, 2014.
DOI: 10.1007/978-3-319-07602-7_1, © Springer International Publishing Switzerland 2014

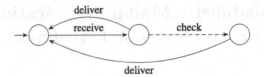

Fig. 1. Modal transition system modeling a simple email system, with an optional behavior: once an email is received it may e.g. be scanned for containing viruses, or automatically decrypted, before it is delivered to the receiver.

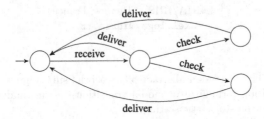

Fig. 2. An implementation of the simple email system in Fig. 1 in which we explicitly model two distinct types of email pre-processing.

been recognized in the ARTIST Network of Excellence and several other related European projects. In fact, modal transition systems have all the ingredients of a complete compositinal specification theory allowing for logical compositions (e.g. conjunction) [15], structural compositions (e.g. parallel) [13] as well as quotienting permitting specifications of composite systems to be transformed into necessary and sufficient specification of components [12]. Thus, modal transition systems have all the benefits of both logical and behavioural specification formalisms [4]. Though modal refinement – like bisimulation – is polynomial-time decidable for finite-state modal transition systems, it only provides a sound but not complete test for the true semantic refinement between modal specification, in terms of set inclusion between their implementation-sets (so-called thorough refinement). For several years, the complexity of thorough refinement – as well as the consistency – between modal specifications was an open problem, which after a series of attempts [1,2,16] was shown to be EXPTIME-complete [3].

2   Probabilistic Modal Specifications

In [14], modal transitions systems were extended into a specification formalism for Markov Chains by the introduction of so-called probabilistic specifications (now known as Interval Markov Chains), where concrete probabilities are replaced with intervals, and with refinement providing a conservative extension or probabilistic bisimulation [17]. However, Interval Markov Chains lack several of the properties required for a complete compositional specification theory; in particular, they are not closed neither under logical nor structural composition. Recently, the extended notion of Constraint Markov Chains [5] was introduced precisely with the purpose of providing these closure properties. A Constraint

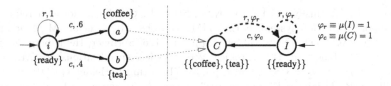

Fig. 3. Implementation PA and specification APA of a coffee machine.

Markov Chain (CMC) is a Markov Chain (MC) equipped with a constraint on the next-state probabilities from any state. Roughly speaking, an implementation for a CMC is thus a MC, whose next-state probability distribution satisfies the constraint associated with each state. The power of constrains can be exploited to obtain closure under any logical/structural composition operation. The complexity of the refinement relation largely depends on the one to solve the constraints – it is at least quadratic (resp. exponential) for syntactic (resp. thorough) refinement. The reader interested in decision probblems for CMCs is redirected to [10, 11].

More recently, the concept of CMC was extended to offer abstractions for Probabilistic Automata (PA), i.e., structures that mix both stochastic and non-deterministic aspects. The work in [7] proposes Abstract Probabilistic Automata, that are a combination of modal transition systems and CMCs, modalities being used to capture the non-determinism in PAs. The model was implemented in the APAC toolset [9] and various decision problems, including stuttering and abstraction, were studied in [8, 19].

Example 2 (taken from [8]). Consider the implementation (left) and specification (right) of a coffee machine given in Fig. 3. The specification indicates that there are two possible transitions from initial state I: a may transition labeled with action r (reset) and a must transition labeled with action c (coin). May transitions are represented with dashed arrows and must transitions are represented with plain arrows. The probability distributions associated with these actions are specified by the constraints φ_r and φ_c, respectively.

3 Future Work

In future work, we intend to combine the APA formalism with the one of timed specifications [6]. This will allows us to reason on timed stochastic systems. Another objective is to exploit the formalism to derive a CEGAR loop for timed stochastic systems.

References

1. Antonik, A., Huth, M., Larsen, K.G., Nyman, U., Wasowski, A.: 20 years of modal and mixed specifications. Bull. EATCS **95**, 94–129 (2008)
2. Antonik, A., Huth, M., Larsen, K.G., Nyman, U., Wasowski, A.: Modal and mixed specifications: key decision problems and their complexities. Math. Struct. Comput. Sci. **20**(1), 75–103 (2010)

3. Beneš, N., Křetínský, J., Larsen, K.G., Srba, J.: Checking thorough refinement on modal transition systems is EXPTIME-complete. In: Leucker, M., Morgan, C. (eds.) ICTAC 2009. LNCS, vol. 5684, pp. 112–126. Springer, Heidelberg (2009)

4. Boudol, G., Larsen, K.G.: Graphical versus logical specifications. In: Arnold, A. (ed.) CAAP 1990. LNCS, vol. 431, pp. 57–71. Springer, Heidelberg (1990)

5. Caillaud, B., Delahaye, B., Larsen, K.G., Legay, A., Pedersen, M.L., Wasowski, A.: Constraint Markov Chains. Theor. Comput. Sci. **412**(34), 4373–4404 (2011)

6. David, A., Larsen, K.G., Legay, A., Nyman, U., Wasowski, A.: Timed i/o automata: a complete specification theory for real-time systems. In: Johansson, K.H., Yi, W. (eds.) HSCC, pp. 91–100. ACM (2010)

7. Delahaye, B., Katoen, J.-P., Larsen, K.G., Legay, A., Pedersen, M.L., Sher, F., Wąsowski, A.: Abstract probabilistic automata. In: Jhala, R., Schmidt, D. (eds.) VMCAI 2011. LNCS, vol. 6538, pp. 324–339. Springer, Heidelberg (2011)

8. Delahaye, B., Katoen, J.-P., Larsen, K.G., Legay, A., Pedersen, M.L., Sher, F., Wasowski, A.: New results on abstract probabilistic automata. In: ACSD, pp. 118–127. IEEE (2011)

9. Delahaye, B., Larsen, K.G., Legay, A., Pedersen, M.L., Wasowski, A.: APAC: a tool for reasoning about abstract probabilistic automata. In: QEST, pp. 151–152. IEEE Computer Society (2011)

10. Delahaye, B., Larsen, K.G., Legay, A., Pedersen, M.L., Wąsowski, A.: Decision problems for interval Markov Chains. In: Dediu, A.-H., Inenaga, S., Martín-Vide, C. (eds.) LATA 2011. LNCS, vol. 6638, pp. 274–285. Springer, Heidelberg (2011)

11. Delahaye, B., Larsen, K.G., Legay, A., Pedersen, M.L., Wasowski, A.: Consistency and refinement for interval Markov Chains. J. Log. Algebr. Program. **81**(3), 209–226 (2012)

12. Goessler, G., Raclet, J.-B.: Modal contracts for component-based design. In: SEFM, pp. 295–303. IEEE Computer Society (2009)

13. Hüttel, H., Larsen, K.G.: The use of static constructs in a modal process logic. In: Meyer, A.R., Taitslin, M.A. (eds.) Logic at Botik 1989. LNCS, vol. 363, pp. 163–180. Springer, Heidelberg (1989)

14. Jonsson, B., Larsen, K.G.: Specification and refinement of probabilistic processes. In: LICS, pp. 266–277 (1991)

15. Larsen, K.G.: Modal specifications. In: Sifakis, J. (ed.) CAV 1989. LNCS, vol. 407, pp. 232–246. Springer, Heidelberg (1990)

16. Larsen, K.G., Nyman, U., Wąsowski, A.: On modal refinement and consistency. In: Caires, L., Vasconcelos, V.T. (eds.) CONCUR 2007. LNCS, vol. 4703, pp. 105–119. Springer, Heidelberg (2007)

17. Larsen, K.G., Skou, A.: Bisimulation through probabilistic testing. Inf. Comput. **94**(1), 1–28 (1991)

18. Larsen, K.G., Thomsen, B.: A modal process logic. In: LICS, pp. 203–210 (1988)

19. Sher, F., Katoen, J.-P.: Compositional abstraction techniques for probabilistic automata. In: Baeten, J.C.M., Ball, T., de Boer, F.S. (eds.) TCS 2012. LNCS, vol. 7604, pp. 325–341. Springer, Heidelberg (2012)

Orchestration

Jayadev Misra[✉]

The University of Texas at Austin, Austin, USA
misra@cs.utexas.edu

Abstract. In this position paper we argue that: (1) large programs should be composed out of components, which are possibly heterogeneous (i.e., written in a variety of languages and implemented on a variety of platforms), (2) the system merely *orchestrates* the executions of its components in some fashion but does not analyze or exploit their internal structures, and (3) the theory of orchestration constitutes the essential ingredient in a study of programming.

Keywords: Program composition · Component-based software construction · Orchestration · Concurrency

1 On Building Large Software Systems

This paper is about a theory of programming, called Orc^1, developed by me and my collaborators [1,7–9,12]. The philosophy underlying Orc is that: (1) large programs should be composed out of components, which are possibly heterogeneous (i.e., written in a variety of languages and implemented on a variety of platforms), (2) the system merely *orchestrates* the executions of its components in some fashion but does not analyze or exploit their internal structures, and (3) the theory of orchestration constitutes the essential ingredient in a study of programming.

I am sorry if I have already disappointed the reader. None of the points made above is startling. Building large systems out of components is as old as computer science; it was most forcefully promulgated by Dijkstra in his classic paper on Structured Programming [2] nearly a half century ago. It is the cornerstone of what is known as object-oriented programming [6,10]. In fact, it is safe to assert that every programming language includes some abstraction mechanism that allows design and composition of components.

It is also well-understood that the internal structure of the components is of no concern to its user. Dijkstra [2] puts it succinctly: "we do not wish to know them, it is not our business to know them, it is our business not to know them!". Lack of this knowledge is essential in order that a component may be replaced by another at a later date, perhaps a more efficient one, without affecting the rest of the program.

---

[1] See http://orc.csres.utexas.edu/ for a description of Orc and its related documentation. A book on Orc is under preparation.

J.L. Fiadeiro et al. (Eds.): FACS 2013, LNCS 8348, pp. 5–12, 2014.
DOI: 10.1007/978-3-319-07602-7_2, © Springer International Publishing Switzerland 2014

Component-based design makes hierarchical program construction possible. Each component itself may be regarded as a program in its own right, and designed to orchestrate its subcomponents, unless the component is small enough to be implemented directly using the available primitive operations of a programming language. Hierarchical designs have been the accepted norm for a very long time.

Where Orc differs from the earlier works is in insisting that programming be a study of composition mechanisms, and *just that*. In this view, system building consists of assembling components, available elsewhere, using a limited set of combinators. The resulting system could itself be used as a component at a higher level of assembly.

There are few restrictions on components. A component need not be coded in a specific programming language; in fact, a component could be a cyber-physical device or a human being that can receive and respond to the commands sent by the orchestration mechanism. Components may span the spectrum in size from a few lines of code, such as to add two numbers, to giant ones that may do an internet search or manage a database. Time scales for their executions may be very short (microseconds) to very long (years). The components may be real-time dependant. A further key aspect of Orc is that the orchestrations of components may be performed concurrently rather than sequentially.

We advocate an *open* design in which only the composition mechanisms are fixed and specified, but the components are not specified. Consequently, even primitive data types and operations on them are not part of the Orc calculus. Any such operation has to be programmed elsewhere to be used as a component. By contrast, most traditional designs restrict the smallest components to the primitives of a fixed language, which we call a *closed* design. Closed designs have several advantages, the most important being that a program's code is in a fixed language (or combinations of languages) and can be analyzed at any level of detail. The semantics of the program is completely defined by the semantics of the underlying programming language. It can be run on any platform that supports the necessary compiler. Perhaps the most important advantage is that the entire development process could be within the control of a team of individuals or an organization; then there are fewer surprises. In spite of these advantages for a closed system design, we do not believe that this is the appropriate model for large-scale programming in the future; we do not believe that a single programming language or a set of conventions will encompass the entirety of a major application; we do not believe that a single organization will have the expertise or resources to build very large systems from scratch, or that a large program will run on a single platform.

The second major aspect of Orc is on its insistence on concurrency in orchestration. Dijkstra [2] found it adequate to program with three simple sequential constructs, sequential composition, a conditional and a looping construct[2].

---

[2] Dijkstra did not explicitly include function or procedure definition. This was not essential for his illustrative examples. In his later work, he proposed nondeterministic selection using guarded commands [3,4] as a construct, though concurrency was not an explicit concern.

However, most modern programming systems, starting from simple desktop applications to mobile computing, are explicitly or implicitly concurrent. It is difficult to imagine any substantive system of the future in purely sequential terms.

We advocate concurrency not as a means to improving the performance of execution by using multiple computers, but for ease in expressing interactions among components. Concurrent interactions merely specify a large number of alternatives in executing a program; the actual implementation may indeed be sequential. Expressing the interactions in sequential terms often limits the options for execution as well as making a program description cumbersome. Components may also be specified for real time execution, say in controlling cyber-physical devices.

Almost all programming is sequential. Concurrency is essential but rarely a substantial part of programming. There will be a very small part of a large program that manages concurrency, such as arbitrating contentions for shared resource access or controlling the proliferation (and interruption) of concurrent threads. Yet, concurrency contributes mightily to complexity in programming. Sprinkling a program with concurrency constructs has proven unmanageable; the scope of concurrency is often poorly delineated, thus resulting in disaster in one part of a program when a different part is modified. *Concurrent program testing can sometimes show the presence of bugs and sometimes their absence.* It is essential to use concurrency in a disciplined manner. Our prescription is to use sequential components at the lowest-level, and orchestrate them, possibly, concurrently.

In the rest of this paper, we argue the case for the orchestration model of programming, and enumerate a specific set of *combinators* for orchestration. These combinators constitute the Orc calculus. Orc calculus, analogous to the λ-calculus, is not a suitable programming language. A small programming language has been built upon the calculus. We have been quite successful in using this notation to code a variety of common programming idioms and some applications.

2   Structure of Orc

2.1   Components, Also Known as *Sites*

Henceforth, we use the term *site* for a component[3].

The notion of a (mathematical) function is fundamental to computing. Functional programming, as in ML [11] or Haskell [5], is not only concise and elegant from a scientist's perspective, but also economical in terms of programming cost. Imperative programming languages often use the term "function" with a broader meaning; a function may have side-effects. A site is an even more general notion. It includes any program component that can be embedded in a larger program, as described below.

---

[3] This terminology is a relic of our earlier work in which web services were the only components. We use "site" more generally today for any component.

The starting point for any programming language is a set of primitive built-in operations or services. Primitive operations in typical programming languages are arithmetic and boolean operations, such as "add", "logical or" and "greater than". These primitive operations are the givens; new operations are built from the primitive ones using the constructs of the language. A typical language has a fixed set of primitive operations. By contrast, Orc calculus has no built-in primitive operation. Any program whose execution can be initiated, and that responds with some number of results, may be regarded as a primitive operation, i.e. a site, in Orc.

The definition of site is broad. Sites could be primitive operations of common programming languages, such as the arithmetic and boolean operations. A site may be an elaborate function, say, to compress a jpeg file for transmission over a network, or to search the web. It may return many results one by one, as in a video-streaming service or a stock quote service that delivers the latest quotes on selected stocks every day. It may manage a mutable store, such as a database, and provide methods to read from or write into the database. A site may interact with its caller during its execution, such as an internet auction service. A site's execution may proceed concurrently with its caller's execution. A site's behavior may depend on the passage of real time.

We regard humans as sites for a program that can send requests and receive responses from them. For example, a program that coordinates the rescue efforts after an earthquake will have to accept inputs from the medical staff, firemen and the police, and direct them by sending commands and information to their hand-held devices. Cyber-physical devices, such as sensors, actuators and robots, are also sites.

Sites may be higher-order in that they accept sites as parameters of calls and produce sites as their results. We make use of many factory sites that create and return sites, such as communication channels. Orc includes mechanisms for defining new sites by making use of already-defined sites.

2.2 Combinators

The most elementary Orc *expression* is simply a site call. A combinator combines two expressions to form an expression. The results published by expressions may be bound to immutable variables. There are no mutable variables in Orc; any form of mutable storage has to be programmed as a site.

Orc calculus has four combinators: "parallel" combinator, as in f|g, executes expressions f and g concurrently and publishes whatever either expression publishes; "sequential" combinator, as in f >x> g, starts the execution of f, binds x to any value that is published by f and immediately starts execution of an instance of g with this variable binding, so that multiple instances of g along with f may be executing concurrently; "pruning" combinator, as in f <x< g, executes f and g concurrently, binds the first value published by g to variable x and then terminates g, here x may appear in f; and "otherwise" combinator, as in f;g, introduces a form of priority-based execution by first executing f, and then g only if f halts without publishing any result.

There is one aspect worth noting even in this very informal description. An expression may publish multiple values just as a site does. For example, each of f and g may publish some number of values, and then f | g publishes all of those values; and (f | g) >x> h executes multiple instances of expression h, an instance for each publication of f | g. The formal meanings of the given combinators have been developed using operational semantics.

2.3   Consequences of Pure Composition

The combinators for composition are agnostic about the components they combine. So, we may combine very small components, such as for basic arithmetic and boolean operations drawn from a library, to simulate the essential data structures for programming. This, in turn, allows creations of yet larger components, say for sorting and searching. Operations to implement mutable data structures, such as for reading or writing to a memory location, can also be included in a program library. A timer that operates in real time can provide the basics for real time programming. Effectively, a general purpose concurrent programming language can be built starting with a small number of essential primitive components in a library. This is the approach taken in the Orc language design.

Even though it is possible to design any kind of component starting with a small library of components, we do not advocate doing so in all cases. The point of orchestration is to reuse components wherever possible rather than building them from scratch, and components built using Orc may not have the required efficiency for specific applications.

3   Concluding Remarks

There is a popular saying that the internet is the computer. That is no less or no more true than saying that a program library is a computer. This computer remains inactive in the absence of a driving program. Orc provides the rudiments of a driving program. It is simultaneously the most powerful language that can exploit available programs as sites, and the least powerful programming language in the absence of sites.

A case against a grand unification theory of programming. It is the dream of every scientific discipline to have a grand unification theory that explains all observations and predicts all experimental outcomes with accuracy. The dream in an engineering discipline is to have a single method of constructing its artifacts, cheaply and reliably. For designs of large software systems, we dream of a single, preferably small, programming language with an attendant theory and methodology that suffices for the constructions of concise, efficient and verifiable programs. As educators we would love to teach such a theory.

Even though we have not realized this dream for all domains of programming, there are several *effective theories* for limited domains. Early examples include boolean algebra for designs of combinational circuits and BNF notation for syntax specification of programming languages. Powerful optimization techniques have been developed for relational database queries. Our goal is to exploit the powers of many limited-domain theories by combining them to solve larger problems. A lowest-level component should be designed very carefully for efficiency, employing the theory most appropriate for that domain, and using the most suitable language for its construction. Our philosophy in Orc is to recognize and admit these differences, and combine efficient low-level components to solve a larger problem. Orc is solely concerned with how to combine the components, not how a primitive component should be constructed.

Bulk vs. Complexity. It is common to count the number of lines of code in a system as a measure of its complexity. Even though this is a crude measure, we expect a system with ten times as many lines of code to be an order of magnitude more complex. Here we are confusing *bulk* with *complexity*; that bulkier a program, the more complex it is. There are very short concurrent programs, say with about 20 lines, that are far more complex than a thousand line sequential program. Concurrency adds an extra dimension to complexity. In a vague sense, the complexity in a sequential program is additive, whereas in a concurrent program it is multiplicative.

The philosophy of Orc is to delegate the bulkier, but less complex parts to components and reserve the complexity for the Orc combinators. Though solvers of partial differential equations can be coded entirely in Orc using the arithmetic and boolean operations as sites, this is not the recommended option. It should be coded in a more suitable language, but concurrent executions of multiple instances of the solvers, with different parameters, for instance, should be delegated to Orc.

Some sweeping remarks about programming. Consider the following scenario. A patient receives an electronic prescription for a drug from a doctor. The patient compares prices at several near-by pharmacies, and chooses the cheapest one to fill the prescription. He pays the pharmacy and receives an electronic invoice which he sends to the insurance company for reimbursement with instructions to deposit the amount in his bank account. Eventually, he receives a confirmation from his bank. The entire computation is mediated at each step by the patient who acquires data from one source, does some minor computations and sends data to other sources.

This computing scenario is repeated millions of times a day in diverse areas such as business computing, e-commerce, health care and logistics. In spite of the extraordinary advances in mobile computing, human participation is currently required in every major step in most applications. This is not because security is the over-riding concern, but that the infrastructure for efficient mediation is largely absent, thus contributing to cost and delay in these applications. We believe that humans can largely be eliminated, or assigned a supporting role, in many applications. Doing so is not only beneficial in terms of efficiency, but also essential if we are to realize the full potential of the interconnectivity among machines, using the services and data available in the internet, for instance. We would prefer that humans advise and report to the machines, rather than that humans direct the machines in each step.

The initial impetus for Orc came from attempting to solve such problems by orchestrating the available web services. Ultimately, languages outgrow the initial motivations of their design and become applicable in a broader domain. Orc is currently designed for component integration and concurrency management in general.

The programming community has had astonishing success in building large software systems in the last 30 years. We routinely solve problems today that were unimaginable even a decade ago. Our undergraduates are expected to code systems that would have been fit for a whole team of professional programmers twenty years ago. What would programs look like in the future? We can try to interpolate. The kinds of problems the programmers will be called upon to solve in the next two decades will include: health care systems automating most of their routine tasks and sharing information across hospitals and doctors (for example, about adverse reaction to drugs); communities and organizations sharing and analyzing data and responding appropriately, all without human intervention; disaster recovery efforts, including responding to anticipated disasters (such as, shutting down nuclear reactors well before there is a need to) being guided by a computer; the list goes on. These projects will be several orders of magnitude larger than what we build today. We anticipate that most large systems will be built around orchestrations of components. For example, a system to run the essential services of a city will not be built from scratch for every city, but will combine the pre-existing components such as for traffic control, sanitation and medical services. Software to manage an Olympic game will contain layer upon layers of interoperating components.

A Critique of Pure Composition. A theory such as Orc, based as it is on a single precept, may be entirely wrong. It may be too general or too specific, it may prove to be too cumbersome to orchestrate components, say in a mobile application, or it may be suitable only for building rapid prototypes but may be too inefficient for implementations of actual systems. These are serious concerns that can not be argued away. We are working to address these issues in two ways: (1) prove results about the calculus, independent of the components, that will establish certain desirable theoretical properties, and (2) supply enough empirical evidence that justifies claims about system building. While goal (1) is largely achievable, goal (2) is a never-ending task. We have gained enough empirical evidence by programming a large number of commonly occurring programming patterns.

References

1. Cook, W., Misra, J.: Computation orchestration: a basis for wide-area computing. J. Softw. Syst. Model. **6**(1), 83–110 (2007)
2. Dahl, O.J., Dijkstra, E.W., Hoare, C.A.R.: Structured Programming. Academic Press, London (1972)
3. Dijkstra, E.W.: Guarded commands, nondeterminacy, and the formal derivation of programs. Commun. ACM **8**, 453–457 (1975)
4. Dijkstra, E.W.: A Discipline of Programming. Prentice-Hall, Englewood Cliffs (1976)

5. Marlow, S. (ed.): Haskell 2010, Language Report (2010). http://www.haskell.org/onlinereport/haskell2010/haskell.html
6. Goldberg, A., Robson, D.: Smalltalk-80: The Language and its Implementation. Addison-Wesley Longman Publishing Co. Inc., Boston (1983)
7. Hoare, T., Menzel, G., Misra, J.: A tree semantics of an orchestration language. In: Broy, M. (ed.) Proceedings of the NATO Advanced Study Institute, Engineering Theories of Software Intensive Systems. NATO ASI Series, Marktoberdorf, Germany (2004). http://www.cs.utexas.edu/users/psp/Semantics.Orc.pdf
8. Kitchin, D., Quark, A., Cook, W., Misra, J.: The Orc programming language. In: Lee, D., Lopes, A., Poetzsch-Heffter, A. (eds.) FMOODS/FORTE 2009. LNCS, vol. 5522, pp. 1–25. Springer, Heidelberg (2009)
9. Kitchin, D., Quark, A., Misra, J.: Quicksort: combining concurrency, recursion, and mutable data structures. In: Roscoe, A.W., Jones, C.B., Wood, K. (eds.) Reflections on the Work of C.A.R. Hoare, History of Computing. Springer (2010) (Written in honor of Sir Tony Hoare's 75th birthday)
10. Meyer, B.: Object-oriented software construction, 2nd edn. Prentice Hall, Upper Saddle River (1997)
11. Milner, R., Tofte, M., Harper, R.: The Definition of ML. The MIT Press, Cambridge (1990)
12. Wehrman, I., Kitchin, D., Cook, W., Misra, J.: A timed semantics of Orc. Theoret. Comput. Sci. **402**(2–3), 234–248 (2008)

Super-Dense Computation in Verification of Hybrid CSP Processes

Dimitar P. Guelev[2], Shuling Wang[1(✉)], Naijun Zhan[1], and Chaochen Zhou[1]

[1] State Key Laboratory of Computer Science, Institute of Software,
Chinese Academy of Sciences, Beijing, China
wangsl@ios.ac.cn
[2] Institute of Mathematics and Informatics,
Bulgarian Academy of Sciences, Sofia, Bulgaria

Abstract. Hybrid Communicating Sequential Processes (HCSP) extends CSP to include differential equations and interruptions. We feel comfortable in our experience with HCSP to model scenarios of the Level 3 of Chinese Train Control System (CTCS-3), and to define a formal semantics for Simulink. The Hoare style calculus of [5] proposes a calculus to verify HCSP processes. However it has an error with respect to super-dense computation. This paper is to establish another calculus for a subset of HCSP, which uses Duration Calculus formulas to record program history, negligible time state to denote super-dense computation and semantic continuation to avoid infinite interval. It is compositional and sound.

Keywords: Hybrid system · Differential invariant · Hybrid CSP · Duration Calculus · Super-dense computation · Hybrid Hoare logic

1 Introduction

Hybrid system combines discrete control and continuous evolution. A continuously evolving plant with discrete control is a typical example. The behaviour of the plant can be defined by a differential equation, say $F(\dot{s}, s, u) = 0$. A computer samples the state of the plant every d time units through a *sensor*, calculates its control parameter u according to the sensed state s and sends back to the plant through an *actuator*. Communicating Sequential Processes (CSP, [4]) provides channels to model the sensor and the actuator, and parallelism to model interaction between the computer and the plant. However CSP lacks a construct to model physical behaviour of the plant. References [3,14] propose a Hybrid CSP (HCSP) and suggest to use HCSP to model hybrid systems. HCSP introduces into CSP continuous variables, differential equations, and interruptions by boundary, timeout and communication. Our experience in using HCSP to describe the scenarios of Level 3, Chinese Train Control System (CTCS-3) [15] and give a formal semantics of Simulink [16] is quite satisfactory, and will be reported in other papers.

J.L. Fiadeiro et al. (Eds.): FACS 2013, LNCS 8348, pp. 13–22, 2014.
DOI: 10.1007/978-3-319-07602-7_3, © Springer International Publishing Switzerland 2014

This paper presents a compositional Hoare style calculus to verify properties of HCSP processes. The calculus has to meet two challenges. The first one is to reason about differential equations. We adopt *differential invariants* from [8,9]. An algorithm which generates a polynomial (in)equality invariant from a polynomial differential equation is developed in [6]. The algorithm is *complete* as it always produces an invariant, provided that one exists. The generation of the polynomial invariant is supported by a symbolic computation tool for semi-algebraic system, DISCOVERER, which is based on the theory invented in [10,11].

Another challenge is how to accommodate *super-dense computation* in the calculus. By *super-dense computation* we mean that computer is much faster than other physical devices and computation time of a computer is therefore negligible, although the temporal order of computations is still there. In the plant control example, the control parameter sent from the computer is supposed to control the state sensed before. The computation time for calculating the new control parameter is neglected.

A Hoare style logic for reasoning about HCSP is firstly proposed by [5], which simply uses the *chop* modality of Duration Calculus (DC) [13] to describe the sequential composition, and point intervals to describe super-dense computations. Unfortunately chop degenerates into *conjunction* at a point interval, and the temporal order of computations disappears. Hence, the monotonicity rule cannot be maintained, and it forms an error of [5]. In this paper we use a dedicated DC state variable N to mark *negligible time*. This idea can be traced back to [1,7]. It is also used in [2], where another Hoare style calculus for HCSP is proposed with different semantic specification. Another approach to deal with super-dense computation is to use pre- and post-conditions as well as history formulas as done in [5], but delete point values in the history formulas in order to maintain the monotonicity rule (see [12] for details).

We also use Hoare triple in our calculus. Triples have the form

$$\{PreH\}Sys\{PostH\},$$

where Sys is an HCSP process, and $PreH$ and $PostH$ are DC formulas to express properties of the *pre-history* and *post-history* of the execution of Sys. A dedicated propositional letter C is used to indicate whether a behaviour defined by a history formula can be further extended.

Structure of the Paper. In Sect. 2, we will introduce the language Hybrid CSP briefly, and then present the calculus for reasoning about Hybrid CSP in Sects. 3 and 4. Finally, we conclude the paper by a discussion about the calculus.

2   Hybrid CSP

Hybrid CSP is an extension of CSP with differential equations and interruptions to model behaviour of hybrid systems.

Notation:
HCSP vocabulary includes:

- a countable set of discrete and continuous variables, which are interpreted as functions from time (non-negative reals) to reals, and
- a countable set of channel names.

HCSP is defined according to the following grammar, where v stands for a variable, s and $\dot{s}$ stand for a vector of variables and their time derivatives, ch stands for channel name, I stands for a non-empty finite set of indices, e and B are arithmetical expression and boolean expression of variables, and d is a positive (real) constant.

$$
\begin{aligned}
P ::=\ & \text{skip} \mid v := e \mid \text{wait } d \mid P; Q \mid B \to P \mid P \sqcup Q \\
& \mid ch?x \mid ch!e \mid \|_{i \in I}(io_i \to P_i) \\
& \mid \langle F(\dot{s}, s) = 0 \& B \rangle \mid \langle F(\dot{s}, s) = 0 \& B \rangle \unrhd_d P \\
& \mid \langle F(\dot{s}, s) = 0 \& B \rangle \unrhd \|_{i \in I}(io_i \to P_i) \\
Sys ::=\ & P \mid P^* \mid Sys_1 \parallel Sys_2
\end{aligned}
$$

Here follows the meaning of each construct:

- skip does nothing and terminates immediately.
- $v := e$ is an atomic assignment.
- wait d does nothing and terminates right after d time units.
- $P; Q$ is the sequential composition of P and Q. It behaves as P first, and then Q after P terminates.
- $B \to P$ behaves like P if B is true. Otherwise it terminates immediately.
- $P \sqcup Q$ is the *internal choice* of CSP. We include this operator to simulate non-deterministic actions.
- $ch?x$ inputs a value over channel ch and stores in x.
- $ch!e$ sends the value of e over channel ch. Here we assume the synchronous communication as defined in CSP.
- $\|_{i \in I}(io_i \to P_i)$ is the *external choice* of CSP. An occurrence of io_i can lead to the execution of P_i, where io_i stands for an input or output.
- $\langle F(\dot{s}, s) = 0 \& B \rangle$ defines a bounded evolution of the differential equation F over s. B is a boolean expression of s, which defines a domain of s in the sense that, if the evolution of s as defined by $F(\dot{s}, s) = 0$ is beyond B, the statement terminates. Otherwise it goes forward.
- $\langle F(\dot{s}, s) = 0 \& B \rangle \unrhd_d P$ behaves like $\langle F(\dot{s}, s) = 0 \& B \rangle$ if it can terminate within d time units. Otherwise, after d (inclusive) time units, it behaves like P.
- $\langle F(\dot{s}, s) = 0 \& B \rangle \unrhd \|_{i \in I}(io_i \to P_i)$ behaves like $\langle F(\dot{s}, s) = 0 \& B \rangle$ until a communication in the following context appears. Then it behaves like P_i immediately after the communication io_i occurs.
- P^* means that the execution of P can be repeated for arbitrarily finitely many times.
- $Sys_1 \parallel Sys_2$ behaves as if Sys_1 and Sys_2 are executed independently except that all communications along the common channels between Sys_1 and Sys_2 are to be synchronized. In order to guarantee that Sys_1 and Sys_2 have no

shared continuous nor discrete variables, and neither shared input nor output channels, we give the following syntactical constraints:

$$(\mathbf{VC}(Sys_1) \cap \mathbf{VC}(Sys_2)) = \emptyset,$$
$$(\mathbf{InChan}(Sys_1) \cap \mathbf{InChan}(Sys_2)) = \emptyset,$$
$$(\mathbf{OutChan}(Sys_1) \cap \mathbf{OutChan}(Sys_2)) = \emptyset,$$

where $\mathbf{VC}(Sys)$ stands for variables of Sys, $\mathbf{InChan}(Sys)$ for input channels of Sys and $\mathbf{OutChan}(Sys)$ for output channels of Sys.

Example: Plant Control (*PLC*)
A computer every d time units senses a plant, calculates the new control according to the sensed state and sends back to the plant. This can be modelled in HCSP as

$$(\langle F(s, \dot{s}, u) = 0 \rangle \trianglerighteq c_{p2c}!s \to c_{c2p}?u)^* \parallel$$
$$(\text{wait } d; c_{p2c}?v; c_{c2p}!contl(v))^*$$

where $contl(v)$ is an expression of v to stand for a calculation of the control parameter corresponding to v, which stores the sensed state.

3   Hoare Triple

The calculus is given in

$$\{PreH\} \ Sys \ \{PostH\},$$

which is similar to the Hoare triple but has *PreH* and *PostH* in Duration Calculus (DC) [13] to record pre-history and post-history of *Sys*.

DC is based on Interval Temporal Logic, and reasons about terms $\int S$, where S is a Boolean function over time (non-negative reals) and $\int S$ is the duration of state S within the reference time interval. We define

$$\ell = \int 1,$$
$$\lceil S \rceil = (\int S = \ell) \wedge (\ell > 0),$$
$$\lceil S \rceil^< = \lceil S \rceil \vee (\ell = 0).$$

Hence, for any given interval, ℓ is the length of the interval, and $\lceil S \rceil$ means that S holds (almost) everywhere in the interval and the interval is not a point one.

A *history formula* is a DC formula, or followed by the propositional letter C to stand for *Continuation*, or a disjunction of such formulas:

$$HF ::= A \mid A^\frown C \mid HF_1 \vee HF_2$$

where A is a DC formula without occurrence of C. *PreH* and *PostH* are history formulas.

Example: Stability of *PLC*

$$\{\lceil Controllable(s, u) \rceil^\frown C\} \ PLC \ \{(\ell > T) \Rightarrow ((\ell = T)^\frown \lceil \mid s - s_{target} \mid < \epsilon \rceil)\}$$

The pre-history requires that the initial state and control are *controllable* and the pre-history can be continued. The post-history concludes that after T time units the plant will be very close to the target (s_{target}).

In order to treat super-dense computation, we introduce N state to stand for *negligible* time. Therefore time is measured by $\int \neg N$.

Example: Stability of PLC becomes

$$\{\lceil Controllable(s,u) \wedge N\rceil\frown C\} \; PLC \; \{((\int \neg N > T) \Rightarrow \\ ((\int \neg N = T)\frown\lceil| s - s_{target} |< \epsilon\rceil)\}$$

4   Axioms and Rules

We introduce for each channel name c two shared states $c!$ and $c?$ to represent the *readiness* of output and input plus a shared variable c to store the message to be passed.

– **Monotonicity**
  If $\{PreH\}Sys\{PostH\}$, $(PreH' \Rightarrow PreH)$ and $(PostH \Rightarrow PostH')$, then

$$\{PreH'\} \; Sys \; \{PostH'\}.$$

– **Disjunction**
  History formula can be restricted to disjunction of DC formulas with or without C as its last part. Correspondingly we can establish the following rule:

$$\text{If } \{PreH_i\} \; Sys \; \{PostH_i\}, \quad i = 1, ..., n,$$
$$\text{then } \{\bigvee_{i=1}^{n} PreH_i\} \; Sys \; \{\bigvee_{i=1}^{n} PostH_i\}$$

This rule can be generalized to the Existential one, such as

$$\text{If } \{PreH\} \; Sys \; \{PostH\}$$
$$\text{then } \{\exists z.PreH\} \; Sys \; \{\exists z.PostH\}$$
$$\text{provided } z \notin \mathbf{VC}(Sys)$$

– **Skip**

$$\{PreH\} \; \text{skip} \; \{PreH\}$$

It means, skip does nothing and terminates immediately.

– **Assignment**
  If $(PreH[(\ell = 0)/C] \Rightarrow \top\frown\lceil Pre[e/x]\rceil)$, then

$$\{PreH\} \; x := e \; \{PreH[(\lceil Pre \wedge \neg\mathbf{Chan}(P) \wedge N\rceil\frown C)/C]\}$$

where we assume that Pre does not contain N nor channel variables, $\mathbf{Chan}(P)$ is $\{c? \mid c \in \mathbf{InChan}(P)\} \cup \{c! \mid c \in \mathbf{OutChan}(P)\}$, and, by $\neg\mathbf{Chan}(P)$, we mean the conjunction of $\neg c$, $c \in \mathbf{Chan}(P)$, assuming that the assignment statement is inside process P.

The hypothesis says that the last period of the pre-history (after ignoring C, i.e. C is replaced by $(\ell = 0)$) can conclude e satisfying Pre. Then the post-history can make sure that x satisfies Pre after the assignment, and no channels are ready for communication during the assignment. By N this rule also shows that an assignment consumes negligible time.

– **Wait**
  If $(PreH[(\ell = 0)/C] \Rightarrow \top \frown \lceil Pre \rceil)$, then

$$\{PreH\} \text{ wait } d \ \{PreH[((\lceil Pre \wedge \neg\mathbf{Chan}(P)\rceil \wedge (\int \neg N = d)) \frown C)/C]\}$$

where $d > 0$, Pre follows the assumption stated in the **Assignment** and so does in the followings. This rule specifies, wait d inherits the last state from $PreH$ and no channel is ready for communication during this waiting period (i.e. non-negligible time passes d).

– **Sequential Composition**
  If $\{PreH_i\}P_i\{PostH_i\}$, $i = 1, 2$, and $PostH_1 \Rightarrow PreH_2$, then

$$\{PreH_1\} \ P_1; P_2 \ \{PostH_2\}$$

– **Conditional**
  1. If $(PreH[(\ell = 0)/C] \Rightarrow \top \frown \lceil B \rceil)$, then

$$\{PreH\} \ B \to P \ \{PostH\}$$

  provided $\{PreH\}P\{PostH\}$.
  2. If $(PreH[(\ell = 0)/C] \Rightarrow \top \frown \lceil \neg B \rceil)$, then

$$\{PreH\} \ B \to P \ \{PreH\}$$

– **Internal Choice**

$$\text{If } \{PreH\} \ P_i \ \{PostH_i\}, \ i = 1, 2$$
$$\text{then } \{PreH\} \ P_1 \sqcup P_2 \ \{PostH_1 \vee PostH_2\}$$

– **Input**

$$\text{If } PreH[(\ell = 0)/C] \Rightarrow \top \frown \lceil Pre \rceil,$$
$$\text{then } \{PreH\} \ c?x \ \{PreH[\text{In}(c, x)/C]\}$$

where

$$\text{WaitIn}(c, x) = \lceil Pre \wedge c? \wedge \neg c! \wedge \neg(\mathbf{Chan}(P) \setminus \{c?\}) \rceil$$
$$\text{SynIn}(c, x) = \lceil (\exists x.Pre) \wedge c? \wedge c! \wedge (x = c) \wedge \neg(\mathbf{Chan}(P) \setminus \{c?\}) \wedge N \rceil \frown$$
$$\lceil (\exists x.Pre) \wedge (x = c) \wedge \neg\mathbf{Chan}(P) \wedge N \rceil$$
$$\text{In}(c, x) = \text{WaitIn}(c, x) \overset{<}{\frown} \text{SynIn}(c, x) \frown C \vee \text{WaitIn}(c, x)$$

An input has to be firstly synchronized by an output that is described through WaitIn. Otherwise the input side will wait forever (i.e. the second disjunct of In cannot be continued). After the synchronization, a message is input to x through c (i.e. $x = c$, as c stores the message), and the other variables do not change (i.e. $\exists x.Pre$). Here, we also assume, the message passing consumes negligible time and after it all channels become not ready for a negligible period to prevent multi-usage of a single message passing event.

– **Output**

$$\text{If } PreH[(\ell = 0)/C] \Rightarrow \top^\frown\lceil Pre\rceil,$$
$$\text{then } \{PreH\} \; c!e \; \{PreH[\text{Out}(c, e)/C]\}$$

where

$$\text{WaitOut(c,e)} = \lceil Pre \wedge c! \wedge \neg c? \wedge \neg(\mathbf{Chan}(P) \setminus \{c!\})\rceil$$
$$\text{SynOut}(c, e) = \lceil Pre \wedge c! \wedge c? \wedge (c = e) \wedge \neg(\mathbf{Chan}(P) \setminus \{c!\}) \wedge N\rceil^\frown$$
$$\lceil Pre \wedge (c = e) \wedge \neg\mathbf{Chan}(P) \wedge N\rceil$$
$$\text{Out}(c, e) = \text{WaitOut}(c, e)^{<\frown}\text{SynOut}(c, e)^\frown C \vee \text{WaitOut}(c, e)$$

A symmetrical explanation can be given for the **Output**.

– **External Choice**

We use $c_1?x_1 \to P_1 \; \| \; c_2?x_2 \to P_2$ to explain this rule.

1. Let $(PreH[(\ell = 0)/C] \Rightarrow \top^\frown\lceil Pre\rceil)$.
2. Waiting Phase:

$$\text{Wait} = \lceil Pre \bigwedge_{i=1}^{2}(c_i? \wedge \neg c_i!) \wedge \neg(\mathbf{Chan}(P) \setminus \{c_1?, c_2?\})\rceil$$

3. Synchronous Phase: for $i = 1, 2$

$$\text{Syn}_i = \lceil (\exists x_i.Pre) \wedge c_i! \wedge c_i? \wedge (x_i = c_i) \wedge \neg(\mathbf{Chan}(P) \setminus \{c_{\bar{i}}?\}) \wedge N\rceil^\frown$$
$$\lceil (\exists x_i.Pre) \wedge (x_i = c_i) \wedge \neg\mathbf{Chan}(P) \wedge N\rceil$$

where, in $c_{\bar{i}}$, $\bar{1} = 2$ and $\bar{2} = 1$.

4. If for $i = 1, 2$

$$\{PreH[(\text{Wait}^{<\frown}\text{Syn}_i{}^\frown C \vee \text{Wait})/C]\} \; P_i \; \{PostH_i\}$$

then we can conclude

$$\{PreH\} \; c_1?x_1 \to P_1 \; \| \; c_2?x_2 \to P_2 \; \{PostH_1 \vee PostH_2\}$$

– **Boundary Interruption**

Given a differential invariant Inv of $\langle F(\dot{s}, s) = 0\&B\rangle$ with initial states satisfying $Init$

$$\text{If } PreH[(\ell = 0)/C] \Rightarrow \top^\frown\lceil Init \wedge Pre\rceil, \text{ then}$$
$$\{PreH\} \; \langle F(\dot{s}, s) = 0\&B\rangle$$
$$\{PreH[(((\lceil Inv \wedge Pre \wedge B \wedge \neg\mathbf{Chan}(P)\rceil^{<\frown}}$$
$$\lceil Pre \wedge \mathbf{Close}(Inv) \wedge \mathbf{Close}(\neg B) \wedge \neg\mathbf{Chan}(P) \wedge N\rceil^\frown C)$$
$$\vee \lceil Inv \wedge Pre \wedge B \wedge \neg\mathbf{Chan}(P)\rceil)/C]\}$$

where Pre does not contain s, and $\mathbf{Close}(G)$ is for the *closure* of G to include the boundary, e.g. $\mathbf{Close}(x < 2) = x \leq 2$.

During the evolution of s, Inv and B must hold and so does Pre for the variables other than s. However, when s stops, it will transit to the consecutive statement immediately (i.e. in negligible time). But, during the transition, $\neg B$ becomes true, or B reaches its boundary and $\mathbf{Close}(\neg B)$ becomes true (if B is closed). This can also argue for Inv.

- **Timeout Interruption**

$$\langle F(\dot{s}, s) = 0 \& B \rangle \trianglerighteq_d Q$$

can be semantically defined as

$$\langle F(\dot{s}, s) = 0, \ \dot{t} = 1 \& (B \wedge t < d) \rangle; ((t = d) \to Q)$$

with 0 as initial value of t.

For the **Boundary Interruption** rule, if we rewrite $\langle F(\dot{s}, s) = 0 \& B \rangle$ into $\langle F(\dot{s}, s) = 0, \ \dot{t} = 1 \& B \rangle$ and can generate a differential invariant which can deduce a range of t, say $Rg(t)$, then we can make sure that the duration of $\int \neg N$ for $\lceil Inv \wedge Pre \wedge B \wedge \neg \mathbf{Chan}(P) \rceil^<$ in the **Boundary Interruption** rule must satisfy $Rg(\int \neg N)$.

- **Communication Interruption**

The rule for $\langle F(\dot{s}, s) = 0 \& B \rangle \trianglerighteq \|_{i \in I}(io_i \to P_i)$ is a combination of the **Boundary Interruption** rule and the **External Choice** rule but quite complicated. Here we use $\langle F(\dot{s}, s) = 0 \rangle \trianglerighteq (c!s \to Q)$ to demonstrate its main idea. Assume Inv is a differential invariant of F for initial values $Init$, and

$$PreH[(\ell = 0)/C] \Rightarrow \top^\frown \lceil Init \wedge Pre \rceil,$$

where Pre does not contain s.

If $\{PreH[((\lceil Inv \rceil \wedge \mathrm{WaitOut}(c, s))^<{}^\frown \mathrm{SynOut}(c, s))^\frown C$
$\vee (\lceil Inv \rceil \wedge \mathrm{WaitOut}(c, s)))/C]\} \ Q \ \{PostH\},$
then $\{PreH\} \ \langle F(\dot{s}, s) = 0 \rangle \trianglerighteq (c!s \to Q) \ \{PostH\}$

Since B is $\top$, s can evolve forever unless an output over c occurs.

- **Repetition**

We use the conventional history invariant as defined below

If $\{InvH\} \ P \ \{InvH\}$
then $\{InvH\} \ P^* \ \{InvH\}$

- **Parallel Composition**

If $\{PreH_i\} \ Sys_i \ \{PostH_i\}$
and $PostH_i[(\ell = 0)/C] \Rightarrow \top^\frown \lceil Post_i \rceil, \ i = 1, 2$
then $\{\bigwedge_{i=1}^2 PreH_i\} \ Sys_1 \ \| \ Sys_2 \ \{\bigwedge_{i=1}^2 PostH_i[\lceil Post_i \rceil/C]\}$

where $Post_i$, $i = 1, 2$ do not contain N and channel variables.

In order to avoid different length and occurrence of N state between parallel processes, we use $\lceil Post_i \rceil$ to fill up $PostH_i$, for $i = 1, 2$.

5 Discussion

1. The calculus can only prove safety property, although it introduces the concept of readiness. It is still a challenge to develop a calculus for liveness property.

2. To prove properties of HCSP processes, we have to find out appropriate differential invariants for various differential equations. Although [6] proposes an algorithm to establish polynomial invariants for polynomial differential equations, the complexity of the algorithm is terribly high. We are making efforts to establish nonlinear invariants with reasonable complexity.
3. In [5], the notation of HCSP includes $(P \trianglerighteq_d Q)$ and $(P \trianglerighteq \|_{i \in I}(io_i \to P_i))$, where P can be an arbitrary HCSP process. The history formulas of the calculus record all details of various HCSP processes. We believe that the calculus can be revised for [5].
4. Intuitively this calculus is sound. A rigorous proof of its soundness is to give HCSP another naive semantics and to prove consistency between the semantics and the calculus.

Acknowledgment. This work has been partly supported by the 973 project with grant No. 2014CB340-700, and the projects from NSFC with grant No. 91118007 and 6110006.

References

1. Guelev, D.P., Van Hung, D.: Prefix and projection onto state in duration calculus. In: Proceedings of TPTS'02, volume 65(6) of ENTCS, pp. 101–119. Elsevier Science (2002)
2. Guelev, D.P., Wang, S., Zhan, N.: Hoare-style reasoning about hybrid CSP in the duration calculus. Technical report ISCAS-SKLCS-13-01, ISCAS (2013)
3. He, J.: From CSP to hybrid systems. In: Roscoe, A.W. (ed.) Proceedings of a Classical Mind: Essays in Honour of C. A. R. Hoare. Prentice-Hall International Series in Computer, pp. 171–189. Prentice-Hall, New Jersey (1994)
4. Hoare, C.A.R.: Communicating Sequential Processes. Prentice-Hall, New Jersey (1985)
5. Liu, J., Lv, J., Quan, Z., Zhan, N., Zhao, H., Zhou, C., Zou, L.: A calculus for hybrid CSP. In: Ueda, K. (ed.) APLAS 2010. LNCS, vol. 6461, pp. 1–15. Springer, Heidelberg (2010)
6. Liu, J., Zhan, N., Zhao, H.: Computing semi-algebraic invariants for polynomial dynamical systems. In: Proceedings of EMSoft'11, pp. 97–106 (2011)
7. Pandya, P.K., Van Hung, D.: Duration calculus of weakly monotonic time. In: Ravn, A.P., Rischel, H. (eds.) FTRTFT 1998. LNCS, vol. 1486, pp. 55–64. Springer, Heidelberg (1998)
8. Platzer, A., Clarke, E.M.: Computing differential invariants of hybrid systems as fixedpoints. In: Gupta, A., Malik, S. (eds.) CAV 2008. LNCS, vol. 5123, pp. 176–189. Springer, Heidelberg (2008)
9. Platzer, A., Quesel, J.-D.: European train control system: a case study in formal verification. In: Proceedings of ICFEM '09, pp. 246–265 (2009)
10. Xia, B., Yang, L.: An algorithm for isolating the real solutions of semi-algebraic systems. J. Symbolic Comput. **34**, 461–477 (2002)
11. Yang, L.: Recent advances on determining the number of real roots of parametric polynomials. J. Symbolic Comput. **28**, 225–242 (1999)

12. Zhan, N., Wang, S., Zhao, H.: Formal modelling, analysis and verification of hybrid systems. In: Liu, Z., Woodcock, J., Zhu, H. (eds.) Unifying Theories of Programming and Formal Engineering Methods. LNCS, vol. 8050, pp. 207–281. Springer, Heidelberg (2013)
13. Zhou, C., Hansen, M.R.: Duration Calculus: A Formal Approach to Real-Time Systems. Springer, Heidelberg (2004)
14. Zhou, C., Wang, J., Ravn, A.P.: A formal description of hybrid systems. In: Alur, R., Henzinger, T.A., Sontag, E.D. (eds.) Hybrid Systems III. LNCS, pp. 511–530. Springer, Heidelberg (1995)
15. Zou, L., Lv, J., Wang, S., Zhan, N., Tang, T., Yuan, L., Liu, Y.: Verifying Chinese train control system under a combined scenario by theorem proving. In: Cohen, E., Rybalchenko, A. (eds.) VSTTE 2013. LNCS, vol. 8164, pp. 262–280. Springer, Heidelberg (2014)
16. Zou, L., Zhan, N., Wang, S., Fränzle, M., Qin, S.: Verifying simulink diagrams via a hybrid Hoare logic prover. In: Proceedings of EMSoft'13, pp. 1–10 (2013)

A Proof-Carrying Code Approach
to Certificate Auction Mechanisms

W. Bai[1,2(✉)], E.M. Tadjouddine[2(✉)], T.R. Payne[1], and S.U. Guan[2]

[1] Department of Computer Science, University of Liverpool, Liverpool, England, UK
{Wei.Bai,T.R.Payne}@liverpool.ac.uk
[2] Department of Computer Science and Software Engineering,
Xi'an Jiaotong-Liverpool University, SIP, Suzhou, China
{Emmanuel.Tadjouddine,Steven.Guan}@xjtlu.edu.cn

Abstract. Whilst it can be highly desirable for software agents to engage in auctions, they are normally restricted to trading within known auctions, due to the complexity and heterogeneity of the auction rules within an e-commerce system. To allow for agents to deal with previously unseen protocols, we present a proof-carrying code approach using CoQ wherein auction protocols can be specified and desirable properties be proven. This enables software agents to automatically certify claimed auction properties and assist them in their decision-making. We have illustrated our approach by specifying both the English and Vickrey auctions; have formalized different bidding strategies for agents; have certified that up to the valuation is the optimal strategy in English auction and truthful bidding is the optimal strategy in Vickrey auction for all agents. The formalization and certification are based on inductive definitions and constructions from within CoQ. This work contributes to solving the problem of open societies of software agents moving between different institutions and seeking to make optimal decisions and will benefit those engaged in agent-mediated e-commerce.

Keywords: CoQ · Proof-carrying code · Certification · e-commerce · Software agents

1 Introduction

One of the major challenges in developing agents that are capable of rational decision making within open, heterogeneous environments, is that of comprehending the rules and social norms that govern the behavior of new institutions. Although much work has addressed interoperability at the communication level (with agent communication languages such as FIPA-ACL, and RDF to underpin recent developments within the Semantic Web [1]) thus *allowing agents to communicate*, the decision of whether or not *the communication is meaningful* is still an open challenge. Agents may understand how to conduct their behavior in certain familiar scenarios, and bid strategically in marketplaces that adhere to certain rules (e.g., an English or Dutch auction). However, such strategies may

J.L. Fiadeiro et al. (Eds.): FACS 2013, LNCS 8348, pp. 23–40, 2014.
DOI: 10.1007/978-3-319-07602-7_4, © Springer International Publishing Switzerland 2014

not be applicable to other markets, such as those based on Vickrey auctions. Within an open and dynamic environment (such as e-commerce), agents might encounter a variety of auction houses, that could form part of an agent mediated e-commerce scenario. It is therefore important for the agent to be able to acquire a deeper model of the marketplaces that they could engage in (other than simply relying in simple classifications) so that they can rationally determine whether or not they should engage in the marketplace.

Agents should be able to query and comprehend the rules that govern an auction house, and verify desirable properties that can be relevant to privacy, security, or economics. This paper focuses on the economic properties, by looking at specifying and verifying game-theoretic properties for single item online auctions. An important game-theoretic property is *strategy-proofness* namely, the existence of a dominant strategy for the players meaning a strategy that is optimal regardless of the game configuration. For example, truthful bidding can be the dominant strategy in certain auction settings. The aim of this paper is to present an approach to help agents to automatically verify desirable properties in online auctions. To this end, we rely on the proof-carrying code (PCC) paradigm [2] to allow for:

- the auctioneer to publish the auction mechanism along with the proofs of desirable properties in a machine readable formalism,
- the potential buyer agent to read the published protocol, make sense of it, and at will, check the proof of a given property by using a simple trusted checker, which makes the automatic checking procedure computationally reasonable.

Our current work focuses on expressing the mechanism and game-theoretic proofs in a machine checkable formalism. We have used CoQ [3], an interactive theorem prover based on inductive definitions and construction wherein the formalizations of English and Vickrey auctions are carried out. Then, different bidding strategies are specified followed by the proofs of a dominant strategy for each bidder.

Previous efforts have explored the use of automatic checking of auction properties. The strategy-proofness property was checked using model checking in [4, 5] but the related computational complexity can be exponential [6]. To handle the computational limits of exhaustive model checking, two property-preserving abstractions are proposed. One is the classical program slicing technique [7]. The other is abstract interpretation [5]. In [8], a distributed computer system infrastructure with a rationality authority that allows for safe consultations among parties is presented. A rationality authority includes the game inventor, participating agents and verifiers, which provide verification services. Game inventors advise the agents about actions and their optimality. Verifiers send their verification procedures to the agents. A typed language which allows for automatic verification that an allocation algorithm is monotonic and therefore truthful is introduced in [9]. Then, a more general-purpose programming language is defined to capture a collection of basic truthful allocation algorithms. This is similar to our current approach as we rely upon the proof-carrying code paradigm and CoQ to allow software agents to achieve reasonable automatic checking of game properties.

Moreover, interactive theorem proving is used to express the proof of desirable properties in a machine-checkable manner. There are two advantages in using an interactive theorem prover [10]. One is that the specification of the desirable properties can be precisely described by the designer. The other is that the proof of a property is machine-checkable. We use the interactive theorem prover CoQ because it has been developed for more than twenty years [11] and is widely used for formal proof development in a variety of contexts related to software and hardware correctness and safety. CoQ has been used to model and verify sequential programs [12] and concurrent programs [13]. In [14], CoQ was used to develop and certify a compiler. A fully computer-checked proof of the Four Colour Theorem was created in [15]. In [16], a CoQ-formalised proof that all non-cooperative, sequential games have a Nash equilibrium point is presented.

This paper is organized as follows. Section 2 describes our certification framework and the scenario of single item auctions. Section 3 describes the formalization of auction mechanisms followed by proofs of desirable properties in Sect. 4. Section 5 discusses the evaluation of our approach and Sect. 6 concludes.

2 Our Certification Framework

The ability for heterogeneous software agents to interoperate between different and open auction houses raise two main questions: how to get agents to operate on previously unseen protocols and how to get agents to automatically check desirable properties that are central to their decision making. In order to solve this difficult problem, we start by looking at models or scenarios allowing us to use a divide-and-conquer paradigm for an incremental solution. A brief overview of our scenario can be stated as follows. Online protocols can be described using some web-based description language; the resulting description is abstracted into CoQ specifications that are used to provide machine-checkable proofs of desirable properties for the protocol at hand. Such a CoQ specification can be turned back into the original web description so as to be read, understood, and checked by a software agent. Such mappings back and forth can be carried out using *abstract interpretation* [17]. Abstract interpretation enables us to analyze the behaviors of a computer system by *safely* approximating its concrete semantics into an abstract one involving a smaller set of values. Note that by safe approximations, we mean approximations that are at least sound allowing us to transpose properties that are true in the abstract domain into the concrete one. For the abstraction, from a web-based description of an auction, we can build up a CoQ-based specification of that auction known as the abstract mapping so that desirable properties can be proved from within the CoQ system. This abstraction approach can solve the problem of heterogeneity of different auction houses by providing a uniform and formalized format of protocols to software agents.

An abstract interpretation is defined as a sound approximated program semantics obtained from a concrete one by replacing the concrete domain of computation and its concrete semantic operations with an abstract domain and corresponding abstract semantic operations. An abstraction is sound if any property that holds in the abstracted program holds also in the concrete program. In the architecture of abstract interpretation, the abstract domain can be concretized back into the concrete domain which means that the concretized abstract context includes the concrete context. The success of abstraction and concretization leads to the correctness of interpretation. Based on abstract interpretation, program transformation frameworks were proposed in [18]. Figure 1 illustrates our use of the abstract interpretation framework. Once a web based auction protocol is abstracted into COQ, desirable properties can be formally proven and the resulting proof is machine-checkable and therefore verifiable by software agents.

In this work, we focus on the verification procedures for some desirable properties of auction mechanisms, which can be specified in COQ. The COQ system is based on a typed lambda calculus [19], which can be taken as a glue specification language into and from which any auction mechanism can be mapped to.

In order to effectively enable automatic checking of desirable properties, we need to take into account the fact that software agents have limited computer resources and may be constrained in their reasoning. On one hand, it is difficult for a software agent to find the best possible or optimal bidding strategy on its own or to optimize its utility out of various strategies in the same way humans might. On the other hand, if the specification of auction protocols and proofs are published in a machine-readable formalism, then automatic checking by software agents can be facilitated and the computational complexity will be reduced. For that purpose, we have relied upon the Proof-Carrying-Code (PCC) ideas since it allows us to shift the burden of proof from the buyer agent to the auctioneer who can spend time to prove a claimed property once for all so that it can be checked by any agent willing to join the auction house.

PCC is a paradigm that enables a computer system to automatically ensure that a computer code provided by a foreign agent is safe for installation and execution. A weakness of the original PCC was that the soundness of the verification condition generator is not proved. To overcome this weakness, *Foundational* PCC (FPCC) [20] provides us with stronger semantic foundations to PCC by generating verification conditions directly from the operational semantics. Figure 2 illustrates our framework that uses FPCC to certify auction properties. At the producer or auctioneer's side, we have the specifications of the auction mechanism along with the proofs of desirable properties in a machine-checkable formalism in the form of a COQ file. The certification procedure works as follows. The buyer agent arriving at the auction house can download its specification

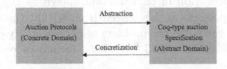

Fig. 1. Framework of abstract interpretation

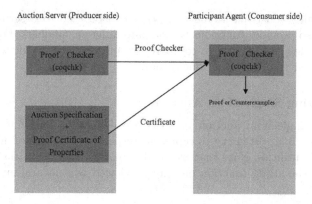

Fig. 2. Applying FPCC to certify auction properties

and the claimed proof of a desirable property. Then, the buyer requests the proof checker *coqhk*, which is a standalone verifier for Coq proofs, to the auctioneer. After the proof checker is installed to the consumer side, the buyer can now perform all verifications of claimed properties of the auction before deciding to join and with which bidding strategy.

We have implemented this FPCC framework from within the Coq system. In our current implementation, we have considered a one-to-many scenario. A single item is allocated using an online auction house. Various buyer agents can enter or leave this house at will, make sense of its mechanism along with some recommended strategies and their associated proofs. Such a recommendation can be for example, truthful bidding is the dominant or optimal strategy for a buyer agent. We then showed how such a desirable property can be proved using two examples of a single item auction: the English and Vickrey auctions. In the remainder of this paper, we basically show how to specify such auctions and its possible strategy-proofness property and how to prove it within Coq. The specifications and proofs are split into different Coq files[1].

3   Formalization of Auction Mechanisms Within Coq

In this section, we define the framework to specify single item auctions. Then, the English and Vickrey auctions are specified respectively. For simplicity, we assume no agents submit the same bid. To specify the English and Vickrey auctions, we start by a framework that is used to describe a single item auction within Coq. Coq uses the keyword **Definition** to define a variable or a function. The keyword **Inductive** is used to provide inductive definitions and **Fixpoint** can be used to define recursive functions in Coq. Coq provides library to define data types, such as the type **nat** which represents natural numbers, the type Z which represents integers and the type **bool** of booleans. When defining a function,

---

[1] Our Coq code is available upon request.

pattern-matching construct match ... with can be used to describe different cases. COQ also provides functions to compare different numbers. For example, function Z_gt_dec can be used to compare two integers and decide whether one integer is greater than the other one or not.

3.1   Specifying Single Item Auction

To specify a single item auction in COQ, we define the following objects as types: Agents, Bid, Utility to represent respectively the set of agents, their bids, and their utilities. Note that Bid is declared as an integer to simplify the calculation of the utility function but can be viewed as a natural number.

```
Definition Agents: = nat.
Definition Bid: = Z.
Definition Utility: = Z.
```

We then describe an inductive relation aRb binding agents with their bids and provide two functions Agent_aRb and Bid_aRb that return respectively the agent and the bid for a given relation.

```
Inductive aRb : Type :=
    Binding : Agents -> Bid -> aRb.

Definition Agent_aRb (r:aRb):Agents :=
  match r with
  | Binding a b => a
  end.

Definition Bid_aRb (r:aRb):Bid :=
  match r with
  | Binding a b => b
  end.
```

To enable us reasoning on the agents' utilities, we define a relation aRu binding agents to their utilities and a handle function Utility_aRu to extract the utility of a given agent.

```
Inductive aRu : Type :=
    AUtility : Agents -> Utility -> aRu.

Definition Utility_aRu (au:aRu):Utility :=
  match au with
  | AUtility a u => u
  end.
```

To eliminate negative bidding, we define a function TestBid allowing us to set any bid that is smaller than zero to zero.

```
Definition TestBid (b:Z):Bid :=
  match Z_gt_dec b 0 with
  | left _ => b
  | right _ => 0
  end.
```

To enable agents to decide whether to bid or not, we have defined a relation flag binding an agent with a boolean value indicating the choice of this agent. If the value is true, then the agent wants to bid, otherwise the agent gives up bidding in the current round. Agents can set their choices based on their bidding strategies by using the function Set_flag.

```
Inductive flag : Type :=
   Choice : Agents -> bool -> flag.

Definition Set_flag (a:Agents)(b:bool) : flag :=
   match b with
   | true => Choice a b
   | false => Choice a b
   end.
```

With the help of `flag`, we can build up the state of the auction by a fixpoint definition of the function `AuctionState`. We use the function `Bool_flag` to get the boolean value associated to each agent. We then store all the flag values into a *List* structure `flaglist`, which is the input to the function `AuctionState`. If `AuctionState` returns true, then the auction will continue, otherwise it stops.

```
Definition Bool_flag (f:flag) : bool :=
   match f with
   | Choice a b => b
   end.

Inductive flaglist : Type :=
   | nil : flaglist
   | cons : flag -> flaglist -> flaglist.

Fixpoint AuctionState (fl:flaglist) : bool :=
   match fl with
   | nil => false
   | cons h nil => match (Bool_flag h) with
                     | false => false
                     | true => true
                     end
   | cons h t => match (Bool_flag h) with
                     | false => AuctionState t
                     | true => true
                     end
   end.
```

Next, we will illustrate our single item auction specification by using the English and Vickrey auctions to show how to specify agents' strategies and how a given strategy profile can be shown to be a dominant strategy equilibrium.

3.2 The English Auction Case

In the English auction, we consider two strategies: First, the agent starts to bid from a lower price up to its valuation termed as `bid_below_to_value`. Second, the agent bids beyond its valuation termed as `bid_beyond_value`.

```
Definition bid_below_to_value (b : Bid) (v : Bid): bool :=
   match Z_le_dec b v with
   | left _ => true
   | right _ => false
   end.

Definition bid_beyond_value (b : Bid) (v : Bid): bool :=
   match Z_gt_dec b v with
   | left _ => true
   | right _ => false
   end.
```

The English auction is a type of sequential auction in which bidders have to beat the current bid. A new bid must be higher than the current one, otherwise it is rejected. To take this into account, we have defined the relation aRboption and used it to return "Accept" or "Reject" for each new bid via the function Compare. Two functions Agent_flag and Find_flag are used to build up the Compare function. Agent_flag returns an agent from one flag. Find_flag searches for the flag of an agent from the list flaglist. The return value (*Choice* 0 %*nat* *false*) is a default value when the flag of an agent cannot be found. The function CurrentWinner returns the winner and its associated bid aRb.

```
Inductive aRboption : Type :=
  | Accept : aRb -> aRboption
  | Reject : aRboption.

Definition Agent_flag (f:flag) : Agents :=
  match f with
  | Choice a b => a
  end.

Fixpoint Find_flag (a:Agents) (fl:flaglist) : flag :=
  match fl with
  | nil => (Choice 0%nat false)
  | cons h t => match beq_nat a (Agent_flag h) with
                | true => h
                | false => Find_flag a t
                end
  end.

Definition Compare (fl:flaglist)(new_aRb current_aRb : aRb) : aRboption :=
  match Bool_flag (Find_flag (Agent_aRb new_aRb) fl) with
  | true => match Z_gt_dec (Bid_aRb new_aRb) (Bid_aRb current_aRb) with
            | left _ => Accept new_aRb
            | right _ => Reject
            end
  | false => Reject
  end.

Definition CurrentWinner (fl:flaglist)(new_aRb current_aRb : aRb) : aRb :=
  match  Compare fl new_aRb current_aRb with
  | Accept n' => n'
  | Reject => current_aRb
  end.
```

The auction ends when all agents have a flag value of false and the winner can be found as the one with the highest bid. Given the agent's valuation v and a payment p, the utility u of an agent is defined as $v - p$ if the agent wins and zero otherwise. This utility function is formalized in Utility_Eng wherein the variable winbid represents the highest bid in the auction.

```
Definition Utility_Eng (winbid:Bid) (b:Bid) (v:Bid) : Utility :=
  match Z_lt_dec b winbid with
  | left _ => 0
  | right _ => v - b
  end.
```

3.3   The Vickrey Auction Case

In a Vickrey auction, also known as second-price sealed-bid auction, all the bidders submit their bids at a time without any knowledge of other bidders' bids. The highest bidder wins but pays the second-highest bid. There are three bidding strategies in this auction: bid truthfully (or its valuation) encoded in the function bid_value, bid below the valuation encoded in the function bid_below_value, and bid beyond the valuation through the function bid_beyond_value.

```
Definition bid_value (b : Bid) (v : Bid): bool :=
   match Z_eq_dec b v with
   | left _ => true
   | right _ => false
   end.

Definition bid_below_value (b : Bid) (v : Bid): bool :=
   match Z_lt_dec b v with
   | left _ => true
   | right _ => false
   end.

Definition bid_beyond_value (b : Bid) (v : Bid): bool :=
   match Z_gt_dec b v with
   | left _ => true
   | right _ => false
   end.
```

We have used the *List* data structure to store the basic elements of aRb. In the definition list of aRb, the binlist type can be described as follows: it is either an empty (bnil) or else a pair of a aRb element and a binlist. This can be described using the notation :: as an infix *bcons* operator for constructing binding lists.

```
Inductive binlist : Type :=
   | bnil : binlist
   | bcons : aRb -> binlist -> binlist.

Notation "x :: l" := (bcons x l) (at level 60, right associativity).
```

The function addsortbid allows us to add and sort a binlist in a descending order. In this recursively defined function, all bindings ($Agents \rightarrow Bid$) are added to the list one by one. Also, the function winbid is used to calculate the winning bid (the head of the sorted binlist). When binlist is empty, it returns a default value ($Binding \quad 0\%nat \quad 0$). The utility u of an agent is defined as $v - sb$ if the agent wins and zero otherwise, where v is the agent's valuation and sb is the second highest bid in the sorted binlist. To calculate the utility of each agent, we need to know the second highest bid in the sorted binlist. The function se_hi_bid finds the second highest bid when there are at least two elements in the sorted binlist. Otherwise, it will return a default value ($Binding \quad 0\%nat \quad 0$).

```
Fixpoint addsortbid (b : aRb) (l : binlist) : binlist :=
   match l with
   | bnil => b :: bnil
   | bcons a l' => match Z_lt_dec (Bid_aRb b)
                     (Bid_aRb a) with
                     | left _ => a :: (addsortbid b l')
                     | right _ => b :: a :: l'
                   end
   end.

Definition winbid (l : binlist) : aRb :=
   match l with
   | bnil => (Binding 0%nat 0)
   | a :: l' => a
   end.
```

```
Definition se_hi_bid (l : binlist) : aRb :=
  match l with
  | bnil => (Binding 0%nat 0)
  | a :: l' => match l' with
                 | bnil => (Binding 0%nat 0)
                 | h :: l'' => h
               end
  end.
```

The `UtilityOfTruthfulBidding` function defines the utility for an agent bidding its valuation v. Recall that the variable sb in this function stands for the second highest bid.

```
Definition UtilityOfTruthfulBidding (v : Bid)
(sb : Bid) : Utility :=
  match Z_le_dec sb v with
  | left _ => v - sb
  | right _ => 0
  end.
```

The utility for an agent in the other two strategies is presented in Algorithm 1. It summarizes the six different conditions giving rise to an agent's utility and is encoded in the function `Utility_OfOtherStrategies`.

```
Definition Utility_OfOtherStrategies (b : Bid) (v : Bid)
      (sb : Bid) : Utility :=
  match Z_gt_dec b v with
  | left _ => match Z_gt_dec sb b with
                | left _ => 0
                | right _ => match Z_le_gt_dec sb v with
                               | left _ => v - sb
                               | right _ => v - sb
                             end
              end
  | right _ => match Z_le_gt_dec sb b with
                 | left _ => v - sb
                 | right _ => match Z_ge_lt_dec sb v with
                                | left _ => 0
                                | right _ => 0
                              end
               end
  end.
```

Algorithm 1. Computation of *Utility_OfOtherStrategies*

Variables:

v: valuation of one agent

b: bid of one agent

sb: second highest bid in the bid list

u: utility of one agent

Different Cases in the definition of *Utility_OfOtherStrategies* :

1. $b > v$
   1.1 $sb > b, u = 0$;
   1.2 $sb \leq v, u = v - sb$;
   1.3 $v < sb \leq b, u = v - sb, u < 0$.
2. $b < v$
   2.1 $sb \leq b, u = v - sb$;
   2.2 $sb \geq v, u = 0$;
   2.3 $b < sb \leq v, u = 0$.

---

4 Certifying Desirable Properties

In the English auction with private values setting, in the sense that bidders know only their own valuation, buyers sequentially submit their bids. The dominant bidding strategy is for a buyer to start bidding from a lower price and keep increasing its bid until its valuation. In a Vickrey auction, the buyers simultaneously submit their bids and a dominant strategy is for the bidder to bid its valuation. We may be interested in additional auction properties, including *collusion-proofness* meaning that agents cannot collude to achieve a favourable outcome to them, or *false-name bidding free* meaning that agents cannot manipulate the outcome by using fictitious names. We may also be interested in showing that the auction is well-defined function and that it is implemented in line with its specification. In this section, we focus on the certification of dominant strategy in both English and Vickrey auctions. To carry out the CoQ proof, all different bidding strategies and their related utilities are examined for comparison. The keyword `Variables` can be used to define local variables in CoQ. We can use the keywords `Hypotheses` and `Lemma` to define Hypotheses and Lemma in a CoQ proof respectively.

4.1 Certification of Dominant Strategy in the English Auction

For the English auction, the dominant strategy is for each buyer to bid up to its valuation. To provide a machine-checkable proof of this fact, we will use the previously defined utility function `Utility_Eng` along with some hypotheses. Algorithm 2 is used to construct the certificate. This algorithm compares two strategies: bid beyond the valuation (b > v) and bid up to the valuation (b <= v). In total, there are three cases of comparison using different hypotheses. In all cases, we see that for a buyer to bid up to its valuation yields an utility that is higher or equal to that obtained when a buyer adopts any other strategy.

Algorithm 2. Proving the Dominant Strategy in the English auction

Variables:
v: valuation of one agent
b: bid of one agent
winbid: the highest bid
u: utility of one agent
Comparison Cases:
1. $b = winbid$,
   $b > v \rightarrow u = v - b < 0$ (If $b \leq v \rightarrow u = v - b \geq 0$, Better);
2. $b < winbid$,
   $b > v \rightarrow u = 0$ (If $b \leq v \rightarrow u = 0$, Same);
3. $b > v, b = winbid \rightarrow u = v - b < 0$ (If $b \leq v, b < winbid \rightarrow u = 0$, Better).

In here, we provide a detailed proof for the first case. The remaining two cases are proved in a similar way. To carry out the CoQ proof of the first case, we started by defining the three variables v, b, and winbid. Recall that v is the valuation of one agent, b is the bid of one agent and winbid is the highest bid in one auction.

Variables $v \quad b \quad winbid \quad : Z.$

As seen in Algorithm 2, the first comparison case is on the condition that one agent wins the auction with bid b. By relying upon this condition, we introduce the hypothesis b = winbid, which means that the bid b is the winning bid in the auction. This hypothesis is defined in CoQ as:

Hypotheses English_hy1 : $b = winbid.$

All of the Lemmas that are proved in this part rely upon this hypothesis. A tactic *omega*, which is a solver of quantifier-free problems in Presburger Arithmetic, i.e. a universally quantified formula made of equations and inequations, is used in the following proofs. In the next step, we prove Lemma 1 to show that bid b is not less than the winning bid winbid.

Lemma 1 (not_b_lt_win). $\sim b < winbid.$

Proof. In **English_hy1**, we have bid b equals to the winning bid winbid. Therefore, bid b is not less than the winning bid winbid. The proof is carried out by using **English_hy1** and the tactic *omega* in CoQ.   □

The following Lemma 2 expresses the fact that if one agent bids up to its valuation (b <= v), it will get an utility of v - b.

Lemma 2 (U_below_to_v). $b <= v \rightarrow \sim b < winbid \rightarrow Utility\_Eng \; winbid \; b \; v = v - b.$

Proof. In here, we use the premises: one agent bids up to its valuation (b <= v) and the previously proved Lemma 1. According to the definition of Utility_Eng, if bid b is less than the winning bid winbid, this agent gets the utility of zero. Otherwise, it gets the utility of v-b. Furthermore, we have proved that bid b is not less than the winning bid winbid in Lemma 1. Consequently, this agent gets the utility of v-b. The proof is finished by a case-splitting following the definition of function Utility_Eng in CoQ.   □

The next Lemma 3 shows that, under the premise (b <= v), the value of v - b is greater or equal to 0.

Lemma 3 (v_min_b_ge_O). $b <= v \rightarrow v - b >= 0.$

Proof. The proof is constructed by using the premise b <= v and the tactic *omega*.   □

Lemma 4 takes Lemmas 2 and 3 as premises, and proves that the utility that the agent gets is greater or equal to 0 when it bids up to its valuation.

Lemma 4 (U_ge_O). $Utility\_Eng \; winbid \; b \; v = v - b \rightarrow v - b >= 0 \rightarrow$ $Utility\_Eng \; winbid \; b \; v >= 0.$

Proof. Lemma 2 indicates that an agent gets the utility of v-b, and Lemma 3 establishes that the value of v-b is greater or equals to 0. By using these two lemmas, we can draw the conclusion that this agent gets a nonnegative utility. The proof is built up by combining the Lemmas 2 and 3 in CoQ.   □

Next, we will calculate and prove that the utility that an agent gets when it bids beyond its valuation under the hypothesis **English_hy1**.

The premises of Lemma 5 are an agent bids beyond its valuation (b > v) and the previously proved Lemma not_b_lt_win. Under these two premises, we can derive the fact that the agent should get the utility of v - b.

Lemma 5 (U_beyond_v). $b > v \rightarrow \sim b < winbid \rightarrow Utility\_Eng\ winbid\ b\ v = v - b$.

Proof. The proof is carried out by combining the premise b > v and Lemma 1. By the definition of Utility_Eng, if bid b is not less than the winning bid winbid, then the agent gets the utility of v-b. Lemma 1 establishes that ~b < winbid is true. So, we have proved that when an agent bids beyond its valuation, it gets utility of v-b. We finish this proof by a case-splitting following the definition of function Utility_Eng in CoQ.   □

Lemma 6 shows that under the premise b > v, the value of v - b is smaller than 0.

Lemma 6 (v_min_b_lt_O). $b > v \rightarrow v - b < 0$.

Proof. The proof is constructed by using the premise b > v and the tactic *omega*.   □

Lemma 7 shows that if an agent bids beyond its valuation, then it will get negative utility.

Lemma 7 (U_lt_O). $Utility\_Eng\ winbid\ b\ v = v - b \rightarrow v - b < 0 \rightarrow Utility\_Eng\ winbid\ b\ v < 0$.

Proof. Lemma 5 shows one agent getting the utility of v-b, and Lemma 6 establishes that the value of v-b is less than 0. Based on these two lemmas, we can conclude that this agent gets a negative utility. The proof is constructed by combining both Lemmas 5 and 6.   □

On the basis of **English_hy1**, Lemma 4 establishes that if one agent bids up to its valuation, then it gets nonnegative utility whereas Lemma 7 shows that an agent will get negative utility if it bids beyond its valuation. As a consequence, we can conclude that for an agent to start bidding from a lower price up to its valuation is a better strategy than for that agent bidding beyond its valuation. This terminates the first case. By proving all the remaining cases, we complete the proof of dominant strategy in the English auction.

4.2   Certification of the Dominant Strategy in Vickrey Auction

Our certification is based on the proof in [21]. Six different cases of bidding strategies are considered and defined in `Utility_OfOtherStrategies`. They are compared against the outcome of the truthful bidding strategy (bidding its valuation). The schema used to construct our machine-checkable proof is shown in Algorithm 3. As in the case of the English auction, we only demonstrate how to construct the COQ proof of the first case in Algorithm 3, since the remaining cases are dealt with in a similar fashion.

Algorithm 3. Proving the Dominant Strategy in Vickrey auction

---

Variables:
v: valuation of one agent
b: bid of one agent
sb: second highest bid in the bid list
u: utility of one agent
Comparison Cases:
1. $sb > b$,
    $b > v \rightarrow u = 0$ (If $b = v \rightarrow u = 0$, Same);
2. $sb \leq v$,
    $b > v \rightarrow u = v - sb$ (If $b = v \rightarrow u = v - sb$, Same);
3. $v < sb \leq b$,
    $u = v - sb < 0$ (If $b = v \rightarrow u = 0$, Better);
4. $sb \leq b$,
    $b < v \rightarrow u = v - sb$ (If $b = v \rightarrow u = v - sb$, Same);
5. $sb \geq v$,
    $b < v \rightarrow u = 0$ (If $b = v \rightarrow u = 0$, Same);
6. $b < sb < v$,
    $u = 0$ (If $b = v \rightarrow u = v - sb > 0$, Better).

Let us start by introducing three variables v, b and sb. The meanings of these variables are listed in Algorithm 3.

Variables v b sb $: Z$.

In the first case of Algorithm 3, we have the hypothesis $sb > b$, meaning that an agent's bid is less than the second highest bid. All of the Lemmas that are proved below are based on this hypothesis.

Hypotheses Vickrey_hy1 : $sb > b$.

The Lemma 8 shows that if one agent bids beyond its valuation (b > v), it will get the utility of zero.

Lemma 8 (Utility_of_CaseOne). $b > v \rightarrow Utility\_OfOtherStrategies\ b\ v$ $sb = 0$.

Proof. We have the premise **b > v**. The definition of **Utility_OfOther Strategies** states that if an agent bids beyond its valuation (**b > v**) and the second highest bid is greater than this agent's bid (**sb > b**), then it gets the utility of zero. The proof is completed by a case-splitting following the definition of function **Utility_OfOtherStrategies** in COQ.   □

So far, we have proved that based on **Vickrey_hy1**, one agent gets the utility of zero if it bids beyond its valuation. Then, we will prove that if one agent bids its valuation, it also gets the utility of zero. To finish this proof, we introduce Lemma 9 in the first step. Lemma 9 shows that **sb** is not smaller or equal to **v** under the premise: **b = v**.

Lemma 9 (not_sb_le_v). $b = v \rightarrow sb > v \rightarrow \sim sb <= v$.

Proof. The COQ proof is constructed by combining the hypothesis **Vickrey_hy1**, the two premises **b = v, sb > v** and the tactic *omega*.   □

The following Lemma 10 shows that when an agent bids its valuation, it gets the utility of zero.

Lemma 10 (Utility_of_Valuation). $\sim sb <= v \rightarrow$ **UtilityOfTruthfu lBidding** $v\ sb = 0$.

Proof. The conclusion of Lemma 9 is used as a premise. Based on the definition of **Utility_OfTruthfulBidding**, if an agent bids its valuation and the second highest bid **sb** is not less than or equal to its valuation **v**, this agent gets the utility of zero. The proof is carried out by a case-splitting following the definition of the function **Utility_OfTruthfulBidding** in COQ.   □

Lemma 11 establishes that under the hypothesis **Vickrey_hy1**, the utility associated with the truthful bidding strategy is the same as that of bidding beyond the valuation for an agent.

Lemma 11 (V_E_SOne). **Utility_OfOtherStrategies** $b\ v\ sb = 0 \rightarrow$ **UtilityOfTruthfulBidding** $v\ sb = 0 \rightarrow$ **Utility_OfOtherStrategies** $b\ v\ sb =$ **UtilityOfTruthfulBidding** $v\ sb$.

Proof. Using the hypothesis **Vickrey_hy1**, we have proved that an agent gets the utility of zero if it bids beyond its valuation in Lemma 8. Moreover, in Lemma 10, if an agent bids its valuation, then it gets the utility of zero. That is to say, this agent gets the same utility, no matter which strategy it uses. The proof is completed by combining Lemma 8 and Lemma 10 in COQ.   □

As mentioned earlier in this section, we do not present the COQ proofs related to the remaining five cases in Algorithm 3 for simplicity of the presentation because these five cases are proved in a similar way. This then completes the COQ certification of truthful bidding be a dominant strategy in Vickrey auction.

5   Discussion

In our current implementation of the FPCC framework to certify auction properties, we have enabled a participating agent to find out desirable properties held by the auction house and to recognize whether a given recommendation is correct or not. For example, suppose a buyer agent visits a *first-price sealed-bid auction* (each agent independently submits a single bid, the highest bidder wins and pays her bid). The server side of this auction house provides this agent with a COQ proof that truthful bidding is a dominant strategy derived from the Vickrey auction. Our system ensures that the proof checker will find a mismatch between the auction specification and the given proof. Thus our implementation enables the buyer agent to find out that *strategyproofness* is not a property of this auction house and that the given proof is wrong. The agent can only check the proof that is related to a well-defined specification, which means that the certificate of dominant strategy in Vickrey auction cannot be used for the English auction for instance. This helps agents distinguish the properties of different auction mechanisms. Our approach can be extended to a broad range of agent-mediated e-commerce systems. For example, we can use this approach to certify whether the winner of the auction is the highest bidder. It also can be applied to verify the communication protocols used by autonomous agents. For the customer who may be concerned by security issues, this approach can be used to verify transaction protocols implemented in an e-commerce system.

One of the limitations of our current work is that an agent cannot understand a previously unseen mechanism unless the specification is part of the common knowledge of this agent. For example, an agent with the knowledge of English auction specification is roaming in the Internet. After this agent arrives at an auction house, it checks the specification of this auction house. The agent can recognize this auction if the specification is an English auction. Otherwise, this agent cannot figure out the type of the auction house. Assume that a human being delegates a task to bid for one item in an English house to a buyer agent. The buyer agent with the knowledge of English auction will join in the English auction house but will ignore any other unrecognized auction house. But, an agent with all the specifications of widely used auction mechanisms can recognize different kinds of auction houses although it requires more computational resources. Nonetheless, it is our intention to extend this implementation by enabling agents to operate on previously unseen protocols by using the semantic web technology so as to build up a shared ontology by the agents and connect this ontology with the COQ formalism in order to enable the verification. Seemingly, Semantic Web Service Language OWL-S is a good Logic-based Language candidate to describe auction mechanisms in a machine understandable formalism.

Note that although, COQ is an interactive theorem prover, we have utilised it to enable automated verification since the proof is constructed only once and agents have to check the correctness of given certificates automatically. Moreover, our approach can be generalised in any kind of auction by making use of ontology based formalism to describe an auction and mapping this description to our COQ specification.

6   Conclusion and Future Work

In this paper, we have used the FPCC framework to e-commerce systems so as to provide certification abilities for software agents. The setting is that of online auction markets wherein agents can move between auction houses. Auction houses can publish their mechanism (auction rules) along with proofs of some desirable properties. Buyer agents can download the auction rules, inquire for a property and get the proof for that property so that the agent can check that a proof is indeed correct. We have demonstrated the feasibility of this FPCC approach by formalizing and checking strategy-proofness for the English and Vickrey auctions from within CoQ. The ability for an agent to verify auction protocols will increase the trust to an online auction house, which in turn may render this kind of trading attractive and boost its market value.

As future work, we will continue implementing the framework that is proposed in this article. We plan to build an auction house using both Semantic Web [1] and the Java Agent DEvelopment Framework (JADE) [22]. Semantic web provides us with a mechanism that can be used by agents to communicate and understand each other. It also enables software agent to provide intelligent access to heterogeneous and distributed information. In this situation, a software agent is an encapsulated computer system in some environment, capable of perceiving and autonomously acting in that environment. JADE is a widely used tool to implement multi-agent systems. It provides mechanisms to create agents, enable agents to execute tasks and make agents communicate with each other. Semantic Web agents can take benefits from Semantic Web technologies in two parts:

– Metadata will be used to identify and extract information from Web sources.
– Ontologies will be used to assist in Web searches, to interpret retrieved information, and to communicate with other agents.

In our scenario, all the information of agents, which are created by JADE, will be translated into an OWL file. Combining the generated auction ontology file with previously defined auction protocol ontology, we can generate an integral Semantic Web Auction system, which is expressed in Semantic Web Languages. Then, this Semantic Web Auction system can be abstracted into CoQ specifications. Wherein FPCC can be used for the verification process.

References

1. Berners-Lee, T., Hendler, J., Lassila, O., et al.: The semantic web. Sci. Am. **284**(5), 28–37 (2001)
2. Necula, G.: Proof-carrying code. In: Proceedings of the 24th ACM SIGPLAN-SIGACT Symposium on Principles of Programming Languages, pp. 106–119. ACM (1997)
3. The Coq Development Team: The coq proof assistant reference manual: Version 8.4 (2012) http://coq.inria.fr

4. Tadjouddine, E.M., Guerin, F.: Verifying dominant strategy equilibria in auctions. In: Burkhard, H.-D., Lindemann, G., Verbrugge, R., Varga, L.Z. (eds.) CEEMAS 2007. LNCS (LNAI), vol. 4696, pp. 288–297. Springer, Heidelberg (2007)
5. Tadjouddine, E., Guerin, F., Vasconcelos, W.: Abstractions for model-checking game-theoretic properties of auctions. In: Proceedings of the 7th International Joint Conference on Autonomous Agents and Multiagent Systems-Volume 3, International Foundation for Autonomous Agents and Multiagent Systems, pp. 1613–1616 (2008)
6. Tadjouddine, E.M.: Computational complexity of some intelligent computing systems. Int. J. Intell. Comput. Cybernetics 4(2), 144–159 (2011)
7. Tip, F.: A survey of program slicing techniques. J. Program. Lang. 3(3), 121–189 (1995)
8. Dolev, S., Panagopoulou, P., Rabie, M., Schiller, E., Spirakis, P.: Rationality authority for provable rational behavior. In: Proceedings of the 30th Annual ACM SIGACT-SIGOPS Symposium on Principles of Distributed Computing, pp. 289–290. ACM (2011)
9. Lapets, A., Levin, A., Parkes, D.: A typed language for truthful one-dimensional mechanism design. Technical report, Computer Science Department, Boston University (2008)
10. Sălcianu, A., Arkoudas, K.: Machine-checkable correctness proofs for intraprocedural dataflow analyses. Electr. Notes Theoret. Comput. Sci. 141(2), 53–68 (2005)
11. Dowek, G., Felty, A., Herbelin, H., Huet, G., Werner, B., Paulin-Mohring, C., et al.: The coq proof assistant user's guide: Version 5.6 (1991)
12. Affeldt, R., Kobayashi, N.: Formalization and Verification of a Mail Server in Coq. In: Okada, M., Pierce, B., Scedrov, A., Tokuda, H., Yonezawa, A. (eds.) ISSS 2002. LNCS, vol. 2609, pp. 217–233. Springer, Heidelberg (2003)
13. Affeldt, R., Kobayashi, N., Yonezawa, A.: Verification of concurrent programs using the coq proof assistant: a case study. IPSJ Digital Courier 1(7), 117–127 (2005)
14. Leroy, X.: Formal verification of a realistic compiler. Commun. ACM 52(7), 107–115 (2009)
15. Gonthier, G.: The four colour theorem: engineering of a formal proof. In: Kapur, D. (ed.) ASCM 2007. LNCS (LNAI), vol. 5081, p. 333. Springer, Heidelberg (2008)
16. Vestergaard, R.: A constructive approach to sequential nash equilibria. Inf. Process. Lett. 97(2), 46–51 (2006)
17. Cousot, P., Cousot, R.: Basic concepts of abstract interpretation. In: Jacquart, R. (ed.) Building the Information Society. IFIP, vol. 156, pp. 359–366. Springer, Heidelberg (2004)
18. Cousot, P., Cousot, R.: Systematic design of program transformation frameworks by abstract interpretation. ACM SIGPLAN Not. 37(1), 178–190 (2002)
19. Barendregt, H.: Lambda calculi with types. In: Abramsky, S., Gabbay, D.M., Maibaum, T.S.E. (eds.) Handbook of Logic in Computer Science, vol. ii. Oxford University Press, Oxford (1992)
20. Appel, A.: Foundational proof-carrying code. In: 16th Annual IEEE Symposium on Logic in Computer Science, Proceedings, pp. 247–256. IEEE (2001)
21. Fudenberg, D., Tirole, J.: Game Theory. MIT Press, Cambridge (1991)
22. Bellifemine, F., Caire, G., Greenwood, D.: Developing Multi-agent Systems with JADE (wiley series in agent technology). Wiley, Chichester (2007)

Towards Verification of Ensemble-Based Component Systems

Jiří Barnat[1], Nikola Beneš[1 (✉)], Tomáš Bureš[2], Ivana Černá[1],
Jaroslav Keznikl[2], and František Plášil[2]

[1] Faculty of Informatics, Masaryk University, Brno, Czech Republic
{xbarnat,xbenes3,cerna}@fi.muni.cz
[2] Faculty of Mathematics and Physics, Charles University in Prague,
Praha, Czech Republic
{bures,keznikl,plasil}@d3s.mff.cuni.cz

Abstract. The relatively new domain of Ensemble-Based Component Systems (EBCS) brings a number of important verification challenges that stem mainly from the dynamism of EBCS. In this paper, we elaborate on our previous work on EBCS verification. In particular, we focus on verification of applications based on the DEECo component model – a representative of EBCS – and evaluate it on a real-life case study. Since our verification technique employs a specialized DEECo semantics to make the verification problem tractable, our goal is to investigate the practical relevance of the properties that can be addressed by the verification. Specifically, we compare the specialized semantics with the realistic general semantics of DEECo to identify verification properties that are preserved by the specialized semantics. We further investigate the tractability of verification of these properties on a real-life case study from the domain of electrical vehicle navigation – one of the key case studies of the EU FP7 project ASCENS.

Keywords: Component-based systems · Component ensembles · Formal verification

1 Introduction

Ensemble-Based Component Systems (EBCS) is a new class of component-based systems, characterized by the fact that the "traditional" component architecture based on explicit bindings is replaced by a composition of components into so-called *ensembles* [6,8]. An ensemble is a first-class concept that addresses the dynamism in software architecture by declaratively capturing the component composition and the corresponding interaction. In particular, this is done by identifying the components to be composed implicitly via a predicate over component states, so that each group of components for which the predicate holds forms an ensemble, and by describing the interaction among the components via a mapping relation among the states of these components. Furthermore, to

J.L. Fiadeiro et al. (Eds.): FACS 2013, LNCS 8348, pp. 41–60, 2014.
DOI: 10.1007/978-3-319-07602-7_5, © Springer International Publishing Switzerland 2014

compensate for the lack of the global system view, the components in EBCS are autonomous entities building on agent-oriented concepts [12] and featuring execution model based on feedback loops (e.g., soft real-time control systems [9]) in order to achieve (self-) adaptive and resilient operation. As an aside, following the agent-oriented paradigm, in EBCS the state of a component is called the component's knowledge. EBCS are thus very appropriate for design and development of highly dynamic autonomous systems that heavily interact with the physical environment – in literature typically termed Cyber-Physical Systems (CPS) [10].

In our previous work, we have introduced a representative of EBCS – the DEECo component model [4,7] (Dependable Emergent Ensembles of Components). In addition to reification of EBCS concepts and language mapping to Java, DEECo comes also with a well-defined semantics [1], which reflects the need for distributed and fully decentralized operation while specifically dealing with components, ensembles, and knowledge. DEECo's semantics is intentionally very general to allow for a number of compliant realizations (i.e., specializations generating strict subsets of traces allowed by the general DEECo semantics) by means of different communication middleware.

The generality of DEECo's semantics however brings about the problems of generating an extensive state space, which is intractable for verification of DEECo-based systems. To alleviate this restriction, we have come up with the Dynamically Communicating Components Language (DCCL) [3] – a specialization of the DEECo's semantics, which by sacrificing some variability in the general DEECo's semantics significantly reduces the state space and thus makes model-checking of DEECo-based applications tractable. Systems described in DCCL can be automatically verified using the explicit-state model checking tool DiVinE [2]. The properties to be verified are to be given as formulae of the Linear Temporal Logic (LTL) [13].

In this paper we evaluate the possibilities of DCCL verification by comparing the general DEECo semantics with DCCL and employing DCCL in a real-life case study from the domain of electrical vehicle navigation which comes from one of our industrial partners in the EU FP7 project ASCENS [11]. In particular, we analyze, which verification properties are preserved by the specialization featured by DCCL and which are not. Thus, we identify classes of properties that may be verified by model checking DCCL-based models. Furthermore, we demonstrate how we employed DCCL for verification of the identified property classes on the case study. Finally, we discuss the scalability limits of the verification by providing estimates of the state space size based on the size of the case study problem.

The rest of the paper is organized as follows. In Sect. 2, we describe the case study and articulate the running example that is used throughout the paper. In Sect. 3, we introduce the main concepts of DEECo and illustrate them on the running example. In Sect. 4 we provide a brief overview of the general DEECo semantics, while describing DCCL in Sect. 5. In Sect. 6, we elaborate on the relation between the general DEECo semantics and DCCL. Consequently, in

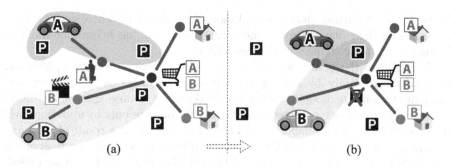

Fig. 1. E-mobility: potential ensembles and their dynamic changes (available parking stations close to respective POIs).

Sect. 7 we demonstrate the DCCL verification on the case study. In Sect. 8 we present a discussion of the experience we have gained while working with the case study. Finally, in Sect. 9 we provide a brief overview of the related work and we conclude the paper in Sect. 10.

2 Case Study

We illustrate the main challenges of EBCS with the help of the electrical vehicle navigation case study – so called e-mobility case study – featured by the ASCENS project, brought to the project by Volkswagen AG [11].

The objective of the e-mobility case study is to coordinate the planning of vehicle journeys in compliance with parking and charging strategies in a highly dynamic and heterogeneous traffic environment, where information is distributed. The case study comprises electric vehicles that have to reach particular Points Of Interest (POIs) within given time constraints. These POIs and their respective constraints are listed in the event calendar of the e-vehicles. E-vehicles are also equipped with sensors of basic capabilities, e.g., monitoring the battery level and energy consumption of the vehicle, but also more sophisticated ones, e.g., monitoring the traffic level along the route. Vehicles can only park and recharge in designated parking spaces and charging lots, organized into parking/charging stations. Vehicles are capable of communicating with each other, as well as parking/charging stations. Such communication is necessary, e.g., in order for a vehicle to obtain the availability of the parking station and potentially reserve a place there. It is important that in this setting no central coordination point is assumed; there is no global control or global planning. Instead, every e-vehicle plans and executes its route individually, based on the data available.

The whole system can be seen as a set of (distributed) nodes, which form ensembles (dynamic communication groups) in order to cooperate on achieving their goal – to allow drivers to arrive at their POIs in time while leveraging the available resources in a close-to-optimal way. This is illustrated in Fig. 1a – each vehicle forms an ensemble with available parking stations close to their respective

POIs. Figure 1b further shows an evolution of the scenario, where vehicles have moved along their planned route and a parking station has become unavailable leading to dynamic changes of the ensembles.

Throughout the paper, we will use a running example that simplifies the e-mobility case study by making the following assumptions: (i) parking and charging stations are modeled together as Parking Lot/Charging Station (PLCS) elements, (ii) vehicles react to changes in the environment only by updating their reserved PLCSs, (iii) availability of PLCSs changes only as a result of reserving a parking place, and (iv) a PLCS will be considered by a vehicle for reservation if it is within a fixed distance to one of the vehicle's POIs. Although simplified, the running example still maintains the important characteristics of the general case study.

We also assume the following conceptual implementation of the running example: (i) each vehicle recurrently aggregates availability information of the relevant PLCSs, e.g., the ones within a fixed distance to one of the vehicle's POIs; (ii) based on this information the vehicle continuously (re-) plans parking/charging periods on a selection of the relevant PLCSs and issues corresponding reservation requests (in the case of re-planning/changes of the selection issues also corresponding cancellation requests); (iii) each PLCS processes its requests and produces confirmations; (iv) having all the reservations confirmed, a vehicle moves towards it's closest destination (while repeating the steps i-iii).

3   DEECo: Key Concepts

Designing a navigation system that targets the case study brings a number of important challenges. In particular: (i) the physical architecture of the system constantly changes as the vehicles/PLCSs might enter/leave the system at any point (e.g., due to low connectivity or physical unavailability); (ii) vehicles and PLCSs have only a partial view over the whole system, according to the information they obtain from components they interact with; and (iii) the trip planning and decision making is decentralized and localized to the vehicles. In this section we illustrate the key concepts of the DEECo component model – a representative of EBCS – on the running example and demonstrate how the challenges listed above are addressed using these concepts. A DEECo-specific implementation of the running example is outlined in Fig. 2 and Fig. 3.

As illustrated in Fig. 2, a component (e.g., lines 7–20) comprises knowledge and processes. Knowledge (lines 8–9) represents the internal data of the component; it can be exposed to the rest of the system via the component's interfaces (e.g., lines 1–2, 7). A process (lines 10–20) is essentially a thread operating upon the component knowledge in a cyclic manner (similar to a feedback loop). For example, Vehicle0123 in Fig. 2 is a component, in which the move process updates the vehicle's next position based on its current position, the route calendar, and the current reservation status. The process is executed periodically every 100 ms. An important restriction of component processes that facilitates autonomy and resilience, is that there is no direct communication (i.e., remote method invocation or message exchange) among components in the system. Each component

```
1   Interface Vehicle:
2       calendar, availabilityList
3
4   Interface PLCS:
5       position, availability
6
7   component Vehicle0123 features Vehicle:
8       knowledge:
9           id, position, calendar, calendarFeasibility, availableParkingLots, reservations, cancellations
10      process computeReservations(In calendar, In availabilityList, Inout reservations, Inout cancellations):
11          function:
12              oldReservations ← reservations
13              reservations ← selectParkingLotsToBeReserved(calendar, availabilityList, oldReservations)
14              cancellations ← determineReservationsToBeCancelled(oldReservations, reservations)
15          scheduling: triggered( changed(availabilityList) )
16      process move(Inout position, In calendar, In reservations)
17          function:
18              if (allPOIsReserved(calendar, reservations))
19                  position ← moveToNextPosition(position, calendar)
20          scheduling: periodic( 100ms )
21          ...
22
23  component PLCS01 features ParkingLot:
24      knowledge:
25          id, position, availability, reservations
26      process processReservations(Inout availability, Inout reservations):
27          function:
28              availability ← reserveFreePlaces(availability, reservations)
29              reservations ← markProcessedReservations(availability, reservations)
30          scheduling: periodic( 2000ms )
31          ...
```

Fig. 2. Example of DEECo components in a DSL

operates solely upon its own knowledge. Nevertheless, a component's knowledge may include it's belief about the knowledge of other components. Updates of this belief are completely externalized into component ensembles, described below.

As illustrated in Fig. 3, an ensemble (e.g., lines 32–40) is a first-class concept that enables dynamic grouping of components and interaction between the components in the group. A component in an ensemble assumes either the role of the unique ensemble coordinator, or the role of one of the potentially multiple members. The role of a component is determined dynamically by the membership condition (lines 35–37) over component interfaces (lines 33–34). For example, PropagateReservationRequests in Fig. 3 is an ensemble, in which a Vehicle and a PLCS form a coordinator-member pair if the Vehicle's reservations include the PLCS. Technically, the run-time platform is responsible for timely evaluation of the condition. As indicated above, the only mechanism for component interaction is updating the interacting components' belief. This is done via the knowledge exchange of an ensemble (lines 38–40). Similar to component processes, knowledge exchange is a cyclic activity that updates the coordinator's belief about the members and vice versa. For example, in PropagateReservationRequests the knowledge exchange updates every 5000 ms the belief of member PLCSs about the relevant reservations of the coordinating Vehicle. Again, the run-time platform is responsible for timely knowledge exchange execution among all components that are in the same ensemble.

```
32  ensemble UpdateAvailabilityInformation:
33      coordinator: Vehicle
34      member: PLCS
35      membership:
36          ∃ poi ∈ coordinator.calendar:
37              distance(member.position, poi.position) ≤ TRESHOLD
38      knowledge exchange:
39          coordinator.availabilityList ← reduce(member.availability)
40      scheduling: periodic( 5000ms )
41
42  ensemble PropagateReservationRequests:
43      coordinator: Vehicle
44      member: PLCS
45      membership:
46          ∃ reservation ∈ coordinator.reservations:
47              reservation.plcsId == member.id ∧ reservation.status == NEW
48      knowledge exchange:
49          member.reservations.add(coordinator.reservations.getNewForPLCS(member.id))
50      scheduling: periodic( 5000ms )
51
52  ensemble PropagateReservationConfirmations:
53      ... // similar to the previous, opposite direction
```

Fig. 3. Example of DEECo ensembles in a DSL

4   General DEECo Semantics

DEECo comes with a well-defined general semantics, which faithfully captures the operation of a DEECo-based application and its run-time platform in real environment by accounting for (a) fully asynchronous, distributed, and decentralized operation of components and ensembles, (b) real-time scheduling, and (c) network specific issues such as communication delays and losses. In this section we describe the general semantics, because it establishes a baseline for verification of DEECo-based applications. Other DEECo semantics aimed at verification (e.g., DCCL) or stemming from implementations of DEECo by employing different communication middleware are further seen as specializations of the general semantics – meaning that they generate only a subset of execution traces permitted by the general semantics.

The general DEECo semantics describes a DEECo-based application as a finite-state non-deterministic automaton, whose states capture the knowledge of the system's components and the transitions correspond to execution of component processes or ensemble knowledge exchange. Note, that although the general DEECo semantics could support infinite knowledge domains, we consider only finite domains. This poses no real limitation, since typical CPS applications are limited in terms of available resources. In particular, we construct the automaton as a Cartesian product of three groups of automata pertaining to: (i) component processes, (ii) knowledge propagation, and (iii) ensemble knowledge exchange.

4.1   Component Processes

A component process is an activity local to a component that atomically reads a subset of the component's knowledge, performs computation on it (possibly performing sensing and actuation), and atomically updates the component's knowledge with the result of the computation. To model this, we associate each process p of each component C with an automaton $A(p)$ – depicted in Fig. 4. The initial state of the automaton is the *idle* state. The transition p_1 corresponds to reading the component knowledge (denoted V_C) into a temporary variable. The transition p_2 reflects both the execution of the process and updating the component's knowledge with the outcome. Such semantics allows for concurrent, asynchronous execution of component processes.

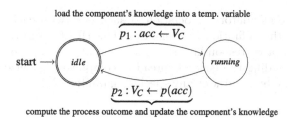

Fig. 4. Component process automaton – $A(p)$

4.2 Knowledge Propagation

As mentioned earlier, components in a DEECo system can only interact via knowledge exchange prescribed by ensemble definitions and realized by the run-time platform. The particulars of distributed communication required to realize knowledge exchange very much depend on the communication middleware used. To keep the execution semantics sufficiently general, we model the distributed communication with relatively few restrictions. In particular, we assume that each component C is associated with an arbitrarily outdated copy of knowledge valuation of any other component C' in the system – the so called C's *view of* C' (denoted as $V_C^{C'}$). Note, that the concept of view is different from belief (the former being a technical means of defining the semantics, the latter expressing the application-specific purpose of a part of component knowledge).

To capture knowledge propagation in terms of updates of component views, we associate a queue $Q_{C_i}^{C_j}$ with each ordered pair of components $C_i, C_j, C_i \neq C_j$, which serves as a communication channel for the knowledge valuations of C_j that are being propagated through the network to become the C_i's view of C_j ($V_{C_i}^{C_j}$). We assume the queue to be an unbounded perfect FIFO queue without errors.

As depicted in Fig. 5, in order to model the actions of knowledge propagation and propagation delays associated with sending and receiving the knowledge valuations over the network, we associate with each queue $Q_{C_i}^{C_j}$ an automaton ($A(Q_{C_i}^{C_j})$). The transition q_1 of this automaton corresponds to sending the knowledge valuation of C_i to C_j in terms of putting it into the queue. In a similar manner, the transition q_2 corresponds to updating C_i's view of C_j ($V_{C_i}^{C_j}$) in terms of retrieving it from the queue.

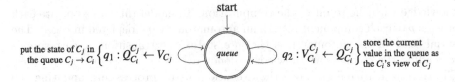

Fig. 5. Knowledge propagation automaton – $A(Q_{C_i}^{C_j})$

Note that the mandatory association of such view with each component is only needed for the definition of semantics. The DEECo run-time framework does not provide a corresponding run-time concept – it only provides a general contract regarding the general spread of component knowledge valuations throughout the system, without any specific guarantees.

4.3   Ensemble Knowledge Exchange

In an ensemble the knowledge exchange takes place always between the coordinator and the members. For the sake of simplicity, in the definition of the semantics, we treat an ensemble as a set of binary relations between a single coordinator and each of the corresponding members.

Note that while the general propagation of knowledge throughout the (distributed) system, modeled via queues, concerns the whole knowledge of the involved components, the ensemble knowledge exchange concerns only certain knowledge fields, specific for the ensemble.

To capture the asynchrony and dependence on knowledge propagation, the knowledge exchange is modeled as a set of component-specific automata locally manipulating the component's knowledge and views.

In particular, as depicted in Fig. 6a, we associate the role of the coordinator (C_i) of an ensemble with an automaton $A_c(E_{C_i}^{C_j})$. Similarly to the process automaton, the process of loading and processing the knowledge is divided into two states – *idle* and *running*, modeling thus asynchronous processing. The transition c_1 corresponds to loading the coordinator's knowledge and it's view of one of the members into temporary variables. The transition c_2 then reflects the storing of the outcome of the knowledge exchange, i.e., the effect of the knowledge transformation T_E associated with the knowledge exchange applied on the temporary variables, in the case the ensemble membership (M_E) holds.

Similarly, we associate the role of a member C_j of the ensemble with an automaton $A_m(E_{C_i}^{C_j})$, as depicted in Fig. 6b. The automaton is very similar to the one in Fig. 6a, with the difference that the member's knowledge and view of the coordinator are interchanged in both T_E and M_E (i.e., C_i and C_j switched the roles in the automaton).

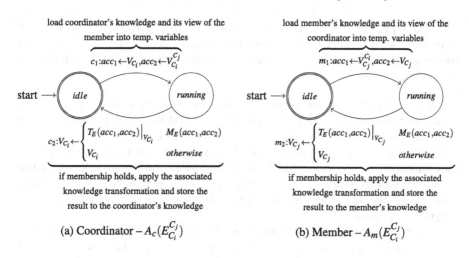

Fig. 6. Ensemble knowledge exchange automaton

4.4   System Semantics

Building on the previously introduced specific automata, we can now define the semantics of a system S consisting of a set of components $\mathbb{C}$, each of which including a set of processes $\mathbb{P}_C$, and a set of ensemble definitions $\mathbb{E}$ via the following automaton:

$$
A(S) = \underbrace{\prod_{C \in \mathbb{C}} \prod_{p \in \mathbb{P}_C} A(p)}_{\substack{\text{processes of all} \\ \text{components}}} \times \underbrace{\prod_{\substack{C_i, C_j \in \mathbb{C} \\ C_i \neq C_j}} A(Q_{C_i}^{C_j})}_{\substack{\text{knowledge propagation} \\ \text{between each two} \\ \text{components}}} \times \underbrace{\prod_{E \in \mathbb{E}} \prod_{\substack{C_i, C_j \in \mathbb{C} \\ C_i \neq C_j}} \left(A_c(E_{C_i}^{C_j}) \times A_m(E_{C_i}^{C_j}) \right)}_{\substack{\text{knowledge exchange between each two} \\ \text{components and for each ensemble}}}
$$

As already indicated in the automaton definition, a system automaton aggregates automata for all the processes of all the components. To capture all the potential ensembles among the components, it also includes a knowledge propagation automaton between each oriented pair of components, as well as both coordinator and member automata for each ensemble definition and each oriented pair of components; i.e., each two components can potentially form a coordinator-member pair of an ensemble. Being completely non-deterministic, the system automaton can also capture system behaviors, that are not realistic w.r.t. real system execution. Therefore, we impose further restrictions on the system automaton in terms of limiting its set of valid execution traces. In particular, as DEECo and EBCS systems in general are soft realtime cyber-physical systems, we focus on realtime properties of the execution traces.

In principle, we allow only those traces of the system automaton that are realistic with respect to a soft-realtime periodic scheduling of the included process/propagation/exchange automata. Namely, we impose the following restrictions:

- Given the duration of the period of a component process, the process has to start and end within each period (i.e., each period the corresponding process automaton has to go from the *idle* to *running* state and back).
- Given the duration of the period and the maximum expected network latency, all knowledge propagation has to be performed within each period with the maximum delay equal to the latency (i.e., each period the corresponding knowledge has to be enqueued, while it is dequeued with a delay at most equal to the latency)
- Similarly to a component process, given the duration of the period, all knowledge exchange has to start and end within each period (i.e., each period all the corresponding coordinator and member automata have to go from the *idle* to *running* state and back).

In a way, these restrictions impose specific "fairness" constraints on the system automaton traces that are brought about by the properties of the run-time platform. Since the technical details are beyond the scope of this paper, we refer an interested reader to [1].

5   DCCL: Semantics Suitable for Verification

Due to the extremely big state space the general DEECo semantics generates, it is not suitable for verification. To accomplish the verification task, we have developed DCCL, which acts as a specialization of the general DEECo semantics that is suitable for LTL model-checking using the model checking tool DiVinE [2].

Compared to the general DEECo semantics, DCCL incorporates certain simplifications to keep the state space reasonably small and the model-checking task thus tractable. In particular, DCCL specializes the general semantics by omitting component views and assuming knowledge propagation to be instant. Furthermore, DCCL restricts the syntactic expressiveness of DEECo in the following way. It allows only one process per component. The set of possible knowledge of a component has to be finite, i.e., we restrict the data of each component to be variables over a finite domain. As already mentioned, this restriction poses no real limitation for typical CPS applications. All processes in the system have to be periodic, synchronously activated and they strictly alternate with knowledge exchange, which is also synchronously activated. We outline the DCCL semantics below, for more details, we refer the reader to [3].

The computation of a DCCL system works in two alternating phases, the *component phase* and the *ensemble phase*. In the component phase, components perform their computation as prescribed by their process description. After the component phase, the system switches to ensemble phase, where the ensemble knowledge exchange is performed. In order to capture various kinds of timing constraints, we provide two different kinds of semantics for the ensemble phase. The first, *fixpoint semantics*, represents a situation in which the knowledge exchange is infinitely faster than the progress of the components' processes, i.e., it takes negligible time. In this semantics, the ensemble phase proceeds as long as there is some knowledge exchange to be done. The second semantics, *timeunit semantics*, is assigned a single number, a time limit ℓ. The ensemble phase then proceeds as in the previous, this time respecting the fact that every component may only take part in as many as ℓ knowledge exchanges.

Formally, we define a labeled transition system $(\Sigma, \mathcal{L}, \rightarrow)$, where Σ is a set of states, $\mathcal{L}$ is a set of labels and $\rightarrow \subseteq \Sigma \times \mathcal{L} \times \Sigma$ is a labeled transition relation. The definition of states depends on the desired semantics. In the fixpoint semantics, a state consists of the knowledge of every component and a marker indicating the current phase.

$$\Sigma_f = K_{C_1} \times \cdots \times K_{C_n} \times \{\mathbf{C}, \mathbf{E}\}$$

In the timeunit semantics, each component includes a time counter whose maximal value is ℓ, the time limit. The ensemble phase marker is also enhanced with a similar counter, called the *round*.

$$\Sigma_\ell = K_{C_1} \times \{0, \ldots, \ell\} \times \cdots \times K_{C_n} \times \{0, \ldots, \ell\} \times (\{\mathbf{C}\} \cup (\{\mathbf{E}\} \times \{1, \ldots, \ell\}))$$

5.1 Component Phase

The progress of the component phase is very straightforward. Each component only possesses a single process and the processes are independent, as they may not touch other components' knowledge. We may thus perform all processes synchronously at once. Formally, whenever σ is a state of our transition system containing the marker $\mathbf{C}$, let σ' denote its modification as follows: All components' knowledge in σ is changed according to the components' processes, the marker is changed to $\mathbf{E}$, and, if the semantics is timeunit, all component time counters as well as the round counter are set to ℓ. We then have the transition $\sigma \xrightarrow{comp} \sigma'$.

5.2 Ensemble Phase

The ensemble phase consists of a number of smaller units, the knowledge exchange steps. Every such step performs the knowledge exchange between one coordinator and one member. The number of steps performed in each ensemble phase depends on the chosen semantics. In a sense, the choice of semantics thus governs the amount of fairness that is provided in the ensemble phase.

Fixpoint Semantics. In the fixpoint semantics, the ensemble phase runs until a fixpoint is reached, i.e., until no more knowledge exchange steps can be performed. Formally, let σ be a state of the transition system containing the ensemble phase marker $\mathbf{E}$. Let us consider all possible combinations of an ensemble

E with membership predicate p and knowledge exchange e, and two components C_i, C_j such that $p(C_i, C_j)$ holds in σ. This means that C_i is currently a coordinator of an ensemble and that C_j is one of its members. For every such triple (E, C_i, C_j), let σ' be the state that is created from σ by changing the knowledge of C_i, C_j according to the knowledge exchange e. We then have the transition $\sigma \xrightarrow{ens(E,C_i,C_j)} \sigma'$. Note that as there might be more triples satisfying the properties above, the evolution of state σ is possibly non-deterministic.

If there is no possible knowledge exchange in the state σ, i.e., no transition from σ has been created according to the above rule, the ensemble phase ends. We represent this by a transition $\sigma \xrightarrow{end} \sigma'$ where σ' is equal to σ with the phase marker changed to $\mathbf{C}$.

Timeunit Semantics. In the timeunit semantics, the number of steps of the ensemble phase is limited with a given number ℓ so that every component takes part in at most ℓ knowledge exchanges during the phase. At the same time, we want to perform as many exchanges as possible. We thus divide the ensemble phase into ℓ rounds, numbered ℓ, $\ell - 1$, ..., 1. In round k, knowledge exchange only occurs if both participants still have k time units left.

Formally, let σ be a state with phase marker $\mathbf{E}$ and its round counter set to k. Let (E, C_i, C_j) satisfy the same property as in the previous semantics with the additional constraint that the time counters of both C_i and C_j are set to k. For every such triple, let σ' be the state that is created from σ by changing the knowledge of C_i, C_j and lowering their time counters to $k - 1$. We then have the transition $\sigma \xrightarrow{ens_k(E,C_i,C_j)} \sigma'$.

Again, if there is no possible exchange in the state σ, the round ends. If $k > 1$, the next round starts. The state σ' is created from σ by changing the round counter, as well as all time counters that have still k units left, to $k - 1$ and we have the transition $\sigma \xrightarrow{round} \sigma'$. If $k = 1$, the ensemble phase ends. The state σ' is created from σ by changing all time counters to zero and changing the phase marker to $\mathbf{C}$. We then have $\sigma \xrightarrow{end} \sigma'$.

6   Relation of DCCL to the General DEECo Semantics

Since DCCL is a simplification of the general DEECo semantics (e.g., while in DEECo processes are fully parallel, in DCCL they are executed synchronously), it is natural that model-checking of a DCCL-based system cannot verify all potential properties that could be expressed over the traces of the general semantics. In this section we thus discuss the relation of the general DEECo semantics and DCCL with respect to analyzable properties. In particular, we identify (i) properties which have equivalent validity under DCCL and general semantics, and (ii) properties which do no have equivalent validity (i.e., they pertain to aspects of the general semantics that are abstracted away by DCCL).

Note also that DCCL is a specialization of the general semantics, which means that DCCL semantics cannot introduce a trace the equivalent of which could not be produced by the general DEECo semantics. (Here, we consider two traces equivalent if they entail the same sequence of knowledge updates.) This means that violation of a property under DCCL implies violation of an equivalent property under the general semantics.

6.1 Realistic Properties That Can Be Verified via DCCL

Based on LTL model-checking procedure [13], we can essentially verify the traditional properties such as safety or liveness for a DCCL-based system, where we consider the model to be an implementation of the system in the DCCL language. Specifically, in our approach the atomic propositions of LTL specification range over component knowledge valuations. In the following, we discuss in more details a classification of properties specific to DEECo concepts that can be verified for DCCL-based models.

Correctness of process execution (P1). Since DCCL explicitly represents the state of a component's knowledge before and after process execution, we can effectively exploit the LTL property checking to verify correctness of the process execution. This is naturally an important concern in DEECo.

Correctness of component interaction protocols (P2). Building on (P1), we can also verify execution of a sequence of component processes and knowledge exchange. This enables us to verify correctness of interaction protocols between components (embodied by the sequence). In DEECo, due to the specifics of the development cycle [4], the correctness of interaction is an important concern as both component processes and ensemble knowledge exchange are developed in isolation and the component interfaces do not provide enough semantic information.

Resilience w.r.t. knowledge inconsistency (P3). In this case, we want to verify that a given system is resilient w.r.t. knowledge inconsistency caused by parallelism of knowledge exchange/component processes (i.e., a component receives up-to-date information from one component while receiving stale information from another, because at the time the information was sent the other component's process has not yet produced the new information). Also, the inconsistencies can be introduced due to variable communication delays. This is an important concern under the general DEECo semantics, since the semantics allows complete parallelism of processes and knowledge exchange (limited only by the realtime constraints) and it imposes little constraints on the communication delays. Although in general the DCCL semantics does not implicitly account for such parallelism/delays, in order to reduce the complexity of a model and its verification, it is possible to capture the parallelism/delays in DCCL explicitly. Specifically, this is done by enabling an execution of a process/knowledge exchange to be non-deterministically skipped, while enforcing fairness (i.e., delayed for a finite number of periods). Technically, this can be done by introducing a specific flag into the relevant components' knowledge and defining an "artificial" ensemble, that manipulates the flag. The other ensembles/processes have to be then modified in such a way, that they will do nothing if the flag is set. The non-deterministic interleaving of knowledge exchange during ensemble phase will then yield two branches (depending, whether the artificial ensemble was evaluated before the others), one where the flag has been set and the corresponding original ensembles/processes did not have any effect (i.e., was delayed), and one where the ensembles/processes proceeded as before, thus simulating non-deterministic delays.

Communication-boundedness of interaction protocols (P4). Building on the timed semantics of DCCL, we can verify whether a particular interaction is communication-bounded – i.e., whether its correctness depends on a particular communication speed. Specifically, we can verify that the system will manifest erroneous behavior if the time limit of the timeunit semantics is too low, while otherwise behaving correctly. Such a situation is realistic w.r.t. the general DEECo semantics, since the semantics does not provide any specific guarantees for the knowledge propagation and network latency. This concern can be critical for certain application that require a high-level of safety and dependability (i.e., some behavior should be correct under arbitrary communication conditions).

6.2   Realistic Properties That Cannot Be Verified via DCCL

Properties related to parallelism of processes and knowledge exchange. Being virtually synchronous, the DCCL semantics does not explicitly allow to verify properties based on parallelism of processes and knowledge exchange, such as race conditions (as allowed by the DEECo semantics). To partially remedy this problem, we can modify the DCCL model so that an execution of a process/knowledge exchange can be non-deterministically skipped, which is the case of (P3). Nevertheless, this still does not reflect complete parallelism.

Properties related to real time. Expanding on the previous point, the DCCL semantics does not allow verification of properties related to real time execution, such as that the periods of processes and knowledge propagation/exchange that have mutual knowledge dependencies are set up correctly, i.e., so that they together provide a satisfactory end-to-end response time. Similar to the previous case, DCCL allows only for a partial solution based on a simple discretization of time, which is the case of (P4).

7   Modeling the Case Study

In order to evaluate DCCL w.r.t. verification of realistic DEECo properties (Sect. 6.1), we have fully modeled the running example presented in Sect. 2, while following the implementation outlined in Sect. 3. Note that the running example retains many important challenges of the realistic, industry-relevant case study, rather than being a mere experimental setting.

Naturally, DCCL introduces a large amount of abstraction w.r.t. the original system behavior. For instance, the time intervals of parking reservations have been discretized into a finite set of time "slots". Similarly, we have also discretized the geographic positions and distance. Moreover, the model includes only a simple and fully deterministic implementation of algorithms for planning vehicle routes, deciding PLCSs for parking, as well as for assigning parking places to vehicles.

To gain a better insight in the impact of concurrency in knowledge exchange, we have modeled two different variants of knowledge exchange of parking requests in the corresponding ensembles. Specifically, these variants are concerned with ordering of the requests coming from multiple parties concurrently. In the first variant, which we will call "standard", the requests are ordered based on their content, thus eliminating the impact of concurrency. In the second variant, which we will call "first-come-first-served", the requests are ordered according to the order in which knowledge exchange was executed, thus emulating the first come first served semantics of message queues.

Note that although we always select particular components/PLCSs in the following examples, in our experiments all the vehicles/PLCSs were symmetric so that the selection of a particular one does not corrupt the generality of the example.

7.1 Verification of Realistic Properties on the Case Study

To illustrate the potential of verifying realistic properties using DCCL on the case study, we have formulated and verified at least one property of each class identified in Sect. 6.1.

Correctness of process execution (P1). As an instance of a (P1) property, we have checked that the process of PLCS, assigning parking places to vehicles, is correct. We have done it by verifying that a PLCS never assigns a single parking space to two vehicles for the same time slot. This property can be expressed via the following LTL formula: G(!v0_assigned_the_same_place_as_v1). The atomic proposition v0_assigned_the_same_place_as_v1 checks in a straightforward way the knowledge of each PLCS, its buffer storing the processed reservation requests in particular, whether the two vehicles (i.e., 0 and 1) have been assigned the same parking place. As an aside, using this property we have been able to localize an error in the parking-place-assignment process of PLCS, which was based on not marking a parking place as occupied after assigning it to a vehicle, and thus assigning it twice.

Correctness of component interaction protocols (P2). As for the (P2) property class, we have verified that whenever a vehicle creates a reservation request, the vehicle gets eventually notified about confirmation or rejection of the request by the corresponding PLCS. This is expressed by the formula G(v0_requests_p0 -> (v0_requests_p0 U v0_request_to_p0_decided)) (again, for convenience we have used a fixed pair vehicle-PLCS). Here, v0_requests_p0 is true whenever the vehicle 0 contains a new parking request for PLCS 0, while v0_request_to_p0_decided is true whenever the vehicle knows the decision of PLCS

0 on its request (be it either confirmation or rejection). Both atomic propositions are simple checks on the knowledge of vehicle 0. This property was verified under the assumption that a PLCS's knowledge can accommodate requests of all relevant Vehicles. Recall that each Vehicle produces a single request for each of its calendar events and waits for the decision.

Resilience w.r.t. interaction inconsistency/delays (P3). Using a (P3) property, we have verified that the system is resilient w.r.t. inconsistency of PLCS-availability information in a vehicle. Specifically, we have done it by verifying the property that a vehicle's reservations are always valid even if its PLCS-availability information is inconsistent due to delays in communication. This is done by verifying the formula G(v0_has_confirmation_for_p0_t0 -> p0_blocks_place_for_v0_t0) in a modified model where the exchange of PLCS availability can be non-deterministically delayed for one ensemble phase. Here, v0_has_confirmation_for_p0_t0 is true whenever vehicle 0 has a confirmed reservation of a place on PLCS 0 for the time slot 0, while p0_blocks_place_for_v0_t0 is true whenever PLCS 0 blocks a parking place for vehicle 0 for the same time slot. Both atomic propositions are simple checks over the corresponding vehicle/PLCS knowledge. The non-determinism is implemented as indicated in Sect. 6.

Communication-boundedness of interaction protocols (P4). As to the class (P4), we have tried to assess the communication-boundedness of the reservation request interaction protocol. For this, we have exploited the property that we have used to illustrate (P2) – G(v0_requests_p0 -> (v0_requests_p0 U v0_request_to_p0_decided)). Under the timeunit semantics, since it limits the number of interactions allowed in a single ensemble phase, the property will not longer hold (for sufficiently small time limits). Thus the interaction protocol concerned with exchanging parking reservation requests is communication bounded. Knowing this, we could improve the design of the vehicle component so that it is resilient w.r.t. this situation. Technically, we have done it by keeping the vehicle idle until it receives a confirmed reservation for all its requests. Note that for example the PLCS-availability exchange protocol is not communication-bounded, as the vehicle does not distinguish whether the availability information is missing because the PLCS is not relevant to any of its POIs or whether it just did not get through due to slow communication.

7.2 Scalability Evaluation

To evaluate the scalability of DCCL w.r.t. the case study, we have measured the size of the state space for different configurations of the case study (i.e., different numbers and initial states of vehicles/PLCSs). Specifically, to obtain comparable results, the configurations enforce the maximum amount of successful interaction expected for the given number of components (i.e., without parking request conflicts).

The scalability of DCCL is illustrated in Fig. 7. As expected, the number of states grows exponentially w.r.t. the number of components in the system. The curve of growth is relatively steep, however, this is acceptable given the complexity of the case study and therefore also the corresponding model. Naturally, the

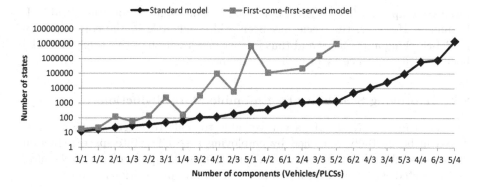

Fig. 7. Scalability of DCCL w.r.t. the case study

first-come-first-served variant of knowledge exchange scales much worse than the standard variant, since it generates much more states at the end of each ensemble phase (capturing different permutations of requests exchanged during the phase). In a similar way, the same configurations yielded a much bigger state space under the timeunit semantics, since the time-constrained prefixes of knowledge exchange sequences produced a lot more different states at the end of each ensemble phase. Since the size of the state space depends on the time limit in a complex way, we have not included this variant in the figure.

8   Discussion

8.1   Lessons Learned

A major asset of our approach to verification of DEECo-based applications is that DCCL is based on the DiVinE model checker, which is a mature, reliable, and well-performing tool with solid supporting infrastructure. This helped especially when verifying a large model including non-trivial behavior, such as the one modeling the case study.

Our experiments show that even after introducing relatively significant simplifications to the execution model (such as synchronous alternation of component/ensemble phases, unlimited time for knowledge exchange under the fixpoint semantics), it is still possible to maintain a rich set of verifiable properties. Specifically, this observation appears to apply not only to DEECo-based systems, but also to EBCS and even cyber-physical systems in general, since they share common basic characteristics. Nevertheless, there are still some aspects of DCCL, such as no explicit support for non-determinism in component processes/knowledge exchange, that introduce unnecessary complexity and thus could be targeted in the future work.

Finally, we argue that when modeling non-trivial examples, the organization of data within the model has a significant impact both on the size of the state space (e.g., fixed index assignment vs. first-come-first-served), as well as in terms of complexity (e.g., regarding formulation of atomic propositions and LTL formulae). However, this issue has been addressed little in the contemporary model-checking approaches and thus further investigation of this topic would be beneficial (for instance by providing guidelines).

8.2 Improving Scalability by Ensemble State Reduction

As shown in Sect. 7, DCCL is not yet able to scale to bigger configurations. This can be partially remedied by employing a specific state-space reduction during ensemble phase. In particular, since none of the properties that we have experimented with relied on a valuation of atomic propositions in an internal ensemble-phase state (i.e., a state that has transitions only from/to states in the same ensemble phase), it should be possible to reduce the state space by eliminating these internal ensemble-phase states. Technically, this can be done by discarding the internal states at the end of each ensemble phase, after all the final states of the phase have been generated.

Nevertheless, as also shown in Sect. 7, the current level of scale still suffices to verify important realistic properties of a modeled system. Also, as supported by our experiments, arguably a large number of important property violations can be detected early, on a reasonably small configuration.

9   Related Work

As to the general domain of EBCS, we are currently not aware of any other approach that would be directly related to DEECo and DCCL. However, there is a number of approaches targeting similar domains; i.e., similar to CPS.

Closest to the area of EBCS, SCEL [8] is targeting a formalization of the semantics of attribute-based communication (i.e., the key concept behind EBCS ensembles) in the domain of formal coordination languages, with the future intention of exploiting the formal semantics for analysis and verification, as well as evaluation on an extensive case study.

When considering the broader domain of real-time embedded systems, which share a number of aspects of CPS, there exists a number of approaches for verification of safety and timing properties. These include well-established languages such as AADL[1], EAST-ADL[2], and VERDE/MARTE[3], which come with a number of related tools (e.g., COMPASS[4]) mainly focusing on timing and dependability analysis, or CHESS[5] methodology and toolset mainly focusing on timing, failure propagation and dependability analysis. The closest to our model-checking of EBCS is the approach of OTHELLO/OCRA [5], which allows for

---

[1] http://www.aadl.info
[2] http://www.east-adl.info
[3] http://www.itea-verde.org
[4] http://compass.informatik.rwth-aachen.de
[5] http://www.chess-project.org

checking of refinement of contracts expressed in a variant of linear-time temporal logics interpreted over hybrid traces (i.e., traces that contain both discrete events and continuous-time state evolution). Although all these approaches and tools target a closely related domain to DCCL, they require a significant shift from the EBCS concepts, thus increasing the effort required for modeling and reducing the value of the verification results.

Our technique of model checking DCCL is built on top of the parallel and distributed explicit-state model checker DiVinE [2]. DiVinE primarily offers the verification of LTL properties by means of the automata-based LTL model checking [13]. DiVinE accepts various input formats, one of them being the binary Common Explicit-State Model Interface (CESMI), which we use for DCCL verification. The translation of a DCCL input file into a CESMI-compliant module is provided via our tool `dccl2cesmi`[6].

10 Conclusion

In this paper, we have discussed the verification possibilities of the DEECo component model, a representative of Ensemble-Based Component Systems (EBCS). In order to make the verification task feasible, we have designed a syntactic and semantic specialization of DEECo called DCCL, verification of which is based on an explicit-state model checker – DiVinE. We have further evaluated the possibilities of DCCL verification on a real-life case study and we have discussed its limitations.

In the future, we would like to focus on two areas. One is that of further extending DCCL to capture more relevant aspects of DEECo, e.g., introducing specific data structures for knowledge-exchange-related tasks. The other area is then that of reducing the state space. DiVinE itself performs certain generic reductions, such as partial order reduction. However, we want to try reductions that are specific to DCCL, such as some kind of symmetry reduction or the reduction of the ensemble steps. In a more distant future, we would like to extend the DCCL verification with quantitative aspect such as probability or precise timing constraints.

Acknowledgments. This work has been supported by the Czech Science Foundation grant project no. P202/11/0312.

References

1. Al Ali, R., Bures, T., Gerostathopoulos, I., Hnetynka, P., Keznikl, J., Kit, M., Plasil, F.: DEECo computational model-I., Technical Report D3S-TR-2013-01, D3S, Charles University in Prague. http://d3s.mff.cuni.cz/publications (2013)
2. Barnat, J., et al.: DiVinE 3.0 – an explicit-state model checker for multithreaded C & C++ programs. In: Sharygina, N., Veith, H. (eds.) CAV 2013. LNCS, vol. 8044, pp. 863–868. Springer, Heidelberg (2013)

---

[6] http://paradise.fi.muni.cz/dccl/

3. Barnat, J., Beneš, N., Černá, I., Petruchová, Z.: DCCL: verification of component systems with ensembles. In: Proceedings of CBSE '13. pp. 43–52. ACM, New York (2013)
4. Bures, T., et al.: DEECo - an ensemble-based component system. In: Proceedings of CBSE '13. ACM, New York (2013)
5. Cimatti, A., Tonetta, S.: A property-based proof system for contract-based design. In: Proceedings of SEAA 2012. IEEE CS, Los Alamitos (2012)
6. Hölzl, M., Rauschmayer, A., Wirsing, M.: Engineering of software-intensive systems: state of the art and research challenges. In: Wirsing, M., Banâtre, J.-P., Hölzl, M., Rauschmayer, A. (eds.) SoftWare-Intensive Systems. LNCS, vol. 5380, pp. 1–44. Springer, Heidelberg (2008)
7. Keznikl, J., et al.: Towards dependable emergent ensembles of components: the DEECo component model. In: Proceedings of WICSA/ECSA'12. IEEE (2012)
8. De Nicola, R., Ferrari, G., Loreti, M., Pugliese, R.: A Language-Based Approach to Autonomic Computing. In: Beckert, B., Bonsangue, M.M. (eds.) FMCO 2011. LNCS, vol. 7542, pp. 25–48. Springer, Heidelberg (2012)
9. Patikirikorala, T., Colman, A., Han, J., Wang, L.: A systematic survey on the design of self-adaptive software systems using control engineering approaches. In: Proceedings of SEAMS 2012 (2012)
10. Rajkumar, R.R., Lee, I., Sha, L., Stankovic, J.: Cyber-physical systems: the next computing revolution. In: Proceedings of DAC'10. pp. 731–736. ACM, New York (2010)
11. Serbedzija, N., Reiter, S., Ahrens, M., Velasco, J., Pinciroli, C., Hoch, N., Werther, B.: Requirement specification and scenario description of the ascens case studies (2011), deliverable D7.1. http://www.ascens-ist.eu/deliverables
12. Shoham, Y., Leyton-Brown, K.: Multiagent Systems: Algorithmic, Game-theoretic, and Logical Foundations. Cambridge University Press, Cambridge (2009)
13. Vardi, M., Wolper, P.: An automata-theoretic approach to automatic program verification (preliminary report). In: Proceedings, Symposium on Logic in Computer Science (LICS'86), pp. 332–344. IEEE Computer Society (1986)

Hierarchical Scheduling Framework Based on Compositional Analysis Using Uppaal

Abdeldjalil Boudjadar[(✉)], Alexandre David, Jin Hyun Kim, Kim G. Larsen,
Marius Mikučionis, Ulrik Nyman, and Arne Skou

Computer Science, Aalborg University, Aalborg, Denmark
jalil@cs.aau.dk

Abstract. This paper introduces a reconfigurable compositional scheduling framework, in which the hierarchical structure, the scheduling policies, the concrete task behavior and the shared resources can all be reconfigured. The behavior of each periodic preemptive task is given as a list of timed actions, which are some of the inputs for the parameterized timed automata that make up the framework. Components may have different scheduling policies, and each component is analyzed independently using UPPAAL. We have applied our framework for the schedulability analysis of an avionics system.

1 Introduction

Embedded systems are involved in many applications, software systems in cars and planes, on which our lives depend. Ensuring the continually correct operation of such systems is an essential task. Avionics and automotive systems consist of both safety-critical and non safety-critical features, which are implemented in components that might share resources (e.g. processors). Resource utilization is still an issue for safety-critical systems, and thus it is important to have both an efficient and reliable scheduling policy for the individual parts of the system. Scheduling is a widely used mechanism for guaranteeing that the different components of a system will be provided with the correct amount of resources. In this paper, we propose a model-based approach for analyzing the schedulability of hierarchical scheduling systems. In fact, our framework is implemented using parameterized timed automata models.

A hierarchical scheduling system consists of a finite set of components, a scheduling policy and (global) resources. Each component, in turn, is the parallel composition of a finite set of entities which are either tasks or other components together with a scheduling policy to manage the component workload. One can remark that we do not consider component local resources. System tasks are instances of the same timed automaton with different input parameters. A special parameter of the task model is a list of timed actions [5], specifying the concrete

---

The research presented in this paper has been partially supported by EU Artemis Projects CRAFTERS and MBAT.

J.L. Fiadeiro et al. (Eds.): FACS 2013, LNCS 8348, pp. 61–78, 2014.
DOI: 10.1007/978-3-319-07602-7_6, © Springer International Publishing Switzerland 2014

behavior of the given task. This list includes abstract computation steps, locking and unlocking resources. Thanks to the parameterization, the framework can easily be instantiated for a specific hierarchical scheduling application. Similarly, each scheduling policy (e.g. EDF: Earliest Deadline First, FPS: Fixed Priority Scheduling, RM: Rate Monotonic) is separately modeled and can be instantiated for any component.

Compositional analysis has been introduced [4,10], as a key model-checking technology, to deal with state space explosion caused be the parallel composition of components. We are applying compositional verification to the domain of schedulability analysis.

We analyze the model in a compositional manner, the schedulability of each component including the top level, is analyzed together with the interface specifications of the level directly below it. In this analysis, we non-deterministically supply the required resources of each component, i.e. each component is guaranteed to be provided its required resources for each period. This fact is viewed by the component entities as a contract by which the component is obliged to supply the required resources, provided by the component parent level, to its sub entities for each period. The main contribution of the paper is combining:

- *a compositional analysis approach* where the schedulability of a system relies on the recursive schedulability analysis of its individual subsystems.
- *a reconfigurable schedulability framework* where a system structure can be instantiated in different configurations to fit different applications.
- *modeling of concrete task behavior* as a sequence of timed actions requiring CPU and resources.

The rest of the paper is structured as follows: Sect. 2 introduces related work. Section 3 is an informal description of the main contribution using a running example. The section gives an overview of both modeling hierarchical scheduling systems and how we perform the schedulability analysis in a compositional way. In Sect. 4, we give the UPPAAL model of our framework where we consider concrete behavior of tasks. Moreover, we show how the compositional analysis can be applied on the model using the UPPAAL and UPPAAL SMC verification engines. Section 5 shows the applicability of our framework, where we analyze the schedulability of an avionics system. Finally, Sect. 6 concludes our paper and outlines the future work.

2   Related Work

Hierarchical scheduling systems were introduced in [7,9]. An analytical compositional framework for hierarchical scheduling systems was presented in [12] as a formal way to elaborate a compositional approach for schedulability analysis of hierarchical scheduling systems [13]. In the same way, the authors of [11] dealt with a hierarchical scheduling framework for multiprocessors based on cluster-based scheduling. They used analytical methods to perform analysis, however both approaches [11,12] have difficulty in dealing with complicated behavior of tasks.

Recent research within schedulability analysis increasingly uses model-based approaches, because this allows for modeling more complicated behavior of systems. The rest of the related work presented in this section focuses on model-based approaches.

In [2], the authors analyzed the schedulability of hierarchical scheduling systems, using a model-based approach with the TIMES tool [1], and implemented their model in VxWorks [2]. They constructed an abstract task model as well as scheduling algorithms, where the schedulability analysis of a component does not only consider the timing attributes of that component but also the timing attributes of the other components that can preempt the execution of the component under analysis.

In [5], the authors introduced a model-based framework using UPPAAL for the schedulability analysis of flat systems. They modeled the concrete task behavior as a sequence of timed actions, each one represents a command that uses processing and system resources and consumes time.

The authors of [3] provided a compositional framework for the verification of hierarchical scheduling systems using a model-based approach. They specified the system behavior in terms of preemptive time Petri nets and analyzed the system schedulability using different scheduling policies.

We combine and extend these approaches [3,5] by considering hierarchy, resource sharing and concrete task behavior, while analyzing hierarchical scheduling systems in a compositional way. Moreover, our model can easily be reconfigured to fit any specific application. Comparing our model-based approach to analytical ones, our framework enables to describe more complicated and concrete systems.

3   Compositional Scheduling Framework

A hierarchical scheduling system consists of multiple scheduling systems in a hierarchical structure. It can be represented as a tree of nodes, where each node in the system is equipped with a scheduler for scheduling its child components.

In this paper, we structure our system model as a set of hierarchical components. Each component, in turn, is the parallel composition of a set of entities (components or tasks) together with a local scheduler and possible local resources. A parent component treats the real-time interface of each one of its child components as a single task with the given real-time interface. The component supplies its child entities with resource allocation according to their real-time interfaces. Namely, each component is parameterized by a period (prd), a budget (budget) specifying the execution time that the component should be provided by its parent level, and a scheduling policy (s) specifying resource allocations that are provided by the component to its child entities. The analysis of a component (scheduling unit) consists of checking that its child entities can be scheduled within the component budget according to the component scheduling policy. A component can be also parameterized by a set of typed resources (R) which serve as component local resources. An example of a hierarchical scheduling system is depicted in Fig. 1.

Tasks represent the concrete behavior of the system. They are parameterized with period (prd), execution time (e), deadline (d), priority (prio) and preemption (p). The execution time (e) specifies the CPU usage time required by the task execution for each period (prd). Deadline parameter (d) represents the latest point in time that the task execution should be done before. The parameter prio specifies the user priority associated to the task. Finally, p is a Boolean flag stating whether or not the task is preemptive.

The task behavior is a sequence of timed actions consuming CPU time and resources. Moreover, task and component parameters prd, budget and e can be single values or time intervals.

3.1 Motivating Example

In this section and throughout the paper, we present the running example shown in Fig. 1 to illustrate our system model of hierarchical scheduling systems, and show the compositional analysis we claim. For the sake of simplicity, we omit some parameters like priorities and resources and only consider single parameter values instead of time intervals.

In this example, the top level System schedules Component1, Component2 with the EDF scheduling algorithm. The components are viewed by the top level System as tasks having timing requirements. Component1, respectively Component2, has the interface (100, 37), respectively (70, 25), as period and execution time. The system shown through this example is schedulable if each component, including the top level, is schedulable. Thus, for the given timing requirements Component1 and Component2 should be schedulable by the top level System according to the EDF scheduling policy. The tasks task1 and task2 should be schedulable, with respect to the timing requirement of Component1 (100, 37), also under the EDF scheduling policy. Similarly, task3, task4 and task5 should be schedulable, with respect to the timing requirements of Component2, under

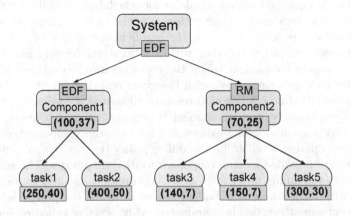

Fig. 1. Example of hierarchical scheduling system.

the RM scheduling policy. The next section presents the compositional analysis of the schedulability of our example.

For a given system structure, we can have many different system configurations. A system configuration consists of an instantiation of the model where each parameter has a specific value. Figure 1 shows one such instantiation.

3.2   Our Analysis Approach

In order to design a framework that scales well for the analysis of larger hierarchical scheduling systems, we have decided to use a compositional approach. Figure 2 shows how the scheduling system, depicted in Fig. 1, is analyzed using three independent analysis steps. These steps can be performed in any order.

The schedulability of each component, including the top level, is analyzed together with the interface specifications of the level directly below it. Accordingly, we will never analyze the whole hierarchy at once. In Fig. 2, the analysis process A consists of checking whether the two components Component1 and Component2 are schedulable under the scheduling policy EDF. In this analysis step, we only consider the interfaces of components in the form of their execution-time (budget) and period, so that we consider the component as an abstract task when performing the schedulability analysis of the level above it. In this way, we consider the *component-composition* problem similarly to [13] but using a non-deterministic supplier model for the interfaces. When performing an analysis step like A1, the resource supplier is not part of the analysis. In order to handle this, we add a non-deterministic supplier to the model. The supplier will guarantee to provide the amount of execution time, specified in the interface of Component1, before the end of the component period. We check all possible ways in which the resources can be supplied to the subsystem in A1. The supplier of each component provides resources to the child entities of that

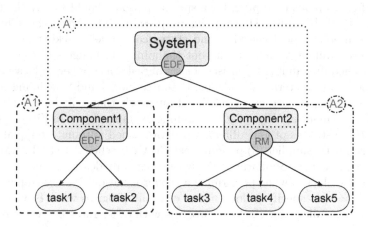

EDF, RM: scheduling policies. A, A1, A2: analysis processes.

Fig. 2. Compositional analysis

component in a non-deterministic way. During the analysis of A1, the supplier non-deterministically decides to start or stop supplying, while still guaranteeing to provide the required amount to its sub entities before the end of the period. The analysis A2 is performed in the same way as A1.

Our compositional analysis approach results in an over-approximation i.e. when performing the analysis of a subsystem, we over-approximate the behavior of the rest of the system. This can result in specific hierarchical scheduling systems that could be schedulable if one considers the entire system at once, but that is not schedulable using our compositional approach. We consider this fact as a design choice which ensures separation of concerns, meaning that small changes to one part of the system does not effect the behavior of other components. In this way, the design of the system is more stable which in turn leads to predictable system behavior. This over-approximation, which is used as a design choice, should not be confused with the over-approximation used in the verification algorithm inside the UPPAAL verification engine (Sect. 4.4). The result can either be *true (false)* or *maybe-not (maybe)*, in the case of *true (false)* the result of the analysis is conclusive and exact.

Thanks to the parameterization of system entities; scheduling policies, preemptiveness, execution times, periods and budgets can all easily be changed. In order to estimate the performance and schedulability of our running example, we have evaluated a number of different configurations of the system. This allows us to choose the best of the evaluated configurations of the system.

4   Modeling and Analysis Using UPPAAL

The purpose of modeling and analyzing hierarchical scheduling systems is to check whether the tasks nested in each component are schedulable, with respect to resource constraints given by the component. This means that the minimum budget of a component supplier, for a specific period, should satisfy the timing requirements of the child tasks. For this purpose, we consider a scheduling unit and use symbolic model checking and statistical model checking methods to check the schedulability, and to find out the minimum budgets of components. In fact, a scheduling unit [13] consists of a set of tasks, a supplier and a scheduler, in [13] known by the terms Workloads, Resource model and Scheduling policy.

This section presents our modeling framework that will be used for the schedulability analysis. We revisit the running example shown in Fig. 1, which is built on the instances of four different UPPAAL timed automata templates: (1) non-deterministic supplier (2) periodic task (3) CPU scheduler (EDF, RM), and (4) resource manager. Similarly to [5], we also use broadcast channels where no sender can be blocked when performing a synchronization. We use stop watches, writing $x' == e$ to specify a clock x that can only progress when e evaluates to 1. UPPAAL also allows for clocks to progress with other rates but we only use 0 and 1.

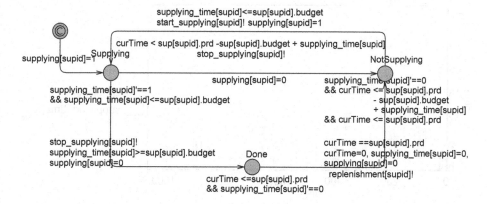

Fig. 3. Non-deterministic supplier template

4.1 Non-Deterministic Supplier Model

In this section, we present some arguments for why it makes sense to use a non-deterministic supplier model in our compositional analysis. The hierarchical scheduling system structure is a set of scheduling components, each one includes a single specific scheduling algorithm and a set of entities (tasks or components). To analyze a single component by means of a compositional manner, it is necessary to consider the interrupted behavior of that component by the other concurrent components within the same system. However, it is hard to capture the interrupting behavior of the other components that influence the component under analysis. For this reason, we introduced a non-deterministic supplier to model all scenarios that the component under analysis can run. Such a non-deterministic fact simulates the influence of the other system components on the execution of the component under analysis.

As mentioned earlier, the non-deterministic supplier is a resource model that provides resources to the component. The scheduling policy within the component then allocates the resources to tasks. It also abstracts the possibility that a task from another part of the system (not part of the current analysis step) could preempt the execution of tasks of the current component.

Figure 3 depicts the UPPAAL template model of the non-deterministic supplier. In fact, the non-deterministic supplier assigns a resource, denoted by rid, to a set of tasks characterized by the timing attributes given in Listing 1.1.

Listing 1.1. Component interface

```
typedef struct {
    time_t          prd;
    time_t          budget;
    tid_t           task_arr[tid_t];
} sup_t;
```

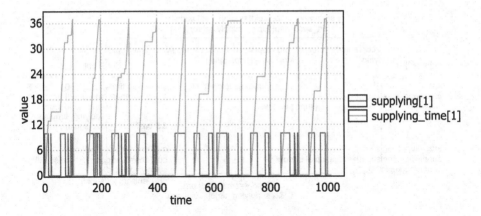

Fig. 4. Supplier's behavior

A resource rid can represent a processing unit (CPU) or a any other system resource, represented in the model by a semaphore. prd is a period and budget is the amount of resources to be provided. The supplier assigns the budget amount of resources to tasks in task_arr[tid_t]. In this model, supplying_time[supid] (supid is the supplier identifier) represents the duration when the supplier provides a resource. start_supplying[supid] and stop_supplying[supid] are broadcast channels that notify tasks of the beginning and completion of the resource supply. curTime denotes the time elapsed since the beginning of the supplier's resource supplying. supplying[supid] contains the supplier's status, 0 (not supplying) or 1 (supplying).

Figure 4 shows one particular resource supply pattern of Component1. supplying_time[1] is increasing while the supplier is providing resources. supplying_time[1] has a long wait while the supplier provides no resource. supplying[1] indicates whether the supplier provides resources or not. Figure 4 shows a nondeterministic supply, in which the values of supplying[1] are irregular in behavior. The amount of resource supplied to tasks can be monitored from the supplying_time[1], which for each period supplies the exact amount of resource, 37 time units, given in the timing interface for Component1.

The supplier provides a resource at the location Supplying (Fig. 3). The transitions between Supplying and NotSupplying are non-deterministically taken until the budget is fulfilled $(supplying\_time[supid] <= sup[supid].budget)$, or the remaining time is equal to the remaining amount of resource to be provided $(curtime <= sup[supid].prd - sup[supid].budget + supplying\_time[supid])$. The supplier stays at the location Supplying to provide the remaining amount of resource when the budget of the supplier is not fully provided, and the remaining time is equal to the remaining amount of resource to be provided.

4.2   Task Model

We only consider a finite set of tasks and refer to them as $T = t_1, t_2, \ldots, t_n$. Each task is defined by the timing attributes given in Listing 1.2.

Listing 1.2. Task data structure

```
typedef struct {
    pri_t          pri;
    time_t         initial_offset;
    time_t         offset;
    time_t         min_period;
    time_t         max_period;
    time_t         deadline;
    time_t         bcet;
    time_t         wcet;
    bool           preemptive;
} task_t;
```

pri is a task priority. initial_offset is an initial offset for the initial release of the task, and offset represents the offset time of each period before the task is released. A task has also best execution time and worst-case execution time.

The timing attributes above are given as a structure associated to a timed automaton template. The task model is given by the template shown in Fig. 5.

Clock exeTime[tid] denotes the execution time in which the task has executed with necessary resources. This clock is a stop-watch and its progress depends on the following condition:

```
int[0,1] isTaskSched() {return rq[rid].element[0] == tid? 1:0;}
```

where j is the resource id, contains the task identifier which is scheduled to use the CPU, and isTaskSched() returns 1 or 0 according to whether the corresponding task is scheduled or not. Thus, exeTime[tid] increases only when isTaskSched() returns 1. A clock tWECT[tid] measures the worst-case execution time for the task. curTime[tid] is the time elapsed since the task arrives. The task is scheduled, according to its priority, by a specific scheduling algorithm. It can execute only when the supplier provides it with resources. That is, the supplier provides a specific resource amount, then a scheduling algorithm assigns the use of that resource to a specific task. Figure 6 shows the timed behavior of task1 and task2; exeTime[1] and exeTime[2] are increasing according to the resource supply from the supplier. They stop increasing when the supplier stops supplying the resource, or their corresponding tasks complete executing within their periods. Clock exeTime[2] starts increasing after exeTime[1] finishes its execution during its period because task2 has a lower priority than task1. running[1] and running[2] indicate whether the tasks are running or not.

4.3   Resource Model and Scheduling

Figure 7 shows both the resource manager template and one scheduling algorithm template. These two templates behave like a function. They process and return data instantaneously after they receive processing requests. Listing 1.3 depicts the structure (a queue) used by the resource manager.

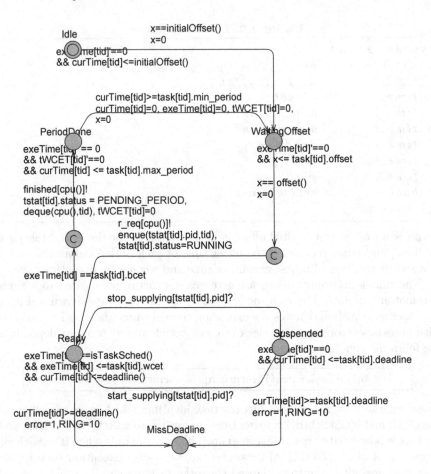

Fig. 5. Task template

Listing 1.3. Resource manager data structure

```
typedef struct {
    int[0,tid_n]    length;
    int[0,LastTid]  element[tid_n+1];
} queue_t;
```

In fact, the resource manager shown in Fig. 7(a) receives a scheduling request from a task, and requests a scheduling algorithm to select the highest priority task. The scheduling model of Fig. 7(b) selects the highest priority task and places it at the first element of the ready queue. The scheduling model acknowledges the resource manager after the selection of a task. At this time, the resource manager notifies the selected task that it is scheduled in order to let it start its execution.

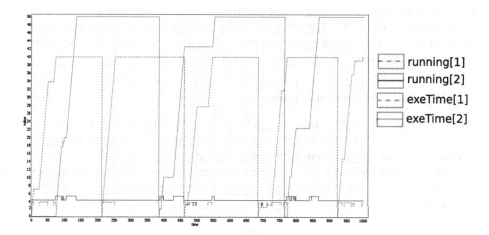

Fig. 6. Task behaviour

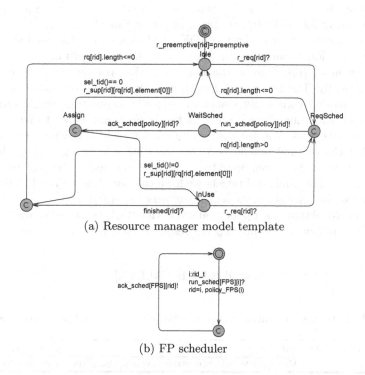

(a) Resource manager model template

(b) FP scheduler

Fig. 7. Resource and scheduling algorithm templates

Thanks to the UPPAAL instantiation mechanism, our system structure can easily be reconfigured. As early mentioned, we have modeled each system entity (task, resource, supplier, scheduling policy) by a template so that if, for example, we need to use a scheduling policy instead of another one, we just replace the scheduling policy name in the system instantiation.

4.4 Symbolic Model Checking

In this section, we explain how to check the schedulability using the symbolic reachability engine of UPPAAL. We consider the system with various configurations in terms of preemptiveness, scheduling policy, etc.

Let us start with an illustration of the schedulability analysis of Component1, depicted in Fig. 1. The components are verified with respect to the following safety property:

$$A[] \text{ error } !=1$$

Here, error is a Boolean variable that will be updated to 1 (true) whenever a task misses its deadline. Thus, this property expresses the absence of deadline violation (i.e. all tasks are schedulable). For a given supplier with a timing requirement (100, 37), the verification results of the component including task1 (250, 40) and task2 (400, 50) are stated below in Table 1.

For the same task set under the EDF scheduling policy, the minimal budget in our verification framework can be greater than the optimal budget of the supplier given in [12]. One of the reasons is that the supplier behaves non-deterministically. The fact that UPPAAL uses an over-approximation technique to analyze models containing stop-watches leads to our framework also being an over-approximation. This results in the answer *maybe-not* to some of our verification attempts. We use the same task set as in [12] where the authors report that the optimal budget is 31 for the EDF scheduling policy, while the minimal budget we have computed to satisfy the same task set by symbolic model checking is 37. The minimal budgets we have computed, for RM scheduling and the same task set, are the same as the budgets presented in [12].

In order to obtain the upper bound on the WCETs of tasks, with respect to the EDF policy and a preemptive resource model, we check the following property:

$$\text{sup: } tWCET[1], tWCET[2]$$

Table 1. Budget evaluation based on scheduling policy and preemptiveness.

Component1	(100, 31)	(100, 37)		(100, 44)
	Preemptive	Preemptive	Non-preemptive	Preemptive
EDF	maybe not	Safe	maybe not	Safe
RM	maybe not	maybe not	maybe not	Safe

where the tWCET[1] and tWCET[2] are stopwatches that are increasing while the corresponding tasks are running. sup is a UPPAAL keyword that refers to a function returning the supprima of the expressions (maximal values in case of integers; upper bounds, strict or not, for clocks). The verification results in tWCET[1] $\leq$ 196 and tWCET[2] $\leq$ 196, signifying that the WCETs of each task is less than or equal to 196. So none of the tasks miss their deadline.

4.5 Statistical Model Checking

As stated in [5], the use of stop-watches in UPPAAL leads to an over-approximation which guarantees that safety properties are valid but reachability properties could be spurious. Thus, symbolic model checking cannot disprove whether tasks are schedulable but only prove when they are schedulable. For that reason, we apply statistical model checking (SMC) to disapprove the schedulability and estimate the minimum budget of the supplier with respect to a specific period.

SMC is a simulation-based approach which estimates the probability for a system to satisfy a property by simulating and observing some of its executions, and then applies statistical algorithms to obtain the result [6]. In this section, we will show a way not only of checking schedulability but also to reason on the execution of tasks.

For our running example, Table 2 shows the query used to evaluate the probability of violating a deadline for runs bounded by 10000 time units regarding different budgets of the supplier. The SMC computed the mentioned results with certain level of confidence and precision, i.e. each result is given as an interval. However, if the lower bound is strictly positive, it guarantees that the checker found at least one witness trace where a task missed its deadline [5]. One may remark that the probability of tasks missing their deadline is much higher when the supplier budget is too small. Note that the possibility that tasks will miss their deadline is between 0.249 and 0.349 for the supplier timing requirement (100,31) of our example.

To visualize a witness of the deadline violation, we can request the checker to generate random simulation runs and show the value of a collection of expressions. For example, run the following query on the system:

$$\text{simulate } 100 \ [<=3000]\{3+\text{running}[1], \text{ exeTime}[1],$$
$$4.5+\text{running}[2], \text{ exeTime}[2]\}: 1: \text{error}==1$$

This query asks the checker to simulate randomly the system execution until the condition error == 1 becomes satisfied, and to generate the task status and the accumulated amount of the resource used by the two tasks.

Table 2. Probability of error estimation with 1 % level of significance.

Component1: EDF	(100, 31)	(100,32)	(100, 33)	(100, 34)	(100,35)
Pr[<=10000](<>error)	[0.249,0.349]	[0.0142,0.114]	[0,0.0987]	[0,0.0987]	[0,0.0987]

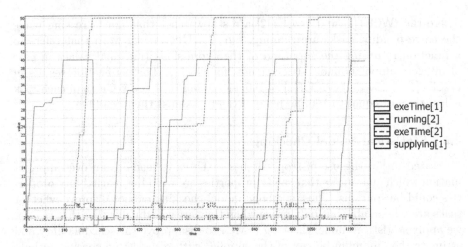

Fig. 8. Unschedulable tasks: task1 misses its deadline at time 1,250.

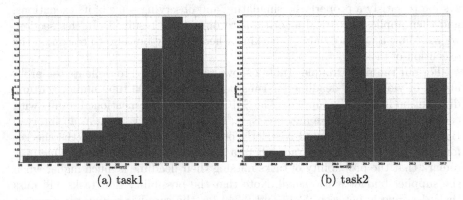

(a) task1   (b) task2

Fig. 9. Probability distribution of the WCET of tasks for the supplier (100, 33)

Figure 8 shows a case where task1 misses the deadline, visualizing the running status of tasks (running[1] and running[2]) in a Gantt chart and the accumulated amount of the resource used by tasks in a period (exeTime[1] and exeTime[2]). Notice that the flat line at the end of the execution of task1 is one value lower than all the previous tops of task1, indicating that this task misses the deadline because of the lack of 1 time unit at time 1,250.

We apply the following queries for different supplier requirements to generate the probability distribution of the worst-case execution time of tasks:

$$E[\text{globalTime} <= 100000; 100] \ (\text{max: tWCET[1]})$$
$$E[\text{globalTime} <= 100000; 100] \ (\text{max: tWCET[2]})$$

The results are shown in Figs. 9 and 10. In fact, Fig. 9 shows the probability distribution of the worst-case execution time of tasks for the supplier timing

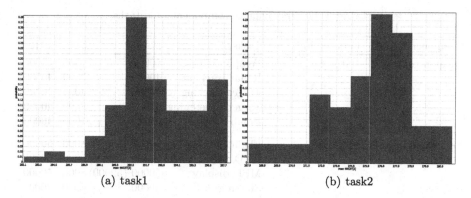

(a) task1   (b) task2

Fig. 10. Probability distribution of the WCET of tasks for the supplier (100, 37)

requirement (100, 33), where task1 and task2 have 210.026 and 292.126 as worst-case execution times. For the supplier timing requirement (100, 37), as shown in Fig. 10, task1 and task2 have 181.304 and 276.121 as worst-case execution times. By means of this reasoning, it can be checked that both cases for the supplier satisfies the task resource requirements and make them schedulable.

5 Case Study

To show the applicability of our compositional framework, we have modeled the avionics system introduced in [3,8], and analyzed its schedulability. The application is a flat composition of 15 tasks declared with different priorities and timing requirements. Depending on the features of tasks, we have structured this application in 3 components. Component 1 (Weapon control) includes 5 tasks concerning the weapon control like bomb button, weapon release, target tracking, etc. Component 2 (Navigation) encapsulates 5 tasks concerning the navigation system whereas component 3 (Controls & displays) includes the basic 5 tasks like display and auto-toggle. Each of the component has a fixed scheduling policy (FPS) and timing requirements (period, budget). The architecture and interfaces of the components, together with the timing attributes of tasks, are depicted in Table 3 where p_i, e_i and d_i are respectively the period, execution time and deadline of tasks. We have also considered shared resources to perform input/output.

In fact, the shared bus for input/output communication is modeled as a particular instance of the processor model. This can easily be extended to model multi-core platforms.

Following the analysis method described in Sect. 3, we associate to each component a non-deterministic supplier. By holding the same timing requirements of tasks as [8], our compositional analysis shows that all components, except the top level one, are schedulable under different scheduling policies with or without preemptiveness. Component 1 is schedulable with at least 89 % of the system

Table 3. Generic avionics components and tasks

Component	Period	Min budget	Tasks	p_i (μs)	e_i(μs)	d_i(μs)
Weapon control	100	89	Weapon release	10000	1000	5000
			Radar tracking	40000	2000	40000
			Target tracking	40000	4000	40000
			Target sweetening	40000	2000	40000
			Bomb button	40000	1000	40000
Navigation	100	90	Flight data	50000 (55000)	8000	50000
			HUD display	50000 (52000)	6000	50000
			MPD display	50000 (52000)	8000	50000
			Steering	80000	6000	8000
			Weapon trajectory	100000	7000	100000
Controls & displays	220	160	Threat display	100000	3000	10000
			AUTO toggle	200000	1000	200000
			Poll RWR	200000	2000	200000
			Reinitiate traject	400000	6000	400000
			Periodic bit	1000000	5000	400000

resources. Component 2 could be schedulable if we provide 90 % of the system resources, whereas Component 3 needs at least 72.7 % of the system resources to being schedulable.

In the top level analysis process (A in Fig. 2), the top level component which consists of a scheduling policy together with the interfaces of the 3 components cannot be scheduled because the sum of the 3 component supplier budgets exceeds 100 % of the resource utilization. This non-schedulability is probably due to the existence of tasks having longer execution time than the deadline of the lowest priority task. Thus, according to our compositional analysis this avionics system is not schedulable. Our schedulability result of this avionics system matches perfectly with the schedulability result obtained in a non-compositional way in [8].

A challenge encountered during this application is the estimation of both period and budget of each supplier such that:

– each supplier provides enough resources to its child tasks.
– the parallel composition of all suppliers is schedulable according to the system level scheduling policy.

We have used a binary search approach to estimate the supplier budgets. In fact, we check the schedulability of a component by giving a supplier budget, and if the schedulability property is not satisfied we increase the budget value and rerun the verification process. A perspective of this work is to study the estimation of time requirements (periods, budgets) of the system intermediate levels in an automatic way, making then the checking process much faster.

6 Conclusions

We have defined a compositional framework for the modeling and schedulability analysis of hierarchical real-time systems. The framework has been instantiated as reusable models given in terms of timed automata which we analyzed using UPPAAL and UPPAAL SMC. The reusable models ensure that when modeling a hierarchical scheduling application, only the concrete task behavior and the hierarchical structure need to be specified by the system engineer. The framework also allows for instant changes of the scheduling policy at each given level in the hierarchy. Comparing our model-based approach to analytical ones, our framework enables the modeling of more complicated and concrete systems. We have successfully applied our compositional framework to model an avionics system and analyze its schedulability. As future work, we plan to study how to estimate the optimal timing requirements of suppliers in an automatic way. We also plan to consider multi-core platforms as well as energy efficiency.

References

1. Amnell, T., Fersman, E., Mokrushin, L., Pettersson, P., Yi, W.: Times: a tool for schedulability analysis and code generation of real-time systems. In: Larsen, K.G., Niebert, P. (eds.) FORMATS 2003. LNCS, vol. 2791, pp. 60–72. Springer, Heidelberg (2004)
2. Behnam, M., Nolte, T., Shin, I., Åsberg, M., Bril, R.: Towards hierarchical scheduling in VxWorks. In: OSPERT 2008, pp. 63–72 (2008)
3. Carnevali, L., Pinzuti, A., Vicario, E.: Compositional verification for hierarchical scheduling of real-time systems. IEEE Trans. Softw. Eng. 39(5), 638–657 (2013)
4. Clarke, E.M., Long, D.E., Mcmillan, K.L.: Compositional Model Checking. MIT Press, Cambridge (1999)
5. David, A., Larsen, K.G., Legay, A., Mikučionis, M.: Schedulability of Herschel-Planck revisited using statistical model checking. In: Margaria, T., Steffen, B. (eds.) ISoLA 2012, Part II. LNCS, vol. 7610, pp. 293–307. Springer, Heidelberg (2012)
6. David, A., Larsen, K.G., Legay, A., Mikučionis, M., Poulsen, D.B., van Vliet, J., Wang, Z.: Statistical model checking for networks of priced timed automata. In: Fahrenberg, U., Tripakis, S. (eds.) FORMATS 2011. LNCS, vol. 6919, pp. 80–96. Springer, Heidelberg (2011)
7. Deng, Z., Liu, J.W.-S.: Scheduling real-time applications in an open environment. In: RTSS, pp. 308–319. IEEE Computer Society (1997)
8. Dodd, R.: Coloured petri net modelling of a generic avionics missions computer. Technical report (2006)
9. Feng, X.A., Mok, A.K.: A model of hierarchical real-time virtual resources. In: Proceedings of the 23rd IEEE Real-Time Systems Symposium, RTSS '02, pp. 26–35. IEEE Computer Society, Washington, DC (2002)
10. Lind-Nielsen, J., Andersen, H.R., Hulgaard, H., Behrmann, G., Kristoffersen, K.J., Larsen, K.G.: Verification of large state/event systems using compositionality and dependency analysis. Formal Meth. Syst. Des. 18(1), 5–23 (2001)
11. Shin, I., Easwaran, A., Lee, I.: Hierarchical scheduling framework for virtual clustering of multiprocessors. In: ECRTS, pp. 181–190. IEEE Computer Society (2008)

12. Shin, I., Lee, I.: Periodic resource model for compositional real-time guarantees. In: RTSS, pp. 2–13. IEEE Computer Society (2003)
13. Shin, I., Lee, I.: Compositional real-time scheduling framework with periodic model. ACM Trans. Embed. Comput. Syst. 7(3), 30:1–30:39 (2008)

Incremental Modeling of System Architecture Satisfying SysML Functional Requirements

Oscar Carrillo, Samir Chouali[✉], and Hassan Mountassir

FEMTO-ST Institute, University of Franche-Comté, Besançon, France
{ocarrill,schouali,hmountas}@femto-st.fr

Abstract. The aim of this work is to propose a methodological approach to model and verify Component-Based Systems (CBS), directly from SysML requirement diagrams, and to ensure formally the architecture consistency of the specified systems. The architecture consistency is guaranteed, when the components that interact in CBS are compatible and all component requirements are preserved by the composition. We propose to exploit functional requirements of CBS, specified with SysML diagrams, and the composition of components to specify incrementally system architecture. Component interfaces are specified with SysML sequence diagrams to capture their behaviors (protocols). From a requirement diagram, we associate atomic requirements, represented as LTL properties, to reusable components satisfying them. LTL properties are verified on the components with SPIN model-checker. Then, we specify system architecture incrementally, with SysML Block Definition Diagram (BDD) and Internal Block Diagram (IBD), by treating, one by one the atomic requirements.

Keywords: System architecture · Requirements · Composition · SysML · Interface automata · Model driven architecture · Verification · LTL properties

1 Introduction

Component-Based Systems (CBS) are widely used in the industrial field, and they are built by assembling various reusable components (third party components), allowing to reduce their development cost. The success of the CBS development is related to the development of complex systems by assembling smaller and simpler components. Generally these systems are made larger because they are developed with software frameworks. However this development is a hard task due to two reasons. The first is the difficulty to decide what to build and how to build it, by considering only system requirements and reusable components. So the question is: how to specify a CBS architecture which satisfies all system requirements? The second reason concerns the compatibility between the set of reusable components that compose the system, which must be guaranteed. Indeed, generally, one exploits reusable components from a component library to construct CBS, so it is necessary to guarantee component compatibility.

J.L. Fiadeiro et al. (Eds.): FACS 2013, LNCS 8348, pp. 79–99, 2014.
DOI: 10.1007/978-3-319-07602-7_7, © Springer International Publishing Switzerland 2014

In this paper we discuss the relationship between system requirements and CBS architecture specification. Our goal is to guide, by the requirements, the CBS specifier to build a consistent system architecture that fulfills all requirements. To reach this goal, we propose to exploit SysML [1], which is a graphical modeling language, widely used in the CBS development. It offers a standard for modeling, specifying and documenting systems. In this work, we exploit SysML requirement diagram to specify and organize system requirements, Sequence Diagram (SD) to describe behavior of components, and Block Definition Diagram (BDD) and Internal Block Diagram (IBD) to specify system architecture. In our previous works [2,3], we exploited BDD, IBD, and SD to verify compatibility between SysML blocks[1]. Particularly in [3], we focused on translating SysML SD to interface automata to verify component compatibility, and in [2] we focused on analyzing the relation between composite blocks and atomic blocks to verify the consistency of a SysML composite blocks. In this context, this paper presents new contributions which are:

- The exploitation of SysML requirement diagram to specify the requirements of CBS.
- The specification of SysML requirements with LTL (Linear Temporal Logic) formulae for their verification on components, thanks to their SD which are translated to Promela by adapting the approach proposed in [4].
- The verification of components compatibility by exploiting the interface automata formalism [5], obtained from SD of components, thanks to the approach proposed in [3]. In this work we adapted the compatibility verification algorithm to handle SysML requirements and to verify also their preservation by the composition.
- The proposition of an incremental approach to construct CBS and to verify their requirements in order to avoid the problem of the combinatorial explosion of the number of states of the verified components. Indeed, the requirement verification is performed on elementary (generally small) components, so we avoid the verification on composite components thanks to the requirements preservation by the composition. This contribution allows to obtain the CBS architecture that fulfills all the requirements. Indeed, this architecture is constructed incrementally and also validated incrementally against to SysML requirements at each step.

Based on SysML requirement diagram and component interfaces, specified with SD, we propose a formal and methodological approach to specify incrementally the system architecture that preserves all the system requirements. So, we propose to treat atomic requirements, extracted from the requirement diagram (provided by the specifier), one by one, to construct a partial architecture, of the system, composed of atomic components and composite components. At each step, we propose to select an atomic requirement (more precise) from a SysML requirement diagram, and choose a component from a library that should satisfy the selected requirement. Then we verify whether the component satisfies the

---

[1] We note that the term used in SysML for components is blocks.

requirement thanks to the LTL formula which specifies the requirement and the Promela program which specifies the component SD (see Sect. 4.3). After that, we verify the compatibility between the selected component, and the selected one in the precedent step, and we verify also the preservation of the requirements treated in the precedent steps. This process ends when all atomic requirements are treated, or when we detect incompatibility between components, or the non preservation of the requirements by component composition. When the process ends correctly, we guarantee the architecture consistency of the final CBS which then fulfills all the requirements.

Our paper is organized as follows: Sect. 2 introduces SysML and the interface automata approach. Section 3 describes our case study. Our approach is presented in Sect. 4, and its illustration on the case study in Sect. 5. In Sect. 6, we present the related works, and we end with conclusion and future works in Sect. 7.

2 Preliminaries

In this section, we introduce the SysML language that we will use in our approach to describe a system, and the interface automata theory that will be used to verify the compatibility between the components that compose that system.

2.1 The SysML Language

SysML (Systems Modeling Language) [1] is a modeling language dedicated to system engineering applications. It was designed as a response to the Request for Proposals (RFP) made in March 2003 by the Object Management Group (OMG) for using UML in Systems Engineering. It was proposed by the OMG and the International Council on Systems Engineering (INCOSE), and it was adopted as standard in May 2006. SysML is a UML 2.0 profile [6] that reuses a subset of its diagrams and adds new features to better fit the needs of systems engineering so that it allows the specification, analysis, design, verification, and validation of a wide range of complex systems.

In this paper we use four of the nine diagrams included in SysML: *Block Definition Diagram (BDD)*: describes the architectural structure of the system as components with their properties, operations, and relationships, *Internal Block Diagram (IBD)*: describes the internal structures of the components, adding parts, and connectors, *Requirement Diagram (RD)*: describes the system requirements and their relationships with other elements, and *Sequence Diagram (SD)*: describes the system behavior as interactions between system components.

2.2 Interface Automata

Interface automata were introduced by Alfaro and Henzinger [5] to specify component interfaces and also to verify component assembly. Each component is described by a single interface automaton. The set of actions is decomposed into three groups: input actions, output actions and internal actions. Input actions allow to model the methods to be called in a component, in which case they are the offered services in a component. These actions are labeled by the character "?". The output actions model the method calls to another component. Therefore, they represent services required by the component. These actions are labeled by the character "!". Internal actions are operations that can be activated locally and are labeled by the character ";". In this work, we exploit interface automata to model interfaces of SysML components (blocks).

Definition 1. *Interface Automata An* interface automaton A *is represented by the tuple* $\langle\ S_A,\ I_A,\ \Sigma_A^I,\ \Sigma_A^O,\ \Sigma_A^H,\ \delta_A\ \rangle$ *such that:*

- S_A *is a finite set of states;*
- $I_A \subseteq S_A$ *is a subset of initial states;*
- Σ_A^I, Σ_A^O, *and* Σ_A^H, *respectively denote the sets of input, output, and internal actions. The set of actions of A is denoted by Σ_A;*
- $\delta_A \subseteq S_A \times \Sigma_A \times S_A$ *is the set of transitions between states.*

We define by $\Sigma_A^I(s)$, $\Sigma_A^O(s)$, $\Sigma_A^H(s)$, respectively the set of input, output, and internal actions at the state s. $\Sigma_A(s)$ represents the set of actions at the state s.

The verification of the assembly of two components (blocks) is obtained by verifying the compatibility of their interface automata. Before this verification, it is necessary to ensure that the interface automata are *composable*.

Two interface automata A_1 and A_2 are *composable* if $\Sigma_{A_1}^I \cap \Sigma_{A_2}^I = \Sigma_{A_1}^O \cap \Sigma_{A_2}^O = \Sigma_{A_1}^H \cap \Sigma_{A_2} = \Sigma_{A_1} \cap \Sigma_{A_2}^H = \emptyset$. We define by $Shared(A_1, A_2) = (\Sigma_{A_1}^I \cap \Sigma_{A_2}^O) \cup (\Sigma_{A_1}^O \cap \Sigma_{A_2}^I)$ the set of actions shared between A_1 and A_2. The verification of the compatibility of two interface automata is based on their synchronized product, $A_1 \otimes A_2$, obtained by synchronizing the interface automata on their shared actions (see Definition 3.4 in [5]).

Two interface automata may be incompatible due to the existence of illegal states in their synchronized product. Illegal states are states from which a shared output action from an automaton can not be synchronized with the same enabled action as input on the other component.

Definition 2. *Illegal States Let A_1 and A_2 be two composable interface automata, the set of* illegal states $Illegal(A_1, A_2) \subseteq S_{A_1} \times S_{A_2}$ *is defined by* $\{(s_1, s_2) \in S_{A_1} \times S_{A_2} \mid \exists a \in Shared(A_1, A_2).((a \in \Sigma_{A_1}^O(s_1) \wedge a \notin \Sigma_{A_2}^I(s_2)) \vee (a \in \Sigma_{A_2}^O(s_2) \wedge a \notin \Sigma_{A_1}^I(s_1)))\}.$

The interface automata approach is considered an optimistic approach, because the reachability of states in *Illegal* (A_1, A_2) does not guarantee the incompatibility of A_1 and A_2. Indeed, in this approach one verifies the existence of an environment that provides appropriate actions to the product $A_1 \otimes A_2$ to avoid illegal states. The states in which the environment can avoid the reachability of illegal states are called compatible states, and are defined by the set $Comp(A_1, A_2)$. This set is calculated in $A_1 \otimes A_2$ by eliminating illegal states, unreachable states, and states that lead to illegal states through internal actions or output actions, called also incompatible states. These states are eliminated by providing a *legal environment* which steers away from the illegal states by generating appropriate inputs. By eliminating these states in $A_1 \otimes A_2$, we obtain the composition $A_1 \parallel A_2$. So the interface automata A_1 and A_2 are compatible *iff* $A_1 \parallel A_2 \neq \emptyset$ [5].

Definition 3. *Composition* *The* composition $A_1 \parallel A_2$ *of two automata* A_1 *and* A_2 *is defined by: (i)* $S_{A_1 \parallel A_2} = Comp(A_1, A_2)$, *(ii)* $I_{A_1 \parallel A_2} = I_{A_1 \otimes A_2} \cap Comp(A_1, A_2)$, *(iii)* $\Sigma_{A_1 \parallel A_2} = \Sigma_{A_1 \otimes A_2}$, *(iv)* $\delta_{A_1 \parallel A_2} = \delta_{A_1 \otimes A_2} \cap (Comp(A_1, A_2) \times \Sigma_{A_1 \parallel A_2} \times Comp(A_1, A_2))$

We call the automaton $A = A_1 \parallel A_2$, the composite automaton.

The verification of the compatibility between a component C_1 and a component C_2 is obtained by verifying the compatibility between their interface automata A_1 and A_2. The main steps of the verification algorithm of the compatibility between A_1 and A_2(the complete algorithm in [5]) are listed as follows: **Compatibility verification algorithm:** (1) verify that A_1 and A_2 are composable. (2) compute the product $A_1 \otimes A_2$. (3) compute the set of illegal states in $A_1 \otimes A_2$. (4) compute the set of incompatible states in $A_1 \otimes A_2$: the states from which the illegal states are reachable by enabling only internal and output actions (one supposes the existence of a helpful environment). (5) compute the composition $A_1 \parallel A_2$ by eliminating from the automaton $A_1 \otimes A_2$, the illegal states, the incompatible states, and the unreachable states from the initial states. (6) if $A_1 \parallel A_2$ is empty then A_1 and A_2 are not compatible, therefore C_1 and C_2 can not be assembled correctly in any environment. Otherwise, A_1 and A_2 are compatible and their corresponding component can be assembled properly.

The complexity of this approach is in time linear on $|A_1|$ and $|A_2|$ [5]. The verification steps in this approach can be performed by the tool *Ptolemy* [7].

3   Case Study

To illustrate our approach, we propose to build the SysML structure that specifies the implementation of a safety vehicle system (case study inspired from [8]). A safety system consists of several sensors all around the car that detect whether a collision occurred. When a car collides with a barrier, there will be a rapid deceleration. Depending on the deceleration values detected by the sensors, a central unit must decide whether or not to inflate the airbag and/or lock the seat-belts.

The associated requirement diagram that specifies the system needs is shown on Fig. 1. In this diagram, the initial requirement $R1$ asks for ensuring passengers lives and it is decomposed into two requirements $R1.1$ and $R1.2$ that ask for two safety devices: an airbag system which must be deployed whenever the car is in a collision, and the seat-belts that must be locked when the sensors detect strong movements, therefore, this last is an atomic requirement as it is not decomposed. On the left side, requirement $R1.1$ is further decomposed into requirements $R1.1.1$, $R1.1.2$, and $R1.1.3$ which are atomic ones. Requirement

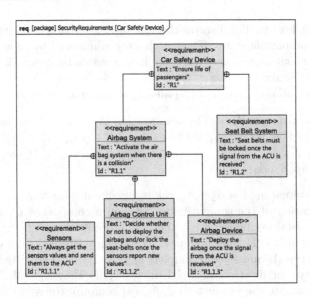

Fig. 1. Requirements refinement for airbag system

$R1.1.1$ asks for the capture and sending of sensor values to an Airbag Control Unit (ACU). Requirement $R1.1.2$ requests an ACU to decide whether or not to deploy the airbag and lock the seat-belts as soon as the sensors report new values. Finally, requirement $R1.1.3$ demands to deploy an airbag device, once the signal from the ACU is received.

4   Our Approach

In Sect. 4.1 we present an overview of our approach by listing its main steps. These steps are then detailed in the following sections.

4.1   Overview

We propose an approach to construct a CBS system and to specify its architecture directly from SysML requirements. Our goal is to obtain a consistent architecture which respects all the specified requirements. To specify this architecture, the software architect exploits a library of reusable components (or blocks). These components are considered as black boxes and described only by their interfaces, specified with sequence diagrams. So, we propose to specify CBS requirements with SysML requirement diagram, then analyze this diagram in order to associate one by one its atomic requirements (can not be decomposed) to software components that satisfy them. The satisfiability is evaluated by performing a formal verification step with a model-checker. Each verified component is tested for compatibility with the other components in the composition and then added to the partial architecture that must preserve the atomic requirements.

In our approach, a CBS is specified with a SysML requirement diagram that shows the functional requirements, and component interfaces describe component protocols by sequence diagrams. The main steps of our approach are described as follows:

1. start by analyzing the SysML requirement diagram to obtain the atomic requirements because they are more precise, and it is easier to find components that satisfy them (see Sect. 4.2).
2. let R_i be the first atomic requirement, let C_i be a component from the component library, described by the sequence diagram SD_i. Specify R_i with the LTL formula F_i and translate SD_i to the Promela code PRO_i, then verify that C_i satisfies R_i by verifying that PRO_i satisfies F_i with the model checker SPIN (see Sect. 4.3). The selection of the component C_i in the library is done by the software architect. However, it is possible to guide this selection (or to automate it) because R_i is a functional requirement, and describes constraints on offered and required services (Input/output actions). These services are also described in component interfaces. So it is easy to extract these services from R_i and to match them with those described in the interfaces. If this step returns *false*, then C_i does not satisfy R_i, therefore one has to obtain the appropriate component in other libraries, or to develop it from scratch.
3. let A_i be the interface automaton describing the component protocol and obtained from the sequence diagram SD_i (see Sect. 4.4).
4. identify the input and output actions in A_i related to R_i (Sect. 4.4).
5. repeat until all the requirements are treated.
   (a) let R_{i+1} be the next atomic requirement, **connected** to R_i (see Definition 6), let C_{i+1} be a component satisfying R_{i+1}, thanks to the LTL formula F_{i+1} and the Promela code PRO_{i+1}. Let A_{i+1} be the interface automaton describing the component protocol.
   (b) identify the set of input and output actions in A_{i+1} related to R_{i+1}.
   (c) verify that C_i and C_{i+1} are compatible thanks to their interface automata, so verify that $A_i \parallel A_{i+1} \neq \emptyset$ (Sect. 2.2).
   (d) verify that the requirements R_i and R_{i+1} are preserved by the composition, so they are satisfied by the composite $C = C_i \parallel C_{i+1}$ (Sect. 4.4).
   (e) define the consistent partial architecture of the system by the composite $C = C_i \parallel C_{i+1}$, according to Definition 7.
   (f) let $C_i = C_i \parallel C_{i+1}$, $A_i = A_i \parallel A_{i+1}$, and $R_i = \{R_i, R_{i+1}\}$.
6. end repeat

According to the main steps of our approach, we validate the final architecture of our CBS when all the atomic requirements are analyzed without problems of component compatibility and/or requirement preservation.

4.2   Analysis of SysML Requirement Diagram

In this section, we specify formally the SysML requirement diagram in order to analyze it and to extract formally the atomic requirements. Then, we show that it is sufficient to a CBS to satisfy only the atomic requirements in order to satisfy all the requirements specified in the requirement diagram. In the following definition we consider two relations of SysML requirement diagram. **Containment**: exploited to decompose a requirement with other ones more precise. **Derivation**: exploited to connect a requirement with other ones which derive from it.

Definition 4. *Requirement diagram specification* We specify a SysML requirement diagram by $RD = \langle IR, SR, RelC, RelD \rangle$ such that:

- *IR: define the set of initial requirements, the first requirements that the specifier defines in the requirement diagram. Generally, they are not precise, and it is necessary to connect them, with the containment relation, to more refined requirements.*
- *SR: the set of all requirements.*
- *RelC $\subseteq SR \times P(SR)$ the relation of containment, where $P(SR)$ is the set of the subsets of SR.*
- *RelD $\subseteq SR \times P(SR)$ the relation of derivation.*

For example in our case study, the specification of the requirement diagram described in Fig. 1 is $RD = \langle IR, SR, RelC, RelD \rangle$, where $IR = \{R1\}$, $SR = \{R1, R1.1, R1.2, R1.1.1, R1.1.2, R1.1.3\}$, $RelC = \{(R1, \{R1.1, R1.2\}), (R1.1, \{R1.1.1, R1.1.2, R1.1.3\})\}$, and $RelD = \emptyset$.

Definition 5. *Atomic requirements* The set of atomic requirements in the requirement diagram specified by $RD = \langle IR, SR, RelC, RelD \rangle$ is the set $AR = \{R | R \in SR, \nexists (R, \{R_i, ... R_n\}) \in RelC\}$

An atomic requirement is a requirement which can not be decomposed. It expresses a constraint on input and output actions which are related to one component (see Sect. 4.4).

The atomic requirements in our case study are (see Fig. 1): $\{R1.1.1, R1.1.2, R1.1.3, R1.2\}$.

Remark 1. To compute the set of atomic requirements, it is necessary to analyze the set SR of all requirements and to identify the requirements that are not related by the relation $RelC$ (containment).

Theorem 1. *Let S be a component-based system, let $RD = \langle IR, SR, RelC, RelD \rangle$ be the specification of a requirement diagram, and let AR be the set of atomic requirements of RD. S satisfies all the requirements in SR iff it satisfies the atomic requirements AR.*

Theorem 1 states that it is sufficient for a system to satisfy the atomic requirements, in order to satisfy all requirements represented in a SysML requirement diagram.

To illustrate the proof of the theorem, we propose a simple requirement diagram presented in Fig. 2. The requirements are connected with a containment relation, with continuous arrows, and a derivation relation, with dashed arrows. So the requirement $R0$ is decomposed in the requirements $R01$ and $R02$. The requirement $R1$ derives from $R0$, and $R2$ derives from $R1$.

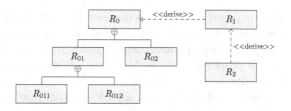

Fig. 2. A SysML requirement diagram

Proof. Due to the semantic of the relation derive in SysML requirement diagram (and also the semantic of requirement diagram), it's obvious to state that a system satisfies all requirements that are specified by a requirement diagram iff it satisfies the initial requirements and all the ones that are derived (linked by the relation derive) directly or indirectly from them. Indeed, the satisfaction of the derived requirements does not guarantee the satisfaction of the initial ones. Since the atomic requirements are either derived (directly or indirectly) from initial requirements, or related by the relation of containment (directly or not) to initial requirements. And due to the semantic of the containment and the derive relations, the satisfaction of atomic requirements leads to the satisfaction of the requirement which are linked to them. Therefore it is sufficient to satisfy atomic requirements to satisfy all requirements. For example in Fig. 2, the requirements to satisfy (initial and derived) are $\{R0, R1, R2\}$. The derived requirements are $R1$ and $R2$, and the initial requirement is $R0$. However to satisfy a requirement composed of other ones, it is sufficient to satisfy the requirements that compose it. This process is repeated until all the atomic requirements are satisfied. So, to satisfy $R0$, it is sufficient to satisfy $R01$ and $R02$. And to satisfy $R01$ it is sufficient to satisfy $R011$ and $R012$. Therefore to satisfy all requirements, it is necessary to satisfy $\{R1, R2, R02, R011, R012\}$, which defines the set of atomic requirements in our requirement diagram.

4.3   Formal Verification of SysML Requirements on System Components

This section presents a formal verification technique based on the approach proposed by V. Lima *et al.* in [4]. This technique proposes to create a Promela-based model from UML interactions expressed in Sequence Diagrams (SD), and uses SPIN model checker [9] to simulate the execution and to verify properties written in Linear Temporal Logic (LTL) [10]. Promela/SPIN was chosen because it provides important concepts for implementing SD: sending and receiving primitives, parallel and asynchronous composition of concurrent processes, and communication channels. Our minor adaptation of the approach proposed by V. Lima *et al.* concerns a particular type of sequence diagrams that we exploit to specify the block behaviors.

We propose to use a particular type of SD with only two lifelines, one for the block and one for the environment. This way, SD can be further translated into interface automata as exposed in [3]. In this diagram the exchanged messages will be the offered services as calls from the environment and the required services as calls to the environment. The main advantage of using SD for verification is that we can verify temporal properties over it. Messages follow a sequence order that we can trace to detect deadlocks or execution of paths. Figures 3 and 5 show the SD for the blocks sensors and ACU, these are blocks from our block library. In these diagrams we notice that there are only two lifelines and messages are sent to/received from the environment.

Verification with SPIN Model Checker. In this paper we exploit and adapt the approach proposed in [4] to translate SD to Promela-based model in order to verify properties with the model-checker SPIN. Table 1 shows the Promela representation of the main elements in SD. Alternative and loop combined fragments are represented as `if` condition and `do` operator in Promela respectively, guard condition is declared globally and the non-deterministic behavior is implemented at `init` time by assigning different values to the guards. Figures 4 and 6 show partially the Promela representation for the sensors SD and ACU SD respectively (due to the lack of space the complete Promela code is not shown in this paper). In both diagrams, we notice that their two lifelines are translated as processes in the Promela code, one process for the block and one other for the environment. Both processes are started at the same time thanks to an atomic call at the main process `init`. We can also notice that *loop* combined fragments are translated as `do` statements and that the *alt* combined fragment in ACU SD is translated as `if` statement where the three possible range values for deceleration are assigned at init time by using an `if` clause, this way, SPIN will choose non-deterministically which of the three values will be used to simulate the system.

Table 1. Mapping of basic concepts from sequence diagrams to Promela

SD element	Promela element	Promela statement
Lifeline	Process	`proctype{...}`
Message	Message	`mtype{m1,...,mn}`
Connector	Communication channel for each message arrow	`chan chanName = [1] of {mtype}`
Send and receive events	Send and receive operations	Send $\Rightarrow$ `ab!m`, Receive $\Rightarrow$ `ab?m`

Alt combined fragment	if condition	`if`
		`::(guard)->ab_p?p;`
		`:: else -> ab_q?q;`
		`fi;`

Loop combined fragment	do operator	`do`
		`::ab_p?p;`
		`od`

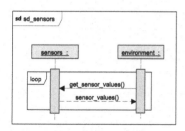

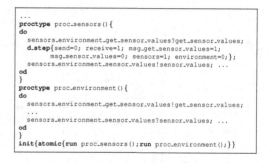

Fig. 3. SD for sensors block   **Fig. 4.** Promela code for sensors block

Once the sequence diagram is translated, the component can be simulated as a SPIN system. However, in order to verify whether the component satisfies a LTL property, the authors propose to use a series of flags to keep track of *who is sending/receiving what message to/from whom* at any time of the execution. In our approach we verify properties over independent components with only two lifelines in their SD, one line for the selected component and the other for the environment. So, we do not use a flag related to *to/from whom* is sent a message as it will always be *the other* lifeline. These flags are updated together at each *send/receive* event using a **d_step** statement. The flags for our example in Fig. 3 will be **send** and **receive** to indicate the performed action, **msg_get_sensor_values** and **msg_sensor_values** to indicate the message exchanged, and **sensors** and **environment** to indicate who performed the action.

After defining the flags to track the execution state of the system, LTL properties can be written as boolean expressions over the flags. In our approach we propose to translate SysML requirements to LTL properties by respecting this formalism with flags. So for example requirement $R1.1.1$ in Fig. 2 can be expressed as: *always after receiving a call to get_sensor_values, the sensor block will send a message with the sensor_values.* The boolean expression, using the flags described before, will be: $\square$((**sensors && receive && msg_get_sensor _values**) $\rightarrow$ $\lozenge$ (**sensors && send && msg_sensor_values**)). Similarly, requirement $R1.1.2$ can be expressed as: *always after receiving a message with the sensor_values, the ACU will send a message deciding to lock the seat-belt, activate the airbag or wait for another call,* and the boolean expression with flags will be: $\square$((**acu && receive && msg_sensor_values**) $\rightarrow$ $\lozenge$ (**acu && send && (msg _reset || msg_act_sb || msg_act_ab**))). These properties are further verified over their corresponding Promela model by using SPIN model checker, which indicates that the properties are satisfied by the blocks. Once a corresponding block is found for a requirement, we continue with another requirement to start building the system architecture.

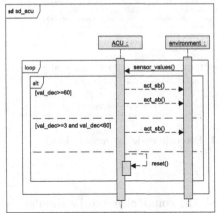

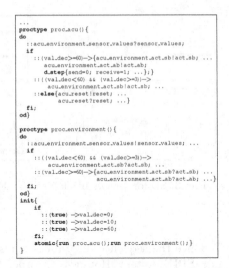

Fig. 5. SD for the ACU block   **Fig. 6.** Promela code for ACU block

4.4   Component Assembly Preserving SysML Requirements

After the verification of the connected atomic requirements on the components, in this section, we specify interface automata from sequence diagrams thanks to the approach proposed in [3], then we propose to compose components and to verify compatibility between them, using their interface automata, by applying the algorithm presented in Sect. 2.2. We propose also to verify, at the same time as the compatibility verification, whether the composition preserves the atomic SysML requirements. Indeed, this verification allows to avoid the requirement verification at the level of the obtained composite component, in order to avoid the state explosion problem for the model checker. Before presenting the algorithm to verify the preservation, we show in the following sections that SysML requirements are related to Input/Output actions of interface automata, and their preservation is related to the preservation by the composition of their related actions.

Relation Between Functional Requirements and Input/Output Actions. The atomic requirements considered in this work concern the functional properties of a CBS. They are related directly to input and output actions of components. Therefore, for each atomic requirement we associate the sets of input and output actions provided by a component.

Let AR be the set of atomic requirements in the specification RD of a requirement diagram. Let R_i be an atomic requirement satisfied by the component C_i. Let A_i be the interface automaton describing the protocol of C_i. So, R_i is associated to input actions $I_{R_i} = \{i_{ri_1}, ..., i_{ri_n}\}$, and output ones $O_{R_i} = \{o_{ri_1}, ..., o_{ri_n}\}$.

For example the first atomic requirement in our case study is $R1.1.1$: *always get the sensor values and send them to the ACU*. It is satisfied by the component

Sensor. The interface automaton of this component is described in Fig. 8. The set of input actions related to $R1.1.1$ is $\{get\_sensor\_values\}$, and the set of output actions is $\{sensor\_values\}$.

The actions related to atomic requirements are formalized by transitions in the interface automata, labeled with these input/output actions.

Definition 6. *Connected requirements Let R and R' be two atomic requirements specified in a SysML requirement diagram. R and R' are related respectively to the set of input actions I_R, and I'_R, and output ones O_R, and O'_R. R and R' are connected iff $I_R \cap O'_R \neq \emptyset$ or $I'_R \cap O_R \neq \emptyset$.*

According to Definition 6 and to the condition of composability of interface automata (see Sect. 2.2), it is obvious to state that two components satisfying two connected atomic requirements are composable. We exploit this definition in our approach: at each iteration i of our approach, we choose an atomic requirement which is connected with the requirement in the iteration $i-1$, in order to compose their components, otherwise the composition is not allowed.

The Interface Automata Composition Does Not Always Guarantee the Preservation of Their Input/Output Actions. In this section, we show that the composition of two interface automata does not guarantee the preservation of their non shared input/output actions in the obtained composite automaton, despite their compatibility. In fact, in the item (iii) of Definition 3, the authors in [5] indicate that the set of actions in the composite automaton $A = A_1 \parallel A_2$ is the same as the set of actions in the synchronized product $A_1 \otimes A_2$, however, the set of transitions in A is not the same as the one in $A_1 \otimes A_2$ (according to Definition 3). Indeed the set of transitions in A is included in the one of $A_1 \otimes A_2$. So, there may be input/output actions in Σ_A which are not associated to transitions in A. In fact according to the optimistic approach of interface automata, despite that A_1 and A_2 are compatible, and $A \neq \emptyset$, there may be shared input/output actions between A_1 and A_2 which do not synchronize, but certainly, there are also shared actions which synchronize (because $A \neq \emptyset$). Thus, the transitions labeled with the shared input/output actions, which do not synchronize, will be eliminated from $A = A_1 \parallel A_2$ because they lead to illegal states. But the related input/output actions (which label the eliminated transitions) remain in the set of actions in A, because the composite component described by the composite automaton A could provide these actions, and with the optimistic approach, one decides that it is compatible, because one supposes the existence of the helpful environment which never enables these actions (for more illustration see the example in [5]).

Verification of the Preservation of the Atomic Requirements by the Composition. In this section, we show the conditions that the composition of components should respect to preserve the requirements of the composed components. And we show also how to verify these conditions by adapting the compatibility verification algorithm of interface automata (see Sect. 2.2).

The preservation of the atomic requirements by the composition of components is necessarily related to the preservation of the input/output actions, associated to these requirements, by the composition of their interface automata. Furthermore, in Sect. 4.4, we indicate that some input/output actions may belong to the set of actions of a composite automaton, but they do not label transitions in this automaton. So, in this case we state that these actions are not preserved.

Condition of Input/Output action preservation: An action *act* (Input or output) is preserved by the composition of two interface automata, A_1 and A_2, iff there is at least one transition in the composite automaton, $A = A_1 \parallel A_2$, which is labeled with *act*. *act* belongs to the set of Input/Output actions in A, when *act* is not shared between A_1 and A_2, and belongs to the internal actions in A otherwise.

Verification algorithm overview: To verify the preservation of atomic requirements by the composition, we propose to adapt the compatibility verification algorithm [5] (Sect. 2.2). We verify whether the transitions labeled with input/output actions, related to atomic requirements, are preserved in the transition set of the obtained composite automaton $A_i \parallel A_{i+1}$. This adaptation consists on: to calculate in the step (2) of the compatibility verification algorithm, the set of transitions in $A_i \otimes A_{i+1}$, noted T, related to the requirements. When we eliminate transitions in the step (5) of the compatibility verification algorithm, we eliminate also these transitions in T. Finally, we verify that all the actions related to the requirements, are associated to at least one transition in T, after the step (6).

We notice that this adaptation does not increase the complexity of the compatibility verification algorithm (this can be easily verifiable). So the complexity of the presented algorithm is $\mathcal{O}|A_i \otimes A_{i+1}|$. However, in order to calculate the time complexity of one step in our approach, we have to consider a component C_c associated to the current requirement to analyze, R_c. This component is selected from the components library specified by the set $C = \{C_1, C_2, ..., C_n\}$. We consider also the sequence diagrams SD_c that specifies the protocol of C_c. In each step we have to verify that the current component satisfies the current requirement thanks to the Promela code of SD_c and to the model checker SPIN. And we verify also the compatibility between the current component and the composite component, C_p, obtained in a precedent step. So the time complexity of one step in our approach is analyzed as follows:

- to select a component from the set C that should satisfy an atomic requirement, the complexity is: $\mathcal{O}(|C|)$
- to verify that C_c satisfies R_c, the complexity is : $\mathcal{O}(|TS_c| \times 2^{|Pc|})$, where TS_c is the automaton calculated by SPIN from the Promela code associated to SD_c (this is the complexity of the LTL model checking), and Pc the LTL formula that specifies the requirement R_c.
- After verifying the atomic current requirement on the component, we verify the compatibility between C_c and C_p and the preservation of the requirements

by the composition. The complexity of this step is : $\mathcal{O}(|A_c \otimes A_p|)$, where A_c and A_p are the interface automata associated respectively to C_c and C_p.

So, to calculate the complexity of the whole approach, we have to consider the complexity of one step and the number of the atomic requirements which defines the number of steps.

To demonstrate the correctness of our approach, we should prove that the composition of two components preserves the atomic requirements iff the composed components are compatible and the input and output actions related to these requirements are preserved according to the condition of preservation of input/output actions. Indeed, each step in the incremental approach is based on the **compatibility** and the **preservation** of the atomic requirements by the composition. So, it is sufficient to show the correctness of a step i in our approach.

Theorem 2. *Let C_i be a component satisfying the atomic requirement R_i and A_i the interface automaton of C_i, let I_i be the set of input actions related to R_i and O_i the output ones. Let C_{i+1} be a component satisfying R_{i+1} and A_{i+1} the interface automaton of C_{i+1}, let I_{i+1} be the set of input actions related to R_{i+1} and O_{i+1} the output ones. The composite component $S = C_i \parallel C_{i+1}$ preserves the requirements $\{R_i, R_{i+1}\}$ iff the interface automata A_i, and A_{i+1}, are compatible, and the input and output actions, I_i, I_{i+1}, O_i, and O_{i+1} are preserved in S.*

Proof. The component C_i satisfies R_i means that the program Promela describing the component behaviors satisfies the LTL property specifying the requirement R_i. In our approach, component behaviors are also described with an interface automaton A_i, and these behaviors are execution paths in the interface automaton. The functional requirement R_i is related to the sets of input/output actions, I_i, O_i, and they express constraints and the order of executing these actions. For example R_i could express: always when C_i enables an input action $i \in I_i$ then it will inevitably enable the output actions $o \in O_i$. So C_i satisfies this requirement iff in all the execution paths in A_i where a transition labeled by i belongs, it will be followed by a transition labeled with o. Since our composition approach preserves at least one of these paths, when the compatibility and the preservation of Input/Output actions hold, then the requirements are preserved.

Indeed, the composite $S = C_i \parallel C_{i+1}$ preserves the input/output actions related to the requirements means that for each input/output actions related to R_i and R_{i+1}, the transitions labeled with these actions are preserved, therefore at least one execution path, in $A_i \parallel A_{i+1}$ containing these transitions is preserved in S. Indeed, we have the following possibilities when A_i and A_{i+1} are compatible and the actions related to R_i and R_{i+1} are preserved (illustration concerning only one action a related to R_i or R_{i+1}):

- if there are no illegal states the preservation is guaranteed, because all the paths are preserved. This case (we have two possibilities) is illustrated in the Fig. 7(a) and (b). In the case (a), we suppose that there is a synchronization between the two automata on the shared action a (related to a requirement),

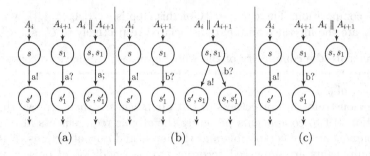

Fig. 7. Proof 2 illustration

so in the composition we obtain a transition labeled with the internal action a. Therefore the action a is preserved and becomes internal. And in the second case (b), we suppose that a is not shared and there is interleaving in the composite automaton, and a is preserved.

- if there are illegal states (and the automata are compatible due the optimistic approach): in this case (see Fig. 7(c)), we suppose that the first automaton provides a shared output action a, in the state s, and the second automaton does not provide the input action a, in $s1$. So we obtain an illegal state and the action a is not enabled in the illegal state $(s, s1)$. In this case we have to verify that a is preserved in other paths of the composite automaton $A_i \parallel A_{i+1}$, with our approach. So, if we find a transition labeled with a, in $A_i \parallel A_{i+1}$, so it is preserved (according to the condition of preservation), and the associated requirement also, otherwise the related requirement is not preserved. So when the preservation of the Input/Output action is verified, then the related requirements are preserved.

4.5   Specification of System Architecture with BDD and IBD Diagrams After the Composition

The construction of a CBS with our approach is based on constructing, at each incremental step, one SysML composite component, which defines a partial architecture of a CBS. This architecture is based on the interface automata of the assembled components and particularly on their shared actions. So, in the following definition, we describe the SysML composite by specifying the relation between SysML BDD and IBD diagrams, and the interface automata describing the behaviors of the composed components.

Definition 7. *SysML Composite component Let C_1 and C_2 be two components, let A_1 and A_2 be their respective interface automata. When A_1 and A_2 are compatible, $A_1 \| A_2 \neq \emptyset$, the composite component C composed of C_1 and C_2, is well formed and it is written $C = C_1 \parallel C_2$. This composite is described with the SysML BDD diagram, BDD_C, composed of the composite block C, and the blocks C_1 and C_2. The interactions between the components C_1 and C_2 are* *described with the SysML IBD diagram, IBD_C such that, IBD_C is composed of the parts[2] C_1 and C_2 which communicate through internal ports, labeled with the names of the synchronized input and output actions, which are shared between A_1 and A_2. The external ports of IBD_C are labeled with the names of actions which are not shared.*

This definition is illustrated in Sect. 5 in Figs. 11 and 12 (BDD and IBD).

5 Illustration on the Case Study

In this section we apply our approach on the case study shown in Sect. 3. As exposed in the approach, we start by analyzing the SysML requirement diagram to obtain the atomic requirements. These requirements are $R1.1.1$, $R1.1.2$, $R1.1.3$, and $R1.2$. Then, we link LTL properties for each of these atomic requirements. These properties are used to verify whether a block in a component library satisfies the requirement in order to match them. For the first requirement $R1.1.1$ we take a sensor block with its associated SD shown in Fig. 3 respectively. This sensor block gets information from several sensors (accelerometers, impact sensors,...) all around the car at each call of the service **get_sensor_values**, and sends them through a service **sensor_values**. These services are respectively the input {**get_sensor_values**} and output actions {**sensor_values**} related to requirement $R1.1.1$. To validate if the block *sensors* satisfies requirement $R1.1.1$, we first describe the requirement as a LTL property like *"always, after the sensors block receives a call for* **get_sensor_values**, *it sends a message* **sensor_values** *to the environment"*. Then we translate the associated SD to a Promela description as exposed in Sect. 4.3, the generated code is not shown here for lack of space. Following the approach of flags from [4], the LTL property in Promela language is:

   □((sensors && receive && msg_get_sensor_values)

      → ◊ (sensors && send && msg_sensor_values))

The next requirement to be analyzed is $R1.1.2$ which is connected to $R1.1.1$. For this requirement, we find the ACU block and its associated SD in Fig. 5, this block offers an input action {**sensor_values**} and requires the output actions {**act_sb,act_ab**} to lock the seat-belts and deploy an airbag respectively, this block analyzes each arrival of sensor values and decides whether the seat-belts must be locked, an airbag must be deployed or wait for another sensor values arrival (**reset** action). To verify if this block satisfies requirement $R1.1.2$, we express it as a Promela description (the generated code is not shown here for lack of space) and the requirement is expressed as a LTL property: *"always after receiving a message with the sensor_values, the ACU will send a message deciding to lock the seat-belt (* **act_sb** *), activate the airbag (* **act_ab** *) or wait for another call (* **reset** *)"*, which expressed in Promela code using flags will be:

   □((acu && receive && msg_sensor_values)

      → ◊ (acu && send && (msg_reset || msg_act_sb || msg_act_ab)))

---

[2] Blocks are instantiated as parts in IBD

These properties are verified using SPIN model-checker which outputs no errors for both models, therefore the models satisfy the properties.

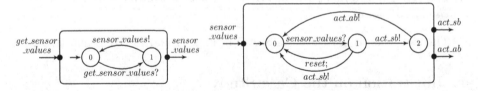

Fig. 8. IA for the sensors block   **Fig. 9.** IA for the ACU

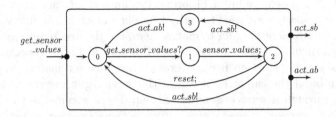

Fig. 10. IA for the composition of sensors and ACU blocks

Then, to link the blocks that satisfy requirements $R1.1.1$ and $R1.1.2$, we verify that they are compatible thanks to their interface automata. These interface automata are generated from SD following the approach in [3], and they are shown in Figs. 8 and 9. To verify compatibility we compute the composition; we use Ptolemy Interface Automata tool [7] which computes the composition of two given interface automata as input. The output composite automaton is shown in Fig. 10, this automaton is not empty, so the blocks Sensors and ACU are compatible. This composition had illegal states that were eliminated automatically by Ptolemy tool, so we have to validate that the actions related to the requirements are still present on the transitions of the composite automaton to guarantee preservation of the requirements over the composition. Looking at the transitions in the composite automaton, we find that the set of input/output actions, related to the requirements, are still present, so the requirements are still preserved over the composition and we can proceed to define a partial architecture of the system, by presenting a BDD with the refinement of an abstract block into the blocks Sensors and ACU, this diagram is presented in Fig. 11.

The interactions between the composed blocks are then described by an IBD (see Fig. 12) where the ports representing the synchronized input and output actions are linked with connectors and the unshared actions are exposed as offered and demanded services of the composition.

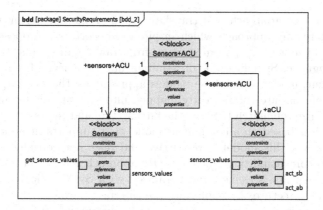

Fig. 11. BDD for the second iteration

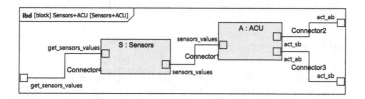

Fig. 12. IBD for the second iteration

Subsequently, we continue adding requirements $R1.1.3$, with related input action {act_ab}, and $R1.2$, with related input action {act_sb}, to our architecture in the same manner, but for lack of space we can not present here these further steps.

6   Related Works

In [11], the authors propose a system modeling approach that combines SysML safety requirements and block diagrams, and the model checking approach to prove that the local behavior of each component contributes to satisfy system requirements. In this work the problem of component compatibility and the preservation of the requirements are not treated.

To construct systems, other approaches take into account all the requirements at once. For example, [12], based on KAOS framework, and in [13] the authors propose an incremental approach by adding structural and behavioral properties into a software architecture. In [14], the authors propose the rCOS method to build a system from requirements to implementation. Our approach is similar to theirs, in the way we use sequence diagrams to express component interfaces, but it lacks the use of a component library to look for third party components and verify their compatibility. The works proposed in [15,16] are based on a behavior tree approach and translate atomic requirements into behavior trees. An interesting approach which inspired our work was proposed in [17], the authors construct the system starting from raw requirements described in a natural language. Specifications of requirements are derived from intermediate requirement models, and these models approximate the raw requirements. These requirements are then directly mapped into system architecture, with a view to maximize the match between the final system and the raw requirements. This approach is based on a component model that supports incremental composition. However this model is restrictive and does not consider component protocols and compatibility verification. Our approach is different and proposes to map requirements, specified and organized with SysML diagrams, directly into system architecture, by exploiting the interface automata formalism and the composition of component interfaces. The construction of system architecture is guided by the requirements, and the preservation of these requirements in the final system is guaranteed by the compatibility of interface automata and the preservation of the component actions linked to the requirements.

7 Conclusion

In reliable applications, it is important to specify a system architecture in accord with the requirement specifications. To achieve this goal, in this paper we proposed an approach to specify system architecture directly from SysML functional requirements. SysML requirement diagram was analyzed to extract its atomic requirements. These requirements were then associated, one by one, to reusable components, and LTL properties representing the requirements were verified on the components. To verify an LTL property, component behavior represented in SD is translated into Promela statements and then verified with the SPIN model-checker. These components were then added to a partial architecture by the composition of their component interfaces described through interface automata. Preservation of requirements over the composition was guaranteed by the conservation of related Input/Output actions on the transitions of the composite automaton. This approach was illustrated by the case study of a safety vehicle system. For future research, further relationships between SysML requirement diagram and formal properties will be investigated, by formalizing requirements with temporal logic formulas in an extended SysML profile. We plan also to integrate our approach as an extension to the TopCased environment [18].

References

1. The Object Management Group (OMG): OMG Systems Modeling Language (OMG SysML) Specification Version 1.2, June 2010. http://www.omg.org/spec/SysML/1.2/
2. Carrillo, O., Chouali, S., Mountassir, H.: Formalizing and verifying compatibility and consistency of sysml blocks. SIGSOFT Softw. Eng. Notes **37**(4), 1–8 (2012)

3. Chouali, S., Hammad, A.: Formal verification of components assembly based on sysml and interface automata. ISSE **7**(4), 265–274 (2011)
4. Lima, V., Talhi, C., Mouheb, D., Debbabi, M., Wang, L., Pourzandi, M.: Formal verification and validation of UML 2.0 sequence diagrams using source and destination of messages. Electron. Notes Theor. Comput. Sci. **254**, 143–160 (2009)
5. de Alfaro, L., Henzinger, T.A.: Interface automata. In: Proceedings of the Ninth Annual Symposium on Foundations of Software Engineering (FSE), pp. 109–120. ACM Press (2001)
6. Object Management Group: The OMG Unified Modeling Language Specification, UML 2.0, July 2005
7. Lee, E.A., Xiong, Y.: A behavioral type system and its application in Ptolemy II. Formal Aspects Comput. **16**(3), 210–237 (2004)
8. National Highway Traffic Safety Administration: Federal Motor Vehicle Safety Standards, September 1998
9. Holzmann, G.J.: Design and Validation of Computer Protocols. Prentice Hall, Englewood Cliffs (1991)
10. Clarke, E.M., Grumberg, O., Peled, D.A.: Model Checking. MIT Press, Cambridge (1999)
11. Pétin, J.F., Evrot, D., Morel, G., Lamy, P.: Combining SysML and formal methods for safety requirements verification. In: 22nd International Conference on Software & Systems Engineering and their Applications, Paris (2010)
12. van Lamsweerde, A.: From system goals to software architecture. In: Bernardo, M., Inverardi, P. (eds.) SFM 2003. LNCS, vol. 2804, pp. 25–43. Springer, Heidelberg (2003)
13. Barais, O., Duchien, L., Le Meur, A.F.: A framework to specify incremental software architecture transformations. In: 31st EUROMICRO Conference on Software Engineering and Advanced Applications, 2005, pp. 62–69 (2005)
14. Chen, Z., Liu, Z., Ravn, A.P., Stolz, V., Zhan, N.: Refinement and verification in component-based model-driven design. Sci. Comput. Program. **74**(4), 168–196 (2009)
15. Dromey, R.G.: From requirements to design: Formalizing the key steps. In: Proceedings of the First International Conference on Software Engineering and Formal Methods, 2003, pp. 2–11 (2003)
16. Dromey, R.G.: Engineering large-scale software-intensive systems. In: ASWEC, pp. 4–6 (2007)
17. Lau, K.-K., Nordin, A., Rana, T., Taweel, F.: Constructing component-based systems directly from requirements using incremental composition. In: Proceedings of 36th EUROMICRO Conference on Software Engineering and Advanced Applications, pp. 85–93. IEEE (2010)
18. Farail, P., Goutillet, P., Canals, A., Le Camus, C., Sciamma, D., Michel, P., Cregut, X., Pantel, M.: The TOPCASED project : a toolkit in open source for critical aeronautic systems design. Ingénieurs de l'automobile **781**, 54–59 (2006)

Formalising Adaptation Patterns for Autonomic Ensembles

Luca Cesari[1,4(✉)], Rocco De Nicola[2], Rosario Pugliese[1], Mariachiara Puviani[3], Francesco Tiezzi[2], and Franco Zambonelli[3]

[1] Università degli Studi di Firenze, Florence, Italy
luca.cesari@unifi.it
[2] IMT Advanced Studies Lucca, Lucca, Italy
[3] Università degli Studi di Modena e Reggio Emilia, Modena, Italy
[4] Università di Pisa, Pisa, Italy

Abstract. Autonomic behavior and self-adaptation in software can be supported by several architectural design patterns. In this paper we illustrate how some of the component- and ensemble-level adaptation patterns proposed in the literature can be rendered in SCEL, a formalism devised for modeling autonomic systems. Specifically, we present a compositional approach: first we show how a single generic component is modelled in SCEL, then we show that each pattern is rendered as the (parallel) composition of the SCEL terms corresponding to the involved components (and, possibly, to their environment). Notably, the SCEL terms corresponding to the patterns only differ from each other for the definition of the predicates identifying the targets of attribute-based communication. This enables autonomic ensembles to dynamically change the pattern in use by simply updating components' predicate definitions, as illustrated by means of a case study from the robotics domain.

1 Introduction

In the era of *autonomic computing* [1], where computer and software systems must manage themselves and their components, (self-)adaptation is a key aspect of software design. Self-adaptation is defined as the ability of a system to autonomously adapt its behaviour and/or structure to dynamic operating conditions [2], so as to preserve its capability of delivering the necessary services with acceptable quality levels. It is a key feature for *ensembles* [3], namely open-ended, large-scale and highly-parallel distributed systems, exhibiting complex interactions and behaviours. In fact, research on self-adaptive systems is attracting more and more attention among those interested in complex distributed systems [4].

Developers of autonomic ensembles have to understand and model not only the functional needs of their systems but also their adaptation needs. In particular, they have to check whether the provided models do offer the expected behaviour or attentively whether they are correct with respect to given specifications.

This work has been partially sponsored by the EU project ASCENS (257414) and by the Italian MIUR PRIN project CINA (2010LHT4KM).

J.L. Fiadeiro et al. (Eds.): FACS 2013, LNCS 8348, pp. 100–118, 2014.
DOI: 10.1007/978-3-319-07602-7_8, © Springer International Publishing Switzerland 2014

At the same time, they have to identify the appropriate architectural schemes for modelling individual components and the whole system as an ensemble of components. The goal of such choice being the guarantee that the adopted architectural scheme is instrumental for attesting that systems do self-adapt without severely undermining their intended functional behaviours.

Building on the large body of work in the area and on our own experience in the engineering of self-adaptive systems [5,6], we have previously identified and framed a few *adaptation patterns*, i.e. key architectural patterns that could be adopted to enforce self-adaptation at the level of individual components and ensembles. Software adaptation can indeed benefit from reuse in a similar way that designing software architectures has benefited from the reuse of software design patterns [7]. We identified context-aware and controllable *service components* (SCs) as the primitive entities to specify self-adaptive systems. In our view, a SC is a well-delimited piece of software (component) that provides a well-defined set of functionalities (services). This approach fits properly with all the software engineering features, namely modularity and reusability, other than simplicity.

Relying on this primitive entities, we have framed the many schemes by which *feedback loops* can be closed around individual SCs or ensembles of SCs, in order to achieve autonomic self-adaptive behaviours [1]. It is, indeed, widely recognized [8–10], especially in the MAPE-K architecture, that the capability of self-adaptation in a system necessarily requires the existence of feedback loops. This implies that, somehow, there exist means to inspect and analyse what is happening in the system (at the level of SCs, SC ensembles or the environment in which they are situated) and have components of the systems react accordingly. Therefore, looking at how these feedback loops appear implicitly or explicitly into SCs or into their ensembles, some categories of patterns can be identified.

Such analysis (extensively described in [11,12]) is still affected by two key limitations. Firstly, the patterns are modelled only in a semi-formal way, via UML diagrams and via a general description of the classes of self-adaptive goals that each pattern can satisfy (as from the SOTA goal-oriented requirements engineering approach [6]). It is then difficult to reason about the exact behaviour and properties of such patterns [13]. Secondly, the issue of rendering the presented patterns in some programming language is simply not considered at the moment.

In this paper, we address the above limitations by using SCEL [14], a formalism devised for modelling autonomic systems, to formalise both SCs of an autonomic ensemble and the adaptation patterns they use. By exploiting attributes associated to a component's interface, we can build patterns of communication that allow SCs to dynamically organise themselves into ensembles and implement specific adaptation patterns. Predicates over such attributes are used to specify the targets of communication actions, thus enabling a sort of *attribute-based* communication. In this way, an ensemble is not a rigid fixed network but rather a highly flexible structure where components linkages are dynamically established according to the chosen adaptation pattern.

Our aim is thus twofold. On the one hand, we show how SCs can enact adaptation by exploiting interfaces and attributes associated to them. On the other hand, we formalise the adaptation patterns via a language with an operational semantics that paves the way to reasoning about them. Our ultimate goal is to provide a sound and uniform set of conceptual and practical guidelines and tools to drive developers of SC ensembles in the engineered exploitation of such mechanisms at the level of abstract system modelling, verification, and implementation.

Moreover, in this work we focus on system components' *linkage*. These connections can change at run-time, thus e.g. enabling the dynamic transition from one adaptation pattern to another, and we take advantage from the SCEL language for modelling these modifications (as shown in Sect. 6). The components' internal logic, comprehensive of their behaviour and feedback loops, is not specified in this work because it plays no role in the modelling of adaptation patterns.

The rest of the paper is organised as follows. In Sect. 2, we introduce some basic notions about service component interfaces and adaptation patterns, while in Sect. 3 we review the main ingredients of SCEL. In Sect. 4, we show how SCs and their environment are rendered in SCEL. These are then exploited in Sect. 5 to express in SCEL the patterns introduced in Sect. 2, and in Sect. 6 to model a robotics case study. Finally, in Sect. 7 we review some strictly related work and in Sect. 8 we hint at directions for future work.

2   Service Components and Adaptation Patterns

We base our categorization of adaptation patterns on a very general model for the interface of the primitive Service Component (SC). Therefore, we begin by introducing some basic notions about SC interfaces and adaptation patterns.

SC interfaces help to better understand how SCs interact and propagate adaptation. A generic SC interface has six ports:

- I - Input: for receiving service requests and responses;
- O - Output: for invoking services or replying to service requests;
- S - Sensor: for sensing the status of other components and of the environment;
- F - Effector: for adapting the behaviour of other components, thus acting as an Autonomic Manager (AM), or for propagating adaptation in the environment;
- E - Emitter: for issuing status information to an AM;
- C - Control: for receiving adaptation orders from an AM.

Notably, the same port may be connected to more than one SC and some ports of given SC can be omitted whenever they do not play any role. In this way, we can characterise families of typical components as exemplified in Fig. 1.

Depending on the SC ports that are enabled and how they are interconnected, different kinds of adaptation patterns can be obtained.

At the level of individual SCs, the categories of adaptation patterns are:

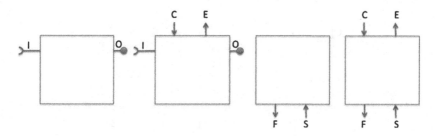

Fig. 1. Examples of SC interfaces of self-adaptive service components, adaptable service components, manager components, and adaptable manager components

- *Reactive SC*: components able to react to environment's changes and not coupled with an explicit feedback loop; instead, such feedback loops exist only implicitly in the interactions of the components with the environment (as in reactive agent and component systems [15]).
- *Autonomic SC*: components explicitly coupled with an external feedback loop that monitors and directs their behaviour (as in most autonomic computing architectures [1,16]). This pattern is shown in Fig. 2 (left), where the autonomic manager *AM* and the service component *SC* are such that:
  - *SC* has an interface appropriate for an adaptable service component;
  - *AM* has an interface appropriate for an adaptable manager component;
  - *AM* senses (along port S) whatever is emitted by *SC* (along port E);
  - *SC* obeys (along port C) *AM*'s control (along port F).
- *Proactive SC*: components that have an internal feedback loop to direct their goal/utility-oriented behaviour (as in intelligent and goal-oriented agents [15]). This pattern is shown in Fig. 2 (right) and differs from the previous one for the following points:
  - the interfaces between *SC* and *AM* are encapsulated;
  - *AM* also monitors *SC*'s input (along port I).

Instead, at the level of SC ensembles, the categories of patterns are:

- *Centralised AM SCs Ensemble*: ensembles in which the overall adaptive behaviour is explicitly designed by means of specifically conceived interaction patterns between components (e.g., choreographies or negotiations [17,18]), and in which mutual interactions implies the existence of feedback loops. This pattern is shown in Fig. 3;
- *P2P AMs SCs Ensemble*: ensembles in which there exists a set of components or "coded behaviours" that have the explicit goals of enforcing a global feedback loop over the ensembles, i.e., of controlling and directing their overall behaviour (as in coordinated systems and electronic institutions [19]);
- *Reactive Stigmergy SCs Ensemble*: ensembles whose overall adaptive activities are not explicitly engineered by design, but for which adaptiveness (and feedback loops) emerges from the interaction of the components with a shared environment (as in pheromone-based [15,20] and field-based [21] approaches). This pattern is shown in Fig. 4.

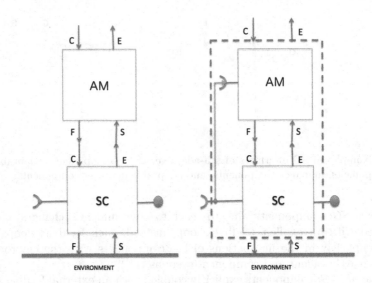

Fig. 2. Autonomic SC pattern and proactive SC pattern

3   SCEL: Software Component Ensemble Language

SCEL (Software Component Ensemble Language) [14,22] is a language for programming service computing systems in terms of service components aggregated
according to their knowledge and behavioural policies. The basic ingredient of
SCEL is the notion of (*service*) *component* $\mathcal{I}[\mathcal{K}, \Pi, P]$ that consists of:

1. An *interface* $\mathcal{I}$ publishing and making available structural and behavioural
   information about the component itself in the form of *attributes*, i.e. names
   acting as references to information stored the component's repository. Among
   them, attribute *id* is mandatory and is bound to the name of the component.
2. A *knowledge repository* $\mathcal{K}$ managing both application data and awareness
   data, together with the specific handling mechanism. The knowledge repository of a component stores also the information associated to its interface,
   which therefore can be dynamically manipulated by means of the operations
   provided by the knowledge repositories' handling mechanisms.
3. *policies* Π regulating the interaction between the different internal parts of
   the component and the interaction of the component with the others.
4. A *process* P, together with a set of process definitions that can be dynamically
   activated. Processes in P execute local computations, coordinate interaction
   with the knowledge repository or perform adaptation and reconfiguration.

The syntax of SCEL is presented in Table 1. SYSTEMS aggregate components
through the *composition* operator $\_ \parallel \_$. It is also possible to restrict the scope
of a name, say n, by using the *name restriction* operator $(\nu n)\_$.

PROCESSES are the active computational units. Each process is built up
from the *inert* process **nil** via *action prefixing* $(a.P)$, *nondeterministic choice*

Table 1. SCELsyntax (Knowledge $\mathcal{K}$, Policies Π, Templates T, and Items t are parameters of the language)

Systems $S ::= \mathcal{I}[\mathcal{K}, \Pi, P] \mid S_1 \parallel S_2 \mid (\nu n)S$	
Processes $P ::= \mathbf{nil} \mid a.P \mid P_1 + P_2 \mid P_1[P_2] \mid X \mid A(\bar{p})$	
Actions $a ::= \mathbf{get}(T)@c \mid \mathbf{qry}(T)@c \mid \mathbf{put}(t)@c \mid \mathbf{fresh}(n) \mid \mathbf{new}(\mathcal{I}, \mathcal{K}, \Pi, P)$	
Targets $c ::= n \mid x \mid \mathsf{self} \mid \mathcal{P} \mid p$	

$(P_1 + P_2)$, *controlled composition* $(P_1[P_2])$, *process variable* (X), and *parametrized process invocation* $(A(\bar{p}))$. The construct $P_1[P_2]$ abstracts the various forms of parallel composition commonly used in process calculi (see [14] for further details). Anyway, in this work, controlled composition will be interpreted as a standard interleaving, which means that in case of parallel processes only one process at a time can perform an action (the others stay still). Process variables can support *higher-order* communication and enable a straightforward implementation of adaptive behaviours [23]. Indeed, they permit to exchange (the code of) a process, and possibly execute it, by first adding an item containing the process to a knowledge repository and then retrieving/withdrawing this item while binding the process to a process variable. We let A to range over a set of parametrized *process identifiers* that are used in recursive process definitions. We assume that each process identifier A has a *single* definition of the form $A(\bar{f}) \triangleq P$, with $\bar{p}$ and $\bar{f}$ denoting lists of actual and formal parameters, respectively.

Processes can perform five different kinds of Actions. Actions $\mathbf{get}(T)@c$, $\mathbf{qry}(T)@c$ and $\mathbf{put}(t)@c$ are used to manage shared knowledge repositories by withdrawing/retrieving/adding information items from/to the knowledge repository identified by c. These actions exploit templates T to select knowledge items t in the repositories. They heavily rely on the used knowledge repository and are implemented by invoking the handling operations it provides. Action $\mathbf{fresh}(n)$ introduces a scope restriction for the name n so that this name is guaranteed to be *fresh*, i.e. different from any other name previously used. Action $\mathbf{new}(\mathcal{I}, \mathcal{K}, \Pi, P)$ creates a new component $\mathcal{I}[\mathcal{K}, \Pi, P]$. Actions $\mathbf{get}$ and $\mathbf{qry}$ may cause the process executing them to wait for the wanted element if it is not (yet) available in the knowledge repository. The two actions differ for the fact that $\mathbf{get}$ removes the found item from the target repository while $\mathbf{qry}$ leaves the repository unchanged. Actions $\mathbf{put}$, $\mathbf{fresh}$ and $\mathbf{new}$ are instead immediately executed.

Different entities may be used as the target c of an action. As a matter of notation, n ranges over component names, while x ranges over variables for names. The distinguished variable self can be used by processes to refer to the name of the component hosting them. The target can also be a *predicate* $\mathcal{P}$ or the name p, exposed as an attribute in the interface of the component, of a predicate that can be dynamically modified. A predicate is a standard boolean-valued expression obtained by applying standard boolean operators to the results returned by the evaluation of relations between component attributes and expressions. We adopt the following conventions about attribute names within predicates.

If an attribute name occurs in a predicate without specifying (via prefix notation) the corresponding interface, it is assumed that this name refers to an
attribute within the interface of the *object* component (i.e., a component that is
a target of the communication action). Instead, if an attribute name occurring
in a predicate is prefixed by the keyword this, then it is assumed that this name
refers to an attribute within the interface of the *subject* component (i.e., the
component hosting the process performing the communication action). E.g., the
predicate this.*status* = "*sending*" $\wedge$ *status* = "*receiving*" is satisfied when the
status of the subject component is *sending* and that of the object is *receiving*.

In actions using a predicate $\mathcal{P}$ to indicate the target (directly or via p),
predicates act as 'guards' specifying *all* components that can be affected by
the execution of the action, i.e. a component must satisfy $\mathcal{P}$ to be the target
of the action. Thus, actions **put**(t)@n and **put**(t)@$\mathcal{P}$ give rise to two different
primitive forms of communication: the former is a *point-to-point* communication,
while the latter is a sort of *group-oriented* communication. The set of components
satisfying a given predicate $\mathcal{P}$ used as the target of a communication action can be
considered as the *ensemble* with which the process performing the action intends
to interact. For example, the names of the components that can be members of
an ensemble can be fixed via the predicate $id \in \{n, m, o\}$. When an action has
this predicate as target, it will act on all components named n, m or o, if any.
Instead, to dynamically characterize the members of an ensemble that are active
and have a battery whose level is higher than *low*, by assuming that attributes
active and *batteryLevel* belong to the interface of any component willing to be
part of the ensemble, one can write *active* = "*yes*" $\wedge$ *batteryLevel* > *low*.

4   Service Components and their Environment in SCEL

We now show how a generic SC is rendered in SCEL. Moreover, since most
scenarios and patterns involve the *environment*, we also point out how it can be
modelled in SCEL. Notably, the parallel composition between a generic SC and
the environment gives rise to the *Reactive SC* pattern introduced in Sect. 2.

Service Components. A generic SC is rendered in SCELas a component
$\mathcal{I}_{SC}[\mathcal{K}_{SC}, \Pi_{SC}, SC]$ with

$$\mathcal{I}_{SC} \triangleq \{(id, sc), (role, \text{"}component\text{"}/\text{"}manager\text{"}/\text{"}environment\text{"}),$$
$$(controlFlag, \text{"}on\text{"}/\text{"}off\text{"}), (emitterFlag, \text{"}on\text{"}/\text{"}off\text{"}),$$
$$(inputFlag, \text{"}on\text{"}/\text{"}off\text{"}), (outputFlag, \text{"}on\text{"}/\text{"}off\text{"}),$$
$$(effectorFlag, \text{"}on\text{"}/\text{"}off\text{"}), (sensorFlag, \text{"}on\text{"}/\text{"}off\text{"}),$$
$$(p_{input}, \mathcal{P}_{input}), (p_{output}, \mathcal{P}_{output}), (p_{emitter}, \mathcal{P}_{emitter}),$$
$$(p_{effector}, \mathcal{P}_{effector}), \ldots\}$$
$$SC \triangleq Control[Sensor[Input[Emitter[Effector[Output[InternalLogic]]]]]]$$

The component exposes in its interface at least twelve attributes. The attribute id
indicates the name of the component, while $role$ is used to define the role of the SC
in a pattern (it can take one of the values *component*, *manager* or *environment*).

Moreover, for each port, the interface contains a flag attribute used to enable (value *on*) or disable (value *off*) the port. Finally, four attributes, i.e. p_{input}, p_{output}, $p_{emitter}$, and $p_{effector}$, are used to refer the predicates $\mathcal{P}_{input}$, $\mathcal{P}_{output}$, $\mathcal{P}_{emitter}$ and $\mathcal{P}_{effector}$, respectively. These predicates can identify single components or ensembles. Specifically, $\mathcal{P}_{input}$ and $\mathcal{P}_{emitter}$ identify the component(s) managing the considered SC, $\mathcal{P}_{output}$ identifies the addressee(s) of the output messages, and $\mathcal{P}_{effector}$ identifies the target of management actions (e.g., to enact adaptation), which can be either components or the environment.

The definition of action targets by means of attributes referring to predicates permits dynamically changing the predicates regulating the communication among SCEL components, which enables the dynamic transition from one adaptation pattern to another. We will come back to this point in Sect. 6.

Each port of the SC is then represented in SCEL as a process *PortName* that manages the data received or sent through the port and acts as a mediator between the external world and the knowledge repository of the component. These processes are executed in parallel with the process *InternalLogic* implementing the internal logic. This latter process, as well as the knowledge $\mathcal{K}_{SC}$ and the policy Π_{SC}, are left unspecified because they do not play any role in the modelling of adaptation patterns. The processes associated to the component's ports follow.

Input. The input data port can receive requests from other components. Its behaviour is expressed in SCEL as follows:

$$Input \triangleq \mathbf{qry}(inputFlag, \text{``on''})@\mathsf{self}.\ \mathbf{get}(\text{``}inputPort\text{''}, ?data, ?replyTo)@\mathsf{self}.$$
$$\mathbf{put}(\text{``}input\text{''}, data, replyTo)@\mathsf{self}.$$
$$\mathbf{put}(\text{``}inputPort\text{''}, data, replyTo)@p_{input}.\ Input$$

This process performs recursively the following behaviour. First, it checks the corresponding flag. If the port is enabled, it retrieves from the knowledge repository of the component an item (tagged with "*inputPort*") containing the input data and a predicate and sends one copy of such information (tagged with "*input*") to the component's internal logic and one copy (tagged with "*inputPort*") to the input port of each component acting as a manager. Indeed, if the SC is self-adaptive (see Fig. 2, right-hand side), its manager(s) must access the information received in input by the SC and, hence, the data received along the input port must be replicated to the manager(s) input port; otherwise, the forwarding of input messages is deactivated by simply setting the predicate referred by p_{input} to *false*. The provided predicate, bound to variable *replyTo*, will be used to respond to the requester(s).

Output. The output port is represented in SCEL as a process that fetches messages (e.g., responses to service requests) and a predicate (identifying, e.g., service requesters) generated by the internal logic, sets this predicate as p_{output} and sends the messages.

$$Output \triangleq \mathbf{qry}(outputFlag, \text{``on''})@\mathsf{self}.\ \mathbf{get}(\text{``}output\text{''}, ?data, ?recipients)@\mathsf{self}.$$
$$\mathbf{get}(p_{output}, ?oldOut)@\mathsf{self}.\mathbf{put}(p_{output}, recipients)@\mathsf{self}.$$
$$\mathbf{put}(\text{``}inputPort\text{''}, data)@p_{output}.\ Output$$

To guarantee a correct identification of the addressee(s), *Output* processes an outgoing response message at a time and we assume that the predicate referred by p_{output} can be modified only by this process. Notably, such assumption only involves processes of the components' internal logic, because the processes associated to the other ports do not modify the predicate, and no adaptation pattern prescribes a specific configuration for it. It is also worth noticing that, in case the same requester sends more than one request simultaneously to the component, the requester has to specify in the request data a correlation identifier that will be then inserted into the response data in order to allow the requester to properly correlate each response to the corresponding request.

Emitter. The emitter port is used to send awareness data to manager(s). The corresponding process is similar to the previous one, except for the item tags and the **put**'s predicate.

$$Emitter \triangleq \mathbf{qry}(emitterFlag, \text{``}on\text{''})@self. \ \mathbf{get}(\text{``}emitter\text{''}, ?data)@self.$$
$$\mathbf{put}(\text{``}sensorPort\text{''}, data)@p_{emitter}. \ Emitter$$

Effector. The effector port is used to enact adaptation on the managed element or to interact with the environment. The corresponding process is similar to the emitter one, except for the item tags and the **put**'s predicate.

$$Effector \triangleq \mathbf{qry}(effectorFlag, \text{``}on\text{''})@self. \ \mathbf{get}(\text{``}effector\text{''}, ?data)@self.$$
$$\mathbf{put}(\text{``}controlPort\text{''}, data)@p_{effector}. \ Effector$$

Sensor. The sensor port is used to sense the status of the component(s) managed by the considered SC or to retrieve information from the environment. The corresponding process gets the data coming from the sensor port and sends it to the component's internal logic:

$$Sensor \triangleq \mathbf{qry}(sensorFlag, \text{``}on\text{''})@self. \ \mathbf{get}(\text{``}sensorPort\text{''}, ?data)@self.$$
$$\mathbf{put}(\text{``}sensor\text{''}, data)@self. \ Sensor$$

Control. The control port is used to receive adaptation orders from manager(s). The corresponding process is similar to the sensor one, except for the item tags.

$$Control \triangleq \mathbf{qry}(controlFlag, \text{``}on\text{''})@self. \ \mathbf{get}(\text{``}controlPort\text{''}, ?data)@self.$$
$$\mathbf{put}(\text{``}control\text{''}, data)@self. \ Control$$

Environment. Since many adaptation patterns involve the environment where SCs are deployed, the environment must be modelled as well in SCEL in order to get a complete specification of patterns. It can be rendered as one or more components, whose precise definition may vary from one scenario to another. A generic environment could be expressed, e.g., as a component $\mathcal{I}_{Env}[\mathcal{K}_{Env}, \Pi_{Env}, Env]$ where its interface is defined as

$$\mathcal{I}_{Env} \triangleq \{(id, env), (role, \text{``}environment\text{''}), \dots\}$$

and a possible sketch of the hosted process is

$$Env \triangleq \ldots \ \mathbf{get}(\text{``}controlPort\text{''}, ?data)@\mathsf{self} \ \ldots$$
$$\ldots \ \mathbf{put}(\text{``}sensorPort\text{''}, newData)@p_{emitter} \ \ldots$$

The environment component receives awareness data from components of the system. Such components should be connected to the environment via their effector and sensor ports, and have to use a predicate definition in their interface such as $(p_{effector}, id = env)$ meaning that name $p_{effector}$ currently refers to predicate $id = env$. Moreover, the environment process provides data to components through their sensor ports by means of the predicate referred by $p_{emitter}$, which dynamically selects the partner(s) of the communication. E.g., if the environment has to communicate with only one component sc, the predicate could be defined as $(p_{emitter}, id = sc)$. Instead, if the environment needs to communicate data to all components of the considered system, it could be used the predicate $(p_{emitter}, role = \text{``}component\text{''})$. As another example, if the environment must interact with a subset of the available components (e.g., those that are currently active), the predicate becomes:

$$(p_{emitter}, role = \text{``}component\text{''} \ \wedge \ status = \text{``}active\text{''})$$

Finally, the environment could comprise multiple SCEL components, such as a room containing various devices (wifi access points, temperature sensors, motion sensors, etc.). In this scenario, each device is an environment component, thus an SC interacting with this 'smart ambient' accesses the environment components appropriate for each specific interaction. For example, the effector predicate is

$$(p_{effector}, role = \text{``}environment\text{''} \ \wedge \ distance(\mathsf{this}.x, \mathsf{this}.y, x, y) <= range)$$

where $(\mathsf{this}.x, \mathsf{this}.y)$ identifies the coordinates of the emitting SC, while (x, y) identifies the coordinates of each environment component within a given range.

5 Adaptation Patterns in SCEL

We show now how the previous concepts can be used to express in SCEL some of the patterns introduced in Sect. 2, that will be exploited in the case study of Sect. 6. We refer to [24] for the SCEL models of the remaining patterns.

In SCEL every pattern results from the composition of the SCEL components corresponding to the involved SCs, AMs and environment[1], and by appropriately tuning the predicate definitions and the interface's attributes. We leave the predicate referred by p_{output} unspecified because it is context-dependent.

---

[1] For the sake of presentation, here we model the environment as a single SCEL component $\mathcal{I}_{Env}[\mathcal{K}_{Env}, \Pi_{Env}, Env]$ (see Sect. 4).

Notably, for any pattern, processes SC and AM running in the SCEL components corresponding to SCs and AMs, respectively, have always the following form:

$$Control[Sensor[Input[Emitter[Effector[Output[InternalLogic]]]]]]$$

Centralized AM SCs Ensemble

Intent. Any SC needs an external feedback loop to adapt. All SCs need to share knowledge and adaptation logic, so they are managed by the same AM.

Context. This pattern can be adopted when:

- an AM is necessary to manage adaptation;
- direct communication between SCs is allowed;
- a centralised feedback loop is more suitable because a single AM has a global vision on the system;
- the ensemble only includes a few, simple components.

Behaviour. This pattern, shown in Fig. 3, is designed around one feedback loop. All components are managed by a single AM that "controls" their behaviour and, by sharing knowledge about them, is able to propagate adaptation.

Consequences. To manage adaptation over the entire system, a single AM is more efficient than multiple ones because it has a global view and knowledge of the system, but it can become a single point of failure.

SCEL description. The pattern is rendered in SCEL as the parallel composition of the components representing the centralized AM, the environment and the SCs:

$$\mathcal{I}_{AM}[\mathcal{K}_{AM}, \Pi_{AM}, AM] \parallel \mathcal{I}_{Env}[\mathcal{K}_{Env}, \Pi_{Env}, Env]$$
$$\parallel \mathcal{I}_{SC_1}[\mathcal{K}_{SC_1}, \Pi_{SC_1}, SC_1] \parallel \mathcal{I}_{SC_2}[\mathcal{K}_{SC_2}, \Pi_{SC_2}, SC_2] \parallel \mathcal{I}_{SC_3}[\mathcal{K}_{SC_3}, \Pi_{SC_3}, SC_3]$$

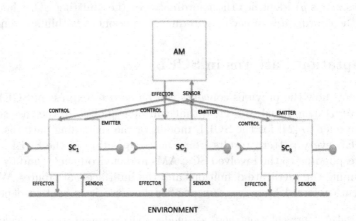

Fig. 3. Centralized AM SCs ensemble

where the interfaces of manger and SCs (with $i \in \{1, 2, 3\}$) are as follows:

- $\mathcal{I}_{AM} \triangleq \{(id, am), (role, \text{"}manager\text{"}),$
  $(controlFlag, \text{"}off\text{"}), (emitterFlag, \text{"}off\text{"}),$
  $(inputFlag, \text{"}on\text{"}), (outputFlag, \text{"}off\text{"}),$
  $(effectorFlag, \text{"}on\text{"}), (sensorFlag, \text{"}on\text{"}),$
  $(p_{input}, false), (p_{output}, \mathcal{P}_{output}), (p_{emitter}, \mathcal{P}_{emitter}),$
  $(p_{effector}, id \in \{sc_1, sc_2, sc_3\})), \ldots\}$

The AM description, in order to work as desired, needs to:
- activate only the sensor, input and effector ports;
- deactivate the forwarding of input messages to other components, by setting the predicate referred by p_{input} to *false*;
- configure the predicate referred by $p_{effector}$ accordingly to communicate only with the three managed SCs (i.e., only by components whose identifier belongs to the set $\{sc_1, sc_2, sc_3\}$).

- $\mathcal{I}_{SC_i} \triangleq \{(id, sc_i), (role, \text{"}component\text{"}),$
  $(controlFlag, \text{"}on\text{"}), (emitterFlag, \text{"}on\text{"}),$
  $(inputFlag, \text{"}on\text{"}), (outputFlag, \text{"}on\text{"}),$
  $(effectorFlag, \text{"}on\text{"}), (sensorFlag, \text{"}on\text{"}),$
  $(p_{input}, id = am), (p_{output}, \mathcal{P}_{output}), (p_{emitter}, id = am),$
  $(p_{effector}, role = \text{"}environment\text{"}), \ldots\}$

The SC description, to be properly controlled by the AM, needs to:
- activate all communication ports;
- configure the predicate referred by p_{input} in order to properly react to the received service requests by forwarding them to the manager am;
- configure the predicate referred by $p_{emitter}$ suitably to send the control data to the manager am;
- configure the predicate referred by $p_{effector}$ so to enable the interaction with the environment (i.e., all components playing the *environment* role).

Reactive Stigmergy SCs Ensemble

Intent. There are several SCs that cannot directly interact with each other. The SCs simply react to the environment and sense the environment changes.

Context. This pattern has to be adopted when:

- the ensemble includes several components;
- the components are very simple, without having a lot of knowledge;
- the environment is frequently changing;
- direct communication between components is disallowed.

Behaviour. This pattern, shown in Fig. 4, has not a direct feedback loop. Each single component acts like a bioinspired component. To satisfy its goal, the SC acts in the environment that senses with its "sensors" and reacts to the changes in it with its "effectors". The different components are not able to communicate one with another, but are able to propagate information (and their actions) in the environment. Hence, they are able to sense the environment changes (e.g., other components reactions) and adapt their behaviour due to these changes.

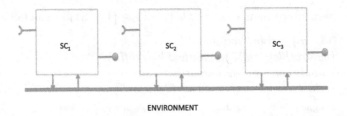

Fig. 4. Reactive Stigmergy SCs ensemble

Consequences. If the component is a proactive one, its behaviour is defined inside it with its internal goal. The behaviour of the whole system cannot be a priori defined. It emerges from the collective behaviour of the ensemble. The components do not require a large amount of knowledge. The reaction of each component is quick and does not need managers since adaptation is propagated via the environment. The interaction model is an entirely indirect one.

SCEL description. The pattern is rendered in SCEL as the parallel composition of the components representing the SCs and their environment:

$$\mathcal{I}_{SC_1}[\mathcal{K}_{SC_1}, \Pi_{SC_1}, SC_1] \ \| \ \mathcal{I}_{SC_2}[\mathcal{K}_{SC_2}, \Pi_{SC_2}, SC_2] \ \| \ \mathcal{I}_{SC_3}[\mathcal{K}_{SC_3}, \Pi_{SC_3}, SC_3]$$
$$\| \ \mathcal{I}_{Env}[\mathcal{K}_{Env}, \Pi_{Env}, Env]$$

where the SCs' interfaces, with $i \in \{1, 2, 3\}$, are as follows:

$$\mathcal{I}_{SC_i} \triangleq \{(id, sc_i), \ (role, \text{``component''}),$$
$$(controlFlag, \text{``off''}), (effectorFlag, \text{``on''}),$$
$$(inputFlag, \text{``on''}), (outputFlag, \text{``on''}),$$
$$(emitterFlag, \text{``off''}), (sensorFlag, \text{``on''}),$$
$$(p_{input}, false), (p_{output}, \mathcal{P}_{output}), (p_{emitter}, \mathcal{P}_{emitter}),$$
$$(p_{effector}, role = \text{``environment''}), \ldots\}$$

The differences w.r.t. the SC description of the previous pattern are as follows:

- control and emitter ports are deactivated (hence, the predicate referred by $p_{emitter}$ is left unspecified because it does not play any role);
- the forwarding of input messages is deactivated by setting the predicate referred by p_{input} to *false*.

6   Adaptation Patterns at Work

A key point about self-adaptation and self-adaptive patterns is the ability of dynamically changing the adaptation pattern in use if some circumstances occur during system lifetime. We illustrate this feature by means of a robotic case study concerning *object transportation*. For this task, robots need to find out objects (e.g., people to assist and rescue in case of disaster) and carry them back to a specific place (e.g., the external of a blazing building). A large number of robots can be used in the unknown environment in order to rapidly satisfy the system's goal. Thus, the most appropriate pattern to be used is the *Reactive Stigmergy SCs Ensemble* one red: the number of robots is large with respect to the size of the area to be explored; danger makes real the necessity to have simple and not too expensive components; the environment is unknown and frequently changing due to the disaster. The suitability of this pattern with respect to other ones, while considering different environment configurations, has been validated in [25] through some simulations carried out using a multi-robot simulator. It has been shown that a fully centralised approach (using the *Centralized AM SCs Ensemble* pattern) is not effective unless the position of all objects is known in advance.

Anyway, in realistic situations a single robot could not be able to carry a victim alone. So, since no pattern can be conveniently adopted for the whole lifetime of the system, in cases a robot collaboration is needed to manage a specific task, a new pattern can be temporary applied for the necessary time. When the satisfaction of the object transportation task must be very short (e.g., in case of victims), the *Centralized AM SCs Ensemble* pattern is the best one. This is because the time for coordinating a single AM and all the other robots is shorter than the time for the coordination and negotiation among all robots (as, e.g., in the *P2P AMs SCs Ensemble* pattern). Thus, when a robot reaches an object that is too heavy, it changes its adaptation pattern becoming an AM. It also contacts other robots (the number that is needed to carry the object) that will change their pattern in order to behave as managed components. The AM then shares information about where the object is and how to carry it to the safe area. Finally, when the task is satisfied, all involved robots change again their pattern for coming back to the *Reactive Stigmergy SCs Ensemble* pattern.

This case study can be modelled in SCEL as follows. During the exploring phase all robots follow the *Reactive Stigmergy SCs Ensemble* pattern, thus each of them is rendered as a SCEL component with the following (excerpt of) interface:

$$\{(id, sc_i), (role, \text{``}component\text{''}), (p_{input}, false),$$
$$(p_{effector}, role = \text{``}environment\text{''}), \ldots\}$$

According to the *separation of concerns* design principle, the internal logic of components here is structured as follows:

$$InternalLogic \triangleq PatternHandler[ApplicationLogic]$$

where *PatternHandler*, that is in charge of changing the pattern when an object is found, is

$$PatternHandler \triangleq$$
get(*"sensor"*, *"objectFound"*, ?*objectData*)@self.*BecomeManager*(*objectData*)
+ **get**(*"input"*, *"changePattern"*, ?*manager*)@self.*BecomeManaged*(*manager*)

while *ApplicationLogic*, that implements the logic for the progress of the computation, is left unspecified as here we are not interested in this part of the internal behaviour of components. Intuitively, if the robot's sensors detect an object in the environment, the event is registered in the component's knowledge and, when the process above consumes it by means of the first **get** action, the execution of process *BecomeManager* is triggered. Similarly, the second **get** action is used to trigger the process *BecomeManaged* to react to a 'change pattern' request coming from another robot that has found an object.

The process *BecomeManager(data)* is defined as follows:

$$\textbf{get}(role, \text{``component''})@\text{self}. \textbf{put}(role, \text{``manager''})@\text{self}.$$
$$\textbf{get}(outputFlag, ?f)@\text{self}. \textbf{put}(outputFlag, \text{``off''})@\text{self}.$$
$$\textbf{get}(p_{effector}, ?oldEff)@\text{self}. \textbf{put}(p_{effector}, id \in S_{data})@\text{self}.$$
$$\textbf{put}(\text{``inputPort''}, \text{``changePattern''}, \text{self})@p_{effector}.$$
$$\textbf{get}(\text{``sensor''}, \text{``taskCompleted''})@\text{self}.RestoreReactiveStigmergy$$

where the set S_{data} of managed components, which are identified by $p_{effector}$, depends on some elaborations on the object *data*. Thus, to become a manager, first the component changes its role, the output port flag[2] and the effector predicate (as defined in Sect. 5). Then, it uses the new definition of this predicate to contact (via a **put** action) the appropriate number of robots that will be managed by it. When the object transportation task is completed, the process *RestoreReactiveStigmergy* is executed to reset the initial pattern.

The process *BecomeManaged(am)*, instead, is defined as follows:

$$\textbf{get}(controlFlag, ?cf)@\text{self}. \textbf{put}(controlFlag, \text{``on''})@\text{self}.$$
$$\textbf{get}(emitterFlag, ?ef)@\text{self}. \textbf{put}(emitterFlag, \text{``on''})@\text{self}.$$
$$\textbf{get}(p_{input}, ?oldInp)@\text{self}. \textbf{put}(p_{input}, id = am)@\text{self}.$$
$$\textbf{get}(p_{emitter}, ?oldEmit)@\text{self}. \textbf{put}(p_{emitter}, id = am)@\text{self}.$$
$$\textbf{get}(\text{``sensor''}, \text{``taskCompleted''})@\text{self}.RestoreReactiveStigmergy$$

This process enables the control and emitter ports, and modifies the predicates associated to the input and emitter ports as required by the *Centralized AM SCs Ensemble* pattern, by using the manager's identifier specified in the 'change pattern' request. Then, when the task is completed, it resets the initial pattern.

Finally, the process *RestoreReactiveStigmergy*, that restores the setting of the initial pattern and reinstalls the pattern handler process, is as follows:

$$\textbf{get}(role, ?oldRole)@\text{self}. \textbf{put}(role, \text{``component''})@\text{self}.$$
$$\textbf{get}(outputFlag, ?of)@\text{self}. \textbf{put}(outputFlag, \text{``on''})@\text{self}.$$
$$\textbf{get}(controlFlag, ?cf)@\text{self}. \textbf{put}(controlFlag, \text{``off''})@\text{self}.$$
$$\textbf{get}(emitterFlag, ?ef)@\text{self}. \textbf{put}(emitterFlag, \text{``off''})@\text{self}.$$
$$\textbf{get}(p_{input}, ?oldInp)@\text{self}. \textbf{put}(p_{input}, false)@\text{self}.$$
$$\textbf{get}(p_{emitter}, ?oldEmit)@\text{self}. \textbf{put}(p_{emitter}, false)@\text{self}.$$
$$\textbf{get}(p_{effector}, ?oldEff)@\text{self}. \textbf{put}(p_{effector}, role = \text{``environment''})@\text{self}.$$
$$PatternHandler$$

---

[2] Indeed, the only difference about ports in the two patterns concerns the output one.

7 Related Works

The interest in engineering self-adaptive systems is growing, as shown by the number of recent surveys and overviews on the topic [4,9,26]. However, a comprehensive and rationally-organized analysis of architectural patterns for self-adaptation is still missing, despite the potential advantages of their use. For example, [27] proposes a classification of modelling dimensions for self-adaptive systems to provide the engineers with a common vocabulary for specifying the self-adaptation properties under consideration and select suitable solutions. However, although this work emphasizes the importance of feedback loops, it does not consider the patterns by which such feedback loops can be organized to promote self-adaptation. [7,28] focus on the mechanisms to perform adaptation actions, and on the various schemes that should be adopted to perform such adaptation actions at run-time and in a safe way. However they overlook the architectural patterns for the feedback loops that can identify and enact adaptation actions. Also [29] introduces the concept of patterns for self-adaptive systems based on control loops. It however focuses on how control loops can enforce adaptivity in a system and does not present a complete set of patterns.

Taking inspiration from control engineering, natural systems and software engineering, [8] presents some self-adaptive architectures that exhibit feedback loops. It also identifies the critical challenges that must be addressed to enable systematic and well-organized engineering of self-adaptive and self-managing software systems. In our work we aim at going further on and describing our patterns using a formalism, namely SCEL. Grounded on earlier works on architectural self-adaptation approaches [2], the FORMS model [30] enables engineers to describe, study and evaluate alternative design choices for self-adaptive systems. FORMS defines a shared vocabulary of adaptive primitives that – while simple and concise – can be used to precisely define arbitrary complex self-adaptive systems and can support engineers in expressing their design choices. This vocabulary is close to our choice of using SCEL to describe patterns, but it is not a formalism and rather has to be considered as a potentially useful complement to our work.

To the best of our knowledge, ours is the first work that addresses the formalisation of adaptation patterns. Rather, a bunch of works in the literature proposes formalisations of *design* patterns that, more in general, are devised to support component-based or object-oriented programming and are not specific for autonomic computing. We took inspiration from [31] and [32] to describe the patterns' template. Two main approaches have been considered: a group of works uses logics as target formalism (e.g., [33] relies on a temporal logic, while [34] on a predicate logic), whereas another group relies on new formalisms specifically devised for modelling design patterns (e.g., [35] uses the design model Abstract Data Views, while [36] proposes the use of Balanced Pattern Specification Language that, anyway, is still based on logics). Other works, as e.g. [37], formalise patterns in terms of graphs. Besides the fact that the above works do not deal with adaptation patterns, they differ from our work also because none of them uses a formalism based on process calculi, like SCEL. An approach using process calculi-like languages, namely CASPIS and COWS, is presented in [38], but it considers *methodological*, rather than *architectural* patterns.

8   Concluding Remarks

This paper reports on the way adaptation patterns for designing autonomic ensembles of SCs can be formalised by using the SCEL language. An application to a robotic case study is also presented, with the twofold aim of demonstrating the practical usage of the formalised adaptation patterns and of showing how dynamic change of adaptation patterns takes place.

From a technical point of view, the main challenge is in providing a compositional formalisation, where each pattern is rendered as the (parallel) composition of the models of the involved primitive components and where the dynamic change of pattern is still dealt with in a compositional way. Compositionality is also the key for allowing heterogeneous patterns to integrate well within the same system. This motivates our choice of using SCEL for defining such formalisation, as it features a form of attribute-based communication that easily permits to express component linkages according to the chosen adaptation pattern and to dynamically adapt them according to a given pattern change.

The objective of the proposed formalisation is to provide an operational semantics for adaptation patterns that paves the way to reasoning about them. This can lead to verifiable development of autonomic SC ensembles from abstract architectural patterns.

In the near future, in order to provide a more concrete evidence of the benefits brought by the proposed formalisation, we plan to implement the formalised adaptation patterns considered in this work in jRESP [14], a Java runtime environment for developing autonomic and adaptive systems according to the SCEL paradigm. A long-term goal, instead, is to integrate in this pattern-based development approach the formal reasoning tools for SCEL programs that are currently under construction. Once also the internal logic of the components (e.g., behaviour, feedback loops) is modelled, this integration will permit to establish qualitative and quantitative properties of individual SCs and their ensembles.

References

1. Kephart, J.O., Chess, D.M.: The vision of autonomic computing. Computer **36**, 41–50 (2003)
2. Weyns, D., Holvoet, T.: An architectural strategy for self-adapting systems. In: SEAMS, p. 3. IEEE (2007)
3. Project InterLink (2007). http://interlink.ics.forth.gr
4. Salehie, M., Tahvildari, L.: Self-adaptive software: landscape and research challenges. ACM Trans. Auton. Adapt. Syst. **4**(2), 14 (2009)
5. Zambonelli, F., Viroli, M.: A survey on nature-inspired metaphors for pervasive service ecosystems. J. Pervasive Comp. and Comm. **7**, 186–204 (2011)
6. Abeywickrama, D.B., Bicocchi, N., Zambonelli, F.: SOTA: towards a general model for self-adaptive systems. In: WETICE, pp. 48–53. IEEE (2012)

7. Gomaa, H., Hashimoto, K.: Dynamic self-adaptation for distributed service-oriented transactions. In: SEAMS, pp. 11–20. IEEE (2012)

8. Brun, Y., et al.: Engineering self-adaptive systems through feedback loops. In: Cheng, B.H.C., et al. (eds.) Software Engineering for Self-Adaptive Systems. LNCS, vol. 5525, pp. 48–70. Springer, Heidelberg (2009)

9. Cheng, B.H.C., et al.: Software engineering for self-adaptive systems: a research roadmap. In: Cheng, B.H.C., et al. (eds.) Software Engineering for Self-Adaptive Systems. LNCS, vol. 5525, pp. 1–26. Springer, Heidelberg (2009)

10. Vromant, P., Weyns, D., Malek, S., Andersson, J.: On interacting control loops in self-adaptive systems. In: SEAMS. ACM (2011)

11. Cabri, G., Puviani, M., Zambonelli, F.: Towards a taxonomy of adaptive agent-based collaboration patterns for autonomic service ensembles. In: CTS, pp. 508–515. IEEE (2011)

12. Puviani, M., Cabri, G., Zambonelli, F.: A taxonomy of architectural patterns for self-adaptive systems. In: C3S2E. ACM (2013)

13. Clarke, E.M., Wing, J.M.: Formal methods: state of the art and future directions. ACM Comput. Surv. **28**(4), 626–643 (1996)

14. De Nicola, R., Loreti, M., Pugliese, R., Tiezzi, F.: SCEL: a language for autonomic computing. Technical report, January 2013. http://rap.dsi.unifi.it/scel/pdf/SCEL-TR.pdf

15. Bordini, R.H., Braubach, L., Dastani, M., Fallah-Seghrouchni, A.E., Gómez-Sanz, J.J., Leite, J., O'Hare, G.M.P., Pokahr, A., Ricci, A.: A survey of programming languages and platforms for multi-agent systems. Informatica (Slovenia) **30**(1), 33–44 (2006)

16. Hariri, S., Khargharia, B., Chen, H., Yang, J., Zhang, Y., Parashar, M., Liu, H.: The autonomic computing paradigm. Clust. Comput. **9**(1), 5–17 (2006)

17. Beam, C., Segev, A.: Automated negotiations: a survey of the state of the art. Wirtschaftsinformatik **39**(3), 263–268 (1997)

18. Jennings, N., Faratin, P., Lomuscio, A., Parsons, S., Wooldridge, M., Sierra, C.: Automated negotiation: prospects, methods and challenges. Group Decis. Negot. **10**(2), 199–215 (2001)

19. Esteva, M., Rodríguez-Aguilar, J.-A., Sierra, C., Garcia, P., Arcos, J.-L.: On the formal specification of electronic institutions. In: Sierra, C., Dignum, F.P.M. (eds.) AgentLink 2000. LNCS (LNAI), vol. 1991, pp. 126–147. Springer, Heidelberg (2001)

20. Kesäniemi, J., Terziyan, V.: Agent-environment interaction in mas-introduction and survey. In: Alkhateeb, F., Maghayreh, E.A., Doush, I.A. (eds.) Multi-Agent Systems: Modeling, Interactions, Simulations and Case Studies. InTech, Vienna (2011)

21. Mamei, M., Zambonelli, F.: Programming pervasive and mobile computing applications: the TOTA approach. ACM Trans. Softw. Eng. Methodol. **18**(4), 1–56 (2009)

22. De Nicola, R., Ferrari, G., Loreti, M., Pugliese, R.: A language-based approach to autonomic computing. In: Beckert, B., Bonsangue, M.M. (eds.) FMCO 2011. LNCS, vol. 7542, pp. 25–48. Springer, Heidelberg (2012). http://rap.dsi.unifi.it/scel/

23. Gjondrekaj, E., Loreti, M., Pugliese, R., Tiezzi, F.: Modeling adaptation with a tuple-based coordination language. In: SAC, pp. 1522–1527. ACM (2012)

24. Cesari, L., De Nicola, R., Pugliese, R., Puviani, M., Tiezzi, F., Zambonelli, F.: Formalising adaptation patterns for autonomic ensembles. Technical report (2013). http://rap.dsi.unifi.it/scel/pdf/patternsInSCEL-TR.pdf

25. Puviani, M., Pinciroli, C., Cabri, G., Leonardi, L., Zambonelli, F.: Is self-expression useful? evaluation by a case study. In: WETICE (2013)
26. Weyns, D., Iftikhar, M., Malek, S., Andersson, J.: Claims and supporting evidence for self-adaptive systems: a literature study. In: SEAMS, pp. 89–98. IEEE (2012)
27. Andersson, J., de Lemos, R., Malek, S., Weyns, D.: Modeling dimensions of self-adaptive software systems. In: Cheng, B.H.C., de Lemos, R., Giese, H., Inverardi, P., Magee, J. (eds.) Software Engineering for Self-Adaptive Systems. LNCS, vol. 5525, pp. 27–47. Springer, Heidelberg (2009)
28. Gomaa, H., Hashimoto, K., Kim, M., Malek, S., Menascé, D.A.: Software adaptation patterns for service-oriented architectures. In: SAC, pp. 462–469. ACM (2010)
29. Weyns, D., et al.: On patterns for decentralized control in self-adaptive systems. In: de Lemos, R., Giese, H., Müller, H.A., Shaw, M. (eds.) Software Engineering for Self-Adaptive Systems. LNCS, vol. 7475, pp. 76–107. Springer, Heidelberg (2013)
30. Weyns, D., Malek, S., Andersson, J.: Forms: Unifying reference model for formal specification of distributed self-adaptive systems. ACM TAAS 7(1), 8 (2012)
31. Gamma, E., Helm, R., Johnson, R., Vlissides, J.: Design Patterns. Addison Wesley, Reading (1995)
32. Ramirez, A., Cheng, B.: Design patterns for developing dynamically adaptive systems. In: SEAMS, pp. 49–58. ACM (2010)
33. Mikkonen, T.: Formalizing design patterns. In: ICSE, pp. 115–124. IEEE (1998)
34. Bayley, I.: Formalising design patterns in predicate logic. In: SEFM, pp. 25–36. IEEE (2007)
35. Alencar, P.S.C., Cowan, D.D., de Lucena, C.J.P.: A formal approach to architectural design patterns. In: Gaudel, M.-C., Wing, Jeannette M. (eds.) FME 1996. LNCS, vol. 1051, pp. 576–594. Springer, Heidelberg (1996)
36. Taibi, T., Ling, D.N.C.: Formal specification of design patterns - a balanced approach. J. Object Technol. 2(4), 127–140 (2003)
37. Bottoni, P., Guerra, E., de Lara, J.: Formal foundation for pattern-based modelling. In: Chechik, M., Wirsing, M. (eds.) FASE 2009. LNCS, vol. 5503, pp. 278–293. Springer, Heidelberg (2009)
38. Wirsing, M., et al.: Sensoria patterns: augmenting service engineering with formal analysis, transformation and dynamicity. In: Margaria, T., Steffen, B. (eds.) ISoLA 2008. CCIS, vol. 17, pp. 170–190. Springer, Heidelberg (2008)

Towards a Failure Model
of Software Components

Ruzhen Dong[1,2]([⊠]) and Naijun Zhan[3]

[1] Dipartimento di Informatica, Università di Pisa, Pisa, Italy
[2] UNU-IIST, Macau, China
dong@di.unipi.it
[3] State Key Laboratory of Computer Science,
Institute of Software, CAS, Beijing, China
znj@ios.ac.cn

Abstract. We present a failure model for software components that describe sequences of services that are provided and required by a component, which may be blocked and therefore result in failures. For any automata-based model introduced in our previous work, there is a corresponding failure model. We show that the failure model is expressive enough to describe non-blockable properties defined in the automata-based models. Plugging operation over failure models is defined and proved to be consistent with the one over automata-based models. A kind of specific components, called coordinators, are introduced to coordinate behaviors of components to avoid failures, and accordingly, coordination operation is defined. Moreover, an algorithm is proposed to generate a coordinator which can filter out sequences of provided service invocations that may cause failures.

Keywords: Component-based design · Interface theory · Failure model · Coordination · Composition

1 Introduction

Component-based software development is set to build large software systems by using existing software components [13,22,28]. In order to facilitate a sound development process across different development teams exploiting existing software components, interface theories [4,5,7,14,18,27] should then define the basic principles for composing several software components based on their interfaces, as the details of their implementations are invisible, and therefore these components are used as a black-box.

In our previous work [8–10], we developed automata-based models describing how a component interacts with its environment via providing and requiring services. We assume *run-to-completeness* of provided service invocations, which means that an invocation of a provided service either is not executed at all, or has to be completed, cannot be interrupted during the execution. The interface

J.L. Fiadeiro et al. (Eds.): FACS 2013, LNCS 8348, pp. 119–136, 2014.
DOI: 10.1007/978-3-319-07602-7_9, © Springer International Publishing Switzerland 2014

model is developed to guarantee that all sequences of services specified should not be blocked. An algorithm that generates an interface model, whose non-blockable behaviors are same as the considered component was invented.

A failure model is presented in this paper, inspired by the failure-divergence semantics of CSP [15, 26]. The model explicitly illustrates the sequences of services that are provided and required, and the services that are refused/blocked after some execution paths by the considered component. The non-blockableness of sequences of service invocations, input-determinism, and plugging operation that are well handled in automata-based models are reconsidered in this failure models. The motivation of this paper is to prove that the failure model can serve as a complete and sound denotational semantic model for component automata.

Two component automata synchronize on the shared events that are provided by one and required by the other. In this paper, we present a plugging operation that plugs a service provider (a component which does not require any services) into the other component. Plugging operation reflects the development process of software systems in practice that primitive components that only provide services are implemented first and then plugged into the components that require these services. A refinement relation based on state simulation [5, 23] is given in [10] and it is suitable for substitution of interface models.

All the provided services specified in the interface of a component should be always available to its environment without any blocking. To the end, certain sequences of services need to be filtered out [3]. A coordinator is simply a deterministic labeled transition system, which serves as a wrapper/adapter to control the sequences of services that are allowed to be called by the environment. The role of coordinators is demonstrated clearly in the coordination operation. Moreover, an algorithm is invented to produce an interface coordinator that can filter out all the possible blockable services and keep all the non-blockable provided traces of the original component.

Related work. The Input/Output(I/O) Automata [20, 21] and the Interface Automata [5–7] are two well known interface theories of components. The compatibility checking is addressed in an optimistic way in Interface Automata [5–7], i.e., two components are compatible if there exists an environment that can make the composition avoid any error state. This hinders the use of components as black-box units in building software components. In contrast, in I/O Automata [20,21], input-enabledness is required, that is that all input should be enabled at any state. Thus, compatibility checking is addressed in a pessimistic way, i.e., the composition should work for any environment. Input-enabbledness assumption is not applicable to reactive components in which there are guards to control service invocations.

The interface model we proposed in our previous work [9,10] is input deterministic that all the services provided by the interface can be called without being blocked if the required services are satisfied. However, all of these are based on operational semantics or game semantics. In this paper, we try to give a denotational description of software components, called failure model, and get some primary results. The denotational model provides a new perspective of software components, an easier way for composition, and more intuitive understanding of input-determinism.

There are some variants of automata based interface theories, e.g., modal transition systems [17,19,24,25], and the corresponding compatibility checking in modal transition systems [11,12,16].

Reo [1,2] is a well known channel-based coordination model and focus mainly on how connectors are composed without considering specific components. In this paper, we use labeled transition system, which is not new, as coordinator to coordinate component models. Components are constrained by coordinators for different uses which shows the flexibility of software components.

Summary of contributions. The contributions of this paper include: (1) a failure model of components that exhibits sequences of non-blockable provided services in a more intuitive way; (2) a coordinator model that is used to coordinate service invocations between components; (3) an algorithm producing a coordinator that filters out all the possible blockable service invocations.

Outline of the paper. The rest of the paper is organized as follows. In Sect. 2, we give a brief view of our previous work [9,10] including component automata, component interface automata, and refinement relation. In Sect. 3, a failure model of components is given, related definitions are discussed, e.g., plugging operation. In Sect. 4, coordinators and coordination are formally defined, and an algorithm producing a coordinator for the interface model is proposed. In Sect. 5, we conclude the paper and discuss future work.

2 Component Automata

In this part, we will give a brief description of the automata-based models of software components introduced in [9,10]. A primitive component consists a provided and required interface which describes the services provided and required by the component, respectively.

The automata-based models are operational structure of components, and in this paper, we present a trace-based model, in which components are modeled as sets of sequences of pairs of provided and required events (called *traces*), and sets of provided events that are refused/blocked after executing the given traces.

2.1 Basic Notions

This part introduces some important notions that will be used throughout this paper.

For any $w_1, w_2 \in \mathcal{L}^*$, the concatenation of w_1 and w_2 is denoted as $w_1 \circ w_2$. Concatenation can be extended to sets of sequences in a standard way, that is, $A \circ B$ is $\{w_1 \circ w_2 \mid w_1 \in A, \ w_2 \in B\}$, where $A, B \subseteq \mathcal{L}^*$ are two sets of sequences of elements from $\mathcal{L}$. Given $a \in L$, we use $w_1 \circ a$ to denote $w_1 \circ \langle a \rangle$. Given a sequence of sets of sequences $\langle A_1, \dots, A_k \rangle$ with $k \geq 0$, we denote $A_1 \circ \cdots \circ A_k$ as

$conc(\langle A_1, \ldots, A_k \rangle)$. We use ϵ to stand for empty sequence $\langle \rangle$. Given a sequence w, we use $last(w)$ to denote the last element of w.

Let t be a pair (x, y), we denote $\pi_1(t) = x$ and $\pi_2(t) = y$. Given any sequence of pairs $tr = \langle t_1, \ldots, t_k \rangle$ and a set of sequences of pairs T, it is naturally extended that $\pi_i(tr) = \langle \pi_i(t_1), \ldots, \pi_i(t_k) \rangle$, $\pi_i(T) = \{\pi_i(tr) \mid tr \in T\}$, where $i \in \{1, 2\}$.

Let $tr \in A$ and $\Sigma \subseteq \mathcal{L}$, $tr|_\Sigma$ is a sequence obtained by removing all the elements that are not in Σ from tr. And we extend this to a set of sequences $T|_\Sigma = \{tr|_\Sigma \mid tr \in T\}$. Similarly, $tr\lceil_\Sigma$ is a sequence obtained by removing all elements in Σ.

Given a sequence of pairs tr, $tr|_P^1$ is a sequence obtained by removing the elements whose first entry is not in P. For a sequence of elements $\alpha = \langle a_1, \cdots, a_k \rangle$, $pair(\alpha) = \langle (a_1, \{a_1\}), \cdots, (a_k, \{a_k\}) \rangle$.

2.2 Component Automata

In this part, we present our automata-based model describing interaction behaviors of components [8–10]. Invocations to provided and required services are modeled as provided and required events, respectively. Internal actions are modeled as internal events. The invocation of a provided service or an internal action will trigger invoking services provided by other components, so the label on a transition step in the formal model consists a provided or internal event and a set of sequences of required events.

Definition 1. *A component automaton is a tuple* $C = (S, s_0, f, P, R, A, \delta)$, *where*

- S *is a finite set of states, and* $s_0 \in S$ *is the initial state,* $f \in S$ *is the error state;*
- P, R, *and* A *are finite sets of provided, required, and internal events, respectively, which are disjoint mutually;*
- $\delta \subseteq (S \setminus \{f\}) \times \Sigma(P, R, A) \times S$ *is the transition relation, where* $\Sigma(P, R, A)$ *is the set of labels, defined as* $(P \cup A) \times (2^{R^*} \setminus \emptyset)$.

Whenever there is $(s, \ell, s') \in \delta$ with $\ell = (w, T)$, we simply write it as $s \xrightarrow{w/T} s'$ and call it a provided transition step if $w \in P$, otherwise internal transition step. We call $s \xrightarrow{a/T} f$ a failure transition. We write $s \xrightarrow{w/} s'$ for $s \xrightarrow{w/\{\epsilon\}} s'$. Component automaton C is called *closed*, if all the transitions are of form $s \xrightarrow{w/\{\epsilon\}} s'$, otherwise, *open*. The internal events are prefixed with ; to differentiate them from the provided events. τ is used to represent any internal event whenever it does not cause confusions. For a state s we use $out(s)$ to denote $\{w \in P \cup A \mid \exists s', w, T.s \xrightarrow{w/T} s'\}$ and $out^\bullet(s) = out(s) \cap P$ and $out^\circ(s) = out(s) \cap A$. We write $s \xrightarrow{w/\bullet} s'$ for $s \xrightarrow{w/T} s'$, when T is not essential. A state s is called *stable*, if $out(s) = out^\bullet(s)$.

Regarding component automata, we need the following definitions and notations,

- a sequence of transitions $s \xrightarrow{\ell_1} s_1 \cdots \xrightarrow{\ell_k} s'$ is called an execution sequence, written as $s \xRightarrow{\ell_1,\ldots,\ell_k} s'$ (possible empty transition if $k = 0$, so $s = s'$ and $s \xRightarrow{\epsilon} s$), and $\langle \ell_1,\ldots,\ell_k \rangle$ is called a *trace* from s to s'. It is also a *trace* of the component if s is the initial state;
- for a sequence sq over $P \cup A$, we write $s \xRightarrow{sq} s'$ if there is a trace tr such that $s \xRightarrow{tr} s'$ and $\pi_1(tr) = sq$;
- a state s' is *internally reachable* from state s, denoted by $intR(s,s')$, if there exists $s \xRightarrow{tr} s'$ such that $\pi_1(tr) \in A^*$. The set of internally reachable states from state s is denoted as $intR^\circ(s)$, and defined by $\{s' \mid intR(s,s')\}$. The set of internally reachable and stable states from s is denoted as $intR^\bullet(s)$ and defined by $\{s' \text{stable} \mid s' \in intR^\circ(s)\}$;
- for a trace tr and a state s, $target(tr, s) = \{s' \mid s \xRightarrow{tr} s'\}$, and $target(tr) = target(tr, s_0)$;
- the set of traces from S is denoted as $\mathcal{T}(s)$ and defined by $\{\langle \ell_1,\ldots,\ell_k \rangle \mid \exists s' \bullet s \xRightarrow{\ell_1,\ldots,\ell_k} s'\}$;
- $\mathcal{T}(s_0)$ is the set of traces of the component automaton C, which is abbreviated as $\mathcal{T}(C)$;
- for a state s, the *provided traces* from s are given by

$$\mathcal{T}_p(s) = \{\pi_1(tr)\downarrow_P \mid tr \in \mathcal{T}(s)\};$$

- the set $\mathcal{T}_p(s_0)$ is called the set of *provided traces* of C, and it is also written as $\mathcal{T}_p(C)$.

2.3 Component Interface Automata

A component automaton describes how the corresponding component interacts with its environment by provided and required services. However, some transitions or executions may be blocked due to non-determinism caused by required traces or internal events. The transitions that may lead to the error state or live lock states should also be forbidden. The non-blockable properties of provided events and provided traces will be discussed in this part.

To the end, we give some basic definitions first, and more details can be found in [8–10]. For simplicity, we fix a component automaton $C = (S, s_0, f, P, R, A, \delta)$ in what follows.

We call a state s *divergent* if there exists a sequence of internal transitions to s from s or s can reach to such kinds of states via a sequence of internal transitions.

Definition 2 (divergent state). *A state s is* divergent, *if there exists sq with $sq \in A^+$ such that $s \xRightarrow{sq} s$ or there exists s', $sq_1 \in A^+$ and $sq_2 \in A^+$ such that $s \xRightarrow{sq_1} s'$ and $s' \xRightarrow{sq_2} s'$.*

Definition 3 (nonrefusal provided event). *For any* $s \in S$, *the set of non-refusal provided events of* s *is*

$$\mathcal{N}(s) = \bigcap_{r \in intR^\bullet(s)} out^\bullet(r) \setminus \{a \mid s \stackrel{sq}{\Longrightarrow} f, sq\lfloor_P = a\}.$$

Definition 4 (non-blockable traces). *A sequence of provided events* $\langle a_1, \cdots, a_k \rangle$ *with* $k \geq 0$ *is non-blockable at state* s, *if* $a_i \in \mathcal{N}(s')$ *for any* $1 \leq i \leq k$ *and* s' *such that* $s \stackrel{tr}{\Longrightarrow} s'$ *with* $\pi_1(tr)\lfloor_P = \langle a_1, \cdots, a_{i-1} \rangle$. *A sequence of pairs* tr *is non-blockable at* s, *if* $\pi_1(tr)\lfloor_P$ *is non-blockable at* s.

$\mathcal{T}_{up}(s)$ and $\mathcal{T}_u(s)$ are used to denote the set of all non-blockable provided traces and non-blockable traces at state s, respectively. $\mathcal{T}_{up}(s)$ and $\mathcal{T}_u(s)$ are also written as $\mathcal{T}_{up}(C)$ and $\mathcal{T}_u(C)$, respectively, when s is the initial state.

Definition 5 (input-determinism). *A component automaton* $C = (S, s_0, f, P, R, A, \delta)$ *is input-deterministic if* f *is not reachable from* s_0 *and for any* $s_0 \stackrel{tr_1}{\Longrightarrow} s_1$ *and* $s_0 \stackrel{tr_2}{\Longrightarrow} s_2$ *with* $\pi_1(tr_1)\lfloor_P = \pi_1(tr_2)\lfloor_P$, *implies* $\mathcal{N}(s_1) = \mathcal{N}(s_2)$.

The following theorem states that all the traces of an input-deterministic component automaton are non-blockable.

Theorem 1. *A component automaton* C *is input-deterministic iff* $\mathcal{T}_p(C) = \mathcal{T}_{up}(C)$.

Hereafter, we simply call C component interface automaton (or interface automaton) if it is input-deterministic. The following algorithm (see in Algorithm 1), given in [10], can construct an interface automaton $\mathcal{I}(C)$ for any given component automaton C.

Theorem 2 (Correctness of Algorithm 1). *The following properties hold for Algorithm 1, for any component automaton* C:

1. *The algorithm always terminates and the error state* f *is not reachable from the initial state;*
2. $\mathcal{I}(C)$ *is an input deterministic automaton;*
3. $\mathcal{T}_u(C) = \mathcal{T}_u(\mathcal{I}(C))$.

2.4 Plugging Operation

Interaction between components through service invocation is modelled as the synchronization of the two corresponding component automata on the shared events that are provided by one and required by the other. The general composition operation is given in [10]. In this part, we focus on the composition between open component automata and closed component automata, called *plugging*.

Definition 6 (plugging). *Given a component automaton* $C_1 = (S_1, s_0^1, f_1, P_1, R_1, A_1, \delta_1)$ *and a closed component automaton* $C_2 = (S_2, s_0^2, f, P_2, R_2, A_2, \delta_2)$,

Algorithm 1. Construction of Interface Automaton $\mathcal{I}(C)$

Input: $C = (S, s_0, f, P, R, A, \delta)$
Output: $\mathcal{I}(C) = (S_I, (Q_0, s_0), f, P, R, A, \delta_I)$, where $S_I \subseteq 2^S \times S$
1: **if** $f \in intR^\circ(s_0)$ **then**
2:     *exit* with $\delta_I = \emptyset$
3: **end if**
4: **Initialization:** $S_I := \{(Q_0, s_0)\}$ with $Q_0 = \{s' \mid s' \in intR^\circ(s_0)\}$; $\delta_I := \emptyset$;
    todo := $\{(Q_0, s_0)\}$; *done* := $\emptyset$
5: **while** *todo* $\neq \emptyset$ **do**
6:     **choose** $(Q, r) \in$ *todo*; *todo* := *todo* $\setminus \{(Q, r)\}$; *done* := *done* $\cup \{(Q, r)\}$
7:     **for each** $a \in \bigcap_{s \in Q} \mathcal{N}(s)$ **do**
8:         $Q' := \bigcup_{s \in Q} \{s' \mid s \xRightarrow{tr} s', \pi_1(tr)\lfloor_P = \langle a \rangle\}$
9:         **for each** $(r \xrightarrow{a/T} r') \in \delta$ **do**
10:           **if** $(Q', r') \notin (todo \cup done)$ **then**
11:             *todo* := *todo* $\cup \{(Q', r')\}$
12:             $S_I := S_I \cup \{(Q', r')\}$
13:           **end if**
14:           $\delta_I := \delta_I \cup \{(Q, r) \xrightarrow{a/T} (Q', r')\}$
15:         **end for**
16:     **end for**
17:     **for each** $r \xrightarrow{w/T} r'$ with $r' \in Q$ and $w \in A$ **do**
18:         $\delta_I := \delta_I \cup \{(Q, r) \xrightarrow{w/T} (Q, r')\}$
19:     **end for**
20: **end while**

C_2 is pluggable to C_1 if $A_1 \cap (P_2 \cup A_2) = \emptyset$, $A_2 \cap (P_1 \cup R_1) = \emptyset$, $P_2 \subseteq R_1$, and $R_2 = \emptyset$. The plugging is $C_1 \ll C_2 = (S, s_0, f, P, R, A, \delta)$, where

- $S = (S_1 \setminus f_1) \times (S_2 \setminus f_2) \cup \{f\}$, where f is the error state of C,
- $s_0 = (s_0^1, s_0^2)$,
- $P = P_1$,
- $R = R_1 \setminus P_2$,
- $A = A_1 \cup A_2$,
- δ is given by the following rule: for any reachable state (s_1, s_2), $s_1 \xrightarrow{w/T} s_1'$
  - $(s_1, s_2) \xrightarrow{w/} f$ if $T\lfloor_{P_2} \nsubseteq T_{up}(s_2)$, otherwise,
  - $(s_1, s_2) \xrightarrow{w/T'} (s_1', s_2')$, where

$$T' = \{sq\lfloor_R \mid sq \in T, s_2 \xRightarrow{tr} s_2' \text{ and } \pi_1(tr)\lfloor_{P_2} = sq\lfloor_{P_2}\}.$$

2.5 Refinement

Refinement is one of the key issues in component based development. It is mainly used for substitution and selection of components at interface level. A refinement relation by state simulation technique [23] is given. The intuitive idea is that a state s' simulates s, if at state s' more provided events are nonrefusal, less required traces are required and the next states following the transitions keep the simulation relation, which is similar to alternating simulation in [5]. We give a brief introduction of *simulation* and *refinement*, and more details can be found in [10].

Definition 7 (simulation). *A binary relation R over the set of states of a component automaton is a simulation iff whenever $s_1 R s_2$:*

- *if $s_1 \xrightarrow{w/T} s_1'$ with $w \in A \cup \mathcal{N}(s_1)$ and $f \notin intR^\circ(s_1')$, there exists s_2' and T' such that $s_2 \xrightarrow{w/T'} s_2'$, where $T' \subseteq T$ and $s_1' R s_2'$,*
- *for any transitions $s_2 \xrightarrow{w/T'} s_2'$ with $w \in A \cup \mathcal{N}(s_1)$ and $f \notin intR^\circ(s_2')$, then there exists s_1' and T such that $s_1 \xrightarrow{w/T} s_1'$, where $T' \subseteq T$ and $s_1' R s_2'$,*
- *$\mathcal{N}(s_1) \subseteq \mathcal{N}(s_2)$,*
- *if $s_2 \xrightarrow{w/} f$ with $w \in A \cup P_1$, then $s_1 \xrightarrow{w/} f$.*

We say that s_2 simulates s_1, written $s_1 \lesssim s_2$, if $(s_1, s_2) \in R$. C_2 refines C_1, written $C_1 \sqsubseteq_{alt} C_2$, if there exists a simulation relation R such that $s_1^0 R s_2^0$ and $P_1 \subseteq P_2$ and $R_2 \subseteq R_1$.

The following theorem shows the trace inclusion properties.

Theorem 3. *Given two component interface automata C_1 and C_2, if $C_1 \sqsubseteq_{alt} C_2$, then $\mathcal{T}_{up}(C_1) \subseteq \mathcal{T}_{up}(C_2)$, and for any non-blockable provided trace $pt \in \mathcal{T}_p(C_1)$, $\mathcal{T}_r^2(pt) \subseteq \mathcal{T}_r^1(pt)$.*

The following corollaries can be obtained from Theorem 5 in [10].

Corollary 1. *Consider four component interface automata C_1, C_1', C_2, and C_2' that C_2 and C_2' are pluggable to C_1 and C_1', respectively, if $C_1 \sqsubseteq_{alt} C_1'$ and $C_2 \sqsubseteq_{alt} C_2'$, then $(C_1 \ll C_2) \sqsubseteq_{alt} (C_1' \ll C_2')$.*

3   Failure Model of Components

The automata-based component model gives the operational descriptions of components. In this section, we propose to develop a denotational description of components. The advantages of denotational models for components are easier for compatibility checking, plugging, and refinement.

In this part, we will give a semantic model of component automata based on traces and provided events that may be refused. The component automata aim at showing interaction behaviors by providing and requiring services with its environment in an operational way, while the failure model of components focuses on traces of the component and the set of provided events that may be refused. The basic idea is inspired by the failure-divergence semantics of CSP [15].

Definition 8 (failures sets of component automata). *Consider component automaton $C = (S, s_0, f, P, R, A, \delta)$, a pair (tr, X) of a trace and a set of the events is called a* failure *of C, if there exists s such that $s_0 \stackrel{tr}{\Longrightarrow} s$ and $X = P \setminus \mathcal{N}(s)$, where s is not divergent nor the failure state f. We use $\mathcal{F}(C)$ to denote the set of failures of C.*

We see that provided events which may lead to the error state or **div** states are refused by the components. This is because the components we consider here aim at providing non-blockable provided services.

3.1   Failure Model of Components

Definition 9 (failure model of components). *A failure model of component M is $(P, R, A, \mathcal{F})$ where*

- *P, R, and A are sets of provided, required, and internal events, respectively;*
- *$\mathcal{F} \subseteq \Sigma(P, R, A)^* \times P$ is the failure set, where $\Sigma(P, R, A) = (P \cup A) \times (2^{R^*} \setminus \emptyset)$. Each $(tr, X) \in \mathcal{F}$ is called a* failure, *satisfying the following conditions:*

  - *if $(tr, X) \in \mathcal{F}$ and $X' \subseteq X$, then $(tr, X') \in \mathcal{F}$;*
  - *if $(tr, X) \in \mathcal{F}$ with $X \neq P$, there exists T, $a \in P \setminus X$, and X' that $(tr \cdot tr' \cdot a/T, X') \in \mathcal{F}$, where $\pi_1(tr') \in A^*$;*
  - *if $(tr \cdot a/T, X) \in \mathcal{F}$ with $a \in A$, then there exists X' such that that $(tr, X') \in \mathcal{F}$.*

The failure model of C is written as $[\![C]\!]_F = (P, R, A, \mathcal{F}(C))$.

Similarly, we define the sets of traces, provided traces, and required traces of failure model M as follows:

$$T(M) = \{tr \mid \exists X \bullet (tr, X) \in \mathcal{F}\}$$
$$T_p(M) = \{\pi_1(tr)\!\downarrow_P \mid tr \in T(M)\}$$
$$T_r(M) = \{\pi_2(tr)\!\downarrow_R \mid tr \in T(M)\}$$

We also give the definition of *input-determinism* and *non-blockableness* in the failure model.

Definition 10 (input-determinism). *A failure model M is* input-deterministic, *if for any $(tr_1, X_1), (tr_2, X_2) \in \mathcal{F}$, $\pi_1(tr_1)\!\downarrow_P = \pi_1(tr_2)\!\downarrow_P$ implies $X_1 = X_2$.*

Definition 11 (non-blockable traces). *Let M be a failure model of component, provided trace $pt = \langle a_0, \cdots, a_k \rangle \in T_p(M)$ is non-blockable, if there does not exist $0 \leq i < k$ and failure (tr, X) that $\pi_1(tr)\!\downarrow_P = \langle a_0, \cdots, a_i \rangle$ and $a_{i+1} \in X$. The set of non-blockable provided traces of M is written $T_{up}(M)$.*

The following theorem states that the failure model of a component automaton $[\![C]\!]_F$ is consistent with component automaton C in the above definition.

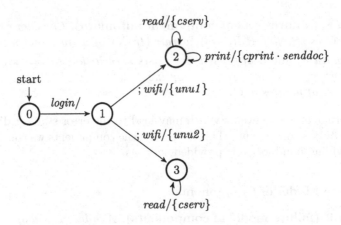

Fig. 1. Execution model of internet connection component C_{ic}

Theorem 4. *Let C be a component automaton and $[\![C]\!]_F$ is the failure model of C, then the following holds*

- $\mathcal{T}(C) = \mathcal{T}([\![C]\!]_F)$, $\mathcal{T}_p(C) = \mathcal{T}_p([\![C]\!]_F)$, $\mathcal{T}_{up}(C) = \mathcal{T}_{up}([\![C]\!]_F)$,
- C *is input-deterministic iff* $[\![C]\!]_F$ *is input-deterministic.*

Example 1. As a demonstrating example, we consider a simple component presented in Fig. 1. It provides the services *login*, *print*, and *read* to the environment, and has an internal service ; *wifi*. The services model the logging into the system, invocation of printing a document, an email service, and automatically connecting the wifi, respectively. The component calls the services *unu1*, *unu2*, *cserv*, *cprint*, and *senddoc*. The first three of them model the searching for a wifi router nearby, connecting to the *unu1* or *unu2* wireless network, and connecting to an application server, respectively. The *cprint* and *senddoc* are services that connect to the printer, sends the document to print and start the printing job. The *print* service is only available for the wifi network *unu1* and *read* can be accessed at both networks.

In Fig. 1, $(\epsilon, \{read, print\})$, $(login/, \{login, print\})$, $(\langle login/, ; wifi/\{unu1\}\rangle$, $\{login\})$,$(\langle login/, ; wifi/\{unu2\}\rangle, \{login, print\})$ are failures.

3.2   Plugging Operation

In this part, we show how two failure models of software components are composed by plugging.

Definition 12 (plugging). *Given failure models $M_1 = (P_1, R_1, A_1, \mathcal{F}_1)$ and $M_2 = (P_2, R_2, A_2, \mathcal{F}_2)$, M_2 is pluggable to M_1 if $A_1 \cap (P_2 \cup A_2) = \emptyset$, $A_2 \cap (P_1 \cup R_1) = \emptyset$, $P_2 \subseteq R_1$, and $R_2 = \emptyset$. The plugging $M_1 \lll M_2$ is a new failure model $(P, R, A, \mathcal{F})$, where*

- $P = P_1$,
- $R = R_1 \setminus P_2$,
- $A = A_1 \cup A_2$,
- $(tr, X_1 \cup X_2) \in \mathcal{F}$, if
  - $(tr_1, X_1) \in \mathcal{F}_1$, $conc(\pi_2(tr_1))|_{P_2} \subseteq T_{up}(M_2)$, and $tr = tr_1\restriction_{P_2}$,
  - $X_2 = \{a \mid \exists X' \bullet (tr_1 \cdot a/T, X') \in \mathcal{F}_1, conc(\pi_2(tr_1 \cdot a/T) \nsubseteq T_{up}(M_2)\}$

The following theorem shows the compositional properties of failure models.

Theorem 5. *Given component C_1 and C_2, if C_2 is pluggable to C_1, then $[\![C_2]\!]_F$ is pluggable to $[\![C_1]\!]_F$, and $[\![C_1]\!]_F \lll [\![C_2]\!]_F = [\![C_1 \lll C_2]\!]_F$.*

3.3 Refinement

We propose a refinement in failure models. The principle is that a refined model provides more non-blockable traces while requiring less required services, and refuses less provided services that are blockable in the provided part.

Definition 13 (failure refinement). *Given two failure models $M_1 = (P_1, R_1, A_1, \mathcal{F}_1)$ and $M_2 = (P_2, R_2, A_2, \mathcal{F}_2)$, M_2 is a refinement of M_1, if*

- $P_1 \subseteq P_2$, $R_2 \subseteq R_1$;
- $T_{up}(M_1) \subseteq T_{up}(M_2)$;
- *given $pt \in T_{up}(M_1)$, for any $(tr_2, X_2) \in \mathcal{F}_2$, there exists $(tr_1, X_1) \in \mathcal{F}_1$ such that $\pi_1(tr_1)|_{P_1} = \pi_1(tr_2)|_{P_2} = pt$, $conc(\pi_2(tr_2)) \subseteq conc(\pi_2(tr_1))$, and $X_2 \subseteq X_1$.*

4 Coordination

The components we consider so far are the basic units for building software systems. In some situations, however, certain services provided by a component need to be restricted due to security polices, budget and so on. In this section, we will introduce a kind of specific components, called *coordinator*, to coordinate services of components.

4.1 Coordinator

We use an online-shopping system shown in Fig. 2 to motivate the need of coordinator.

Example 2. Consider an online marketplace system which provides a consumer-to-consumer platform for retail stores. It consists of stores and a payment component trusted by both stores and clients. The store component, called *eStore*, presented in Fig. 2(i). It provides services *select*, *pay'*, and *deliver*, which model selecting items, obtaining the money from payment component, and delivering the paid items to the clients, respectively. The payment component, called

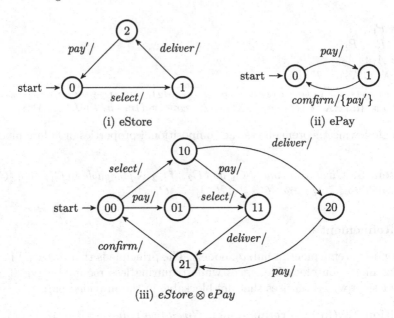

(i) eStore

(ii) ePay

(iii) $eStore \otimes ePay$

Fig. 2. Online shopping system

ePay shown in Fig. 2(ii) provides services *pay* and *confirm* which model receiving money from the clients and being confirmed by the client after the items are received. It requires service *pay′* that the component will transfer the money to the store. The composition of *eStore* and *ePay* is in Fig. 2(iii).

In the above example, provided trace ⟨*select · deliver*⟩ is allowed, which means that the store may not get paid even if it delivers the items bought by the clients. So such online marketplace system is unsafe for the store retailers. We introduce a kind of specific components, called *coordinator*, to filter out services provided by components that should not be allowed. A coordinator is modeled as a labeled transitions system, the formal definition is given below.

Definition 14 (Coordinator). *A coordinator F is a deterministic labeled transition system (Q, q_0, E, σ), where*

- *Q is the set of states with $q_0 \in Q$ as the initial state,*
- *E is the set of active events,*
- *σ is a set of transition.*

Similarly, the set of traces of coordinator F, written as $\mathcal{T}(F)$, is $\{\langle a_0, a_1, \cdots, a_k \rangle \mid q_0 \xrightarrow{a_0} \cdots \xrightarrow{a_k} q_{k+1}\}$.

Example 3. In order to filter out the unexpected provided traces in Fig. 2(iii), we can exploit coordinator F shown in Fig. 3.

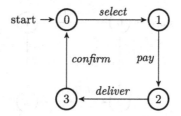

Fig. 3. Coordinator F

4.2 Parallel Composition of Coordinators

Now we define the parallel composition of coordinators. Since coordinators only show the sequences of services that are allowed, two coordinators do not communicate directly. Two coordinators are composable, if they do not have active events in common. Thus, the parallel composition of two coordinators is simply the interleaving execution of the actions of the individual coordinators.

Definition 15 (Parallel composition of coordinators). *Given two coordinators* $F_1 = (Q_1, q_0^1, E_1, \delta_1,)$ *and* $F_1 = (Q_2, q_0^2, E_2, \delta_2,)$, *if* $E_1 \cap E_2 = \emptyset$, *the parallel composition* $F_1 \parallel F_2$ *results in another coordinate* (Q, q_0, E, δ), *where*

- $Q = Q_1 \times Q_2$ *and* $q_0 = (q_0^1, q_0^2)$,
- $E = E_1 \cup E_2$,
- δ *is given by the rule,* $(q_1, q_2) \xrightarrow{a} (q_1', q_2') \in \delta$ *if either*
  - $q_1 = q_1'$ *and* $q_2 \xrightarrow{a} q_2'$ *is a transition of* F_2, *or*
  - $q_2 = q_2'$ *and* $q_1 \xrightarrow{a} q_1'$ *is a transition of* F_1.

The following theorem shows that the traces of $F_1 \parallel F_2$ can be obtained from the traces of F_1 and F_2.

Theorem 6. *Given two composable coordinators* F_1 *and* F_2, $\mathcal{T}(F_1 \parallel F_2) = \{sq \in E^* \mid sq\lfloor_{E_1} \in \mathcal{T}(F_1), sq\lfloor_{E_2} \in \mathcal{T}(F_2)\}$.

4.3 Coordination Operation

Components are coordinated in the way that all the sequences of services provided should also obey the constraint of the coordinators. The formal definition is given below.

Definition 16 (Coordination). *Given a component automaton* $C = (S, s_0, P, R, A, \delta)$ *and a coordinator* $F = (Q, q_0, E, \sigma)$ *such that* $E \subseteq P$, *the coordination of* C *by* F, *denoted by* $C \ltimes F$, *derives another component automaton* $(S', s_0', P', R', \delta')$, *where*

- $S' = S \times Q$,
- $s_0' = (s_0, q_0)$,
- $P' = P$,

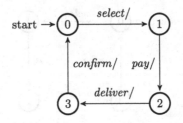

Fig. 4. Coordination of $(eStore \otimes ePay) \ltimes F$

- $R' = R$,
- δ' is a set of transitions complying with the following rules:
  - if $s \xrightarrow{w/T} s'$ and $t \xrightarrow{w} t'$, then $(s,t) \xrightarrow{w/T} (s',t')$,
  - $s \xrightarrow{w/T} s'$ with $w \notin E$, then $(s,t) \xrightarrow{w/T} (s',t)$.

Theorem 7. *The failures of $C \ltimes F$ is $\mathcal{F}(C \ltimes F) = \{(tr, D \cup D') \mid (tr, D) \in \mathcal{F}(C), \pi_1(tr)\lfloor_E \in \mathcal{T}(F), D' = \{d \mid \pi_1(tr)\lfloor_E \cdot d \notin \mathcal{T}(F)\}\}$.*

Example 4. Now, we can see how the component $eStore \otimes ePay$ shown in Fig. 2(iii) is coordinated by coordinator in Fig. 3. The result is presented in Fig. 4.

4.4 Synthesizing Interface Coordinator for Component Automata

In this part, we will show that given any component automaton C, there exits a coordinator F such that coordination of C by F is equivalent with the component interface automaton $\mathcal{I}(C)$ constructed by Algorithm 1.

We now present a procedure in Algorithm 2 that, given a component automaton, constructs a coordinator which only records non-blockable provided traces. The basic idea is similar to the construction of a deterministic automaton from a non-deterministic one, and the only difference is that in the algorithm only the deterministic traces are kept.

Three key correctness properties of the algorithm are stated in the following theorem.

Theorem 8 (Correctness of Algorithm 2). *Given any component automaton C, the following properties hold for Algorithm 2:*

- *the algorithm always terminates,*
- *$\mathcal{G}(C)$ is deterministic,*
- *$\mathcal{T}(\mathcal{G}(C)) = \mathcal{T}_{up}(C)$.*

Proof. The termination of the algorithm is obtained, because *todo* will eventually be empty: the size of power set of state S is bounded, only fresh state is added to *todo*, and for each iteration of the loop a state from *todo* is removed.

Assume that there exists $q \xrightarrow{a} q_1$ and $q \xrightarrow{a} q_1$, then from Algorithm 2, we $q_1 = q_2 = \{s' \mid s \xRightarrow{tr} s', \text{with} s \in q, \pi_1(tr)\lfloor_P = a\}$. So $\mathcal{G}(C)$ is deterministic.

Algorithm 2. Construction of Interface coordinator

Input: $C = (S, s_0, P, R, A, \delta)$
Output: $\mathcal{G}(C) = (Q, q_0, E, \sigma)$
 1: **Initialization:** $q_0 = \{s' \mid s' \in intR^\circ(s_0)\}, Q := \{q_0\}, E := P, \sigma := \emptyset, todo := \{q_0\}$
 2: **while** $todo \neq \emptyset$ **do**
 3:   **choose one** $q \in todo$ **and** $todo := todo \setminus \{q\}$
 4:   **for each** $a \in \bigcap_{s \in q} \mathcal{N}(s)$ **do**
 5:     let q' be $\{s' \mid s \xrightarrow{tr} s', \text{with } s \in q, \pi_1(tr)\!\restriction_P = a\}$
 6:     **if** $q' \notin Q$ **then**
 7:       add q' to Q and $todo$
 8:     **end if**
 9:     $\sigma := \sigma \cup \{q \xrightarrow{a} q'\}$.
10:   **end for**
11: **end while**

We first prove that, for any non-blockable provided trace pt of C, there exists $q_0 \xrightarrow{pt} q$ in $\mathcal{G}(C)$ with $q = \{s' \mid s_0 \xrightarrow{tr} s', \pi_1(tr)\!\restriction_P = pt\}$ by induction on the length of pt. The base case is obvious that $q_0 = \{s' \mid s' \in intR^\circ(s_0)\}$. Consider non-blockable trace $sq \cdot a$, so there exists q_1 that $q_1 = \{s' \mid s_0 \xrightarrow{tr} s', \pi_1(tr)\!\restriction_P = sq\}$ and $q_0 \xrightarrow{sq} q_1$. Since $sq \cdot a$ is non-blockable, $a \in \mathcal{N}(s')$ for $s' \in q_1$. From Loop (Line 4–10) in Algorithm 2, we see $q'_1 = \{s' \mid s \xrightarrow{tr} s', \text{with } s \in q_1, \pi_1(tr)\!\restriction_P = a\}$, so $q_0 \xrightarrow{sq \cdot a} q'_1$ and $q'_1 = \{s' \mid s_0 \xrightarrow{tr} s', \pi_1(tr)\!\restriction_P = sq \cdot a\}$ by hypothesis induction. From above, we see $\mathcal{T}_{up}(C) \subseteq \mathcal{T}(\mathcal{G}(C))$.

Next we prove that sq is non-blockable in C, for any $q_0 \xrightarrow{sq} q$, and $q = \{s' \mid s_0 \xrightarrow{tr} s', \pi_1(tr)\!\restriction_P = sq\}$. The base case follows that ϵ is non-blockable in C. Consider $q_0 \xrightarrow{sq' \cdot a} q_2$, then, there exists $q_0 \xrightarrow{sq'} q_1$ and $q_1 \xrightarrow{a} q_2$. By hypothesis induction, $q_1 = \{s' \mid s_0 \xrightarrow{tr} s', \pi_1(tr)\!\restriction_P = sq'\}$ and sq' is non-blockable. $sq' \cdot a$ is non-blockable, since $a \in \mathcal{N}(r)$ for any $r \in q_1$. And $q_2 = \{s' \mid s_0 \xrightarrow{tr} s', \pi_1(tr)\!\restriction_P = sq' \cdot a\}$. From above, we see $\mathcal{T}(\mathcal{G}(C)) \subseteq \mathcal{T}_{up}(C)$.

So, $\mathcal{T}(\mathcal{G}(C)) = \mathcal{T}_{up}(C)$. $\qquad\square$

We can obtain the following corollary from Theorems 7 and 8.

Corollary 2. *Given a component automaton* C, $\mathcal{T}_u(C) = \mathcal{T}(C \ltimes \mathcal{G}(C))$

Example 5. The component automaton in Fig. 1 is not input-deterministic. A coordinator shown in Fig. 5(i) is obtained by Algorithm 2. We use state a as shorthand for $\{1, 2, 3\}$. The coordination of $C_{ic} \ltimes \mathcal{G}(C)$ is given in Fig. 5(ii).

5 Conclusion and Future Work

In this paper, we proposed a denotational semantic model for software components, called *failure model*, and discussed how to handle traces, non-blockablness, input-determinism, plugging operations in a failure model. In particular, we proved that these notions are consistent with their counterparts in the operational settings.

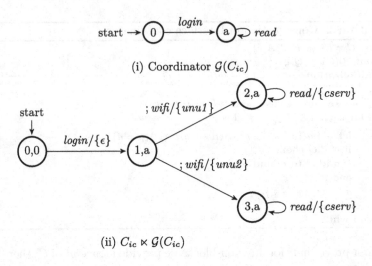

(i) Coordinator $\mathcal{G}(C_{ic})$

(ii) $C_{ic} \ltimes \mathcal{G}(C_{ic})$

Fig. 5. Coordination of component C_{ic} by a synthesized coordinator

Future work. There are several open problems left for future work. Firstly, refinement relation based on failure models and the relation with the refinement defined on component automata need further studied. Secondly, more general composition operation instead of plugging needs to be given for failure models. Thirdly, algebraic properties of composition such as associative, commutative, distributive of coordination over composition are also important. In addition, it deserves to extend these untimed theories to timed settings.

Acknowledgments. This work was funded in part by the projects 2014CB340700, NSFC-61103013 and NSFC-91118007 from the Natural Science Foundation of China, GAVES and PEARL funded by Macau Science and Technology Development. We thank Prof. Zhiming liu for his inspiring comments and discussions. We also thank the anonymous reviewers for their valuable comments.

References

1. Arbab, F.: Reo: a channel-based coordination model for component composition. Math. Struct. Comput. Sci. **14**, 329–366 (2004)
2. Arbab, F., Baier, C., Rutten, J., Sirjani, M.: Modeling component connectors in reo by constraint automata: (extended abstract). Electron. Notes Theor. Comput. Sci. **97**(0), 25–46 (2004)
3. Castagna, G., Gesbert, N., Padovani, L.: A theory of contracts for web services. ACM Trans. Program. Lang. Syst. **31**(5), 19:1–19:61 (2009)
4. Chen, Z., Liu, Z., Ravn, A.P., Stolz, V., Zhan, N.: Refinement and verification in component-based model-driven design. Science of Computer Programming **74**(4), 168–196 (2009). (special Issue on the Grand Challenge)
5. De Alfaro, L., Henzinger, T.: Interface automata. ACM SIGSOFT Softw. Eng. Notes **26**(5), 109–120 (2001)

6. De Alfaro, L., Henzinger, T.: Interface-based design. Eng. Theor. Softw.-Intensive Syst. **195**, 83–104 (2005)
7. de Alfaro, L., Henzinger, T.A.: Interface theories for component-based design. In: Henzinger, T.A., Kirsch, C.M. (eds.) EMSOFT 2001. LNCS, vol. 2211, pp. 148–165. Springer, Heidelberg (2001)
8. Dong, R., Faber, J., Ke, W., Liu, Z.: rCOS: defining meanings of component-based software architectures. In: Liu, Z., Woodcock, J., Zhu, H. (eds.) Unifying Theories of Programming and Formal Engineering Methods. LNCS, vol. 8050, pp. 1–66. Springer, Heidelberg (2013)
9. Dong, R., Faber, J., Liu, Z., Srba, J., Zhan, N., Zhu, J.: Unblockable compositions of software components. In: Proceedings of the 15th ACM SIGSOFT Symposium on Component Based Software Engineering, CBSE '12, pp. 103–108. ACM, New York (2012)
10. Dong, R., Zhan, N., Zhao, L.: An interface model of software components. In: Liu, Z., Woodcock, J., Zhu, H. (eds.) ICTAC 2013. LNCS, vol. 8049, pp. 159–176. Springer, Heidelberg (2013)
11. Emmi, M., Giannakopoulou, D., Păsăreanu, C.S.: Assume-guarantee verification for interface automata. In: Cuellar, J., Maibaum, T., Sere, K. (eds.) FM 2008. LNCS, vol. 5014, pp. 116–131. Springer, Heidelberg (2008)
12. Giannakopoulou, D., Pasareanu, C.S., Barringer, H.: Assumption generation for software component verification. In: ASE, pp. 3–12. IEEE Computer Society (2002)
13. Jifeng, H., Li, X., Liu, Z.: Component-based software engineering. In: Van Hung, D., Wirsing, M. (eds.) ICTAC 2005. LNCS, vol. 3722, pp. 70–95. Springer, Heidelberg (2005)
14. He, J., Li, X., Liu, Z.: A theory of reactive components. Electr. Notes Theor. Comput. Sci. **160**, 173–195 (2006)
15. Hoare, C.: Communicating sequential processes. Commun. ACM **21**(8), 666–677 (1978)
16. Larsen, K.G., Nyman, U., Wasowski, A.: Interface input/output automata. In: Misra, J., Nipkow, T., Sekerinski, E. (eds.) FM 2006. LNCS, vol. 4085, pp. 82–97. Springer, Heidelberg (2006)
17. Larsen, K.G., Nyman, U., Wasowski, A.: Modal I/O automata for interface and product line theories. In: De Nicola, R. (ed.) ESOP 2007. LNCS, vol. 4421, pp. 64–79. Springer, Heidelberg (2007)
18. Liu, Z., Morisset, C., Stolz, V.: rCOS: theory and tool for component-based model driven development. In: Arbab, F., Sirjani, M. (eds.) FSEN 2009. LNCS, vol. 5961, pp. 62–80. Springer, Heidelberg (2010)
19. Lüttgen, G., Vogler, W.: Modal interface automata. In: Baeten, J.C.M., Ball, T., de Boer, F.S. (eds.) TCS 2012. LNCS, vol. 7604, pp. 265–279. Springer, Heidelberg (2012)
20. Lynch, N.A., Tuttle, M.R.: Hierarchical correctness proofs for distributed algorithms. In: PODC, pp. 137–151 (1987)
21. Lynch, N.A., Tuttle, M.R.: An introduction to input/output automata. CWI Quarterly **2**(3), 219–246 (1989)
22. Mcilroy, D.: Mass-produced software components. In: Buxton, J.M., Naur, P., Randell, B. (eds.) Proceedings of Software Engineering Concepts and Techniques, pp. 138–155. NATO Science Committee, January 1969
23. Milner, R.: Communication and Concurrency. Prentice Hall International (UK) Ltd., Hertfordshire (1995)

24. Raclet, J., Badouel, E., Benveniste, A., Caillaud, B., Legay, A., Passerone, R.: Modal interfaces: unifying interface automata and modal specifications. In: Proceedings of the Seventh ACM International Conference on Embedded Software, pp. 87–96. ACM (2009)
25. Raclet, J.B., Badouel, E., Benveniste, A., Caillaud, B., Legay, A., Passerone, R.: A modal interface theory for component-based design. Fundam. Inf. **108**(1–2), 119–149 (2011)
26. Roscoe, A.: The Theory and Practice of Concurrency. Prentice Hall, Upper Saddle River (1998)
27. Sifakis, J.: A framework for component-based construction. In: Third IEEE International Conference on Software Engineering and Formal Methods, SEFM 2005, pp. 293–299. IEEE (2005)
28. Szyperski, C.: Component Software: Beyond Object-Oriented Programming. Addison-Wesley, Boston (1997)

Formally Reasoning on a Reconfigurable Component-Based System — A Case Study for the Industrial World

Nuno Gaspar[1,2,3]([✉]), Ludovic Henrio[2], and Eric Madelaine[1,2]

[1] INRIA Sophia Antipolis, Valbonne, France
{Nuno.Gaspar,Eric.Madelaine}@inria.fr
[2] University of Nice Sophia Antipolis,
CNRS, I3S, UMR 7271, 06900 Sophia Antipolis, France
Ludovic.Henrio@cnrs.fr
[3] ActiveEon S.A.S, Sophia Antipolis, France
http://www.activeeon.com/

Abstract. The modularity offered by component-based systems made it one of the most employed paradigms in software engineering. Precise structural specification is a key ingredient that enables their verification and consequently their reliability. This gains special relevance for *reconfigurable* component-based systems.

To this end, the *Grid Component Model* (GCM) provides all the means to define such reconfigurable component-based applications. In this paper we report our experience on the formal specification and verification of a reconfigurable GCM application as an industrial case study.

Keywords: Component-based systems · Autonomous systems · Formal methods · Reconfiguration · Model-checking

1 Introduction

Meeting the demands of our modern society requires special care when designing software. Applications are expected to be full-featured, performant and reliable. Moreover, for distributed applications high-availability is also cause of concern. Taming this complexity makes the use of modular techniques mandatory. To this end, the modularity offered by component-based systems made it one of the most employed paradigms in software engineering.

Embracing this approach enables structural specifications, thus leveraging formal verification. This gains special relevance for *reconfigurable* component-based systems. Indeed, while offering systems with an higher availability, the ability to evolve at runtime inherently increases the complexity of an application, making its formal verification a challenging task.

J.L. Fiadeiro et al. (Eds.): FACS 2013, LNCS 8348, pp. 137–156, 2014.
DOI: 10.1007/978-3-319-07602-7_10, © Springer International Publishing Switzerland 2014

1.1   Context

This work occurs in the context of the Spinnaker project, a French collaborative project between INRIA and several industrial partners, where we intend to contribute for the widespread adoption of RFID-based technology. To this end, our contribution comes with the design and implementation of a nonintrusive, flexible and reliable solution that can integrate itself with other already deployed systems. Specifically, we developed the HYPERMANAGER, a general purpose monitoring application with autonomic features. This was built using GCM/ProActive[1] — a Java middleware for parallel and distributed programming that follows the principles of the GCM component model. For the purposes of this project, it had the goal to monitor the E-Connectware[2] (ECW) framework in a loosely coupled manner.

For the sake of clarity let us describe one of the real life scenarios faced in a industrial context. An hotel needs to keep track of the bed sheets used by their customers. Every bed sheet used has an embedded RFID sensor chip that uniquely identifies it. At every shift, the hotel maids go through all the rooms recovering these bed sheets and putting them in a laundry cart. By reaching the end of the rooms' corridor, the laundry cart emits to another physical device running the ECW Gateway software the bed sheets' identifiers. For each corridor there might be several laundry carts and one device running the ECW Gateway. After receiving the bed sheets' identifiers the ECW Gateways emit this information along with their own identifier to yet another physical device running the ECW Server. Once the information reaches the top of this hierarchy it can be used to whatever purpose, namely bed sheets traceability.

Abstracting away this particular scenario, one can see it in a hierarchical manner as depicted by Fig. 1.

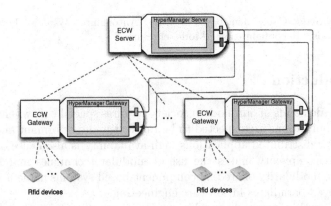

Fig. 1. Hierarchical representation of our case study

---

[1] http://proactive.activeeon.com/index.php
[2] http://www.tagsysrfid.com/Products-Services/RFID-Middleware

Regarding the previously described scenario, this hierarchical view should pose no doubt. For each of the N floors of the hotel there are M laundry carts that communicate in a *one-to-one* style with a gateway. On the other hand, the gateways communicate with the server on a *n-to-one* style. Moreover, there is also the need to cope for possible maintenance issues. For instance, in the case of malfunction of some device running the ECW Gateway, it may be required to replace it or add a new one in order to avoid any overloading.

The architecture depicted by Fig. 1 also includes the HyperManager application. Indeed, it is deployed alongside the pre-existent distributed system, performing its monitoring on all ECW components. The careful reader will notice that the flow of requests go both from the HyperManager Server to the Hyper-Manager Gateway, and vice-versa. Indeed, these follow the *pull* and *push* styles of communication, respectively. More details regarding these mechanisms will be discussed at a later stage.

1.2 Contributions

This paper discusses an industrial case study of a reconfigurable monitoring application. On the one hand, it should be noted that we aim at real-life applications, indeed, our models go upto the intricacies of the middleware itself. This has the direct consequence of promoting the use of formal methods within the industry.

On the other hand, we go beyond previous work [5] by including reconfiguration capabilities. This yields bigger state-spaces and inherently new issues to deal with. Investigating the feasibility of such undertakings is within the scope of this paper too. To the best of our knowledge this is the first work addressing the challenges of behavioural specification and verification of reconfigurable component-based applications.

1.3 Organisation of the Paper

The remaining of this paper is organised as follows. Section 2 gives the main ingredients of our behavioural semantics for specifying GCM applications. Then, Sect. 3 presents our general purpose monitoring application — THE HYPERMAN-AGER. Section 4 details its simplified behavioural model, i.e. without support for structural reconfigurations, and its proven properties. The impact of adding reconfiguration capabilities is discussed in Sect. 5. Related work is discussed in Sect. 6. For last, Sect. 7 concludes this paper.

2 A Behavioural Semantics for GCM Applications

This section provides a brief overview of the behavioural semantics modelling GCM/ProActive applications by relying on the *pNets* formalism. For the sake of space we omit some of the underlying definitions. For a detailed account of its intricacies the interested reader is pointed to [1].

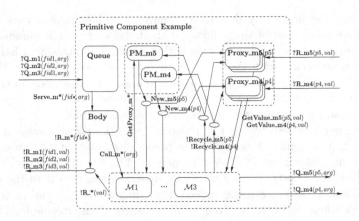

Fig. 2. pNet representing a primitive component

As an illustrative example, the internals of a GCM primitive component featuring three service methods — m_1, m_2 and m_3 — and two client methods — m_4 and m_5 — are depicted by Fig. 2.

Invocation on service methods — $Q\_m_{i,\ i \in \{1,2,3\}}$ — go through a Queue, that dispatches the request — Serve_m* — to the Body. Serving the request consists in performing a Call_m* to the adequate service method, represented by the $\mathcal{M}_i$ boxes in the figure. Once a result is computed, a synchronized R_m* action is emitted. This synchronization occurring between the service method and the Body stems from the fact that GCM primitive components are mono-threaded. Moreover, the careful reader will notice the $fid_{i,\ i \in \{1,2,3\}}$ in the figure. These are called *futures* and act as promises for replies, leveraging asynchrony between components.

Service methods interact with external components by means of client interfaces. This requires obtaining a proxy — GetProxy_m*, New_$m_{i,\ i \in \{4,5\}}$ — in order to be able to invoke client methods — $Q\_m_{i,\ i \in \{4,5\}}$. The reply — R_$m_{i,\ i \in \{4,5\}}$ — goes to the proxy used to call the external component. Then, a GetValue_$m_{i,\ i \in \{4,5\}}$ is performed in order to access the result in the method being served. Finally, Recycle_$m_{i,\ i \in \{4,5\}}$ actions can be performed in order to release the proxies.

The behaviour of the Queue and the Body elements should pose no doubt. The former acts as priority queue with a *First in, First Out* (FIFO) policy, raising an exception if its capacity is exceeded. The latter dispatches the requests to the appropriate method and awaits its *return*, thus preventing the service of other requests in parallel.

The handling of proxies however, is not as straightforward and deserves a closer look. Figures 3 and 4 illustrate the behaviour of the Proxies and Proxy Managers, respectively. Upon reception of a New_m_i action, a Proxy waits for the reply of the method invoked with it — R_m —, making thereafter its result

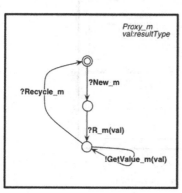

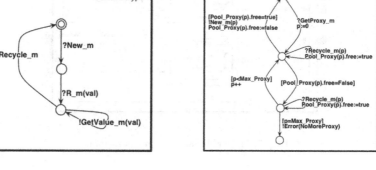

Fig. 3. Behaviour of proxy

Fig. 4. Behaviour of the proxy manager

available — GetValue_m. The proxy becomes then available on the reception of a Recycle_m action.

The behaviour of the Proxy Manager is slightly more elaborated. This maintains a *pool* of proxies, keeping track of those available and those already allocated. On the reception of a GetProxy_m action, it activates a new proxy — New_m — if there is one available. Should that not be the case, an Error(NoMoreProxy) action is emitted. As expected, a Recycle_m action frees a previously allocated proxy.

3   The HyperManager

The HYPERMANAGER is a general purpose monitoring application that was developed in the context of the Spinnaker project[3]. The goal was to deliver a modular solution that would be capable of monitoring a distributed application and react to certain events. As such, the HYPERMANAGER is itself a distributed application, deployed alongside the target application to monitor.

Generally, when performing a monitoring task in an application one may consider two types of events: *pull* and *push*. The former stands for the usual communication scenario where the request comes from the client and then responded by the server. The latter however, is when the server *pushes* data to clients independently from a client's request. Both styles of communication are employed in the HYPERMANAGER application.

As illustrated by Fig. 5, the server (composite) component of the HYPERMANAGER application features three primitive components that are responsible for the application logic. Each possesses one or several service methods that

---

[3] Project OSEO ISIS. http://www.spinnaker-rfid.com/

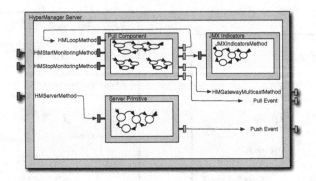

Fig. 5. HyperManager server component

stand for their functionalities and are modelled by *labelled transition systems* (LTSs).

The JMX Indicators component features only one service method: it accepts requests about a particular JMX[4] indicator and replies its status. This encapsulates business code and interacts directly with ECW.

The Pull Component however, includes three service methods and four client interfaces. As the component's name indicates, it is responsible for *pulling* information and emitting it as *pull events*. The service methods HMStartMonitoring-Method and HMStopMonitoringMethod are responsible for starting and stopping the *pulling* activity, respectively. Typically, these are the methods called by the administrator. The remaining service method, HMLoopMethod, may pose some doubt. Indeed, it is called from one of its own client's interface. Being a PROACTIVE application, it follows the active object paradigm where explicit threading is discouraged. As such, making a method *loop* is achieved by making this method sending itself a request before concluding its execution.

While in the monitoring loop, the HMLoopMethod method *pulls* information regarding its own local JMX indicators and those of its gateways via a *multicast* client interface. The last remaining client interface serves the purpose of reporting the *pulled* information as *pull* events.

Last, the Server Primitive component receives *push* information from the HM Gateways — typically to alert the occurrence of some anomaly — and emits it as *push* events. In our implementation both *push* and *pull* events are then displayed in some application with a graphical interface for administration purposes.

The description of the HYPERMANAGER's gateway component follow the same spirit. Figure 6 depicts its constitution.

It is also composed by three primitive components. As expected, the JMX Indicators component has the same semantics as described above.

The Push Component features the same service methods as the Pull Component. Its semantics however, are slightly different. While *looping* it will check for

---

[4] JMX is the standard protocol used for monitoring Java applications.

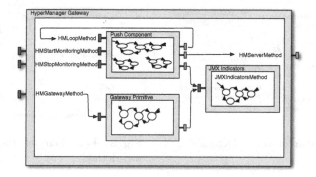

Fig. 6. HyperManager gateway component

the status of its JMX indicators, and communicate with the HYPERMANAGER server if some anomaly is encountered — which will then trigger a *push* event.

As for the Gateway Primitive component, its sole purpose is to reply to the *pulling* requests from HYPERMANAGER server.

4 HyperManager's Behavioural Model

Modelling the HYPERMANAGER in the behavioural semantics *pNets* [1] requires us to provide a behaviour for each service method. In the following we illustrate this by providing an *user-version* LTS for all of them — i.e. we omit all the machinery involving futures and proxies. Moreover, for more material on this case study the reader is invited to its companion website[5].

Regarding our modelling and verification *workflow*, we build the behavioural models by encoding the involved processes in the Fiacre specification language [3]. Then, the FLAC compiler translates it to LOTOS [4]. From there we can use the CADP toolbox [9]. Typically, we use bcg_open for state-space generation — in conjunction with distributor if performing it on a distributed setting —, svl scripts for managing state-space replication, label renaming and build products of transition systems. For last, evaluator4 for model-checking the state-space against MCL (Model Checking Language) [13] formulas — an extension of the alternation-free regular μ-calculus with facilities for manipulating data.

To optimize the size of the model, the composite components have no request queue and requests are directly forwarded to the targeted primitive component. This has no influence in the system's semantics as the primitives' request queues are sufficient for dealing with asynchrony and requests from the sub-components are directly dispatched too. Moreover, we set the primitive components with re-entrant calls with a queue of size 2, and the remaining of size 1.

---

[5] http://www-sop.inria.fr/members/Nuno.Gaspar/HyperManager.php

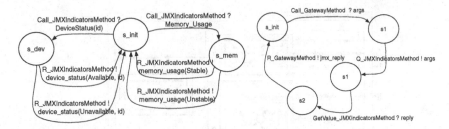

Fig. 7. Behaviour of the JMXIndicatorsMethod

Fig. 8. Behaviour of the HMGatewayMethod

4.1   The HM Gateway

The JMX Indicators primitive component only features one service method: JMXIndicatorsMethod. Its behaviour is modelled by Fig. 7. For the sake of simplicity, we only model two types of indicators: *MemoryUsage* and *DeviceStatus*. The latter takes into account an identifier, returning its availability status. This relates to the status of a RFID reader transmitting to the ECW Gateway. While the former simply returns the stability status of the memory.

The service method offered by the Gateway Primitive component has also a fairly simple behaviour. It is illustrated by Fig. 8. It acts merely as a request forwarder for the JMX Indicators component.

Regarding the Push Component, the HMStartMethod and HMStopMethod methods enable/disable the *looping* process. This is achieved by a shared variable among processes that acts as a *flag*. Invoking HMStartMethod will set the *flag* variable **started** to *true* and perform an invocation to HMLoopMethod. On the other hand, HMStopMethod will set the *flag* to *false*. Their behaviour is rather trivial and therefore omitted for the sake of space. In practice, the involved labels are GuardQuery, GuardReply?b:bool, SetFalse and SetTrue; their meaning should be obvious from their names.

The last remaining service method to describe is the most interesting one — the *loop* method.

As illustrated by Fig. 9, the actual *looping* only occurs if the *flag* variable **started** is set to TRUE, otherwise a simple *return* without performing any significant action is made.[6] While *looping*, the JMX indicators are checked. Should an anomaly be detected a report is made to the HM Server. Last, before *returning* a request is sent to itself — Q_HMLoopMethod — in order to be able to continue *looping* while the *flag* variable evaluates to *true*.

Model Generation and Proven Properties. Table 1 illustrates the relevant information concerning the HM Gateway's state-space built using the CADP toolbox. The model is generated with two RFID readers.

---

[6] For the sake of clarity, *communications actions* are written in black, while *local* computations are written in blue. Their intended meaning should pose no doubt.

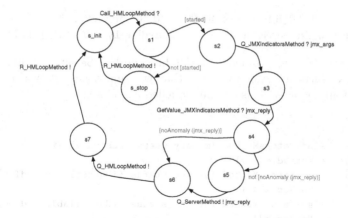

Fig. 9. Behaviour of the HMLoopMethod at the gateway level

Table 1. Numbers regarding the gateway model

	States	Transitions	File size (mb)
hmgateway.bcg	14.931.628	147.485.103	∼295
hmgateway-min.bcg	14.931.628	147.485.103	∼296

The entry suffixed by -min means that minimization by branching *bisimulation* was applied. We note that the minimization process fails to produce a reduced transition system. This is due to the fact that we do not hide any *communication action* and all transitions are visible[7]. However, there is an increase in the file size even though the number of states and transitions remained equal. This is justified by the fact that bcg_min inserts information in the produced file stating that it came from a minimization process. In any case, this overhead is rather negligible.

Having this state-space generated we can now prove some properties regarding the expected behaviour of the model. Specifying properties of interest in MCL is a rather intuitive task due to its expressiveness and conciseness. Its main ingredients include patterns extracting data values from LTS actions, modalities on transition sequences described using extended regular expressions and programming language constructs.

For instance, one could wonder about this rather unusual *looping* mechanism. Once setting the *flag* to *true* — accomplished by Q_HMStartMethod —, the *looping* continues until a request to stop monitoring is received. That is, there is no path in which the *flag* evaluates to *false* without the occurrence of a Q_HMStopMethod.

---

[7] It is worth noticing that the FLAC compiler translates shared variables and internal communications into τ-transitions. These will therefore disappear from the LTS if subject to minimization.

Property 1.   ["Q_HMStartMethod" . "Q_HMLoopMethod" .
        (not"Q_HMLoopMethod")* . "GuardReply !FALSE"] false

Naturally, we also want to avoid overloading the HM Server with unnecessary messages. As such, we want to ensure that we cannot *push* data if not in the presence of an anomaly. This can be modelled as follows:

Property 2.

```
[ ((not "R_JMXIndicatorsMethod !memory_usage (Unstable)")* .
      "Q_ServerMethod.*")  |
  ((not "R_JMXIndicatorsMethod !device_status ((Unavailable, IdTwo))")* .
      "Q_ServerMethod.*")  |
  ((not "R_JMXIndicatorsMethod !device_status ((Unavailable, IdOne))")* .
      "Q_ServerMethod.*")
] false
```

Both properties are naturally proved *true*.

4.2   The HM Server

Similarly as seen for the HM Gateway component, the HM Server component also features a JMX Indicators primitive component. This however, is naturally not endowed with indicators for the RFID devices statuses. Technically, we attach to the LTS modelling its behaviour (Fig. 7) a context that constraints its requests. Moreover, HMStartMethod and HMStopMethod methods exhibit the same behaviour as described above.

As seen above, upon detection of an anomaly, the HM Gateway component *push*es the relevant information to the HM Server. Then, it is emitted as a *push* event as depicted by Fig. 10. The careful reader will notice that the emitted event also contains the information regarding the HM Gateway from which the anomaly originated. This should come as no surprise as there can be several of them, and properly identifying the source of an abnormal situation is of paramount importance.

As depicted by Fig. 11, the *looping* process for the HM Server proceeds in a similar fashion as the one from the HM Gateway: the *flag* variable **started**'s valuation determines whether we enter the *looping* process or if we just *return*. While *looping* we *pull* information from the local JMX indicators and emit it as a *pull* event.

Moreover, via a multicast interface information is *pulled* from the connected gateways. This, will emit as many *pull* events as the number of connected gateways. Last, a request to itself is performed in order to continue *looping*.

Model Generation and Proven Properties. Table 2 illustrates the relevant information concerning HM Server's state-space.

As in the case of the HM Gateway model, the minimization process failed to produce a smaller state-space. However, this time we get a 9 % increase in the

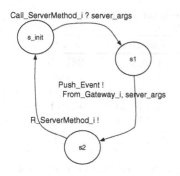

Fig. 10. Behaviour of the HMServerMethod

Fig. 11. Behaviour of the HMLoopMethod at the server level

Table 2. Numbers regarding the server model

	States	Transitions	File size (mb)
hmserver.bcg	12.787.376	187.589.422	∼363
hmserver-min.bcg	12.787.376	187.589.422	∼396

file size, not so much negligible as the increase noticed for the HM Gateway's state-space.[8]

A rather trivial property we can expect to hold is that we can reach a state which *explodes* one of the request queues. This can be modelled in MCL as follows:

Property 3. < true* . 'QueueException_ServerPrimitive !.*'> true

As mentioned above, we omitted all the machinery involving proxies while describing the service methods' behaviour. However, this is naturally included in the generated model. For instance, the HMLoopMethod method needs to request a proxy in order to be able to invoke JMX Indicators's service method. This is naturally encoded as follows:

Property 4. [(not "GetProxy_JMXIndicatorsMethod.*")* .
        "Q_JMXIndicatorsMethod.*"] false

As expected, both properties hold in the model.

4.3   System Product, Model Generation and Proven Properties

We attempted to generate a system product constituted by two HM Gateways and one HM Server components. However, even on a machine with 90 GB of RAM, we experienced the so common state-space explosion phenomena.

---

[8] In fact, we encountered another peculiar situation where minimization produced a smaller state-space, yet a bigger file size: http://cadp.forumotion.com/t374-bcg-file-size-after-minimization.

Table 3. Relevant numbers regarding the generated model

	States	Transitions	File size
hmgateway-min-w-hidden.bcg	14.931.628	147.485.103	~287 mb
hmgateway-min-w-hidden-min.bcg	409.374	4.007.232	~8.5 mb
hmserver-min-w-hidden.bcg	12.787.376	187.589.422	~375 mb
hmserver-min-w-hidden-min.bcg	5.761.504	85.157.420	~179 mb
SystemProduct.bcg	342.047.684	3.026.114.393	~5.27 gb
SystemProduct-min.bcg	259.340.044	2.396.896.830	~4.83 gb

This arises often in the analysis of complex systems. To this end, *communication hiding* comes as an efficient and pragmatic approach for tackling this issue. Indeed, it allows to specify the *communication actions* that need not to be observed for verification purposes, thus yielding more tractable state-spaces.

Table 3 illustrates the effects of applying this technique to the model. The sole *communication actions* being hidden are the ones involved in (1) the request transmission from the Queue to the adequate method — Serve_ and Call_ —, (2) the proxy machinery —GetProxy_, New_ and Recycle_ —, and (3) finally in the *guard* of the *looping* methods — GuardQuery, GuardReply, SetFalse and SetTrue.

The lines suffixed by -hidden indicate the results obtained by *hiding* the mentioned *communication actions* in the *minimized* HM Gateway and HM server state-spaces. For both, no effect is noticed on the size of the LTS. However, there is a decrease in the file size. This is due to the fact that the *hiding* process yields several τ-transitions, which facilitates file compression. This has the consequence of leveraging the subsequent *minimization* process. Indeed, we even obtain a reduction by two orders of magnitude (!) for the HM Gateway state-space.

The HYPERMANAGER comes as a monitoring application that should be able to properly trace the origin of an anomaly. As such, one behavioural property that we expect to hold is that whenever an abnormal situation is detected by a HM Gateway, it is *fairly inevitable* to be reported as a *push event* that correctly identifies its origin.

First, we shall use MCL's macro capabilities to help us build the formula:

```
macro GETVALUE_1_MEMORY () =
  "GetValue_JMXIndicatorsMethod_Push_1 !memory_usage (Unstable)"
end_macro

macro PUSH_1_MEMORY ()       =
  ("Push_Event (FirstGateway, UnstableMemoryUsage)")
end_macro

...
```

The above macros should be self-explanatory. The former represents the detection of an anomaly coming from the first HM Gateway — the model is instantiated with two HM Gateways, thus we differentiate their actions by suffixing them adequately. The latter stands for the emission of the *push* event corresponding to that anomaly. The macros for the remaining relevant actions are defined analogously.

Moreover, we define the following macro generically encoding the *fair inevitability* that after an *anomaly* the system emits a *push*.

```
macro FAIRLY_INEVITABLY_A_PUSH (ANOMALY, PUSH) =
    [ true* . "ANOMALY" . (not "PUSH")* ]
            < (not PUSH)* . PUSH > true
end_macro
```

Having the macros defined, we can now write the formula of interest:

Property 5.

```
(FAIRLY_INEVITABLY_A_PUSH(GETVALUE_1_MEMORY, PUSH_1_MEMORY) and
 FAIRLY_INEVITABLY_A_PUSH(GETVALUE_2_MEMORY, PUSH_2_MEMORY) and
 FAIRLY_INEVITABLY_A_PUSH(GETVALUE_1_DEVICE_1, PUSH_1_DEVICE_1) and
 FAIRLY_INEVITABLY_A_PUSH(GETVALUE_1_DEVICE_2, PUSH_1_DEVICE_2) and
 FAIRLY_INEVITABLY_A_PUSH(GETVALUE_2_DEVICE_1, PUSH_2_DEVICE_1) and
 FAIRLY_INEVITABLY_A_PUSH(GETVALUE_2_DEVICE_2, PUSH_2_DEVICE_2)
)
```

As expected, this property holds for the model.

5   The Case Study Reloaded: On Structural Reconfigurations

As seen so far, the HyperManager acts as a monitoring application with two styles of communication: *pull* and *push*. However, it also needs to cope with structural reconfigurations. This means that at runtime the architecture of the application can evolve by, say, establishing new bindings and/or removing existing ones.

For GCM applications *bind* and *unbind* operations are handled by the component owning the *client* interface that is supposed to be reconfigurable. This should come as no surprise, indeed, it follows the same spirit as in object-oriented languages: an object holds the reference to a target object; it is this object that must change the reference it holds.

In our case-study, these reconfigurations can occur both at the server level — when *pulling* data from the bound gateways —, and at gateway level — when *pushing* data to the server. The difference lies at the fact that the server communicates via a *multicast* interface, unlike the gateways that establish a standard *1-to-1* communication. Therefore, these are dealt in a different manner.

5.1   HM Reconfigurable Gateway

Let us first illustrate how a *singleton client* reconfigurable interface is modelled in *pNets*. As depicted by Fig. 12, for each client reconfigurable interface there exists a *binding controller*.

Indeed, we allow for reconfigurations by defining two new request messages for the *binding* and *unbinding* of interfaces. These are delegated to a binding

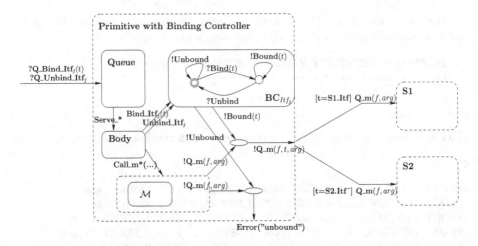

Fig. 12. Binding controller

Table 4. Gateway with reconfigurable interface

	States	Transitions	File size (gb)
hmgateway-reconfig.bcg	354.252.868	4.178.400.886	~8.45
hmgateway-reconfig-min.bcg	354.104.012	4.176.956.686	~8.54

controller that upon method invocation over these reconfigurable interfaces will check if they are indeed bound, emitting an error if it is not the case. Moreover, the target of the invocation is decided by checking its passed reference. For this reason one must know statically what are the possible target interfaces that a reconfigurable interface can be bound too.

In practice, to the HM Gateway model discussed in Subsect. 4.1 we add the request messages Q_Bind_ServerMethod and Q_Unbind_ServerMethod. Since we only have one reconfigurable interface we can avoid adding an explicit parameter — unlike shown in Fig. 12, where we demonstrate a more general case. Moreover, since the gateways can only be bound to one target — the server — the *binding controller* only needs to keep a state variable regarding its *connectedness*.

As expected, these changes have a considerable impact in the size of the model. This is illustrated by Table 4.

All the properties proven in Subsect. 4.1 still hold for this new HM Gateway model, with a natural overhead in *model-checking* them in a much bigger state-space. However, for this new model we are more interested in addressing the reconfiguration capabilities. For instance, provided that the interface is bound, it will not yield an Unbound action upon method invocation.

Property 6.

```
< true* . "Q_Bind_ServerMethod". (not "Q_Unbind_ServerMethod")* .
"Q_ServerMethod" . (not "Q_Unbind_ServerMethod")* . "Unbound" > true
```

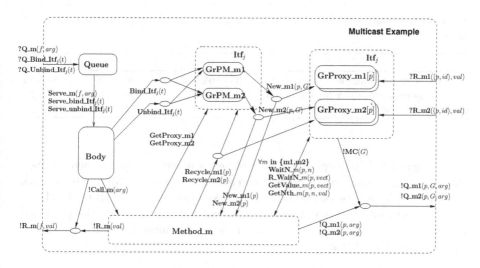

Fig. 13. pNet example for reconfigurable multicast interface

Table 5. Server with reconfigurable *multicast* interface

	States	Transitions	File size (gb)
hmserver-reconfig.bcg	931.640.080	16.435.355.306	∼32.93

The above property is proved *false*. This indicates that provided that the interface is bound, a path yielding an Unbound action without the occurrence of a Q_Unbind_ServerMethod will not occur.

5.2 HM Reconfigurable Server

As an illustrative example, the *pNet* of a primitive component featuring a reconfigurable client *multicast* interface and two service methods — m_1 and m_2 — is depicted by Fig. 13.

In short, the machinery involved for dealing with this kind of interfaces mainly differs from reconfigurable *singleton* interfaces in that we must keep track of the target's connectedness status. Indeed, the emission of a new proxy — New_$m_{i,i \in \{1,2\}}$ — is synchronized in a similar manner, however we also transmit the current status of the *multicast* interface (i.e. the G variable in the figure). This status will be taken into account when invoking one of the client methods — Q_$m_{i,i \in \{1,2\}}$. In practice, G is a boolean vector whose element's valuation determine the interface's connectedness.

Table 5 demonstrates the impact of adding reconfiguration capabilities to the HM Server model.

Table 6. Relevant numbers regarding the generated model with reconfigurable interfaces

	States	Transitions	File size
hmgateway-reconfig-min-w-hidden.bcg	354.104.012	4.176.956.686	∼8.15 gb
hmgateway-reconfig-min-w-hidden-min.bcg	11.090.974	127.799.874	∼283.5 mb
hmserver-reconfig-min-w-hidden.bcg	931.640.080	16.435.355.306	∼31.28 gb

The generated state-space for the HM Server model nearly attained 1 billion states.[9] Our attempts to *minimize* it revealed to be unsuccessful due to the lack of memory. These were carried out on a workstation with ∼90 GB of RAM.

It is worth noticing that while we were not able to *minimize* the produced state-space, we were still able to *model-check* it against the same properties discussed in Subsect. 4.2.

5.3   Model Generation and Proven Properties

As seen in Subsect. 4.3, building the product of the system already showed to be delicate. Abstraction techniques such as *communication hiding* were already required to build the system. Thus, it should come as no surprise that we face the same situation here.

However, it should be noted that the *hiding* process itself, produced little effect on the file size, and no effect on the state-spaces. It mainly acted as a means to leverage the subsequent *minimization* process, allowing for a very significant state-space reduction. Table 6 illustrates the results obtained by following the same approach as above.

We obtained a significant state-space reduction for the HM Gateway model, but we were unable to *minimize* the HM Server. Indeed, *communication hiding* may leverage state-space reduction, but still requires that the *minimization* process is able to run, therefore not solving the lack of memory issue. This is a rather embarrassing situation as we would expect a significant state-space reduction as well for the HM Server.

While *communication hiding* revealed to be a valuable tool, *minimization* is still a bottleneck if the input state-space is already too big. Thus, we need to shift this burden to the lower levels of the hierarchy. Indeed, both HM Server and HM Gateway components are the result of a product between their primitive components. Moreover, these are themselves the result of a product between their internals – request queue, body, proxies ...

---

[9] As mentioned in Subsect. 4.2, for the HM Server model, the JMX Indicators component is generated with a context not including the request of device statuses. Previous experiments not considering this context produced a HM Server model with the following characteristics: 4.148.563.680 states, with 74.268.977.628 transitions, on a 154.2 GB file. It is interesting to note the huge impact that (the lack of) a contextual state-space generation on one of its components can provoke.

Table 7. Relevant numbers regarding the generated model with reconfigurable interfaces

	States	Transitions	File size
hidden-hmgateway-reconfig.bcg	3.483.000	43.193.346	~85.46 mb
hidden-hmgateway-reconfig-min.bcg	3.073.108	39.373.968	~83.95 mb
hidden-hmserver-reconfig.bcg	210.121.904	3.890.791.694	~7.52 gb
hidden-hmserver-reconfig-min.bcg	177.604.848	3.288.937.718	~6.61 gb
SystemProduct-reconfig.bcg	3.054.464.649	38.680.270.695	~74.16 gb

Table 7 illustrates the results obtained by hiding the same communication actions as in the above approaches, but before starting to build any product.

Indeed, following this approach proved to be fruitful as we were able to generate the system product. Yet, *minimization* remained still out of reach. Nevertheless, we are still in a position to *model-check* some properties of interest. For instance, *pulling* information via a *multicast* emission is now predicated with a boolean array whose element's valuation determines its connectedness. As an example, a rather simple *liveness* property is the following one:

Property 7.

```
<true* . "Q_GatewayMulticastMethod !ARRAY(FALSE FALSE) !MemoryUsage"> true
```

Initially, both HM Gateways are bound, the above property tell us that we can indeed unbind both of them.

6   Related Work

The maturity attained by the CADP toolbox made it a reference tool among the formal methods community. Several case studies have been published, namely industrial ones addressing other goals than verification. For instance, in [8] Coste et al. discuss performance evaluation for systems and networks on chips. More closely related with our work we must refer the experiments presented in [7]. A dynamic reconfiguration protocol is specified and model-checked, however their focus is on the reconfiguration protocol itself rather than reconfigurable applications.

Indeed, many works can be found in the literature embracing a behavioural semantics approach for the specification and verification of distributed systems. Yet, literature addressing the aspects of reconfigurable applications remains scarce.

Nevertheless, we must cite the work around BIP (Behaviour, Interaction, Priority) [2] — a framework encompassing rigorous design principles. It allows the description of the coordination between components in a layered way. Moreover, it has the particularity of also permitting the generation of code from its models. Yet, structural reconfigurations are not supported.

Another rather different approach that we must refer is the one followed by tools specifically tailored for architectural specifications. For instance, in [11] Inverardi et al. discusses CHARMY, a framework for designing and validating architectural specifications. It offers a full featured graphical interface with the goal of being more *user friendly* in an industrial context. Still, architectural specifications remain of static nature.

Looking at the interactive theorem proving arena we can also find some related material. In [6] Boyer et al. propose a reconfiguration protocol and prove its correctness in the Coq Proof Assistant [15]. This work however, focuses on the protocol itself, and not in the behaviour of a reconfigurable application. Moreover, in [10] we presented Mefresa — a *Mechanized Framework for Reasoning on Software Architectures*. This work discusses a formal specification and a (re)configuration language for GCM architectures. All the involved machinery and underlying formal semantics are mechanized in Coq. However, at the current stage of development its main focus is on the reasoning at the architectural level.

7   Final Remarks

In the realm of component-based systems, behavioural specification is among the most employed approaches for the rigorous design of applications. It leverages the use of model-checking techniques, by far the most widespread formal method in the industry. Yet, verification in the presence of structural reconfigurations remains still a rather unaddressed topic. This can be justified by the inherent complexity that such systems impose. However, reconfiguration plays a significant role for the increase in systems availability, and is a key ingredient in the autonomic computing arena, thus tackling its demands should be seen of paramount importance.

In this paper we discussed the specification and formal verification of a reconfigurable monitoring application as an industrial case study. Several lessons can be drawn from this work.

The Spinnaker project gave us the opportunity to promote the use of formal methods within the industry. As expected, the interaction with our industrial partners revealed to be a demanding task. Common budgetary issues (time allocation, hirings, ...) of such projects and lack of prior formal methods' exposure by our partners were some of the barriers to overcome. This was further aggravated by the fact that software development was playing a little part in the overall project budget, and therefore not a main priority.

Nevertheless our experience revealed to be fruitful. We were able to witness the general curiosity on the use of formal methods by the industry, and increase our understanding on the needs and obstacles for its broader adoption. Indeed, collaborative projects of this nature allow the industry to *test the waters* and expose researchers to real-world scenarios. However, bridging the gap between the industry's expectation and the current state of the art still remains as a challenge for the research community. To this end, recent work on Vercors [12] aims at bringing intuitive specification languages and graphical tools for the non-specialists.

Concerning our task at hand, modelling the HYPERMANAGER application upto the intricacies of the middleware led us to a combinatorial explosion in the number of states. This, is further exasperated by the inclusion of reconfigurable interfaces. Even the use of compositional and contextual state-space generation techniques revealed to be insufficient. While this could be solved by further increasing the available memory in our workstation, it is worth noticing that this approach is not always feasible in practice. This bottleneck can be alleviated by performing the synchronization product in a *distributed* manner. Alas, this is not supported by the CADP toolbox. Alternatively, CADP supports τ-reduction algorithms that reduce *on-the-fly* the existent τ-transitions. While this approach was successfully applied in [5], its practical effects for this case study remain as future work.[10] Moreover, handling such big state-spaces teaches us the importance of automation regarding model generation. Indeed, debugging can be a daunting task due to the inherent complexity and size of the involved models. Regarding this issue we must refer that we plan on tackling behavioural specification concerns within the Mefresa framework as future work. This will leverage the use of deductive reasoning in a usual model-checking context as demonstrated in [14], and thus relax the burden of dealing with huge state-spaces.

At last, as usual in the realm of formal verification, we conclude that abstraction is the key. Taking advantage of CADP's facilities for *communication hiding*, one can specify actions that need not to be observed for the verification purposes, which further enhances the effects of a subsequent minimization by branching *bisimulation*. This illustrates the pragmatic rationale of formal verification by model-checking — the most likely reason behind its acceptance in the industry.

Acknowledgements. The authors are grateful to Frédéric Lang from the INRIA Vasy team for troubleshooting with the CADP toolbox and the semantics of the Fiacre specification language. Moreover, our *ingénieur experts* Arthur Mbonyinshuti and Bartlomiej Szejna deserve a mention for technical assistance regarding CADP's license management and the implementation of THE HYPERMANAGER, respectively.

References

1. Ameur-Boulifa, R., Henrio, L., Madelaine, E., Savu, A.: Behavioural semantics for asynchronous components. RR RR-8167, December 2012
2. Basu, A., Bensalem, S., Bozga, M., Combaz, J., Jaber, M., Nguyen, T.-H., Sifakis, J.: Rigorous component-based system design using the BIP framework. IEEE Softw. **28**(3), 41–48 (2011)

---

[10] It is worth mentioning that the immediate concerns and goals for this case study were more aimed at convincing our industrial partners on the ease of use of our verification workflow.

3. Berthomieu, B., Bodeveix, J.P., Filali, M., Garavel, H., Lang, F., Peres, F., Saad, R., Stoecker, J., Vernadat, F.: The syntax and semantics of FIACRE. RR (2009)
4. Bolognesi, T., Brinksma, E.: Introduction to the iso specification language lotos. Comput. Netw. ISDN Syst. **14**(1), 25–59 (1987)
5. Ameur-Boulifa, R., Halalai, R., Henrio, L., Madelaine, E.: Verifying safety of fault-tolerant distributed components. In: Arbab, F., Ölveczky, P.C. (eds.) FACS 2011. LNCS, vol. 7253, pp. 278–295. Springer, Heidelberg (2012)
6. Boyer, F., Gruber, O., Pous, D.: Robust reconfigurations of component assemblies. In: Proceedings of the 2013 International Conference on Software Engineering, ICSE '13. IEEE Press (2013)
7. Aguilar Cornejo, M., Garavel, M., Mateescu, R., De Palma, N.: Specification and verification of a dynamic reconfiguration protocol for agent-based applications. In: Zielinski, K., Geihs, K., Laurentowski, A. (eds.) New Developments in Distributed Applications and Interoperable Systems. IFIP. Springer, Heidelberg (2001)
8. Coste, N., Hermanns, H., Lantreibecq, E., Serwe, W.: Towards performance prediction of compositional models in industrial GALS designs. In: Bouajjani, A., Maler, O. (eds.) CAV 2009. LNCS, vol. 5643, pp. 204–218. Springer, Heidelberg (2009)
9. Garavel, H., Lang, F., Mateescu, R., Serwe, W.: CADP 2010: a toolbox for the construction and analysis of distributed processes. In: Abdulla, P.A., Leino, K.R.M. (eds.) TACAS 2011. LNCS, vol. 6605, pp. 372–387. Springer, Heidelberg (2011)
10. Gaspar, N., Henrio, L., Madelaine, E.: Bringing Coq into the world of GCM distributed applications. Int. J. Parallel Program. (HLPP'2013 Special Issue). doi:10.1007/s10766-013-0264-7 (2013)
11. Inverardi, P., Muccini, H., Pelliccione, P.: Charmy: an extensible tool for architectural analysis. In: ESEC-FSE'05, ACM SIGSOFT Symposium on the Foundations of Software Engineering. Research Tool Demos, 5–9 September 2005
12. Kulankhina, O.: A graphical specification environment for GCM component-based applications. Ubinet master internship report, INRIA (2013)
13. Mateescu, R., Thivolle, D.: A model checking language for concurrent value-passing systems. In: Cuellar, J., Sere, K. (eds.) FM 2008. LNCS, vol. 5014, pp. 148–164. Springer, Heidelberg (2008)
14. Sprenger, C.: A verified model checker for the modal mu-calculus in coq. In: Steffen, B. (ed.) Tools and Algorithms for the Construction and Analysis of Systems. LNCS, vol. 1384. Springer, Heidelberg (1998)
15. The Coq Development Team. The Coq Proof Assistant Reference Manual (2012)

A General Trace-Based Framework
of Logical Causality

Gregor Gössler$^{(\boxtimes)}$ and Daniel Le Métayer

INRIA Grenoble – Rhône-Alpes, Montbonnot-Saint-Martin, France
gregor.goessler@inria.fr

Abstract. In component-based safety-critical embedded systems it is
crucial to determine the cause(s) of the violation of a safety property,
be it to issue a precise alert, to steer the system into a safe state, or
to determine liability of component providers. In this paper we present
an approach to blame components based on a single execution trace
violating a safety property P. The diagnosis relies on counterfactual
reasoning ("what would have been the outcome if component C had
behaved correctly?") to distinguish component failures that actually con-
tributed to the outcome from failures that had little or no impact on the
violation of P.

1 Introduction

In a concurrent, possibly embedded and distributed system, it is often crucial
to determine which component(s) caused an observed failure. Understanding
causality relationships between component failures and the violation of system-
level properties can be especially useful to understand the occurrence of errors
in execution traces, to allocate responsibilities, or to try to prevent errors (by
limiting error propagation or the potential damages caused by an error).

The notion of causality inherently relies on a form of counterfactual reasoning: basically the goal is to try to answer questions such as "would event e_2 have
occurred if e_1 had not occurred?" to decide if e_1 can be seen as a cause of e_2
(assuming that e_1 and e_2 have both occurred, or could both occur in a given
context). But this question is not as simple as it may look:

1. First, we have to define what could have happened if e_1 had not occurred, in
   other words what are the *alternative worlds*.
2. In general, the set of alternative worlds is not a singleton and it is possible
   that in some of these worlds e_2 would occur while in others e_2 would not
   occur.
3. We also have to make clear what we call an event and when two events
   in two different traces can be considered as similar. For example, if e_1 had
   not occurred, even if an event potentially corresponding to e_2 might have
   occurred, it would probably not have occurred at the same time as e_2 in the
   original sequence of events; it could also possibly have occurred in a slightly
   different way (for example with different parameters, because of the potential
   effect of the occurrence of e_1 on the value of some variables).

J.L. Fiadeiro et al. (Eds.): FACS 2013, LNCS 8348, pp. 157–173, 2014.
DOI: 10.1007/978-3-319-07602-7_11, © Springer International Publishing Switzerland 2014

Causality has been studied in many disciplines (philosophy, mathematical logic, physics, law, etc.) and from different points of view. In this paper, we are interested in causality for the analysis of execution traces in order to establish the origin of a system-level failure. The main trend in the use of causality in computer science consists in mapping the abstract notion of event in the general definition of causality proposed by Halpern and Pearl in their seminal contribution [12] to properties of execution traces. Halpern and Pearl's model of causality relies on a counterfactual condition mitigated by subtle contingency properties to improve the accurateness of the definition and alleviate the limitations of the counterfactual reasoning in the occurrence of multiple causes. While Halpern and Pearl's model is a very precious contribution to the analysis of the notion of causality, we believe that a fundamentally different approach considering traces as first-class citizens is required in the computer science context considered here: The model proposed by Halpern and Pearl is based on an abstract notion of event defined in terms of propositional variables and causal models expressed as sets of equations between these variables. The equations define the basic causality dependencies between variables (such as $F = L_1$ or L_2 if F is a variable denoting the occurrence of a fire and L_1 and L_2 two lightning events that can cause the fire). In order to apply this model to execution traces, it is necessary to map the abstract notion of event onto properties of execution traces. But these properties and their causality dependencies are not given a priori, they should be derived from the system under study. In addition, a key feature of trace properties is the temporal ordering of events which is also intimately related to the idea of causality but is not an explicit notion in Halpern and Pearl's framework (even if notions of time can be encoded within events). Even though this application is not impossible, as shown by [4], we believe that definitions in terms of execution traces are preferable because (a) in order to determine the responsibility of components for an observed outcome, component traces provide the relevant granularity, and (b) they can lead to more direct and clearer definitions of causality.

As suggested above, many variants of causality have been proposed in the literature and used in different disciplines. It is questionable that one single definition of causality could fit all purposes. For example, when using causality relationships to establish liabilities, it may be useful to ask different questions, such as: "could event e_2 have occurred in some cases if e_1 had not occurred?" or "would event e_2 have occurred if e_1 had occurred but not e_1'?". These questions correspond to different variants of causality which can be perfectly legitimate and useful in different situations. To address this need, we propose two definition of causality relationships that can express these kinds of variants, called *necessary* and *sufficient* causality.

The framework introduced here distinguishes a set of black-box components, each equipped with a specification. On a given execution trace, the causality of the components is analyzed with respect to the violation of a system-level property. In order to keep the definitions as simple as possible without losing generality — that is, applicability to various models of computation and communication —, we provide a language-based formalization of the framework. We believe that our general, trace-based definitions are unique features of our framework.

Traces can be obtained from an execution of the actual system, but also as counter-examples from model-checking. For instance, we can model-check whether a behavioral model satisfies a property; causality on the counter-example can then be established against the component specifications.

2 Modeling Framework

In order to focus on the fundamental issues in defining causality on execution traces we introduce a simple, language-based modeling framework.

Definition 1 (Component signature). *A component signature C_i is a tuple (Σ_i, S_i) where Σ_i is an alphabet and $S_i \subseteq \Sigma_i^*$ is a prefix-closed specification (set of allowed behaviors) over Σ_i.*

A component signature is the abstraction of an actual component that is needed to apply the causality analysis introduced here. Similarly, a system signature is the abstraction of a system composed of a set of interacting components.

Definition 2 (System signature). *A system signature is a tuple (C, Σ, B, ρ) where*

- *$C = \{C_1, ..., C_n\}$ is a finite set of component signatures $C_i = (\Sigma_i, S_i)$ with pairwise disjoint alphabets;*
- *$\Sigma \subseteq \Sigma_1' \times ... \times \Sigma_n'$ is a system alphabet with $\Sigma_i' = \Sigma_i \cup \{\epsilon\}$ is a distinct element denoting that C_i does not participate in an interaction $\alpha \in \Sigma$;*
- *$B \subseteq \Sigma^* \cup \Sigma^\omega$ is a prefix-closed behavioral model;*
- *$\rho \subseteq \left(\bigcup_i \Sigma_i\right) \times \left(\bigcup_i \Sigma_i\right)$ is a relation modeling information flow among components.*

The behavioral model B is used to express assumptions and constraints on the possible (correct and incorrect) behaviors. The relation ρ models possible information flow among components. Intuitively, $(a, b) \in \rho$ means that any occurrence of a may influence the next occurrence of b (possibly in the same interaction), e.g., by triggering or constraining the occurrence of b, or by transmitting information.

Notations. Given a trace $tr = \alpha_1 \cdot \alpha_2 \cdots \in \Sigma^*$ and an index $i \in \mathbb{N}$ let $tr[1..i] = \alpha_1 \cdots \alpha_i$, let $tr[i] = \alpha_i$, and $tr[i...] = \alpha_i \alpha_{i+1} \cdots$. Let $|tr|$ denote the length of tr. For $\alpha = (a_1, ..., a_n) \in \Sigma$ let $\alpha[k] = a_k$ denote the action of component k in α ($a_k = \epsilon$ if k does not participate in α); for $w = \alpha_1 \cdots \alpha_k \in \Sigma^*$ and $i \in \{1, ..., n\}$ let $\pi_i(w) = \alpha_1[i] \cdots \alpha_k[i]$ (where ϵ letters are removed from the resulting word).

For the sake of compactness of notations we define composition $\| : \Sigma_1^* \times ... \times \Sigma_n^* \to \Sigma^*$ such that $w_1 \| ... \| w_n = \{ w \in \Sigma \mid \forall i = 1, ..., n : \pi_i(w) = w_i \}$, and extend $\|$ to languages.

2.1 Logs

A (possibly faulty) execution of a system may not be fully observable; therefore we base our analysis on *logs*. A log of a system $S = (C, \Sigma, B, \rho)$ with components $C = \{C_1, ..., C_n\}$ of alphabets Σ_i is a vector $\boldsymbol{tr} = (tr_1, ..., tr_n) \in \Sigma_1^* \times ... \times \Sigma_n^*$ of component traces such that there exists a trace $tr \in \Sigma^*$ with $\forall i = 1, ..., n :$ $tr_i = \pi_i(tr)$. A log $\boldsymbol{tr} \in \mathcal{L}$ is thus the projection of an actual system-level trace $tr \in B$. This relation between the actual execution and the log on which causality analysis will be performed allows us to model the fact that only a partial order between the events in tr may be observable rather than their exact precedence.[1]

Let $\mathcal{L}(S)$ denote the set of logs of S. Given a log $\boldsymbol{tr} = (tr_1, ..., tr_n) \in \mathcal{L}(S)$ let $\boldsymbol{tr}^\uparrow = \{tr \in B \mid \forall i = 1, ..., n : \pi_i(tr) = tr_i\}$ be the set of behaviors resulting in $\boldsymbol{tr}$.

Definition 3 (Consistent specification). *A consistently specified system is a tuple $(S, \mathcal{P})$ where $S = (C, \Sigma, B, \rho)$ is a system signature with $C = \{C_1, ..., C_n\}$ and $C_i = (\Sigma_i, \mathcal{S}_i)$, and $\mathcal{P} \subseteq B$ is a prefix-closed property such that for all traces $tr \in B$,*

$$(\forall i = 1, ..., n : \pi_i(tr) \in \mathcal{S}_i) \implies tr \in \mathcal{P}$$

Under a consistent specification, property $\mathcal{P}$ may be violated only if at least one of the components violates its specification. Throughout this paper we focus on consistent specifications.

3 Motivating Example

Consider a database system consisting of three components communicating by message passing over point-to-point FIFO buffers. Component C_1 is a client, C_2 the database server, and C_3 is a journaling system. The specifications of the three components are as follows:

$\mathcal{S}_1$: sends a lock request lock to C_2, followed by a request m to modify the locked data.

$\mathcal{S}_2$: receives a write request m, possibly preceded by a lock request lock. Access control is optimistic in the sense that the server accepts write requests without checking whether a lock request has been received before; however, in case of a missing lock request, a conflict may be detected later on and signaled by an event x. After the write, a message journ is sent to C_3.

$\mathcal{S}_3$: keeps receiving journ events from C_2 for journaling.

The system is modeled by the system signature (C, Σ, B, ρ) where $C = \{C_1, C_2, C_3\}$ with component signatures $C_i = (\Sigma_i, \mathcal{S}_i)$, and

---

[1] It is straight-forward to allow for additional information in traces $tr \in B$ that is not observable in the log, by adding to the cartesian product of Σ another alphabet that does not appear in the projections. For instance, events may be recorded with some timing uncertainty rather than precise time stamps [23].

- $\Sigma_1 = \{a, m!, lock!\}$, $\Sigma_2 = \{m?, journ!, x, lock?\}$, and $\Sigma_3 = \{b, journ?\}$, where m! and m? stand for the emission and reception of a message m, respectively, and a, b, and x are internal events;
- $\mathcal{S}_1 = \{lock!.m!\}^2$, $\mathcal{S}_2 = \{lock?.m?.journ!, m?.journ!.x\}$, and $\mathcal{S}_3 = \{journ?^i \mid i \in \mathbb{N}\}$;
- $\Sigma = (\Sigma_1 \times \{\epsilon\} \times \{\epsilon\}) \cup (\{\epsilon\} \times \Sigma_2 \times \{\epsilon\}) \cup (\{\epsilon\} \times \{\epsilon\} \times \Sigma_3)$: component actions interleave;
- $B = \{w \in \Sigma^* \cup \Sigma^\omega \mid \forall u, v : w = u.v \implies (|u|_{m?} \leq |u|_{m!} \wedge |u|_{journ?} \leq |u|_{journ!} \wedge |u|_{lock?} \leq |u|_{lock!} \wedge w$ respects lossless FIFO semantics)$\}$ (where $|u|_a$ stands for the number of occurrences of a in w): communication buffers are point-to-point FIFO queues;
- $\rho = \{(m!, m?), (journ!, journ?), (lock!, lock?)\}$: any component may influence another component's state only by sending a message that is received by the latter.

We are interested in the global safety property $\mathcal{P} = \Sigma_{ok}^* \cup \Sigma_{ok}^\omega$ with $\Sigma_{ok} = \Sigma \setminus \{(\epsilon, x, \epsilon)\}$ modeling the absence of a conflict event x. It can be seen that if all three components satisfy their specifications, x will not occur.

Figure 1 shows the log $tr = (tr_1, tr_2, tr_3)$. In the log, tr_1 violates $\mathcal{S}_1$ at event a and tr_3 violates $\mathcal{S}_3$ at b. The dashed lines between m! and m?, and between journ! and journ? stand for communications.

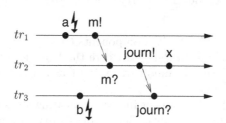

Fig. 1. A scenario with three component logs.

In order to analyze which component(s) caused the violation of $\mathcal{P}$ we can use an approach based on *counterfactual reasoning*. Informally speaking,

- C_i is a *necessary cause* for the violation of $\mathcal{P}$ if in all executions where C_i behaves correctly and all other components behave as observed, $\mathcal{P}$ is satisfied.
- Conversely, C_i is a *sufficient cause* for the violation of $\mathcal{P}$ if in all executions where all incorrect traces of components other than C_i are replaced with correct traces, and the remaining traces (i.e., correct traces and the trace of C_i) are as observed, $\mathcal{P}$ is still violated.

---

[2] For the sake of readability we omit the prefix closure of the specifications in the examples.

Applying these criteria to our example we obtain the following results:

If C_1 had worked correctly, it would have produced the trace $tr_1' = \text{lock!} \cdot \text{m!}$. This gives us the counterfactual scenario consisting of the traces $\boldsymbol{tr'} = (tr_1', tr_2, tr_3)$. However, this scenario is not consistent as C_1 now emits lock, which is not received by C_2 in tr_2. According to B, the FIFO buffers are not lossy, such that lock would have been received before m if it had been sent before m. By vacuity (as no execution yielding the traces $\boldsymbol{tr'}$ exists), C_1 is a necessary cause and C_3 is a sufficient cause according to our definitions above. While the first result matches our intuition, the second result is not what we would expect. As far as C_2 is concerned, it is not a cause since its trace satisfies $\mathcal{S}_2$.

Why do the above definitions fail to capture causality? It turns out that our definition of counterfactual scenarios is too narrow, as we substitute the behavior of one component (e.g., tr_1 to analyze sufficient causality of C_3) without taking into account the impact of the new trace on the remainder of the system. When analyzing causality "by hand", one would try to evaluate the effect of the altered behavior of the first component on the other components. This is what we will formalize in the next section.

4   Causality Analysis

In this section we improve our definition of causality of component traces for the violation of a system-level property. We suppose the following inputs to be available:

- A system signature (C, Σ) with components $C_i = (C_i, \Sigma_i)$.
- A log $\boldsymbol{tr} = (tr_1, ..., tr_n)$. In the case where the behavior of two or more components is logged into a common trace, the trace of each component can be obtained by projection.
- A set $\mathcal{I} \subseteq \{1, ..., n\}$ of component indices, indicating the set of components to be jointly analyzed for causality. Being able to reason about *group causality* is useful, for instance, to determine liability of software vendors that have provided several components.

4.1   Temporal Causality

As stated in the introduction, the temporal order of the events has an obvious impact on causality relations. We use Lamport's temporal causality [17] to over-approximate the parts of a log that are impacted by component failures. This technique will allow us, in the next section, to give counterfactual definitions of causality addressing the question of "what would have been the outcome if the failure of component C had not occurred?".

Given a trace $tr \in B$ let $tr_i = \pi_i(tr)$. The trace tr is analyzed as follows, for a fixed set $\mathcal{I}$ of components to be checked.

Definition 4 (Cone of influence, $\mathcal{C}(\boldsymbol{tr}, \mathcal{I})$). *Given a consistently specified system* $(S, \mathcal{P})$ *with* $S = (C, \Sigma, B, \rho)$, $C = \{C_1, ..., C_n\}$, *and* $C_i = (\Sigma_i, \mathcal{S}_i)$, *a log*

$tr \in \mathcal{L}(S)$, and a set of component indices $\mathcal{I} \subseteq \{1, ..., n\}$, let $g_i : \mathbb{N} \to \{\bot, \top\}$ be a function associating with the length of each prefix of tr_i a value in $\{\bot, \top\}$ (with $\bot < \top$). Let $(g_1^*, ..., g_n^*)$ be the least fixpoint of

$$
g_i(\ell) = \begin{cases}
\top \;\; if(\ell = \min\{k \mid tr_i[1..k] \notin \mathcal{S}_i\} \land i \in \mathcal{I}) \lor \\
\quad (\exists k < \ell : g_i(k) = \top) \lor \\
\quad (\exists tr' \in \boldsymbol{tr}^\uparrow \; \exists j, k, m, n : m \le n \land k = |\pi_j(tr'[1..m])| \land \\
\quad \ell = |\pi_i(tr'[1..n])| \land g_j(k) = \top \land (tr'[m][j], tr'[n][i]) \in \rho \land \\
\quad tr_i[1..\ell - 1] \in \mathcal{S}_i) \\
\bot \;\; otherwise
\end{cases}
$$

for $i \in \{1, ..., n\}$ and $1 \le \ell \le |tr_i|$. Let $\mathcal{C}(\boldsymbol{tr}, \mathcal{I}) = (c_1, ..., c_n)$ such that

$$
\forall i = 1, ..., n : c_i = \min\left(\{|tr_i| + 1\} \cup \{\ell \mid g_i^*(\ell) = \top\}\right)
$$

The cone of influence *spanned by the components* $\mathcal{I}$ *is the vector of suffixes* $tr_i[c_i...]$ *of the component traces.*

That is, as soon as a component $i \in \mathcal{I}$ violates $\mathcal{S}_i$ on a prefix $tr_i[1..\ell]$, g_i is set to $\top$ (first line). Once $g_i(k) = \top$, it remains $\top$ for all larger indices (second line). Each time a component i participates in an interaction $\beta = tr'[n]$ for some possible trace tr' on which another component j has previously participated in an interaction $\alpha = tr'[m]$ after a prefix of length k such that $g_j(k) = \top$ and $(\alpha[j], \beta[i]) \in \rho$, then g_i is set to $\top$, provided that the prefix of tr_i satisfied $\mathcal{S}_i$ before (third line). The last condition $tr_i[1..\ell - 1] \in \mathcal{S}_i$ means that a possibly incorrect behavior of C_i following an endogenous violation of $\mathcal{S}_i$ is blamed on C_i rather than on the components in $\mathcal{I}$.

The cone of influence spanned by the components $\mathcal{I}$ is the vector of suffixes of the component traces starting with the first component action that may have been impacted by the behavior of the components $\mathcal{I}$ starting in one of their failures. For the sake of simplicity we will refer to $\mathcal{C}(\boldsymbol{tr}, \mathcal{I})$ as the cone.

Example 1. Figure 2 shows the cones $\mathcal{C}(\boldsymbol{tr}, \{1\}) = (1, 1, 3)$ and $\mathcal{C}(\boldsymbol{tr}, \{2, 3\}) = (3, 4, 1)$ for the example of Sect. 3 and Fig. 1.

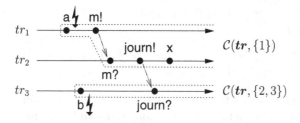

Fig. 2. The scenario with the cones $\mathcal{C}(\boldsymbol{tr}, \{1\})$ and $\mathcal{C}(\boldsymbol{tr}, \{2, 3\})$, respectively.

4.2 Logical Causality

Using the cone of influence defined above we are able to define, for a given log *tr* and set of component indices $\mathcal{I}$, the set of *counterfactual traces* modeling *alternative worlds* in which the failures $F_\mathcal{I}$ of components in $\mathcal{I}$ do not happen, and the behavior of the remaining components is as observed in *tr* up to the part lying inside the cone spanned by $F_\mathcal{I}$.

Definition 5 (Counterfactuals). *Let* $\mathbf{tr} = (tr_1, ..., tr_n) \in \mathcal{L}$, $\mathbf{C} = (c_1, ..., c_n)$ *be a cone of influence, and* $\mathbf{S} = (\mathcal{S}_1, ..., \mathcal{S}_n)$.

$$\sigma(\mathbf{tr}, \mathbf{C}, \mathbf{S}) = \{ tr' \in B \mid \forall i : pr_i \text{ is a prefix of } \pi_i(tr') \wedge \tag{1}$$
$$(pr_i \in \mathcal{S}_i \implies \pi_i(tr') \in \mathcal{S}_i) \wedge \tag{2}$$
$$(pr_i \notin \mathcal{S}_i \implies \pi_i(tr') = pr_i) \wedge \tag{3}$$
$$(c_i = |tr_i| + 1 \implies \pi_i(tr') = pr_i) \} \tag{4}$$

where $pr_i = tr_i[1..c_i - 1]$.

Intuitively, σ returns the set of alternative behaviors $tr' \in B$ where for each component i, the prefix pr_i before entering c_i matches its logged behavior in tr_i (line 1), and if the prefix is correct and a strict prefix of tr_i then the suffix is substituted such that the whole behavior of i in trace tr' is correct (line 2); otherwise pr_i is not extended in the alternative behavior (lines 3 and 4). The rationale behind Definition 5 is to compute the set of *alternative worlds* where the failures spanning $\mathcal{C}$ do not occur. To this end we have to prune out their possible impact on the logged behavior, and substitute with correct behaviors. Prefixes violating their specifications (line 3) and component traces that never enter the cone (line 4) are not extended since we want to determine causes for system-level failures observed in the log, rather than exhibiting causality chains that are not complete yet and whose consequence would have shown only in the future.

Definition 6 (Necessary cause). *Given*

- *a consistently specified system* $(S, \mathcal{P})$ *with* $S = (C, \Sigma, B, \rho)$, $C = \{C_1, ..., C_n\}$, *and* $C_i = (\Sigma_i, \mathcal{S}_i)$,
- *a log* $\mathbf{tr} \in \mathcal{L}$ *such that* $\mathbf{tr}^\uparrow \cap \mathcal{P} = \emptyset$, *and*
- *an index set* $\mathcal{I}$,

let $\mathbf{C} = \mathcal{C}(\mathbf{tr}, \mathcal{I})$. *The set of traces indexed by* $\mathcal{I}$ *is a necessary cause for the violation of* $\mathcal{P}$ *by* $\mathbf{tr}$ *if* $\sigma(\mathbf{tr}, \mathbf{C}, \mathbf{S}) \subseteq \mathcal{P}$.

That is, the set of logs indexed by $\mathcal{I}$ is a necessary cause for the violation of $\mathcal{P}$ if in the observed behavior where the cone spanned by the incorrect behaviors of $\mathcal{I}$ is replaced by a correct behavior, $\mathcal{P}$ is satisfied. In other words, if the components in $\mathcal{I}$ had satisfied their specifications, and all components had behaved as in the logs before entering the cone, then $\mathcal{P}$ would have been satisfied.

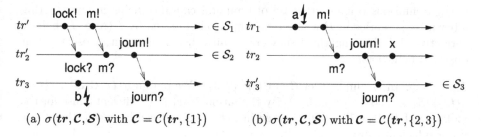

(a) $\sigma(\boldsymbol{tr}, \boldsymbol{C}, \boldsymbol{S})$ with $\boldsymbol{C} = \mathcal{C}(\boldsymbol{tr}, \{1\})$ (b) $\sigma(\boldsymbol{tr}, \boldsymbol{C}, \boldsymbol{S})$ with $\boldsymbol{C} = \mathcal{C}(\boldsymbol{tr}, \{2,3\})$

Fig. 3. The scenario where the cone (a) $\mathcal{C}(\boldsymbol{tr}, \{1\})$ and (b) $\mathcal{C}(\boldsymbol{tr}, \{2,3\})$ is substituted with suffixes satisfying the component specifications.

According to the construction of the cone of influence, this definition of necessary causality makes the assumption that the violation of a component specification $\mathcal{S}_j$ within the cone of other components $\mathcal{I}$, $j \notin \mathcal{I}$, cannot be blamed for certain on component j.

Example 2. Coming back to Example 1, let $\boldsymbol{C} = \mathcal{C}(\boldsymbol{tr}, \{1\})$. We have $\sigma(\boldsymbol{tr}, \boldsymbol{C}, \boldsymbol{S}) = \mathcal{S}_1 \| \mathcal{S}_2 \| \{tr_3\}$, as shown in Fig. 3(a). According to Definition 6, tr_1 is a necessary cause for the violation of $\mathcal{P}$ since $\mathcal{P}$ is satisfied in $\sigma(\boldsymbol{tr}, \boldsymbol{C}, \boldsymbol{S})$. It can be shown that tr_3 is not a necessary cause.

The definition of *sufficient causality* is dual to necessary causality, where in the alternative worlds we remove the failures of components *not in $\mathcal{I}$* and verify whether $\mathcal{P}$ is *still violated*.

For a set of traces S, let $\sup S = \{s \in S \mid \forall t \in S : s$ is not a strict prefix of $t\}$.

Definition 7 (Sufficient cause). *Given*

- *a consistently specified system $(S, \mathcal{P})$ with $S = (C, \Sigma, B, \rho)$, $C = \{C_1, ..., C_n\}$, and $C_i = (\Sigma_i, \mathcal{S}_i)$,*
- *a log $\boldsymbol{tr} \in \mathcal{L}$ with $\boldsymbol{tr}^\uparrow \cap \mathcal{P} = \emptyset$, and*
- *an index set $\mathcal{I}$,*

let $\overline{\mathcal{I}} = \{1, ..., n\} \backslash \mathcal{I}$ and $\boldsymbol{C} = \mathcal{C}(\boldsymbol{tr}, \overline{\mathcal{I}})$. The set of traces indexed by $\mathcal{I}$ is a sufficient cause for the violation of $\mathcal{P}$ by $\boldsymbol{tr}$ if

$$\left(\sup \sigma(\boldsymbol{tr}, \boldsymbol{C}, \boldsymbol{S})\right) \cap \mathcal{P} = \emptyset$$

That is, the set of logs indexed by $\mathcal{I}$ is a sufficient cause for the violation of $\mathcal{P}$ if in the observed behavior where the cone spanned by the violations of specifications by the complement of $\mathcal{I}$ is replaced by a correct behavior, the violation of $\mathcal{P}$ is inevitable (even though $\mathcal{P}$ may still be satisfied for non-maximal counterfactual traces). In other words, even if the components in the complement $\overline{\mathcal{I}}$ of $\mathcal{I}$ had satisfied their specifications and no component had failed in the cone spanned by the failures of $\overline{\mathcal{I}}$, then $\mathcal{P}$ would still have been violated. The inclusion of infinite traces in the behavioral model B (Definition 2) ensures the least upper bound of the set of counterfactual traces to be included in B.

In Definitions 6 and 7 the use of temporal causality helps in constructing alternative scenarios in B where the components indexed by $\mathcal{I}$ (resp. $\overline{\mathcal{I}}$) behave correctly while keeping the behaviors of all other components close to their observed behaviors.

Example 3. In Example 2 let $\mathcal{C} = \mathcal{C}(tr, \{2,3\})$. We obtain $\sigma(tr, \mathcal{C}, \mathcal{S}) = \{tr_1\}$ $\|\{tr_2\}\|\mathcal{S}_3$, as shown in Fig. 3(b). By Definition 7, tr_1 is a sufficient cause for the violation of $\mathcal{P}$ since $\mathcal{P}$ is still violated in $\sigma(tr, \mathcal{C}, \mathcal{S})$. It can be shown that tr_3 is not a sufficient cause.

Properties. The following results show that our analysis does not blame any set of innocent components, and that it finds a necessary and a sufficient cause for every system-level failure.

Theorem 1 (Soundness). *Each cause contains an incorrect trace.*

Proof (sketch). Consider a set $\mathcal{I} \subseteq \{i \mid tr_i \in \mathcal{S}_i\}$. We show that the set of traces indexed by $\mathcal{I}$ is not a necessary, nor sufficient cause for the violation of $\mathcal{P}$ by $tr = (tr_1, ..., tr_n)$.

For necessary causality, counterfactuals are computed by substituting the cone $\mathcal{C} = \mathcal{C}(tr, \mathcal{I})$ spanned by the failures of components in $\mathcal{I}$. If all of them satisfy their specifications, then the cone is empty, so $\sigma(tr, \mathcal{C}, \mathcal{S}) = tr^\uparrow$, and $\mathcal{I}$ is not a necessary cause according to Definition 6.

For sufficient causality, counterfactuals are computed by substituting the cone $\mathcal{C} = \mathcal{C}(tr, \overline{\mathcal{I}}) = (c_1, ..., c_n)$ spanned by the failures of components in $\overline{\mathcal{I}}$. If all components in $\mathcal{I}$ satisfy their specifications, then $\sigma(tr, \mathcal{C}, \mathcal{S}) \subseteq \mathcal{P}$ since ρ — and thus, $\mathcal{C}(tr, \overline{\mathcal{I}})$ — captures the possible impact of failures by components in $\overline{\mathcal{I}}$, and $(S, \mathcal{P})$ is a consistently specified system. Moreover, $\mathcal{C}$ is constructed as a *cut* of the global execution, such that there exists a system-level trace $tr \in B$ with $\forall i : \pi_i(tr) = tr_i[1..c_i - 1]$. Therefore, $\sigma(tr, \mathcal{C}, \mathcal{S}) \neq \emptyset$. Thus, $\mathcal{I}$ is not a sufficient cause according to Definition 7.   □

Theorem 2 (Completeness). *Each violation of $\mathcal{P}$ has a necessary and a sufficient cause.*

Proof (sketch). Consider a log $tr = (tr_1, ..., tr_n)$ and let $\mathcal{I} = \{i \mid tr_i \notin \mathcal{S}_i\}$. Due to the duality of necessary and sufficient causality, the proof of completeness for necessary (resp. sufficient) causality is similar to the proof of soundness for sufficient (resp. necessary) causality:

For necessary causality, let $\mathcal{C} = \mathcal{C}(tr, \mathcal{I})$. We have $\sigma(tr, \mathcal{C}, \mathcal{S}) \subseteq \mathcal{P}$, thus $\mathcal{I}$ is a necessary cause for the violation of $\mathcal{P}$ by tr.

For sufficient causality, let $\mathcal{C} = \mathcal{C}(tr, \overline{\mathcal{I}})$. By the choice of $\mathcal{I}$ this cone is empty. We thus have $\sigma(tr, \mathcal{C}, \mathcal{S}) = tr^\uparrow$, thus $\sigma(tr, \mathcal{C}, \mathcal{S}) \cap \mathcal{P} = \emptyset$. It follows that $\mathcal{I}$ is a sufficient cause for the violation of $\mathcal{P}$ in tr.   □

5   Application to Synchronous Data Flow

In this section we use the general framework to model a synchronous data flow example, and illustrate a set of well-known phenomena studied in the literature.

Consider a simple filter that propagates, at each clock tick, the input when it is stable in the sense that it has not changed since the last tick, and holds the output when the input is unstable. Using LUSTRE [11]-like syntax the filter can be written as follows:

$$change = false \rightarrow in \neq pre(in)$$

$$h = pre(out)$$

$$out = \begin{cases} in \text{ if } \neg change \\ h \text{ otherwise} \end{cases}$$

That is, component *change* is initially *false*, and subsequently *true* if and only if the input *in* has changed between the last and the current tick. *h* latches the previous value of *out*; its value is $\perp$ ("undefined") at the first instant. *out* is equal to the input if *change* is false, and equal to *h* otherwise. Thus, each signal consists of an infinite sequence of values, e.g., $change = \langle change_1, change_2, ... \rangle$. A log of a valid execution is for instance

in	0	0	3	2	2
change	*false*	*false*	*true*	*true*	*false*
h	$\perp$	0	0	0	0
out	0	0	0	0	2

We formalize the system as follows.

- $\Sigma_{ch} = \mathbb{R} \times \mathbb{B} \times \mathbb{N} \times \{\text{ch}\}$ where the first two components stand for the value of the input to and output from *change*, the third component is the index of the clock tick, and ch is a tag we will use to distinguish the alphabets of different components. Similarly, let $\Sigma_h = \mathbb{R} \times (\mathbb{R} \cup \{\perp\}) \times \mathbb{N} \times \{\text{h}\}$ and $\Sigma_{out} = \mathbb{R} \times \mathbb{R} \times \mathbb{B} \times \mathbb{R} \times \mathbb{N} \times \{\text{out}\}$.

- $S_{ch} = \{(r_1, r_2, ...) \in \Sigma_{ch}^* \mid r_i = (in_i, change_i, i, \text{ch}) \wedge change_1 = false \wedge (i \geq 2 \implies change_i = in_{i-1} \neq in_i)\}$ is the specification of *change*. Similarly, $S_h = \{(r_1, r_2, ...) \in \Sigma_h^* \mid r_i = (out_i, h_i, i, \text{h}) \wedge (i \geq 2 \implies h_i = out_{i-1})\}$ and

$$S_{out} = \Big\{ (r_1, r_2, ...) \in \Sigma_{out}^* \mid r_i = (in_i, h_i, change_i, out_i, i, \text{out}) \wedge$$

$$out_i = \begin{cases} in_i \text{ if } \neg change_i \\ h_i \text{ otherwise} \end{cases} \Big\}$$

- $\Sigma = \{(r_{ch}, r_h, r_{out}) \in \Sigma_{ch} \times \Sigma_h \times \Sigma_{out} \mid r_{ch} = (in^{ch}, change, i_1, \text{ch}) \wedge r_h = (out^h, h, i_2, \text{h}) \wedge r_{out} = (in^{out}, h^{out}, ch^{out}, out, i_3, \text{out}) \mid i_1 = i_2 = i_3\}$ is the system alphabet (where all components react synchronously).

in	0	0	1	2
change	false	false	false	false
h	⊥	0	-1	-3
out	0	0	1	2

(a) tr^1: early preemption.

in	0	0	0	0
change	false	false	_true_	_true_
h	⊥	0	-1	1
out	0	0	-1	1

(b) tr^2: joint causation.

Fig. 4. Two logs of faulty executions.

- $B = \{(r_1, r_2, ...) \in \Sigma^* \cup \Sigma^\omega \mid \forall i : r_i = ((in_i^{ch}, change_i, i_1, \mathsf{ch}), (out_i^h, h_i, i_2, \mathsf{h}),$ $(in_i^{out}, h_i^{out}, ch_i^{out}, out_i, i_3, \mathsf{out})) \wedge in_i^{ch} = in_i^{out} \wedge change_i = ch_i^{out} \wedge out_i^h = out_i \wedge h_i = h_i^{out}\}$ is the set of possible behaviors, meaning that connected flows are equal.
- $\rho = \{((\cdot, \cdot, i, \mathsf{in}), (\cdot, \cdot, i, \mathsf{ch})),\ ((\cdot, \cdot, i, \mathsf{in}), (\cdot, \cdot, i, \mathsf{out})),\ ((\cdot, \cdot, i, \mathsf{ch}), (\cdot, \cdot, i, \mathsf{out})),$ $((\cdot, \cdot, i, \mathsf{h}), (\cdot, \cdot, i, \mathsf{out})),\ ((\cdot, \cdot, i, \mathsf{out}), (\cdot, \cdot, i+1, \mathsf{h})) \mid i \geq 1\}$ models the data dependencies.
- $\mathcal{P} = \{(r_1, r_2, ...) \in B \mid \forall i : r_i = (..., (..., out_i, ...)) \wedge out_i = out_{i+1} \vee out_{i+1} = out_{i+2}\}$ is the stability property, meaning that there are no two consecutive changes in output.

Figure 4 shows four logs of faulty executions (where connected signals only appear once, and the tick number and identity tags are omitted).

Consider Fig. 4a. Two components violate their specifications (incorrect values are underlined): _change_ and _h_, both at the third instant. The stability property $\mathcal{P}$ is violated at the fourth output. Let us apply our definitions to analyze causality of each of the two faulty components.

1. In order to check whether _change_ is a necessary cause, we first compute the cone spanned by the violation by _change_ as $\mathcal{C}(tr^1, \{change\}) = (3, 5, 3)$. Thus, the prefixes of the component traces before entering the cone are as shown in Fig. 5a. Next we compute the set of counterfactuals, according to Definition 5, as $(tr')^\uparrow$, where tr' is shown in Fig. 5b. $\mathcal{P}$ is still violated by the (unique) counterfactual trace, hence _change_ is not a necessary cause.
   We can show, using the same construction, that _h_ is a sufficient cause for the violation of $\mathcal{P}$.
2. In order to check whether _change_ is a sufficient cause, we first compute the cone spanned by the violation by _h_ as $\mathcal{C}(tr^1, \{h\}) = (5, 3, 3)$. That is, the cone encompasses the last two values of _h_ and _out_. Due to _change_ being (incorrectly) _false_, the only possible counterfactual trace according to Definition 5 is $\sigma(tr^1, \mathcal{C}, \mathcal{S}) = (tr_{change}, tr'_h, tr_{out})^\uparrow$ where tr_{change} is as observed in tr^2, $tr'_h = (\bot, 0, 0, 1)$, and $tr'_{out} = (0, 0, 1, 2)$. $\mathcal{P}$ is still violated by the unique counterfactual trace, hence _change_ is a sufficient cause.
   We can show, using the same construction, that _h_ is not a necessary cause for the violation of $\mathcal{P}$.

in	0	0	1	2
change	false	false		
h	⊥	0	-1	-3
out	0	0		

in	0	0	1	2
change	false	false	true	true
h	⊥	0	-1	-3
out	0	0	-1	-3

(a) tr^1 after removing $C(tr^1, \{change\})$.

(b) tr' such that $(tr')^\uparrow = \sigma(tr^1, C, S)$

Fig. 5. Computing necessary causality of *change* for the violation of P in tr^1.

The example of log tr^1 shows two phenomena called *over-determination* (there are two sufficient causes, one of which would have sufficed to violate P) and *early preemption*: the causal chain from the violation of S_h to the violation of P is interrupted by the causal chain from the violation of S_{change} to the violation of P, since due to *change* being *false*, the incorrect value of h is discarded in the computation of *out* in log tr^1.

Figure 4b shows a case of *joint causation*: both *change* and h are necessary causes for the violation of P in tr^2, but none of them alone is a sufficient cause.

6   Related Work

Causality has been studied for a long time in different disciplines (philosophy, mathematical logic, physics, law, etc.) before receiving an increasing attention in computer science during the last decade. Hume discusses definitions of causality in [13]:

> Suitably to this experience, therefore, we may define a cause to be an object, followed by another, and where all the objects similar to the first are followed by objects similar to the second. Or in other words where, if the first object had not been, the second never had existed.

In computer science, various approaches to causality analysis have been developed recently. They differ in their assumptions on what pieces of information are available for causality analysis: a model of causal dependencies, a program as a black-box that can be used to replay different scenarios, the observed actual behavior (e.g. execution traces, or inputs and outputs), and/or the expected behavior (that is, component specifications). Existing frameworks consider different subsets of these entities. We cite the most significant settings and approaches for these settings.

A Specification and an Observation. In the preliminary work of [8], causality of components for the violation of a system-level property under the BIP interaction model [2,9] has been defined using a rudimentary definition of counterfactuals where only faulty traces are substituted but not the parts of other component traces impacted by the former. This definition suffered from the conditions for causality being true by vacuity when no consistent counterfactuals exist. A similar approach is used in [22] for causality analysis in real-time systems.

With a similar aim of independence from a specific model of computation as in our work, [21] formalizes a theory of diagnosis in first-order logic. A *diagnosis* for an observed incorrect behavior is essentially defined as a minimal set of components forming a sufficient cause.

A Causal Model. Reference [12] proposes what has become the most influential definition of causality for computer science so far, based on a model over a set of propositional variables partitioned into *exogenous* variables $\mathcal{U}$ and *endogenous* variables $\mathcal{V}$. A function $\mathcal{F}_X$ associated with each variable $X \in \mathcal{V}$ uniquely determines the value of X depending on the value of all variables in $(\mathcal{U} \cup \mathcal{V}) \backslash \{X\}$. These functions define a set of *structural equations* relating the values of the variables. The equations are required to be *recursive*, that is, the dependencies form an acyclic graph whose nodes are the variables. The observed values of a set X of variables is an *actual cause* for an observed property φ if with different values of X, φ would not hold, and there exists a context (a *contingency*) in which the observed values of X entail φ. With the objective of better representing causality in processes evolving over time, *CP-logic* defines actual causation based on probability trees [3].

In [14], fault localization and repair in a circuit with respect to an LTL property are formulated as a game between the environment choosing inputs and the system choosing a fix for a faulty component.

A Model and a Trace. In several applications of Halpern and Pearl's SEM, the model is used to encode and analyze one or more execution traces, rather than a behavioral model.

The definition of actual cause from [12] is used in [4] to determine potential causes for the first violation of an LTL formula by a trace. As [12] only considers a propositional setting without any temporal connectors, the trace is modeled as a matrix of propositional variables. In order to make the approach feasible in practice, an over-approximation is proposed. In this approach, the structure of the LTL formula is used as a model to determine which events may have caused the violation of the property.

Given a counter-example in model-checking, [10] uses a distance metric to determine a cause of the property violation as the difference between the error trace and a closest correct trace.

An approach to fault localization in a sequential circuit with respect to a safety specification in LTL is presented in [6]: given a counter-example trace, a propositional formula is generated that holds if a different behavior of a subset of gates entails the satisfaction of the specification.

A Set of Traces. Reference [15] extends the definition of actual causality of [12] to totally ordered sequences of events, and uses this definition to construct from a set of traces a fault tree. Using a probabilistic model, the fault tree is annotated with probabilities. The accuracy of the diagnostic depends on the number of traces used to construct the model. An approach for on-the-fly causality checking is presented in [19].

An Input and a Black Box. Delta debugging [24] is an efficient technique for automatically isolating a cause of some error. Starting from a failing input and a passing input, delta debugging finds a pair of a failing and a passing input with minimal distance. The approach is syntactical and has been applied to program code, configuration files, and context switching in schedules. By applying delta debugging to *program states* represented as *memory graphs*, analysis has been further refined to program semantics. Delta debugging isolates failure-inducing causes in the *input* of a program, and thus requires the program to be available.

7   Conclusion

We have presented a general approach for causality analysis of system failures based on component specifications and observed component traces. Applications include identification of faulty components in black-box testing, recovery of critical systems at runtime, and determination of the liability of component providers in the aftermath of a system failure.

This article opens a number of directions for future work. First of all, we will instantiate and implement the framework for specific models of computation and communication, such as Timed Automata [1] and functional programs. The tagged signal model [18] provides a formal basis for representing such models in our framework. In order to make the definitions of causality effectively verifiable, we will reformulate them as operations on symbolic models, and use efficient data structures such as the event structures used in [5] for distributed diagnosis.

At design time, the code of the components can be instrumented so as to log relevant information for analyzing causality with respect to a set of properties to be monitored. For instance, precise information on the actual (partial) order of execution can be preserved by tagging the logged events with vector clocks [7, 20]. Generally speaking, appropriate instrumentation of the code enables more precise causality analysis. We intend to further investigate this aspect of ensuring *accountability* [16] by design in future fork.

In this paper we assume only the logs to be available. However, in some situations such as post-mortem analysis the (black-box) components may be available, in which case counterfactual scenarios could be replayed on the system to evaluate their outcome more precisely. In the same vein, an alternative behavior of the control part of a closed-loop systems is likely to impact the physical process, as in our cruise control example: a counterfactual trace with different brake or throttle control will impact the speed of the car. This change should be propagated through a model of the physical process to make the counterfactual scenario as realistic as possible.

References

1. Alur, R., Dill, D.L.: A theory of timed automata. Theoret. Comput. Sci. **126**, 183–235 (1994)
2. Basu, A., Bensalem, S., Bozga, M., Combaz, J., Jaber, M., Nguyen, T.-H., Sifakis, J.: Rigorous component-based system design using the BIP framework. IEEE Softw. **28**(3), 41–48 (2011)
3. Beckers, S., Vennekens, J.: Counterfactual dependency and actual causation in cp-logic and structural models: a comparison. In: Kersting, K., Toussaint, M. (eds.) STAIRS. Frontiers in Artificial Intelligence and Applications, vol. 241, pp. 35–46. IOS Press (2012)
4. Beer, I., Ben-David, S., Chockler, H., Orni, A., Trefler, R.J.: Explaining counterexamples using causality. Formal Methods Syst. Des. **40**(1), 20–40 (2012)
5. Fabre, E., Benveniste, A., Haar, S., Jard, C.: Distributed monitoring of concurrent and asynchronous systems. Discrete Event Dyn. Syst. **15**(1), 33–84 (2005)
6. Fey, G., Staber, S., Bloem, R., Drechsler, R.: Automatic fault localization for property checking. IEEE Trans. CAD Integr. Circ. Syst. **27**(6), 1138–1149 (2008)
7. Fidge, C.J.: Timestamps in message-passing systems that preserve the partial ordering. In: Raymond, K. (ed.) Proceedings of the ACSC'88, pp. 56–66 (1988)
8. Gössler, G., Le Métayer, D., Raclet, J.-B.: Causality analysis in contract violation. In: Barringer, H., Falcone, Y., Finkbeiner, B., Havelund, K., Lee, I., Pace, G., Roşu, G., Sokolsky, O., Tillmann, N. (eds.) RV 2010. LNCS, vol. 6418, pp. 270–284. Springer, Heidelberg (2010)
9. Gössler, G., Sifakis, J.: Composition for component-based modeling. Sci. Comput. Prog. **55**(1–3), 161–183 (2005)
10. Groce, A., Chaki, S., Kroening, D., Strichman, O.: Error explanation with distance metrics. STTT **8**(3), 229–247 (2006)
11. Halbwachs, N., Caspi, P., Raymond, P., Pilaud, D.: The synchronous dataflow programming language Lustre. Proc. IEEE **79**(9), 1305–1320 (1991)
12. Halpern, J.Y., Pearl, J.: Causes and explanations: a structural-model approach. part I: Causes. Br. J. Philos. Sci. **56**(4), 843–887 (2005)
13. Hume, D.: An Enquiry Concerning Human Understanding (1748)
14. Jobstmann, B., Staber, S., Griesmayer, A., Bloem, R.: Finding and fixing faults. J. Comput. Syst. Sci. **78**(2), 441–460 (2012)
15. Kuntz, M., Leitner-Fischer, F., Leue, S.: From probabilistic counterexamples via causality to fault trees. In: Flammini, F., Bologna, S., Vittorini, V. (eds.) SAFE-COMP 2011. LNCS, vol. 6894, pp. 71–84. Springer, Heidelberg (2011)
16. Küsters, R., Truderung, T., Vogt, A.: Accountability: definition and relationship to verifiability. In: ACM Conference on Computer and Communications Security, pp. 526–535 (2010)
17. Lamport, L.: Time, clocks, and the ordering of events in a distributed system. CACM **21**(7), 558–565 (1978)
18. Lee, E.A., Sangiovanni-Vincentelli, A.: A framework for comparing models of computation. IEEE Trans. Comput. Aided Des. Integr. Circuits Syst. **17**(12), 1217–1229 (1998)
19. Leitner-Fischer, F., Leue, S.: Causality checking for complex system models. In: Giacobazzi, R., Berdine, J., Mastroeni, I. (eds.) VMCAI 2013. LNCS, vol. 7737, pp. 248–267. Springer, Heidelberg (2013)
20. Mattern, F.: Virtual time and global states of distributed systems. In: Cosnard, M. (ed.) Proceedings of the Workshop on Parallel and Distributed Algorithms, pp. 215–226. Elsevier (1988)

21. Reiter, R.: A theory of diagnosis from first principles. Artif. Intell. **32**(1), 57–95 (1987)
22. Wang, S., Ayoub, A., Kim, B.G., Gössler, G., Sokolsky, O., Lee, I.: A causality analysis framework for component-based real-time systems. In: Legay, A., Bensalem, S. (eds.) RV 2013. LNCS, vol. 8174, pp. 285–303. Springer, Heidelberg (2013)
23. Wang, S., Ayoub, A., Sokolsky, O., Lee, I.: Runtime verification of traces under recording uncertainty. In: Khurshid, S., Sen, K. (eds.) RV 2011. LNCS, vol. 7186, pp. 442–456. Springer, Heidelberg (2012)
24. Zeller, A.: Why Programs Fail. Elsevier, Amsterdam (2009)

Axioms and Abstract Predicates on Interfaces in Specifying/Verifying OO Components

Ali Hong[✉], Yijing Liu, and Zongyan Qiu[✉]

LMAM and Department of Informatics, School of Mathematics,
Peking University, Beijing, China
{hongali,liuyijing,qzy}@math.pku.edu.cn

Abstract. Abstraction is essential in component-based design and implementation of systems, however, it brings also challenges to the formal specification and verification. In this paper we develop a framework to support the abstract specification for the interfaces of components and their interactions, and the related verification. We show also that the abstract specification on the interface-level can be used to enforce correct implementations of the components. We take one practical application of the well-known MVC architecture as a case study. Although our work focuses on the OO based programs, some concepts and techniques developed in the work might be useful more broadly.

Keywords: Component · Specification · Verification · Abstract predicate · Axiom · MVC

1 Introduction

Component-based design and composition have been widely respected and used in implementing large-scale software systems. The related methodologies emphasize abstraction, interaction based on clear and abstract interfaces, separation of interfaces from implementations, interchangeability of components, etc. The main ideas of these techniques are information hiding, modularity, insulation, and so on, to support more flexible and robust development and integration of complex systems.

Separation of interfaces from concrete components is one of the most important techniques in component-based system (CBS) development. Interfaces serve as a layer to insulate components and a media to connect them, and provide enough information to the clients. This separation makes twofold benefits: on one hand, clients are designed only based on interfaces of the components which they use, that make them independent of details of the components. On the other hand, the components to be used need only to implement the interfaces that may provide wider design choices.

Supported by NNSF of China, Grant No. 61272160, 61100061, and 61202069.

J.L. Fiadeiro et al. (Eds.): FACS 2013, LNCS 8348, pp. 174–195, 2014.
DOI: 10.1007/978-3-319-07602-7_12, © Springer International Publishing Switzerland 2014

However, although the interface-based techniques are very useful and effective in supporting good component design and flexible integration, they bring also challenges to formal specification and verification. In common practice, interface declarations provide only syntactic and typing information. For verifying behaviors of systems, we must include semantic specifications for interfaces. How and in which form the specifications are provided becomes a new problem, due to an obvious quandary: for one thing, we need to protect the abstraction provided by the component interfaces, thus the specification should not leak details of the implementation. For another, we need the specifications to provide enough information for the behaviors of the components, to support the reasoning of their clients. Obviously, if the specification involves real implementation details, it will block the modification and replacement of the components, or ask for re-specifying/re-verifying large portion of the system on account of modification, either in the development or in the maintenance.

In this paper, we present an approach for specifying a group of co-related OO components abstractly by giving the specifications for their interfaces. The specifications consist of two aspects: a pair of abstract pre/post conditions which is expressed upon abstract predicates (named *specification predicates*) for each method, and a group of *axioms* over the predicates which describes relations over different predicates thus gives constraints on the implementations over methods and classes.

Based on our previous work [20], we build the theoretical foundation and define how a program with these specifications is correct. We give some new rules to form a more complete inference system for reasoning OO programs, then whether a group of classes forms a correct implementation of a group of relative interfaces can be proved. Also, we support the proof for client codes based only on the interfaces. As the proof involves no information from the implementation, modular verification is well achieved. We illustrate our approach by specifying and verifying a simple multiplication calculator designed following the MVC architecture and built upon closely co-related interfaces and classes. Due to the page limit, we leave some details in our report [9].

In the rest of the paper, we will analyze the problems with a MVC calculator in more details in Sect. 2, and introduce the concept *axioms* and basic languages in Sect. 3. We build the formal framework in Sect. 4, and then show the case study in Sect. 5. At last, we discuss some related work and conclude in Sect. 6. The basic inference rules of the framework are given in Appendix A.

2 Abstractly Specify/Verify Co-related Components: Problem

To give an intuition for the problem of this study, we use a simple MVC (Model-View-Controller) architecture design for an integer-multiplication calculator displayed in Fig. 1. This MVC calculator consists of three components. A model component which is independent of views, encapsulates the application logic (such as multiplying and reset algorithms, and so on) of the calculator. A view

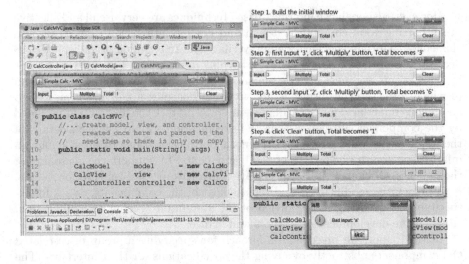

Fig. 1. An execution of the MVC multiplication calculator

component requests the product value from the model and represents it in a certain style. And a controller component listens to user actions on the view and passes it to the model. Here the view is designed as a user interface with two buttons for detecting user requests to the model by the controller, where "Multiply" for multiplication and "Clear" for reset; and two textboxes for representing user-input integer in "Input" and the product value (also as one multiplier for the next multiplying) in "Total".

We show an execution of this calculator by several steps as in Fig. 1 (the right side). First, we run the program and get an initial frame with a default value 1 for "Total" and blank "Input". Second, we input an integer 3 for "Input" and click the "Multiply" button to call the model to multiply 3 and 1, and immediately the "Total" value becomes 3. Third, we input another integer 2 and click "Multiply" again, and this time the "Total" becomes 6 (that is $2 \star 3$). Then, we click "Clear" button to reset "Total" to its initial value 1. Noninteger inputs like char 'a' would be caught as exceptions by reporting a message like in the lower right corner of Fig. 1.

As the view styles of a model could be various (e.g., text-based, graphical, or web interface) and would not affect the intrinsic properties (e.g., separating model from its views, interactions among three components) of MVC architecture, we simplify the user-interface view in Fig. 1 and let the views output total values textually in our case. Further, to make this MVC calculator more extensible, modular and reusable, we abstract it with interfaces as depicted in Fig. 2. Three interface declarations with method signatures (the right part) are respectively given for the components. For example, *MI* is the interface of model,

i1) A MVC architecture consists of three components: one model, several views and one controller;

i2) Model embeds application logic and relative data state;

i3) Views can register on a model, flush themselves accordingly, and paint in each of their own way;

i4) Controller deals with user inputs, passes it for updating model that further affects all related views.

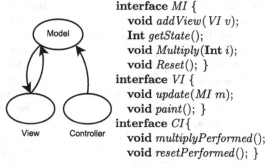

```
interface MI {
    void addView(VI v);
    Int getState();
    void Multiply(Int i);
    void Reset(); }
interface VI {
    void update(MI m);
    void paint(); }
interface CI{
    void multiplyPerformed();
    void resetPerformed(); }
```

Fig. 2. MVC architecture and component interfaces for multiplication calculator

having a method *Multiply(i)* for multiplying input i^1 and a certain integer (e.g., the current value displaying in "Total" textbox when inputting *i*), a method *Reset()* for resetting total value, *addView(v)* adding a view onto the model, *getState()* returning the current state value, etc. Three components here are closely related: views register on some model, the controller deals with user inputs and asks its model to update the state (i.e., total value), the model then notifies all registered views for its state change, and the views need to get model's state after notified, etc. But, how can we specify these independent of the implementations?

We follow the ideas of abstract predicates [4,16,18] and Separation Logic, and introduce predicate *model(m, vs, st)* to assert that model *m* has a registered view set *vs* and a state *st*, *view(v, m, st)* to assert view *v* has registered on *m* and its state is *st*, and *controller(c, m, st)* to assert controller *c* monitors *m* and its state is *st*. We specify the MVC interfaces as given in Fig. 3 according to the (informal) requirements, where we have some additional predicates which will be explained below. Here we use a brief form "⟨*pre*⟩⟨*post*⟩" after each method signature to represent the pre/post conditions instead of more common pair "**requires** *pre*; **ensures** *post*;". In addition, the types for predicate parameters are omitted, which can be added in real implementations.

The specification of *addView* in *MI* says that the calling view will be added into the view set of the model, and its state will be updated following the model. The specification of *getState* means that it simply returns the state of the model. For methods *Multiply* and *Reset*, things become more complex, because the methods will not only affect the model, but also its related views. We introduce a predicate *MVs(m, vs, st)* to assert the state of a bundle of one model and its

---

[1] Here we assume that, all inputs *i* and return values which are declared as primitive **Int** in our case are actually of **BigInteger** type in Java. Because as defined in Java Language Specification, semantics of arithmetic operations in **BigInteger** exactly mimic those of Java's integer arithmetic operators. We simply use **Int** type to declare and operate big integers, while the overflow error by multiplying two big integers can be eliminated.

interface MI {
  void $addView(VI\ v)$
  $\langle model(\textbf{this}, vs, st) * view(v, \textbf{this}, -)\rangle$
  $\langle model(\textbf{this}, vs \cup \{v\}, st) *$
    $view(v, \textbf{this}, st)\rangle;$
  Int $getState()$ $\langle model(\textbf{this}, vs, st)\rangle$
  $\langle model(\textbf{this}, vs, st) \wedge \text{res} = st\rangle;$
  void $Multiply(\textbf{Int}\ i)$
  $\langle MVs(\textbf{this}, vs, st)\rangle$
  $\langle \exists st' \cdot MVs(\textbf{this}, vs, st')$
    $\wedge\ st' = product(st, i)\rangle;$
  void $Reset()$ $\langle MVs(\textbf{this}, vs, st)\rangle$
  $\langle MVs(\textbf{this}, vs, 1)\rangle;$ }

interface VI {
  void $update(MI\ m)$
  $\langle view(\textbf{this}, m, -) * model(m, vs, st)\rangle$
  $\langle view(\textbf{this}, m, st) * model(m, vs, st)\rangle;$
  void $paint()$
  $\langle view(\textbf{this}, m, st)\rangle\langle view(\textbf{this}, m, st)\rangle;$ }
interface CI {
  void $multiplyPerformed()$
  $\langle MVC(\textbf{this}, m, vs, st)\rangle$
  $\langle \exists st' \cdot MVC(\textbf{this}, m, vs, st')\rangle;$
  void $resetPerformed()$
  $\langle MVC(\textbf{this}, m, vs, st)\rangle$
  $\langle MVC(\textbf{this}, m, vs, 1)\rangle;$ }

Fig. 3. Interfaces with formal specifications for MVC arch.

related views, thus *Multiply* and *Reset* modify this state as desired. Predicate $product(st, i)$ encapsulates the algorithm of multiplying st and i. Method *update* in *VI* is called by a model that will flush the view's state and cause some other related actions (e.g., the view painting by method *paint*). At last we consider *multiplyPerformed* and *resetPerformed* in *CI* which can be called by clients of the MVC components. They brings also problems, because both will affect all components here. To specify states of this bundle of components, we introduce another predicate $MVC(c, m, vs, st)$ to assert that we have a bundle of a controller c, a model m, a set of views vs with internal state st. These specifications go the similar way as shown in literature, e.g. [6], and ours [20].

Having the interface declarations, we can go ahead to define classes to implement them, and then build concrete MVC instance(s), and write client codes to use the implementation. We postpone the implementation for a moment, and first consider some client codes and their verifications. Because interfaces should be fences for hiding implementation details, on the semantic side, we should support verifying client codes without knowing the implementation details of the interfaces.

Figure 4 gives a client method, where we assume some implementing classes have been built. From its formal parameters, we get a pair of connected model and controller objects, and require the result state satisfies assertion $\exists r_1, r_2 \cdot MVC(c, m, \{r_1, r_2\}, 1)$. *View* and *View$_2$* are classes implementing *VI*. For the constructor of *View*, we assume it satisfies a specification $\{model(m, vs, st)\}$ $View(m)\{model(m, vs \cup \{\textbf{this}\}, st) * view(\textbf{this}, m, st)\}$. Here **this** refers to the new created object which is assigned to variable v by "$v = \textbf{new}\ View(m);$". It is similar for *View$_2$*.

For verifying the client method, we list a part of reasoning in Fig. 5. The constructions go well, then we meet problems in line (5'). To step into the while loop and verify the first command $c.multiplyPerformed()$ according to the specification of $multiplyPerformed()$ in interface *CI*, we need to check whether the current program state specified in line (5") not only satisfies the loop

void *buildviews* $(MI\ m,\ CI\ c)$ $\langle \exists i \cdot model(m, \emptyset, i) * controller(c, m, i) \rangle$
$$\langle \exists r_1, r_2 \cdot MVC(c, m, \{r_1, r_2\}, 1) \rangle \ \{$$

    $VI\ v_1 =$ **new** $View(m);$ // add a new view to model m
    Int $n = 1;$
    while $(n < 4)\{$ $c.multiplyPerformed();$ // process a user input for multiply
        $n{+}{+};$ $\}$
    $VI\ v_2 =$ **new** $View_2(m);$ // add another view to model m
    $c.resetPerformed();$ // process another user input for reset
$\}$

Fig. 4. A client procedure using the MVC architecture

(1) $\{\exists i \cdot model(m, \emptyset, i) * controller(c, m, i)\}$
(2) $VI\ v_1 =$ **new** $View(m);$
(3) $\{\exists i, r_1 \cdot v_1 = r_1 \wedge model(m, \{r_1\}, i) * view(r_1, m, i) * controller(c, m, i)\}$
(4)   **Int** $n = 1;$
(5) $\{\exists i, r_1 \cdot v_1 = r_1 \wedge n = 1 \wedge model(m, \{r_1\}, i) * view(r_1, m, i) * controller(c, m, i)\}$
(5$'$) $\{\exists i, r_1, n_1 \cdot v_1 = r_1 \wedge n = 1 \wedge n = n_1 \wedge n_1 < 4 \wedge model(m, \{r_1\}, i)*$
       $view(r_1, m, i) * controller(c, m, i)\}$
              $\Downarrow$???
(5$''$) $\{\exists i, r_1, n_1 \cdot v_1 = r_1 \wedge n = 1 \wedge n = n_1 \wedge n_1 < 4 \wedge \underline{MVC(c,\ \underline{[1]},)\ \underline{[2]}}\}$
(6)   **while** $(n < 4)\{$
(7) $\{\exists i', r_1, n_1' \cdot v_1 = r_1 \wedge n = n_1' \wedge n_1' < 4 \wedge \underline{MVC(c,\ \underline{[1']})\ \underline{[2']}}\}$ **[Loop Invariant]**
(8) $c.multiplyPerformed();$
     ......

Fig. 5. Verification of the client code

condition but also assertions like $MVC(\ldots)$ with some parameters. Moreover, a loop invariant containing $MVC(\ldots)$ should be inferred in line (7). However, with the abstract specifications, we cannot deduce out a $MVC(\ldots)$ assertion from an assertion building of predicate symbols $model(\ldots)$, $view(\ldots)$, $controller(\ldots)$. Neither can we know what are the things to fill segments [1], [2], [1'] and [2'], then we cannot go ahead. This means clearly that something is missed in our specifications.

In reasoning component-based programs, such problems are common. Because we want to have interfaces independent of implementations to support flexible system designs and replaceable components, the specifications on the interface-level can be written only in terms of some abstract symbols, here the predicate names and parameters. Although we have some intentions for each symbol, abstract expressions cannot reveal them in the method specifications. Besides, verifying client codes based on the specifications asks for more information about the components, but we cannot expose the predicate definitions which are closely related to the implementations that have not presented yet or may be multiple ones for a given interface.

To solve the problem here, adding an assertion like "$(model(m, vs, st) * (\circledast_{v \in vs} view(v, m, st)) * controller(c, m, st)) \Leftrightarrow MVC(c, m, vs, st)$" to the specifications seems helpful. By applying it on (5') with parameter substitutions $(\{r_1\}, i/vs, st)$, we can easily infer the desired assertion in (5") to be like $\exists i, r_1, n_1 \cdot v_1 = r_1 \wedge n = 1 \wedge n = n_1 \wedge n_1 < 4 \wedge MVC(c, m, \{r_1\}, i)$ and the loop invariant $\exists i', r_1, n'_1 \cdot v_1 = r_1 \wedge n = n'_1 \wedge n'_1 < 4 \wedge MVC(c, m, \{r_1\}, i')$ in line (7). Then the following proof can go on. However, to ensure the soundness of our proof, we should prove such added assertion is true with regard to the given implementation before using it in code reasoning. In the following, we will call these assertions *axioms*, and present a framework on how to specify them, how to verify programs with *specification predicates* and axioms, and how to apply them in proving implementations and client codes.

3   Axioms and Languages

In our framework, a specification predicate is abstract on the interface level, which may have a definition in each class that implements the interface. On the other hand, an *axiom* is a logic statement expressed based on constants, logical variables, and predicates combined by logic connectors and quantifiers. It gives restrictions and/or relations over abstract predicates. Similar to the situation in the First-Order Logic, a set of axioms defines what is its "model". Here a "model" should be a set of class definitions with specifications, where relative predicates get their definitions.

As in other logic, to have a model, a set of axioms should be consistent.

Definition 1 (Consistency of Axioms). *Assume $\mathcal{A}_G$ is the set of axioms of program G. $\mathcal{A}_G$ is consistency, if $\mathcal{A}_G \nvdash \mathbf{false}$.*

An inconsistent set of axioms cannot have any implementation. However, due to the incompleteness of the inference system for our logic (similar to the classical Separation Logic), the inconsistency is generally undecidable. We can also define non-redundancy for a set of axioms, however, that is not important and thus omitted.

To conduct the design for components, we declare a set of interfaces to outline the system, and specify methods using pre/post conditions based on abstract predicates. Then we use axioms to restrict/relate the predicates, which put further restrictions on implementations. How to choose predicates and axioms is the matter of the designers' thoughts about the requirements. The axioms describe general properties of the later-coming implementations. Another important role of axioms is to support abstract-level reasoning for client codes. In this aspect, two forms of axioms are most important: implications and equivalences, because they support the *substitution rule* in reasoning.

Now we give a brief introduction to our assertion and programming language VeriJ. More details about it can be found in our report [9].

The assertion language in VeriJ is a Separation Logic (SL) revised to fit the needs of OO programs, as given in Fig. 6 (upper part). Here are variables (v),

$$\rho ::= bool\_exps \mid r_1 = r_2 \mid r : T \mid r <: T \mid v = r \qquad \eta ::= \mathbf{emp} \mid r_1.a \mapsto r_2 \mid \mathsf{obj}(r, T)$$
$$\psi ::= \rho \mid \eta \mid p(\bar{r}) \mid \neg\psi \mid \psi \vee \psi \mid \psi * \psi \mid \psi -\!\!* \psi \mid \circledast_i \psi_i \mid \exists r \cdot \psi$$

$$T ::= \mathbf{Bool} \mid \mathbf{Object} \mid \mathbf{Int} \mid C \mid I \qquad\qquad P ::= \mathbf{def}\ p(\mathbf{this}, \bar{r})$$
$$v ::= \mathbf{this} \mid x \qquad\qquad\qquad\qquad\qquad\qquad M ::= T\ m(\overline{T\ z})$$
$$e ::= \mathbf{true} \mid \mathbf{false} \mid \mathbf{null} \mid v \mid numeric\_exps \qquad L ::= \mathbf{interface}\ I\ [:\ \bar{I}]\ \{\overline{P;\ M\ [\pi]};\}$$
$$b ::= \mathbf{true} \mid \mathbf{false} \mid e < e \mid e = e \mid \neg b \mid b \vee b \qquad K ::= \mathbf{class}\ C : C\ [\triangleright\bar{I}]\ \{\ \overline{T\ a};$$
$$c ::= \mathbf{skip} \mid x := e \mid v.a := e \mid x := v.a \qquad\qquad \overline{P : \psi};\ C(\overline{T\ z})\ [\pi]\ \{\overline{T\ y};\ c\}$$
$$\quad\mid\ x := (C)v \mid x := v.m(\bar{e}) \mid x := \mathbf{new}\ C(\bar{e}) \qquad \overline{M\ [\pi]\ \{\overline{T\ y};\ c\}}\ \}$$
$$\quad\mid\ \mathbf{return}\ e \mid c; c \mid \mathbf{if}\ b\ c\ \mathbf{else}\ c \mid \mathbf{while}\ b\ c$$
$$\pi ::= \langle\psi\rangle\langle\psi\rangle \qquad\qquad A ::= \mathbf{axiom}\ \psi \qquad G ::= \bar{A};\ \overline{(L \mid K)}\ K$$

Fig. 6. VeriJ assertion and programming language with specification annotations

constants, numeric and boolean expressions. ρ denotes pure (heap-free) assertions and η the heap assertions, where r denotes references which serve as logical variables here. We have classical SL connectors, where $\psi_1 * \psi_2$ asserts that the current heap (satisfying $\psi_1 * \psi_2$) can be split into two parts, while one satisfies ψ_1 and the other satisfies ψ_2; and $\psi_1 -\!\!* \psi_2$ asserts that if any heap satisfying ψ_1 is added to current heap, the combined heap would satisfy ψ_2. $\circledast_i$ is the iterative version of $*$. There are some OO specific assertion forms: $r : T$ and $r <: T$ assert the object which r refers to is exactly of the type T or a subtype of T; and $\mathsf{obj}(r, T)$ asserts the heap contains exactly an object of type T and r refers to it. We use over-lined form to represent sequences, as in predicate application $p(\bar{r})$. We may extend it with set or other mathematical notations as needed.

VeriJ is a subset of sequential Java (μJava [21]) with specifications as annotations, especially predicate definitions, method specifications and axioms (lower part of Fig. 6). Here C denotes class name, I for interface name, a and m for field and method names respectively. We omit Java access control issues. Here are some explanations:

– **def** $p(\mathbf{this}, \bar{r})$ declares a specification predicate with signature $p(\mathbf{this}, \bar{r})$, whose body ψ in a class may be directly defined or inherited from the superclass. **this** is always explicitly written as the first parameter of predicates to denote the current object. Sub-interfaces inherit predicate declarations. Predicates are used in method specifications and axioms to provide abstraction.
– **axiom** ψ introduces an axiom ψ into the global scope, while all variables are implicitly universal-quantified, and can be instantiated in axiom application. No program variables are allowed in axioms. We will give more details in Sect. 4.
– π is a pair of specification for constructors or methods in the form of $\langle pre \rangle \langle post \rangle$. Specifications in a supertype can be inherited or overridden in subtypes. When a method does not have an explicit specification, it may inherit several specification pairs from the supertypes of its class. If a non-overriding method is not explicitly specified, the default specification "$\langle \mathbf{true} \rangle \langle \mathbf{true} \rangle$" is assumed. In addition, we assume sub-interface will not redeclare the same methods as in its super-interfaces.

- As in Java, each class has a superclass, possibly **Object**, but may implement
  zero or more interfaces. A class can define some specification predicates and
  if it implements an interface which declares some predicates, it must directly
  define each predicate with a body or inherit one from its superclass. We assume
  all methods are public. For simplicity method overloading is omitted here.
- A program G consists of a sequence of axiom definitions, and then a sequence
  of class and interface declarations, where at least one class presents.

For typing and reasoning a program G, a static environment Γ_G, or simply Γ
without ambiguity, is built to record useful information in G. We need also
type-checking specification parts in programs, e.g., a predicate definition body
involves only its parameters; each predicate in an axiom is an application of
some declared predicate in some interfaces; the pre/post conditions of a method
are well-formed; predicates declared in an interface must be realized in its implementation classes, etc. For these, we may introduce types into specifications. The
environment construction and type-checking are routine and are ignored here.
We will only consider well-typed programs below, and assume some components
of Γ are usable: $\Theta(C.m)$ fetches the body of method m in class C, $\Pi(T.m)$
gives the method specification(s) of m in type T; $\Phi(C.p(\mathbf{this}, \overline{r}))$ gets the body
assertion of p in class C; and $\mathcal{A}$ is the set of all axioms in G.

We assume that in a program, each predicate is uniquely named (this can
be achieved by suitable renaming). Thus, if several definitions for one predicate
name p appear in different classes, they are local definitions for p fitting the
needs of each individual class. We assume all definitions for p have the same
signature, that is, no overloading.

4   Verifying Programs wrt Axioms and Method Specifications

In this section, we develop the framework for reasoning VeriJ programs with specifications, especially interface-based design and axioms. We extend the inference
rule set developed in our previous work [17,20] (Ref. Appendix A).

4.1   Verifying Implementations wrt Axioms

Because of the possible existence of subclass overriding and multi-implementing
classes for one interface, multiple definitions for the same predicate are common
in programs. On the other hand, axioms are global properties/requirements over
a program. To judge whether a group of classes obeys a set of axioms, we should
define clearly what the predicate applications denote in axioms. We can obtain
predicate definitions from Γ. However, as a predicate may have multiple definitions, we must determine which of them is used to unfold a specific predicate
application. Thus we define a substitution for a predicate application in a program as follows:

Definition 2 (Predicate Application Substitution). *Suppose p is a specification predicate, and $\{C_j\}_{j=1}^{k}$ is the set of classes in program G where p is defined. We define the expansion for the application $p(r, \overline{r'})$ in axioms as a substitution:*

$$\delta_{p,\Gamma} \;\widehat{=}\; [\; \textstyle\bigvee_j (r : C_j \wedge \mathsf{fix}(C_j, p(r, \overline{r'}))) \;/\; p(r, \overline{r'}) \;] \tag{1}$$

where:

$$\mathsf{fix}(D, \psi) = \begin{cases} \neg\mathsf{fix}(D, \psi'), & \textit{if } \psi \textit{ is } \neg\psi'; \\ \mathsf{fix}(D, \psi_1) \otimes \mathsf{fix}(D, \psi_2), & \textit{if } \psi \textit{ is } \psi_1 \otimes \psi_2, \textit{where} \otimes \in \{\vee, *, -\!\!*\}; \\ \exists r \cdot \mathsf{fix}(D, \psi'), & \textit{if } \psi \textit{ is } \exists r \cdot \psi'; \\ D.q(r_0, \overline{r}), & \textit{if } \psi \textit{ is } q(r_0, \overline{r}); \\ \psi, & \textit{otherwise.} \end{cases} \tag{2}$$

We substitute application $p(r, \overline{r'})$ in axioms by a disjunction, while each element consists of a type assertion $(r : C_j)$ and a type fixed body generated by fix. Because the body may contain applications of other predicate(s) or recursive application(s) of the same predicate, we need to fix their meaning by type and also avoid infinite expansion. Here fix carries on type D down over the formula. The special $D.q$ form is used to suspend the unfolding thus prevent infinite expansion. We introduce the following rule to enable further unfolding and a new round of the fixing:

$$\frac{\Phi(D.q(\mathbf{this}, \overline{r})) = \psi}{\Gamma \vdash D.q(r_0, \overline{r'}) \Leftrightarrow \mathsf{fix}(D, \psi)[r_0, \overline{r'}/\mathbf{this}, \overline{r}]} \quad \text{(EXPAND)}$$

For a predicate set Ψ, we define the substitution for Ψ based on all the substitutions for $p \in \Psi$. Based on Definition 2, we have the following definition to connect axioms with interface and class declarations in a program.

Definition 3 (Well-Supported Axiom). *Suppose N is a sequence of class/interface declarations, and ψ is an axiom mentioning only types and relative predicates defined in N. We say ψ is* well supported *by N, if $\Gamma_N \models \psi\delta_{\mathsf{preds}(\psi),\Gamma_N}$.*

Here Γ_N provides predicate definitions, and $\delta_{\mathsf{preds}(\psi),\Gamma_N}$ is the substitution built from $\mathsf{preds}(\psi)$ (a subset[2] of predicates occurring in ψ,) according to Definition 2, and used to obtain the assertion to be validated. Because $\delta_{\mathsf{preds}(\psi),\Gamma_N}$ is completely determined by Γ_N, we will write the fact simply as $\Gamma_N \models \psi$. Generally, for a set of axioms $\mathcal{A}$, we say $\mathcal{A}$ is *well supported* by N and write $\Gamma_N \models \mathcal{A}$, if $\Gamma_N \models \psi$ for every $\psi \in \mathcal{A}$.

Now we define whether a program G with its axiom set $\mathcal{A}$ is *well-axiom-constrained*:

---

[2] We can obtain it from the complete set of predicates in the axiom by analyzing the axiom formula based on the given implementation. Not all predicates need to be unfolded in constructing the substitution for proving the axiom.

Definition 4 (Well-Axiom-Constrained Program). *A program* $G = (\overline{A}; N)$ *is a well-axiom-constrained program, if* $\Gamma_N \models \mathcal{A}$, *where* $\mathcal{A}$ *is built from* $\overline{A}$.

Note that both well-supported and well-axiom-constrained are semantic concepts. As a version of separation logic, we have given a set of inference rules for our logic and proven its soundness result in [17], which contains the basic inference rules for FOL and SL (of course, it is incomplete as the classical SL). Because of the soundness, we can use the rules to prove the well-supported (and well-axiom-constrained) property by a two-step procedure:

1. Construct a substitution for each axiom in the program according to Definition 2, and use it to obtain a logic formula to be proven;
2. Try to use the inference rules to prove the formulas obtained in Step-1.

If we can prove an axiom ψ under environment Γ_N by the above procedure, we know that ψ is well-supported by N, and will write this fact as $\Gamma_N \vdash \psi$. We take it similar for $\Gamma_N \vdash \Psi$. Due to the soundness result, if $\Gamma_N \vdash \Psi$, then $\Gamma_N \models \Psi$.

Because axioms are state-independent assertions (i.e., free of program variables), to prove whether an axiom is supported by a program, we need at most consulting predicate definitions. After the proving, we know that the axioms are globally true over the implementation, thus can safely apply them in reasoning client programs which utilize the objects via the interfaces. We will demonstrate this in next section.

Now we give some properties that might facilitate the verification of axioms. First, we can verify axioms one by one, or in groups:

Lemma 1. *Assume* $\Gamma_N \vdash \Psi$ *and* $\Gamma_N \vdash \Psi'$, *then* $\Gamma_N \vdash \Psi \cup \Psi'$.   □

Then we give some cases of program extension with unchanged axiom set. We will use $N \nmid \Psi$ to mean N contains no declaration/definition of predicates in Ψ.

Lemma 2. *Assume* $\Gamma_N \vdash \Psi$, *and* N' *is a sequence of interface declarations. If* NN' *is still a well-typed declaration sequence, then* $\Gamma_{NN'} \vdash \Psi$.

If $\Gamma_N \vdash \Psi$, *for a sequence of interface/class declarations* N' *where* $N' \nmid \Psi$ *and* $N N'$ *is still a well-typed declaration sequence, then* $\Gamma_{NN'} \vdash \Psi$.

If $\Gamma_N \vdash \Psi$ *and* $\Gamma_{N'} \vdash \Psi'$, *where* $N \nmid \Psi'$ *and* $N' \nmid \Psi$, *and* $N N'$ *is still a well-typed declaration sequence, then* $\Gamma_{NN'} \vdash \Psi \cup \Psi'$.   □

If some *client classes* use existing classes and support another set of axioms, they fall into the last case, and can be directly combined with the existing classes (and axioms), because their verifications do not touch other implementation details.

However, in general case, adding a new class onto existing class/interface sequence may bring proof obligations wrt some related axioms. If this new comer also supports these related axioms (if any), we call it "a proper extension class" wrt existing components. Here we use *proper* instead of *correct* because we have not verified the methods in the classes according to their specifications yet. We can check whether an extension class is *proper* by the following definition:

Definition 5 (Proper Extension Class). *If* $\Gamma_N \vdash \Psi$, K *is a class declaration, and* $N K$ *is still well-typed. We say* K *is a* proper extension class *wrt* (Ψ, N), *if*

(1) $K \nmid \Psi$; *or*
(2) K *provides a definition(s) for one (or more) predicate(s) appearing in an axiom subset* Ψ_1 *in* Ψ, *and* $\Gamma_{NK} \vdash \Psi_1$.

Then for the well-supported axioms Ψ in existing components (Ψ, N), we have,

Lemma 3. *If* $\Gamma_N \vdash \Psi$ *and* K *is a proper extension class wrt* (Ψ, N), *then* $\Gamma_{NK} \vdash \Psi$.

If $\Gamma_N \vdash \Psi$, N' *is a sequence of class/interface declarations, and for any class declaration* K *in* N' *such that* $N' = N'_1 K N'_2$, K *is a proper extension class with respect to* $(\Psi, N N'_1)$, *then* $\Gamma_{NN'} \vdash \Psi$. $\qquad\qquad\square$

These Lemmas are simple, and we leave their proofs in our report [9].

4.2   Verifying Methods and Behavioral Subtyping

The second part of verification is relatively common: to verify that each method satisfies its specifications, i.e., the components are correctly implemented. We have given a set of rules for method verification, and list them in Appendix A with brief explanations.

Because of the existence of interfaces, multi-implementation, and inheritance, a class definition takes generally the form:

$$\textbf{class } C : B \ \triangleright \ I_1, \ldots, I_k \ \{\ldots \ T \ m(\ldots)[\langle P \rangle \langle Q \rangle]\{\ldots\} \ \ldots\} \qquad (3)$$

where class C inherits B as its superclass and implements interfaces $I_1, \ldots, I_k$. For the m, it can be a new one, or one overriding another definition for m accessible in B; and it can be defined with an explicit specification $\langle P \rangle \langle Q \rangle$, or inherit its specifications from B, or even from the interfaces. In addition, the definition should implement specification(s) for m in the interfaces, if exist(s). Also, C may inherit a method from B (but not define it) to implement a declared method in some interface(s) $(I_i(s))$.

An available method in class C may have a definition with explicit specification in C, or only a definition and inherited specifications from C's supertypes, or an inherited definition with also inherited specification from its superclass. These facts tell us that two interrelated problems must be resolved in verifying a method: (1) determining a specification and using it to verify the method body; (2) verifying that the method fits the need of both the superclass and the implemented interfaces. We consider them in the following, and first introduce some notations and definitions.

We think an interface defines a type, and a class defines a type with implementation. We will use $C, B, \ldots$ for class names, I for interface names, T for type names, to avoid simple conditions. We use $(T, T') \in \textsf{super}$ to mean that

T' is a direct supertype of T, and $T <: T'$ as the transitive and reflective closure of super. We use $\text{super}(C)$ to get all supertypes of C, thus for example (3), $\text{super}(C) = \{I_1, \ldots, I_k, B\}$. When C implements $I_1, I_2, \ldots$, and defines method m without giving a specification, m in C may have multiple specifications if more than one of the I_i has specifications for m. We write $\langle\varphi\rangle\langle\psi\rangle \in \Pi(T.m)$ in semantic rules to mean that $\langle\varphi\rangle\langle\psi\rangle$ is one specification of m in T, and write $\Pi(T.m) = \langle\varphi\rangle\langle\psi\rangle$ when $\langle\varphi\rangle\langle\psi\rangle$ is the only specification.

In semantics, we use $\Gamma, C, m \vdash \psi$ to state that ψ holds in method m of class C under Γ. Clearly, here ψ must be a state-independent formula. We use $\Gamma, C, m \vdash \{\varphi\}c\{\psi\}$ to say that command c in m of C satisfies the pair of precondition φ and postcondition ψ. We write $\Gamma \vdash \{\varphi\}C.m\{\psi\}$ (or $\Gamma \vdash \{\varphi\}C.C\{\psi\}$) to state that $C.m$ (or the constructor of C) is correct wrt $\langle\varphi\rangle\langle\psi\rangle$ under Γ. For methods with multiple specifications, we use $\Gamma \vdash C.m \triangleright \Pi(C.m)$ to say that $C.m$ is correct wrt its every specification.

For OO programs, behavioral subtyping is crucial in verification. To introduce it here, we define a refinement relation between method specifications.

Definition 6 (Refinement of Specification). *Given two specifications* $\langle\varphi_1\rangle\langle\psi_1\rangle$ *and* $\langle\varphi_2\rangle\langle\psi_2\rangle$, *we say that the latter refines the former in context* Γ, C, *iff there exists an assertion* R *which is free of program variables, such that* $\Gamma, C \vdash (\varphi_1 \Rightarrow \varphi_2 * R) \wedge (\psi_2 * R \Rightarrow \psi_1)$. *We use* $\Gamma, C \vdash \langle\varphi_1\rangle\langle\psi_1\rangle \sqsubseteq \langle\varphi_2\rangle\langle\psi_2\rangle$ *to denote this fact. For multiple specifications* $\{\pi_i\}_i$ *and* $\{\pi'_j\}_j$, *we say* $\{\pi_i\}_i \sqsubseteq \{\pi'_j\}_j$ *iff* $\forall i \, \exists j \cdot \pi_i \sqsubseteq \pi'_j$.

Liskov and Wing [15] defined the condition for specification refinement as $\varphi_1 \Rightarrow \varphi_2 \wedge \psi_2 \Rightarrow \psi_1$. We extend it by considering the storage extension (specified in R) and multiple specifications as above. It follows also the *nature refinement order* proposed by Leavens and Naumann [13].

The behavioral subtyping relation should also be verified for interfaces with inheritance relations. Assume I has a super-interface I', and method m in I has a new specification $\langle\varphi\rangle\langle\psi\rangle$ overriding its counterpart $\langle\varphi'\rangle\langle\psi'\rangle$ in I', we must verify $\Gamma, I \vdash \langle\varphi'\rangle\langle\psi'\rangle \sqsubseteq \langle\varphi\rangle\langle\psi\rangle$ holds on the logic level, because of no method body involved.

Now we can define a class to be *correct* with two aspects of proof obligations wrt given specifications. That is, every defined method meets its specifications, and each subclass is a behavioral subtype of its superclass. We will use the inference rules listed in Appendix A to prove these. Note that in the rules for methods, we include premises for verifying the behavioral subtyping relation.

Definition 7 (Correct Class). *A class C defined in program G is correct, iff,*

- *for each method m defined in C, we have $\Gamma_G \vdash C.m \triangleright \Pi(C.m)$, and for the constructor of C with $\Pi_G(C.C) = \langle\varphi\rangle\langle\psi\rangle$, we have $\Gamma_G \vdash \{\varphi\}C.C\{\psi\}$;*
- *if C is defined as a subclass of class D in G, then C is a behavioral subtype of D.*

Then, we define a program with axioms to be *correct* as follows:

Definition 8 (Correct Program). *Program G is correct, iff,*

(1) G is well-axiom-constrained according to Definition 4.
(2) Each class C defined in G is correct according to Definition 7.

It is easy to conclude, our extended verification framework with axioms of VeriJ is sound because the assertion logic used and all inference rules have been proven sound.

5   Case Study

Having the enriched specification and verification framework, in this section we will reexamine the MVC example discussed in Sect. 2, to see how the problems mentioned there can be tackled naturally and the two roles of axioms.

5.1   Specifying the MVC Architecture

Following the guideline in Fig. 2, we have declared interfaces *MI, CI, VI* in Fig. 3 to embody the calculator design. Some specification predicates with respective purposes as we explained have been introduced to form a foundation for formal method specification. Each predicate should have a declaration, as "**def** *model*(**this**, vs, st);" in the interface, but we omit them here to save space. These declarations introduce predicate names with parameters, all as abstract symbols, and their concrete meaning (possibly multiple) will be defined later in implementing class(es) of the interfaces.

However, not any definition for the predicates is acceptable, and some predicates may have interconnections with others. In order to reflect our anticipation in correctly specifying the calculator requirements, preventing wrong implementations, and providing enough information for client verifications, we need to constrain definitions of the predicates in later implementations and their correct uses in specifications by revealing their relations or properties. Applying our approach in Sect. 4, we specify a set of axioms labeled as [a1–a3] according to the requirements in Fig. 2:

$$\textbf{axiom } MVC(c, m, vs, st) \Leftrightarrow model(m, vs, st) * (\circledast_{v \in vs} view(v, m, st)) \quad \text{[a1]}$$
$$* \, controller(c, m, st);$$
$$\textbf{axiom } MVs(m, vs, st) \Leftrightarrow model(m, vs, st) * (\circledast_{v \in vs} view(v, m, st)); \quad \text{[a2]}$$
$$\textbf{axiom } MVC(c, m, vs, st) \Leftrightarrow MVs(m, vs, st) * controller(c, m, st); \quad \text{[a3]}$$

The axioms form a part of specifications to capture important interactions or properties of the MVC architecture, and constrain the forthcoming implementations. Semantically, any implementation should fulfill them, and the definitions for the methods declared in the interfaces must obey these constraints which will generate proof obligations. In this way, although the interfaces provide no behavior definitions, their implementations have been connected formally by the predicates and axioms.

In Fig. 7, we give four classes *Model, Controller, View* and *View$_2$* which implement the interfaces and form an implementation of the MVC calculator. We

```
class Model ▷ MI{                           void paint(){
  def model(this, vs, st) :                    Int n = this.vtotal;
    this.total ↦ st * this.views ↦ vs;        System.out.println("Product is: ")+n; }}
  def MVs(this, vs, st) :                   class View₂ ▷ VI{
    model(this, vs, st) * (⊛ᵥ∈ᵥₛview(v, this, st));  def view(this, m, st) :
  def product(n, m) : n * m;                    this.model ↦ m * this.vtotal ↦ (st + 1);
  Int total; List⟨VI⟩views;                   MI model; Int vtotal;
  Model()⟨emp⟩⟨model(this, ∅, 1)⟩           View₂(MI m)⟨model(m, vs, st)⟩
  { this.total = 1;                           ⟨model(m, vs ∪ {this}, st)*
    this.views = new ArrayList⟨VI⟩(); }        view(this, m, st)⟩ {...}
  Int getState(){ Int s;                     void update(MI m){
    s = this.total; return s; }               if (m==this.model)
  void addView(VI v){                            this.vtotal = m.getState() + 1;
    views.add(v); v.update(this); }            this.paint(); }
  void Multiply(Int i){                       void paint(){...}
    this.total = this.total * i; this.Notify(); }  }
  void Reset() {                            class Controller ▷ CI{
    this.total = 1; this.Notify(); }          def controller(this, m, st) :
  void Notify()⟨model(this, vs, st)*          this.model ↦ m * this.state ↦ st;
  (⊛ᵣ∈ᵥₛview(r, this, st')))⟩⟨MVs(this, vs, st)⟩  def MVC(this, m, vs, st) :
  { for(VI v : views) v.update(this); }       model(m, vs, st) * (⊛ᵥ∈ᵥₛview(v, m, st))*
}                                               controller(this, m, st);
class View ▷ VI{                             MI model; Int state;
  def view(this, m, st) :                     Controller(MI m) ⟨model(m, vs, st)⟩
    this.model ↦ m * this.vtotal ↦ st;        ⟨controller(this, m, st) * model(m, vs, st)⟩
  MI model; Int vtotal;                       { this.model = m; this.state = m.getState(); }
  View(MI m) ⟨model(m, vs, st)⟩              void multiplyPerformed(){
  ⟨model(m, vs ∪ {this}, st) * view(this, m, st)⟩  Scanner scan = new Scanner(System.in);
  { this.model = m; this.vtotal = 0;          System.out.print("Enter a number: ");
    m.addView(this); }                        Int i = scan.nextInt(); model.Multiply(i);
  void update(MI m){                          Int j = model.getState(); this.state = j; }
    if (m==this.model)                       void resetPerformed(){
      this.vtotal = m.getState();             this.state = 1; model.Reset(); }
    this.paint(); }                        }
```

Fig. 7. An implementation of the MVC calculator interfaces

use class *Scanner* in package "java.util.Scanner" and call its method *nextInt()* to get an integer from the input stream for multiplying. Abstractly, we specify method *Scanner.nextInt()* as "⟨**true**⟩⟨∃n · res = n⟩". All predicates declared in the interfaces are defined with bodies in relative classes that give also specific meaning for the axioms. For example, axiom [a1] tells the whole MVC can be divided into a model object, its controller object and its view-object set; Importantly, [a1] requires the states of these interactive objects must be synchronous to be the abstract state *st* as in the whole case. [a2] means the model-views aggregate structure consists of a model object and its view-object set with a synchronous state; and [a3] says the whole MVC can also be viewed as consisting of a model-views aggregate structure with a controller object with a synchronized state.

5.2 Verifying Implementations with Axioms and Method Specifications

Now we consider verifying the implementation before reasoning client codes. Definition 8 lists two parts of work for concluding the correctness of the implementation: (1) checking it supports axioms [a1-a3] by applying the two-step

Proving *View.View*(**m**) :
{*model*(*m, vs, st*)}
this.*model* = *m*; **this**.*vtotal* = 0;
{*model*(*m, vs, st*)∗
  this.*model* ↦ *m* ∗ **this**.*vtotal* ↦ 0}
{*model*(*m, vs, st*) ∗ *view*(**this**, *m*, 0)}
[Rule [H-DPRE](*View.view*(. . .))]
m.*addView*(**this**);
{*model*(*m, vs* ∪ {**this**}, *st*)∗
  view(**this**, *m, st*)}

Proving *Controller.resetPerformed*() :
{*MVC*(**this**, *m, vs, st*)}
{*MVs*(*m, vs, st*) ∗ *controller*(**this**, *m, st*)}
[Axiom [a3][**this**/*c*] (R/L)]
{*MVs*(*m, vs, st*) ∗ **this**.*model* ↦ *m*∗
  this.*state* ↦ *st*}
[Rule [H-DPRE](*Controller.controller*(. . .))]
this.*state* = 1;
{*MVs*(*m, vs, st*) ∗ **this**.*model* ↦ *m*∗
  this.*state* ↦ 1}
{*MVs*(*m, vs, st*) ∗ *controller*(**this**, *m*, 1)}
[Rule [H-DPRE](*Controller.controller*(. . .))]
model.Reset();
{*MVs*(*m, vs*, 1) ∗ *controller*(**this**, *m*, 1)}
{*MVC*(**this**, *m, vs*, 1)}
[Axiom [a3][**this**/*c*] (L/R)]

Proving *Controller.multiplyPerformed*() :
{*MVC*(**this**, *m, vs, st*)}
Scanner scan = **new** *Scanner*(System.in);
System.out.print("Enter a number: ");

Int *i* = *scan.nextInt*();
{∃*n* · *i* = *n* ∧ *MVC*(**this**, *m, vs, st*)}
{∃*n* · *i* = *n* ∧ *MVs*(*m, vs, st*)∗
  controller(**this**, *m, st*)}
[Axiom [a3][**this**/*c*] (R/L)]
model.Multiply(*v*);
{∃*n, st'* · *i* = *n* ∧ *st'* = *product*(*st, i*)∧
  MVs(*m, vs, st'*) ∗ *controller*(**this**, *m, st*)}
{∃*n, st'* · *i* = *n* ∧ *st'* = *product*(*st, i*)∧
  model(*m, vs, st'*) ∗ (⊛*v*∈*vs* *view*(*v, m, st'*))∗
  controller(**this**, *m, st*)}
[Axiom [a2][*st'*/*st*] (R/L)]
Int *j* = *model.getState*();
{∃*n, st'* · *i* = *n* ∧ *st'* = *product*(*st, i*) ∧ *j* = *st'*
  ∧*model*(*m, vs, st'*) ∗ (⊛*v*∈*vs* *view*(*v, m, st'*))
  ∗*controller*(**this**, *m, st*)}
{∃*n, st'* · *i* = *n* ∧ *st'* = *product*(*st, i*) ∧ *j* = *st'*
  ∧*model*(*m, vs, st'*) ∗ (⊛*v*∈*vs* *view*(*v, m, st'*))
  ∗**this**.*model* ↦ *m* ∗ **this**.*state* ↦ *st*}
[Rule [H-DPRE](*Controller.controller*(. . .))]
this.*state* = *j*;
{∃*n, st'* · *i* = *n* ∧ *st'* = *product*(*st, i*) ∧ *j* = *st'*
  ∧*model*(*m, vs, st'*) ∗ (⊛*v*∈*vs* *view*(*v, m, st'*))
  ∗**this**.*model* ↦ *m* ∗ **this**.*state* ↦ *j*}
{∃*n, st'* · *i* = *n* ∧ *st'* = *product*(*st, i*)∧
  model(*m, vs, st'*) ∗ (⊛*v*∈*vs* *view*(*v, m, st'*))∗
  controller(**this**, *m, st'*)}
[Rule [H-DPRE](*Controller.controller*(. . .))]
{∃*n, st'* · *i* = *n* ∧ *st'* = *product*(*st, i*)∧
  MVC(**this**, *m, vs, st'*)}
[Axiom [a3][**this**/*c*] (L/R)]
{∃*st'* · *MVC*(**this**, *m, vs, st'*)}

Fig. 8. The verification of three methods

procedure given in Sect. 4; (2) checking each declared method satisfies its specifications. Due to limited space, we only give detailed proofs of axiom [a1] and called methods by client here, and leave other proofs in our report [9], where we give also some discussions about the proof steps which may be deduced interactively or automatically in a proof assistant.

For axiom [a1], we construct a substitution under Γ of the implementation:

$$\delta_{\{MVC, controller\}, \Gamma} \;\widehat{=}\; [$$
$$c : Controller \wedge \mathsf{fix}(Controller, MVC(c, m, vs, st))/MVC(c, m, vs, st),$$
$$c : Controller \wedge \mathsf{fix}(Controller, controller(c, m, st))/controller(c, m, st)]$$

That is because only class *Controller* defines predicates $MVC(\dots)$ and $controller(\dots)$. By applying this substitution on the assertion of [a1] (simply denoted as ψ), we get the following logic formula (4) to prove,

$$\psi\delta_{\{MVC, controller\}, \Gamma} = c : Controller \wedge \mathsf{fix}(Controller, MVC(c, m, vs, st))$$
$$\Leftrightarrow model(m, vs, st) * (\circledast_{v \in vs} view(v, m, st)) * \qquad (4)$$
$$c : Controller \wedge \mathsf{fix}(Controller, controller(c, m, st))$$

Using the definition of fix and inference rules, we know

$$c : Controller \wedge \mathsf{fix}(Controller, MVC(c, m, vs, st)) \Leftrightarrow Controller.MVC(c, m, vs, st)$$

and similar for fix($Controller, controller(\dots)$). Thus we can reduce (4) to:

$$Controller.MVC(c, m, vs, st) \Leftrightarrow model(m, vs, st) * (\circledast_{v \in vs} view(v, m, st)) * \\ Controller.controller(c, m, st) \tag{5}$$

Then, from Γ, we have $\Phi(Controller.MVC(\mathbf{this}, m, vs, st)) = model(m, vs, st) * controller(\mathbf{this}, m, st) * (\circledast_{v \in vs} view(v, m, st))$. Using rule [EXPAND], we get

$$Controller.MVC(c, m, vs, st) \Leftrightarrow \text{fix}(Controller, model(m, vs, st)* \\ (\circledast_{v \in vs} view(v, m, st)) * controller(\mathbf{this}, m, st))[c/\mathbf{this}]$$
$$\Leftrightarrow (\text{fix}(Controller, model(m, vs, st)) * \text{fix}(Controller, \circledast_{v \in vs} view(v, m, st))* \\ \text{fix}(Controller, controller(\mathbf{this}, m, st)))[c/\mathbf{this}]$$
$$\Leftrightarrow model(m, vs, st) * (\circledast_{v \in vs} view(v, m, st))* \\ Controller.controller(\mathbf{this}, m, st)[c/\mathbf{this}]$$
$$\Leftrightarrow model(m, vs, st) * (\circledast_{v \in vs} view(v, m, st)) * Controller.controller(c, m, st)$$

Thus, we have proven that [a1] is well supported. With similar proofs for other axioms in our report [9], we conclude all the axioms are well-supported by the implementation, then the axioms can be used in verifying the implementation and client codes.

We give detail proofs of methods $View.View(m)$, $Controller.resetPerformed()$ and $Controller.multiplyPerformed()$ in Fig. 8, because they are called in the illustrating client method. In the proof, labels like "[Rule [H-DPRE]($View.view(\dots)$)]" mean applying the inference rule [H-DPRE] (listed in Fig. 10 in Appendix A) on predicate $view(\dots)$ to unfold/fold its definition in class $View$; and "[Axiom [a3] [$\mathbf{this}/c$] (R/L)]" means using axiom [a3] from its left side (L) to right side (R) by substituting parameter c to $\mathbf{this}$. Steps without explicit labels normally use simple inference rules. Finally, we conclude these three methods are correct.

Having proven that all axioms are well-supported and all methods satisfy their specifications, we know the implementation is correct for the MVC architecture.

5.3 Verifying Client Methods

At last, we resolve the verification of the client method in Fig. 9, by using the above extended specifications on interfaces including axioms [a1-a3] and similar labels as in method verifications. It shows that, we can finish the verification of the client now, thus it makes a correct application of the MVC calculator.

6 Related Work and Conclusion

In this paper, we focus on specifying and verifying OO programs which are built on interactive components through clearly defined interfaces. We propose the axioms to relate abstract predicates for the specification of interfaces. These axioms semantically constrain the implementations and interactions in component-based systems (CBSs), and support the verification of clients which

(1) $\{\exists i \cdot model(m, \emptyset, i) * controller(c, m, i)\}$
(2) $VI\ v_1 = \mathbf{new}\ View(m);$
(3) $\{\exists i, r_1 \cdot v_1 = r_1 \land model(m, \{r_1\}, i) * view(r_1, m, i) * controller(c, m, i)\}$
(4) $\mathbf{Int}\ n = 1;$
(5) $\{\exists i, r_1 \cdot v_1 = r_1 \land n = 1 \land model(m, \{r_1\}, i) * view(r_1, m, i) * controller(c, m, i)\}$
(5′) $\{\exists i, r_1, n_1 \cdot v_1 = r_1 \land n = 1 \land n = n_1 \land 1 < 4 \land model(m, \{r_1\}, i) *$
           $view(r_1, m, i) * controller(c, m, i)\}$
(5″) $\{\exists i, r_1, n_1 \cdot v_1 = r_1 \land n = 1 \land n = n_1 \land n_1 < 4 \land MVC(c, m, \{r_1\}, i)\}$
           [Axiom [a1] [$\{r_1\}, r_1, i/vs, v, st$] (L/R)]
(6) $\mathbf{while}\ (n < 4)$
(7) $\{\ \{\exists i', r_1, n_1' \cdot v_1 = r_1 \land n = n_1' \land n_1' < 4 \land MVC(c, m, \{r_1\}, i')\}$ [—loop invariant]
(8) $c.multiplyPerformed();$
(9) $\{\exists i'', r_1, n_1' \cdot v_1 = r_1 \land n = n_1' \land n_1' < 4 \land MVC(c, m, \{r_1\}, i'')\}$
(10) $n++;$
(11) $\{\exists i'', r_1, n_1', n_2 \cdot v_1 = r_1 \land n = n_2 \land n_2 = n_1' + 1 \land n_2 \leq 4 \land MVC(c, m, \{r_1\}, i'')\}$
(11′) $\{\exists i'', r_1, n_2 \cdot v_1 = r_1 \land n = n_2 \land n_2 \leq 4 \land MVC(c, m, \{r_1\}, i'')\}\ \}$
(12) $\{\exists j, r_1 \cdot v_1 = r_1 \land n = 4 \land MVC(c, m, \{r_1\}, j)\}$
(12′) $\{\exists j, r_1 \cdot v_1 = r_1 \land model(m, \{r_1\}, j) * view(r_1, m, j) * controller(c, m, j)\}$
           [Axiom [a1][$\{r_1\}, r_1, j/vs, v, st$] (R/L)]
(13) $VI\ v_2 = \mathbf{new}\ View_2(m);$
(14) $\{\exists j, r_1, r_2 \cdot v_1 = r_1 \land v_2 = r_2 \land model(m, \{r_1, r_2\}, j) * view(r_1, m, j)*$
           $view(r_2, m, j) * controller(c, m, j)\}$
(14′) $\{\exists j, r_1, r_2 \cdot v_1 = r_1 \land v_2 = r_2 \land MVC(c, m, \{r_1, r_2\}, j)\}$[Axiom [a1][$\{r_1, r_2\}, j/vs, st$] (L/R)]
(15) $c.resetPerformed();$
(16) $\{\exists r_1, r_2 \cdot v_1 = r_1 \land v_2 = r_2 \land MVC(c, m, \{r_1, r_2\}, 1)\}$
(16′) $\{\exists r_1, r_2 \cdot MVC(c, m, \{r_1, r_2\}, 1)\}$

Fig. 9. The correct proof of the client method

are defined based on interfaces abstractly (i.e., without consulting the concrete implementations nor the hidden predicate definitions) and modularly (i.e., avoiding reverification).

In the enriched foundation of framework VeriJ, we require checking each system implementation in two aspects: first the well-supportedness of each axiom, and then the correctness of each method with its specifications. Behavioral subtyping property is also ensured by checking specification refinement relations. Further we well support information hiding and extensibility in specifying and verifying OO programs.

To our limited knowledge, there exist some works on specifying and reasoning CBSs in different ways. Leavens *et al.* [11] combined model variables [3] and model programs to specify interfaces of CBSs, and extended the behavioral subtyping concept for CBSs. However, they only pointed out subtypes should obey the specifications of instance methods, no formalization details for the modular reasoning was given. Henzinger *et al.* [5] gave a type system for component interaction by checking component compatibility with some interface automata but touched no real semantics. Our idea requires compatible components to meet both method specifications and global axioms specified in/on interfaces. Their refinement is only from the interface designs to implementations, without behavioral subtyping as what we consider. Aguirre and Maibaum [1] used algebraic specification of Guttag *et al.* [8] with temporal logic to define the ADTs of components, and specified interactions of components in special specification modules. Except the axioms relating actions of components in the ADTs, they also gave some axioms independent of particular subsystem declarations to express properties of their class instances and associations. Poetzsch-Heffter and Schäfer [19] adopted model variables and pure methods in specifying interfaces of encapsulated components too. They specified invariants expressing properties of components but the behavioral subtype relation for components was absent.

On the other side, *object invariants* in JML [10] and Spec# [2], and *axioms* in MultiStar [22] are also specified to constrain subclasses through specification inheritance as ours act. However, compared with axioms, object invariants are less abstract and less powerful because: (1) they only hold at particular program points in operations while axioms hold always; (2) they constrain operations but axioms constrain logical data abstractions; (3) verifications for axioms which are done ahead of method verifications do not involve methods, but invariants do; (4) axioms are expressed as logical predicates, but invariants are in term of fields and pure methods in implementation; etc. Moreover, Dafny, an automatic program verifier for functional correctness developed by Leino [14], uses invariants in terms of valid mathematical functions and ghost variables, but it supports neither subtyping nor interface-based design.

Using the technique of abstract predicate family of Parkinson and Bierman [18], Van Staden and Calcagno [22] expressed separately properties for individual classes and entire multiple hierarchies correspondingly in *exports* and *axioms* in MultiStar. We uniform their two kinds into our axioms, where each predicate application encapsulates all its polymorphic definitions in implementations and its meaning can be determined by applying fix function and inference rules. Differing from *exports* in MultiStar, we can inherit individual properties to restrict subclasses. As we can inherit and reuse predicate definitions from superclass, our specification and verification is less complex but more modular. Still, we avoid infinite expansion of recursive predicate definitions in proving axioms and method specifications which is not considered in MultiStar. *Exports* in jStar [6] expressed interactive objects from different classes and enabling client verifications, however, it cannot restrict subclasses.

As future work, we would investigate more challenges [12] such as object invariant, frame problem in specifying and verifying OO programs. We attempt to apply our approach for more interactive programs like design patterns [7], web applications, etc. Meanwhile, we are working on implementing our theoretical framework using Coq.

A   Inference Rules of VeriJ Framework

In this appendix, we give a brief introduction on the inference rules for verifying VeriJ programs. More details can be found in [16, 20].

Basic inference rules are given in Fig. 10. We skip explaining many simple rules here. Rules [H-DPRE], [H-SPRE] are key to show our idea that specification predicates have scopes, thus may have multi-definitions crossing the class hierarchy for the polymorphism. If a predicate invoked is in scope (in its class or the subclasses), it can be unfolded to its definition. These rules support hiding implementation details in predicate definition. However, these two rules are

[H-THIS] $\Gamma, T, m \vdash \mathbf{this} : T$ [H-SKIP] $\Gamma \vdash \{\varphi\}\mathbf{skip}\{\varphi\}$ [H-ASN] $\Gamma \vdash \{\varphi[e/x]\}x := e; \{\varphi\}$

[H-MUT] $\Gamma \vdash \{v = r_1 \wedge e = r_2 \wedge r_1.a \mapsto -\}v.a := e; \{v = r_1 \wedge e = r_2 \wedge r_1.a \mapsto r_2\}$

[H-LKUP] $\Gamma \vdash \{v = r_1 \wedge r_1.a \mapsto r_2\}x := v.a; \{x = r_2 \vee v = r_1 \wedge r_1.a \mapsto r_2\}$

[H-CAST] $\Gamma \vdash \{v = r \wedge r <: N\}x := (N)v; \{x = r\}$ [H-RET] $\Gamma \vdash \{\varphi[e/\mathbf{res}]\}\mathbf{return}\ e; \{\varphi\}$

[H-SEQ] $\dfrac{\Gamma \vdash \{\varphi\}c_1\{\psi\}, \quad \Gamma \vdash \{\psi\}c_2\{R\}}{\Gamma \vdash \{\varphi\}c_1\ c_2\{R\}}$ [H-COND] $\dfrac{\Gamma \vdash \{b \wedge \varphi\}c_1\{\psi\}, \quad \Gamma \vdash \{\neg b \wedge \varphi\}c_2\{\psi\}}{\Gamma \vdash \{\varphi\}\mathbf{if}\ b\ c_1\ \mathbf{else}\ c_2\{\psi\}}$

[H-ITER] $\dfrac{\Gamma \vdash \{b \wedge I\}c\{I\}}{\Gamma \vdash \{I\}\mathbf{while}\ b\ c\{\neg b \wedge I\}}$ [H-FRAME] $\dfrac{\Gamma, C, m \vdash \{\varphi\}c\{\psi\} \quad \mathsf{FV}(R) \cap \mathsf{MD}(c) = \emptyset}{\Gamma, C, m \vdash \{\varphi * R\}c\{\psi * R\}}$

[H-CONS] $\dfrac{\Gamma, C, m \vdash \varphi \Rightarrow \varphi', \quad \Gamma, C \vdash \psi' \Rightarrow \psi \quad \Gamma, C, m \vdash \{\varphi'\}c\{\psi'\}}{\Gamma, C, m \vdash \{\varphi\}c\{\psi\}}$ [H-EX] $\dfrac{\Gamma, C, m \vdash \{\varphi\}c\{\psi\} \quad r\ \text{is free in}\ \varphi, \psi}{\Gamma, C, m \vdash \{\exists r \cdot \varphi\}c\{\exists r \cdot \psi\}}$

[H-OLD] $\dfrac{\forall\langle\varphi\rangle\langle\psi\rangle \in \Pi(T.m) \bullet \Gamma, T, m \vdash (\overline{z} = \overline{r} \wedge \varphi[\overline{r}/\overline{z}]) \Rightarrow \psi'}{\Gamma, T, m \vdash \psi'[\mathbf{old}(e)/e]}$ [H-SPRE] $\dfrac{C <: D, \quad \Phi(D.p(\mathbf{this}, \overline{a})) = \psi}{\Gamma, C, m \vdash D.p(r, \overline{r'}) \Leftrightarrow \mathsf{fix}(D, \psi)[r, \overline{r'}/\mathbf{this}, \overline{a}]}$

[H-DPRE] $\dfrac{r : D, \quad C <: D, \quad \Phi(D.p(\mathbf{this}, \overline{a})) = \psi}{\Gamma, C, m \vdash p(r, \overline{r'}) \Leftrightarrow \psi[r, \overline{r'}/\mathbf{this}, \overline{a}]}$ [H-PDPRE] $\dfrac{r : D, \quad \Phi(D.p(\mathbf{this}, \overline{a})) = \psi}{\Gamma, C, m \vdash p(r, \overline{r'}) \Leftrightarrow \psi[r, \overline{r'}/\mathbf{this}, \overline{a'}]}$

Fig. 10. Basic inference rules

different. [H-DPRE] says if r is of type D, then in any subclass of D, $p(r, \overline{r'})$ can be unfolded to the body of p in D. [H-SPRE] is for the static binding, where $\mathsf{fix}(D, \psi)$ (in combine with $D.p(r, \overline{r'})$) gives the *instantiation* of ψ in D (seeing Sect. 4), and provides a static explanation for ψ. In fact, [H-SPRE] is the typed version of [EXPAND] given in Sect. 4; [H-DPRE] and [H-PDPRE] are similar but deal with dynamic binding.

Rules related to methods and constructors are given in Fig. 11, where we assume a default side-condition that local variables $\overline{y}$ are not free in φ, ψ, that can be provided by renaming. The rules reflect our idea in Sect. 4.2 and divide three cases in verifying methods. They ensure the behavioral subtyping property in a program.

[H-MTHD1] is for verifying methods with a specification (and a definition). It demands that $C.m$'s body meets its specification, and asks to check the refinement between specification of m in C with each of C's supertypes, if exist. Here we promote Π to type set, thus $\Pi(\mathsf{super}(C))(m)$ gives specifications for m in C's supertypes. If there is no, this check is true by default. [H-MTHD2] is for verifying methods defined in classes without specifications. [H-MINH] is for verifying inherited methods. [H-CONSTR] for constructors is similar. However, a constructor cannot have multi-specifications. Here $\mathsf{raw}(\mathbf{this}, C)$ specifies **this** refers to a newly created raw object of type C, and then c modifies its state, where $\mathsf{raw}(r, C)$ has a definition:

$$\mathsf{raw}(r, C) \triangleq \begin{cases} \mathsf{obj}(r, C), & N\ has\ no\ field \\ r : C \wedge (r.a_1 \mapsto \mathsf{nil}) * \cdots * (r.a_k \mapsto \mathsf{nil}), & \text{fields of } C \text{ is } a_1, \ldots, a_k \end{cases}$$

Last two rules are for method invocation and object creation. Note that $T.n$ may have multiple specifications, and we can use any of them in proving client code. Due to the *behavioral subtyping*, it is enough to do the verification by

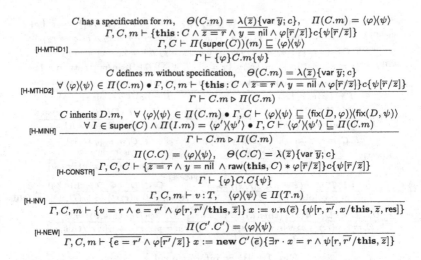

$$C \text{ has a specification for } m, \quad \Theta(C.m) = \lambda(\overline{z})\{\text{var } \overline{y}; c\}, \quad \Pi(C.m) = \langle\varphi\rangle\langle\psi\rangle$$

[H-MTHD1]
$$\frac{\Gamma, C, m \vdash \{\text{this}: C \wedge \overline{z = r} \wedge y = \text{nil} \wedge \varphi[\overline{r}/\overline{z}]\}c\{\psi[\overline{r}/\overline{z}]\}}{\Gamma, C \vdash \Pi(\text{super}(C))(m) \sqsubseteq \langle\varphi\rangle\langle\psi\rangle}$$
$$\frac{}{\Gamma \vdash \{\varphi\}C.m\{\psi\}}$$

[H-MTHD2]
$$C \text{ defines } m \text{ without specification}, \quad \Theta(C.m) = \lambda(\overline{z})\{\text{var } \overline{y}; c\}$$
$$\frac{\forall \langle\varphi\rangle\langle\psi\rangle \in \Pi(C.m) \bullet \Gamma, C, m \vdash \{\text{this}: C \wedge \overline{z = r} \wedge y = \text{nil} \wedge \varphi[\overline{r}/\overline{z}]\}c\{\psi[\overline{r}/\overline{z}]\}}{\Gamma \vdash C.m \triangleright \Pi(C.m)}$$

[H-MINH]
$$C \text{ inherits } D.m, \quad \forall \langle\varphi\rangle\langle\psi\rangle \in \Pi(C.m) \bullet \Gamma, C \vdash \langle\varphi\rangle\langle\psi\rangle \sqsubseteq \langle\text{fix}(D, \varphi)\rangle\langle\text{fix}(D, \psi)\rangle$$
$$\frac{\forall I \in \text{super}(C) \wedge \Pi(I.m) = \langle\varphi'\rangle\langle\psi'\rangle \bullet \Gamma, C \vdash \langle\varphi'\rangle\langle\psi'\rangle \sqsubseteq \Pi(C.m)}{\Gamma \vdash C.m \triangleright \Pi(C.m)}$$

[H-CONSTR]
$$\Pi(C.C) = \langle\varphi\rangle\langle\psi\rangle, \quad \Theta(C.C) = \lambda(\overline{z})\{\text{var } \overline{y}; c\}$$
$$\frac{\Gamma, C, C \vdash \{\overline{z = r} \wedge y = \text{nil} \wedge \text{raw}(\text{this}, C) * \varphi[\overline{r}/\overline{z}]\}c\{\psi[\overline{r}/\overline{z}]\}}{\Gamma \vdash \{\varphi\}C.C\{\psi\}}$$

[H-INV]
$$\frac{\Gamma, C, m \vdash v : T, \quad \langle\varphi\rangle\langle\psi\rangle \in \Pi(T.n)}{\Gamma, C, m \vdash \{v = r \wedge \overline{e = r'} \wedge \varphi[r, \overline{r'}/\text{this}, \overline{z}]\} \, x := v.n(\overline{e}) \, \{\psi[r, \overline{r'}, x/\text{this}, \overline{z}, \text{res}]\}}$$

[H-NEW]
$$\frac{\Pi(C'.C') = \langle\varphi\rangle\langle\psi\rangle}{\Gamma, C, m \vdash \{\overline{e = r'} \wedge \varphi[\overline{r'}/\overline{z}]\} \, x := \text{new } C'(\overline{e})\{\exists r \cdot x = r \wedge \psi[r, \overline{r'}/\text{this}, \overline{z}]\}}$$

Fig. 11. Inference rules related to methods and constructors

the declared type of variable v. Because [H-INV] refers to only specifications, recursive methods are supported.

Here we see how the information given by the developers affects verification. A method specification is a specific requirement and induces some special proof obligations. It connects the implementation with surrounding world: the implemented interfaces, the superclass, and the client codes. When no specification is given, we need to verify more by considering all the possibilities.

References

1. Aguirre, N., Maibaum, T.: A temporal logic approach to component-based system specification and reasoning. In: Proceedings of the 5th ICSE Workshop on Component-Based Software Engineering. Citeseer (2002)
2. Barnett, M., Leino, K.R.M., Schulte, W.: The spec# programming system: an overview. In: Barthe, G., Burdy, L., Huisman, M., Lanet, J.-L., Muntean, T. (eds.) CASSIS 2004. LNCS, vol. 3362, pp. 49–69. Springer, Heidelberg (2005)
3. Cheon, Y., Leavens, G., Sitaraman, M., Edwards, S.: Model variables: cleanly supporting abstraction in design by contract. Softw. Pract. Experience 35(6), 583–599 (2005)
4. Chin, W.N., David, C., Nguyen, H.H., Qin, S.: Enhancing modular OO verification with separation logic. In: POPL'08, pp. 87–99. ACM (2008)
5. De Alfaro, L., Henzinger, T.A.: Interface automata. In: ESEC/FSE'01, vol. 26, pp. 109–120. ACM (2001)
6. Distefano, D., Parkinson, M.J.: jStar: towards practical verification for java. In: OOPSLA'08, pp. 213–226. ACM (2008)
7. Gamma, E., Helm, R., Johnson, R., Vlissides, J.: Design Patterns, Elements of Reusable Object-Oriented Software. Addison-Wesley, Reading (1994)
8. Guttag, J.V., Horowitz, E., Musser, D.R.: Abstract data types and software validation. Commun. ACM 21(12), 1048–1064 (1978)

9. Hong, A., Liu, Y., Qiu, Z.: Axioms and abstract predicates on interfaces in specifying/verifying OO components. Technical report, School of Mathamatics, Peking University (2013). https://github.com/zyqiu/tr/blob/master/OO-components-rep.pdf

10. Leavens, G.T., Baker, A.L., Ruby, C.: Preliminary design of JML: a behavioral interface specification language for Java. ACM SIGSOFT Softw. Eng. Notes 31(3), 1–38 (2006)

11. Leavens, G.T., Dhara, K.K.: Concepts of behavioral subtyping and a sketch of their extension to component-based systems. In: Leavens, G.T., Sitaraman, M. (eds.) Foundations of Component-Based Systems, Chap. 6, pp. 113–135. Cambridge University Press, Cambridge (2000)

12. Leavens, G.T., Leino, K.R.M., Müller, P.: Specification and verification challenges for sequential object-oriented programs. Formal Aspects Comput. 19, 159–189 (2007)

13. Leavens, G.T., Naumann, D.A.: Behavioral subtyping is equivalent to modular reasoning for object-oriented programs. Technical Report, Department of Computer Science, Iowa State University (2006)

14. Leino, K.R.M.: Dafny: an automatic program verifier for functional correctness. In: Clarke, E.M., Voronkov, A. (eds.) LPAR-16 2010. LNCS (LNAI), vol. 6355, pp. 348–370. Springer, Heidelberg (2010)

15. Liskov, B., Wing, J.M.: A behavioral notion of subtyping. ACM Trans. Program. Lang. Syst. 16(6), 1811–1841 (1994)

16. Liu, Y., Hong, A., Qiu, Z.: Inheritance and modularity in specification and verification of OO programs. In: TASE'11, pp. 19–26. IEEE Computer Society (2011)

17. Yijing, L., Zongyan, Q.: A separation logic for OO programs. In: Barbosa, L.S., Lumpe, M. (eds.) FACS 2010. LNCS, vol. 6921, pp. 88–105. Springer, Heidelberg (2012)

18. Parkinson, M.J., Bierman, G.M.: Separation logic, abstraction and inheritance. In: POPL'08, pp. 75–86. ACM (2008)

19. Poetzsch-Heffter, A., Schäfer, J.: Modular specification of encapsulated object-oriented components. In: de Boer, F.S., Bonsangue, M.M., Graf, S., de Roever, W.-P. (eds.) FMCO 2005. LNCS, vol. 4111, pp. 313–341. Springer, Heidelberg (2006)

20. Zongyan, Q., Ali, H., Yijing, L.: Modular verification of OO programs with interfaces. In: Aoki, T., Taguchi, K. (eds.) ICFEM 2012. LNCS, vol. 7635, pp. 151–166. Springer, Heidelberg (2012)

21. Qiu, Z., Wang, S., Long, Q.: Sequential μJava: Formal foundations. Technical Report 2007-35, School of Mathamatics, Peking University (2007). http://www.mathinst.pku.edu.cn/index.php?styleid=2

22. Van Staden, S., Calcagno, C.: Reasoning about multiple related abstractions with multistar. In: OOPSLA'10, pp. 504–519. ACM (2010)

A Framework for Handling
Non-functional Properties
Within a Component-Based Approach

Jean-Michel Hufflen[✉]

FEMTO-ST (UMR CNRS 6174) & University of Franche-Comté,
16, Route de Gray, 25030 Besançon Cedex, France
jmhuffle@femto-st.fr

Abstract. We describe a framework that allows us to manage evolution of software assembled by means of a component-based approach. We start from information about the components of a software architecture, written using an ADL. Several versions of the same component may coexist within a kind of repository, we show how such a repository is organised. Then we explain how our framework allows us to help designers when they have to choose among several versions of a component, regarding non-functional properties. We can also deal with some replacement operations when such software is reconfigured dynamically.

Keywords: Component-based approach · Model transformations · Non-functional properties · Configuration family · Design time vs run time · Dynamic reconfiguration

1 Introduction

Component-based approaches have reached some maturity since they have been shown successful for the development of large software systems, especially embedded systems. In particular, this approach seems to be suitable for systems with high-safety requirements, such as time-constrained response or availability of requested services. If we consider 'practical' results, this approach has led to the implementation of many *toolboxes*, encompassing tools assisting developers for the conception of different parts at design time, tools for deriving programs and assembling them, tools allowing dynamic reconfiguration at run time. Some examples are UniFrame [18], Fractal [1], SOFA[1] 2 [2], SCA[2] [19,20]. Each of these tools is based on a *component model* and the architecture of a component system is described by means of an ADL[3], most often using XML[4]-like syntax.

This work has been partially funded by the Labex ACTION, ANR-11-LABX-01-01.

[1] **SOF**tware **A**ppliances.
[2] **S**ervice **C**omponent **A**rchitecture.
[3] **A**rchitecture **D**efinition **L**anguage.
[4] e**X**tensible **M**arkup **L**anguage.

J.L. Fiadeiro et al. (Eds.): FACS 2013, LNCS 8348, pp. 196–214, 2014.
DOI: 10.1007/978-3-319-07602-7_13, © Springer International Publishing Switzerland 2014

As shown in [7], these component models have many similarities but also principal differences. In addition, they have been developed with different aims. Among these principal differences, we can notice the specification and processing of *non-functional properties*[5]. As examples, SCA uses annotations referring to *policy sets* [21], Fractal allows some non-functional properties to be handled at run time in order for a system's components to be reconfigured dynamically—an example using a component's electrical power is given in [9]—but such properties cannot be specified at design time within the configuration files handled by Fractal/ADL.

The problems addressed in this article are related to the management of configuration *families*. We build such a family by starting from specifications of architectures, each describing a component system. Such specifications are written using an ADL such as Fractal. These descriptions are supposed to be *alternatives* implementing the same service. They are *merged* in order to share common subparts as far as possible and build relationships among subcomponents of such alternatives as precisely as possible. Within our framework, we are able to deal with non-functional properties, we can use them to build a 'best' architecture of components and export it using an ADL such as Fractal or SCA.

In Sect. 2, we precisely explain why our approach is original and why it *complements* existing approaches and tools. Then we introduce our component model and our notion of *repository* after a short example motivating them. We also express the requirements and the implementation of our tools. Then Sect. 3 describes the successive stages of our approach, with particular focus on our merge operation and our management of non-functional properties. Then Sect. 4 discusses some points about our framework. Last, we mention our future plans in Sect. 5.

2   Our Framework

2.1   Motivation

The toolboxes mentioned above—UniFrame, Fractal, SOFA, SCA—use configuration files that describe *one* architecture of *one* component system. In fact, some tools—e.g., Fractal or SOFA—allow a component to be derived from a more abstract one, so we could express that several components are derived from a common basis and are implementations of the same service. Such a *modus operandi* is related to a *top-down* approach: a common abstract interface is developed, and there may be *several* ways to refine it. Our approach proceeds from another starting point: we are given several versions of a component architecture, possibly developed by different teams. These versions are supposed to implement the same service and we have to choose one of them. Maybe a configuration is better; another possible solution is that the best architecture is achieved

---

[5] Some authors [5,15] use the term *extra-functional properties* instead. Let us recall that functional requirements specify what a system is supposed to do whereas non-functional properties express what a system is supposed to be.

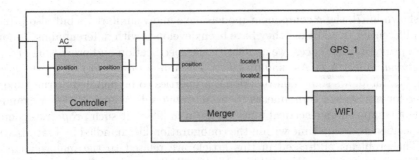

Fig. 1. Architecture of the location component.

by replacing some subcomponents of an architecture by subcomponents originating from another architecture. Such replacement can be done at design time, it also be performed at run time, in case of a dynamic reconfiguration, if a subcomponent fails and must be replaced by another.

An example motivating this approach has been provided by the TACOS[6] project. This project concerned the development of urban vehicles with new functionalities and services, following the CyCab concept. In this framework, a *location* composite component—a *composite* component consists of assembling sub-components into a kind of black box—has been designed as part of this land transportation system. This complete composite component uses two positioning systems—GPS[7] and Wifi—a controller and a merger. Each positioning system is composed of an atomic positioning component and a software component to validate perceived data. The validation components transfer the positioning data to the merger if they are precise enough. The merger applies a particular algorithm to merge data obtained from positioning systems. Roughly speaking, the goal of this algorithm is to ensure that the level of reliability must not decrease between two locations unless the operation updating the context is called. Finally, the controller's purpose is to request and to acknowledge the receipt of positioning data. In fact, *several* versions of this location component were designed within the TACOS project. The first version, described above, is pictured in Fig. 1. A second version, given in Fig. 2, uses another GPS component, a GSM[8] positioning system, and a WIFI comparable with Fig. 1's. No version appeared undoubtedly better than the other, and there was much debate inside the working group in charge of this component in order to choose among these versions. From a technical point of view, these versions were designed in Fractal/ADL[9], which does not allow non-functional properties to be handled at design time. But studying such properties could be useful for this choice.

---

[6] **T**rustworthy **A**ssembling of **C**omponents: fr**O**m requirements to **S**pecification. More details about this project can be found in [3] or at http://tacos.loria.fr.

[7] **G**lobal **P**ositioning **S**ystem.

[8] **G**lobal **S**ystem for **M**obile communications.

[9] Fractal was used within the TACOS project.

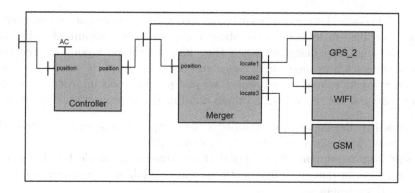

Fig. 2. Alternative architecture of Fig. 1.

2.2   A Tool Complementing Other Services

To help designers to perform the choice between the two versions of the location component, a first idea was to translate Fractal/ADL specifications into descriptions of component architectures suitable for SCA. This task would have been quite easy by means of an XSLT[10] stylesheet. That would have been a kind of transformation model, which would have allowed us to study some non-functional properties. But in SCA, some non-functional properties are predefined, some are not handled. Even if it quite illusory to handle *any* non-functional property— they are so diverse—we aimed to study these properties without giving any privilege to particular ones *a priori*. The same criticism holds for other tools such as UniFrame or SOFA 2, so using them seemed to us to be too restrictive and we plan to design our own architecture description language.

However we did not aim to put into action a new toolbox which would be comparable with Fractal or SCA. We just aimed to provide additional services to users of such a toolbox. That is why we designed a new ADL, TACOS+/XML, allowing us to express component architectures originally designed with tools such as Fractal, such a description being enriched with additional annotations in our language. We start from descriptions written using an ADL, translate them into our language, merge them into a kind of *repository*, and can export an description usable by the original toolbox. Since building the final architecture description from several versions can result from examining non-functional properties, our language allows us to deal with such properties when a final configuration is built. In addition, we can perform some mixing: importing a description from an ADL and exporting it using another ADL, merging several descriptions written using different ADLs, etc.

TACOS+/XML has been designed in order to be able to specify any non-functional property *a priori*, with its possible associated values. Our goal is not to measure such properties: we do not handle components themselves and our

---

[10] e**X**tensible **S**tylesheet **L**anguage **T**ransformations, the language of transformations used for XML documents [24].

approach is static. Our goal is to organise and use such information—computed by tools or filled in by end-users—about components to compute globally such properties and help designers when they have to choose among alternatives. Minimising such a property may cause another property to be maximised, it is up to developers to express *strategies*, we just provide tools in order to validate such strategies. Let us go back to these non-functional properties, these may:

- supplied by developers, an example is the complexity property, expressed by means of expressions such that $\mathcal{O}(n^2)$ or $\mathcal{O}(\log n)$;
- result from measurement performed at run-time, e.g., the electrical power,
- be constraints that an implementation must fulfill, an example is the time-constrained response.

Of course, our approach is mainly accurate for non-functional properties that result from measurements. But if a constraint has not been fulfilled at run time, we can report that and use our system to find possible replacement.

2.3   Repository of Components

Hereafter we explain how our component model is organised. Let S be a set of *class names*[11], a *component* C is defined by:

- there pairwise-disjoint sets of *parameters*[12] P_C, input port names I_C, and output port names O_C;
- the class t_C of the service implemented by the component;
- additional functions which allow us to get access to the class of a parameter or port ($\tau_C : P_C \cup I_C \cup O_C \rightarrow S$), or to a parameter's value ($v_C : P_C \rightarrow \bigcup_{s \in S} s$);
- the set *sub-c$_C$* of its subcomponents if the C component is composite.

A composite component cannot have parameters[13]. Of course, the binary relation 'is a subcomponent of' must be a DAG[14].

The components of an architecture are elements of a set CP. The *bindings* of ports are couples of output and input port names, being the same type. In addition, we also handle an *is-alt-of* binary relation: if C_0 and C_1 are components, C_0 *is-alt-of* C_1 means that C_0 can be replaced by C_1; in addition to this intuitive definition, we will show at Sect. 3.1 how this relation is built; of course, it is an equivalence relation.

Non-functional properties are modelled by a *nfp* set of partial functions starting from CP. For example, the non-functional property related to electrical power is a partial function from CP to $\mathbb{R}^+$ (the set of non-negative real numbers). The range of such a function must be totally ordered.

---

[11] In the sense used in object-oriented programming.

[12] Some authors use the term 'attributes' instead. A parameter is related to an internal feature, e.g., the maximum number of messages a component can process.

[13] ... but its simple subcomponents can.

[14] **D**irect **A**cyclic **G**raph.

```
1  <tacos:components ...>
2    <tacos:general-metadata roots="d2e2">
3      <dc:title>...</dc:title>
4      ...
5    </tacos:general-metadata>
6    <tacos:component-specifications>
7      <tacos:composite-component id="d2e2">
8        <tacos:path value="location.Location" wrt="Location.fractal"/>
9        ...
10       <tacos:refers-to ref="d2e15"/>
11       ...
12     </tacos:composite-component>
13     ...
14     <tacos:component id="d2e15">
15       <tacos:path value="merger" wrt="d2e2"/>
16       <tacos:port ref="location.Position" role="output" name="position"/>
17       <tacos:port ref="location.Locate1" role="input" name="locate1"
18                   optional="true"/>
19       <tacos:port ref="location.Locate2" role="input" name="locate2"
20                   optional="true"/>
21       <tacos:port ref="location.Locate3" role="input" name="locate3"
22                   optional="true"/>
23       <tacos:implements ref="location.MergerImpl"/>
24       <tacos:nonfunctional-properties>
25         <nfp:complexity>O(n)</nfp:complexity>
26         <nfp:energy-consumption
27           compute="http://tacos.univ-fcomte.fr/electric-power.xsl"
28           args="cp='d2e15'" href="..."/>
29         <nfp:reliability
30           check-up="http://tacos.univ-fcomte.fr/reliability-check-up"
31           args="..." href="..."/>
32       </tacos:nonfunctional-properties>
33       <tacos:technical-metadata/>
34       <tacos:imported from="Fractal"/>
35     </tacos:component>
36   </tacos:component-specifications>
37   ...
38   <tacos:binding-specifications>
39     <tacos:binding from="position" to="position" server="d2e15"
40                    client="d2e6"/>
41     ...
42   </tacos:binding-specifications>
43 </tacos:components>
```

Fig. 3. Example of TACOS+/XML specification.

An example of specification using our TACOS+/XML language is given in Fig. 3. We can see that this description is organised into a *repository* of components. The name of the components at the top level is given by the **roots** attribute of the **tacos:general-metadata** element. We can also remark that this specification has been derived from a Fractal/ADL specification: this information has been put by means of the **tacos:imported** element (cf. line 34). The original specification is pictured in Fig. 4. It is easy to see that Fig. 3's text— except for the **tacos:nonfunctional-properties** element (lines 24–32)—has been got from Fig. 4's text by means of a *tree transformation*. Such a transformation is clearly syntactic, but we put a constraint into action. Informally, given an import to TACOS+/XML, we *must* be able to restore the original text. Formally, let $\mathcal{L}_{ADL}$ be the set of texts expressed using the ADL language, and $\mathcal{L}_{TACOS+/XML}$ be the set of texts expressed using the TACOS+/XML language, the

```
1  <definition name="location.Location">
2   ...
3    <component name="merger" definition="location.Merger">
4      <interface name="position" role="server"
5                 signature="location.Position"/>
6        <interface name="locate1" role="client" contingency="optional"
7                 signature="location.Locate1"/>
8        <interface name="locate2" role="client" contingency="optional"
9                 signature="location.Locate2"/>
10       <interface name="locate3" role="client" contingency="optional"
11                 signature="location.Locate3"/>
12     <content class="location.MergerImpl"/>
13   </component>
14   ...
15   <binding client="..." server="merger.position"/>
16   ...
17 </definition>
```

Fig. 4. Fractal/ADL specification Localisation.fractal (excerpt).

transformation $f : \mathcal{L}_{\text{ADL}} \to \mathcal{L}_{\text{TACOS}+/\text{XML}}$ is valid if there exists a left inverse transformation $g : \mathcal{L}_{\text{TACOS}+/\text{XML}} \to \mathcal{L}_{\text{ADL}}$ such that $g \circ f = id_{\mathcal{L}_{\text{ADL}}}$.

Practically, we implement these transformation functions in XSLT. In fact, XML/XSLT techniques have been recognised as not providing adequate mechanisms to support model transformation problems: when there is loss of information due to the expressive power of the source and target languages, the mechanism has to store in an *ad hoc* structure, as mentioned in [22, Ch. 16]. This *ad hoc* structure is modelled by the `tacos:imported` element. In practice, this element is empty for specifications originating from Fractal/ADL, and contains the specification of policy sets for specifications originating from SCA. Measurements of non-functional properties included into the original specification—as allowed by UniFrame—are put under the `tacos:nonfunctional-properties` element.

Let us remark that the existence of a right inverse f holds only for the TACOS+/XML texts without `tacos:nonfunctional-properties` elements. In addition, this composition property holds up to a bijective renaming of component names. If we consider Fig. 3's text, we can see that the transformation function puts new names for components—as an example, cf.lines 7 and 14, the `id` attribute, the original name used by the Fractal/ADL specification, is retained by means of a *path* information: the `value` attribute of the `tacos:path` element, see lines 8 and 15—: that allows us to merge specifications even if the same name is used for different components, as we will show in Sect. 3.1. In other words, there exists a right inverse g_0 of f, that is, such that $f \circ g_0 \simeq id_{\mathcal{L}_{\text{TACOS}+/\text{XML}}^{nfp=\varnothing}}$, where '$\simeq$' means 'equals up to a bijective renaming of port names' and $\mathcal{L}_{\text{TACOS}+/\text{XML}}^{nfp=\varnothing}$ is the set of texts expressed using the TACOS+/XML language, without any occurrence of the `tacos:nonfunctional-properties` element. If the target ADL allows some non-functional properties to be expressed, the properties it knows are specified into the result after a transformation of a TACOS+/XML text.

TACOS+/XML uses *four* namespaces, here are the prefixes we use:

- `tacos` is for TACOS+/XML's main namespace: in particular, the elements specifying components belong to it;

- nfp is for the namespace devoted to non-functional properties;
- dc and dcterms are for *metadata* belonging to the *Dublin Core* [11]; the dc prefix is for basic elements: we use these Dublin Core elements as sons of the tacos:general-metadata element: dc:title for the study's title, dc:creator for the user performing this study, dc:date, ... the dcterms prefix introduces elements of the *Qualified Dublin Core*: we use these elements for *relationships* among component specifications. Originally, the Dublin Core aims to provide interoperable metadata standards that support a broad range of purposes and business models. In particular, some elements of the Qualified Dublin Core are very suitable for relationships among component specifications:

dcterms:hasVersion	dcterms:isReplacedBy
dcterms:isFormatOf	dcterms:isRequiredBy
dcterms:isPartOf	dcterms:isVersionOf
dcterms:isReferencedBy	...

3 The Different Stages of Our Approach

The *modus operandi* we put into action is pictured in Fig. 5. We explain it by starting from Fractal/ADL specifications, but it is the same for texts originating from other ADLs. At Step (1), an XSLT stylesheet is applied to a component specification written using Fractal/ADL and results in a text in TACOS+/XML. Let us mention that this tree transformation flattens out a composite component's specification[15]. A second version—or alternative—of the software may be designed using Fractal/ADL and converted into a TACOS+/XML file. More versions may be processed, as pictured by dashed boxes. At Step (2), all the TACOS+/XML files built during the previous step are merged into one family. This merge operation is described in Sect. 3.1.

Step (3) consists in adding information about non-functional properties, more precisely about the properties that can be determined statically or filled in by end-users (for example, the complexity property). At Step (4), we choose the 'best' component, regarding non-functional properties—we explain our *modus operandi* in Sect. 3.2—and the result is a TACOS+/XML specification describing this 'best' configuration. At Step (5), this 'best' configuration can be expressed in Fractal/ADL by using another XSLT stylesheet. That is, the specification of this configuration is exported using the Fractal/ADL format.

Fractal is now ready to assemble the parts of the 'best' component, and run a simulation of it. This simulation may enrich the knowledge about the non-functional properties that evolve whilst the program is running. That causes the master TACOS+/XML file to be updated, this is Step (6). Step (7) allows users to perform dynamic replacement of a component by another, regarding non-functional properties again. Our framework does not perform such replacement

---

[15] In Fractal/ADL, a composite component is described by a tree of descriptions of its subcomponents, whereas a TACOS+/XML text is a set of component descriptions, a composite component referring to its subcomponents, as shown in Fig. 3.

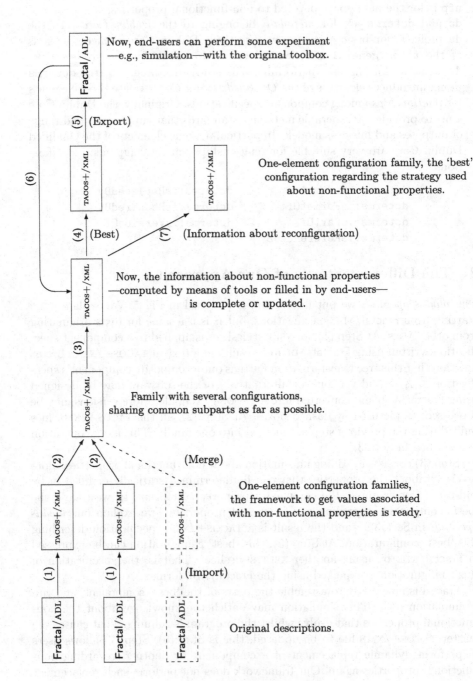

Fig. 5. *Modus operandi.*

```
1  <merge:setting xmlns:merge="http://tacos.loria.fr/merge">
2    <merge:force component-ref-id="..." component-ref-id-0="...">
3      <!-- "Ref-ids" are new names, put when the importation was performed. -->
4      <merge:ports port-ref="..." port-ref-0="..."/>
5      <merge:signatures ref="..." ref-0="..."/>
6    </merge:force>
7    <merge:dont-force component-ref-id="..." component-ref-id-0="..."/>
8  </merge:setting>
```

Fig. 6. Customising the merge function.

directly since it only can be made by the tool in charge of assembling and running the system—e.g., Fractal or SCA—but our framework may help developers to choose which replacements have to be performed.

Of course, let us assume that we would like to interface TACOS+/XML with a new environment, the component specification of this environment being written in an $\mathcal{L}$ language, which is an ADL. Then we have to write two programs—using XSLT or another language—: one from $\mathcal{L}$ to TACOS+/XML and another from TACOS+/XML to $\mathcal{L}$, with the constraint mentioned in Sect. 2 about the left inverse of the transformation from $\mathcal{L}$ to TACOS+/XML. Our approach is general... provided that we are able to program some connection with particular environments. But, in practice, these environments handle the same kind of information: input and output ports, service names, bindings between ports, etc. So these programs are quite easy to write, as we experienced them with Fractal and SCA. Besides, the goal is to be able to deal with some non-functional properties not handled by the environment we start from. As abovementioned, SCA allows the specification of constraints related to time constraints and security, but many other non-functional properties are not handled.

3.1   The Merge Operation

Roughly speaking, our merge operation aims to share the common subparts of some configuration families, as far as possible. In addition, components that are supposed to implement the same functionality but are not identical are bound each together, that is, we express that such a component can be replaced by another. In other words, this merge operation aims to share common TACOS+/XML specifications as far as possible, and also to extend the relation *is-alt-of* as far as possible. Let us recall that when a component is imported into a TACOS+/XML repository, this component is given a unique name, the original name being accessible as the *path* information (cf. Fig. 3). So several components having the same original name can coexist in a TACOS+/XML configuration family. During the merge operation, such namesake components are supposed to implement the same functionality, but end-users can redefine that as shown in Fig. 6. In other words, our merge operation can be customised, its default behaviour being intuitive. When the merge operation is launched, it aims to merge the components that are roots—given by the **roots** attribute (cf. Sect. 2)—and the components that are supposed to implement the same service. The *modus operandi* is given in Fig. 7 using a pseudo-algorithmic language. We use:

- '$x \leftarrow \cup\, y$' for '$x \leftarrow x \cup y$';
- '$\texttt{update-bindings}(\mathcal{C}_0, \mathcal{C}_1)$' causes all the bindings from or to the $\mathcal{C}_0$ component and recursively from or to its subcomponents to be substituted by bindings from or to the $\mathcal{C}_1$ component and its subcomponents;
- '$\texttt{find-same-service-as}(\mathcal{C}, \mathcal{C}\text{-}set)$'—where $\mathcal{C}$ is a component and $\mathcal{C}\text{-}set$ a set of components—which returns a component of $\mathcal{C}\text{-}set$ supposed to implement the same service as $\mathcal{C}$ if such a component exists[16], the value null otherwise.

```
merge(𝒞₀,𝒞₁)  ⟶    // 𝒞₀ and 𝒞₁ are TACOS+/XML specifications.
  if 𝒞₀ = 𝒞₁   // The same specification is shared.
    then update-bindings(𝒞₁,𝒞₀) ; return 𝒞₀ ;
    else if P𝒞₀ = P𝒞₁ ∧ I𝒞₀ = I𝒞₁ ∧ O𝒞₀ = O𝒞₁ ∧ τ𝒞₀ = τ𝒞₁ ∧ t𝒞₀ = t𝒞₁
      then    // Only the parameters' values are different. Let us recall that
              // composite components do not have parameters, so we can merge
              // subcomponents regardless parameters' values.
        return join(𝒞₀,𝒞₁) ∪ merge-subcomponents(𝒞₀,𝒞₁) ;
      else return (𝒞₀,𝒞₁) ;    // Two different components, no alternative.
    end if ;
end ;

join(𝒞₀,𝒞₁)  ⟶    // Two different components, but one can replace the other.
  is-alt-of ←∪ (𝒞₀,𝒞₁) ; return (𝒞₀,𝒞₁) ;
end ;

merge-subcomponents(𝒞₀,𝒞₁)  ⟶
  result ← () ; 𝒞-set₀ ← sub-c𝒞₀ ; 𝒞-set₁ ← sub-c𝒞₁ ;
  foreach 𝒞 in 𝒞-set₀ do
    𝒞ₙ ← find-same-service-as(𝒞,𝒞-set₁) ;
    if 𝒞ₙ = null then result ←∪ 𝒞 ;
    else result ←∪ merge(𝒞,𝒞ₙ) ; 𝒞-set₁ ← 𝒞-set₁ \ {𝒞ₙ} ;
    end if ;
  end foreach ;
  result ←∪ 𝒞-set₁ ; return result ;
end ;
```

Fig. 7. Merging specifications of components.

As an example, if this merge operation is applied to the configurations depicted in Figs. 1 and 2, it results in the repository consisting of:

- the simple components Controller, Merger, GPS_1, GPS_2, Wifi, GSM.;
- Figs. 1's and 2's composite components, as roots of this family;
- metadata expressing that the last two composite components—known as d2e15 and d2e16 within TACOS+/XML specifications (cf. Fig. 3)—are alternatives, e.g.:

---

[16] That is, having the same original name as $\mathcal{C}$ w.r.t. the default behaviour, as explained above.

```
<tacos:component id="d2e15">
   ...
   <tacos:technical-metadata>
      <dcterms:alternative>d2e16</dcterms:alternative> ...
   </tacos:technical-metadata>
   ...
</tacos:component>
```

In fact, this merge operation is quite close to what is done by means of rules in the EML[17] language [14], but ours returns two results: a set of components and an update of the *is-alt-of'* relation and of the bindings.

3.2   Using Information About Non-functional Properties

As abovementioned, non-functional properties are very diverse. Some must be checked at run time, for example, time-constrained responses related to real-time systems. Some result from measurement performed at run-time, for example, the *reliability* property, which may be defined as the mean time between failures, or the *speed's performance*, which often results from an average of measurements when this component is in service. Some can be determined statically—for example, the *complexity* of a program—or may be predictable—for example, the *energy consumption* of a GPS. If we consider the types of the possible values for non-functional properties, they are very diverse, too: let us recall that the complexity is usually expressed by means of symbolic expressions such as $\mathcal{O}(n^2)$ or $\mathcal{O}(n \log n)$ whereas the other properties we have just mentioned above can be expressed using decimal numbers. As another difficulty, there is no universal evaluation function for all kinds of non-functional properties, as mentioned in [27]. Some non-functional properties may apply for simple components, or can be *aggregated* in the case of composite components, in which case the aggregation function takes results for subcomponents and computes a global value for the composite component. There is also a notion of *dynamic aggregation*, studied in [27], in the sense that some properties may vary dynamically, for example, the speed's performance. In such a case, the dynamic aggregation method aims to return a final score from individual successive ones.

In our framework, we assume the existence of a function summarising the non-functional properties of interest for the current project. The range of this function must be a totally ordered set and we try to maximise this function. For example, let us assume that we are only interested in the *reliability* of a component, this property being measured by a positive decimal number, so the range is $\mathbb{R}^+$ and the order used may be '$\leq$' since we are obviously interested in maximising this property's value. As a second example, the values of the *power* property used by [9] are low, medium and high. In such a case, if we are interested to minimize this power, the order $\preceq_p$ used must be the reflexive and transitive closure of high $\preceq_p$ medium $\preceq_p$ low. As a third example, more ambitious, let us

---

[17] Epsilon Merging Language.

assume that we are interested first in reliability, second in complexity. That is, if the reliability of two versions of a component are equivalent, we choose the component with the minimal complexity. Let C be the set of expressions denoting algorithm complexity—e.g., $\mathcal{O}(n^2)$, $\mathcal{O}(n \log n)$, see above—C being ordered by a relation $\preceq_C$ such that $\mathcal{O}(n^2) \preceq_C \mathcal{O}(n \log n)$, i.e., $\mathcal{O}(n \log n)$ is a better value for complexity than $\mathcal{O}(n^2)$. In this second case, the range is the cartesian product $\mathbb{R}^+ \times C$ and the global order relation $\preceq_g$ is a variant of the lexicographic order, used within dictionaries:

$$(r_1, c_1) \preceq_g (r_2, c_2) \overset{\text{def}}{\Longleftrightarrow} (r_1 < r_2) \vee (r_1 = r_2 \wedge c_1 \preceq_C c_2)$$

for $r_1, r_2 \in \mathbb{R}^+$, $c_1, c_2 \in C$.

Within our terminology, the function summarising non-functional properties is called a **digest**. A digest is not a policy model because a policy model defines both some situations and the actions to be performed in such cases. A digest expresses a *strategy* to choose 'better' components. If trying to improve a property causes another property to get more bad, it is up to the digest to manage such situations. Of course, digests are user-defined, that is, each project has its own digest. Syntactically, a digest is a function that can be used by an XSLT 2.0 stylesheet, under the name `tacos:le-digest` and has the following look:

```
<xsl:function name="tacos:le-digest"as="xsd:boolean">
  <xsl:param name="c0"as="element(tacos:composite-component)"/>
  <xsl:param name="c1"as="element(tacos:composite-component)"/>
  <!--  First computes the digests of c0 and c1, then compares them.   -->
  ...
</xsl:function>
```

This function should implement a total and strict[18] order. More precisely, when this program is called, the users must make precise the components for which the digest is applied. For example, if you want to organise the best configuration around several versions of the `Merger` component, just make precise:

$$... \text{basename="Merger"}$$

—according to our terminology, a *basename* is a common name used by several versions of Fractal for alternative components, it is distinct from a TACOS+/XML identifier—and the program will look for the best value about a `Merger` component, provided that a complete composite component—whose root belongs to the value associated with the **roots** attribute of a family—can be build around this 'best' component. This **basename** parameter can be dropped out if only global non-functional properties for the complete roots are of in interest.

If there is a list of several alternative components for which the digest is to be applied, we sort this list according to this digest. Then we go to a possible root (a composite component's top), step by step, and repeat this operation.

---

[18] That is, an *irreflexive*, antisymmetric, and transitive relation, e.g. '$<$' for natural numbers.

```
1  <xsl:variable name="the-table" as="element(tacos:nfp-power)*">
2    <nfp:power for="i2e2">80.</nfp:power>
3    <nfp:power for="...">...</nfp:power>
4  </xsl:variable>
5
6  <xsl:function name="nfp:get-power" as="xsd:float">
7    <xsl:param name="the-id" as="xsd:IDREF"/>
8    <xsl:variable
9       name="content"
10      select=
11      "id($the-id)/tacos:nonfunctional-properties/nfp:energy-consumption"
12      as="element(nfp:energy-consumption)?"/>
13    <xsl:choose>
14      <xsl:when test="empty($content)">
15        <xsl:variable name="first-pass"
16                      select="$the-table[nfp:power[data(@for) eq $the-id]]"
17                      as="element(nfp:power)?"/>
18        <xsl:value-of
19          select="if (empty($first-pass)) then
20                     sum(for $id in tacos:refers-to/@to
21                         return nfp:get-power(data($id))) else
22                     data($first-pass)"/>
23      </xsl:when>
24      <xsl:otherwise><xsl:value-of select="data($content)"/></xsl:otherwise>
25    </xsl:choose>
26  </xsl:function>
27
28  <xsl:function name="tacos:le-digest" as="xsd:boolean">
29    <xsl:param name="c0" as="element(tacos:composite-component)"/>
30    <xsl:param name="c1" as="element(tacos:composite-component)"/>
31    <xsl:value-of select="nfp:get-power(c0) gt nfp:get-power(c1)"/>
32  </xsl:function>
```

Fig. 8. XSLT functions for the electric power of a component and using that as a digest.

It may lead to ruling out some impossible associations of components. Finally, we go to the descendants not yet explored and repeat this operation again. At the last step, we return the first element of the list we have just got, this first element has the 'better' value for the digest. This *modus operandi* cannot fail since any component belongs to a realisable configuration[19], before it was merged with others. In fact, the answer may be an 'original' configuration or may mix components belonging to several original configurations. This procedure may lead to combinatorial explosion, but we confess that we have experienced it on small- and medium-sized systems, leaving this problem for a future revision.

As a more complete example, let us assume that among several versions of a component, we aim to minimise the electrical power. In this case, we express that a C_1 version is better than a C_0 version if the electrical power of C_0 is greater than C_1's. That is shown in Fig. 8, lines 28–32.

Within TACOS+/XML texts, the whole information concerning non-functional properties is grouped under the tacos:nonfunctional-properties element. The values associated with some properties have to be filled in by users, in which case this is the contents of the corresponding element: an example is given by the complexity property, modelled by the nfp:complexity element.

---

[19] This is a strong hypothesis, but realistic, since such 'original' configurations have been designed by means of tools such as Fractal or SCA.

If the value can be computed by a program at design time, we use the compute attribute, as shown for the energy-consumption property. If the value results from benchmarks done at run time, we use the check-up attribute. In these last two cases:

- the values associated with attributes compute or check-up are URIs[20] identifying the program;
- the result of such a program is stored into a file whose pathname is given by the href attribute.

If the value associated with attributes compute or check-up is an XSLT stylesheet, it is applied to the complete TACOS+/XML text, and the args attribute gives additional information to supply; as an example, the electric power of a component pictured in Fig. 3 can be computed by an XSLT function as shown in Fig. 8: this function—which can be viewed as an aggregation function—uses a look-up table for the electric power of simple components, and the electric power of a composite component is supposed to be the sum of the electric power of every subcomponent. This scheme is frequent for the evaluation of some non-functional properties. An aggregation function is superseded by values given by means of a look-up table.

Considering the classification given in [7], our management of non-functional properties is related to *exogeneous* management since we do not handle components themselves, we just refer to a specification of knowledge about them. Let us look at Fig. 8: if there is no information associated with a component specification under the tacos:nonfunctional-properties element—that is, the whole knowledge about electrical power is included into the variable the-table and the function nfp:get-power—an exogeneous system-wide management is implemented. This *modus operandi* is supersed by a non-empty content under the tacos:nonfunctional-properties element, in which case an exogeneous management per collaboration is put into action. Using both tables and information associated with component specifications allow some refinement to be implemented: by default, values associated with component specifications are used, but within particular contexts, these values may be refined by using tables or other structures; even if the implementation is not the same, the approach is close to what is shown in [15].

4   Discussion

At first glance, what has been done with TACOS+/XML may seem to be worthwhile exercises using XML. Anyway, we use XML in an accurate way, that is, as a central formalism for information interchange. We could have built databases of component specifications and dealt with them using a language like SQL[21] in order to select 'better' components, but it would have been more complicated

---

[20] Uniform Resource Identifier.
[21] Structured Query Language.

for designers to specify digests in order to compare components regarding non-functional properties. The same, the specification of possible values associated with non-functional properties by XML Schema [25] may be viewed as a worthwhile exercise. However, as far as we know, that is the most advanced attempt of specifying non-functional properties, in the sense that we have specified a precise taxonomy that may be checked by means of a validator.

A merge operation working on component models has been studied in [4] about the evolution of component-based software. This operation is related to versioning software, it pursues the same goals than our merge operation in the sense that it aims to share common subparts, but does not deal with alternatives as done by our relation *is-alt-of*.

Considering the diversity of non-functional properties, it seems to be impossible to put a universal scheme into action. Moreover, articles and reports studying these properties in general—e.g., [6,12,23]—do not agree about a common classification. We do not pretend to propose such a solution, but we have defined a framework that allows knowledge about the non-functional properties of components to be organised—provided that the values of a property belong to a totally ordered set—and to put into action the two ways to implement exogeneous management, as defined in [15]. Some non-functional properties have been studied within this framework: reliability, and efficiency regarding the result of profiling tools such as the gprof analysis tool of GNU[22] for programs written in C++ or JRat for classes developed in Java. These non-functional properties, based on simulations, are evaluated at run time, so we are able to analyse programs in order to influence the choice of better components if the system has to evolve. This direction seems to us to be very promising. Other tools, more specialised in handling non-functional properties are presently in β-test and will be available soon. They include simple examples of properties computed statically, for example, the XSLT function calculating the electric power of a component and given in Fig. 8 and some examples of order relations among digests.

If we see non-functional properties as *annotations*, comparable work has been done as part of [16] or about the UniFrame toolbox. But if such annotations have to be updated whilst the program is running, only predefined properties can be handled. Our system requires intervention from designers but allows them to put into action their own non-functional properties, their own criteria. Of course, it may be difficult to express a digest, especially if several properties are combined, but until now we have succeeded in doing that for our examples.

5 Conclusion and Future Work

The schemas defining the TACOS+/XML language are available in [13], with all our XSLT stylesheets, in particular, those allowing Fractal/ADL and SCA texts to be imported and exported. In addition, we could also import a specification using Fractal/ADL and export it using SCA, or *vice versa*; we have just tried this feature, but it seems to us to be promising. In such a case, the fact that information

---

[22] Recursive acronym: GNU's Not UNIX.

is not lost is ensured by our first transformation into TACOS+/XML, as explained in Sect. 2. We plan to replace some XSLT stylesheets by more efficient implementations using algorithmic languages: for example, the merge operation, and a revised version of our selection operation, that would use heuristics related to NP problems if the number of components is high. Since starting configurations are actual implementations of a service, our selection of the 'best' configuration w.r.t. a digest may return a starting configuration or a mixing of components belonging to several configurations. This implies that any component belonging to a configuration family may work without additional constraint about hardware or components accompanying it. A next version of our selection procedure could take into account such constraints.

It can be viewed that we have focused on flexibility at design time mainly. We plan to study how our tools may be usable for flexibility at run time, as mentioned at the end of Sect. 3. Besides, we have implemented the checking of the structural refinement relation defined in [8,10], we plan to add this relation to our metadata. We will have to extend the definition of these metadata, since the Dublin Core is unable to model refinement relations. This refinement relation may be viewed as a possible replacement relation, but not as an alternative because such refinement is not symmetric: we can only replace an abstract specification by a more refined one. Last but not least, some recent works use languages and tools related to the Semantic Web in order to model services, including the description of non-functional properties. Examples are OWL-S[23] [17] and WSMO[24] [26], a survey can be found in [28]. An interesting way could be the integration of uch tools based on the Semantic Web to our framework.

Acknowledgements. Many thanks to the first version's referees, who suggested me constructive improvement. I also thank Olga Kouchnarenko, who encouraged me for this work.

References

1. Bruneton, É., Coupaye, T., Stefani, J.-B.: The Fractal Component Model (2004). http://fractal.objectweb.org/specification/index.html
2. Bures, T., Hnetynka, P., Plasil, F.: SOFA 2.0: Balancing advanced features in a hierarchical component model. In: Proceedings of SERA 2006, pp. 40–48, Aug 2006
3. Chouali, S., Dormoy, J., Hammad, A., Hufflen, J.-M., Mouelhi, S., Kouchnarenko, O., Mountassir, H., Tatibouët, B., et al.: Assemblage des composants digne de confiance : de l'ingénierie des besoins aux spécifications formelles. Génie Logiciel **95**, 13–18 (2010)
4. Cicchetti, A., Ciccozzi, F., Lévêque, T., Pierantonio, A.: On the concurrent versioning of metamodels and models: challenges and possible solutions. In: Proceedings of IWMCP'11, pp. 16–25. ACM, New York (2011)

---

[23] Ontology Web Language—Semantics.
[24] Web Service Modelling Ontology.

5. Cicchetti, A., Ciccozzi, F., Lévêque, T., Sentilles, S.: Evolution management of extra-functional properties in component-based embedded systems. In: Proceedings of CBSE, pp. 93–102 (2011)
6. Colin, S., Maskoor, A., Lanoix, A., Souquières J., Hammad, A., Dormoy, J., Hufflen, J.-M., Kouchnarenko, O., Mountassir, H., Lecomte, S., Petit, D., Poirriez, V.: A synthesis of existing approaches to specify non-functional properties. Deliverable L2 1.1, tacos project (ANR-06-SETI-017) (2008)
7. Crnković, I., Sentilles, S., Vulgarakis, A., Chaudron, M.R.V.: A classification framework for software component models. IEEE Trans. Softw. Eng. **37**(5), 593–615 (2011)
8. Dormoy, J.: Contributions à la spécification et à la vérification des reconfigurations dynamiques dans les systèmes à composants. Ph.D. thesis, Université de Franche-Comté (2011)
9. Dormoy J., Koucharenko, O.: Event-based adaptation policies for Fractal components. In: Proceedings of AICSSA (2010)
10. Dormoy, J., Kouchnarenko, O., Lanoix, A.: When structural refinement of components keeps temporal properties over reconfigurations. In: Giannakopoulou, D., Méry, D. (eds.) FM 2012. LNCS, vol. 7436, pp. 171–186. Springer, Heidelberg (2012)
11. Dublin Core Metadata Initiative (2008). http://dublincore.org
12. Glinz, M.: On non-functional requirements. In: Proceedings of RE 07, New-Delhi, India, Oct 2007
13. Hufflen, J.-M.:TACOS+/XML and its toolbox (2011). http://lifc.univ-fcomte.fr/home/~jmhufflen/texts/tacos-plus/
14. Kolovos, D.M., Paige, R.F., Polack, F.A.C.: Model comparison: a foundation for model composition and model transformation testing. In: Proceedings of GaMMa '06, Shangai, China, May 2006
15. Lévêque, T., Sentilles, S.: Refining extra-functional property values in hierarchical component models. In: Proceedings of CBSE 2011, pp. 83–92 (2011)
16. OMG. UML Profile for marte (2008) http://www.omgmarte.org/Documents/Specifications/08-06-09.pdf
17. OWL-S: Semantic markup for web services (2005) http://www.daml.org/services/owl-s/1.1/overview/
18. Raje, R.R., Bryant, B.R., Auguston, M., Olson, A.M., Burt, C.C.: A unified approach for integration of distributed heterogeneous software components. In: Proceedings of the 2001 Monterey Workshop Engineering Automation for Software Intensive System, Integration, pp. 109–119 (2001)
19. Service Component Architecture: Java component implementation specification (2007). http://www.osoa.org/download/attachments/35/SCA_JavaComponentImplementation_V100.pdf?version=1
20. Service Component Architecture: Assembly model specificiation (2007). http://www.osoa.org/download/attachments/35/SCA_AssemblyModel_V100.pdf?version=1
21. Service Component Architecture: Policy framework (2007). http://www.osoa.org/download/attachments/35/SCA_Policy_Framework_V100.pdf?version=1
22. van Bommel, P. (ed.): Transformation of Knowledge, Information and Data: Theory and Applications. Idea Group Inc, Hershey (2007)
23. van Eenoo, C., Hylooz, O., Khan, K.M.: Addressing non-functional properties in software architecture using ADL. In: Proceedings of the Sixth Australasian Workshop on Software System Architectures (2005)

24. Kay, M.H.: W3C. xsl Transformations (xslt). Version 2.0. w3c Recommendation (2007). http://www.w3.org/TR/2007/WD-xslt20-20070123
25. W3C: XML Schema (2008). http://www.w3.org/XML/Schema
26. Roman, D., Lausen, H., Keller, U.: WSMO: Web Service Modelling Ontology (2006). http://www.wsmo.org/TR/d2/v1.3/
27. Yu, H.Q., Reiff-Marganiec, S.: Non-functional property based service selection: a survey and classification of approaches. In: Non-Functional Properties and Service Level Agreements in Service-Oriented Computing Workshop, Dublin (2008)
28. Yu, L.: Semantic Web and Semantic Web Services. Chapman & Hall, Boca Raton (2007)

Using Daikon to Prioritize and Group Unit Bugs

Nehul Jain[1], Saikat Dutta[2], Ansuman Banerjee[1]([⊠]), Anil K. Ghosh[1],
Lihua Xu[3], and Huibiao Zhu[4]

[1] Indian Statistical Institute, Kolkata 700108, India
{ansuman,akghosh}@isical.ac.in
[2] Jadavpur University, Kolkata 700032, India
[3] Department of Computer Science and Technology,
East China Normal University, Shanghai 200241, China
lhxu@cs.ecnu.edu.cn
[4] Software Engineering Institute, East China Normal University,
Shanghai 200241, China
hbzhu@sei.ecnu.edu.cn

Abstract. Unit testing and verification constitute an important step in
the validation life cycle of large and complex multi-component software
code bases. Many unit validation methods often suffer from the problem
of false failure alarms, when they analyse a component in isolation and
look for errors. It often turns out that some of the reported unit failures
are *infeasible*, i.e. the valuations of the component input parameters that
trigger the failure, though feasible on the unit module in isolation, cannot
occur in practice considering the integrated code, in which the unit-
under-test is instantiated. In this paper, we consider this problem in the
context of a multi-function software code base, with a set of unit level
failures reported on a specific function. We present here an automated
two-stage failure classification and prioritization strategy that can filter
out false alarms and classify them accordingly. Early experiments show
interesting results.

1 Introduction

Professional coding practices advocate the development of a large complex software code base as a collection of components, instead of a single monolithic
piece. Each component is developed to support a specific functionality and is
expected to be instantiated in different contexts inside the integrated software.
Each component typically has a set of input parameters, appropriate valuations
to which determine the context in which it is to be instantiated. The execution
of the entire software is the organized orchestration of the control and data flow
induced by the top level code, with inline component instantiations in between
to implement the top level design objective. Such modular design styles not only
facilitate development but also diagnosis and debug.

Verifying correctness of a software code at a large scale has always been a
grand challenge. Traditional test methods typically run out of steam, considering

J.L. Fiadeiro et al. (Eds.): FACS 2013, LNCS 8348, pp. 215–233, 2014.
DOI: 10.1007/978-3-319-07602-7_14, © Springer International Publishing Switzerland 2014

the fact that the number of test cases arising out of the possible orchestrations of the different components and their instantiations, is beyond the limit of what they can achieve in reasonable time. Formal verification methods, on the other hand, attempt at exhaustive verification of abstractions of the underlying infinite software state space, with limits on the amount of promise they can deliver. The complex state space arising out of the possible interleavings and instantiations, typically give rise to an enormous analysis space, traversal of which is infeasible in practice.

A popular approach often found to be successful in practice is modular testing or verification. A modular approach essentially treats each module in isolation and tries to come up with an exhaustive guarantee on its functional correctness. Unit testers typically target some coverage criterion and generate test cases to achieve a reasonable proportion of them within the testing duration. A number of unit bugs are expected to be revealed as an outcome of this exercise, leading to possible refinements of the buggy modules. Formal approaches for modular analysis essentially attempt to analyze (either symbolically or explicitly) every possibility of the presence of a bug inside the unit, and attempt to prove their presence, usually guided by an assertion violation or reachability of error labels. This can possibly lead to some quick unit level violations, which can be diagnosed and fixed.

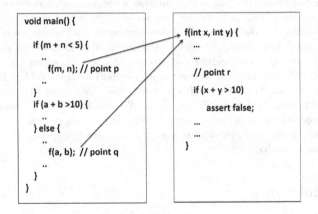

Fig. 1. Infeasible failure

While modular approaches are quick and scalable in finding unit bugs, they often suffer from the problem of false failure alarms. A failure reported by a unit tester may actually be infeasible, that is, the test data that triggered the failure, although reasonable when looking at the unit-under-test in isolation, are outside of their boundaries when considering the integrated software code. Similarly, failures received from a formal verifier analyzing an unit in isolation, may actually be spurious, considering the fact that the state pointed to may be unreachable in the integrated code base, or the failure run may not actually occur. In both the cases, these false alarms received from a unit level verifier, need to be diagnosed and analyzed for correctness. False alarms may lead to needless fixes, which has to be avoided.

In this paper, we consider this problem in the context of a multi-function software code base, with a set of unit level failures reported on a specific function. Figure 1 shows one such infeasible failure. The function f $(intx, inty)$ may report failures for unit tests which drive input values such that the condition $(x+y > 10)$ is met at point r. However, when put in the context of $main$, it is called at program points p and q, where the input sets (m, n) and (a, b) have their value constraints. It is clearly evident that due to the guard conditions at the points from which f is called, the error triggering condition can actually never happen in practice. Therefore, this failure is spurious and needs to be filtered out.

To get around this problem, a number of approaches propose to enrich the unit level verifier with more knowledge about the calling environment [6]. It is acknowledged that an exhaustive scalable verification solution at the integrated system level is not easy to achieve, and unit validation is a much needed step before attempting to scale up to the system level. Researchers have suggested enriching the unit verifier with as much knowledge about the unit's instantiating environment as possible to get around the false alarms. On one extreme, several researchers have looked at the possibility of unit verification in universal environments, assuming all valuations and combinations of the unit parameters in all scenarios. While this leads to better theoretical guarantees, this is not a viable option, considering the complexity of the associated verification problems. On the other extreme, several articles report the possibility of refinement style of reasoning, which may start with zero knowledge about the instantiating environment, and incrementally add as much revealed in the false verification steps. None of these approaches have been reported to be successful at the large scale.

A viable alternative to get around the problem of false alarms, is to possibly analyze and rule out the failures which exhibit call sequences/valuations, which will never occur in the integrated code. While it is possible for the developer to actually achieve this in practice, the number of such scenarios may be overwhelming and end up in a needlessly painstaking exercise. Moreover, in a distributed development environment, and a concurrent code base, it may actually be an infeasible proposition to do this.

The motivation of our work is as follows. Each reported failure can be best analyzed from the perspective of the information about the calling environment that the failure assumes. Failures which depict scenarios that are in more conformance to the calling environment, should be examined with more priority, since they possibly depict true bugs. The ones, which assume calling valuations that contradict common knowledge about the function's environment, are more likely to be spurious. Moreover, many of the failures may actually relate to similar flows in the code, and need not be separately examined. Intuitively, the infeasible failures tend to be similar and can be grouped together because they are relatively likely to relate to similar input constraint violations. Inspecting one failure within the group yields information about the others. For example, if the failures in one group are perfectly correlated, then classifying one effectively

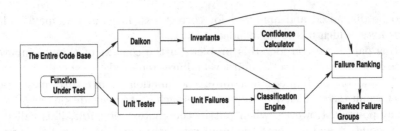

Fig. 2. The overall architecture of our framework

classifies them all. If one failure is identified as infeasible, so are the others and can be skipped. If one failure relates to a true bug, so may be the others and need to be examined. The objective of this work is to assign ranks to a given set of failures based on their likelihood of being true. We present in this work, an automated framework for classification and prioritization of unit failures. Our proposed methodology has two main steps.

- In the first stage, we use Daikon [9] to identify input constraints on the function under test, by mining invariants on the function boundary. Each invariant thus generated is assigned a confidence.
- In the second stage, we associate a belief value to each failure by analyzing the invariants the failures are in conflict with, and the respective confidence values. Failures with similar characteristics are put into the same classification group and assigned the same belief value. The idea behind this is motivated by the fact that failures conflicting with the same invariants might be manifestations of similar errors. The belief values enable us assign priorities to the failures and help us prioritize the bug fixing activity.

Figure 2 shows an overview of the overall architecture of our framework. This work is inspired by a similar article on ranking and classifying counterexamples produced for hardware logic code bugs in [14]. We performed an empirical evaluation of our framework on the replace program, which is a part of Siemens Benchmark Suite [3]. early experiments demonstrate that our proposed method works well in practice.

The rest of this paper is organized as follows. In Sect. 2, we illustrate our overall approach on a motivating example. Section 3 presents the detailed methodology. Section 4 presents our implementation, while Sect. 5 is a discussion on our evaluation results. Section 6 presents a review of related work. Section 7 concludes the paper.

2   Overview

In this section, we present an overview of our approach using an illustrative example, as shown in Figs. 3 and 4. The example consists of the *main* routine, along with two functions, namely, *div_by_f* and *gcd*.

```
1  //Program: S, Targeted module:
       div_by_f ( int  c,  int  f)
2
3  int  main(int  argc  ,char* argv []){
4
5       int  s,t,a,v;
6
7       scanf("%d %d %d",&s,&t,&a);
8
9       v = gcd(s,t);
10
11      x = div_by_f(s, v);
12
13      switch(a)
14      {
15          case 1:
16              x = div_by_f(t, v);
17              break;
18
19          case 2:
20              x = div_by_f(s, v);
21              break;
22
23          case 3:
24              x = div_by_f(s+t, v);
25              break;
26
27          case 4:
28              x = div_by_f(s*t, v*v);
29              break;
30      }
31      assert(x != 0);
32      return 0;
33  }
```

Fig. 3. main

```
1  // function-under-test
2  int div_by_f (int  c,  int  f) {
3       int  i = 0, result;
4
5       if (c > 0){
6           i = c + 20*f;
7           printf("%d",i);
8       }
9
10      if (i%f != 0 || f == 0)
11          return 0;  // error
12
13      result = i/f;
14
15      if(result < 0)
16          return 0;  // error
17
18      return result;
19  }
20
21  // gcd function
22  int gcd(int  u,  int  v) {
23      int  t;
24      if(v == 0) v = u;
25      while (v) {
26          t = u;
27          u = v;
28          v = t % v;
29      }
30      u = u < 0 ? -u : u;
31      /* abs(u) */
32
33      return u == 0 ? 1: u;
34  }
```

Fig. 4. function-under-test

We consider the case when the function *div_by_f* is being verified in isolation. This function is expected to compute a function of the input parameters c and f and return a non-zero value. We wish to verify whether the function code guarantees that the value returned is always non-zero. A scenario in which this function returns zero is considered a failure and needs to be examined.

If we look at *div_by_f* in isolation, it is evident that there are multiple ways in which this function can end up returning a value 0. A unit validation tool (a unit tester like CUTE/CREST [16,17] or a model checker like BLAST [11]), working on *div_by_f* in isolation, can end up generating scenarios (valuations of c and f), which induce a flow of control in *div_by_f* that reach the *return 0* statements. Following are some valuations generated, all of which lead to failures.

- c = 11,   f = 2
- c = -189, f = 9
- c = 10,   f = 0

The unit verifier, having no knowledge of the conditions under which a call to *div_by_f()* is made, looks at all the above as valid failures. Let us now look

```
1   =========================================
2   ..div_by_f():::ENTER
3
4   f >= 1              confidence = 0.9
5
6   c % f == 0          confidence = 0.7
7   =========================================
```

Fig. 5. Invariants generated by Daikon

closely at the failures, and examine if these valuations are at all possible, when the function is considered as part of *main*, and not an isolated piece of code. Indeed, each program point in *main*, from where this function is called, may present different valuations and contexts, which in turn may induce different flows inside *div_by_f*. A close examination of *main*, reveals that there are some invariants which are guaranteed to hold whenever *div_by_f* is called, no matter from which point in *main*. This immediately allows us to analyze the earlier reported failures in a more informed setting. Consider failure 1 for example. This is never possible in the current piece of code, since at all invocation points of *div_by_f* inside main, the condition $c \% f == 0$ is ensured since either f is the gcd of c and some other number or f is a factor of c.

Our Strategy: Our objective is to classify the failures as real or spurious. We use two main steps to do this, namely (a) Invariant Mining and (b) Failure Belief assignment and classification. Below, we explain briefly how this works on the above example.

Invariant Mining: A program invariant is a property that is true at a particular program point or points [9]. Despite their advantages, invariants are usually missing from programs. An alternative to expecting programmers to fully annotate code with invariants is to automatically infer likely invariants from the program itself. Invariant detection recovers a hidden part of the design space: the invariants that hold over all possible executions. This can be done either statically or dynamically. Static analysis examines the program text and reasons over the possible executions and runtime states. Static approaches are not scalable and hence not used widely in practice. A dynamic invariant detector runs a program, observes the values that the program computes, and then reports properties that were true over the observed executions. It does not suffer from the scalability drawbacks faced by static analysis and so complements static analysis. Our work, in this paper, uses Daikon [9], a dynamic invariant miner.

Invariants at the interface of *div_by_f*() are mined using Daikon. Invariants capture conditions on inputs fed to *div_by_f*() by *main*, and thus give the details of the environment for *div_by_f*() provided by *main*. Since the invariants are mined dynamically from execution traces of the program, each invariant has an associated confidence. The confidence assignment method is discussed in detail in the following section. Dynamic invariants, as mined on the example on inputs c, f of function *div_by_f*(*int c, int f*) are given in Fig. 5.

Failure Belief assignment and classification: Based on the dynamic invariants and their confidence values, we associate a belief value to each failure, based on their conflicts with the invariant set. The intuition behind this measure will be explained in the following section. Failures which contradict invariants of high confidence are given lower belief values. Also, failures which conflict with exactly the same set of invariants are put into one classification group.

We now consider each failure for *div_by_f*(*int c, int f*) and illustrate the belief assignment step.

Failure 1: $[c = 11, f = 2]$

When *div_by_f*() is called with this valuation, the inputs contradict the input constraints imposed by the invariant $c \% f == 0$. We want to associate a belief to this failure based on what we know of the environment. If this failure has to be true, then the high confidence invariant (reported with confidence 0.7) from Daikon has to be false. Hence, the belief of this failure to be real is calculated to be 0.3 using the following expression:

$$[1 - confidence(c \% f == 0)]$$

Failure 2: $[c = -189, f = 9]$

The input valuation does not contradict any of the input constraints imposed by the invariants and is likely to be real. We give a belief of 1.0 to failures that do not contradict any of the invariants.

Failure 3: $[c = 10, f = 0]$

This input valuation contradicts both the invariants $c \% f == 0$ and $f >= 1$. This failure can be true only when both the invariants are false in the same execution. We thus combine the likelihood of *both* the invariants to be false in the expression below. In this case, the belief evaluates to .03 using the following expression:

$$[1 - confidence(c \% f == 0)] * [1 - confidence(f >= 1))]$$

Thus, when presenting these failures to a developer for debugging, they will be presented in the following order:

```
unit-under-test:div_by_f()
[c = -189, f = 9]:    belief = 1.0    rank = 1
[c = 11, f = 2]:      belief = 0.3    rank = 2
[c = 10, f = 0]:      belief = 0.03   rank = 3
```

The first failure is presented as the most promising one since it does not contradict any invariant known from the function environment, and hence has a high likelihood to be a real failure. The third failure, on the other hand, contradicts two high confidence invariants, and is less likely to be real.

3   Detailed Methodology

This section presents the proposed formal approach behind our methodology.
Given:

1. A software code-base $\mathcal{B}$
2. A function $\mathcal{G}$ invoked from different points in $\mathcal{B}$
3. A set of unit failures $\mathcal{F} = \{F_i\}$ reported on $\mathcal{G}$ when examined in isolation

Our objective:

– To group failures into families
– To associate a belief metric with each failure, and order these families based on the belief measure.

Our methodology has three main steps:

– Invariant Mining
– Confidence Assignment to Invariants
– Failure classification and belief assignment

In the following subsections, we describe each of the above steps in detail.

3.1   Invariant Mining

We use Daikon, a dynamic invariant miner to mine dynamic invariants on the interface of $\mathcal{G}$. $\mathcal{B}$ interacts with $\mathcal{G}$ by passing variables as input to $\mathcal{G}$. By mining invariants on this interface, we get a summary of the environment provided by $\mathcal{B}$ to $\mathcal{G}$. We consider multiple test cases on $\mathcal{B}$, and collect the corresponding execution traces of $\mathcal{B}$. These traces are used as input to Daikon to get invariants on inputs of $\mathcal{G}$.

3.2   Confidence Assignment to Invariants

Given a set of dynamic invariants reported by Daikon, we now need to assign a confidence measure to each invariant, which expresses the likelihood of it being true in the actual code. Since the invariants are based on observed patterns in the execution dump, the confidence should be based on the extent of the different program control and data flow exercised by the tests used for collecting program executions on which Daikon works. If the proportion of program possibilities explored is low, the invariants should be assigned low confidence values, since any unexplored program path may render the invariant false. Also, the confidence assignment measure needs to take into account the number of ways an invariant can be satisfied in reality, and the proportion of the satisfying valuations encountered in the executions. It is worthwhile to note an important guarantee that Daikon gives: for a reported invariant $\mathcal{I}$, no instance satisfying the negation of $\mathcal{I}$ has been observed. As noted in [1], Daikon has a metric for confidence assignment, which has some inherent weaknesses. We therefore, devised our own confidence assignment metric, as explained below.

We want to associate a confidence measure to each of the mined invariants. As noted above, these reported invariants do not have a single evidence of their violation in our execution traces. Given a reported invariant $\mathcal{I}$, there are multiple ways of satisfying $\mathcal{I}$, some (but may not be all) of which have been observed on the execution traces. Consider, for example, the invariant $x > 5$, where x is an integer, which can take any integral value between -8 and 8. There are 3 values of x which satisfy this invariant, namely, 6, 7, and 8. Hence, the number of distinct satisfying valuations we can witness on the execution traces is 3. However, it may be the case that we actually encounter multiple occurrences of some of the satisfying valuations, which should ideally boost our confidence. Also, we would like to see occurrences of all the 3 satisfying scenarios in the execution runs. Hence, a good confidence measure ψ should consider the following factors:

- ψ should increase with the number of instances of a satisfying valuation
- ψ should also increase with the diversity of the observed valuations that satisfy the invariant.

We first define a confidence measure for each of the satisfying scenarios and then we aggregate the coefficients corresponding to all the satisfying scenarios that satisfy the invariant. Our confidence measure for a particular scenario is similar to the idea of Bayesian strength function proposed in [10]. Let p be the probability that when a particular scenario is observed, there will be no violation in the execution traces. In Bayesian analysis, instead of considering p to be fixed and non-random, one considers a prior distribution $\pi(p)$ for p. As in [10], we consider this prior to be uniform over the (0,1) interval, i.e. $\pi(p) = 1$ for $p \in [0, 1]$. Note that this prior is non-informative, and it gives no preference to any particular value of p. Now, let us define a random variable X that denotes the number of times the scenario is observed. Suppose that, we have observed this scenario n times, and in none of these cases, any violation is reported. Given a value of p, the probability of this event is given by $P(X = n \mid p) = p^n$. Now, given that event, we compute the posterior distribution of p and calculate $P(p > \alpha \mid X = n)$, the conditional probability that p exceeds a threshold α (typically α lies in the (0.5,1) interval), which is given by

$$\psi_\alpha(n) = P(p > \alpha \mid X = n) = \int_\alpha^1 p^n dp / \int_0^1 p^n dp = 1 - \alpha^{n+1}.$$

It is clear from the above definition that $\psi_\alpha(n)$ takes values in the $[1 - \alpha, 1]$ interval. It takes the minimum value $1 - \alpha$ when $n = 0$, gradually increases with

n, and takes a value close to 1 when n is large. If there are k such scenarios that satisfy the invariant and the i-th ($i =, 2, \ldots, k$) scenario is observed n_i times, the belief coefficient for the invariant is given by

$$\psi_\alpha(n_1, n_2, \ldots, n_k) = \sum_{i=1}^{k} \psi_\alpha(n_i)/k = \frac{1}{k} \sum_{i=1}^{k} (1 - \alpha^{n_i+1}).$$

Note that k is finite, since we are dealing with invariants over finite domain data types. Like $\psi_\alpha(n)$, $\psi_\alpha(n_1, n_2, \ldots, n_k)$ also takes values in the $[1 - \alpha, 1]$ interval, and it is strictly monotonically increasing function of its arguments. Since $\psi_\alpha(n_1, n_2, \ldots, n_k)$ is symmetric in its arguments, it gives equal importance to all satisfying scenarios. Also note that $\psi_\alpha(n_1, n_2) > \psi_\alpha(0, n_1 + n_2) = \psi_\alpha(n_1 + n_2, 0)$, which indicates that instead of observing the same scenario repeatedly, we prefer to observe different scenarios relatively less of number of times. Therefore, this confidence measure also takes care of the coverage of the scenarios satisfying the invariant.

For a reported invariant $\mathcal{I}$, we enumerate the number of satisfying scenarios possible, and count the actual number of occurrences of each of these scenarios. The expression above allows us to assign a confidence to $\mathcal{I}$, as a function of α.

3.3   Failure Classification and Belief Assignment

For each failure $\mathcal{F}_i$, we now examine the invariants to assign a belief measure to it. A failure in conflict with a large set of invariants is less likely to be real. The idea behind this is that invariants serve as our eyesight to the environment provided by the entire code base. If a failure is not in agreement with this environment, then it is possibly a false failure which is not feasible. The additional issue to be addressed when using dynamic invariants instead of static is, although dynamic invariants hold across all the traces from which they are mined, a dynamic invariant may not hold across an execution which is not yet seen. To address this issue, we use the confidence measure associated with each dynamic invariant (as explained above), to compute the belief measure (i.e. the likelihood) of a failure.

Assigning a Belief Measure to a Failure: Given a failure $\mathcal{F}_i$ and a set of dynamic invariants $\mathcal{I} = \mathcal{I}_j$, each associated with a confidence $\psi(\mathcal{I}_i)$, we compute the belief of $\mathcal{F}_i$ in two steps, as below.

- *Identify the invariants which are in conflict with $\mathcal{F}_i$:* If the failure is true, then the conflicting invariants must all be untrue. Let $\mathbb{CI}_{\mathcal{F}_i}$ be the set of invariants in $\mathcal{I}$ which are in conflict with $\mathcal{F}_i$.
- *Calculate the belief of $\mathcal{F}_i$:* If $\mathbb{CI}_{\mathcal{F}_i}$ is empty, then we associate a belief measure of 1.0 to the failure, as in Failure 2 in our example in Sect. 2. Otherwise, the belief on $\mathcal{F}_i$ is computed as:

$$\pi(\mathcal{F}_i) = \Pi_{I_j \in \mathbb{CI}_{\mathcal{F}_i}} (1 - \psi(I_j))$$

The intuitive meaning of this metric is as follows. If any of the invariants in $\mathbb{CI}_{\mathcal{F}_i}$ is valid, then $\mathcal{F}_i$, which contradicts it, cannot be a real failure. Therefore, based on available evidence, $\mathcal{F}_i$ can be a real failure, if each invariant in $\mathbb{CI}_{\mathcal{F}_i}$ is not valid. $\psi(I_j)$ models the likelihood that I_j is valid based on available evidence, and hence $\pi(\mathcal{F}_i)$ computes the joint probability that all invariants in $\mathbb{CI}_{\mathcal{F}_i}$ are invalid. Π denotes the product operation.

In the approach proposed in this paper, we assume that the invariants are independent of each other, and hence the joint probability distribution is as given above.

Failure Classification Groups: All failures in conflict with exactly the same set of invariants are put together in a classification group. In other words, two failures $\mathcal{F}_i$ and $\mathcal{F}_j$ with $\mathbb{CI}_{\mathcal{F}_i} = \mathbb{CI}_{\mathcal{F}_j}$ are put into the same classification group. Each member in the same group has the same belief measure, and therefore, the group is assigned the same measure.

The groups are ranked according to their belief measures and presented arranged in priority order. The highest belief failure group is assigned the rank 1.

4 Implementation

Our framework includes the following steps: invariant mining, confidence assignment, failure grouping and ranking. In addition, we also used unit testing tools (CREST [16] and KLEE [2]) to generate the unit failures. If the unit failures are already available, this step is not needed. We explain the detail of the failure generation step below, followed by a detailed discussion of the rest.

4.1 Failure Extraction

We explain here our experience with CREST. The steps with KLEE are somewhat different and excluded here due to lack of space. Crest [5] is an open source Concolic Testing Engine for C, a reimplementation of CUTE (Concolic Unit Testing Engine) [16]. It uses CIL (C Intermediate Language written in Ocaml) to insert instrumentation code into a given program and perform symbolic execution in parallel with concrete execution to explore all feasible program paths. It uses Yices [4] to solve symbolic constraints and generate inputs which enable CREST to explore unique paths. At present, it supports only linear and integer arithmetic and has no support for pointers/dereferences and bitwise operators.

For testing with CREST, we need to include crest.h in the target program and use CREST_type(x) to mark symbolic variables, where type can be int, short, char, unsigned_int, unsigned_char or unsigned_short. Then crestc (crest compiler) is to be run on the target source code to enable CREST perform instrumentation. Once this is done, run_crest (which performs the symbolic execution for crest based on the provided parameters) will run the program executable with a search strategy. CREST provides 5 search strategies, namely, depth first search, nearest uncovered branch first, random-negated branch randomly selected, uniform_random and random_input.

By default CREST produces one input file and one coverage file which contains the last input and branch coverage information. *We tweaked the source code of CREST in our work to make CREST output multiple input combinations and coverage information for all runs in a separate file.*

4.2   Invariant Mining

Daikon [9] is a dynamic invariant detector which reports likely program invariants in C, C++, Java, and Perl programs, and in record-structured data sources. It is easy to extend Daikon to other applications. It generates only those invariants whose confidence is above the threshold value set (we set it to 0 to get all invariants) and outputs the confidence associated with each invariant so produced. Examples of invariants include being constant $(x = a)$, non-zero $(x \neq 0)$, being in a range $(a \leq x \leq b)$, linear relationships $(y = ax + b)$, ordering $(x \leq y)$, functions from a library $(x = fn(y))$, containment $(x \in y)$, sortedness $(x \ is \ sorted)$, and many more.

For each test case for $\mathcal{B}$, we first run the kvasir front-end tool (also known as instrumenter or tracer) on the software $\mathcal{B}$ which results in production of separate *.dtrace* and *.decls* files corresponding to the execution trace for each test case. Before using kvasir, the software has to be compiled with the $gdwarf - 2$ flag enabled to produce $DWARF - 2$ format debugging information along with the program. A *.dtrace* file contains information about a particular execution of the program, the values of the program variables at each program point. A *.decls* file consists of the information about what variables and functions exist in a program, along with information grouping the variables into abstract types.

Next we use java *daikon.Daikon* to produce a single *.inv* file which contains all invariants found over all the execution traces in binary format. There are numerous control, optimization and debugging options available with Daikon that have been used to produce suitable invariants for our purpose. The confidence threshold was set to 0 so that we can work with all kinds of invariants. For our program, we focused on only a targeted unit module and mined invariants over the module interface.

4.3   Confidence Assignment, Failure Grouping and Ranking

Once the invariants are obtained, we also collect the different scenarios encountered in support of each invariant in the execution run. We also compute the number of satisfying scenarios possible for each invariant, and hence, we have all the information to compute our confidence measure. We do this using a simple Java routine.

For the purpose of grouping and ranking, we designed a simple Java program which takes the failures, the invariants along with the confidence values as input, and produces the set of failure groups arranged in decreasing order of belief values.

5   Evaluation

We now report our experience in using our method for grouping and ranking failures on the replace program (written in C) from the Siemens Benchmark Suite [3].

Generating Unit Failures with CREST: We considered *replace* as the top level code $\mathcal{B}$. The replace program searches for the occurrence of a given string in a file and replaces it by another given string and displays the result to standard output. We tested the function *dodash*() (unit function $\mathcal{G}$) in the replace program and found that it contains some stack smashing errors and a few memory out of bound errors for particular combination of inputs. The function *dodash*() has 6 parameters: two integer pointers, two character arrays, one character and one integer. For testing with CREST, we declare all these variables as symbolic using $CREST\_type(x)$ where type is the variable data type. We fix the length of two character arrays at 5 for this setup as CREST cannot symbolically create arrays of arbitrary length. Also it must be remembered that CREST cannot support pointers/dereferences. So we created two integers and made them symbolic using CREST. Then we used the address of those integers as inputs to *dodash*(). Given below is the instrumented code for running CREST. This will further clarify our methodology.

```
main()
{
    char delim;
    char src[5];
    int i;
    char dest[5];
    int j;
    int maxset;

    CREST_char(delim);
    CREST_char(src[0]);
    CREST_char(src[1]);
    CREST_char(src[2]);
    CREST_char(src[3]);
    CREST_char(src[4]);
    CREST_int(i);
    CREST_char(dest[0]);
    CREST_char(dest[1]);
    CREST_char(dest[2]);
    CREST_char(dest[3]);
    CREST_char(dest[4]);
    CREST_int(j);
    CREST_int(maxset);
    dodash(delim, src, &i, dest, &j, maxset);
}
```

We compiled the code using CREST using *crestc* (crest compiler).

> crestc replace.c -o replace

The next step was to *run_crest* over the executable file thus produced.

> run_crest ./replace 1000 -dfs

Here 1000 refers to the maximum number of iterations that CREST must use during path exploration using the depth first search strategy (specified here by dfs flag). CREST, by default, produces a single input and coverage file with the information about the last iteration only. We edited the source code of CREST to make it produce input and coverage information for input valuations and branch coverage information produced during each iteration of CREST, corresponding to multiple executions. In 58 of these executions (produced by CREST and KLEE), the program produced stack smashing and memory out-of-bound errors and the program was terminated. We extracted these 58 test cases from the *inputs* file and used them as failures for our work.

Invariant Mining with Daikon: The next step was to mine invariants over the interface of the function *dodash*() using Daikon. We used the test cases provided by the Siemens benchmark suite to train Daikon. We used the kvasir front end tool to produce *.decls* and *.dtrace* files for each run of the program. Invariants were mined from the generated trace and declaration files combined. We set the confidence threshold to 0, so that Daikon reports back all kinds of invariants found. In addition, we used the option *-ppt-select-pattern = "dodash*"* to force Daikon report only the invariants found over the program points corresponding to our target function *dodash*(). An additional option, *config_option daikon.Daikon.print_sample_totals = true* was enabled to print the total number of all kinds of samples (variable values) found during the operation. All invariants found at the entry and exit points of the function *dodash*() over all executions were reported.

It is quite expected that the nature and number of the invariants will vary with increase in the number of executions. The number of invariants drops as more executions are encountered, since many of them encounter refutations with new program paths and valuations being explored. Figure 6 shows the results of our invariant mining exercise. The vertical axis plots the number of invariants, while the horizontal axis shows the number of Daikon runs used for mining. As shown in the figure, Daikon reported 13 invariants when 100 executions were considered, but the number dropped gradually and finally reached 6 when 5000 program executions were considered.

Confidence Measures of Invariants: Not only does the number of invariants vary, the confidence measures vary as well with the number of Daikon runs. Figure 7 shows the confidence plot for the 6 invariants surviving after 5000 Daikon runs (as shown in Fig. 6). The confidence values for the invariants *delim == 93* and *maxset == 100* are same, hence, they are indistinguishable in the plot. For this experiment, we scaled up the confidence values for the first four

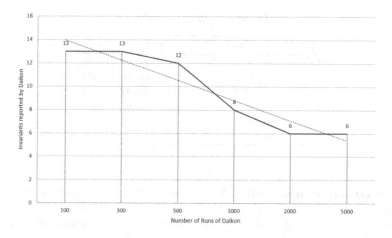

Fig. 6. Number of invariants reported by Daikon

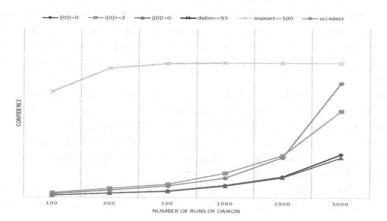

Fig. 7. Confidence Plot

invariants (as per Table 1) to demonstrate how the confidence values change with increasing runs.

The exact confidence values found for each of the 6 invariants is shown in Table 1. In the program being tested, i and j are pointers to integers. Daikon represents the values pointed to by i and j as i[0] and j[0] respectively. Also Daikon, being based on Java platform, represents the two character arrays 'src' and 'dest' as two strings and reports an invariant (src < dest) based on the lexicographical comparison of the two strings, 'src' and 'dest' are therefore, not positions of char arrays in memory as is the usual case in the C language.

It may be noted that the confidence measures were calculated only for invariants involving variables with finite domains. For example, in C, integers are allotted a size of 32 bits. Invariants involving pointers were not considered in this work.

Table 1. Confidence values

Inv no.	Invariant	Confidence
1	$i[0] \neq 0$	0.0100000064206967
2	$i[0] \geq 2$	0.0100000128413934
3	$j[0] \neq 0$	0.0100000059285127
4	src < dest	0.0102976672794117
5	delim == 93	1.0
6	maxset == 100	1.0

Failure Grouping and Belief Assignment: We now report on the failure grouping and belief assignment activity for the 58 failures considered by us. Figure 8 shows the number of groups formed with increasing number of Daikon runs. Each group consists of 1 or more of the 58 failures. It is interesting to note that initially, 10 groups were formed by collecting failures in conflict with exactly the same set of invariants. The number of groups remains same for less than 1000 runs (though a few invariants get dropped). As the number of runs increases, beyond 1000, the number of groups formed drops to 9 (due to some invariants being falsified leading to groups getting merged) and remains so till 5000 runs.

Table 2 shows the details of the 9 groups formed, considering all the 5000 executions. Column 1 of the table reports the group number, while the next column reports the set of invariants (out of the 6 reported at the end of 5000 executions as in Table 1) that this group is in conflict with. The third column shows the number of failures belonging to the group, while the final column is the belief value assigned to it by our method.

Out of the 58 failures considered, 15 were actually real failures (verified by us). All these 15 failures were in group 6, which was assigned a likelihood measure

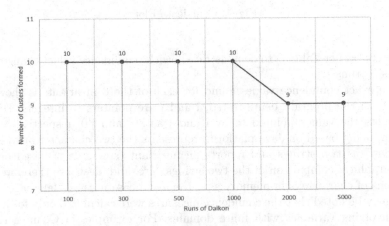

Fig. 8. Classification grouping plot

Table 2. Failure Group details

Group no.	Inv. contradicted by the group/(inv no.)	Group size	Belief
1	3, 6, 4, 5	1	0.0
2	4, 5, 6	6	0.0
3	1, 2, 4, 5, 6	5	0.0
4	1, 2, 3, 4, 5	4	0.0
5	5, 6	1	0.0
6	4	15	0.99
7	1, 2, 4, 5	3	0.0
8	1, 2, 3, 4, 5, 6	12	0.0
9	1, 2, 4, 6	11	0.0

of 0.99. All the other groups (containing the remaining 43 failures) were assigned the likelihood value 0 by our method, which were actually spurious.

6 Related Work

There has been quite a number of research attempts towards test case prioritization and clustering. Test case prioritization techniques are typically heuristics as it may be a difficult objective, with the goal to optimize rate of fault detection. Various heuristics that have already been explored for a specific objective function [15] are randomized ordering, prioritizing in order of coverage of branches, prioritizing in order of coverage of branches not yet covered, prioritizing in order of total probability of exposing faults, prioritizing in order of total probability of exposing faults adjusted to consider effects of previous tests prioritizing in order of coverage of statements, prioritizing in order of coverage of statements not yet covered. Many more have been suggested in [8].

Since a large number of reported bugs or crashes tend to be false alarms, prioritizing reported bugs has also been extensively discussed. Often, many factors are considered to indicate the importance of a bug to be diagnosed, such as the complexity of the method the bug relates to, the correlations among certain bugs, the frequency of certain bug patterns, the feedback from inspectors. A lot of research articles propose to learn from historical results, such as techniques reported in [12,13,19]. EFindBugs [19] clusters bug reports based on identified bug patterns, whereas Feedback-Ranking [13] utilizes code locality to infer correlations among reported bugs. On the other hand, researchers in [12] predict correlations from method calls. Both ReBucket [7] and the technique reported by Seo and Kim [18] analyze crash stack traces and call stacks to identify whether certain crash reports are related to the same bug. Crash reports are then clustered based on their related bugs.

Our work has notable differences with those proposed in literature. Our approach dynamically groups and orders unit bugs based on their trigger inputs, and utilize the collected information to cluster and prioritize test data. The idea of ranking counterexamples has been proposed in [14] for ranking counterexamples produced in a module checking flow. The overall approach presented in this work is closely similar, with a different ranking metric used by us. In addition, we address the problem in a generic software validation framework and our results are inspired by unit testing in software.

7 Conclusion

This paper presents a grouping and prioritization framework for unit failures produced on a program module. We use the knowledge obtained from a dynamic invariant miner to assign a belied measure to each failure, and group similar failures. Finally, we order the failure groups according to their likelihood values. Experimental results are promising on one benchmark that we used for this work. We are currently evaluating our method on more benchmarks. We believe that our method will have good benefits in filtering spurious failure alarms in a unit validation environment.

Acknowledgement. This work was partially supported by The Open Project of Shanghai Key Laboratory of Trustworthy Computing (No. 07dz22304201201).

References

1. Daikon Invariant Detector. http://groups.csail.mit.edu/pag/daikon/download/doc/daikon.html
2. Klee. http://klee.llvm.org/
3. Siemens Benchmarks. http://pleuma.cc.gatech.edu/aristotle/Tools/subjects/
4. The yices smt solver. http://yices.csl.sri.com/
5. Burnim, J., Sen, K.: Heuristics for scalable dynamic test generation. In: ASE, pp. 443–446 (2008)
6. Chaki, S., Clarke, E., Giannakopoulou, D., Psreanu, C.S.: Abstraction and assume-guarantee reasoning for automated software verification. Technical report (2004)
7. Dang, Y., Wu, R., Zhang, H., Zhang, D., Nobel, P.: Rebucket: a method for clustering duplicate crash reports based on call stack similarity. In: ICSE, pp. 1084–1093 (2012)
8. Elbaum, S.G., Malishevsky, A.G., Rothermel, G.: Test case prioritization: a family of empirical studies. IEEE Trans. Softw. Eng. **28**(2), 159–182 (2002)
9. Ernst, M.D., Perkins, J.H., Guo, P.J., McCamant, S., Pacheco, C., Tschantz, M.S., Xiao, C.: The daikon system for dynamic detection of likely invariants. Sci. Comput. Program. **69**(1–3), 35–45 (2007)
10. Ghosh, A.K., Chaudhuri, P., Murthy, C.A.: On visualization and aggregation of nearest neighbor classifiers. IEEE Trans. Pattern Anal. Mach. Intell. **27**(10), 1592–1602 (2005)
11. Henzinger, T.A., Jhala, R., MAjumdar, R., Sutre, G.: Lazy abstraction. In: POPL, pp. 58–70 (2002)
12. Kim, D., Wang, X., Kim, S., Zeller, A., Cheung, S.C., Park, S.: Which crashes should I fix first?: predicting top crashes at an early stage to prioritize debugging efforts. IEEE Trans. Softw. Eng. **37**(3), 430–447 (2011)

13. Kremenek, T., Ashcraft, K., Yang, J., Engler, D.R.: Correlation exploitation in error ranking. In: SIGSOFT FSE, pp. 83–93 (2004)
14. Mitra, S., Banerjee, A., Dasgupta, P.: Formal methods for ranking counterexamples through assumption mining. In: DATE, pp. 911–916 (2012)
15. Rothermel, G., Untch, R.H., Chu, C., Harrold, M.J.: Test case prioritization: an empirical study. In: ICSM, pp. 179–188 (1999)
16. Sen, K., Agha, G.: CUTE and jCUTE: concolic unit testing and explicit path model-checking tools. In: Ball, T., Jones, R.B. (eds.) CAV 2006. LNCS, vol. 4144, pp. 419–423. Springer, Heidelberg (2006)
17. Sen, K., Marinov, D., Agha, G.: Cute: a concolic unit testing engine for c. In: ESEC/SIGSOFT FSE, pp. 263–272 (2005)
18. Seo, H., Kim, S.: Predicting recurring crash stacks. In: ASE, pp. 180–189 (2012)
19. Shen, H., Fang, J., Zhao, J.: Efindbugs: effective error ranking for findbugs. In: ICST, pp. 299–308 (2011)

Adapting Component-Based Systems
at Runtime via Policies with Temporal Patterns

Olga Kouchnarenko[1,2] and Jean-François Weber[1(✉)]

[1] FEMTO-ST CNRS and University of Franche-Comté, Besançon, France
{okouchnarenko,jfweber}@femto-st.fr
[2] Inria/Nancy-Grand Est, Villers-les-Nancy, France

Abstract. Dynamic reconfiguration allows adding or removing components of component-based systems without incurring any system downtime. To satisfy specific requirements, adaptation policies provide the means to dynamically reconfigure the systems in relation to (events in) their environment. This paper extends event-based adaptation policies by integrating temporal requirements into them. The challenge is to reconfigure component-based systems at runtime while considering both their functional and non-functional requirements. We illustrate our theoretical contributions with an example of an autonomous vehicle location system. An implementation using the Fractal component model constitutes a practical contribution. It enables dynamic reconfigurations guided by either enforcement or reflection adaptation policies.

1 Introduction

Dynamic reconfiguration is a mechanism that allows components of component-based systems to be added to or removed without incurring any system downtime. The challenge is to build or maintain trustworthy systems which satisfy both functional and non-functional requirements.

Let us illustrate the adaptation and reconfiguration needs on a characteristic example inspired from a real case study in the land transportation domain. The example concerns the Cybercar concept, a public transport system with automated driving capabilities. Within the autonomous vehicle case study, a location composite component — a critical part of land transportation systems — is made up of different positioning systems, like GPS or Wi-Fi. Thanks to adaptation policies, the location composite component architecture can be modified to use either GPS, Wi-Fi, or GPS+Wi-Fi positioning systems, depending on some non-functional properties, such as available energy.

Recent implementations to support the development of component-based systems, like those for the Fractal reference implementation Julia[1] or for GCM[2], tend to provide mechanisms for the execution of high-level adaptation policies.

This work has been partially funded by the Labex ACTION, ANR-11-LABX-01-01.

[1] http://fractal.objectweb.org/julia/index.html
[2] http://gridcomp.ercim.org/

J.L. Fiadeiro et al. (Eds.): FACS 2013, LNCS 8348, pp. 234–253, 2014.
DOI: 10.1007/978-3-319-07602-7_15, © Springer International Publishing Switzerland 2014

Adaptation polices implemented in Tangram4Fractal [1], triggered by qualitative expressions of fuzzy logic (e.g., "power is *low*"), do not allow expressing temporal constraints. In [2,3], the authors have introduced a component-based system model equipped with either (*a*) adaptation policies using qMEDL[3] logic [4] or (*b*) a linear temporal logic, called FTPL[4], expressing architectural constraints, events, and temporal patterns [3]. FTPL, based on Dwyer's work on patterns and scopes [5], and being more expressive than qMDEL at providing temporal schemas, this paper proposes to bridge the gap between [2] and [3].

Our main contribution is the use of FTPL logic for triggering adaptation policies and specifying behaviours of the system under scrutiny. As a practical contribution, we have implemented these more expressive adaptation policies to guide and control dynamic reconfigurations via enforcement and reflection adaptation policies. When a violation of a property is detected, the reflection's purpose is to reconfigure the system to mitigate, if possible, the failure, whereas the enforcement aims to circumvent property violations.

Furthermore, as temporal properties often cannot be evaluated to true or false during the system execution, and so cannot, *a fortiori*, the extended policies, this paper addresses this question by evaluating at runtime, in a progressive manner, both temporal properties and extended policies. To this end, like in RV-LTL [6], in addition to *true* and *false* values, *potential true* and *potential false* values are used whenever an observed behaviour has not yet led to an acceptance or a violation of the property under consideration.

Layout of the paper. Section 2 introduces our motivating example, a component model, and its operational semantics, while Sect. 3 covers a temporal pattern logic over reconfiguration sequences. In Sect. 4, linear temporal patterns are integrated into adaptation policies. The evaluation at runtime of both temporal properties and extended—reflection and enforcement—adaptation policies is presented in Sect. 5. We show that these mechanisms guarantee a system's behaviour allowed by the initial system specification (correctness result). Finally, an implementation allowing the user to deal with the Fractal component model is described in Sect. 6. Section 7 presents our conclusion.

2   Motivating Example and Background

Component models can be very heterogeneous. Most of them consider software components that can be seen as black boxes (or grey boxes if some of their inner features are visible) having fully described interfaces. Behaviours and interactions are specified using components' definitions and their interfaces. In this section, after introducing a motivating example, we revisit the architectural reconfiguration model introduced in [3,7]. In general, the system configuration is the specific definition of the elements that define or prescribe what a system

---

[3] qMEDL is a flavor of MEDL used to express quantity of resource properties.

[4] FTPL stands for TPL (Temporal Pattern Language) prefixed by 'F' to denote its relation to Fractal-like components and to first-order integrity constraints over them.

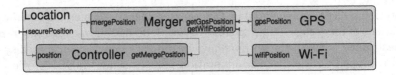

Fig. 1. The location component in Fractal

is composed of, while a reconfiguration can be seen a transition from a configuration to another.

Motivating Example. The development, validation, and certification of a new type of urban vehicles with fully or partially automated driving capabilities, like CyCab [8] or Cristal[5] aimed at replacing the private car, are a challenging issue. These distributed and embedded systems require the expression of functional as well as non-functional properties, for example time-constrained response, QoS, and availability of required services.

A positioning system is a critical part of a land transportation system. Many positioning systems have been proposed over the past few years. Among them, we can mention GPS, GALILEO or GLONASS positioning systems which belong to the Global Navigation Satellite Systems (GNSS, for short). Other localisation systems have been designed using various technologies, like Wireless personal networks such as Bluetooth, sensors, GNSS repeaters, or visual landmarks.

Figure 1 gives an abstract view of a composite location component developed within the Fractal component framework. This component includes several positioning systems, like GPS or Wi-Fi, a controller, and a merger. Each positioning system is composed of an atomic positioning component and a software component to validate perceived data. The validation components transfer the positioning data to the merger if they are precise enough. The merger applies a particular algorithm to merge data obtained from positioning systems. Finally, the controller's purpose is to request and to acknowledge the receipt of positioning data.

Moreover, there is a need to make the system's architecture evolve at runtime. Reconfigurations, however, must not happen at any but suitable circumstances. The location composite component architecture can be modified to use, e.g., either GPS, or Wi-Fi, or GPS+Wi-Fi positioning systems, depending on some non-functional properties, such as available energy, and the events from the current indoor/outdoor environment. For example, the following requirement "After the GPS component has been removed, the level of energy has to be greater than 33 % before this component is added back" makes use of temporal and architectural constraints to allow the "with GPS" reconfiguration. Then, thanks to adaptation policies, several possible reconfigurations can be determined, and the most suitable reconfiguration can be chosen. For example, when the available energy makes both reconfigurations "with GPS" and "with GPS+Wi-Fi"

---

[5] http://www.projet-cristal.net/

possible within an adaptation policy, this policy can be used to put system's priorities to the "with GPS+Wi-Fi" reconfiguration, for more reliability.

Configurations. Following [3], we define a configuration to be a set of architectural elements (components, required or provided interfaces, and parameters) together with relations to structure and to link them.

Definition 1 (Configuration). *A configuration c is a tuple* $\langle Elem, Rel \rangle$ *where*

- $Elem = Components \uplus Interfaces \uplus Parameters \uplus Types$ *is a set of architectural elements, such that*
  - *Components is a non-empty set of the core entities, i.e., components;*
  - $Interfaces = RequiredInts \uplus ProvidedInts$ *is a finite set of the (required and provided) interfaces;*
  - *Parameters is a finite set of component parameters;*
  - $Types = ITypes \uplus PTypes$ *is a finite set of the interface types and the parameter data types;*
- $Rel = \begin{cases} Container \uplus ContainerType \uplus Contingency \\ \uplus Parent \uplus Binding \uplus Delegate \uplus State \uplus Value \end{cases}$
  is a set of architectural relations which link architectural elements, such that
  - $Container : Interfaces \uplus Parameters \rightarrow Components$ *is a total function giving the component which supplies the considered interface or the component of a considered parameter;*
  - $ContainerType : Interfaces \uplus Parameters \rightarrow Types$ *is a total function that associates a type to each (required or provided) interface and to each parameter;*
  - $Contingency : RequiredInts \rightarrow \{mandatory, optional\}$ *is a total function indicating whether each required interface is mandatory or optional;*
  - $Parent \subseteq Components \times Components$ *is a relation linking a sub-component to the corresponding composite component*[6]*;*
  - $Binding : ProvidedInts \rightarrow RequiredInts$ *is a partial function which binds together a provided interface and a required one;*
  - $Delegate : Interfaces \rightarrow Interfaces$ *is a partial function to express delegation links;*
  - $State : Components \rightarrow \{started, stopped\}$ *is a total function giving the status of instantiated components;*
  - $Value : Parameters \rightarrow \{t | t \in PType\}$ *is a total function which gives the current value of each parameter.*

Example 1. To illustrate our model, the example of Fig. 1 is described in Fig. 2.

We also introduce a set CP of configuration propositions on the architectural elements and the relations between them. These properties are specified using first-order logic formulae [9]. The interpretation of functions, relations, and predicates over $Elem$ is done according to basic definitions in [9] and Definition 1.

---

[6] For any $(p, q) \in Parent$, we say that q has a sub-component p, i.e., p is a child of q. Shared components (sub-components of multiple enclosing composite components) can have more than one parent.

$$
\begin{aligned}
Components &= \{controller, gps, location, merger, wifi\} \\
ProvidedInts &= \{gpsPosition, mergePosition, position, securePosition, wifiPosition\} \\
RequiredInts &= \{getGpsPosition, getMergePosition, getWifiPosition\} \\
Parameters &= \{GpsPowerUsage, Power, Trust, WifiPowerUsage\} \\
Types &= \{MergePosition, Position, SecurePosition, int\} \\
Container &= \{gpsPosition \mapsto gps, mergePosition \mapsto merger, position \mapsto controller, \\
&\qquad securePosition \mapsto location, wifiPosition \mapsto wifi, \\
&\qquad getGpsPosition \mapsto merger, getMergePosition \mapsto controller, \\
&\qquad getWifiPosition \mapsto merger, GpsPowerUsage \mapsto merger, \\
&\qquad Power \mapsto controller, Trust \mapsto merger, WifiPowerUsage \mapsto merger\} \\
ContainerType &= \{getGpsPosition \mapsto Position, getMergePosition \mapsto MergePosition, \\
&\qquad getWifiPosition \mapsto Position, gpsPosition \mapsto Position, \\
&\qquad mergePosition \mapsto MergePosition, position \mapsto SecurePosition, \\
&\qquad securePosition \mapsto SecurePosition, wifiPosition \mapsto Position, Trust \mapsto int, \\
&\qquad GpsPowerUsage \mapsto int, Power \mapsto int, WifiPowerUsage \mapsto int\} \\
Contingency &= \{getGpsPosition \mapsto optional, getMergePosition \mapsto mandatory, \\
&\qquad getWifiPosition \mapsto optional\} \\
Parent &= \{(controller, location), (gps, location), (merger, location), (wifi, location)\} \\
Binding &= \{gpsPosition \mapsto getGpsPosition, mergePosition \mapsto getMergePosition, \\
&\qquad wifiPosition \mapsto getWifiPosition\} \\
Delegate &= \{position \mapsto securePosition\} \\
State &= \{controller \mapsto started, gps \mapsto started, location \mapsto started, merger \mapsto started, \\
&\qquad wifi \mapsto started\} \\
Value &= \{GpsPowerUsage \mapsto 3, Power \mapsto 95, Trust \mapsto 0, WifiPowerUsage \mapsto 2\}
\end{aligned}
$$

Fig. 2. Configuration of the example of Fig. 1

Let $\mathcal{C} = \{c, c_1, c_2, \ldots\}$ be a set of configurations. We introduce an *interpretation* function $l : \mathcal{C} \to CP$ which gives the largest conjunction of $cp \in CP$ evaluated to true on $c \in \mathcal{C}$. We say that a configuration $c = \langle Elem, Rel \rangle$ satisfies $cp \in CP$, written $[\![\, c \models cp \,]\!] = \top$, when $l(c) \Rightarrow cp$. In this case, cp is valid on c. Otherwise, c does not satisfy cp, written $[\![\, c \models cp \,]\!] = \bot$.

Among all the configuration propositions, there are constraints common to all the component-based system architectures. They define *consistent* configurations. For example, two bound interfaces must have the same interface type and their suppliers must be sub-components of the same composite. These consistency constraints are respectively expressed by $\forall\, ip \in ProvidedInts, ir \in RequiredInts.$ $(Binding(ip) = ir \Rightarrow ContainerType(ip) = ContainerType(ir))$, and $\forall\, ip \in ProvidedInts, ir \in RequiredInts.$

$$
\left(Binding(ip) = ir \Rightarrow \left(\exists\, c \in Components. \left(\begin{matrix} (Container(ip), c) \in Parent \\ \wedge (Container(ir), c) \in Parent \end{matrix} \right) \right) \right)
$$

The reader interested in consistency constraints is referred to [7].

Reconfigurations. Reconfigurations make the component-based architecture evolve dynamically. They are combinations of primitive operations such as instantiation/destruction of components; addition/removal of components; binding/ unbinding of component interfaces; starting/stopping components; setting parameter values of components. The normal running of different components also changes the architecture, e.g., by modifying parameter values or stopping components. Let $\mathcal{R}_{run} = \mathcal{R} \cup \{run\}$ be a set of evolution operations, where $\mathcal{R}$ is a finite set of reconfiguration operations, and run is the name of a generic action used to represent all the running operations of the component-based system.

Definition 2 (Reconfiguration model). *The operational semantics of component-based systems with reconfigurations is defined by the labelled transition system* $S = \langle C, C^0, \mathcal{R}_{run}, \rightarrow, l \rangle$ *where* $C = \{c, c_1, c_2, \ldots\}$ *is a set of configurations,* $C^0 \subseteq C$ *is a set of initial configurations,* $\rightarrow \subseteq C \times \mathcal{R}_{run} \times C$ *is the reconfiguration relation, and* $l : C \rightarrow CP$ *is a total interpretation function.*

Let us note $c \xrightarrow{ope} c'$ for $(c, ope, c') \in \rightarrow$, and $c \xrightarrow{ope}$ when there is a target configuration c' such that $c \xrightarrow{ope} c'$. Given the model $S = \langle C, C^0, \mathcal{R}_{run}, \rightarrow, l \rangle$, an evolution path (or a path for short) σ of S is a sequence of configurations $c_0, c_1, c_2, \ldots$ such that $\forall i \geq 0.\ \exists\ ope_i \in \mathcal{R}_{run}.(c_i \xrightarrow{ope_i} c_{i+1})$. We write $\sigma(i)$ to denote the i-th configuration of σ. The notation σ_i denotes the suffix path $\sigma(i), \sigma(i+1), \ldots$, and σ_i^j denotes the segment path $\sigma(i), \sigma(i+1), \ldots, \sigma(j-1), \sigma(j)$. Let Σ denote the set of paths, and Σ^f ($\subseteq \Sigma$) the set of finite paths. A configuration c' is reachable from c when there is a path $\sigma = c_0, c_1, \ldots, c_n$ in Σ^f s.t. $c = c_0$ and $c' = c_n$. An execution is a path σ in Σ s.t. $\sigma(0) \in C^0$.

3 FTPL: A Temporal Logic for Dynamic Reconfigurations

In this section, we briefly recall the FTPL logic introduced in [3]. Inspired by [10,11], we present a new *progressive* semantics for FTPL properties evaluation at runtime, where, unlike [12], the evaluation of a trace or temporal property at any given state of a path σ is based on its evaluation at the previous state.

3.1 Syntax and Notations

Basically, constraints on the architectural elements and the relations between them are specified as configuration propositions defined in Sect. 2. In addition, the proposed logic contains external events, as well as events from reconfiguration operations, temporal properties, and, finally, trace properties embedded into temporal properties. Let $Prop_{FTPL}$ denote the set of the FTPL formulae obeying the FTPL grammar given below. Let us first give the FTPL syntax.

```
<FTPL>   ::= <tpp> | <events> | cp
<tpp>    ::= after <events> <tpp> | before <events> <trp> | <trp> until <events> | <trp>
<trp>    ::= always cp | eventually cp | <trp> ∧ <trp> | <trp> ∨ <trp>
<events> ::= <event>,<events> | <event>
<event>  ::= ope normal | ope exceptional | ope terminates | ext
```

In order to give the semantics for these formulae, we introduce the set $\mathbb{B}_4 = \{\bot, \bot^p, \top^p, \top\}$, where $\bot, \top$ stand resp. for *false* and *true* values, and $\bot^p, \top^p$ for *potential false* and *potential true* values. As in [6], we consider $\mathbb{B}_4$ together with the truth non-strict ordering relation $\sqsubseteq$ satisfying $\bot \sqsubseteq \bot^p \sqsubseteq \top^p \sqsubseteq \top$. On $\mathbb{B}_4$ we define the unary operation $\neg$ as $\neg\bot = \top$, $\neg\bot^p = \top^p$, $\neg\top^p = \bot^p$, $\neg\top = \bot$, and we define two binary operations $\sqcup, \sqcap$ resp. as the minimum and maximum interpreted wrt. $\sqsubseteq$. Thus, $(\mathbb{B}_4, \sqsubseteq)$ is a finite *de Morgan* lattice but not a Boolean lattice.

3.2   FTPL Basic Semantics

FTPL semantics is basic for events and configuration propositions, and runtime-oriented for other properties. We write $[\![\sigma(i) \models cp]\!]$ to denote the evaluation of the configuration proposition cp in $\mathbb{B}_4{}^7$ at the i-th configuration of the path σ.

External events (like events in [13]) occur instantaneously and can be seen as invocations of methods performed by (external) sensors when a change is detected in their environment. For each external event ext that may occur on a given execution path σ, we define (a) a guard cp_{ext}, which is a first-order logic formula over the parameters specified in the invocation of the method ext, and (b) an assertion $eval_\sigma$, valued in $\mathbb{B}_2$. Intuitively, if, at or before the i-th and after the $i-1$-th state (or, if $i = 0$, at the first state) of an execution path σ, there is at least one occurrence of ext s.t. $cp_{ext} = \top$ then $eval_\sigma(cp_{ext}, i) = \top$, otherwise $eval_\sigma(cp_{ext}, i) = \bot$.

The following definition present FTPL semantics for (a) reconfiguration events —"ope **normal**" (resp. "ope **exceptional**") when a reconfiguration ope terminates normally (resp. abnormally) or "ope **terminates**" when ope terminates regardless of its result—, (b) external events, and (c) lists of events. We write $[\![\sigma(i) \models e]\!]$ to denote the evaluation of the event (resp. list of events) e in $\mathbb{B}_4$ at the i-th configuration of the path σ.

Definition 3 (FTPL Events Semantics). *Let ope be a reconfiguration operation, ext an external event, e an event, and events a list of events.*
The interpretation of the events at the i-th state of the path σ is defined by:

$$[\![\sigma(i) \models ope\ \mathbf{normal}]\!] = \begin{cases} \top & if\ i > 0 \wedge \sigma(i-1) \neq \sigma(i) \wedge \sigma(i-1) \overset{ope}{\rightarrow} \sigma(i) \\ \bot & otherwise. \end{cases}$$

$$[\![\sigma(i) \models ope\ \mathbf{exceptional}]\!] = \begin{cases} \top & if\ i > 0 \wedge \sigma(i-1) = \sigma(i) \wedge \sigma(i-1) \overset{ope}{\rightarrow} \sigma(i) \\ \bot & otherwise. \end{cases}$$

$$[\![\sigma(i) \models ope\ \mathbf{terminates}]\!] = [\![\sigma(i) \models ope\ \mathbf{normal}]\!] \sqcup [\![\sigma(i) \models ope\ \mathbf{exceptional}]\!]$$

$$[\![\sigma(i) \models ext]\!] = eval_\sigma(cp_{ext}, i)$$

$$[\![\sigma(i) \models e, events]\!] = [\![\sigma(i) \models e]\!] \sqcup [\![\sigma(i) \models events]\!]$$

3.3   FTPL *Progressive* Semantics

Let $\sigma \in \Sigma$ be a path. Given an FTPL property from $Prop_{FTPL}$, its value on σ is given by the interpretation function $[\![\_ \models \_]\!] : \Sigma \times Prop_{FTPL} \rightarrow \mathbb{B}_4$ defined below by induction. In order to evaluate, in a *progressive* fashion, FTPL expressions at runtime, without consulting a complete history of FTPL properties' evaluation (like in [12]), we introduce the following notations. Let $\phi_\sigma = [\![\sigma \models \phi]\!]$ be the evaluation of an FTPL formula where ϕ is a list of events, a trace property, or a temporal property. We denote $\phi_\sigma(i)$ the evaluation of ϕ on σ, at the i-th state of the path.

Furthermore, following [5], if the scope of an FTPL property ϕ is restricted to the suffix path σ_k, $k \geq 0$, we write $\phi_{\sigma_k} = [\![\sigma_k \models \phi]\!]$ for such a restriction, and

---

[7] Since $\mathbb{B}_2 \subset \mathbb{B}_4$, the evaluation $[\![c \models cp]\!]$ of the configuration proposition $cp \in CP$ on the configuration c detailed on p. 5 is considered to be valued in $\mathbb{B}_4$.

$\phi_{\sigma_k}(i)$ for the evaluation in $\mathbb{B}_4$ of this restriction at the i-th state of σ, where $i \geq k$. Then, the evaluation of ϕ on the path σ ($\phi_\sigma = [\![\sigma \models \phi]\!]$), is similar to the evaluation of ϕ on the suffix path σ_0 starting at the first configuration, wich is $\phi_{\sigma_0} = [\![\sigma_0 \models \phi]\!]$. For the sake of simplicity, we also write $cp_{\sigma_k}(i) = [\![\sigma_k(i) \models cp]\!]$.

Definition 4 (FTPL Runtime Progressive Trace Properties Semantics). *Let cp be a configuration proposition, ϕ (resp. φ) a trace property of the form $\phi = $ always cp (resp. $\varphi = $ eventually cp). We define $\phi_{\sigma_k}(i)$ (resp. $\varphi_{\sigma_k}(i)$), the evaluation in $\mathbb{B}_4$ of $[\![\sigma_k \models \phi]\!]$ (resp. $[\![\sigma_k \models \varphi]\!]$) at the i-th state of σ when the scope is restricted to σ_k, by:*

- for $i = k$, $\phi_{\sigma_k}(k) = \top^p \sqcap cp_\sigma(k)$; $\varphi_{\sigma_k}(k) = \bot^p \sqcup cp_\sigma(k)$
- for $i > k$, $\phi_{\sigma_k}(i) = \phi_{\sigma_k}(i-1) \sqcap cp_\sigma(i)$; $\varphi_{\sigma_k}(i) = \varphi_{\sigma_k}(i-1) \sqcup cp_\sigma(i)$

Furthermore, let ψ_1 and ψ_2 be two trace properties, then:
$$[\![\sigma_k \models \psi_1 \wedge \psi_2]\!] = [\![\sigma_k \models \psi_1]\!] \sqcap [\![\sigma_k \models \psi_2]\!] \; ; \; [\![\sigma_k \models \psi_1 \vee \psi_2]\!] = [\![\sigma_k \models \psi_1]\!] \sqcup [\![\sigma_k \models \psi_2]\!]$$

On the scope starting at the k-th state of σ, if at state k one has $cp_\sigma(k) = \top$ (resp. $cp_\sigma(k) = \bot$), the trace property **always** cp (resp. **eventually** cp) is evaluated to $\top^p$ (resp. $\bot^p$); otherwise, it is evaluated to $\bot$ (resp. $\top$). Then, for $i > k$, at the i-th state of σ, **always** cp (resp. **eventually** cp) is evaluated to the minimum (resp. maximum), interpreted wrt. $\sqsubseteq$, of (a) its evaluation at the previous state and (b) $cp_\sigma(i)$. Table 1 shows an example of the evaluation of such trace properties.

Table 1. Evaluation of trace properties

Let be $\phi = $ **always** $\neg cp$ and $\varphi = $ **eventually** cp

i	k	$k+1$	$k+2$	$k+3$	$k+4$	$k+5$	$k+6$	$k+7$	$k+8$	$\cdots$
$cp_\sigma(i)$	$\bot$	$\bot$	$\bot$	$\bot$	$\bot$	$\top$	$\bot$	$\bot$	$\bot$	$\cdots$
$\phi_{\sigma_k}(i)$	$\top^p$	$\top^p$	$\top^p$	$\top^p$	$\top^p$	$\bot$	$\bot$	$\bot$	$\bot$	$\bot$
$\varphi_{\sigma_k}(i)$	$\bot^p$	$\bot^p$	$\bot^p$	$\bot^p$	$\bot^p$	$\top$	$\top$	$\top$	$\top$	$\top$

Definition 5 (FTPL Runtime Progressive Lists of Events Semantics). *Let e be a list of events. We define $e_{\sigma_k}(i)$, the evaluation in $\mathbb{B}_4$ of $[\![\sigma_k \models e]\!]$ at the i-th state of σ when the scope is restricted to σ_k, by:*

- for $i = k$, $e_{\sigma_k}(k) = [\![\sigma_k(k) \models e]\!]$
- for $i > k$, $e_{\sigma_k}(i) = [\![\sigma_k(i) \models e]\!] \sqcup (\top^p \sqcap e_{\sigma_k}(i-1))$

Intuitively, the expression $[\![\sigma(i) \models e]\!] \sqcup (\top^p \sqcap e_{\sigma_k}(i-1))$ evaluates to $\top$ if there is an occurrence of e at configuration i, and to $\bot$ (resp. $\top^p$) if there is no occurrence of e at configuration i and no (resp. at least one) occurrence of e happening before configuration i on the scope starting at configuration k.

Definition 6 (FTPL Runtime Progressive Temporal Properties Semantics). *Let tpp be a temporal property, trp a trace property, e a list of events,*

ϕ (resp. φ, ψ) a temporal property of the form $\phi = $ **after** e tpp (resp. $\varphi = $ **before** e trp, $\psi = $ trp **until** e). We define $\phi_{\sigma_k}(i)$ (resp. $\varphi_{\sigma_k}(i)$, $\psi_{\sigma_k}(i)$), the evaluation in $\mathbb{B}_4$ of $[\![\sigma_k \models \phi]\!]$ (resp. $[\![\sigma_k \models \varphi]\!]$, $[\![\sigma_k \models \psi]\!]$) at the i-th state of σ when the scope is restricted to σ_k, by: for $i \geq k$,

$$\phi_{\sigma_k}(i) = \left(\prod_{j \in \mathcal{I}_{\sigma_k^i}(e)} tpp_{\sigma_j}(i) \right) \sqcap \mathsf{T}^p \quad \begin{array}{l} \textit{where } \mathcal{I}_{\sigma_k^i}(e) = \{j | k \leq j \leq i \wedge [\![\sigma(j) \models e]\!] = \mathsf{T}\} \\ \textit{represents the set of indexes for an occurrence of } e. \end{array}$$

$$\varphi_{\sigma_k}(i) = \begin{cases} \mathsf{T}^p & \textit{if } e_{\sigma_k}(i) = \perp \vee i = k \\ \perp & \textit{if } e_{\sigma_k}(i) = \mathsf{T} \wedge trp_{\sigma_k}(i-1) \in \{\perp, \perp^p\} \\ \varphi_{\sigma_k}(i-1) & \textit{otherwise} \end{cases}$$

$$\psi_{\sigma_k}(i) = \begin{cases} \mathsf{T}^p & \textit{if } trp_{\sigma_k}(i) \neq \perp \wedge e_{\sigma_k}(i) = \mathsf{T} \wedge \ e_{\sigma_k}(i-1) = \perp \wedge \ trp_{\sigma_k}(i-1) \in \{\mathsf{T}^p, \mathsf{T}\} \\ \perp^p & \textit{if } trp_{\sigma_k}(i) \neq \perp \wedge (e_{\sigma_k}(i) = \perp \vee i = k) \\ \perp & \textit{if } trp_{\sigma_k}(i) = \perp \vee (e_{\sigma_k}(i) = \mathsf{T} \wedge \ trp_{\sigma_k}(i-1) \in \{\perp, \perp^p\}) \\ \psi_{\sigma_k}(i-1) & \textit{otherwise} \end{cases}$$

By definition, the evaluation of $\phi = $ **after** e tpp is either (a) T^p as long as e does not occur or if tpp is evaluated to T^p or T on each suffix of the path starting at an occurrence of e, or (b) $\perp$ if on any of these suffixes tpp is evaluated to $\perp$, or (c) $\perp^p$, otherwise.

For $\varphi = $ **before** e trp, its evaluation is either (a) T^p if e has not occurred yet, or (b) $\perp$ if for each occurrence of e, trp is evaluated to $\perp$ or $\perp^p$ on the segment starting at the beginning of the considered scope and ending at the previous $i-1$-th configuration on the σ path. Otherwise, ϕ at the i-th configuration is evaluated to its value at the previous $i-1$-th configuration.

Intuitively, the $\psi = $ trp **until** e property can be seen as being evaluated similarly to **before** e trp, but with the two following exceptions: (a) when trp is evaluated to $\perp$, ψ is evaluated to $\perp$; otherwise, (a) on the beginning part of the scope and as long as e has not occurred, ψ is evaluated to $\perp^p$.

Finally, we say that a reconfiguration model $S = \langle \mathcal{C}, \mathcal{C}^0, \mathcal{R}_{run}, \rightarrow, l \rangle$ satisfies a property $\phi \in Prop_{FTPL}$, written $S \models \phi$, if $\forall \sigma.(\sigma \in \Sigma(S) \wedge \sigma(0) \in \mathcal{C}^0 \Rightarrow \phi_\sigma = \mathsf{T})$.

Table 2 shows the evaluation of the temporal property ϕ which is always $\perp^p$ except on and after the configuration when the event *entry* occurs until the configuration preceding the occurrence of the event *exit* where it is T^p. Note that the event *entry* occurs at both the j-th and the l-th configurations whereas the evaluation of $e = start, exit$ is T at configurations 0 and k, hence $\phi_{\sigma_0}(i) = \varphi_{\sigma_0}(i)$ for $i < k$, and $\phi_{\sigma_0}(i) = \varphi_{\sigma_0}(i) \sqcap \varphi_{\sigma_k}(i)$ for $i \geq k$.

3.4   FTPL Expressiveness

We should note that FTPL trace properties are either (a) a subset of safety properties, as **always** cp, or, (b) a subset of guarantee properties, as **eventually** cp, or (c) conjunctions and disjunctions of properties from these subsets (safety and guarantee properties). Consequently, according to the *safety-progress* hierarchy [14,15], they are included in obligation properties which represent a subset of response properties. In [16] the issue of enforceable properties, originally

Table 2. Detail of the evaluation of "**after** $start, exit$ ($\top^p$ **until** $entry$)"

Let be $e = start, exit$, $\varphi = \top^p$ **until** $entry$, $\phi =$ **after** $start, exit$ ($\top^p$ **until** $entry$) = **after** e φ

i	0	1	$\cdots$	$j-1$	j	$j+1$	$\cdots$	$k-1$	k	$k+1$	$\cdots$	$l-1$	l	$l+1$	$\cdots$
$[\sigma(i) \models start]$	$\top$	$\bot$	$\cdots$	$\bot$	$\bot$	$\bot$	$\cdots$	$\bot$	$\bot$	$\bot$	$\cdots$	$\bot$	$\bot$	$\bot$	$\cdots$
$[\sigma(i) \models entry]$	$\bot$	$\bot$	$\cdots$	$\bot$	$\top$	$\bot$	$\cdots$	$\bot$	$\bot$	$\bot$	$\cdots$	$\bot$	$\top$	$\bot$	$\cdots$
$[\sigma(i) \models exit]$	$\bot$	$\bot$	$\cdots$	$\bot$	$\bot$	$\bot$	$\cdots$	$\bot$	$\top$	$\bot$	$\cdots$	$\bot$	$\bot$	$\bot$	$\cdots$
$[\sigma(i) \models e]$	$\top$	$\bot$	$\cdots$	$\bot$	$\bot$	$\bot$	$\cdots$	$\bot$	$\top$	$\bot$	$\cdots$	$\bot$	$\bot$	$\bot$	$\cdots$
$\mathcal{I}_{\sigma_0^i}(e)$	$\{0\}$	$\{0\}$	$\cdots$	$\{0\}$	$\{0\}$	$\{0\}$	$\cdots$	$\{0\}$	$\{0,k\}$	$\{0,k\}$	$\cdots$	$\{0,k\}$	$\{0,k\}$	$\{0,k\}$	$\cdots$
$entry_{\sigma_0}(i)$	$\bot$	$\bot$	$\cdots$	$\bot$	$\top$	$\top^p$	$\cdots$	$\top^p$	$\top^p$	$\top^p$	$\cdots$	$\top^p$	$\top$	$\top^p$	$\cdots$
$\varphi_{\sigma_0}(i)$	$\bot^p$	$\bot^p$	$\cdots$	$\bot^p$	$\top^p$	$\top^p$	$\cdots$	$\top^p$	$\top^p$	$\top^p$	$\cdots$	$\top^p$	$\top^p$	$\top^p$	$\cdots$
$entry_{\sigma_k}(i)$	$\times$	$\times$	$\cdots$	$\times$	$\times$	$\times$	$\cdots$	$\times$	$\bot$	$\bot$	$\cdots$	$\bot$	$\top$	$\top^p$	$\cdots$
$\varphi_{\sigma_k}(i)$	$\times$	$\times$	$\cdots$	$\times$	$\times$	$\times$	$\cdots$	$\times$	$\bot^p$	$\bot^p$	$\cdots$	$\bot^p$	$\top^p$	$\top^p$	$\cdots$
$\phi_{\sigma_0}(i)$	$\bot^p$	$\bot^p$	$\cdots$	$\bot^p$	$\top^p$	$\top^p$	$\cdots$	$\top^p$	$\bot^p$	$\bot^p$	$\cdots$	$\bot^p$	$\top^p$	$\top^p$	$\cdots$

addressed because of infinite sequences, is extended to finite and infinite properties at runtime. It is then established that enforceable properties are exactly response properties. Hence, FTPL trace properties, as a subset of obligation properties, are enforceable as well.

Before ending this section, let us mention (infinite) renewal properties [17], a superset of safety properties also containing some liveness properties, that can be enforced by *edit-automata* as runtime monitors. Intuitively, a property is a *renewal property* if every valid infinite sequence of actions has infinitely many valid prefixes. This is exactly the case of response properties [15]. FTPL trace properties being, as established above, response properties, they are also renewal properties and can then be enforced by edit-automata. Consequently, FTPL temporal properties, acting as scopes [5] of trace properties, can also be enforced in the same way.

4   Integrating Temporal Properties into Adaptation Policies

Although one of the main advantages of reconfigurable component-based systems is the ability of the system's architecture to evolve at runtime, reconfigurations must not happen at any but in suitable circumstances. In order to supervise and to dynamically influence component-based systems reconfigurations, this section introduces adaptation policies indicating reconfigurations suitable to perform, and rules that can impact on the architecture of the component-based system model.

To take into account some resource constraints, events in the system environment, or even properties over sequences of reconfigurations, we propose to extend adaptation policies by integrating FTPL properties into them. For that, adaptation policies exploit the above-mentioned properties and their domains. Each domain defines its specific vocabulary to qualify associated properties, based on the evaluation of the architectural or temporal constraints. Adaptation policies are defined by: (*a*) architectural reconfiguration operations to specify the possible modifications of the architecture; and (*a*) adaptation rules to link the properties concerning the component-based system and the need[8] to activate a reconfiguration. We adapt definitions in [1,2] to fit in with our component-based system model semantics, when extending them with temporal properties.

Definition 7 (Adaptation Policies). *Let S be a reconfiguration model, and Ftype a set of fuzzy types. Given $\sigma(i) \in C$, a finite set AP of adaptation policies for $\sigma(i)$ is composed of elements $A = \langle R_N, R_R \rangle$, where:*

- $R_N \subseteq \mathcal{R}$ *is a finite (non-empty) set of architectural reconfiguration names,*
- $R_R = \{\langle F, B, G, I \rangle\}$ *is a finite (non-empty) set of adaptation rules, where*
  - *$F \in Ftype$ is a fuzzy type,*
  - *$B \subseteq \{\phi_\sigma(i) = value \mid \phi \in Prop_{FTPL} \wedge value \in \mathbb{B}_4\}$ is a set of properties in $Prop_{FTPL}$ evaluated in $\mathbb{B}_4$ on $\sigma(i)$,*
  - *$G \subseteq \{cp_\sigma(i) = value \mid cp \in CP \wedge value \in \mathbb{B}_2\}$ is a set of configuration propositions in CP evaluated in $\mathbb{B}_2$ on $\sigma(i)$,*
  - *$I \subseteq R_N \times F$ is a relation between reconfigurations and fuzzy values.*

Let us denote $B_{\sigma(i)}$ (resp. $G_{\sigma(i)}$) the conjunction of the properties evaluations in B (resp. guards evaluations in G) on $\sigma(i)$.

To illustrate adaptation policies with events, let us suppose that the system where the location component is running can dynamically support the removal or the addition of either the GPS and the Wi-Fi components. Of course, at any given time there should be at least one of these components present. In certain cases, however, it can be beneficial to remove one of these components.

For example, when the energy level of the vehicle is low, the Wi-Fi component can be removed, and then added back when the internal batteries are recharged. Furthermore, when the vehicle enters a "Wi-Fi area" where there is no GPS signal available, it is suitable to remove the GPS component, which can be added back after exiting such an area. Figure 3 displays the `cycabgps` adaptation policy, which is written using a syntax inspired by Tangram4Fractal [1] adaptation policies. This policy influences the `addgps` and `removegps` reconfigurations to respectively add or remove the GPS component. It uses three events (lines 3–5): *start* (that occurs only when the adaptation policy becomes effective) and *entry* (resp. *exit*) that occurs when the vehicle enters (resp. exits) a "Wi-Fi area".

Example 2. For the adaptation policy in Fig. 3, we have the architectural reconfigurations set $R_N = \{\texttt{addgps}, \texttt{removegps}\}$ and $Ftype = \{\{\texttt{low}, \texttt{medium}, \texttt{high}\}\}$ which contains all the fuzzy types used in this policy. For the adaptation rule spanning lines 23–25, we have, using the notation of Definition 7, $F = \{\texttt{low}, \texttt{medium}, \texttt{high}\}$, $B = \{\textbf{after } start, exit \ (\top^p \textbf{ until } entry) = \top^p\}$, $G = \{gps \in Components \wedge wifi \in Components = \top\}$, and finally $I = \{(\texttt{removegps}, \texttt{high})\}$. This adaptation rule expresses that when the expression in B holds (i.e., the vehicle is within a "Wi-Fi area" - cf. Table 2 for details of the evaluation), if both the GPS and the Wi-Fi components are present, then the utility of removing the GPS component, by invoking the `removegps` reconfiguration, is high.

---

[8] As in [1,2], we use a fuzzy value (e.g., in {low, medium, high}) to express this need.

```
 1 policy cycabgps              18
 2                              19 when (Power < 33) = FALSE4
 3   event entry                20   if (gps in Components and
 4   event exit                        wifi in Components) = TRUE
 5   event start                21   then utility of removegps is low
 6                              22
 7 when (after start,exit (     23 when (after start,exit (
     P_TRUE4 until entry))=P_TRUE4    P_TRUE4 until entry))=P_TRUE4
 8   if (gps in Components) = FALSE 24  if (gps in Components and
 9   then utility of addgps is low      wifi in Components) = TRUE
10                              25   then utility of removegps is high
11 when (Power < 33) = TRUE4    26
12   if (gps in Components) = FALSE 27 when (Power < 33) = TRUE4
13   then utility of addgps is low 28  if (gps in Components and
14                                     wifi in Components) = TRUE
15 when (Power < 33) = FALSE4    29   then utility of removegps is high
16   if (gps in Components) = FALSE 30
17   then utility of addgps is high 31 end policy
```

Fig. 3. cycabgps adaptation policy

Let $S = \langle \mathcal{C}, \mathcal{C}^0, \mathcal{R}_{run}, \rightarrow, l \rangle$ be a reconfiguration model and AP_S a finite set of adaptation policies for S. We now define how the adaptation policies affect the behaviour of the component-based system model.

Definition 8 (Restriction by Adaptation Policies). *The restriction of S by adaptation policies in AP_S is defined as $S \triangleleft AP_S = \langle \mathcal{C} \triangleleft AP_S, \mathcal{C}^0 \triangleleft AP_S, \mathcal{R}_{run}, \rightarrow, l \rangle$, where $\mathcal{C} \triangleleft AP_S$ is the least set s.t. if $c \in \mathcal{C}$ and $A \in AP_S$ then $c \triangleleft A \in \mathcal{C} \triangleleft AP_S$, $\mathcal{R}_{run} \cap (\cup_{A \in AP_S} R_N) \neq \emptyset$, $l : \mathcal{C} \triangleleft AP_S \rightarrow CP$ is a total interpretation function, and for every $ope \in \mathcal{R}_{run}$, the transition relation $\rightarrow \in \mathcal{C} \triangleleft AP_S \times \mathcal{R}_{run} \times \mathcal{C} \triangleleft AP_S$ is the least set of triples $(c \triangleleft A, ope, c' \triangleleft A)$ satisfying the following rules:*

$$[ACT1] \quad \frac{c \xrightarrow{ope} c'}{c \triangleleft A \xrightarrow{ope} c' \triangleleft A} \quad (ope \in \bigcup_{A \in AP_S} R_N) \wedge B_c \wedge G_c$$

$$[ACT2] \quad \frac{c \xrightarrow{ope} c'}{c \triangleleft A \xrightarrow{ope} c' \triangleleft A} \quad ope \notin \bigcup_{A \in AP_S} R_N$$

This definition means that all the configurations in $\mathcal{C} \triangleleft AP_S$ are reachable from initial configurations by either reconfiguration operations obeying adaptation policies (Rule *[ACT1]*), or by normal reconfigurations which are not involved in the adaptation policy (Rule *[ACT2]*).

5 Runtime Policy Evaluation

Given a component-based system and a set of adaptation policies, a problem occurring while applying adaptation policies is to ensure that the reconfigurations (of a component-based system obeying the policies) conform to the specified reconfigurations. More formally, for two component-based systems modelled by S and $S \triangleleft AP_S$, the problem is to decide whether the behaviour of S obeying its adaptation policies in AP_S is also a behaviour of S. To address this problem, we propose to use the ready simulation notion [18].

Definition 9 (Ready Simulation). *Let S_1 and S_2 be two reconfiguration models over $\mathcal{R}_{run}$. A binary relation $\simeq \; \subseteq \mathcal{C}_1 \times \mathcal{C}_2$ is a ready simulation iff, for all ope in $\mathcal{R}_{run}$, $(c_1, c_2) \in \simeq$ implies*

(i) *Whenever $(c_1, ope, c_1') \in \rightarrow_1$, then there exists $c_2' \in \mathcal{C}_2$ such that (c_2, ope, c_2') $\in \rightarrow_2$ and $(c_1', c_2') \in \simeq$.*

(ii) *Whenever $c_1 \overset{ope}{\not\rightarrow}$, then $c_2 \overset{ope}{\not\rightarrow}$.*

We say that S_1 and S_2 are ready-similar, written $S_1 \simeq S_2$, if $\forall c_1^0 \in \mathcal{C}_1^0 \exists c_2^0 \in \mathcal{C}_2^0.(c_1^0, c_2^0) \in \simeq$. Following [18], we keep the ready-set definition for S as *readies* $(c) = \{ope \mid ope \in \mathcal{R}_{run} \wedge c \overset{ope}{\rightarrow}\}$. A useful fact follows immediately from Definition 9: $(c_1, c_2) \in \simeq$ implies *readies*(c_1) = *readies*(c_2). Consequently, it is enough to show the disequality of the ready-sets to show that the ready simulation does not hold between two configurations.

To be able to establish whether $S \lhd AP_S \simeq S$ or not, and thus to provide a correctness result concerning the restriction by adaptation policies, we consider the following decision problem.

Adaptation Problem

Input: Component-based system modelled by $S = \langle \mathcal{C}, \mathcal{C}^0, \mathcal{R}_{run}, \rightarrow, l \rangle$, $c \in \mathcal{C}$, and the set $AP \subseteq AP_S$ of adaptation policies for c.
Output: true if $\forall A \in AP, c \lhd A \simeq c$, and **false** otherwise.

For the component-based system under its adaptation policies, we define the ready set wrt. Definition 8 by: *readies*$(c \lhd A) = \{ope \mid ope \in \mathcal{R}_{run} \setminus \cup_{A \in AP} R_N \wedge c \overset{ope}{\rightarrow}\} \cup \{ope \mid (ope \in \cup_{A \in AP} R_N) \wedge B_c \wedge G_c \wedge c \overset{ope}{\rightarrow}\}$. Then, again, it is easy to see that $c \lhd A \simeq c$ implies *readies*$(c \lhd A)$ = *readies*(c). Both S and $S \lhd AP_S$ being infinite state systems, the simulation problem is undecidable in general. However, when the ready sets are different, we can reach a conclusion. Consequently,

Proposition 1. *The adaptation problem is semi-decidable.*

The adaptation policies can be used for specifying reflection or enforcement mechanisms. The notion of reflection means that any unwanted behaviour triggers a corrective reconfiguration through an adaptation policy. The notion of enforcement, exposed in the `AdaptEnfor` algorithm in Fig. 4, means that no reconfiguration that would lead the system to behave in an unwanted way is allowed. This algorithm uses as inputs (1) a generic component-based system *gcbs*—an object used to manage a component-based system regardless of the design/development framework, and, (2) an array, v, containing candidate reconfigurations ordered by priority. Each of the variables *currentConf*, *targetConf*, and *endConf* represents a configuration while the variable r designates a reconfiguration[9].

This algorithm contains five functions: (a) `retrieveConf(s)` returns the configuration of the generic component-based system s; (b) `size(v)` returns the size

---

[9] In `AdaptEnfor` Algorithm, $\equiv$ can be implemented by various (pre-)congruence relations—set equality for *Elem* and *Rel* in Definition 1, structural refinement in [19], or other relations compatible with the reconfiguration relation.

```
 1  (*AdaptEnfor*)
 2  Input
 3     gcbs  (*generic component-based system*)
 4     v     (*array of candidate reconfigurations ordered by priority*)
 5  Variables
 6     currentConf,
 7     targetConf,
 8     endConf: configuration
 9     r: reconfiguration
10  Begin
11     currentConf := retrieveConf(gcbs)
12     WHILE (size(v) > 0) DO
13        r := getNextElement(v)
14        remove(v, r)
15        targetConf := applyReconf(currentConf, r)
16        IF (preserveEnforProps(targetConf)) DO
17           applyToSystem(targetConf, gcbs)
18           endConf := retrieveConf(gcbs)
19           IF (endConf ≡ targetConf) DO
20              sendEvent(r, normal)
21              break
22           ELSE
23              applyToSystem(currentConf, gcbs)
24              endConf := retrieveConf(gcbs)
25              IF (endConf ≡ currentConf) DO
26                 sendEvent(r, exceptionnal)
27                 break
28              ELSE
29                 systemExit
30              FI
31           FI
32        FI
33     ENDWHILE
34  End
```

Fig. 4. Algorithm AdaptEnfor

of the array v; (c) getNextElement(v) returns the next element of the array v; (d) applyReconf(c, r) returns the resulting configuration when the reconfiguration r is applied to the configuration c; (e) preserveEnforProps(c) returns $\top$ if every enforcement property loaded holds on the configuration c, $\bot$ otherwise. Finally, there are also five procedures used within this algorithm: (a) remove(v, e) removes the element e of the array v; (b) applyToSystem(c, s) initiates a reconfiguration of the system s to reach a configuration c; (c) sendEvent (r, arg) sends the event "r **normal**" or "r **exceptional**", where r is a reconfiguration, and arg stands for "normal" or "exceptional"; (d) **break** exits the current "while" loop; (e) systemExit terminates the current run of the program.

Let us add that the way we enforce properties on adaptation policies supports the *soundness* and *transparency* principles [20]. Given a set of properties to enforce at runtime, the mechanism we use is (a) *sound* because it prevents (by not entering in the IF statement's body at line 16) the occurrence of reconfigurations that would lead the system to violate, at the next state of execution, the properties to enforce, (b) *transparent* because it allows (by entering in the IF statement's body at line 16) the occurrence of reconfigurations (if any) that put the system in a state complying with these properties.

The "while" loop starting at line 12 in Fig. 4 ends when the size of the array v becomes equal to 0. Since, on every loop iteration, the size of v is only decremented (line 14), this algorithm always terminates.

Proposition 2. *The* `AdaptEnfor` *algorithm always terminates.*

When the `AdaptEnfor` algorithm terminates with no reconfiguration operation available to be applied to the current configuration, i.e., when the v size becomes equal to 0 in the "while" loop, it means that the set $\{ope \mid (ope \in \bigcup_{A \in AP} R_N) \wedge B_c \wedge G_c \wedge c \xrightarrow{ope}\}(\subseteq readies(c \triangleleft A))$ is empty. In this case, as every adaptation policy for c specifies at least one adaptation rule for a reconfiguration operation, the ready sets of c and $c \triangleleft A$ are different. This way the `AdaptEnfor` algorithm allows answering the adaptation problem with **false**. Moreover,

Theorem 1 (Correctness). *If a configuration c is not reachable in S then, for any AP_S, it is not reachable in $S \triangleleft AP_S$.*

Correctness is clear because when we forget the B and G parts of an adaptation policy A from AP_S restricting a behaviour of $S \triangleleft AP_S$, we get a behaviour of S.

Reflection can be applied in a way similar to the enforcement mechanism presented above. The main difference is that, whereas enforcement prevents the occurrence of specific reconfigurations to avoid unwanted behaviours before they actually happen, reflection allows the detection of such behaviours and triggers corrective actions in the form of reconfigurations performed through adaptation policies. Such actions can range up to the total stop of the system in case of the detection of behaviours that would justify it.

6   Implementation and Case Study

This section describes an implementation developed in Java for the dynamic reconfiguration of component-based systems guided by adaptation policies. A case study shows the result of our experiment on the location component of the CyCab given in Fig. 1.

As shown in Fig. 5, in a nutshell, our implementation uses three controllers: (*a*) the *event controller* receives events, stores them, and flushes then after they have been sent to a requester, (*b*) the *reflection controller* sends events to the *event controller* when a property of a reflection policy is violated, and (*a*) the *adaptation policy controller* manages reconfigurations, as well as, adaptation and enforcement policies as in the `AdaptEnfor` algorithm displayed in Fig. 4.

In addition, an *event handler* is used to receive events from an external source and to send them to the *event controller*. All interactions with the *component-based system* (implemented using Fractal in our case) take place through the *generic component-based system manager*, a set of Java classes developed in such a way that they can be used regardless of the framework used to design the *component-based system* without modifying its code.

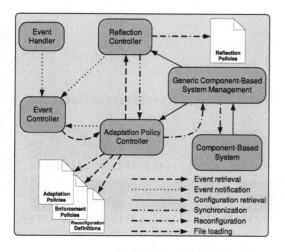

Fig. 5. Implementation architecture

Since we want our implementation to be independent of a particular component-based framework, only a few classes implementing Java interfaces of the *generic component-based system manager* use API specific to the *component-based system* framework. This way, the controllers of Fig. 5 not being Fractal-based, our implementation can manage various component-based frameworks. The synchronization between *adaptation policy* and *reflection* controllers coupled with the way events are managed allows the controllers to operate together under the *perfect synchrony hypothesis* [21].

When running the implementation, each reconfiguration is simulated (cf. line 15 of the AdaptEnfor algorithm, Fig. 4), starting with the ones with higher priority. The first one which does not violate any property from an enforcement policy is applied (lines 16 and 17). If the reconfiguration ends normally the event "r normal" (line 20), where r is the name of the above-mentioned reconfiguration, is sent to the *event controller*. If the reconfiguration ends with an error, the previous configuration is rolled back and the event "r exceptional" (line 26) is sent to the *event controller*. Events sent by the *reflection controller* to the *event controller* are caught by the *adaptation policy controller* that apply corrective actions using appropriate adaptation policies.

Figure 6 provides the results obtained by running our implementation with the location component of the CyCab given in Fig. 1. The top chart illustrates the evolution of the energy level, while the middle (resp. bottom) chart shows the presence (value 1) or the absence (value 0) of the GPS (resp. Wi-Fi) components. Note that the rate of energy consumption is related to the presence or absence of the GPS and Wi-Fi component. When the vehicle enters (resp. exits) a "Wi-Fi area", the event entry (resp. exit) is sent to the *event controller*, as shown by vertical segments on Fig. 6 at configurations 66 and 134 (resp. 78 and 147).

When the energy level goes below 10, a reflection policy triggers a reconfiguration (chargeBattery) that has the effect to update the energy level to 100. Just before configuration 100, a Fractal API has been used to artificially set the energy level to a negative value, this triggers (through a reflection policy) the reconfigurations stopCycab and chargeBattery that respectively stop the location composite component and update the energy level to 100. The location composite component being stopped, the energy level does not decrease until configuration 116 when it is restarted.

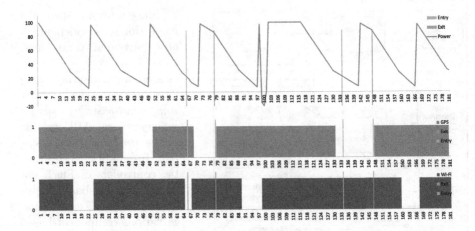

Fig. 6. Experiment with the location component

The `cycabgps` (Fig. 3) (resp. `cycabwifi`) adaptation policy, favours the removal of the GPS (resp. Wi-Fi) component when the energy is low, and favours its addition when the energy level is medium to high. Furthermore, when the CyCab is in a "Wi-Fi area", `cycabgps` (resp. `cycabwifi`) favours the removal of the GPS (resp. addition of the Wi-Fi) component.

At configuration 66, the CyCab enters a "Wi-Fi area" having only the GPS component present. The *reflection controller*, detecting that the vehicle is within a "Wi-Fi area" without the Wi-Fi component, sends, to the *event controller*, the `reflectionNoWifiInWifiArea` event. At the next configuration, as a consequence of the retrieval of this event the *adaptation policy controller* initiates the `addwifi` reconfiguration which adds and starts the Wi-Fi component. Then, at the following configuration, the application of the `cycabgps` adaptation policy (Fig. 3) by the *adaptation policy controller* causes the removal of the GPS component through the `removegps` reconfiguration. At configuration 134, the CyCab enters a "Wi-Fi area" having only the Wi-Fi component present. When the level of energy becomes high (configuration 142), in application of `cycabgps`, the GPS component is not added. As soon as the vehicle exits the "Wi-Fi area" (configuration 79 and 148), since the level of energy is high, the GPS component is added back.

Outside of a "Wi-Fi area", the Wi-Fi (resp. GPS) component is removed at configurations 15, 64, 89, and 159 (resp. 37 and 130), as a result of the application of adaptation policies, because the level of energy becomes low. Still outside of a "Wi-Fi area", when there is only one component present (among the Wi-Fi and GPS components), the other is added when the level of energy is medium to high (configurations 24, 50, 79, 99, 148, and 167).

These experimental results show that extending adaptation policies with temporal patterns provides the specifier with means allowing to better — in comparison with [1,2,4] — comprehend and control the component-based system's behaviour. Because the frequency at which adaptation occurs depends on the system under scrutiny, this parameter must be specified as a user-defined parameter. In a future development it will be possible to specify that adaptation needs to happen in some bounded time.

Of course, it should be possible to come up with a finite encoding of the bounded version of our example to use techniques for finite state systems. Our point, however, is to evaluate temporal and architectural constraints over changeable architectures at runtime. One can imagine new components, not even implemented at the beginning of the run, to be added at execution time. This, indeed, can lead to infinite behaviours.

7 Related Work and Conclusion

7.1 Related Work

The analysis of systems whose topology evolves over time is a challenging topic. Tangram4Fractal [1] presents a qualitative approach of adaptation policies, but disallow the use of temporal properties. The work in [2] shows an evolution of Tangram4Fractal that permits adaptation policies based on a qMEDL logic [4] to use external events. Architectural constraints, however, cannot be expressed with qMEDL.

The FTPL logic, expressing temporal and architectural constraints, is introduced in [3]. It is based on Dwyer's work on patterns and scopes [5] and uses specifications inspired by [22]. Nevertheless, this version of FTPL does not support external events and cannot always be evaluated at runtime.

Like Bounded Model Checking [23] (BMC for short), our approach may produce counterexamples when detecting property violation. Moreover, when no violation is detected, both approaches are incomplete for the safety properties. However, for some liveness properties, for example **eventually**, the satisfaction can be established. It is also possible to establish the satisfaction of some safety properties within the appropriate scope [5,22]. Similar to [7] using BMC, we can validate architectural or temporal properties over instantiated reconfigurable systems; this validation is size-bounded and partial.

Evaluation of FTPL properties at runtime is detailed in [12]. This version of FTPL, however, does not support the use of external events. Furthermore, to allow easier runtime evaluation, we use a *progressive* semantics inspired by [10,11]. This semantics, unlike the one in [12], takes fully into account the usage of scopes [5,22]

Our implementation for handling reflection is somehow similar to the steering performed with the MaCS framework in [13]. The coupled PEDL and MEDL scripts act as the event and adaptation controllers in our implementation while the SADL script acts as our reflection controller. No enforcement is provided in MaCS.

In [24], only runtime verification is performed; there is no adaptation mechanism. Nevertheless, by using locations spanning over several components, the specifications considered for BIP systems allow, similar to our approach, describing global behaviours of the system. Dissimilar to our approach where the code of the component-based system under scrutiny is not modified, RV-BIP slightly modifies components and thus may not allow the component reusability; in this case, the separation of concerns principle would not be respected.

The work in [25] allows runtime monitoring of temporal properties for component interfaces. When components come with an abstract behavioural model, they can be considered as grey boxes rather than black boxes. Our approach, not limited to monitoring interactions of component interfaces with an external application, works in both cases.

7.2 Conclusion

As component-based systems evolve at runtime, and as a behaviour in which the runtime temporal property evaluation becomes false might be not acceptable, this paper has proposed to integrate temporal properties into adaptation policies, and to supervise—at runtime—the reconfiguration execution allowed by the adaptation policies. Inspired by proposals in [6], this paper continues with a four-valued logic allowing to characterize the "potential" properties (un)satisfiability. In addition, the four-valued logic helps in guiding the reconfiguration process, namely in choosing the next reconfiguration operation to be applied. A prototype Java implementation of the algorithm for verifying and enforcing FTPL properties integrated into the adaptation policies has been developed, as a proof of concept.

As a future work, we plan to investigate a decentralized method to evaluate adaptation policies and temporal formulae by progression, as in [10]. On the implementation side, a future direction is to handle component-based systems using the FraSCAti [26] framework.

References

1. Chauvel, F., Barais, O., Plouzeau, N., Borne, I., Jézéquel, J.: Composition et expression qualitative de politiques d'adaptation pour les composants Fractal. In: Actes des Journées nationales du GDR GPL 2009 (2009)
2. Dormoy, J., Kouchnarenko, O.: Event-based adaptation policies for fractal components. In: IEEE/ACS International Conference on Computer Systems and Applications 2010, AICCSA 2010, pp. 1–8. IEEE (2010)
3. Dormoy, J., Kouchnarenko, O., Lanoix, A.: Using temporal logic for dynamic reconfigurations of components. In: Barbosa, L.S., Lumpe, M. (eds.) FACS 2010. LNCS, vol. 6921, pp. 200–217. Springer, Heidelberg (2012)
4. Gonnord, L., Babau, J.P.: Quantity of resource properties expression and runtime assurance for embedded systems. In: IEEE/ACS International Conference on Computer Systems and Applications 2009, AICCSA 2009, pp. 428–435. IEEE (2009)
5. Dwyer, M.B., Avrunin, G.S., Corbett, J.C.: Patterns in property specifications for finite-state verification. In: ICSE, pp. 411–420 (1999)
6. Bauer, A., Leucker, M., Schallhart, C.: Comparing LTL semantics for runtime verification. J. Log. Comput. **20**, 651–674 (2010)

7. Lanoix, A., Dormoy, J., Kouchnarenko, O.: Combining proof and model-checking to validate reconfigurable architectures. ENTCS **279**, 43–57 (2011)
8. Baille, G., Garnier, P., Mathieu, H., Pissard-Gibollet, R.: The INRIA Rhône-Alpes CyCab. Technical Report RT-0229, INRIA (1999)
9. Hamilton, A.G.: Logic for Mathematicians. Cambridge University Press, Cambridge (1978)
10. Bauer, A., Falcone, Y.: Decentralised LTL monitoring. In: Giannakopoulou, D., Méry, D. (eds.) FM 2012. LNCS, vol. 7436, pp. 85–100. Springer, Heidelberg (2012)
11. Bacchus, F., Kabanza, F.: Planning for temporally extended goals. Ann. Math. Artif. Intell. **22**, 5–27 (1998)
12. Dormoy, J., Kouchnarenko, O., Lanoix, A.: Runtime verification of temporal patterns for dynamic reconfigurations of components. In: Arbab, F., Ölveczky, P.C. (eds.) FACS 2011. LNCS, vol. 7253, pp. 115–132. Springer, Heidelberg (2012)
13. Kim, M., Lee, I., Shin, J., Sokolsky, O., et al.: Monitoring, checking, and steering of real-time systems. ENTCS **70**, 95–111 (2002)
14. Manna, Z., Pnueli, A.: A hierarchy of temporal properties (invited paper, 1989). In: Proceedings of the 9th ACM Symposium on Principles of Distributed Computing, pp. 377–410. ACM (1990)
15. Chang, E., Manna, Z., Pnueli, A.: Characterization of temporal property classes. In: Kuich, W. (ed.) Automata, Languages and Programming. LNCS, vol. 623, pp. 474–486. Springer, Heidelberg (1992)
16. Falcone, Y., Fernandez, J.-C., Mounier, L.: Runtime verification of safety-progress properties. In: Bensalem, S., Peled, D.A. (eds.) RV 2009. LNCS, vol. 5779, pp. 40–59. Springer, Heidelberg (2009)
17. Ligatti, J., Bauer, L., Walker, D.: Run-time enforcement of nonsafety policies. ACM TISSEC **12**, 19:1–19:41 (2009)
18. Bloom, B., Istrail, S., Meyer, A.R.: Bisimulation can't be traced. In: Ferrante, J., Mager, P. (eds.) POPL, pp. 229–239. ACM Press (1988)
19. Dormoy, J., Kouchnarenko, O., Lanoix, A.: When structural refinement of components keeps temporal properties over reconfigurations. In: Giannakopoulou, D., Méry, D. (eds.) FM 2012. LNCS, vol. 7436, pp. 171–186. Springer, Heidelberg (2012)
20. Ligatti, J., Bauer, L., Walker, D.: Edit automata: enforcement mechanisms for run-time security policies. Int. J. Inf. Secur. **4**, 2–16 (2005)
21. Jantsch, A.: Modeling Embedded Systems and SoC's: Concurrency and Time in Models of Computation. Morgan Kaufmann, San Francisco (2004)
22. Trentelman, K., Huisman, M.: Extending JML specifications with temporal logic. In: Kirchner, H., Ringeissen, Ch. (eds.) AMAST 2002. LNCS, vol. 2422, pp. 334–348. Springer, Heidelberg (2002)
23. Biere, A., Cimatti, A., Clarke, E.M., Strichman, O., Zhu, Y.: Bounded model checking. Adv. Comput. **58**, 117–148 (2003)
24. Falcone, Y., Jaber, M., Nguyen, T.-H., Bozga, M., Bensalem, S.: Runtime verification of component-based systems. In: Barthe, G., Pardo, A., Schneider, G. (eds.) SEFM 2011. LNCS, vol. 7041, pp. 204–220. Springer, Heidelberg (2011)
25. Kähkönen, K., Lampinen, J., Heljanko, K., Niemelä, I.: The LIME interface specification language and runtime monitoring tool. In: Bensalem, S., Peled, D.A. (eds.) RV 2009. LNCS, vol. 5779, pp. 93–100. Springer, Heidelberg (2009)
26. Seinturier, L., Merle, P., Rouvoy, R., Romero, D., Schiavoni, V., Stefani, J.B.: A component-based middleware platform for reconfigurable service-oriented architectures. Softw. Pract. Exper. **42**, 559–583 (2012)

Automatic Component Deployment in the Presence of Circular Dependencies

Tudor A. Lascu, Jacopo Mauro$^{(\boxtimes)}$, and Gianluigi Zavattaro

FOCUS team, Department of Computer Science/INRIA,
University of Bologna, Bologna, Italy
{lascu,jmauro,zavattar}@cs.unibo.it

Abstract. In distributed systems like clouds or service oriented frameworks, applications are typically assembled by deploying and connecting a large number of heterogeneous software components, spanning from fine-grained packages to coarse-grained complex services. The complexity of such systems requires a rich set of techniques and tools to support the automation of their deployment process. By relying on a formal model of components, we describe a sound and complete algorithm for computing the sequence of actions allowing the deployment of a desired configuration. Moreover, differently from other proposals in the literature, our technique works even in the presence of circular dependencies among components. We give a proof for the polynomiality of the devised algorithm, thus guaranteeing efficiency and effectiveness of automatic tools for component deployment based on our algorithm.

1 Introduction

Deploying software component systems is becoming a critical challenge, especially due to the advent of Cloud Computing technologies that make it possible to quickly run complex distributed software systems on-demand on a virtualized infrastructure, at a fraction of the cost which was necessary just a few years ago. When the number of software components needed to run the application grows, and their interdependencies become too complex to be manually managed, it is necessary for the system administrator to use high-level languages for specifying the expected minimal system requirements, and then rely on tools that automatically synthesize the low-level deployment actions necessary to actually realize a correct and complete system configuration that satisfies such requests.

Recent works have introduced formalisms which focus on this automation aspect of the deployment process, like the Juju initiative within Ubuntu [15] or the Engage system [13]. According to the Juju approach, the system administrator decides which are the high-level services needed in the system and how they should be reciprocal connected, and then the actual deployment is realized by low-level scripts. Similarly, in Engage it is possible to indicate only the relevant services which are needed and their interdependencies, and then the entire system is automatically completed and the actual deployment is synthesized.

Work partially supported by Aeolus project, ANR-2010-SEGI-013-01.

J.L. Fiadeiro et al. (Eds.): FACS 2013, LNCS 8348, pp. 254–272, 2014.
DOI: 10.1007/978-3-319-07602-7_16, © Springer International Publishing Switzerland 2014

One of the limitations of the Engage system is that component interdependencies cannot be circular. This limitation follows from the fact that Engage synthesizes the deployment plan by performing a topological visit of a graph representing the component dependencies: the presence of cycles would forbid to complete such visit. Nevertheless, in many cases, the assumption on the absence of circular dependencies is not admissible. As a first example, we can mention package-based software distributions where circularities are frequent (see [9] for a list of circular dependencies among packages in Debian). Another example of circularity is between replicated database services. For instance, in order to realize a MySQL master-slave replication [4], the master needs from the slave some authentication information (like the IP address), while the slave needs to receive from the master a dump of the database.

In this paper, we address the problem of automatic synthesis of deployment plans in the presence of component circular dependencies. To study the problem we consider the Aeolus component model [12], that enriches traditional component models, based on require/provide ports, with an internal *state machine* that describes the component life-cycle. Each internal state can activate only some of the ports at the component interface. Automatizing a deployment plan consists in specifying a sequence of low-level actions like creation/deletion of components, port binding/unbinding, and internal state changes, that reaches a configuration with at least one component in a specific target internal state. The Aeolus model has been introduced to study the computational boundaries of deployment automation. In the full Aeolus model it is possible to specify *conflicts* among components and also *capacity constraints*, i.e. for each provided port how many requirements it can satisfy, and for each require port how many different instances of a complementary provide port are needed. In [12] we have proved that the deployment problem is undecidable for the full Aeolus model. On the contrary, if capacity constraints are not considered, we have proved in [11] that the problem turns out to be decidable, but it is Exp-Space hard. In order to allow efficient algorithms for automatic deployment, in this paper we further simplify the Aeolus model by removing also conflicts. Juju and Engage also, abstract away from conflicts and this is useful, for instance in Engage, to complete partial configurations simply by adding new components without having to check whether these are incompatible with already present components.

Paper contribution. The novel solution for automatic component deployment that we propose in this paper is based on an algorithm divided in three distinct phases. In a first phase the existence of a plan is checked by performing a forward symbolic *reachability analysis* of all possible reachable states of the components. If the target state is reachable, a second phase of *abstract planning* generates a graph that indicates the kinds of internal state change actions that are necessary, and the causal dependencies among them. Causal dependencies reflect, for instance, the fact that a component should enter a state enacting a provide port before another component enters a state requiring that port. In the third phase of *plan generation* an adaptive topological sort of the abstract plan is performed. By adaptive, we mean that the abstract plan could be rearranged during the topological sort if component duplication is needed. Component duplication is used to deal with those cases in which more instances of the same kind of component must be contemporaneously deployed, in different states, in order to enact different ports at the same time.

The algorithm is described in detail, and its correctness and completeness is proved. By correctness we mean that in all the system configurations traversed during the execution of the deployment plan, each active require port is guaranteed to be connected to a corresponding active provide port. By completeness we mean that if it is possible to reach the required final configuration, our algorithm is guaranteed to return a corresponding deployment plan. Finally, we show the polynomial complexity of our algorithm.

In this paper we present the formalization of our algorithm, the correctness and completeness proof, and the complexity analysis; in a related paper [18] we present a proof of concept implementation.

Paper structure. In Sect. 2 we report the Aeolus component model and the formalization of the component deployment problem. In Sect. 3 we present our novel solution to this problem, and in Sect. 4 we provide the correctness, completeness and computational complexity results for the given algorithm. Finally, in Sect. 5 we discuss related work and draw some concluding remarks.

2   The Aeolus Component Model

In this section we introduce the fragment of the Aeolus model used to frame the problem addressed. The Aeolus model, defined in [12], is a formal model of components, specifically tailored to describe both fine grained software components, like packages to be installed on a single (virtual) machine, and coarse grained ones, like services, obtained as composition of distributed and properly connected sub-services. The problem that we address in this paper is finding a plan, i.e. a correct sequence of actions, that, given a universe of components, leads to a configuration where a target component is in a given state.

A component is a grey-box showing relevant internal states and the actions that can be acted on the component to change state during deployment. Each state activates provide and require ports representing resources that the component provides and needs. Active require ports must be bound to active provide ports of other components.

As an example consider, for instance, the task of configuring a *master-slave replication*, typically used to scale a MySQL deployment over two servers. The master node must be created, installed and configured, and put in running mode to start serving external requests. To activate the slave, an initial *dump* of the data stored in the master is needed. Moreover, the master has to authorize the slave. This is a circular dependency between master and slave, since the latter requires the dump of the former that, on its turn, requires the IP address of the slave to grant its authorization. The Aeolus model for the master and slave component is shown in Fig. 1.

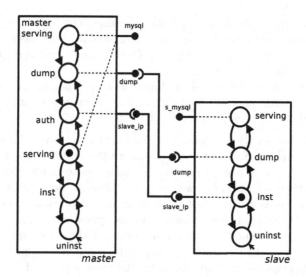

Fig. 1. MySQL master-slave components according to the Aeolus model

The master component has 5 states, an initial uninst state followed by inst and serving. In serving state, it activates the provide port mysql. When replication is needed, in order to enter the final master serving state, it first traverses the state auth that requires the IP address from the slave, and the state dump to provide the dump to the slave. The slave component has instead 4 states, an initial uninst state and 3 states which complement those of the master during the replication process.

We now move to the formal definition of the Aeolus component model. It is based on the notion of *component type*, used to specify the behaviour of a particular kind of component. In the following, $\mathcal{I}$ denotes the set of port names and $\mathcal{Z}$ the set of components.

Definition 1 (Component type). *The set $\mathcal{T}_{flat}$ of component types ranged over by $T, \mathcal{T}_1, \mathcal{T}_2, \ldots$ contains 4-ples $\langle Q, q_0, T, D \rangle$ where:*

- *Q is a finite set of states containing the initial state q_0;*
- *$T \subseteq Q \times Q$ is the set of transitions;*
- *D is a function from Q to a pair $\langle \mathbf{P}, \mathbf{R} \rangle$ of port names (i.e. $\mathbf{P}, \mathbf{R} \subseteq \mathcal{I}$) indicating the provide and require ports that each state activates. We assume that the initial state q_0 has no requirements (i.e. $D(q_0) = \langle \mathbf{P}, \emptyset \rangle$).*

We now define configurations that describe systems composed by components and their bindings. Each component has a unique identifier, taken from the set $\mathcal{Z}$. A configuration, ranged over by $\mathcal{C}_1, \mathcal{C}_2, \ldots$, is given by a set of component types, a set of components in some state, and a set of bindings.

Definition 2 (Configuration). *A configuration $\mathcal{C}$ is a 4-ple $\langle U, Z, S, B \rangle$ where:*

- *$U \subseteq \mathcal{T}_{flat}$ is the finite universe of the available component types;*

- $Z \subseteq \mathcal{Z}$ is the set of the currently deployed components;
- S is the component state description, i.e. a function that associates to components in Z a pair $\langle T, q \rangle$ where $T \in U$ is a component type $\langle Q, q_0, T, D \rangle$, and $q \in Q$ is the current component state;
- $B \subseteq \mathcal{I} \times Z \times Z$ is the set of bindings, namely 3-ple composed by a port, the component that provides that port, and the component that requires it; we assume that the two components are distinct.

Notation. We write $\mathcal{C}[z]$ as a lookup operation that retrieves the pair $\langle T, q \rangle = S(z)$, where $\mathcal{C} = \langle U, Z, S, B \rangle$. On such a pair we then use the postfix projection operators .type and .state to retrieve T and q, respectively. Similarly, given a component type $\langle Q, q_0, T, D \rangle$, we use projections to decompose it: .states, .init, and .trans return the first three elements; .$P(q)$ and .$R(q)$ return the two elements of the $D(q)$ tuple. Moreover, we use .prov (resp. .req) to denote the union of all the provide ports (resp. require ports) of the states in Q. When there is no ambiguity we take the liberty to apply the component type projections to $\langle T, q \rangle$ pairs. *Example*: $\mathcal{C}[z].R(q)$ stands for the require ports of component z in configuration $\mathcal{C}$ when it is in state q.

A configuration is correct if all the active require ports are bound to active provide ports.

Definition 3 (Correctness). *Let us consider the configuration $\mathcal{C} = \langle U, Z, S, B \rangle$.*

We write $\mathcal{C} \models_{req} (z, r)$ to indicate that the require port of component z, with port r, is bound to an active port providing r, i.e. there exists a component $z' \in Z \setminus \{z\}$ such that $\langle r, z', z \rangle \in B$, $\mathcal{C}[z'] = \langle T', q' \rangle$ and r is in $T'.P(q')$.

The configuration $\mathcal{C}$ is correct if for every component $z \in Z$ with $S(z) = \langle T, q \rangle$ we have that $\mathcal{C} \models_{req} (z, r)$ for every $r \in T.R(q)$.

We now formalize how configurations evolve by means of actions.

Definition 4 (Actions). *The set $\mathcal{A}$ contains the following actions:*

- *stateChange(z, q, q') changes the state of the component $z \in \mathcal{Z}$ from q to q'*
- *bind(r, z_1, z_2) creates a binding between the provide port $r \in \mathcal{I}$ of the component z_1 and the require port r of z_2 $(z_1, z_2 \in \mathcal{Z})$;*
- *unbind(r, z_1, z_2) deletes the binding between the provide port $r \in \mathcal{I}$ of the component z_1 and the require port r of z_2 $(z_1, z_2 \in \mathcal{Z})$;*
- *new$(z : T)$ creates a new component of type T in its initial state. The new component is identified by a unique and fresh identifier $z \in \mathcal{Z}$;*
- *del(z) deletes the component $z \in \mathcal{Z}$.*

The execution of actions is formalized by means of a labeled transition system on configurations, which uses actions as labels.

Definition 5 (Reconfigurations). *Reconfigurations are denoted by transitions $\mathcal{C} \xrightarrow{\alpha} \mathcal{C}'$ meaning that the execution of $\alpha \in \mathcal{A}$ on the configuration $\mathcal{C}$ produces a new configuration $\mathcal{C}'$. The transitions from a configuration $\mathcal{C} = \langle U, Z, S, B \rangle$ are defined as follows:*

$$\mathcal{C} \xrightarrow{stateChange(z,q,q')} \langle U, Z, S', B \rangle$$
if $\mathcal{C}[z]$.state $= q$ and
$(q, q') \in \mathcal{C}[z]$.trans and
$$S'(z') = \begin{cases} \langle \mathcal{C}[z].\text{type}, q' \rangle & \text{if } z' = z \\ \mathcal{C}[z'] & \text{otherwise} \end{cases}$$

$$\mathcal{C} \xrightarrow{bind(r,z_1,z_2)} \langle U, Z, S, B \cup \langle r, z_1, z_2 \rangle \rangle$$
if $\langle r, z_1, z_2 \rangle \notin B$
and $r \in \mathcal{C}[z_1].\text{prov} \cap \mathcal{C}[z_2].\text{req}$

$$\mathcal{C} \xrightarrow{unbind(r,z_1,z_2)} \langle U, Z, S, B \setminus \langle r, z_1, z_2 \rangle \rangle$$
if $\langle r, z_1, z_2 \rangle \in B$

$$\mathcal{C} \xrightarrow{new(z:T)} \langle U, Z \cup \{z\}, S', B \rangle$$
if $z \notin Z$, $T \in U$ and
$$S'(z') = \begin{cases} \langle T, T.\text{init} \rangle & \text{if } z' = z \\ \mathcal{C}[z'] & \text{otherwise} \end{cases}$$

$$\mathcal{C} \xrightarrow{del(z)} \langle U, Z \setminus \{z\}, S', B' \rangle$$
if $S'(z') = \begin{cases} \perp & \text{if } z' = z \\ \mathcal{C}[z'] & \text{otherwise} \end{cases}$ and
$B' = \{ \langle r, z_1, z_2 \rangle \in B \mid z \notin \{z_1, z_2\} \}$

We can now define a *deployment plan* as a sequence of actions that transform a correct configuration without violating correctness along the way.

Definition 6 (Deployment plan). *A* deployment plan P *is a sequence of reconfigurations* $\mathcal{C}_0 \xrightarrow{\alpha_1} \mathcal{C}_1 \xrightarrow{\alpha_2} \cdots \xrightarrow{\alpha_m} \mathcal{C}_m$ *such that* $\mathcal{C}_i$ *is correct, for* $0 \le i \le m$.

As an example of a deployment plan let us consider the configuration depicted in Fig. 1. If we want to activate the slave, a possible deployment plan that allows to do so requires to perform two consecutive state changes in the master to reach the dump state. At this point, the slave component can reach the serving state performing first the state change into the dump state and then into the serving state. Note that every action in the deployment plan will correspond to one or more concrete instructions. For instance, the state change from the serving to the auth state in the master corresponds to issue the command `grant replication slave on *.* to user@'slave_ip'`.

We now have all the ingredients to define the *deployment problem*, that is our main concern: given an universe of component types, we want to know whether and how it is possible to deploy at least one component of a given component type T in a given state q.

Definition 7 (Deployment problem). *The* deployment problem *has as input an universe* U *of component types, a component type* T_t, *and a target state* q_t. *The output is a deployment plan* P $= \mathcal{C}_0 \xrightarrow{\alpha_1} \mathcal{C}_1 \xrightarrow{\alpha_2} \cdots \xrightarrow{\alpha_m} \mathcal{C}_m$ *such that* $\mathcal{C}_0 = \langle U, \emptyset, \emptyset, \emptyset \rangle$ *and* $\mathcal{C}_m[z] = \langle T_t, q_t \rangle$, *for some component* z *in* $\mathcal{C}_m$, *if there exists one. Otherwise, it returns a negative answer, stating that no such a plan exists.*

Notice that the restriction to consider one component in a given state is not limiting: one can easily encode any given final configuration by adding dummy provide ports enabled only by the required final states and a dummy component that requires all such provides. For instance, Fig. 2 depicts the dummy target component that in inst state requires the presence of both an active master and an active slave.

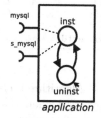

Fig. 2. Target

3   Solving the Deployment Problem

The algorithm that we present for solving the deployment problem is a chain of three phases: *reachability analysis, abstract planning* and *plan generation*. Each phase works on a representation of the meaningful information output by the previous one. Namely, the *reachability analysis* produces a reachability graph where the component types to be used in the deployment plan are selected in combination with their internal states and the necessary bindings that will have to be established between the activated provide and require ports. If the target is reachable, the subsequent *abstract planning* phase produces a graph where nodes represent deployment actions and arcs denote precedence constraints among them. Finally, the *plan generation* phase synthesizes the deployment plan.

3.1   Reachability Analysis

The aim of the first phase is to check if the target can be obtained starting from an initial empty configuration. This is achieved through a forward symbolic reachability analysis that relies on an abstract representation of components. For each component its individual identity as well as the number of its instances are ignored, keeping only its component type and its state $\langle \mathcal{T}, q \rangle$. Also, we abstract away from individual bindings without considering *delete* actions. The abstraction on the bindings is possible since we can safely assume that, given a set of components, all complementary ports on two distinct components are bound. Delete actions are superfluous since the presence of one component does not hinder the reachability of a state in another component.

Algorithm 1. Reachability graph construction

1: $Nodes_0 = \{\langle \mathcal{T}, \mathcal{T}.\text{init} \rangle \mid \mathcal{T} \in U\}$; $provPort = \bigcup_{\langle \mathcal{T}, q \rangle \in Nodes_0} \{\mathcal{T}.\mathbf{P}(q)\}$; $i = 0$;
2: **repeat**
3:     $i = i + 1$;
4:     $Arcs_i, Nodes_i = \emptyset$;
5:     **for all** $\langle \mathcal{T}, q \rangle \in Nodes_{i-1}$ **do**
6:         **for all** $(q, q') \in \mathcal{T}.\text{trans}$ **do**
7:             **if** $\mathcal{T}.\mathbf{R}(q') \subseteq provPort$ **then**
8:                 $Nodes_i.\text{add}(\langle \mathcal{T}, q' \rangle)$;
9:     **for all** $\langle \mathcal{T}, q \rangle \in Nodes_i$ **do**
10:         $provPort.\text{add}(\mathcal{T}.\mathbf{P}(q))$;
11:     $Nodes_i = Nodes_{i-1} \cup Nodes_i$;
12:     **for all** $\langle \mathcal{T}, q \rangle \in Nodes_{i-1}, \langle \mathcal{T}, q' \rangle \in Nodes_i$ **do**
13:         **if** $(q, q') \in \mathcal{T}.\text{trans}$ **then**
14:             $Arcs_i.\text{add}(\langle \mathcal{T}, q' \rangle \longrightarrow \langle \mathcal{T}, q \rangle)$;
15:         **if** $q == q'$ **then**
16:             $Arcs_i.\text{add}(\langle \mathcal{T}, q' \rangle \cdots\cdots \langle \mathcal{T}, q \rangle)$;
17: **until** $Nodes_{i-1} == Nodes_i$

Algorithm 1 creates a *reachability graph* that visually could be seen as a pyramid where the top level contains all the component types in their initial state and, at every step, a new level is produced by adding new component type-state pairs, reachable from the ones at the previous level (see the grey part of Fig. 3). $Nodes_i$ is the set of the type-state pairs at level i, while $Arcs_i$ represents the possible ways a type-state pair can be obtained; $x \longrightarrow y$ means that component state y, at level $i+1$, is obtained from x at level i by a state change, otherwise y is a copy of x (denoted as $x \cdots\!\!\cdot y$). $ProvPort$ is a set containing the ports provided by the components. Initially, it contains the ports provided by all components in their initial state (line 1) and then it is incrementally augmented with the ports provided by the newly added components (lines 9–10). The new type-state pairs to be added are computed by checking if all their requirements are satisfied by at least one component state at the previous level (lines 5–8). Finally, variable $Arcs_i$ is updated (lines 13–16), listing all the possible ways a type-state pair can be obtained. The generation of levels proceeds until a fix-point is reached (line 17). Termination is guaranteed by the fact that the number of possible type-state pairs is finite and at every cycle at least a new pair is added to the $Node_i$ set. When the fix-point is reached, if the last set does not contain the target component type-state pair, a plan to achieve the goal does not exist and we do not execute the subsequent phases of the algorithm.

Once all pairs have been generated, starting from the target pair at the bottom of the pyramid, a selection procedure is carried out in order to pick the pairs to be employed in the deployment plan. The selection is performed by means of a bottom-up visit of the reachability graph as described in Algorithm 2.

Algorithm 2. Component Selection

1: $SNodes_n = \{\langle \mathcal{T}_{target}, q_{target}\rangle\}$;
2: **for** $i = n$ downto 1 **do**
3:    $SNodes_{i-1} = SArcs_{i-1} = \emptyset$;
4:    **for all** $\langle \mathcal{T}, q\rangle \in SNodes_i$ **do**
5:       $\langle \mathcal{T}', q'\rangle = $ heuristic_parent$(\langle \mathcal{T}, q\rangle, i)$;
6:       $SNodes_{i-1}$.add$(\langle \mathcal{T}', q'\rangle)$;
7:       $SArcs_{i-1}$.add$(\langle\langle \mathcal{T}', q'\rangle, \langle \mathcal{T}, q\rangle\rangle)$;
8:       **for all** $r \in \mathcal{T}.R(q)$ **do**
9:          $\langle \mathcal{T}', q'\rangle = $ heuristic_prov$(\langle \mathcal{T}, q\rangle, r, i)$;
10:          $SNodes_{i-1}$.add$(\langle \mathcal{T}', q'\rangle)$;
11:          $SReq$.add$(\langle \mathcal{T}', q'\rangle \xrightarrow{r} \circ \langle \mathcal{T}, q\rangle)$;

From the bottom level (that we denote with n) we proceed upward selecting the pairs used to deploy the pairs at the lower level. Variables $SNodes_i$ and $SArcs_i$ denote, respectively, the selected components state pairs at level i and how these pairs are obtained. From the last level only the target pair is selected (line 1). For every selected component at level $i + 1$, we select at level i one of its predecessors and we store this choice in variables $SNodes_{i-1}$ and $SArcs_{i-1}$ (lines 5–7). Since there may be more than one possible choice, we rely for the decision on heuristics, here abstracted by function heuristic_parent. The decision at this point could affect the length of the deployment plan. A study of the best heuristics is out of the scope of this paper; we leave this task for future work. For an example of a possible heuristic we refer to [18].

For every require port needed by the selected pairs of level $i+1$ that are not copies, we select a pair at level i that is able to activate a complementary provide port. This choice is recorded in $SNodes_{i-1}$ and $SReq$ (lines 10–11). In particular, $SReq$ maintains the indication of the kinds of binding between provide and require ports of components that will be used in the plan to be subsequently synthesized; these dependencies are represented by arcs $\langle T', q' \rangle \overset{r}{\multimap} \langle T, q \rangle$ where $\langle T', q' \rangle$ is the component type-state pair that activates the provide port r, while $\langle T, q \rangle$ activates the complementary require port. Even in this case there is usually more than one possible alternative in the selection of the type-pair that can provide the requested port. As before, we rely on an heuristics, dubbed `heuristic_prov`, to decide which pair is used as a provider.

Figure 3 depicts the output of this first phase for the MySQL master-slave example. The grey and black part is the reachability graph generated by Algorithm 1, while the part only in black is a possible selection done by Algorithm 2. For space reasons, master, slave and application are denoted by M, S and A respectively, and each state is referred by its initial upper-case letter: U for uninst, I for inst, S for serving, A for auth, D for dump and MS for master serving.

The first level of Fig. 3 contains components M, S and A in their initial states. At the second level, two pairs are added: component M in I and component S in I, derived respectively from M in U and S in U. At level 3, pair $\langle M, S \rangle$ is added. At next step, pair $\langle M, A \rangle$ can also be added since it derives from $\langle M, S \rangle$ and its requirement on the interface $slave\_ip$ is fulfilled by $\langle S, I \rangle$, appearing at previous level. The generation of the reachability graph proceeds as depicted until the pair $\langle A, I \rangle$ is added: this is the last level as no new type-state pairs can be generated.

The selection procedure starts from the target node, $\langle A, I \rangle$ in the last level. There is only one possible derivation for $\langle A, I \rangle$ and so $\langle A, U \rangle$ is selected as its origin. Since $\langle A, I \rangle$ requires two interfaces, r_mysql and s_mysql, provided by $\langle M, RS \rangle$ and $\langle S, S \rangle$, these providers are also selected. The selection process continues until all components at the top level are selected.

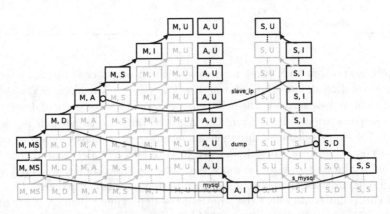

Fig. 3. Reachability graph and component selection for the running example.

3.2   Abstract Planning

The abstract plan specifies the life-cycle of all component types employed in the deployment of the target state. It can be seen as a directed graph where nodes represent either a *new*, *del*, or *stateChange* action, and arcs represent action precedence constraints. Every node is tagged by a triple denoting an action: $\langle z, q, q' \rangle$ for a *stateChange* from state q to q' of instance z; $\langle z, \varepsilon, q_0 \rangle$ for a *new* action of instance z (in state q_0), and $\langle z, q, \varepsilon \rangle$ for *del* action on the instance z (in state q). Precedence arcs are of three kinds: (i) $\longrightarrow$: precedence of *stateChange* actions on the same instance; (ii) $\overset{r}{\dashrightarrow}$: precedence of instances that provide a resource r w.r.t instances requiring it; (iii) $\overset{r}{\dashrightarrow}$: precedence of an instance requiring a port r w.r.t. actions that deactivate it.

Algorithm 3. Abstract Plan Generation

1: $Paths = \texttt{getMaxPaths}(Nodes_0, \ldots, Nodes_n);$
2: $Act = \emptyset;\ InstMap = \{\ \};$
3: **for all** $(\langle \mathcal{T}, q_0 \rangle, \ldots, \langle \mathcal{T}, q_h \rangle) \in Paths$ **do**
4:     $inst = \texttt{getFreshName}();$
5:     $InstMap[inst] = \mathcal{T};$
6:     $Act.\texttt{add}(\langle inst, \varepsilon, q_0 \rangle);\ Act.\texttt{add}(\langle inst, q_h, \varepsilon \rangle);$
7:     **for all** $i \in [0..h-1]$ **do**
8:         $Act.\texttt{add}(\langle inst, q_i, q_{i+1} \rangle)$
9:     $Prec.\texttt{add}(\langle\langle inst, \varepsilon, q_0 \rangle \longrightarrow \langle inst, q_0, q_1 \rangle\rangle);$
10:    $Prec.\texttt{add}(\langle\langle inst, q_{h-1}q_h \rangle \longrightarrow \langle inst, q_h, \varepsilon \rangle\rangle);$
11:    **for all** $i \in [0..h-2]$ **do**
12:       $Prec.\texttt{add}(\langle\langle inst, q_i, q_{i+1} \rangle \longrightarrow \langle inst, q_{i+1}, q_{i+2} \rangle\rangle);$
13: **for all** $\langle \langle \mathcal{T}, q' \rangle \overset{r}{\multimap} \langle \mathcal{T}', s' \rangle \rangle \in SReq$ **do**
14:    **for all** $n_1 == \langle i_1, s, s' \rangle \in Act\ .\ InstMap[i_1] == \mathcal{T}'$ **do**
15:       **let** $n_2 = \langle i_2, q, q' \rangle \in Act$ **where** $InstMap[i_2] == \mathcal{T}$ **in**
16:           $Prec.\texttt{add}(n_2 \overset{r}{\dashrightarrow} n_1)$
17:           **let** n'_1 **where** $n_1 \longrightarrow n'_1$ **in**
18:           **repeat**
19:              **let** $n'_2 = \langle i_2, q', q'' \rangle$ **where** $n_2 \longrightarrow n'_2$ **in**
20:                **if** $q' \neq \varepsilon \wedge r \in \mathcal{T}.P(q')$ **then**
21:                   $n_2 = n'_2$
22:              **until** $q'' == \varepsilon \vee r \notin \mathcal{T}.P(q')$
23:           $Prec.\texttt{add}(n'_1 \overset{r}{\dashrightarrow} n_2)$

Algorithm 3 is used to derive the abstract plan. To generate an abstract plan we consider an instance for every maximal path that starts from a type-state pair in the top level and reaches a type-state that is not a copy. For instance, as shown in Fig. 3, for the master-slave example there are three maximal paths: one for the master (starting from $\langle \mathsf{M}, U \rangle$ and ending in $\langle \mathsf{M}, MS \rangle$), one for the dummy component and one for the slave (starting from $\langle \mathsf{S}, U \rangle$ and ending in $\langle \mathsf{S}, S \rangle$). The computation of the maximal paths is performed by the function `getMaxPaths` (line 1). Variables Act and $Prec$ are used to store the actions of the abstract plan and the precedence constraints, respectively.

The first loop (lines 3–12) is used to generate the nodes of the abstract plan and the precedence constraints $\longrightarrow$ among them. First of all, a new fresh name for the instance is generated (line 4) and is associated to the component type

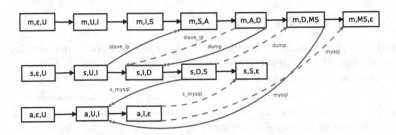

Fig. 4. Abstract plan for the running example.

of the instance using the map $InstMap$ (line 5). After that, nodes corresponding to the creation and deletion of the instance are added (line 6), as well as
nodes representing intermediate state changes (line 8). The last part of the loop
(lines 9–12) is used to generate the precedence arcs $\longrightarrow$.

The second loop, starting at line 13, adds for every dependency arc, selected
in the reachability graph, a pair of $\twoheadrightarrow$ and $--\rightarrow$ arcs. In particular, lines 17–23
apply a relaxation of the $\overset{r}{--\rightarrow}$ arc, since if a port r is provided also by successor
states, then we can relax the constraint imposed by the $--\rightarrow$ arc by setting its
destination to the last successor node that still provides r.

Figure 4 displays the abstract plan for the running example. The rows rep-
resent the life-cycles of master, slave and application, respectively. The $\overset{slave\_ip}{\twoheadrightarrow}$
from $\langle s, U, I \rangle$ to $\langle m, S, A \rangle$ expresses the fact that the $stateChange$ of slave from
uninstalled to installed must precede the $stateChange$ of master from serving to
auth because state auth of server requires interface $slave\_ip$, provided by slave
in state installed. The twin $--\rightarrow$ arc states that master must switch from auth to
dump before slave switches from installed to dump, as this state ceases providing
interface $slave\_ip$, otherwise its requirement would become unfulfilled. Following
the same principle we can interpret the pair of arcs $\langle m, A, D \rangle \twoheadrightarrow \langle s, I, D \rangle$ and
$\langle s, D, S \rangle --\rightarrow \langle m, D, MS \rangle$ for interface $dump$. Finally, the target is represented by
node $\langle a, U, I \rangle$, namely application entering state installed. This state requires two
interfaces, $mysql$ and s_mysql provided respectively by master in state master
serving and slave in state serving. Two $\twoheadrightarrow$ arcs (together with their $--\rightarrow$ counterparts) are thus added with destination $\langle a, U, I \rangle$, one from $\langle s, D, S \rangle$ and the other
one from $\langle m, D, MS \rangle$.

3.3 Plan Generation

The main idea for the synthesis of a concrete deployment plan is to visit the
nodes of the abstract plan in topological order until the target component is
reached. Visiting a node consists of performing that action. Moreover, in order
to properly satisfy component requirements, when an incoming $\twoheadrightarrow$ is encountered
a, new binding should be created, and when an outgoing $--\rightarrow$ is encountered, the
corresponding binding should be deleted.

Algorithm 4. Plan synthesis

```
 1: Plan = [ ]; ToVisit = [ ]; finished = false;
 2: for all n = ⟨i, x, y⟩ ∈ Act do
 3:     if no_incoming_edges(n) then
 4:         Plan.append(new(i : InstMap[i]));
 5:         ToVisit.push(n);
 6: repeat
 7:     repeat
 8:         ⟨i, x, y⟩ = ToVisit.pop();
 9:         if x == ε then
10:             PROCESSINSTANCEEDGE(⟨i, x, y⟩)
11:         else if y == ε then
12:             PROCESSREDEDGES(⟨i, x, y⟩)
13:             Plan.append(del(i));
14:         else
15:             Plan.append(stateChange(⟨i, x, y⟩));
16:             PROCESSREDEDGES(⟨i, x, y⟩)
17:             PROCESSBLUEEDGES(⟨i, x, y⟩)
18:             PROCESSINSTANCEEDGE(⟨i, x, y⟩)
19:         if InstMap[i] == T_{target} ∧ y == q_{target} then finished = true;
20:         Act.remove(⟨i, x, y⟩);
21:     until ToVisit == [ ] ∨ finished
22:     if ¬finished then
23:         n = Duplicate();
24:         ToVisit.push(n);
25: until finished
26:
27: procedure PROCESSINSTANCEEDGE(⟨i, x, y⟩)
28:     let n ∈ Act where ⟨i, x, y⟩ ⟶ n ∈ Prec in
29:         Prec.remove(⟨i, x, y⟩ ⟶ n);
30:         if no_incoming_edges(n) then ToVisit.push(n);
31: procedure PROCESSBLUEEDGES(⟨i, x, y⟩)
32:     for all ⟨i, x, y⟩ ↠ ⟨i', x', y'⟩ ∈ Prec do
33:         Plan.append(bind(r, i, i')); Prec.remove(⟨i, x, y⟩ ↠ ⟨i', x', y'⟩);
34:         if no_incoming_edges(⟨i', x', y'⟩) then ToVisit.push(⟨i', x', y'⟩);
35: procedure PROCESSREDEDGES(⟨i, x, y⟩)
36:     for all ⟨i, x, y⟩ --↠ ⟨i', x', y'⟩ ∈ Prec do
37:         Plan.append(unbind(r, i', i)); Prec.remove(⟨i, x, y⟩ --↠ ⟨i', x', y'⟩);
38:         if no_incoming_edges(⟨i', x', y'⟩) then ToVisit.push(⟨i', x', y'⟩);
```

Algorithm 4 builds the plan adding actions to a list called *Plan*. Nodes can be visited if they do not have precedence constraints, i.e. incoming arcs. Function no_incoming_edges is used to check this condition. Visitable nodes are stored in a stack, named *ToVisit*. As soon as a node becomes visitable it is pushed onto *ToVisit* in order to be later processed.

The algorithm relies on three auxiliary procedures, ProcessInstanceEdge, ProcessBlueEdges and ProcessRedEdges, aimed at dealing respectively with ⟶, ↠ and --↠ edges, the three kinds of edges present in the abstract plan. Given a node of the abstract plan, procedures ProcessRedEdges and processBlueEdges deal with its outgoing --↠ and ↠ arcs. They add *unbind* and *bind* actions to the *Plan* list and remove the corresponding arcs from the abstract plan. Moreover, if the removal of an arc makes a node visitable, they add it to the *ToVisit* stack. Similarly, procedure processInstanceEdge removes the precedence arc ⟶, adding its target node to the *ToVisit* stack if it has no incoming arcs.

266   T.A. Lascu et al.

At the beginning, all initial nodes are pushed on $ToVisit$ (lines 2–5) and a *new* action is added to the plan for every initial node (line 4). The algorithm then proceeds considering one action $a = \langle i, x, y \rangle$ at a time in $ToVisit$ until the target node is encountered or $ToVisit$ becomes empty. If a is an initial node its outgoing precedence arcs are removed by calling procedure processInstanceEdge (line 10). If, instead, a is a final node its outgoing red arcs are first transformed into *unbind* actions, via procedure processRedEdges (line 12), and then the corresponding *del* action is added to the plan (line 13). Finally, if a is an intermediate node, a *stateChange* action is added to the plan (line 15). The a outgoing red, blue and precedence arcs are then removed from the abstract plan by calling in sequence the auxiliary procedures ProcessRedEdges, ProcessBlueEdges, and ProcessInstanceEdge (lines 16–18). At the end of the inner loop, variable $finished$ is set to true if the target node is encountered (line 19) and the node a is removed from the abstract plan (line 20).

Note that the topological visit could not reach the target if a cycle is present in the abstract plan. This happens when an instance is required to perform a state change as well as provide a port that the state change deactivates. In these cases, it is necessary to duplicate the instance: one new copy remains in the state, thus keeping the provide port active, and in this way the original instance is allowed to perform the state change. Lines 22–24 deal with the duplication process, calling function Duplicate in Algorithm 5.

Algorithm 5. Duplicate

1: **function** DUPLICATE
2:     let $n = \langle i, x, y \rangle \in Act$ **where** $y \neq \varepsilon \wedge \nexists n' \in Act$. $(n' \longrightarrow n \in Prec \vee n' \overset{r}{\longrightarrow} n \in Prec)$ **in**
3:         $i' = $ getFreshName(); $InstMap[i'] = InstMap[i]$; $Act.$add($\langle i', x, \varepsilon \rangle$);
4:         **for all** $n' \overset{r}{\dashrightarrow} \langle i, x, y \rangle \in Prec$ **do**
5:             $Prec.$remove($n' \overset{r}{\dashrightarrow} \langle i, x, y \rangle$); $Prec.$add($n' \overset{r}{\dashrightarrow} \langle i', x, \varepsilon \rangle$);
6:         **for** $(j = Plan.size() - 1; j \geq 0; j = j - 1)$ **do**
7:             **if** $Plan[j] == bind(r, i, z)$ **then** $Plan[j] = bind(r, i', z)$;
8:             **else if** $Plan[j] == bind(r, z, i)$ **then** $Plan.$insert($bind(r, z, i'), j$);
9:             **else if** $Plan[j] == unbind(r, i, z)$ **then** $Plan[j] = unbind(r, i', z)$;
10:            **else if** $Plan[j] == unbind(r, z, i)$ **then** $Plan.$insert($unbind(r, z, i'), j$);
11:            **else if** $Plan[j] == new(i : T)$ **then** $Plan.$insert($new(i : T), j$);
12:            **else if** $Plan[j] == stateChange(\langle i, x, y \rangle)$ **then**
13:                $Plan.$insert($stateChange(\langle i', x, y \rangle, j$);
14:     **return** $\langle i, x, y \rangle$;

The Duplicate function first identifies a state change node $\langle i, x, y \rangle$ with only incoming $\dashrightarrow$ arcs (line 2). i is the instance to duplicate until the node preceding $\langle i, x, y \rangle$. A fresh name i' is assigned to identify the new instance and the delete node of i' is added to the set of actions (line 3). All $\dashrightarrow$ arcs incoming into $\langle i, x, y \rangle$ are redirected towards the new node $\langle i', x, \varepsilon \rangle$ (lines 4–5). Then, the actions already performed on i are duplicated in order to perform them also on the new instance i' (lines 6–13). The actions *new* and *stateChange* of i' are added to the plan immediately after the *new* and *stateChange* actions of i (lines 11, 13). Similarly, *bind* and *unbind* actions where i requires something from another instance, are replicated (lines 8, 10). The *bind* and *unbind* actions where i instead provides something for other instances, are replaced with bind and unbind actions involving i' instead of i (lines 7, 9).

The Duplicate function returns the node $\langle i, x, y \rangle$; notice that this node is immediately added to the $ToVisit$ stack since, after the duplication procedure, it has no precedence constraints. Algorithm 4 eventually terminates since the number of duplications needed to reach the target component is bound by the number of actions in the original abstract plan.

As an example, starting from the abstract plan of Fig. 4, the tool exploiting the previously described algorithms generates the following deployment plan[1].

```
Plan[1]  = [Create instance slave:Slave]
Plan[2]  = [Create instance master:Master]
Plan[3]  = [Create instance application:Application]
Plan[4]  = [master : change state from uninst to inst]
Plan[5]  = [master : change state from inst to serving]
Plan[6]  = [slave : change state from uninst to inst]
Plan[7]  = [slave : bind port slave_ip to master]
Plan[8]  = [master : change state from serving to auth]
Plan[9]  = [master : change state from auth to dump]
Plan[10] = [master : unbind port slave_ip from slave]
Plan[11] = [master : bind port dump to slave]
Plan[12] = [slave : change state from inst to dump]
Plan[13] = [slave : change state from dump to serving]
Plan[14] = [slave : unbind port dump from master]
Plan[15] = [slave : bind port s_mysql to application]
Plan[16] = [master : change state from dump to master serv.]
Plan[17] = [master : bind port mysql to application]
Plan[18] = [application : change state from uninst to inst]
```

4   Formal Analysis of the Algorithm

In this section we prove that the proposed algorithm, called *DeploymentPlanner* in the following, is sound and complete, i.e. it produces a correct deployment plan if and only if it exists. Moreover, we prove that it runs in polynomial time w.r.t. the size of the problem.

Theorem 1 (Soundness). *Given a universe of components U, a component type $\mathcal{T}_t$, and a target state q_t, if the DeploymentPlanner algorithm computes a sequence of actions $\alpha_1, \ldots, \alpha_m$, then $\langle U, \emptyset, \emptyset, \emptyset \rangle \xrightarrow{\alpha_1} \mathcal{C}_1 \xrightarrow{\alpha_2} \ldots \xrightarrow{\alpha_m} \mathcal{C}_m$ is a deployment plan for $\mathcal{T}_t$ in state q_t.*

---

[1] For more information related to the developed tool and use cases involving also duplication we defer the interested reader to [18].

Proof. $\langle U, \emptyset, \emptyset, \emptyset \rangle$ is the empty configuration and therefore it is correct by definition. $\langle \mathcal{T}_t, q_t \rangle$ is contained in $\mathcal{C}_m$ since Algorithm 4 terminates when the state change to obtain $\langle \mathcal{T}_t, q_t \rangle$ is added to the plan. To prove the thesis we have to show that every reconfiguration action preserves correctness. This can be proven by cases on the kind of α_j action. If α_j is a bind or new action, correctness is preserved since these two actions do not violate any requirement.

If $\alpha_j = stateChange(i, x, y)$ then α_j may invalidate correctness in two ways: either i stops providing a port p, needed by someone else or state y of i requires a port r, not provided in $\mathcal{C}_j$. In the first case, if i' is the component requiring p, by Algorithm 3 there is an arc $\xrightarrow{p}$ from i to i', that goes from a predecessor of $\langle i, x, y \rangle$ to a node of i'. Together with it, a twin $\dashrightarrow$ arc, from i' to i, is added, that has $\langle i, x, y \rangle$ as destination. This guarantees that an *unbind* action is added to the plan before the $stateChange(i, x, y)$, thus i' does not require p any longer, and so correctness is ensured. For the second case, if i in y requires a port r, then, for the same reason as above, there exists an $\overset{r}{\dashrightarrow}$ arc from a successor of $\langle i, x, y \rangle$ in i, to one node of i'. Thus a twin $\xrightarrow{r}$ arc exists, from i' to a predecessor of $\langle i, x, y \rangle$ in i, meaning that the corresponding *bind* action is added to the plan before the $stateChange(i, x, y)$ action, and correctness is not violated.

Let us consider the case $\alpha_j = unbind(r, i', i)$. It does not violate correctness since by Algorithm 4 we add an *unbind* action for every $\langle i, x, y \rangle \overset{r}{\dashrightarrow} \langle i', x', y' \rangle$ arc. This ensures that instance i, that required r, has already stopped requiring it.

Similarly, if $\alpha_j = del(i)$, it may violate correctness by deleting a component that still provides a needed port. This, however, is never the case because delete actions have just $\overset{r}{\dashrightarrow}$ incoming arcs. Therefore, by Algorithm 4, this action is performed only after all instances requiring r have stopped requiring it.   □

The second result shows that the algorithm is complete, i.e. if a deployment plan exists, then the algorithm will eventually find one. To prove completeness we rely on the following lemma, stating that all circularities in the abstract plan contain at least an $\dashrightarrow$ arc. This key property guarantees, in presence of circularities, the existence of a node that has as only $\dashrightarrow$ incoming arcs. This is the node chosen by Algorithm 5 for duplication, to eliminate a cycle and proceed with the topological visit.

Lemma 1. *Every cycle in the abstract plan contains at least an $\dashrightarrow$ arc.*

Proof. (By contradiction). Assume that the cycle contains just $\twoheadrightarrow$ and $\longrightarrow$. If an $\longrightarrow$ arc belongs to the cycle this means that during the reachability analysis a component type-state pair of a higher level required a port from a type-state pair in a lower level. This is impossible by construction. Hence the cycle contains only $\twoheadrightarrow$ arrows. This means that the actions involved in the cycle are just state changes. Moreover the type-state pairs obtained with these state changes are mutually dependent, i.e. the component z_1 to reach a state q_1 needs something provided by z_2 in state q_2 and, vice versa, the component z_2 to reach q_2 needs something provided by z_1 in q_1. By Algorithm 1 mutually dependent type-state cannot be obtained.   □

Theorem 2 (Completeness). *Given an universe of components U, a component type T_t, and a target state q_t, if a solution exists to the deployment problem on input $I = (U, T_t, q_t)$, then algorithm DeploymentPlanner returns a deployment plan for I.*

Proof. Since by hypothesis there is a sequence of create and state change actions that allow the deployment of T_t in state q_t, during the reachability analysis the component state pair $\langle T_t, q_t \rangle$ is obtained. A correct plan will be produced (Thm. 1) assuming that the abstract plan and plan generation phases terminate. The former terminates because given the reachability graph, the maximal number of maximal paths is finite. The latter terminates because duplication will be needed at most k^2 times, where k is the number of component type-state pairs in the last level of the reachability graph. Indeed, to reach the target component state pair, potentially all the state changes and create actions of the abstract plan could be visited. When there is a cycle that forbids the visit of a state change action, as a direct consequence of Lemma 1, there is at least a state change action that has only $\dashrightarrow$ incoming arcs. The duplication procedure removes all the cycles involving that action without creating new ones. The topological visit can therefore proceed and it eventually terminates since at every duplication at least a state change could be performed and the number of state change actions in the abstract plan is finite and fixed. □

As a final result we prove that *DeploymentPlanner* runs in polynomial time.

Theorem 3 (Complexity). *The DeploymentPlanner algorithm runs in polynomial time.*

Proof. Let us denote with k the total number of possible component type-state pairs, with b the maximal number of predecessors of a type-state pair, and with h the maximal number of ports. Every level of the reachability graph has no more than k type-state pairs. At every level one or more type-state pairs are added, hence the reachability analysis terminates and in the pyramid there are at most $k + 1$ levels. To build a new level from a previous one it is necessary to filter the successors of the components in the previous level by checking if their requirements are satisfied. Since a component has at most k successors and requires at most h ports, the cost of building a level is $O(hk^2)$. The pyramid has at most $k + 1$ levels, hence Algorithm 1 runs in $O(hk^3)$ time.

To select the bindings and the components (Algorithm 2), for every type-state pair at most h ports and b parent pairs need to be considered. Since in every level there could be potentially k pairs and the total number of pairs in the reachability graph is $O(k^2)$, Algorithm 2 takes $O(bhk^3)$ time.

The computation of the maximal paths in Algorithm 3 can be performed in $O(k^3)$ since there are at most k^2 maximal paths of length k. The generation of the abstract plan can be done in $O(hk^2)$ since there could be at most k^2 actions, each of them having no more than $h + 1$ outgoing precedence constraints.

Algorithm 4 relies on duplicating an instance whenever the topological visit gets stuck, due to precedence constraint cycles. In the worst case, a duplication is needed for every node of every instance and to detect which node to duplicate all the nodes could be visited. Since every node has at most $2hk^2 + 1$ incoming arcs, detecting the node to duplicate has a worst case cost of $O(hk^4)$. The duplication procedure may update the plan adding or modifying at most an action for every node and binding involving the instance to duplicate. Since an instance could be involved in k actions and every action has up to $2hk^2 + 1 + h$ (incoming and outgoing) arcs, the cost to perform a duplication is $O(hk^3)$. Therefore, in the worst case, the cost of all duplications is $O(hk^4)$.

The topological visit of the abstract plan is linear w.r.t. the number of nodes and thus requires $O(k^3)$ steps.

Summing up, the *DeploymentPlanner* algorithm has a total complexity of $O(bhk^3) + O(hk^4)$, which considering b bound by k, amounts to $O(hk^4)$.   □

5   Related Work and Conclusions

In this work we address the problem of finding a suitable technique to automatize the deployment of complex systems assembled from a large number of interconnected components. We propose an algorithm that computes in polynomial time the actions needed to deploy such a system and prove soundness and completeness of this novel approach.

To describe a system we adopt the Aeolus component model [12]. According to it, components are grey-boxes with provide and require ports and with an associated automaton, describing the component life-cycle, and expressing for each internal state the corresponding ports that are (de)activated. The idea to specify a component by means of a black-box with an interface that exhibits to the (outside) environment its behavior is widely adopted. For instance, the standard definition of component in the UML specification [1] sees components as black-boxes that may provide and require certain interfaces. This sometimes is not enough and the inner structure of a component must be also considered. The use of automata as a formal model is a natural choice as testified, for instance, by interface automata [8,17]. These models allow to develop formal verification methods for properties of interest but, differently from our approach, they focus on checking component compatibility and behavior refinement. The FraSCAti [23] platform, by leveraging on a concise and expressive description of a complex software system, defined by the Fractal component model [5], develops a framework for managing the deployment of applications in the cloud. It is up to the system designer, however, to select the components and to realize their interconnection. Process calculi approaches are also used to model software components, e.g. [3,6,19,22]. The focus of these approaches, however, is not on deployment but rather on modeling interaction and communication between components.

Industrial tools such as [7,15,16,20,21,24] are available to ease the deployment of software. They allow to automatize the process of carrying out the deployment of components on a pool of machines, provided a deployment plan is known in advance.

Related to our work are [10,14] that compute final configurations solving a Constraint Satisfaction Problem. Both these works however do not provide a sequence of actions to reach the desired configuration.

Engage [13] uses automata to specify a component's behaviour and it is able to deploy the resources completing a target partial configuration. However, it relies on the assumption that the dependency graph is acyclic, meaning that circular dependencies among components are not admitted.

Closely related is [2] that proposes an heuristic-based algorithm to remove build dependency cycles for bootstrapping a Linux software distribution. The building order of the packages is generated using a topological sort of a graph. However, differently from our work, one of the assumptions is that once a package is recompiled, its older version is no longer required.

A proof of concept implementation of the *DeploymentPlanner* algorithm has been developed and described in [18] with some preliminary validation modeling more complex use cases. Results are encouraging as the tool is able to produce plans in less than a minute, for scenarios involving hundreds of components. As future work we intend to study the impact of the selection heuristics on the length of the deployment plan. We deem that with the right heuristics the number of components involved in the plan could be greatly reduced. We aim to further refine the current technique by considering also reconfiguration plans, dealing with cases in which the initial configuration has already some deployed components. Finally, we would like to take into account conflicts, producing in a reasonable amount of time plans that do not violate them or minimize the time windows where a system is inconsistent.

References

1. OMG Unified Modeling Language (UML), Superstructure, V2.4.1
2. Abate, P., Johannes, S.: Bootstrapping software distributions. In: CBSE'13, pp. 131–142. ACM (2013)
3. Achermann, F., Nierstrasz, O.: A calculus for reasoning about software composition. Theor. Comput. Sci. **331**(2–3), 367–396 (2005)
4. Baron, S., Peter, Z., Vadim, T., Jeremy, Z.D., Arjen, L., Balling, D.J.: High Performance MySQL, 2nd edn. O'Reilly, Sebastopol (2008)
5. Bruneton, E., Coupaye, T., Leclercq, M., Quéma, V., Stefani, J.-B.: The FRACTAL component model and its support in Java. Softw. Pract. Exper. **36**(11–12), 1257–1284 (2006)
6. Bundgaard, M., Hildebrandt, T.T., Godskesen, J.C.: A CPS encoding of name-passing in higher-order mobile embedded resources. Theor. Comput. Sci. **356**(3), 422–439 (2006)
7. Burgess, M.: A site configuration engine. Comput. Syst. **8**(2), 309–337 (1995)
8. De Alfaro, L., Henzinger, T.A.: Interface automata. In: ACM SIGSOFT Software Engineering Notes, vol. 26, pp. 109–120. ACM (2001)
9. Circular Build Dependencies: http://wiki.debian.org/CircularBuildDependencies (2013). Accessed June 2013
10. Di Cosmo, R., Lienhardt, M., Treinen, R., Zacchiroli, S., Zwolakowski, J.: Optimal provisioning in the cloud. Technical report, Aeolus project, June 2013. http://hal.archives-ouvertes.fr/hal-00831455

11. Di Cosmo, R., Mauro, J., Zacchiroli, S., Zavattaro, G.: Component reconfiguration in the presence of conflicts. In: Fomin, F.V., Freivalds, R., Kwiatkowska, M., Peleg, D. (eds.) ICALP 2013, Part II. LNCS, vol. 7966, pp. 187–198. Springer, Heidelberg (2013)
12. Di Cosmo, R., Zacchiroli, S., Zavattaro, G.: Towards a formal component model for the cloud. In: Eleftherakis, G., Hinchey, M., Holcombe, M. (eds.) SEFM 2012. LNCS, vol. 7504, pp. 156–171. Springer, Heidelberg (2012)
13. Fischer, J., Majumdar, R., Esmaeilsabzali, S.: Engage: a deployment management system. In: PLDI'12: Programming Language Design and Implementation, pp. 263–274. ACM (2012)
14. Hewson, J.A., Anderson, P., Gordon, A.D.: A declarative approach to automated configuration. In: LISA '12: Large Installation System Administration Conference, pp. 51–66 (2012)
15. Juju, devops distilled. https://juju.ubuntu.com/ (2013). Accessed June 2013
16. Kanies, L.: Puppet: next-generation configuration management. login: USENIX Mag. **31**(1), 19–25 (2006)
17. Larsen, K.G., Nyman, U., Wąsowski, A.: Interface input/output automata. In: Misra, J., Nipkow, T., Sekerinski, E. (eds.) FM 2006. LNCS, vol. 4085, pp. 82–97. Springer, Heidelberg (2006)
18. Lascu, T.A., Mauro, J., Zavattaro, G.: A planning tool supporting the deployment of cloud applications. In: ICTAI 2013, pp. 213–220. IEEE (2013)
19. Montesi, F., Sangiorgi, D.: A model of evolvable components. In: Wirsing, M., Hofmann, M., Rauschmayer, A. (eds.) TGC 2010. LNCS, vol. 6084, pp. 153–171. Springer, Heidelberg (2010)
20. Opscode: Chef. http://www.opscode.com/chef/ (2013). Accessed June 2013
21. Puppet Labs: Marionette Collective. http://docs.puppetlabs.com/mcollective/ (2013). Accessed June 2013
22. Schmitt, A., Stefani, J.-B.: The kell calculus: a family of higher-order distributed process calculi. In: Priami, C., Quaglia, P. (eds.) GC 2004. LNCS, vol. 3267, pp. 146–178. Springer, Heidelberg (2005)
23. Seinturier, L., Merle, P., Fournier, D., Dolet, N., Schiavoni, V., Stefani, J.-B.: Reconfigurable SCA Applications with the FraSCAti Platform. In: IEEE SCC, pp. 268–275. IEEE (2009)
24. VMWare: Cloud Foundry, deploy & scale your applications in seconds. http://www.cloudfoundry.com/ (2013). Accessed June 2013

Modeling and Analysis of Component Connectors in Coq

Yi Li and Meng Sun[✉]

LMAM and Department of Informatics, School of Mathematical Sciences,
Peking University, Beijing, China
waircorner@pku.edu.cn, sunmeng@math.pku.edu.cn

Abstract. Connectors have emerged as a powerful concept for composition and coordination of concurrent activities encapsulated as components and services. Compositional coordination languages, like Reo, serve as a means to formally specify and implement connectors. They support large-scale distributed applications by allowing construction of complex component connectors out of simpler ones. In this paper, we present a new approach to modeling and analysis of Reo connectors via Coq, a proof assistant based on high-order logic and λ-calculus. Basic notions in Reo, like nodes and channels, are defined by inductive types. By tracing the data streams, we can simulate the behavior and output of a given Reo connector. Besides, with prerequisite axioms given, we can automatically prove connectors' properties using the Coq proof assistant.

Keywords: Coordination · Reo · Connector · Coq · Analysis

1 Introduction

Nowadays, due to the increasing size and complexity of software systems, component-based development has become a prominent paradigm in software engineering, where components are designed to work independently. Necessary interfaces are provided, by which we can organize these components as a whole system [22]. Typically, complex component-based systems are heterogeneous and geographically distributed, usually exploit communication infrastructures. Their topology varies and components can, at any moment, connect to or detach from them. The development of such systems requires a coordination model that formalizes the orchestration among the components. Coordination models are used to describe software middleware, which combines independent components into an organic whole [12]. Compositional coordination models and languages provide a "glue code" that interconnects the constituent components and organizes the mutual interactions among them in a distributed processing environment. They support large-scale distributed systems by allowing construction of complex component connectors out of simpler ones. As an example, Reo [2,10] offers a powerful glue language for implementation of coordinating component connectors. Primitive connectors called *channels* in Reo, such as synchronous channels and FIFO channels, can be composed to build circuit-like connectors which

J.L. Fiadeiro et al. (Eds.): FACS 2013, LNCS 8348, pp. 273–290, 2014.
DOI: 10.1007/978-3-319-07602-7_17, © Springer International Publishing Switzerland 2014

serve as the glue code to exogenously coordinate the behavior of components in component-based systems.

The importance of formal verification for connectors is more and more prevalent in recent years. The rapid growth in terms of complexity of the computing infrastructures that underly and accompany the evolution of complex systems has made it harder to have confidence on their correctness. Being able to establish that a system behaves as it is supposed to is now more delicate than ever. In this paper, we aim to provide an approach to formally model and analyze Reo connectors using Coq, a proof assistant based on high-order logic and λ-calculus [11]. The proof assistant makes it possible to simulate the behavior of a given connector, and prove its properties automatically. The basic idea of our approach is to model the behavior of a Reo connector by the set of input data streams and output data streams on every node of the connector, and to prove the connector's properties by the help of the Coq proof assistant with some prerequisite axioms provided.

With the help of interaction pattern and automatic searching, Coq is able to decrease the workload of proving process to a pretty low level. Now it has been widely used in various fields, such as logic, automata theory and algorithm. Comparing with existing works, modeling Reo via the Coq proof assistant has the following advantages:

Higher Abstract Level. We can describe Reo connectors more abstractly and symbolically simulate their behavior in Coq environment, through their properties instead of exact concrete values. For example, in simulation of a system's operational state, concrete data is indispensable in traditional languages. However, we can define abstract input data in Coq and describe them via mathematical properties, through which we can prove properties of corresponding output data.

Complete Proof System. In many existing works, the correct-checking process is realized as a step-limited simulation. An approximating conclusion is given by comparison between standard answer and simulation result [16]. This can be improved by using the Coq proof assistant, where we can describe the correctness of our system by a theorem, and finally give it a complete proof precisely.

Powerful Tool Support. Coq has a rich set of tactics which can provide help to verify properties of component connectors efficiently.

The paper is structured as follows. After this general introduction, we briefly summarize the coordination language Reo in Sect. 2. Section 3 presents our modeling approach briefly. Section 4 shows some examples of modeling Reo connectors and proving their properties in Coq. In Sect. 5, we present some related works and compare them with our approach. Finally, Sect. 6 concludes with some further research directions.

The source code of the connector model in Coq can be found online [23].

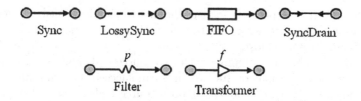

Fig. 1. Some basic channels in Reo

2   Reo Coordination Model

In this section we provide a brief introduction to Reo [2]. Reo is a channel-based exogenous coordination model wherein complex coordinators, called connectors, are compositionally built out of simpler ones. Exogenous coordination imposes a purely local interpretation on each inter-components communication, engaged in as a pure I/O operation on each side, that allows components to communicate anonymously, through the exchange of untargeted passive data. We summarize only the main concepts in Reo here. Further details about Reo and its semantics can be found elsewhere [2,8,10].

Connectors serve to provide the protocol that controls and organizes the communication, synchronization and cooperation among the components that they interconnect. Each connector consists of one or more primitive connectors, called channels, through which data items flow. Each channel has two channel ends. Channels ends of different channels are glued together on nodes to compose the channels to construct complex connectors. There are two types of channel ends defined in Reo: source end and sink end. A source channel end accepts data into its channel, and a sink channel end dispenses data out of its channel. It is noteworthy that both channel ends for one channel can be of the same type (both are sink ends or both are source ends, see SyncDrain in Fig. 1 as an example). Figure 1 shows the graphical representation of some simple channel types that are often used.

The behavior of these Reo channels are listed as follows:

FIFO1. Asynchronous channel with a source end, a sink end and a buffer. When the buffer is empty and a data item is written to its source end, FIFO1 can save data item in the buffer and the write operation will be executed successfully. Then a take operation will be performed on its sink end later. When the buffer is full, any write operation to its source end will be suspended until the date item in the buffer is taken out from its sink end.

Sync. Synchronous channel with a source end and a sink end. A write operation to the source end can be performed when it is ready for a take operation on its sink end and the data item being accepted on its source end is immediately dispensed on its sink end. The write operation will be suspended if the sink end is not ready for the take operation.

LossySync. Synchronous channel similar to Sync but not reliable. A write operation is always executed successfully once the data item arrives at its source end. If it is possible for the channel to simultaneously dispense the data item through its sink end, the channel transfers the data item. Otherwise the data item is lost.

SyncDrain. Synchronous channel with two source ends and no sink end. The pair of write operations on its two ends can succeed only simultaneously. If there are two data items arrive at both source ends, they will be accepted and lost simultaneously. Otherwise one write operation will be suspended until the other one arrives.

Filter. Synchronous channel with a filter pattern p which is a set of data values. It transfers only those data items that match with the pattern p and loses the rest. A write operation on the source end succeeds only if either the data item to be written does not match with the pattern p or the data item matches the pattern p and it can be taken synchronously via the sink end of the channel.

Transformer. Synchronous channel with a function f which is a mapping from the set of data items to the set itself. A write operation to the source end can be performed when the channel is ready for a take operation on its sink end. Then the data item d being accepted on its source end is immediately transformed to a new data item $f(d)$ which is dispensed on its sink end. The write operation will be suspended if the sink end is not ready for the take operation.

There are some more exotic channels permitted in Reo. For example, the P-producer is a variant of a synchronous channel whose source end accepts any data item, but the value dispensed through its sink end is always a data element $d \in P$. An asynchronous drain accepts data items through its source ends and loses them, but never simultaneously. The synchronous and asynchronous spouts are duals to the drain channels, as they have two sink ends and no source ends. Note that Reo places no restriction on the behavior of a channel and thus allows an open-ended set of different channel types to be used simultaneously together. This allows engineers to define their own channels with custom semantics.

Complex connectors are constructed by composing simpler ones via the join and hiding operations. Channels are joined together in nodes. The set of channel ends coincident on a node is disjointly partitioned into the sets of source and sink channel ends that coincide on the node, respectively. Nodes are categorized into source, sink and mixed nodes, depending on whether all channel ends that coincide on a node are source ends, sink ends or a combination of the two. The hiding operation is used to hide the internal topology of a component connector. The hidden nodes can no longer be accessed or observed from outside. A complex connector has a graphical representation which is a finite graph where the nodes are labeled with pair-wise disjoint, non-empty sets of channel ends, and the edges represent the connecting channels. The behavior of a Reo connector is formalized by means of the data-flow at its sink and source nodes. Intuitively, the source nodes of a connector are analogous to the input ports, and the sink nodes to the output ports of a component, while mixed nodes are its hidden internal details. Components cannot connect to, read from, or write to mixed nodes.

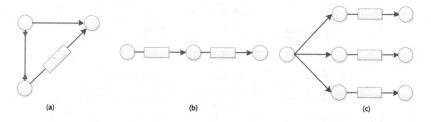

Fig. 2. Examples of connectors with multiple channels

Instead, data-flow through mixed nodes is totally specified by the connectors they belong to.

Figure 2 shows some examples for constructing complex connectors from basic channels. Figure 2(a) describes an alternator connector, which consists of 3 basic channels: a SyncDrain, a synchronous channel and a FIFO1 channel. There are two source nodes for input operations and one sink node which can only be used for output in the connector. An input on either of the two source nodes will remain pending at least until there is one input on both of the two source nodes; it is only then that both of the input operations can succeed simultaneously (because of the SyncDrain between the two source nodes). For an input to the synchronous channel to succeed, there must be a matching output on the sink node, at which time the data item input to the channel is transferred and consumed at the sink node. Simultaneously, the data item received by input to the FIFO1 channel is transferred into the buffer of the FIFO1 channel which is initially empty. As long as this data item remains in the buffer, no other data items can be input to either of the two source nodes. The only possible behavior for the connector at this moment is to consume the contents in the buffer of the FIFO1 channel and output it on the sink node. Once this happens, the connector returns back to its initial state and the cycle can repeat itself. Thus the behaviour of this connector can be seen as imposing an order on the flow of the data items written to the two source nodes through the sink node. The sequence of data items that appear through the sink node consists of zero or more repetitions of the pairs of data items that are input to the two source nodes, in an alternating order. Figure 2(b) describes a FIFO2 connector, whose behavior is identical to a FIFO1 channel, except that it will be prevented from accepting data items from input when its bounded capacity is full (the two buffers are both occupied by some data items). We can build a general FIFOn connector similarly, which keeps a n-capacity buffer while the data items follow the first-in-first-out rule. Figure 2(c) describes a 3-dispatcher that will distribute copies of the data item being received from input to the three sink nodes, with a buffer for every output.

3   Modeling Reo in Coq

In this section, we show how connectors in Reo are modeled in Coq. In most of existing works, primitive notions, such as channel or node, are regarded as the core concepts. What we adopt here is a data-centered modeling designation

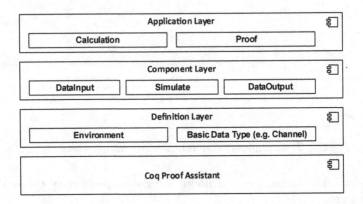

Fig. 3. System framework

where the concept 'data packet' in network protocol plays a key role and will be introduced in more detail later. In our approach, a table is created to record all data items' positions and targets, by changing of which the system's state is updated. The new method, on one hand, is more consistent with Reo's design purpose, describing the data-flow relationship between inputs and outputs. On the other hand, it provides more convenience for theorem proving.

3.1 System Framework

The system consists of four layers, as shown in Fig. 3:

1. Coq proof Assistant: the bottom layer where all codes are written in Coq system;
2. Definition Layer: all data structures and abstract data types are described in this layer;
3. Component Layer: a series of functions is provided in this layer, such as data input and output, state transition, etc.;
4. Application Layer: several interfaces are provided here, by which users can define their own connector and prove its properties.

3.2 Modeling of Basic Notions

Basic Data Type: Reo aims to formalize the notion of connectors that coordinates the interactions and communications among components. The basic concepts in Reo, such as node, channel, data, etc., are defined here and form the basis of our system.

1. Node: A node is an atomic concept. It is not necessary to describe its details but declare it as an inductive type. Besides, we make an one-to-one mapping between nodes and natural numbers to check whether two nodes are same or not.

```
Inductive Node : Set := CreateNode : nat -> Node.
```

2. Data: It can be defined as either a new abstract type or a pre-defined type in Coq. In our approach we use the inductive type to describe data items. Multiple constructors are permitted in inductive types, thus we can have different data types in our model. If a new data type is needed, we just need to add corresponding constructors and axioms for making proofs. This approach makes the system more flexible and extensible.

```
Inductive Data : Set :=
 | NatData : nat -> Data
 | Empty : Data.
```

3. Channel: Channel is a basic concept in Reo, the simplest form of connectors. Each channel has a ChannelType, which is an inductive type describing the type of the channel. Here we only provide a list of some basic channel types. This list is extensible according to user's requirement. Once a new channel type is needed, we can add corresponding constructors and axioms to the system. A natural number is used to denote the index of the channel, which is unique. One channel has two ports, each of them is a reference to a single node.

```
Inductive ChannelType : Set :=
 | Sync
 | Fifo
 | SyncDrain
 | LossySync
 | Filter : Pattern -> ChannelType
 | Transformer : DataFunc -> ChannelType.

Definition Channel : Set :=
ChannelType * nat * Node * Node.
```

4. Time: There are two kinds of time models: continuous model and discrete model. Usually the measurement of time is actually a discrete process with accuracy limitation, and in our approach time is just a logic concept. Therefore we adopt the discrete model which is easier for implementation: In state list S_i, the index i means that this state is presented in time i. No particular data structure is necessary to describe this.

Position: Position is a notion different from Location defined in Reo, which is just a physical concept and has no effect on the computation [2]. Here position refers to the point where data items exist (node or buffer in specific channel). We use an inductive type to describe positions:

```
Inductive Position : Set :=
 | NODE_POS : Node -> Position
 | BUFF_POS : Channel -> Position.
```

Note that from the coding perspective, every channel c has its $BUFF\_POS_c$. However, each of the basic channels except the FIFO1 channel has no buffer.

Data Packet: Data Packets are basic units of data items. A data packet refers to a data item that actually exists in some place and is described as a pair, which consists of the content and position of the data item.

```
Inductive DataPack : Set :=
 RealDP: Data -> Position -> DataPack.
```

Command: External interventions to a running connectors are defined as commands. An external intervention is an instruction given by some actor from outside of the connector to change the connector's state. For example, to input some data to a specific node. In our current system model, the only available command is data-input. A command is described by an inductive type. Therefore, it is easy to be expanded without large-scale modification to the source code.

```
Inductive Command : Set :=
 | Push : Data -> Node -> Command.
```

Timed Data Streams: Every timed data stream is described by a stream (defined in Coq.Lists.Stream) of data items. If the index of an element in the stream is i, then the data item appears at time i. In our system, the input and output data on every node are given by timed data streams. And a series of nodes' data together are described as a list of data streams (defined as DStreams). When we describe a connector, it is enough to represent all nodes' input and output contents in the whole process.

```
Definition DStream : Set := Stream Data.
Definition DStreams : Set := list DStream.
```

Environment: Environment is the core concept in our system. An environment refers to the runtime environment of a data flow including the data flow itself. In other words, an environment is a complete description of a connector and it's running state. The definition of an environment is as follows:

```
Definition Environment : Set :=
   (list Channel) * (list Node) * (list DataPack) *
   (list Node).
```

In this definition, the first part 'list Channel' is a list of channels. All the channels in the connector are stored here. The second part 'list Node' is a list describing all the nodes in the connector. The third part 'list DataPack' is a list of data packets, being used to describe every data packet that exists in the current environment. Finally, the last 'list Node' is a list representing the output nodes of a connector. In every round of simulation, data items in output nodes will be taken away and sent to the list of output data streams. Then the output nodes will be set to empty, preparing for new data arriving.

3.3   Description of System's Behaviour

Here we first show the behavior of basic channels in the model, and then describe the behavior of our system in a top-down logical order.

Simulating Channel Behavior: For the synchronous channel, the system first checks the target position. If it is empty, then the data packet will be put into the position. Otherwise, the original data packet will be kept in the queue. The behavior for lossy synchronous channel is similar. When the target position is empty then the data packet is put into the position. But the data packet will be discarded if the position is not available. For the FIFO1 channel, the buffer is first checked. If the buffer is empty, then the data packet is put into the buffer. Otherwise, the original data packet will be kept in the queue. For the SyncDrain channel, If the target position is empty, the data packet is thrown away. Otherwise, it will be kept in the original place.

For a certain data packet d staying in the node n. Suppose l is a set of adjacency channels:

$$l = \{c \in Channels \mid n = source(l) \vee (n = sink(l) \wedge l = SyncDrain)\}$$

A test will be executed on channels in l by the function $isAbleIterate$. A data item d will be dispatched to every channel $c \in l$ only when write operations can be applied on all these channels. Otherwise d will be kept in the data packet list.

State Migration: The computation process is shown in Fig. 4. When every round starts, we get the input data at that time and normalize them as commands. Then the commands are sent to data packet list. After that, a standard dispatching process will be executed on all data packets in the connector.

```
Definition SubFuncSim (env:Environment)
               (dsm:DataStreamMatrix)(s:nat) :=
   GainOutput (NextDPList (ApplyCommands env
                         (GetCommandList dsm s))).
```

Generation and Application of Data Commands: In the computation process, a list of data streams (with type DStreams) should be provided by

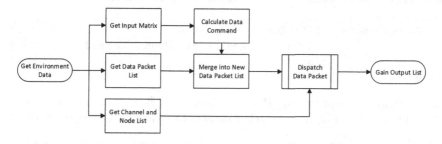

Fig. 4. Simulation of environment state migration

users, which keeps the information of all nodes' input data flows. In this step, we check every node n_i under certain environment. If n_i is empty, we grab the corresponding data stream's head element, otherwise the data stream won't be changed. These grabbed data items, together with their target positions, are normalized as data commands and then be executed uniformly.

```
Fixpoint GetCommands (e:Environment)(ds:DStreams)(n:nat):=
 match ds with
 | nil => (nil, nil)
 | l::r =>
   if (isEmpty e (CreateNode n)) then
     match (GetCommands e r (n + 1)) with
     | (cl,dl)=>((Push(hd l)(CreateNode n))::cl,(tl l)::dl)
     end
   else
     match (GetCommands e r (n + 1)) with
     | (cl, dl) => (cl, l :: dl)
     end
 end.
```

Obviously if there are n positions in the connector, then the length of command list, thanks to the inserted Empty data, must be n. So we have to create a function CommandFilter for filtering the command list.

```
Fixpoint CommandFilter (cl:CommandList) : CommandList :=
 match cl with
 | nil => nil
 | l::r => match l with
           | Push Empty _ => CommandFilter r
           | Push (NatData _) _ => l::(CommandFilter r)
           | Push (BoolData _) _ => l::(CommandFilter r)
           end
 end.
```

After being filtered, the commands are directly applied to the data packet list. Further operations will be performed when the data packets are dispatched.

```
Definition ApplyCommand (e:Environment)(c:Command) :=
 match c with
 | Push dt nd => if (isEmpty e nd) then
                    AddData e (RealDP dt (NODE_POS nd))
                 else e
 end.
```

Data Packets Dispatching Process: The basic flow graph of data packets dispatching is shown in Fig. 5. The key points of this process are listed as follows:

– In the dispatching process of a data packet $(data, position)$, first we get the adjacency channel list of $position$ and check if write operations succeed on

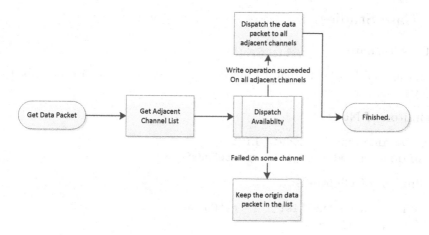

Fig. 5. The iterate process of data packet dispatching

every channel in the list (The checking function is defined as *isAbleIterate*). If passed, the data packet will be dispatched, otherwise the data packet will be kept in the data packet list.

- A write operation on Sync channel s succeeds only if the sink node of s is empty.
- Similarly, a write operation on Fifo succeeds only if the buffer is empty. Besides, if the data packet is in some buffer, its adjacent channel list contains only the Fifo channel itself.
- A write operation on SyncDrain channel will succeed under two conditions: a data packet exists in another end of this channel; the data packet is able to be dispatched.
- While dispatching a data packet, if the channel is SyncDrain and there is a data packet existing at another port, then the data packet will be dropped directly. Or if the channel is LossySync, then we check if the target node is empty or not. If it is empty then a data packet will be sent to the target, otherwise the data packet will be dropped.
- For a Filter channel with pattern p, writing operations (with data d) succeed if $p(d) = false$ or the sink node is empty.
- Transformer channel's writable prerequisites is exactly same as Sync.
- For node N, if there exists a data packet in the data packet list with position denoted by N, this means that the last dispatching job on node N hasn't been finished yet. Obviously some writing operation is suspended and N is still in the state of being occupied, and any writing operation to N won't be executed successfully.
- If node N is an output node, there is no channel whose source end coincides with N, then any data packet on N can't be dispatched. The data packet is kept until being grabbed to the output streams. If N is an output node but not in the OutputList of its environment, then the data packet transferred to this node will be blocked.

4   Case Studies

4.1   Alternator

In our approach, the alternator connector as shown in Fig. 2(a) is described as follows:

Definiton of Nodes:

```
(* Definitions of Nodes' List *)
Definition nodeList_1 := createNodeSq 3.
```

Definition of Channels:

```
Definition channelList_1 := getChannels (
  (Sync, 0, 1) ::
  (SyncDrain, 0, 2) ::
  (Fifo, 2, 1) ::
  nil
).
```

Definition of Output List:

```
Definition outpList_1 := createNodeLst (1::nil).
```

Now we can define the environment as follows:

```
Definition ENV_1 := (channelList_1 , nodeList_1,
                     nil: list DataPack, outpList_1).
```

Assume that dataflows on the two source nodes are (A, B, C) and (D, E, F), respectively. Then the state list of this connector can be described as in Fig. 6. After input to the system being provided, we can get the following result in 10 units of time:

```
NatData a :: NatData d ::
NatData b :: NatData c ::
NatData e :: NatData f :: nil
```

4.2   Distributor Connector

For the distributor as shown in Fig. 2(c), we will prove its isotonicity while distributing data items. The connector construction process is similarly to the previous example and will be omitted here.

First we give the input streams and define some axioms:

```
Parameters a b : nat.
Definition inputStream_2 : DStreams :=
  ((NatData a) ::: ((NatData b) ::: Nil)) ::
  nil.
Axiom Condition : a > b.
```

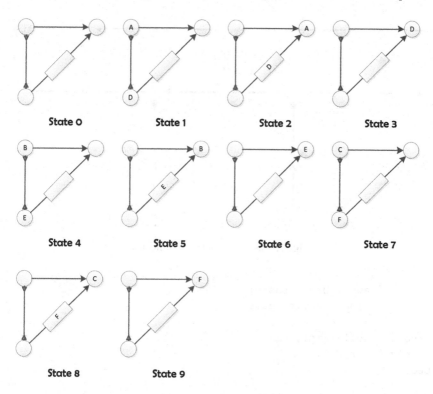

State 0   State 1   State 2   State 3

State 4   State 5   State 6   State 7

State 8   State 9

Fig. 6. States of the alternator connector

Then we define the ordered property of stream and relevant axioms:

```
Parameter Ordered : Stream Data -> Prop.
Axiom Order_Basic :
forall (d:Data)(s:Stream Data),
  (Larger d (hd s) /\ Ordered s) -> Ordered (d ::: s).
Axiom Order_Nil : Ordered Nil.
```

Besides, for convenience we defined another lemma *EmptyLem*, which is used to remove the empty data items in the stream. Now we'll prove that the output stream is ordered.

```
Definition Run_2 (t:nat) :=
getOutput (Simulate ENV_2 inputStream_2 t).
Definition Str := nth 1 (Run_2 10) Nil.

Theorem Example : Ordered Str.
Proof.
 repeat (
        repeat (apply EmptyLem);
```

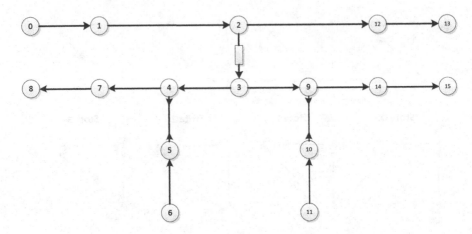

Fig. 7. Task transaction connector

```
        apply Order_Basic;
        simpl; split; auto
      ).
  repeat (apply EmptyLem).
  apply Order_Nil.
Qed.
```

4.3   Task Transaction Connector

A task transaction connector[1] is shown in Fig. 7. Task sequences are pushed in node 0 and user actions are changed via node 6 and node 11. Every task will be send to node 13 after they are performed and if there is confirm or abandon signal (data flow in relevant nodes), another copy of the task will be sent to the connector again.

Definiton of Nodes:
```
(* Definitions of Nodes' List *)
Definition nodeList_3 := createNodeSq 16.
```

Definition of Channels:
```
Definition channelList_3 := getChannels (
  (Sync, 0, 1)        :: (Sync, 1, 2) ::
  (Fifo, 2, 3)        :: (Sync, 3, 4) ::
  (SyncDrain, 4, 5) :: (Sync, 6, 5) ::
  (Sync, 4, 7)        :: (Sync, 7, 8) ::
  (Sync, 3, 9)        :: (Sync, 2, 12) ::
  (Sync, 12, 13)      :: (SyncDrain, 9, 10) ::
  (Sync, 11, 10)      :: (Sync, 9, 14) ::
  (Sync, 14, 15)      :: nil).
```

---

[1] This connector is a simplification of one example provided in [17].

Definition of Output List:

```
Definition outpList_3 := createNodeLst (8::13::15::nil).
```

Now we can define the environment as follows:

```
Definition ENV_3 := (channelList_3 , nodeList_3,
                     nil: list DataPack,
                     outpList_3).
```

To prove properties of this connector, first we define and abstract type *TimeProp* : *nat* → *Prop*. It is used to describe properties about time. For example, the following definition is used to describe if the task has been confirmed on some time. Besides, we define *TimeBefore* to describe if a property is satisfied before a certain time.

```
Definition Confirmed : TimeProp := fun (n:nat) =>
  match nth 1 (SingleOutp n) Empty with
  | Empty => False
  | _ => True
  end.
```

With a confirm action given in input stream, we can prove that *Confirmed* will be satisfied in 5 time units.

```
Definition ConfirmedBefore := TimeBeforeProp Confirmed.
Goal (TimeBeforeProp Confirmed 5).
Proof.
  apply TimeBefore.
  try (exists 1; right; compute; auto; fail).
  try (exists 2; right; compute; auto; fail).
  try (exists 3; right; compute; auto; fail).
  try (exists 4; right; compute; auto; fail).
Qed.
```

5 Related Work

There are a plethora of formal models for Reo. For example, a coalgebraic semantics for Reo in terms of relations on infinite Timed Data Streams (TDS) has been developed by Arbab and Rutten [8], TDS model the possible flows of data on connector nodes, assigning a time to each interaction (input or output of one data element). The causality between input and output is not clear in this approach, and there is no tool support for simulation or verification. An operational semantics for Reo using Constraint Automata (CA) is provided by Baier et al. [10], and later the symbolic model checker Vereofy is developed [9] which can be used to check CTL-like properties. However, modeling unbounded primitives or even bounded primitives with unbounded data domains is impossible with finite constraint automata. Bounded large data domains cause an explosion in the constraint automata model which becomes problematic. A model for Reo connectors based on the idea of coloring a connector with possible data flows to resolve synchronization and exclusion constraints is presented by Clarke et al. [13]. Unlike the coalgebraic and operational semantics, data sensitive behavior, which is supported by filters in Reo, are not captured by the coloring approach.

Series of research have been made on translation from Reo to other formal models, such as Alloy [16], Maude [21], mCRL2 [18], UTP [1,20], etc. The translation from Reo to Alloy in [16] is rather simple and no working tool is provided. The work in [21] provides an operational semantics for Reo using Maude rewriting logic. Later in [1] the UTP model is implemented also using Maude. One of the main advantages of Maude is that it provides a single framework that facilitates the use of a wide range of formal methods. Furthermore, one can experiment with the "search" facility of Maude, or with its LTL model-checker in order to perform verification. However, by using Coq, we can simply take advantage of already existing efficient implementations of data structures like *streams* and *lists* (which are the basic ingredients in the theory of connectors as shown in [8]) and the corresponding functions to manipulate them. While working with Maude one needs to adapt to the basic constructions provided by the system or implement new ones.

6   Conclusion and Future Work

In this paper, we described the approach of formalizing the coordination model Reo in the proof assistant Coq. We implement a set of basic channels in Reo, which can be used to construct complex connectors. With the system, we can describe connectors consists of basic channels and nodes, simulate the connector's behavior, i.e., the transformation sequence between its states. Besides, when related axioms are given, we can prove the properties of a connector via the Coq Proof Assistant. Properties of connectors are defined as Goals in Coq and by applying axioms provided by users, the Coq proof assistant can make it easy to derive the goals from the axioms. The system can be easily reused and extended for more channel types in Reo and open to user-defined channels with custom semantics.

In the current system, we describe the channels' action patterns directly instead of describing its properties, thus we cannot give proof for some universal properties. To solve this problem, we can replace the descriptions of channels' action patterns (Definition) by description of channels' property (Axiom), and add a series of tactics to make proofs automatically. However, this will make it rather difficult to compute detailed result. So we should judge the comparative usage occasion and user's requirement to choose how to implement the system.

A family of tools for Reo have been developed under the Eclipse platform, which is called the Eclipse Coordination Tools (ECT) [6,14]. Integrating our system with the Eclipse Coordination Tools is of special interest and in our scope. The main task is to make a transformation of the graphical representation of connectors in ECT to our formalization of connectors in Coq. Incorporating real-time (and other QoS) constraints on connectors [3–5,7,19] into the Coq model is another interesting topic in our future work as well. What is very interesting for us is the complementary nature of theorem provers and other verification approaches like model checking. Although this is not a completely new topic [15], we need to explore the relationship between our work and model checking approaches like [18].

Acknowledgement. The work was partially supported by the National Natural Science Foundation of China under grant no. 61202069 and 61272160, and Research Fund for the Doctoral Program of Higher Education of China under grant no. 201200011 20103.

References

1. Aichernig, B.K., Arbab, F., Astefanoaei, L., de Boer, F.S., Meng, S., Rutten, J.J.M.M.: Fault-based test case generation for component connectors. In: Proceedings of TASE 2009, pp. 147–154. IEEE Computer Society (2009)
2. Arbab, F.: Reo: a channel-based coordination model for component composition. Math. Struct. Comput. Sci. **14**(3), 329–366 (2004)
3. Arbab, F., Baier, C., de Boer, F., Rutten, J.: Models and temporal logical specifications for timed component connectors. Softw. Syst. Model. **6**(1), 59–82 (2007)
4. Arbab, F., Chothia, T., Meng, S., Moon, Y.-J.: Component connectors with QoS guarantees. In: Murphy, A.L., Vitek, J. (eds.) COORDINATION 2007. LNCS, vol. 4467, pp. 286–304. Springer, Heidelberg (2007)
5. Arbab, F., Chothia, T., van der Mei, R., Meng, S., Moon, Y.J., Verhoef, C.: From coordination to stochastic models of QoS. In: Field, J., Vasconcelos, V.T. (eds.) COORDINATION 2009. LNCS, vol. 5521, pp. 268–287. Springer, Heidelberg (2009)
6. Arbab, F., Koehler, C., Maraikar, Z., Moon, Y.-J., Proença, J.: Modeling, testing and executing Reo connectors with the eclipse coordination tools. In: Preliminary proceedings of FACS 2008 (2008)
7. Arbab, F., Meng, S., Moon, Y.-J., Kwiatkowska, M., Qu, H.: Reo2mc: a tool chain for performance analysis of coordination models. In: Proceedings of the 7th Joint Meeting of the European Software Engineering Conference and the ACM SIGSOFT Symposium on The Foundations of Software Engineering, pp. 287–288. ACM (2009)
8. Arbab, F., Rutten, J.J.M.M.: A coinductive calculus of component connectors. In: Wirsing, M., Pattinson, D., Hennicker, R. (eds.) WADT 2003. LNCS, vol. 2755, pp. 34–55. Springer, Heidelberg (2003)
9. Baier, C., Blechmann, T., Klein, J., Klüppelholz, S., Leister, W.: Design and verification of systems with exogenous coordination using vereofy. In: Margaria, T., Steffen, B. (eds.) ISoLA 2010, Part II. LNCS, vol. 6416, pp. 97–111. Springer, Heidelberg (2010)
10. Baier, C., Sirjani, M., Arbab, F., Rutten, J.: Modeling component connectors in Reo by constraint automata. Sci. Comput. Program. **61**, 75–113 (2006)
11. Bertot, Y., Castéran, P.: Interactive Theorem Proving and Program Development: Coq'Art: The Calculus of Inductive Constructions. Springer, Berlin (2004)
12. Ciancarini, P.: Coordination models and languages as software integrators. ACM Comput. Surv. (CSUR) **28**(2), 300–302 (1996)

13. Clarke, D., Costa, D., Arbab, F.: Connector colouring I: synchronisation and context dependency. Sci. Comput. Program. **66**, 205–225 (2007)
14. Eclipse Coordination Tools. http://reo.project.cwi.nl/
15. Halpern, J.Y., Vardi, M.Y.: Model checking vs. theorem proving: a manifesto. In: Artificial intelligence and mathematical theory of computation, pp. 151–176. Academic Press Professional, San Diego (1991)
16. Khosravi, R., Sirjani, M., Asoudeh, N., Sahebi, S., Iravanchi, H.: Modeling and analysis of Reo connectors using alloy. In: Lea, D., Zavattaro, G. (eds.) COORDINATION 2008. LNCS, vol. 5052, pp. 169–183. Springer, Heidelberg (2008)
17. Kokash, N., Arbab, F.: Formal design and verification of long-running transactions with eclipse coordination tools. IEEE Trans. Serv. Comput. **6**(2), 186–200 (2013)
18. Kokash, N., Krause, Ch., de Vink, E.: Reo + mCRL2: a framework for model-checking dataflow in service compositions. Formal Aspects Comput. **24**(2), 187–216 (2012)
19. Meng, S.: Connectors as designs: the time dimension. In: Proceedings of TASE 2012, pp. 201–208. IEEE Computer Society (2012)
20. Meng, S., Arbab, F., Aichernig, B.K., Aştefănoaei, L., de Boer, F.S., Rutten, J.: Connectors as designs: modeling, refinement and test case generation. Sci. Comput. Program. **77**(7), 799–822 (2012)
21. Mousavi, M.R., Sirjani, M., Arbab, F.: Formal semantics and analysis of component connectors in Reo. Electron. Notes Theor. Comput. Sci. **154**(1), 83–99 (2006)
22. Ramasubbu, N., Balan, R.K.: Globally distributed software development project performance: an empirical analysis. In: Proceedings of the 6th Joint Meeting of the European Software Engineering Conference and the ACM SIGSOFT Symposium on The Foundations of Software Engineering, pp. 125–134. ACM (2007)
23. Source code of the Coq development. http://www.math.pku.edu.cn/teachers/sunm/rc/Main.v

On the Complexity of Input Output Conformance Testing

Neda Noroozi[1(✉)], Mohammad Reza Mousavi[2], and Tim A.C. Willemse[1]

[1] Eindhoven University of Technology, Eindhoven, The Netherlands
[2] Center for Research on Embedded Systems, Halmstad University,
Halmstad, Sweden
n.noroozi@tue.nl, m.r.mousavi@hh.se, t.a.c.willemse@tue.nl

Abstract. Input-output conformance (ioco) testing is a well-known app-roach to model-based testing. In this paper, we study the complexity of checking ioco. We show that the problem of checking ioco is PSPACE-complete. To provide a more efficient algorithm, we propose a more restricted setting for checking ioco, namely with deterministic models and show that in this restricted setting ioco checking can be performed in polynomial time.

1 Introduction

Motivation. Testing is a major part of the software development process and, together with debugging, accounts for more than half of the development cost and effort [14]. Model-based testing is a structured and rigorous discipline of testing, which is likely to improve the current practice of testing [17,23,24]. Input-output conformance (**ioco**) testing is a well-known formal approach to model-based testing, which is used extensively in various practical applications, see [5,13] and the references therein, and which has been the subject of much theoretical research, see [21] and the references therein.

In this paper, we study the complexity of checking **ioco**, a topic which—as far as we could trace—has not been addressed in the literature. Our study sheds some light on the theoretical boundaries for this popular notion and possible enhancements in its efficiency and efficacy by considering restricted forms of specifications and implementations.

We first show that the upper bound on the complexity of checking **ioco** is exponential in the size of the model. This is as expected due to the trace-based nature of (the intensional definition of) **ioco**. We show that this exponential com-plexity bound is indeed tight, by proving that the problem is PSPACE-complete. This means that, unless the complexity class hierarchy from P to PSPACE col-lapses, the exponential time complexity in deciding **ioco** is unavoidable in the worst case. Next, we identify a more restricted setting for checking **ioco** which still admits a polynomial time algorithm. In this restricted setting, implemen-tations are still permitted to behave non-deterministically, but specifications

J.L. Fiadeiro et al. (Eds.): FACS 2013, LNCS 8348, pp. 291–309, 2014.
DOI: 10.1007/978-3-319-07602-7_18, © Springer International Publishing Switzerland 2014

must be deterministic. In order to obtain this result, we first give a coinductive (simulation-like) definition of **ioco** for deterministic specifications and we subsequently show that it can be decided in polynomial time.

Our study is based on the intensional representation of **ioco**, which allows for defining exact complexity bounds on checking conformance. The complexity bounds for the intensional representation also hold for the extensional representation, but it remains to be checked under which conditions these bounds can be realized in the practical setting by using test-cases.

Compositional testing concerns about testing of composite systems consisting of communication components which can be separately tested. Though **ioco** lacks the compositionality property in general, several researches were conducted to adapt **ioco** for compositional testing. In [6,9,15] some variants of **ioco** have been introduced for testing of component-based systems. Our results in this paper can be easily adapted and applied for those relations as well. For instance, in [6], a variant of **ioco** for testing components is introduced such that the correctness of the integration of the conformed components is guaranteed. That aforementioned relation coincides with the standard **ioco** for a restricted class of specification, namely deterministic models.

Related work. Our polynomial time algorithm for checking **ioco** (for deterministic models) is inspired by [18], which is based on the reduction of checking **ioco** into the **NHORNSAT** problem [8]. The coinductive definition of **ioco**, which is an important means for this result, is akin to the alternating refinement [4] of Interface Automata [3] (see also [1,10]). In [22], it is shown that for deterministic models and implementations, alternating refinement coincides with **ioco**. In this paper, we show that our coinductive definition of **ioco** coincides with **ioco** for deterministic models (and possibly nondeterministic implementations). In a recent paper [10], a simulation-like relation, called iocos, is presented. It is shown that iocos is finer than **ioco**.

In [11], the author proves that testing conformance under asynchronous communication is in general EXPTIME-hard. Then, by restricting to a particular class of models, called observable IOTSs, the author gives a polynomial time algorithm for checking conformance under asynchronous FIFO communication. (The problem remains equally hard for observable models under arbitrary asynchronous communication.) Apart from being in the asynchronous setting, the notion of conformance used in [11] differs from **ioco** (e.g., its theory does not treat quiescence).

Structure of the Paper. In Sect. 2, we recall some basic definitions regarding labeled transition systems and the input-output conformance relation. In Sect. 3, we study the complexity of checking **ioco**. In order to obtain more efficient bounds for checking conformance of deterministic models, we first give a coinductive definition of **ioco** in Sect. 4 and use this definition in Sect. 5 to show that in this restricted setting, conformance checking is indeed possible in polynomial time. We conclude the paper in Sect. 6.

2   Preliminaries

In this section, we briefly repeat the definitions of the formal models used in our context for specifying system behavior, as well as the notion of input-output conformance testing. Throughout this paper, we use variants of Labeled Transition Systems (LTSs) for modeling the behavior of specifications and implementations. The LTS model assumes that systems can be represented using a set of states and transitions, labeled with events or actions, between such states. The events leading to new states can be observed by the tester, but the states cannot be inspected. We assume the presence of a special action, denoted by τ, which models an event that is unobservable to the tester.

Definition 1 (LTS). *A labeled transition system (LTS) is a 4-tuple $\langle S, L, \rightarrow, \bar{s} \rangle$, where S is a set of states, L is a finite alphabet of actions that does not contain the internal action τ, $\rightarrow \subseteq S \times (L \cup \{\tau\}) \times S$ is the transition relation, and $\bar{s} \in S$ is the initial state.*

Throughout this section, we assume a fixed yet arbitrary LTS $\langle S, L, \rightarrow, \bar{s} \rangle$. We tend to refer to LTSs by referring to their initial state, i.e., $\bar{s}$ in the case of the above mentioned LTS. Let $s, s' \in S$ and $x \in L \cup \{\tau\}$. In line with common practice, we write $s \xrightarrow{x} s'$ rather than $(s, x, s') \in \rightarrow$. Furthermore, we write $s \xrightarrow{x}$ whenever $s \xrightarrow{x} s'$ for some $s' \in S$, and $s \xnrightarrow{x}$ when not $s \xrightarrow{x}$. The transition relation is generalized to a relation over a sequence of actions by the following deduction rules:

$$\frac{}{s \xrightarrow{\epsilon}{}^* s} \qquad \frac{s \xrightarrow{\sigma}{}^* s'' \quad s'' \xrightarrow{x} s' \quad x \neq \tau}{s \xrightarrow{\sigma x}{}^* s'} \qquad \frac{s \xrightarrow{\sigma}{}^* s'' \quad s'' \xrightarrow{\tau} s'}{s \xrightarrow{\sigma}{}^* s'}$$

We tacitly adopt the same notational conventions both for $\rightarrow$ and $\rightarrow^*$.

An LTS $\bar{s}$ is said to be *deterministic* if the set of states reached after executing any sequence of actions is always a singleton set; that is, for all $s, s', s'' \in S$ and all $\sigma \in L^*$, if $s \xrightarrow{\sigma}{}^* s'$ and $s \xrightarrow{\sigma}{}^* s''$ then $s' = s''$.

A state in the LTS $\bar{s}$ is said to *diverge* if it is the source of an infinite sequence of τ-labeled transitions. The LTS $\bar{s}$ is *divergent* if one of its reachable states diverges. Throughout this paper, we confine ourselves to non-divergent LTSs.

Definition 2. *Let $s' \in S$ and $S' \subseteq S$. The set of* traces, enabled actions *and* weakly enabled actions *for s and S' are defined as follows:*

- $\mathsf{traces}(s) = \{\sigma \in L^* \mid s \xrightarrow{\sigma}{}^*\}$, *and* $\mathsf{traces}(S') = \bigcup_{s' \in S'} \mathsf{traces}(s')$.

- $\mathsf{init}(s) = \{x \in L \cup \{\tau\} \mid s \xrightarrow{x}\}$, *and* $\mathsf{init}(S') = \bigcup_{s' \in S'} \mathsf{init}(s')$.

- $\mathsf{Sinit}(s) = \{x \in L \mid s \xrightarrow{x}{}^*\}$, *and* $\mathsf{Sinit}(S') = \bigcup_{s' \in S'} \mathsf{Sinit}(s')$.

Input, output, Quiescence and Suspension Traces. When engaging in interaction with another system, the actions of an LTS are often assumed to be partitioned into two subcategories, reflecting which of the systems has the initiative in executing the action. Output actions are under the control of the system, whereas input actions are under the control of the environment of the system. We refine the LTS model to reflect this distinction in initiative.

Definition 3 (IOLTS). *An input-output labeled transition system (IOLTS) is a tuple* $\langle S, I, U, \to, \bar{s} \rangle$ *such that the tuple* $\langle S, L, \to, \bar{s} \rangle$ *is an LTS in which the alphabet* L *is partitioned into a set* I *of inputs and a set* U *of outputs, i.e.* $L = I \cup U$.

Testers often not only have the power to observe the events produced by an implementation, but also can observe the *absence* of events, or *quiescence* [21]. A state $s \in S$ is said to be *quiescent* if it does not produce outputs and it is *stable*, that is, it cannot, through internal computations, evolve to a state that *is* capable of producing outputs. Formally, state s is quiescent, denoted $\delta(s)$, whenever init$(s) \subseteq I$. In order to formally reason about the observations of inputs, outputs and quiescence, we introduce the set of *suspension traces*. To this end, we first generalize the transition over a sequence of input, output and quiescence actions. Let L_δ denote the set $L \cup \{\delta\}$.

$$\frac{s \xrightarrow{\sigma}{}^* s'}{s \overset{\sigma}{\Longrightarrow} s'} \qquad \frac{\delta(s)}{s \overset{\delta}{\Longrightarrow} s} \qquad \frac{s \overset{\sigma}{\Longrightarrow} s'' \quad s'' \overset{\rho}{\Longrightarrow} s'}{s \overset{\sigma\rho}{\Longrightarrow} s'}$$

The following definition formalizes the set of suspension traces.

Definition 4. *Let* $s \in S$ *and* $S' \subseteq S$. *The set of* suspension traces *for* s, *denoted by* Straces(s) *is defined as the set* $\{\sigma \in L_\delta^* \mid s \overset{\sigma}{\Longrightarrow}\}$; *we set* Straces$(S') = \bigcup_{s' \in S'}$ Straces(s').

Input-Output Conformance Testing with Quiescence. Tretmans' **ioco** testing theory [21] is a formal approach to conformance testing. It assumes that the behavior of implementations can be described adequately using a class of IOLTSs, called *input output transition systems*; this assumption is the so-called *testing hypothesis*. Input output transition systems are essentially plain IOLTSs with the additional assumption that inputs can always be accepted.

Definition 5 (IOTS). *Let* $\langle S, I, U, \to, \bar{s} \rangle$ *be an IOLTS. A state* $s \in S$ *is* input-enabled *iff* $I \subseteq$ Sinit(s); *the IOLTS* $\bar{s}$ *is an* input output transition system *(IOTS) iff every state* $s \in S$ *is input-enabled. The class of input output transition systems ranging over inputs* I *and outputs* U *is denoted* IOTS(I, U).

While the **ioco** testing theory assumes input-enabled implementations, it does not impose this requirement on specifications. This facilitates testing using partial specifications, i.e., specifications that are under-specified. To simplify presenting the input-output conformance relation (**ioco**), we first introduce the formal definitions below.

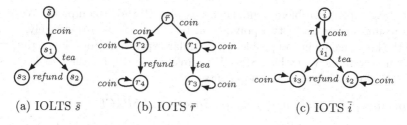

Fig. 1. A specification $\bar{s}$ of a tea vending machine, a correct implementation $\bar{r}$ and an incorrect implementation $\bar{i}$.

Definition 6. *Let* $\langle S, I, U, \rightarrow, \bar{s} \rangle$ *be an IOLTS. Let* $s \in S$, $S' \subseteq S$ *and let* $\sigma \in L_\delta^*$.

- *s* after $\sigma = \{s' \in S \mid s \overset{\sigma}{\Rightarrow} s'\}$, *and* S' after $\sigma = \bigcup_{s' \in S'} s'$ after σ.

- $\mathsf{out}(s) = \{x \in L_\delta \setminus I \mid s \overset{x}{\Rightarrow}\}$, *and* $\mathsf{out}(S') = \bigcup_{s' \in S'} \mathsf{out}(s')$.

The **ioco** conformance relation [21] is then defined as follows.

Definition 7 (ioco). *Let* $\langle Q, I, U, \rightarrow, \bar{r} \rangle$ *be an IOTS representing a realization of a system, and let IOLTS* $\langle S, I, U, \rightarrow, \bar{s} \rangle$ *be a specification. We say that* $\bar{r}$ *is input output conform with specification* $\bar{s}$, *denoted by* $\bar{r}$ **ioco** $\bar{s}$, *iff*

$$\forall \sigma \in \mathsf{Straces}(\bar{s}) : \ \mathsf{out}(\bar{r} \text{ after } \sigma) \subseteq \mathsf{out}(\bar{s} \text{ after } \sigma)$$

Example 1. Consider the IOLTSs pictured in Fig. 1. The IOLTS $\bar{s}$ is a specification of a vending machine which sells tea. After receiving a coin, it either delivers tea or refunds the coin. The IOLTS $\bar{r}$ is a formal model of a possible implementation of this vending machine. Upon receiving a coin, the machine $\bar{r}$ chooses non-deterministically between serving tea or refunding the coin. Note that IOLTS $\bar{r}$ is input-enabled, because it accepts input action *coin* (as the only input action) at every state. The set $\mathsf{Straces}(\bar{s})$ is given by the regular expression $(\delta^*) \mid (\delta^* coin) \mid (\delta^* coin(tea \mid refund)\delta^*)$. Clearly, for all $\sigma \in \mathsf{Straces}(\bar{s})$, we have $\mathsf{out}(\bar{r}$ after $\sigma) \subseteq \mathsf{out}(\bar{s}$ after $\sigma)$. Thus, $\bar{r}$ **ioco** $\bar{s}$.

The IOLTS $\bar{i}$ is a formal model of an implementation of a malfunction vending machine. After receiving a coin, it either delivers tea, refunds the coin or does nothing. Similar to IOTS $\bar{r}$, it accepts input action *coin* at every state. Thus, the IOLTS $\bar{i}$ is input-enabled. Consider the trace *coin* after which $\mathsf{out}(\bar{s}) = \{refund, tea\}$ while $\mathsf{out}(\bar{i}) = \{refund, tea, \delta\}$. As a result, we find that $\bar{i}$ **io/co** $\bar{s}$.

3 Conformance Checking for Nondeterministic Models

In this section, we study the complexity of input-output conformance checking in full generality. We prove that, in the general case, checking **ioco** is PSPACE-complete. To this end, we first show that checking **ioco** is in PSPACE. Subsequently, we show that checking **ioco** is at least as hard as other canonical

PSPACE-complete problems and hence, is also PSPACE-complete. We prove these results by means of two polynomial time reductions, respectively, to and from the language inclusion problem for regular expressions (or NFAs); the latter problem is well-known to be PSPACE-complete; see [19] for the classical result and [2,16] for some recent developments.

Theorem 1. *The problem of checking* **ioco** *is in PSPACE.*

Proof. We prove the thesis by showing that the problem of checking **ioco** for input-enabled specifications is reducible to the language inclusion problem of NFAs with ϵ-moves (hereafter simply referred to as NFAs) in polynomial time. Observe that without loss of generality we can restrict our attention to the problem of checking **ioco** for input-enabled specifications. Indeed, for a non input-enabled specification A_2, we can construct an input-enabled specification $\bar{A}_2$ in polynomial time such that for any implementation A_1, we have A_1 **ioco** A_2 iff A_1 **ioco** $\bar{A}_2$. The construction uses a standard angelic completion, adding missing input transitions to A_2 that lead to fresh input-enabled states that accept all outputs and quiescence.

Assume that, for $i \in \{1, 2\}$, we have IOTSs A_i of the form $\langle S_i, I, U, \rightarrow_i, \bar{s}_i \rangle$. Our reduction proceeds as follows. We define NFAs $A_i' = \langle Q_i, \Sigma, \Delta_i, q_i, F \rangle$ as follows:

- $Q_i = S_i$ is the set of states,
- $\Sigma = L_\delta \cup \{\epsilon\}$ where $L_\delta = I \cup U \cup \{\delta\}$ is the common alphabet,
- $\Delta_i = \{(q, a, q') \mid q \xrightarrow{a} q' \wedge a \in L\} \cup \{(q, \epsilon, q') \mid q, q' \in S_i \wedge q \xrightarrow{\tau} q'\} \cup \{(q, \delta, q) \mid q \in S_i \wedge \delta(q)\}$ is the transition relation, which is that of the corresponding IOTS union with δ-labeled self-loop for single and each quiescent state.
- $q_i = \bar{s}_i$ is the initial state, and
- $F = Q_i$ is the set of final states.

Note that the above reduction is carried out linearly in the size of the transition relations of A_1 and A_2. Moreover, observe that $L(A_1') = \mathsf{Straces}(A_1)$ and $L(A_1') = \mathsf{Straces}(A_2)$. We next proceed by showing that A_1 **ioco** A_2 if and only if $L(A_1') \subseteq L(A_2')$. We prove the contraposition of both implications separately.

- Assume that A_1 **io$\not$co** A_2. By definition of **ioco** there is a suspension trace σ in specification A_2 such that for some output x, $\sigma x \in \mathsf{Straces}(A_1)$, but $\sigma x \notin \mathsf{Straces}(A_2)$. Since $L(A_1') = \mathsf{Straces}(A_1)$ and $L(A_2') = \mathsf{Straces}(A_2)$ we find $L(A_1') \not\subseteq L(A_2')$.
- Assume $L(A_1') \not\subseteq L(A_2')$. Then there is a word $\sigma \in L(A_1') \setminus L(A_2')$. Without loss of generality, assume $\sigma = \rho x$ for some $\rho \in L(A_1') \cap L(A_2')$ and $x \in \Sigma$. Since $L(A_1') = \mathsf{Straces}(A_1)$ and $L(A_2') = \mathsf{Straces}(A_2)$, we have $\rho x \in \mathsf{Straces}(A_1) \setminus \mathsf{Straces}(A_2)$. We distinguish two cases:

  • Suppose $x \in I$. Since, A_2 is input-enabled, we know that $\rho a \in \mathsf{Straces}(A_2)$ for all $a \in I$. In particular, $\rho x \in \mathsf{Straces}(A_2)$, contradicting $\rho x \notin \mathsf{Straces}(A_2)$. Therefore, $x \in I$ cannot be the case.
  • Suppose $x \in U \cup \{\delta\}$. Therefore, $x \in \mathsf{out}(\bar{s}_1 \text{ after } \rho)$ but $x \notin \mathsf{out}(\bar{s}_2 \text{ after } \rho)$. By definition of **ioco** relation we have A_1 **io$\not$co** A_2.

We next establish that the problem of checking **ioco** is in fact PSPACE-complete.

Theorem 2. *The problem of checking **ioco** is PSPACE-complete.*

Proof. We prove the thesis by providing a linear reduction of the PSPACE-complete language inclusion problem for regular expressions to checking **ioco**. Every regular expression can be translated linearly to a language equivalent NFA, following Kleene's theorem. In particular, we may assume that the language-equivalent NFA of a regular expression has one initial and one final state, all states are reachable from the initial state and can reach the final state, there is no incoming transition to the initial state and no outgoing transition from the final state (e.g., by applying Thompson's algorithm for converting regular expressions to NFAs [20]).

Formally, let RE_1 and RE_2 be two regular expressions over alphabet Σ and assume A_1 and A_2 are the language-equivalent NFAs for RE_1 and RE_2. The inclusion problem of regular expressions of RE_1 and RE_2 is equivalent to the problem whether $L(A_1) \subseteq L(A_2)$. As stated above, we may assume that NFA A_i is of the form $\langle Q_i, \Sigma \cup \{\epsilon\}, \Delta_i, q_i, \{f_i\}\rangle$. We define IOTSs $A_i' = \langle S_i, I, U, \to_i, \bar{s}_i\rangle$ as follows:

- $S_i = Q_i$,
- $I = \{i\}$, where $i \notin \Sigma$ is a fresh symbol,
- $U = \Sigma$,
- $\to_i = \{(q, a, q') \mid (q, a, q') \in \Delta_i \wedge a \in \Sigma\} \cup \{(q, \tau, q') \mid (q, \epsilon, q') \in \Delta_i\} \cup \{(q, i, q) \mid q \in Q_i\}$, i.e., the transition relation is that of the corresponding automaton union with i-labeled self-loops for each and every state,
- $\bar{s}_i = q_i$.

Note that the two IOLTSs A_1' and A_2' obtained from the above reduction are input-enabled, because $\{i\} \subseteq \mathsf{Sinit}(s)$ for all s in both A_1' and A_2'. Moreover, the accepting states in A_1 and A_2 are the only quiescent states in A_1' and A_2'. We proceed to show that language inclusion of A_1 in A_2 can be decided by checking for **ioco**; that is, we prove $L(A_1) \subseteq L(A_2)$ if and only if $A_1' \,\textbf{ioco}\, A_2'$. The contraposition of each implication is again proved separately.

- Assume that $L(A_1) \not\subseteq L(A_2)$. Thus, there is a word $\sigma \in \Sigma^*$ such that $\sigma \in L(A_1)$ but $\sigma \notin L(A_2)$. Therefore, the accepting state f_1 in NFA A_1 is reachable after σ. By construction, the state f_1 state in A_1' is quiescent. Thus, $\delta \in \mathsf{out}(A_1' \text{ after } \sigma)$. We distinguish two cases.
  - Suppose there is a state in automaton A_2 which is reachable after σ. Thus, $\sigma \in \mathsf{Straces}(A_2')$. Since $\sigma \notin L(A_2)$, we know that A_2 does not reach its accepting state f_2 after σ. Therefore, $\delta \notin \mathsf{out}(A_2' \text{ after } \sigma)$. Since $\delta \in \mathsf{out}(A_1' \text{ after } \sigma)$ and $\sigma \in \mathsf{Straces}(A_2')$, we find that $A_1' \,\text{io\!/\!co}\, A_2'$, which was to be shown.
  - Assume there is no state in automaton A_2 that is reachable after σ. Then also $\sigma \notin \mathsf{Straces}(A_2')$. Let $\rho x \in \Sigma^+$ be a prefix of σ such that $\rho \in \mathsf{Straces}(A_2')$ but $\rho x \notin \mathsf{Straces}(A_2')$. Note that such a prefix must exist. Since $\sigma \in \mathsf{Straces}(A_1')$, we find that $\rho x \in \mathsf{Straces}(A_1')$. Therefore $A_1' \,\text{io\!/\!co}\, A_2'$, which was to be shown.

– Assume that $A'_1 \text{ io\!\!\!/co } A'_2$. Thus, there is a $\sigma \in \mathsf{Straces}(A'_1) \cap \mathsf{Straces}(A'_2)$ and an output $x \in \Sigma \cup \{\delta\}$ such that $\sigma x \in \mathsf{Straces}(A'_1)$ but $\sigma x \notin \mathsf{Straces}(A'_2)$.
We first define the projection operator $_{-\downarrow}$ over the sequences in $\Sigma \cup \{i, \delta\}$. Let $\gamma \in (\Sigma \cup \{i, \delta\})^*$ and $a \in \Sigma \cup \{i, \delta\}$. Then $(\gamma a)_\downarrow = (\gamma)_\downarrow a$ when $a \in \Sigma$, and $(\gamma a)_\downarrow = (\gamma)_\downarrow$ otherwise.

Since, by construction, only transitions labeled with an action in Σ invoke state changes in IOLTS A'_1, for all γ we have $(A'_1 \text{ after } \gamma) = (A'_1 \text{ after } \gamma_\downarrow)$, and, similarly for A'_2. Therefore, without loss of generality we may assume that $\sigma x = (\sigma x)_\downarrow$; i.e., $\sigma x \in (\Sigma \cup \{\delta\})^*$. We distinguish two cases, based on the type of x.

- Assume that $x \in \Sigma$. Since $\sigma x \in \mathsf{Straces}(A'_1) \cap \Sigma^*$, there is a state in A_1 that is reachable after σx. Since the accepting state f_1 in A_1 is reachable from every all states in A_1, there must be a $\rho \in \Sigma^*$ such that $\sigma x \rho \in L(A_1)$. From $\sigma x \notin \mathsf{Straces}(A'_2)$ and $\sigma x \in \Sigma^*$ we can deduce that no state in A_2 can be reached via the word σx. Consequently, the extended word $\sigma x \rho$ is also not accepted by A_2; i.e., $\sigma x \rho \notin L(A_2)$. Since $\sigma x \rho \in L(A_1)$, we conclude that $L(A_1) \not\subseteq L(A_2)$.
- Assume that $x \notin \Sigma$; it then follows that $x = \delta$. Thus, $\delta \in \mathsf{out}(A'_1 \text{ after } \sigma)$. By our construction, a δ-labeled transition is enabled only at state f_1 in A'_1 and state f_2 in A'_2. From this, it follows that word σ is accepted by A_1, i.e., $\sigma \in L(A_1)$. Following a similar line of reasoning, we conclude from $\delta \notin \mathsf{out}(A'_2 \text{ after } \sigma)$ that the word σ is not accepted by A_2, i.e., $\sigma \notin L(A_2)$. But then $L(A_1) \not\subseteq L(A_2)$, which we needed to show.

Since the reduction we used is linear in the size of A_1 and A_2 and since checking **ioco** conformance is in PSPACE (Theorem 1), it follows that checking **ioco** conformance is PSPACE-complete.

Example 2. Consider automata A_1 and A_2 over $\Sigma = \{a\}$ depicted in Fig. 2. Automata A_1 and A_2 accept regular languages a and aa^*, respectively. Thus, $L(A_1) \subset L(A_2)$. Now consider the IOLTS's A'_1 and A'_2 in Fig. 2 with $\{a\}$ as the output alphabets and $\{i\}$ as the set of inputs. Observe that IOLTS's A'_1 and A'_2 can be obtained from A_1 and A_2 according to the reduction algorithm presented in the proof of Theorem 2. Both models are input-enabled because they have a transition labeled with i as the only input action at every state.

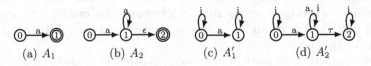

    (a) A_1 (b) A_2 (c) A'_1 (d) A'_2

Fig. 2. NFA's A_1 and A_2 represents the regular expression a and aa^* respectively. IOLTS's A'_1 and A'_2 depicts two input-enabled IOLTS's over the language $L = I \cup U$, where $I = \{i\}$ and $U = \{a\}$

The set $\mathsf{Straces}(A_2')$ is given by the regular expression $(i^*)\,|\,(i^*a\,(a|i)^*(\delta|i)^*)$. It is clear that $A_1'\ \mathbf{ioco}\ A_2'$, because for all $\sigma \in \mathsf{Straces}(A_2')$, $\mathsf{out}(A_1'\ \text{after}\ \sigma) \subseteq \mathsf{out}(A_2'\ \text{after}\ \sigma)$.

4   Coinductive Definition of IOCO

In the previous section, we showed that checking **ioco** is in general inefficient and requires exponential time and space (in the size of the specification). In the next section, we show that checking **ioco** can be performed in polynomial time when specifications are deterministic. To accommodate proving this result, we first show that checking **ioco** for deterministic specifications reduces to checking a simulation-like preorder which we call *coinductive* **ioco** in this section. This preorder closely resembles *alternating refinement* [4] for Interface Automata [3].

Definition 8 (Coinductive ioco). *Let deterministic IOLTS $\langle S, I, U, \to_s, \bar{s}\rangle$ be a specification, and let IOTS $\langle Q, I, U, \to, \bar{r}\rangle$ be an implementation. A binary relation $R \subseteq Q \times S$ is called a coinductive **ioco** relation from $\bar{r}$ to $\bar{s}$ when $(\bar{r}, \bar{s}) \in R$ and for each $(q, p) \in R$, then*

- *(Input simulation) if $p \xrightarrow{a}_s p'$, for $a \in I$, then $(q\ \text{after}\ a) \neq \emptyset$ and for all $q' \in q$ after a, we have $(q', p') \in R$*
- *(Output simulation) if $q \xRightarrow{a} q'$, and $a \in U \cup \{\delta\}$, then $a \in \mathsf{out}(p)$ and for all $p' \in p$ after a, we have $(q', p') \in R$.*

*We write $q \preceq p$, when there exists a coinductive **ioco** relation relating q to p.*

If the intent is clear from the context, we will simply say that a relation is a coinductive **ioco** relation rather than a coinductive **ioco** relation from $\bar{r}$ to $\bar{s}$.

The following theorem is the main result of this section.

Theorem 3. *For deterministic specifications, coinductive **ioco** and **ioco** coincide.*

Before giving the proof of the theorem, we need to show the correctness of the lemma given below.

Lemma 1. *Let deterministic IOLTS $\langle S, I, U, \bar{s}, \to_s\rangle$ be a specification, and let IOTS $\langle Q, I, U, \bar{r}, \to\rangle$ be an implementation. Let $R \subseteq S \times Q$ be a coinductive **ioco** relation, and let $\sigma \in \mathsf{Straces}(\bar{s}) \cap \mathsf{Straces}(\bar{r})$ with length $n \geq 1$. Then, $(q, p) \in R$ for all $p \in (\bar{s}\ \text{after}\ \sigma)$ and $q \in (\bar{r}\ \text{after}\ \sigma)$.*

Proof. Because R is a coinductive **ioco** relation, we have $(\bar{r}, \bar{s}) \in R$. We proceed with an induction on the length of σ.

- For the base case, assume that $\sigma \in L_\delta$ is a suspension trace of length 1. We distinguish two cases. Suppose that $\sigma \in I$. Following the *input simulation* condition with $(\bar{r}, \bar{s}) \in R$, we immediately find that $(q, p) \in R$ for $p \in (\bar{s}\ \text{after}\ \sigma)$ and $q \in (\bar{r}\ \text{after}\ \sigma)$. Suppose $\sigma \in U \cup \{\delta\}$. It follows from the *output simulation* condition together with $(\bar{r}, \bar{s}) \in R$ and the fact that $\bar{s}$ is deterministic that $(q, p) \in R$ for all $p \in (\bar{s}\ \text{after}\ \sigma)$ and $q \in (\bar{r}\ \text{after}\ \sigma)$. Both cases lead to the desired result.

– Assume that the induction hypothesis holds for all sequences of length $n-1$ and consider a sequence $\sigma \in \mathsf{Straces}(\bar{s}) \cap \mathsf{Straces}(\bar{r})$ with length $n \geq 2$. We may assume that σ is of the form ρa. Let $q, q' \in Q$ be arbitrary states such that $\bar{r} \overset{\rho}{\Rightarrow} q' \overset{a}{\Rightarrow} q$ (we know these exist since $\sigma \in \mathsf{Straces}(\bar{r})$). Likewise, there are unique $p, p' \in S$ such that $\bar{s} \overset{\rho}{\Rightarrow}_s p' \overset{a}{\Rightarrow}_s p$ (note that unicity follows from the fact that $\bar{s}$ is deterministic). Following the induction hypothesis, we have that $(q', p') \in R$. Therefore, the pair (q', p') satisfies the input and output simulation conditions. We distinguish two cases. Suppose that $a \in I$. Due to the *input simulation* condition, we find that $(q, p) \in R$. Suppose that $a \in U \cup \{\delta\}$; then $(q, p) \in R$ follows from the *output simulation* condition. Therefore, $(q, p) \in R$ for arbitrary $p \in (\bar{s} \text{ after } \sigma)$ and $q \in (\bar{r} \text{ after } \sigma)$.

Now, we are in the position to give the proof of Theorem 3.

Proof (Theorem 3). The proof of each implication is given separately.

– We suppose that $\bar{r} \mathbf{ioco} \, \bar{s}$, then we show that there is no binary relation R such that $(\bar{r}, \bar{s}) \in R$ and R is such that the input and output simulation conditions hold for all pairs $(q, p) \in R$. By definition of **ioco**, we know that there exists a sequence $\sigma \in \mathsf{Straces}(\bar{r}) \cap \mathsf{Straces}(\bar{s})$ and there exits an output x such that $\sigma x \in \mathsf{Straces}(\bar{r})$ but $\sigma x \notin \mathsf{Straces}(\bar{s})$. We distinguish two cases; $\sigma = \epsilon$ and $\sigma \in L_\delta^+$.
  - Suppose that $\sigma = \epsilon$. Clearly, the pair $(\bar{r}, \bar{s})$ violates the output simulation condition, because $\bar{r} \overset{x}{\Rightarrow}$, whereas $\bar{s} \overset{x}{\not\Rightarrow} s$. Therefore, there can be no relation R that simultaneously satisfies the required simulation properties *and* $(\bar{r}, \bar{s}) \in R$.
  - Suppose $\sigma \in L_\delta^+$. Towards a contradiction, assume that there is a coinductive **ioco** relation R. Thus, $(\bar{r}, \bar{s}) \in R$. It follows from $\sigma x \in \mathsf{Straces}(\bar{r})$ that there is some $q \in (\bar{r} \text{ after } \sigma)$ such that $x \in \mathsf{out}(q)$. Since $\bar{s}$ is deterministic, from $\sigma \in \mathsf{Straces}(\bar{s})$ we find that there is some unique $p \in S$ such that $\bar{s} \overset{\sigma}{\Rightarrow}_s p$. Because $\sigma x \notin \mathsf{Straces}(\bar{s})$, we find that $x \notin \mathsf{out}(p)$. From Lemma 1, we obtain that $(q, p) \in R$. However, the pair (q, p) violates the output simulation condition since $q \overset{x}{\Rightarrow}$ but $p \overset{x}{\not\Rightarrow} s$. This contradicts the assumption that there is a coinductive **ioco** relation R.
– We suppose that $\bar{r} \, \mathbf{ioco} \, \bar{s}$. We construct the relation $R = \{(\bar{r}, \bar{s})\} \cup \{(q, p) \mid \exists \sigma \in L_\delta^+ \bullet \bar{r} \overset{\sigma}{\Rightarrow} q \wedge \bar{s} \overset{\sigma}{\Rightarrow}_s p\}$. We proceed to show that R is a coinductive **ioco** relation. Clearly, $(\bar{r}, \bar{s}) \in R$. So it suffices to show that for arbitrary pair $(q, p) \in R$ the input and output simulation conditions are met. We assume arbitrary pair $(q, p) \in R$. Thus, there exists $\sigma \in L_\delta^*$ such that $\bar{r} \overset{\sigma}{\Rightarrow} q$ and $\bar{s} \overset{\sigma}{\Rightarrow} p$. Because $\bar{r}$ is input-enabled, q has a matching (weak) transition for any input action performed by p, i.e., for all $a \in I$ such that $p \overset{a}{\Rightarrow}_s$, q after $a \neq \emptyset$. By definition of R, we find that $(q', p') \in R$ for an action $a \in I$ such that $p \overset{a}{\Rightarrow}_s p'$ and any $q \overset{a}{\Rightarrow} q'$. Thus, (q, p) satisfies the input simulation condition. Using $\bar{r} \, \mathbf{ioco} \, \bar{s}$, by construction of R, we know that $\mathsf{out}(q) \subseteq \mathsf{out}(p)$. Combining this observation with the definition of R results in $(q', p') \in R$ for all actions $a \in U \cup \{\delta\}$ for which $p \overset{a}{\Rightarrow}_s p'$ and $q \overset{a}{\Rightarrow} q'$. Thus, (q, p) also satisfies the output

simulation condition. Hence, the pair (q, p) fulfills both input and output simulation conditions which was to be shown.

Since R satisfies both simulation conditions and $(\bar{r}, \bar{s}) \in R$, we find that R is a coinductive **ioco** relation.

Following Theorem 3, we say that a coinductive **ioco** relation R is a *witness* for $\bar{r}$ **ioco** $\bar{s}$.

Example 3. Consider the IOLTS's $\bar{s}$ and $\bar{r}$ presented in Fig. 1 on p. 295. We define the binary relation $R = \{(\bar{r}, \bar{s}), (r_1, s_1), (r_2, s_1), (r_3, s_2), (r_4, s_3)\}$. Clearly, for all pair of states $(q, p) \in R$, the two input and output simulation conditions presented in Definition 8 are satisfied. Thus, the relation R is an **ioco** coinductive relation and it is also a witness for $\bar{r}$ **ioco** $\bar{s}$.

Now, consider the IOLTS $\bar{i}$ depicted in Fig. 1: Because out($\bar{i}$ after *coin*) $\not\subseteq$ out($\bar{s}$ after *coin*), it is clearly obtained that $\bar{i}$ io/co $\bar{s}$. Therefore, we find that there is no binary relation from $\bar{i}$ to $\bar{s}$ such that $(\bar{i}, \bar{s}) \in R$ and the two input and output simulation conditions hold for any pair $(q, p) \in R$. However, we for the sake of contradiction assume that there is a relation R' such that $(\bar{i}, \bar{s}) \in R'$ and R' is such that for any $(q, p) \in R'$, the two conditions in Definition 8 holds. Regarding the input simulation condition, $(\bar{i}, \bar{s}) \in R'$ implies that $(i_1, s_1) \in R'$ as well. We know from the properties of R', that s_1 has to simulate all the outputs produced by i_1. While observation of quiescence is not possible at s_1, via an internal transition i_1 can reach to a quiescent state. Therefore, (i_1, s_1) violates the output simulation condition which contradicts with the assumption that all pairs in R' respect the output simulation condition.

5   Conformance Checking of Deterministic Specifications

In this section, we give a polynomial-time algorithm for deciding the coinductive **ioco** relation defined in the previous section. The results obtained in the remainder of this section can be adapted in a straightforward manner to some other conformance relations in the **ioco** family, such as uioco [6]. Our algorithm is inspired by [18] and is based on the reduction of checking **ioco** into the **NHORNSAT** problem [8].

5.1   NHORNSAT Problem

The *satisfiability* problem for Boolean formulas is a typical (in fact, the first identified) NP-complete problem. In a restricted setting, however, the problem becomes decidable in polynomial time.

Definition 9 ((N)HORNSAT). *A boolean clause (a disjunction of literals) containing of at most one positive literal is called a Horn clause. We call the conjunction of Horn clauses a Horn formula. The satisfiability of a Horn formula is known as **HORNSAT**. Similarly, checking the satisfiability of a conjunction of clauses containing of at most one negative literal is called **NHORNSAT**.*

The *size* of a **(N)HORNSAT** instance is defined as the total number of occurrences of literals in the given formula. It is well-known that **(N)HORNSAT** is decidable in polynomial time in the size of the **(N)HORNSAT** instance [8].

5.2   Reducing IOCO to NHORNSAT

Throughout this section, we assume that we have an IOTS $\langle Q, I, U, \bar{r}, \rightarrow \rangle$ and a deterministic IOLTS $\langle S, I, U, \bar{s}, \rightarrow_s \rangle$. We assume p, p', p'' are states in S and q, q', q'' are states in Q. The algorithm, which we will present shortly, intuitively uses the following encoding:

1. positive literals X_{qp} model that q is (purportedly) related to p by a coinductive **ioco** relation,
2. negative literals $\overline{X_{qp}}$ model that the pair (p, q) cannot be in a coinductive **ioco** relation, and
3. implication clauses $X_{qp} \Rightarrow X_{q'p'}$, which are shorthand for $\overline{X_{qp}} \vee X_{q'p'}$, model that the pair (p, q) can be in a coinductive **ioco** relation only if (q', p') is in the same relation.

The reduction of checking for a coinductive **ioco** relation to **NHORNSAT** is presented in Algorithm 1: this algorithm constructs a negative Horn formula F such that F is satisfiable if and only if there exists a coinductive **ioco** relation R from $\bar{r}$ to $\bar{s}$.

The algorithm takes an implementation $\bar{r}$ and a deterministic specification $\bar{s}$ as input. We assume that for $\bar{r}$, the generalized transition relation $\Rightarrow$ from $\rightarrow$ of $\bar{r}$ has been computed. This requires a pre-processing step of $\bar{r}$, involving a transitive closure computation, see e.g. [12]. Computing $\Rightarrow$ can be done in polynomial time.

It is easy to see that the algorithm terminates. In each iteration, of the outer loop, the set $V \subseteq \{X_{qp} \mid q \in Q, p \in S\}$ strictly increases and $C \subseteq \{X_{qp} \mid q \in Q, p \in S\} \setminus V$ is a loop invariant. The algorithm thus terminates after at most $|Q| \times |S|$ iterations of the outer loop. Since the set of actions L_δ is finite, termination of the two inner loops is also guaranteed. It is equally easy to see that the formula that is constructed is a **NHORNSAT** formula.

Example 4. Reconsider IOLTSs $\bar{s}$ and $\bar{i}$ in Fig. 1 on p. 295. As we concluded in Example 1, $\bar{i}$ **ioco** $\bar{s}$ because, e.g. out($\bar{i}$ after *coin*) $\not\subseteq$ out($\bar{s}$ after *coin*). Therefore, the **NHORNSAT** instance obtained from Algorithm 1 must be unsatisfiable. The formula F generated by Algorithm 1 is the following:

$$X_{\bar{i}\bar{s}} \wedge (X_{\bar{i}\bar{s}} \Rightarrow X_{\bar{i}\bar{s}}) \wedge (X_{\bar{i}\bar{s}} \Rightarrow X_{i_1 s_1}) \wedge (X_{\bar{i}\bar{s}} \Rightarrow X_{\bar{i}s_1}) \wedge (X_{i_1 s_1} \Rightarrow X_{i_2 s_2})$$
$$\wedge (X_{i_1 s_1} \Rightarrow X_{i_3 s_3}) \wedge \overline{X_{i_1 s_1}} \wedge \overline{X_{\bar{i}s_1}} \wedge (X_{i_2 s_2} \Rightarrow X_{i_2 s_2}) \wedge (X_{i_3 s_3} \Rightarrow X_{i_3 s_3})$$

Indeed, it is easily seen that the obtained formula F is unsatisfiable: for F to be satisfiable, $X_{\bar{i}\bar{s}}$ must be **True**, which means that $X_{i_1 s_1}$ must be **True**, but that means that $\overline{X_{i_1 s_1}}$ is **False**.

Algorithm 1. ioco-NHORN

1: **procedure ioco-NHORN**$(\bar{s}, \bar{r})$
2:     $F \leftarrow X_{\bar{r}\bar{s}}$ ▷ Positive literal $X_{\bar{r}\bar{s}}$ is added to Formula F.
3:     $C \leftarrow \{X_{\bar{r}\bar{s}}\}$ ▷ Set of unprocessed variables
4:     $V \leftarrow \emptyset$ ▷ Set of processed variables
5:     **while** $C \neq \emptyset$ **do**
6:         Choose $X_{qp} \in C$
7:         $V \leftarrow V \cup \{X_{qp}\}$
8:         $C' \leftarrow \emptyset$
9:         **for** $a \in \text{init}(p) \cap I$ **do**
10:             **if** $(q \text{ after } a) \neq \emptyset$ **then**
11:                 Choose $p' \in p$ after a ▷ Due to determinism, $|p \text{ after } a| = 1$
12:                 $F \leftarrow F \wedge \bigwedge_{q' \in (q \text{ after } a)}(X_{qp} \Rightarrow X_{q'p'})$ ▷ Input simulation condition
13:                 $C' \leftarrow C' \cup \{X_{q'p'} \mid q' \in q \text{ after } a\}$ ▷ Add unprocessed variables
14:             **else**
15:                 $F \leftarrow F \wedge \overline{X_{qp}}$ ▷ Violation of input simulation
16:             **end if**
17:         **end for**
18:
19:         **for** $a \in \text{out}(q)$ **do**
20:             **if** $a \in \text{out}(p)$ **then**
21:                 Choose $p' \in p$ after a ▷ Due to determinism, $|p \text{ after } a| = 1$
22:                 $F \leftarrow F \wedge \bigwedge_{q' \in (q \text{ after } a)}(X_{qp} \Rightarrow X_{q'p'})$ ▷ Output simulation condition
23:                 $C' \leftarrow C' \cup \{X_{q'p'} \mid q' \in q \text{ after } a\}$ ▷ Add unprocessed variables
24:             **else**
25:                 $F \leftarrow F \wedge \overline{X_{qp}}$ ▷ Violation of output simulation
26:             **end if**
27:         **end for**
28:         $C \leftarrow C \cup (C' \setminus V)$;
29:     **end while**
30:
31:     **return** F ▷ The final negative HORN formula
32: **end procedure**

Next, reconsider IOLTS $\bar{r}$ of Fig. 1. We know from Example 1 that $\bar{r} \textbf{ ioco } \bar{s}$. The formula F generated by Algorithm 1 is the following:

$$X_{\bar{r}\bar{s}} \wedge (X_{\bar{r}\bar{s}} \Rightarrow X_{\bar{r}\bar{s}}) \wedge (X_{\bar{r}\bar{s}} \Rightarrow X_{r_1 s_1}) \wedge (X_{\bar{r}\bar{s}} \Rightarrow X_{r_2 s_1}) \wedge (X_{r_1 s_1} \Rightarrow X_{r_3 s_2})$$
$$\wedge (X_{r_2 s_1} \Rightarrow X_{r_4 s_3}) \wedge (X_{r_3 s_2} \Rightarrow X_{r_3 s_2}) \wedge (X_{r_4 s_3} \Rightarrow X_{r_4 s_3})$$

Clearly, the constructed formula is satisfiable: assigning **True** to all literals is a satisfying assignment.

5.3   Correctness of the Reduction Algorithm

The constructed formula F by Algorithm 1 has two key properties that together ensure the correctness of our algorithm. First, the existence of a coinductive

ioco relation R implies satisfiability of F. This follows from the observation that from any coinductive **ioco** relation R the truth assignment ν for F defined by assigning **True** to every variable X_{qp} appearing in F for which $(q, p) \in R$, and assigning **False** to all remaining variables in F is a witness to the satisfiability of F. Second, satisfiability of F implies the existence of a coinductive **ioco** relation R. In a nutshell, this follows from the observation that for any given satisfying assignment ν of F, the binary relation $R \subseteq Q \times S$ defined by $(p, q) \in R$ iff variable X_{qp} appears in F and $X_{pq} = $ **True** in ν, is a coinductive **ioco** relation. We first prove these two properties, and then state our main theorem claiming correctness of the algorithm.

Proposition 1. *Let $\langle S, I, U, \rightarrow_s, \bar{s} \rangle$ be a deterministic IOLTS and let $\langle Q, I, U, \rightarrow, \bar{r} \rangle$ be an arbitrary IOTS. Let F be the **NHORNSAT** instance from Algorithm 1. If $\bar{r} \preceq \bar{s}$ then F is satisfiable.*

The correctness of the above-given proposition results from the following lemma. This lemma essentially states that the presence of a negative literal $\overline{X_{qp}}$ in formula F indicates the pair (q, p) can never be related by a coinductive **ioco** relation.

Lemma 2. *Let F be the formula obtained from Algorithm 1, and let X_{pq} be an arbitrary variable. If F contains the literal $\overline{X_{pq}}$, then no coinductive **ioco** relation R for which $(q, p) \in R$ exists.*

Proof. Towards a contradiction, assume there is a coinductive **ioco** relation R such that $(q, p) \in R$. In our algorithm, the literal $\overline{X_{qp}}$ is only added to F under one of the following two conditions:

1. there is an input action $a \in \text{init}(p)$ while q after $a = \emptyset$,
2. there is an output action $a \in \text{out}(q)$ while $a \notin \text{out}(p)$.

We first assume that $\overline{X_{qp}}$ is generated because of the first case, i.e., there is an input $a \in \text{init}(p)$ for which q after $a = \emptyset$. Then the pair $(q, p) \in R$ does not meet the input simulation condition of Definition 8, contradicting the fact that the pair (q, p) can be in a coinductive **ioco** relation R. Next, assume that $\overline{X_{qp}}$ is generated because of the second case. Following the same line of reasoning, the presence of $(q, p) \in R$ violates the output simulation condition, contradicting that R is a coinductive **ioco** relation.

Next, we return to proving Proposition 1.

Proof (Proposition 1). Consider a coinductive **ioco** relation $R \subseteq Q \times S$. Let ν be a truth assignment for the variables in F defined as follows:

$$\nu(X_{qp}) = \begin{cases} \textbf{True} & \text{if } (q, p) \in R \\ \textbf{False} & \text{otherwise} \end{cases}$$

Since $(\bar{r}, \bar{s}) \in R$, we know that the single literal clause $X_{\bar{r}\bar{s}}$ evaluates to **True**. Next, consider the other two types of clauses that are introduced in formula F: single negative literal clauses and implication clauses.

- Clauses of the form $\overline{X_{qp}}$. Due to Lemma 2 we have $(q,p) \notin R$ whenever the negative literal clause $\overline{X_{qp}}$ is added to F in line 15 or line 25. By definition we then have $\nu(X_{qp}) = \textbf{False}$. Consequently, a negative literal clause $\overline{X_{qp}}$ in F evaluates to **True**.
- Clauses of the form $X_{qp} \Rightarrow X_{q'p'}$. We distinguish the cases when $(q,p) \notin R$ and $(q,p) \in R$.
  - Assume that $(q,p) \notin R$. By definition of ν, we have $\nu(X_{qp}) = \textbf{False}$. Then the clause $X_{qp} \Rightarrow X_{q'p'}$ immediately evaluates to **True** under ν.
  - Suppose that $(q,p) \in R$. Thus $\nu(X_{qp}) = \textbf{True}$. Therefore the clause $X_{qp} \Rightarrow X_{q'p'}$ evaluates to **True** only if $\nu(X_{q'p'}) = \textbf{True}$. The implication clause $X_{qp} \Rightarrow X_{q'p'}$ in Algorithm 1 is added to F in line 12 when there is some input $a \in \text{init}(p)$ or in line 22 when there is some output $a \in \text{out}(q)$ for which $q' \in q$ after a and $p' \in p$ after a. From these observations, and the fact that R is a coinductive **ioco** relation it follows that $(q',p') \in R$. But then, by definition of ν, we have $\nu(X_{q'p'}) = \textbf{True}$, which was to be shown. As a result, implication clauses in F of the form $X_{qp} \Rightarrow X_{q'p'}$ evaluate to **True**.

Since there are no other types of clauses in F, formula F evaluates to **True** under ν.

The proposition below formalizes the second property of algorithm **ioco**-NHORN.

Proposition 2. *Let $\langle S, I, U, \to_s, \bar{s} \rangle$ be a deterministic IOLTS and let $\langle Q, I, U, \to , \bar{r} \rangle$ be an arbitrary IOTS. Let F be the **NHORNSAT** instance from Algorithm 1. If F is satisfiable, then $\bar{r} \preceq \bar{s}$.*

Proof. Let ν be a truth assignment such that formula F evaluates to **True**. We construct a binary relation $R \subseteq S \times Q$ as follows:

$$R = \{(q,p) \mid \text{variable } X_{qp} \text{ occurs in } F \text{ and } \nu(X_{qp}) = \textbf{True}\}$$

We proceed by showing that R is a coinductive **ioco** relation. Clearly, since the single literal $X_{\bar{r}\bar{s}}$ occurs in F and F is satisfiable, we have $\nu(X_{\bar{r}\bar{s}}) = \textbf{True}$. By definition, we then have $(\bar{r}, \bar{s}) \in R$.

Let $(q,p) \in R$ be an arbitrary pair. By definition, this means that $\nu(X_{pq}) = \textbf{True}$. Observe that this means that formula F cannot contain the single negative literal $\overline{X_{qp}}$. We next show that the pair $(q,p) \in R$ meets both the input and output simulation conditions:

- *Ad* input simulation. Suppose that $p \xrightarrow{a}_s p'$ for some $a \in I$. Since F does not contain the negative literal $\overline{X_{qp}}$, we know that q after $a \neq \emptyset$ (line 10). Therefore, F contains implication clauses of the form $X_{qp} \Rightarrow X_{q'p'}$ where $q' \in q$ after a and $p' \in p$ after a. Since, F evaluates to **True** under ν, also $X_{qp} \Rightarrow X_{q'p'}$ evaluates to **True** under ν. Since $q' \in q$ after a is chosen arbitrarily, we find that $\nu(X_{q'p'}) = \textbf{True}$ for all $q' \in q$ after a. Then by construction, $(q',p') \in R$ for all $q' \in q$ after a.

- *Ad* output simulation. Suppose that $q \overset{a}{\Rightarrow} q'$ for some $a \in U \cup \{\delta\}$. Following the same line of reasoning as in the above case, we find that the pair (q, p) meets the output simulation condition.

An immediate consequence of the preceding two propositions is the following theorem, stating that our reduction algorithm for checking **ioco** is sound.

Theorem 4. *Let $\langle S, I, U, \rightarrow_s, \bar{s} \rangle$ be a deterministic IOLTS and let $\langle Q, I, U, \rightarrow, \bar{r} \rangle$ be an arbitrary IOTS. Let F be the **NHORNSAT** instance from Algorithm 1. Then F is satisfiable if and only if $\bar{r}$ **ioco** $\bar{s}$.*

Proof. Following Propositions 1 and 2, we know that the formula F obtained from Algorithm 1 is satisfiable if and only if there is a coinductive **ioco** relation. Combined with Theorem 3 we find that formula F is satisfiable if and only if $\bar{r}$ **ioco** $\bar{s}$.

5.4   Complexity Analysis

We next analyze the complexity of Algorithm 1. Since **NHORNSAT** is decidable in linear time [8], proving that we can decide that a possibly nondeterministic implementation conforms to a deterministic specification in polynomial time only requires showing that the Negative Horn formula F can be constructed in polynomial time.

Theorem 5. *Let $\langle S, I, U, \rightarrow_s, \bar{s} \rangle$ be a deterministic IOLTS and let $\langle Q, I, U, \rightarrow, \bar{r} \rangle$ be an arbitrary IOTS for which $\Rightarrow$ has been computed. Algorithm 1 constructs formula F, which is of size $O(|S| \times |Q|^2 \times |L_\delta|)$ in time $O(|S| \times |Q|^2 \times |L_\delta|)$.*

Proof. To facilitate writing the proof, we first introduce some auxiliary notation. Let d_a^s denote the cardinality of the set of states reachable from a state t after executing an a-labeled transition, i.e., $d_a^t = |t \text{ after } a|$.

The main loop of Algorithm 1 iterates over the set of variables of the form X_{qp}, for $q \in Q$ and $p \in S$. This means there are at most $|Q| \times |S|$ iterations. The complexity of a single iteration is given by the sum of the complexity of the two inner loops (lines 9–17 and lines 19–27).

Since the size of a clause $\overline{X_{qp}}$ is smaller than the size of an implication clause introduced in line 12 or line 22, the size of the constructed clause in each iteration of one of the inner loops is bounded from above by $2 \times d_a^q$ for each $a \in I$ for the first inner loop, and $2 \times d_a^q$ for each $a \in U \cup \{\delta\}$. The cumulative size of the generated clauses in the first inner loop is therefore bounded from above by $2 \times \sum_{a \in I} d_a^q$ and the cumulative size of the generated clauses in the second inner loop is bounded from above by $2 \times \sum_{a \in U \cup \{\delta\}} d_a^q$.

Thus, the cumulative size of the clauses added in each iteration of the outer loop is at most $2 \times (\sum_{a \in I} d_a^q + \sum_{a \in U \cup \{\delta\}} d_a^q) = 2 \times \sum_{a \in L_\delta} d_a^q$. Assuming that for all $q \in Q$ and all $p \in S$, all variables X_{qp} are inspected, the total size of the **NHORNSAT** instance is bound from above as follows:

$$\sum_{p \in S} \sum_{q \in Q} (2 \times \sum_{a \in L_\delta} d_a^q)$$
$$\leq^\dagger \sum_{p \in S} \sum_{q \in Q} (2 \times \sum_{a \in L_\delta} |Q|)$$
$$= 2 \times |S| \times |Q|^2 \times |L_\delta|$$

Observe that at †, we used the fact that d_a^q is bounded from above by the size of the state space of $\bar{r}$, i.e., $|Q|$. Hence, the size of formula F is $O(|S| \times |Q|^2 \times |L_\delta|)$. Since we assume that $\Rightarrow$ has been computed, all operations involving $\Rightarrow$, such as _ after _ and out(_) require constant time. Constructing formula F can therefore also be done in time $O(|S| \times |Q|^2 \times |L_\delta|)$.

The theorem below states the complexity of deciding **ioco** for deterministic specifications and possibly non-deterministic implementations.

Theorem 6. *Let $\langle S, I, U, \to_s, \bar{s} \rangle$ be a deterministic IOLTS and let $\langle Q, I, U, \to, \bar{r} \rangle$ be an arbitrary IOTS. Deciding whether $\bar{r}$ **ioco** $\bar{s}$ for deterministic specifications $\bar{s}$ and possibly non-deterministic implementations $\bar{r}$ can be done in $O(|L_\delta| \times |Q|^{2.3727}) + O(|S| \times |Q|^2 \times |L_\delta|)$.*

Proof. Generating and solving the NHORN formula F obtained from Algorithm 1 requires $O(|S| \times |Q|^2 \times |L_\delta|)$, see Theorem 6 combined with the fact that F can be solved in time linear in the size of F. A precondition to the algorithm is that $\Rightarrow$ has been computed from $\to$. Following [12], this can be done in $O(|L_\delta| \times |Q|^{2.3727})$.

When both implementation and specification are deterministic, the time complexity of our algorithm reduces to $O(|S| \times |\to|)$. Note that in this case, the computation of $\Rightarrow$ only requires augmenting the transition relation with δ transitions, which can be done in $O(|\to|)$.

6 Conclusion

In this paper, we studied the complexity of checking input-output conformance (**ioco**). We proved that the problem of checking conformance is PSPACE-complete. Then, we presented a coinductive definition of **ioco** in the restricted setting of deterministic models and through a reduction to **NHORNSAT**, presented a polynomial-time algorithm for checking **ioco** in this setting.

We plan to investigate the application of our algorithm in Sect. 5 to checking alternating simulation. Currently, the best known algorithm for this purpose is proposed in [7], which is a game-based algorithm for deterministic models. The solution provided in this paper may offer an alternative for the existing algorithms for checking alternating refinement relation, but it must be checked to see whether the runtime complexity of the resulting algorithm would be comparable to that of existing algorithms.

Acknowledgments. We thank Sarmen Keshishzadeh and Jeroen Keiren (both TU/e) for feedback on earlier drafts of this paper.

References

1. Aarts, F., Vaandrager, F.: Learning I/O automata. In: Gastin, P., Laroussinie, F. (eds.) CONCUR 2010. LNCS, vol. 6269, pp. 71–85. Springer, Heidelberg (2010)
2. Abdulla, P.A., Chen, Y.-F., Holík, L., Mayr, R., Vojnar, T.: When simulation meets antichains. In: Esparza, J., Majumdar, R. (eds.) TACAS 2010. LNCS, vol. 6015, pp. 158–174. Springer, Heidelberg (2010)
3. de Alfaro, L., Henzinger, T.A.: Interface automata. In: Proceedings of FSE/ESEC'01, pp. 109–120. ACM (2001)
4. Alur, R., Henzinger, T.A., Kupferman, O., Vardi, M.Y.: Alternating refinement relations. In: Sangiorgi, D., de Simone, R. (eds.) CONCUR 1998. LNCS, vol. 1466, pp. 163–178. Springer, Heidelberg (1998)
5. Asaadi, H.R., Khosravi, R., Mousavi, M.R., Noroozi, N.: Towards model-based testing of electronic funds transfer systems. In: Arbab, F., Sirjani, M. (eds.) FSEN 2011. LNCS, vol. 7141, pp. 253–267. Springer, Heidelberg (2012)
6. van der Bijl, M., Rensink, A., Tretmans, J.: Compositional testing with ioco. In: Petrenko, A., Ulrich, A. (eds.) FATES 2003. LNCS, vol. 2931, pp. 86–100. Springer, Heidelberg (2004)
7. Chatterjee, K., Chaubal, S., Kamath, P.: Faster algorithms for alternating refinement relations. In: Proceedings of the CSL'12. LIPIcs, vol. 16, pp. 167–182. Dagstuhl (2012)
8. Dowling, W.F., Gallier, J.H.: Linear-time algorithms for testing the satisfiability of propositional horn formulae. JLAP 1(3), 267–284 (1984)
9. Frantzen, L., Tretmans, J.: Model-based testing of environmental conformance of components. In: de Boer, F.S., Bonsangue, M.M., Graf, S., de Roever, W.-P. (eds.) FMCO 2006. LNCS, vol. 4709, pp. 1–25. Springer, Heidelberg (2007)
10. Gregorio-Rodríguez, C., Llana, L., Martínez-Torres, R.: Input-Output Conformance Simulation (iocos) for Model Based Testing. In: Beyer, D., Boreale, M. (eds.) FORTE 2013 and FMOODS 2013. LNCS, vol. 7892, pp. 114–129. Springer, Heidelberg (2013)
11. Hierons, R.M.: The complexity of asynchronous model based testing. TCS **451**, 70–82 (2012)
12. Kanellakis, P.C., Smolka, S.A.: CCS expressions, finite state processes, and three problems of equivalence. Inf. Comput. **86**(1), 43–68 (1990)
13. Mostowski, W., Poll, E., Schmaltz, J., Tretmans, J., Wichers Schreur, R.: Model-based testing of electronic passports. In: Alpuente, M., Cook, B., Joubert, Ch. (eds.) FMICS 2009. LNCS, vol. 5825, pp. 207–209. Springer, Heidelberg (2009)
14. Myers, G.J., Badgett, T., Sandler, C.: The Art of Software Testing, 3rd edn. Wiley, New York (2011)
15. Noroozi, N., Mousavi, M.R., Willemse, T.A.C.: Decomposability in input output conformance testing. In: Proceedings of MBT'13. EPTCS, vol. 111, pp. 51–66 (2013)
16. Ploeger, B.: Improved verification methods for concurrent systems. Ph.D. thesis, TU/Eindhoven (2009)
17. Pretschner, A.: One evaluation of model-based testing and its automation. In: Proceedings of ICSE'05, pp. 722–723. ACM (2005)
18. Shukla, S.K., Hunt III, H.B., Rosenkrantz, D.J., Stearns, R.E.: On the complexity of relational problems for finite state processes (extended abstract). In: Meyer auf der Heide, F., Monien, B. (eds.) ICALP 1996. LNCS, vol. 1099, pp. 466–477. Springer, Heidelberg (1996)

19. Stockmeyer, L.J., Meyer, A.R.: Word problems requiring exponential time: preliminary report. In: Proceedings STOC'73, pp. 1–9. ACM (1973)
20. Thompson, K.: Regular expression search algorithms. CACM **11**(6), 419–422 (1968)
21. Tretmans, J.: Model based testing with labelled transition systems. In: Hierons, R.M., Bowen, J.P., Harman, M. (eds.) FORTEST. LNCS, vol. 4949, pp. 1–38. Springer, Heidelberg (2008)
22. Veanes, M., Bjorner, N.: Alternating simulation and ioco. STTT **14**(4), 387–405 (2012)
23. Veanes, M., Campbell, C., Grieskamp, W., Schulte, W., Tillmann, N., Nachmanson, L.: Model-based testing of object-oriented reactive systems with Spec Explorer. In: Hierons, R.M., Bowen, J.P., Harman, M. (eds.) FORTEST. LNCS, vol. 4949, pp. 39–76. Springer, Heidelberg (2008)
24. Vishal, V., Kovacioglu, M., Kherazi, R., Mousavi, M.R.: Integrating model-based and constraint-based testing using SpecExplorer. In: Proceedings MoTiP'12, pp. 219–224. IEEE (2012)

Compatibility Checking
for Asynchronously Communicating Software

Meriem Ouederni[1]([⊠]), Gwen Salaün[2], and Tevfik Bultan[3]

[1] Toulouse INP, IRIT, Toulouse, France
meriem.ouederni@irit.fr
[2] LIG, Grenoble INP, Inria, Montbonnot Saint-Martin, France
gwen.salaun@inria.fr
[3] UCSB, Santa Barbara, USA
bultan@cs.ucsb.edu

Abstract. Compatibility is a crucial problem that is encountered while constructing new software by reusing and composing existing components. A set of software components is called compatible if their composition preserves certain properties, such as deadlock freedom. However, checking compatibility for systems communicating asynchronously is an undecidable problem, and asynchronous communication is a common interaction mechanism used in building software systems. A typical approach in analyzing such systems is to bound the state space. In this paper, we take a different approach and do not impose any bounds on the number of participants or the sizes of the message buffers. Instead, we present a sufficient condition for checking compatibility of a set of asynchronously communicating components. Our approach relies on the synchronizability property which identifies systems for which interaction behavior remains the same when asynchronous communication is replaced with synchronous communication. Using the synchronizability property, we can check the compatibility of systems with unbounded message buffers by analyzing only a finite part of their behavior. We have implemented a prototype tool to automate our approach and we have applied it to many examples.

1 Introduction

A widely accepted view in software development is that the software systems should be built by reusing and composing existing pieces of code. Moreover, recent trends in computing technology promote development of software applications that are intrinsically concurrent and distributed. For example, service-oriented computing promotes development of Web-accessible software systems that are composed of distributed services that interact with each other by exchanging messages over the Internet. Cyber-physical systems, on the other hand, involve integration of physical and computational components that interact in a variety of ways to implement a common functionality. Finally, pervasive systems combine large numbers of sensors and computational elements integrated into everyday environment and require their coordination in a dynamic setting. All these computing paradigms

J.L. Fiadeiro et al. (Eds.): FACS 2013, LNCS 8348, pp. 310–328, 2014.
DOI: 10.1007/978-3-319-07602-7_19, © Springer International Publishing Switzerland 2014

involve concurrent execution of distributed components that are required to interact with each other to achieve a shared goal.

A central problem in composing distributed components is checking their compatibility. Compatibility checking is used to identify if composed components can interoperate without errors. This verification is crucial for ensuring correct execution of a distributed system at runtime. Compatibility errors that are not identified during the design phase can make a distributed system malfunction or deadlock during its execution, which can result in delays, financial loss, and even physical damage in the case of cyber-physical systems.

In this paper, we focus on the compatibility checking problem for closed systems involving composition of distributed components. We call the components that participate in a composed system *peers*. A set of peers is compatible if, when they are composed, they satisfy a certain property. We call such a property a compatibility notion. It is worth observing that the compatibility problem depends on several parameters: the behavioral model used to describe the peers (finite state machines, Petri nets, etc.), the communication model (synchronous *vs.* asynchronous, pairwise *vs.* broadcast/multicast, ordered *vs.* unordered buffers, lossy channels, etc.), and the compatibility notion. In this paper, we use Labeled Transition Systems (LTSs) to describe peer behaviors. We focus on pairwise asynchronous communication model (which corresponds to message-based communication via FIFO buffers). Pairwise communication means that each individual message is exchanged between two peers (no broadcast communication). As for compatibility, there are several compatibility notions existing in the literature. Here, we focus on two widely used notions, namely deadlock-freedom (*DF*) [15] and unspecified receptions (*UR*) [11,34]. A set of peers is *DF* compatible if their composition does not contain any deadlock, i.e., starting from their initial states peers can either progress by following transitions in their respective LTSs or terminate if they are in final states. A set of peers is *UR* compatible if they do not deadlock and for each message that is sent there is a peer that can receive that message.

Most results in the literature for verifying the compatibility of behavioral models assume two interacting peers and synchronous communication, e.g., [9,13,15,34]. However, asynchronous communication is more suitable than synchronous communication in a distributed setting, since asynchronous communication is non-blocking. In asynchronous communication the sender does not have to wait for the receiver when it needs to emit a message. Analyzing asynchronously communicating systems is more complicated than synchronously communicating systems since it is necessary to represent the contents of the message buffers during analysis of a system that uses asynchronous communication. Moreover, asynchronous communication with unbounded message buffers leads to infinite state spaces. This means that, in general, verification techniques based on explicit state space exploration will not be sound for such systems. Analysis of asynchronously communicating systems has been investigated extensively during the last 30 years, e.g., [11,14,24,26,31]. A common approach used in analyzing asynchronously communicating systems is to bound the state space by bounding the number of cycles, peers, or buffers. Bounding buffers to an arbitrary size during its execution is not a satisfactory solution since, if at some point buffers' sizes change (due to changes in memory requirements for example), it is not possible to know how the system would behave compared to its former version and new unexpected errors can show up. This is the case for instance of the simplified news server protocol shown in Fig. 1. Transitions are labeled with either emissions (exclamation marks) or receptions (question marks). Initial states are marked with incoming half-arrow and final states have no outgoing transitions. With buffer size 1, the system executes correctly (no deadlock). However, if we increase the buffer size to 2, a deadlock appears when the news server sends message sendnews! followed by stop!. In that situation, the news server is in a final state, but the reader is not able to read the stop message from its buffer and cannot interact properly with the news server.

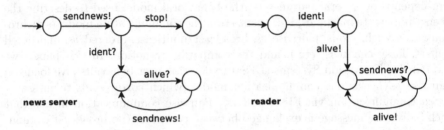

Fig. 1. Motivating example (1)

Figure 2 shows another simple example involving three peers: a client (cl), a server (sv), and a database (db), which exchange three messages request, result, and log. Peer sv receives a request, sends a result, and loops. Peer cl sends a request, receives a result, sends a log message, and loops. Peer db receives log messages. If we try to generate the LTS corresponding to the composition of these three peers interacting asynchronously through unbounded buffers, this results in an infinite state system. Indeed, the peers sv and cl can loop infinitely, and the peer db can consume from its input buffer whenever it wants, meaning that its buffer can grow arbitrarily large. Analyzing such system is therefore a complicated task (undecidable in general [11]), and to the best of our knowledge, existing approaches cannot analyze compatibility of such systems, because they cannot handle systems that communicate with asynchronous communication via unbounded buffers.

It was recently shown that it is decidable to check certain properties of distributed systems interacting asynchronously through unbounded buffers using the *synchronizability* property [3,4]. A set of peers is synchronizable if and only if the system generates the same sequences of messages under synchronous and unbounded asynchronous communication (considering only the ordering of the send actions and ignoring the ordering of receive actions). It was shown that synchronizability can be verified by checking the equivalence of synchronous

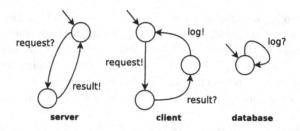

Fig. 2. Motivating example (2)

and 1-bounded asynchronous (where buffer sizes are bounded to be 1) versions of the given system [3,4]. Hence, synchronizability checking can be achieved using equivalence checking techniques for finite state spaces, although the system consisting of peers interacting asynchronously can result in infinite state spaces. For example, the system described in Fig. 2 is synchronizable because the synchronous system consists of sequences of interactions on request, result, and log, and this order is the same in the 1-bounded asynchronous system considering only send actions. Focusing only on send actions and ignoring receive actions makes sense for checking synchronizability because: (i) send actions are the actions that transfer messages to the network and are therefore observable, (ii) receive actions correspond to local consumptions by peers from their buffers and can therefore be considered to be local and private information.

In this paper, we propose a new approach for checking the compatibility of a set of peers interacting asynchronously through unbounded FIFO buffers. Peers are described using LTSs and exhibit their internal behaviors in these models (e.g., replacing conditional constructs with non-deterministic choices of internal actions). Compatibility checking relies on synchronizability, which ensures that the synchronous system behaves like the asynchronous one for any buffer size. Thus, we can check the compatibility on the synchronous version of the system and the results hold for the asynchronous versions. We propose a branching notion of synchronizability to take internal actions present in the peer models into account. We also need to check that the system is *well-formed*, meaning that every message sent to a buffer will be eventually consumed. We show that our approach can be used to check *DF* and *UR* compatibility. Many systems involving loops do respect the synchronizability property. Thus, these systems can be analyzed using the approach proposed in this paper, whereas they could not be analyzed using existing approaches. This is the case for the example given in Fig. 2. This set of peers is synchronizable and the synchronous system is deadlock-free for instance. Therefore, we can conclude using our result that the asynchronous version of this system is also deadlock-free compatible even if buffers are unbounded.

Our approach is fully automated through an encoding of the peer model into the process algebra LOTOS [23], one of the input languages of the CADP verification toolbox [19]. By doing so, we can reuse all CADP tools and particularly state space exploration tools for generating synchronous and asynchronous systems, equivalence checking techniques for verifying synchronizability, and model checking techniques for searching deadlocks. We have validated our approach on many case studies, most of them borrowed from real-world scenarios found in the literature. The evaluation shows that (i) most systems are synchronizable and can be analyzed using our approach, and (ii) this check is achieved in a reasonable time (seconds for examples involving up to ten peers, and minutes for systems up to 18 peers).

Our contributions with respect to earlier results on formal analysis of behavioral models for synchronizability and compatibility checking are the following:

- A general framework for verifying the compatibility of synchronizable systems interacting asynchronously through unbounded buffers;
- A generalization of synchronizability and well-formedness results to branching time equivalences for peer models involving internal actions;
- A fully automated tool support that implements the presented approach for checking asynchronous compatibility.

The organization of the rest of this paper is as follows. Section 2 defines our models for peers and their composition. Section 3 presents a branching notion of synchronizability. In Sect. 4, we present our solution for checking asynchronous compatibility. Section 5 illustrates our approach on a case study. Section 6 describes our tool support and experiments we carried out to evaluate our approach. Finally, Sect. 7 reviews related work and Sect. 8 concludes.

2   Behavioral Models

2.1   Peer Model

We use Labeled Transition Systems (LTSs) for modeling peers. This behavioral model defines the order in which a peer executes the send and receive actions.

Definition 1 (Peer). *A peer is an LTS* $\mathcal{P} = (S, s^0, \Sigma, T)$ *where S is a finite set of states, $s^0 \in S$ is the initial state, $\Sigma = \Sigma^! \cup \Sigma^? \cup \{\tau\}$ is a finite alphabet partitioned into a set of send messages, receive messages, and the internal action, and $T \subseteq S \times \Sigma \times S$ is a transition relation.*

We write $m!$ for a send message $m \in \Sigma^!$ and $m?$ for a receive message $m \in \Sigma^?$. We use the symbol τ (tau in figures) for representing internal activities. A transition is represented as $(s, l, s') \in T$ where $l \in \Sigma$.

Finally, we assume that peers are deterministic on observable messages meaning that if there are several transitions going out from one peer state, and if all the transition labels are observable, then they are all different from one another. However, nondeterminism can result from internal actions when several transitions (at least two) outgoing from a same state are labeled with τ.

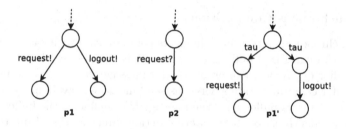

Fig. 3. p1 and p2 are deadlock-free; p1' and p2 deadlock

It is crucial to represent internal activities in the peer model using τ actions, particularly when we reason in terms of synchronous communication. These internal actions are used to model internal choices, that is, if/while constructs in programming languages for instance. Figure 3 shows a simple example where we see that two peers p1 and p2 are deadlock-free if we do not explicitly show the internal actions. If we consider an abstraction closer to reality by modeling the internal actions, we observe that the peers (p1' and p2) actually deadlock.

2.2 Synchronous Composition

The synchronous composition of a set of peers corresponds to the system in which the peer LTSs communicate using synchronous communication. In this context, a communication between two peers occurs if both agree on a synchronization label, i.e., if one peer is in a state in which a message can be sent, then the other peer must be in a state in which that message can be received. One peer can evolve independently from the others through an internal action.

Definition 2 (Synchronous Composition). *Given a set of peers* $\{\mathcal{P}_1, \dots, \mathcal{P}_n\}$ *with* $\mathcal{P}_i = (S_i, s_i^0, \Sigma_i, T_i)$, *the synchronous composition* $(\mathcal{P}_1 \mid \dots \mid \mathcal{P}_n)$ *is the labeled transition system* $LTS_s = (S_s, s_s^0, \Sigma_s, T_s)$ *where:*

- $S_s = S_1 \times \dots \times S_n$
- $s_s^0 \in S_s$ *such that* $s_s^0 = (s_1^0, \dots, s_n^0)$
- $\Sigma_s = \cup_i \Sigma_i$
- $T_s \subseteq S_s \times \Sigma_s \times S_s$, *and for* $s = (s_1, \dots, s_n) \in S_s$ *and* $s' = (s_1', \dots, s_n') \in S_s$

(interact) $s \xrightarrow{m} s' \in T_s$ *if* $\exists i, j \in \{1, \dots, n\}$ *where* $i \neq j : m \in \Sigma_i^! \cap \Sigma_j^?$ *where*

$\exists\, s_i \xrightarrow{m!} s_i' \in T_i$, *and* $s_j \xrightarrow{m?} s_j' \in T_j$ *such that* $\forall k \in \{1, \dots, n\}, k \neq i \wedge k \neq j \Rightarrow s_k' = s_k$

(internal) $s \xrightarrow{\tau} s' \in T_s$ *if* $\exists i \in \{1, \dots, n\}, \exists\, s_i \xrightarrow{\tau} s_i' \in T_i$ *such that* $\forall k \in \{1, \dots, n\}, k \neq i \Rightarrow s_k' = s_k$

2.3 Asynchronous Composition

In the asynchronous composition, the peers communicate with each other asynchronously through FIFO buffers. Each peer $\mathcal{P}_i$ is equipped with an unbounded message buffer Q_i. A peer can either send a message $m \in \Sigma^!$ to the tail of the receiver buffer Q_j at any state where this send message is available, read a message $m \in \Sigma^?$ from its buffer Q_i if the message is available at the buffer head, or evolve independently through an internal action. Since reading from the buffer is not considered as an observable action, it is encoded as an internal action in the asynchronous system.

Definition 3 (Asynchronous Composition). *Given a set of peers* $\{\mathcal{P}_1, \ldots, \mathcal{P}_n\}$ *with* $\mathcal{P}_i = (S_i, s_i^0, \Sigma_i, T_i)$, *and* Q_i *being its associated buffer, the asynchronous composition* $((\mathcal{P}_1, Q_1) \parallel \cdots \parallel (\mathcal{P}_n, Q_n))$ *is the labeled transition system* $LTS_a = (S_a, s_a^0, \Sigma_a, T_a)$ *where:*

- $S_a \subseteq S_1 \times Q_1 \times \ldots \times S_n \times Q_n$ *where* $\forall i \in \{1, \ldots, n\}$, $Q_i \subseteq (\Sigma_i^?)*$
- $s_a^0 \in S_a$ *such that* $s_a^0 = (s_1^0, \epsilon, \ldots, s_n^0, \epsilon)$ *(where* ϵ *denotes an empty buffer)*
- $\Sigma_a = \cup_i \Sigma_i$
- $T_a \subseteq S_a \times \Sigma_a \times S_a$, *and for* $s = (s_1, Q_1, \ldots, s_n, Q_n) \in S_a$ *and* $s' = (s_1', Q_1', \ldots s_n', Q_n') \in S_a$

  (send) $s \xrightarrow{m!} s' \in T_a$ *if* $\exists i, j \in \{1, \ldots, n\}$ *where* $i \neq j : m \in \Sigma_i^! \cap \Sigma_j^?$, *(i)* $s_i \xrightarrow{m!} s_i' \in T_i$, *(ii)* $Q_j' = Q_j m$, *(iii)* $\forall k \in \{1, \ldots, n\} : k \neq j \Rightarrow Q_k' = Q_k$, *and (iv)* $\forall k \in \{1, \ldots, n\} : k \neq i \Rightarrow s_k' = s_k$

  (consume) $s \xrightarrow{\tau} s' \in T_a$ *if* $\exists i \in \{1, \ldots, n\} : m \in \Sigma_i^?$, *(i)* $s_i \xrightarrow{m?} s_i' \in T_i$, *(ii)* $m Q_i' = Q_i$, *(iii)* $\forall k \in \{1, \ldots, n\} : k \neq i \Rightarrow Q_k' = Q_k$, *and (iv)* $\forall k \in \{1, \ldots, n\} : k \neq i \Rightarrow s_k' = s_k$

  (internal) $s \xrightarrow{\tau} s' \in T_a$ *if* $\exists i \in \{1, \ldots, n\}$, *(i)* $s_i \xrightarrow{\tau} s_i' \in T_i$, *(ii)* $\forall k \in \{1, \ldots, n\} : Q_k' = Q_k$, *and (iii)* $\forall k \in \{1, \ldots, n\} : k \neq i \Rightarrow s_k' = s_k$

We use LTS_a^k to define the *bounded asynchronous composition*, where each message buffer is bounded to size k. The definition of LTS_a^k can be obtained from Definition 3 by allowing send transitions only if the message buffer that the message is being written to has less than k messages in it.

3 Branching Synchronizability and Well-Formedness

Although peers are represented with finite models, their parallel execution could be an infinite state system due to the communication over unbounded buffers. This makes the exhaustive analysis of all executed communication traces impossible and most verification tasks in this setting are undecidable [11]. However, this issue can be avoided for systems that are synchronizable, i.e., if the sequences of send actions generated by the peer composition remains the same under synchronous and asynchronous communication semantics. Thus, the *synchronizability* condition [4] enables us to analyze asynchronous systems, even those generating an infinite state space, using the synchronous version of the given system (which has a finite state space). The results presented below show that synchronizability can be checked by bounding buffers to $k = 1$ and comparing interactions in the synchronous system with the interactions in the asynchronous system.

In this paper, the peer model and corresponding compositions take internal behaviors into account. Therefore, we need to extend synchronizability to branching time semantics [32][1]. This is crucial for considering models closer to reality (see Fig. 3) and for analyzing the internal structure to detect possible issues at this level. In this paper, we refer to branching equivalence as $\equiv_{br}$.

Definition 4 (Branching Synchronizability). *Given a set of peers* $\{\mathcal{P}_1, \ldots, \mathcal{P}_n\}$, *their synchronous composition* $LTS_s = (S_s, s_s^0, L_s, T_s)$, *and their asynchronous composition* $LTS_a = (S_a, s_a^0, L_a, T_a)$, *we say that* LTS_a *is branching synchronizable,* $\mathcal{SYNC}_{br}(LTS_a)$, *if and only if* $LTS_s \equiv_{br} LTS_a$.

Theorem 1. *A* LTS_a *defined over a set of peers* $\{\mathcal{P}_1, \ldots, \mathcal{P}_n\}$ *is branching synchronizable if and only if* $LTS_s \equiv_{br} LTS_a^1$. *In other words:* $LTS_s \equiv_{br} LTS_a^1 \Leftrightarrow LTS_s \equiv_{br} LTS_a$

Proofs of the theorems from this section are available on the first author Webpage.

Below we define the well-formedness property and present two theorems related to well-formedness.

Definition 5. *An asynchronous system is well-formed if and only if every message that is sent is eventually consumed.*

Given a labeled transition system LTS_a defined over a set of peers $\{\mathcal{P}_1, \ldots, \mathcal{P}_n\}$, we use $\mathcal{WF}(LTS_a)$ to denote that LTS_a is well-formed.

Theorem 2. *A synchronizable system* LTS_a *is well-formed if and only if* LTS_a^1 *is well-formed, i.e.,* $\mathcal{WF}(LTS_a^1) \Leftrightarrow \mathcal{WF}(LTS_a)$.

Theorem 3. *Every asynchronous system* LTS_a *that is branching synchronizable and composed of observationally deterministic peers is always well-formed.*

4   Compatibility

In this section, we present how to check the compatibility of a set of peers communicating asynchronously over unbounded FIFO buffers. This problem is undecidable in the general case [11] since unbounded buffers may lead to infinite state spaces. We present the compatibility checking for synchronous communication, and then show how we extend these results to asynchronous communication. We first focus on DF and UR compatibility notions. We use DF to detect blocking

---

[1] We assume that the reader is familiar with branching time bisimulations, refer to [32] otherwise.

behaviors where system remains infinitely in a pending state with no further execution. We use UR to detect cases where some emissions are never received. As a second step, we show how other compatibility notions can also be considered such as bidirectional complementarity and goal oriented compatibility (BC and GOC for short, respectively). BC requires that every emission must be received and every message that is expected to be received must be sent during peer communication. GOC describes a temporal logic-based compatibility (expressed in Linear Time Logic for example), that must be respected by the peers. It is worth noting that here we focus on checking properties related to ordering of message exchanges among peers, leaving properties such as state reachability out of the scope of this paper.

4.1   Synchronous Compatibility

Given n communicating peers described using LTSs $(S_i, s_i^0, \Sigma_i, T_i)$, we define a *global state* as a tuple of states $(s_1, \ldots, s_n)$ where s_i is the current state of LTS_i. We refer to a label l as a message in Σ together with its direction ($d \in \{!, ?\}$), i.e., $l = m!|m?$. Two labels $l_1 = m_1 d_1$ and $l_2 = m_2 d_2$ are considered *compatible*, *lab-comp*(l_1, l_2), if and only if $m_1 = m_2$ and $\overline{d_1} = d_2$ where $\overline{!} =?$ and $\overline{?} =!$.

Compatibility checking requires to verify the interaction at every global state *reachable* during system execution. Reachability returns the set of global states that n interoperating peers can reach from a current global state $(s_1, \ldots, s_n)$ through independent evolutions (internal behaviors) or synchronizations.

The DF compatibility is defined as follows. Given a set of peers, we call them DF compatible if and only if, starting from their initial global state, they can always evolve until reaching a global state where every peer state has no outgoing transition (correct termination).

The UR compatibility is defined as follows. Given a set of peers, we call them UR compatible if, when one peer can send a message at a reachable state, there is another peer which must eventually receive that emission, and the system is deadlock-free. A set of peers can be compatible even if one peer is able to receive a message that cannot be sent by any of the other peers, i.e., there might be additional receptions. It is also possible that one peer holds an emission that will not be received by its partners as long as the state from which this emission goes out is unreachable when those peers interact together.

More details about these compatibility notions (DF and UR but also BC and GOC) as well as their formal definitions can be found in [17].

4.2   Asynchronous Compatibility

In this section we present sufficient conditions for checking asynchronous compatibility. The behaviors of synchronizable systems remain identical for any buffer size, therefore, we can check compatibility of synchronizable systems using existing techniques for checking synchronous compatibility. A set of communicating peers $\{P_1, \ldots, P_n\}$ is asynchronous compatible if the following conditions hold:

- **Synchronizability.** Peer composition LTSs are branching synchronizable (Theorem 1).
- **Well-formedness.** Every message sent to a buffer is eventually consumed (Theorems 2 and 3).
- **Compatibility.** The set of peers is compatible under synchronous communication semantics (Sect. 4.1).

In the rest of this section, we define the asynchronous DF and UR compatibility (DF_a and UR_a for short, resp.) and we finally show how our asynchronous checking can be generalized to check other notions, e.g., BC_a and OGC_a.

Deadlock-Freedom. An asynchronous system LTS_a defined over a set of peers $\{P_1, \ldots, P_n\}$, is DF_a compatible if $\mathcal{SYNC}_{br}(LTS_a)$ and $\mathcal{WF}(LTS_a)$, and the corresponding LTS_s is DF (referred to as $DF(LTS_s)$).

Theorem 4. $(\mathcal{SYNC}(LTS_a) \wedge \mathcal{WF}(LTS_a) \wedge DF(LTS_s)) \Rightarrow DF_a(LTS_a)$

Proof. $LTS_s \equiv_{br} LTS_a$ follows from $\mathcal{SYNC}(LTS_a)$ (Theorem 1). Then, we have $DF(LTS_s) \Rightarrow DF_a(LTS_a)$. ∎

Unspecified Receptions. Although both DF and UR compatibility are different under the synchronous communication semantics, in the asynchronous setting, they can be checked similarly. Recall that UR compatibility requires us to check that (i) every reachable sent message must be received (*i.e.*, consumed from the buffer where it has been stored), and (ii) the system must be deadlock-free.

Theorem 5. $(\mathcal{SYNC}(LTS_a) \wedge \mathcal{WF}(LTS_a) \wedge DF(LTS_s)) \Rightarrow UR_a(LTS_a)$

Proof. Condition (i) for UR compatibility is ensured by well-formedness. Thus, this claim follows directly from UR compatibility definition and Theorem 1. ∎

Property 1. Our condition for checking DF_a and UR_a is not a necessary condition.

Proof. Let us consider the example given in Fig. 4. The asynchronous system starts with an interleaving of both emissions that can be executed in peer 1 and peer 2, whereas no synchronization is possible under synchronous communication. Thus, this example is not synchronizable and we cannot conclude anything about its compatibility. Yet the asynchronous version of this system is deadlock-free compatible. As a result, our condition for asynchronous compatibility is sufficient but not necessary. ∎

Note that finding a necessary and sufficient condition for asynchronous compatibility of behavioral peers is still an open problem.

Generalization. The former results can be generalized to define a sufficient condition for verifying any notion of compatibility CN_a on synchronizable systems. Examples of other notions that can be derived are BC_a and OGC_a. For instance, OGC_a can be formalized in terms of liveness and safety properties, e.g., $G(\phi \Rightarrow F\psi)$ and $G(\neg\phi)$ in LTL, resp.

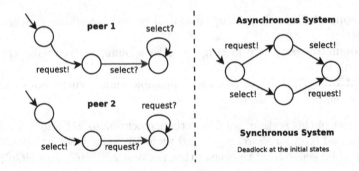

Fig. 4. Asynchronous but not synchronous DF compatible example

Theorem 6. $(\mathcal{SYNC}(LTS_a) \wedge \mathcal{WF}(LTS_a) \wedge CN(LTS_s)) \Rightarrow CN_a(LTS_a)$

Proof. The claim follows from Theorems 1 and 3.   ∎

Complexity. The complexity of our asynchronous compatibility checking lies on the cost of checking the synchronizability and the compatibility on the synchronous composition. Branching bisimulation complexity is $O(S' \times T')$ [20] where S' and T' are the total number of states and transitions in LTS_s and LTS_a^1. As for compatibility checking, given n LTSs (S, s^0, Σ, T), $S = \prod_{i=1}^{n} |S_i|$ represents an upper bound of the number of possible global states, and $T = \sum_{i=1}^{n} |T_i|$ represents an upper bound for the number of transitions available from any particular global state. S and T are greater than or equal to the number of states reachable from $(I_1, \ldots, I_n)$. Both UR_a and DF_a compatibilities have a time complexity of $O(S \times T)$ and BC_a has a time complexity of $O(S^2 \times T^2)$.

5 Illustrative Example

We consider a simplified version of a Web application involving four peers: a client, a Web interface, a Web server, and a database. Figure 5 shows the peer LTSs. The *client* starts with a request (request!), and expects an acknowledgment (ack?). Then, the client either interacts with the Web server as long as it needs (access!), or decides to terminate its processing (terminate!). This internal choice is modeled using a branching of internal actions. Finally, the client waits for an invoice (invoice?). The *server* first receives a setup request (setup?). Then, the server is accessed by the client (access?) and it expects to either be released (free?) or receive an alarm if an error occurs (alarm?). Finally, the server submits information to be stored (log!), e.g., start/end time and used resources. Every time a client request is received (request?), the *interface* triggers a setup request (setup!) and sends back an acknowledgment (ack!) to the client. Then, if a termination message is received (terminate?), the interface asks the Web server to be freed (free!). If an error occurs (error?), the interface sends an alarm message (alarm!). Finally, the *database* waits for some information to be stored (log?).

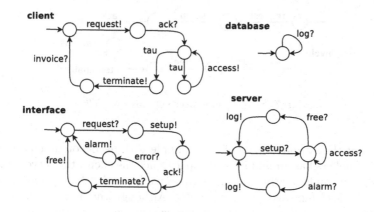

Fig. 5. Peer LTSs

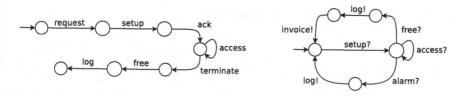

Fig. 6. Synchronous peer composition, V1 (left), Web server peer, V2 (right)

Synchronizability. LTS_s and LTS_a^1 are branching equivalent and therefore $\mathcal{SYNC}_{br}(LTS_a)$. Figure 6 (left) shows LTS_s, where transitions are labeled with the messages on which the peers can synchronize as presented in Definition 2.

Well-Formedness. The set of peers are observationally deterministic and $\mathcal{SYNC}_{br}(LTS_a)$, hence $\mathcal{WF}(LTS_a)$.

Synchronous Compatibility. This system cannot be compatible *wrt. DF, UR,* and *BC* notions since the peers deadlock at the last state in Fig. 6 (left). In that situation, all peers are in their initial states and may continue interacting with each other, except the client, which is expecting an invoice that is not provided by any of the partners.

Asynchronous Compatibility. Since LTS_a is branching synchronizable and well-formed, we can use results for synchronous compatibility for this system. The system is not DF_a and UR_a compatible because there is a deadlock in LTS_s. We can fix this issue by, e.g., adding the missing invoice! message to the server peer (Fig. 6, right). Thus, the new system is branching synchronizable (see the resulting synchronous composition in Fig. 7), well-formed, and LTS_s is deadlock-free, so it is DF_a and UR_a compatible. However, LTS_a is still not compatible *wrt. BC_a,* because there are still messages, e.g., error? in the interface peer, that have no counterpart in any other peer. This issue could also be detected using *GOC* compatibility and checking the following LTL formula: $LTS_s \models \Diamond \Box$error.

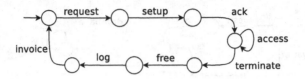

Fig. 7. Synchronous peer composition, V2

Note that the second version of our example with peers communicating over unbounded buffers has an infinite state space since the client, the server, and the interface peers can loop arbitrary many times while the database peer does never consume the log? messages from its buffer. Although this is not a finite state system, we can analyze it using the techniques we propose in this paper.

6   Tool Support and Evaluation

Our approach for checking the asynchronous compatibility is fully automated. This is achieved by a translation we implemented from peer models to the LOTOS process algebra. The CADP verification toolbox [19] accepts LOTOS as input and provides efficient tools for generating LTSs from LOTOS specifications and for analyzing these LTSs using equivalence and model checking techniques, which enable us to check all the notions of compatibility presented in this paper.

6.1   LOTOS Encoding

LOTOS [23] is an abstract formal language for specifying concurrent processes, communicating via messages. We chose LOTOS because (i) it provides expressive operators for encoding LTSs and generating their compositions, and (ii) it is supported by state-of-the-art verification tools (CADP) that can be used for analyzing LOTOS specifications. With regards to compatibility checking, we first encode peer LTSs into LOTOS processes following the state machine pattern (one process is generated per state in the LTS). Each peer comes with an input buffer. Buffers are processes, which interact with the peers and store/handle messages using classic structures (lists) and operations on them (add, remove, etc.). Finally, we use the LOTOS parallel composition for specifying the synchronous and asynchronous composition of peers.

Based on this encoding, we first use state space exploration tools to generate LTSs corresponding to the LOTOS specification, in particular for synchronous and 1-bounded asynchronous system. Then, we check the synchronizability condition using branching equivalence checking, and finally we check compatibility conditions using the deadlock-freedom check or model checking of properties written in MCL [29], which subsumes both LTL and CTL.

6.2   Experiments

We carried out experiments on a Mac OS machine running on a 2.53 GHz Intel dual core processor with 4 GB of RAM. Our database of examples includes 160 examples of communicating systems: 10 case studies taken from the literature (Web services, cloud computing, e-commerce, etc.), 86 examples of Singularity channel contracts [1], which is a contract notation for Microsoft's Singularity operating system, and 64 hand-crafted examples. We emphasize that out of the 96 real-world examples, only 5 are not branching synchronizable and well-formed. Thus, 91 examples out of 96 can be analyzed using our approach.

Tables 1, 2, and 3 present experiments for some examples from our database. Each table considers DF_a compatibility for illustration purposes, but we recall that DF_a is equivalent to UR_a for asynchronous systems. Each table shows, for each example, the number of peers, the total number of transitions and states involved in these peers, the size of the synchronous system, the size of the 1-bounded asynchronous system, the compatibility result ("$\sqrt{}$" denotes that the system is compatible, "$\times$" denotes that the system is not compatible, and "-" denotes that the system does not satisfy the sufficient condition, i.e., it is not synchronizable), the successive time for computing the synchronous and 1-bounded asynchronous system, and for checking synchronizability and deadlock-freedom, respectively.

We can see that analyzing the examples given in Tables 1 and 2 only takes a few seconds. This is due to systems involving a reasonable number of peers (up to 6 in Table 1), which results in quite small LTSs, even for the 1-bounded asynchronous composition (up to 100 states and 200 transitions in Table 1).

Table 3 presents a few examples with more than 10 peers. The number of interacting peers is the main factor of state space explosion, because it induces more parallelism in the corresponding composition. The cost in terms of computation time mainly lies on the generation of the 1-bounded asynchronous system, that is compiling LOTOS code into LTSs by enumerating all the possible behaviors (interleavings of concurrent emissions/receptions) and minimizing the resulting LTS using CADP tools. In particular, reducing LTSs with respect to a branching relation needs a certain amount of time (see examples 0115, 0153, and 0159). In contrast, checking synchronizability and deadlock-freedom using equivalence and model checking techniques takes only few seconds because LTSs obtained after reduction are much smaller.

We have also made a few experiments, increasing the buffer size (k = 5, k = 10, etc.). We have observed that the resulting, reduced LTS remains the same due to the synchronizability property, but the generation time increases because there are more possibilities of adding/removing messages from buffers. Consequently, computation time for our solution is much lower than approaches using arbitrary bounds for buffers.

7   Related Work

One of the first approaches on compatibility checking is proposed by Brand and Zafiropulo [11]. It defines the unspecified receptions compatibility notion

Table 1. Case studies from the literature

Example	|peers|	$\|T\|/\|S\|$	LTS_s $\|T\|/\|S\|$	LTS_a^1 $\|T\|/\|S\|$	DF Comp.	Analysis time Gen. (s)	Sync. (s)	DF(s)
Supply Chain Management Application [7]	6	20/25	20/17	216/97	×	5.05	0.35	0.15
Health System [12]	6	21/20	10/11	22/21	×	4.48	1.99	2.26
Cloud System [21]	4	19/15	10/9	29/22	×	4.65	2.25	1.88
Cloud System (V2) [21]	4	20/16	12/10	78/43	√	4.44	1.96	1.60
Sanitary Agency [30]	4	37/27	26/21	159/100	-	4.76	2.28	-
E-Marketplace [18]	3	8/11	6/7	15/14	√	4.35	1.96	1.49
Filter Collaboration [34]	2	10/11	10/10	14/14	√	4.18	2.22	1.51
Car Rental [8]	4	17/17	9/9	59/44	-	4.99	2.04	-
Client/Server [11]	2	10/6	9/6	19/14	-	4.68	2.09	-
Airline Ticket Reservation [33]	2	9/9	7/7	15/13	×	4.30	2.01	1.49

Table 2. Singularity channels contracts [1]

Example	|peers|	$\|T\|/\|S\|$	LTS_s $\|T\|/\|S\|$	LTS_a^1 $\|T\|/\|S\|$	DF Comp.	Analysis time Gen.	Sync. (s)	DF(s)
Smb Client Manager	2	40/18	21/10	41/30	√	6.83 s	3.30	2.53
Calculator	2	12/10	7/6	13/12	√	6.89 s	2.40	2.51
File System Controller	2	16/10	9/6	17/14	√	6.87 s	2.21	2.30
Tcp Contract	2	8/8	5/5	9/9	√	6.61	2.55	2.26
Pipe Multiplex Control	2	4/4	2/2	5/5	√	6.44 s	2.10	2.27
Udp Connection Contract	2	134/60	69/32	136/99	√	7.26 s	2.52	2.14
IP Contract	2	64/28	33/15	65/47	√	7.07	2.30	2.23
Routing Contract	2	44/20	23/11	45/33	√	6.65 s	2.10	2.27
Reservation Session	2	16/12	9/7	23/19	-	6.66 s	2.37	-
Tpm Contract	2	38/24	20/13	44/35	-	6.80	2.36	-

Table 3. Hand-crafted examples

Example	|peers|	$\|T\|/\|S\|$	LTS_s $\|T\|/\|S\|$	LTS_a^1 $\|T\|/\|S\|$	LTS_a red. $\|T\|/\|S\|$	DF Comp.	Analysis Time Gen.	Red.	Sync. (s)	DF (s)
0097	9	19/19	103/27	1,543/387	98/26	√	4.59 s	2.2 s	2.45	1.43
0101	14	42/29	4,277/649	334,379/54,433	3,402/486	√	1 min 15 s	4 min 2 s	2.46	1.80
0115	16	48/41	14,754/1,945	2,332,812/326,593	11,664/1,458	√	3 min 34 s	11 min 33 s	2.44	1.45
0153	18	38/38	4,616/577	1,179,656/147,457	4,608/576	√	7.51 s	18 min 52 s	2.60	1.43
0159	20	45/43	15,561/1,729	7,962,633/884,737	15,552/1,728	√	24.28 s	5 h 58 min	2.62	1.64

for interaction protocols described using Communicating Finite State Machines (CFSMs). This work focuses on the compatibility of n interacting processes executed in parallel and exchanging messages via FIFO buffers. When considering unbounded buffers, the authors show that the resulting state spaces may be infinite, and the problem becomes undecidable.

The approaches used in [6,15] deal with two kinds of processes compatibility, namely *optimistic* and *pessimistic* notions. De Alfaro and Henzinger [15] argue for the use of the optimistic notion that considers two processes P_1 and P_2 (I/O automata) as compatible if there is an environment that can *properly* communicate with their composite process. Note that an environment is also composed of one or more processes. A proper communication holds if the composition of the interface product $P_1 \otimes P_2$ with its environment is deadlock-free. The approach introduced in [6] addresses the pessimistic notion which states that two processes P_1 and P_2 are compatible if no deadlock occurs between P_1 and P_2, in *any* environment of $P_1 \otimes P_2$. Bauer et al. [5] defines an asynchronous compatibility for modal I/O transition systems. The authors do not propose any decision criterion but they claim that this verification is undecidable in the general case due to the buffering mechanism which may lead to infinite state spaces.

Haddad et al. [22] treats different compatibility problems for non-ordered buffers and for open systems using Petri nets. References [25,27,28,31] rely on an extension of Petri nets, namely open nets to model and verify behavioral interfaces of processes described as workflows, assuming asynchronous communication over message buffers. This model provides a graphical representation, and can be computed from existing programming languages. Martens et al. [28] rely on the *usability* concept to analyze the compatibility of processes represented as workflows. This compatibility notion is an environment-aware compatibility where two processes A and B are considered compatible if there is an environment E, which uses the composed system $A \otimes B$. In such a case, $A \otimes B$ is considered usable, meaning that its composition with E is deadlock-free. The condition, yet necessary, is not sufficient in the case of n processes. A similar compatibility definition used in the literature is that of *controllability* [25,27,31]. A process A is controllable if it has a compatible partner B in the sense that the composite process $A \otimes B$ is deadlock-free. As far as asynchronous semantics is considered, controllability has proven to be undecidable for unbounded open nets. For implementing controllability, the authors require that open nets are bounded and satisfy k-limited communication, for some given k. Consequently, using a Petri net-based model requires a much higher computational and space complexity than our approach.

Darondeau et al. [14] identify a decidable class of systems consisting of non-deterministic communicating processes that can be scheduled while ensuring boundedness of buffers. Abdulla *et al.* [2] propose some verification techniques for CFSMs. They present a method for performing symbolic forward analysis of unbounded *lossy* channel systems. Jeron and Jard [24] propose a sufficient condition for testing unboundedness, which can be used as a decision procedure for checking reachability for CFSMs. In [26], the authors present an incomplete boundedness test for communication channels in Promela and UML RT models. They also provide a method to derive *upper bound* estimates for the maximal occupancy of each individual message buffer. More recently, [16] proposed a causal chain analysis to determine upper bounds on buffer sizes for multi-party sessions with asynchronous communication. Recently, Bouajjani and Emmi [10] consider a bounded analysis for message-passing programs, which does not limit the number of communicating processes nor the buffers' size. However, they limit the number of communication cycles. They propose a decision procedure for reachability analysis when programs can be sequentialized. By doing so, program analysis can easily scale while previous related techniques quickly explode.

8 Conclusion

In this paper, we have presented results that go beyond all existing works on checking the compatibility of systems communicating asynchronously by message exchange over unbounded buffers. In our approach, we do not have any restrictions on the number of participants, on the presence of communication cycles in behavioral models, or on the buffer sizes. Instead, we focus on the class of synchronizable systems and propose a sufficient condition for analyzing asynchronous compatibility. This results in a generic framework for verifying whether a set of peers respect some property such as deadlock-freedom or unspecified receptions. In order to obtain these results for peer models involving internal behaviors, we have extended synchronizability results to branching time. Finally, we have implemented a prototype tool which enables us to automatically check the asynchronous compatibility using the CADP toolbox, and we have conducted experiments on many examples. In the future we plan to develop techniques for enforcing the asynchronous compatibility of a set of peers when the compatibility check fails, by automatically generating a set of distributed controllers as advocated in [21] for enforcing choreography realizability.

References

1. Singularity Design Note 5: Channel Contracts. Singularity RDK Documentation (v1.1) (2004). http://www.codeplex.com/singularity
2. Abdulla, P.A., Bouajjani, A., Jonsson, B.: On-the-fly analysis of systems with unbounded, lossy FIFO channels. In: Hu, A.J., Vardi, M.Y. (eds.) CAV1998. LNCS, vol. 1427, pp. 305–318. Springer, Heidelberg (1998)
3. Basu, S., Bultan, T.: Choreography conformance via synchronizability. In: Proceedings of WWW'11, pp. 795–804. ACM Press (2011)
4. Basu, S., Bultan, T., Ouederni, M.: Deciding choreography realizability. In: Proceedings of POPL'12, pp. 191–202. ACM (2012)
5. Bauer, S.S., Hennicker, R., Janisch, S.: Interface theories for (A)synchronously communicating modal I/O-transition systems. In: Proceedings of FIT'10, EPTCS, vol. 46, pp. 1–8 (2010)
6. Bauer, S.S., Mayer, P., Schroeder, A., Hennicker, R.: On weak modal compatibility, refinement, and the MIO workbench. In: Esparza, J., Majumdar, R. (eds.) TACAS 2010. LNCS, vol. 6015, pp. 175–189. Springer, Heidelberg (2010)

7. Beyer, D., Chakrabarti, A., Henzinger, T.: Web service interfaces. In: Proceedings of WWW'05, pp. 148–159. ACM (2005)
8. Bianculli, D., Giannakopoulou, D., Pasareanu, C.S.: Interface decomposition for service compositions. In: Proceedings of ICSE'11, pp. 501–510. ACM (2011)
9. Bordeaux, L., Salaün, G., Berardi, D., Mecella, M.: When are two web services compatible? In: Shan, M.-C., Dayal, U., Hsu, M. (eds.) TES 2004. LNCS, vol. 3324, pp. 15–28. Springer, Heidelberg (2005)
10. Bouajjani, A., Emmi, M.: Bounded phase analysis of message-passing programs. In: Flanagan, C., König, B. (eds.) TACAS 2012. LNCS, vol. 7214, pp. 451–465. Springer, Heidelberg (2012)
11. Brand, D., Zafiropulo, P.: On communicating finite-state machines. J. ACM 30(2), 323–342 (1983)
12. Bucchiarone, A., Melgratti, H., Severoni, F.: Testing service composition. In: Proceedings of ASSE'07 (2007)
13. Canal, C., Pimentel, E., Troya, J.M.: Compatibility and inheritance in software architectures. Sci. Comput. Program. 41(2), 105–138 (2001)
14. Darondeau, P., Genest, B., Thiagarajan, P.S., Yang, S.: Quasi-static scheduling of communicating tasks. In: van Breugel, F., Chechik, M. (eds.) CONCUR 2008. LNCS, vol. 5201, pp. 310–324. Springer, Heidelberg (2008)
15. de Alfaro, L., Henzinger, T.: Interface automata. In: Proceedings of ESEC/FSE'01, pp. 109–120. ACM Press (2001)
16. Deniélou, P.-M., Yoshida, N.: Buffered communication analysis in distributed multiparty sessions. In: Gastin, P., Laroussinie, F. (eds.) CONCUR 2010. LNCS, vol. 6269, pp. 343–357. Springer, Heidelberg (2010)
17. Durán, F., Ouederni, M., Salaün, G.: A generic framework for N-protocol compatibility checking. Sci. Comput. Program. 77(7–8), 870–886 (2012)
18. Foster, H., Uchitel, S., Kramer, J., Magee, J.: Compatibility verification for web service choreography. In: Proceedings of ICWS'04. IEEE Computer Society (2004)
19. Garavel, H., Lang, F., Mateescu, R., Serwe, W.: CADP 2010: a toolbox for the construction and analysis of distributed processes. In: Abdulla, P.A., Leino, K.R.M. (eds.) TACAS 2011. LNCS, vol. 6605, pp. 372–387. Springer, Heidelberg (2011)
20. Groote, J.F., Vaandrager, F.W.: An efficient algorithm for branching bisimulation and stuttering equivalence. In: Michael, S.P. (ed.) ICALP 1990. LNCS, vol. 443, pp. 626–638. Springer, Heidelberg (1990)
21. Güdemann, M., Salaün, G., Ouederni, M.: Counterexample guided synthesis of monitors for realizability enforcement. In: Chakraborty, S., Mukund, M. (eds.) ATVA 2012. LNCS, vol. 7561, pp. 238–253. Springer, Heidelberg (2012)
22. Haddad, S., Hennicker, R., Møller, M.H.: Channel properties of asynchronously composed Petri nets. In: Colom, J.-M., Desel, J. (eds.) PETRI NETS 2013. LNCS, vol. 7927, pp. 369–388. Springer, Heidelberg (2013)
23. ISO/IEC. LOTOS – A Formal Description Technique Based on the Temporal Ordering of Observational Behaviour. International Standard 8807, ISO (1989)
24. Jéron, T., Jard, C.: Testing for unboundedness of FIFO channels. Theor. Comput. Sci. 113(1), 93–117 (1993)
25. Kaschner, K., Wolf, K.: Set algebra for service behavior: applications and constructions. In: Dayal, U., Eder, J., Koehler, J., Reijers, H.A. (eds.) BPM 2009. LNCS, vol. 5701, pp. 193–210. Springer, Heidelberg (2009)
26. Leue, S., Mayr, R., Wei, W.: A scalable incomplete test for message buffer overflow in Promela models. In: Graf, S., Mounier, L. (eds.) SPIN 2004. LNCS, vol. 2989, pp. 216–233. Springer, Heidelberg (2004)

27. Lohmann, N.: Why does my service have no partners? In: Bruni, R., Wolf, K. (eds.) WS-FM 2008. LNCS, vol. 5387, pp. 191–206. Springer, Heidelberg (2009)
28. Martens, A., Moser, S. Gerhardt, A., Funk, K.: Analyzing compatibility of BPEL processes. In: Proceedings of AICT/ICIW'06, pp. 147–156. IEEE Computer Society (2006)
29. Mateescu, R., Thivolle, D.: A model checking language for concurrent value-passing systems. In: Cuellar, J., Sere, K. (eds.) FM 2008. LNCS, vol. 5014, pp. 148–164. Springer, Heidelberg (2008)
30. Salaün, G., Bordeaux, L., Schaerf, M.: Describing and reasoning on web services using process algebra. Int. J. Bus. Process. Integr. Manage. 1(2), 116–128 (2006)
31. van der Aalst, W.M.P., Mooij, A.J., Stahl, C., Wolf, K.: Service interaction: patterns, formalization, and analysis. In: Bernardo, M., Padovani, L., Zavattaro, G. (eds.) SFM 2009. LNCS, vol. 5569, pp. 42–88. Springer, Heidelberg (2009)
32. van Glabbeek, R.J., Weijland, W.P.: Branching time and abstraction in bisimulation semantics. J. ACM 43(3), 555–600 (1996)
33. Wong, P., Gibbons, J.: Verifying business process compatibility. In: Proceedings of QSIC'08, pp. 126–131. IEEE Computer Society (2008)
34. Yellin, D.M., Strom, R.E.: Protocol specifications and component adaptors. ACM Trans. Program. Lang. Syst. 19(2), 292–333 (1997)

Layered Reduction for Modal Specification Theories

Arpit Sharma(✉) and Joost-Pieter Katoen(✉)

Software Modeling and Verification Group,
RWTH Aachen University, Aachen, Germany
{arpit.sharma,katoen}@cs.rwth-aachen.de

Abstract. Modal transition systems (MTSs) are a well-known formalism used as an abstraction theory for labeled transition systems (LTSs). MTS specifications support compositionality together with a step-wise refinement methodology, and thus are useful for component-oriented design and analysis of distributed systems. This paper proposes a state-space reduction technique for such systems that are modeled as a network of acyclic MTSs. Our technique is based on the notion of layered transformation. We propose a layered composition operator for acyclic MTSs, and prove the communication closed layer (CCL) laws. Next, we define a partial order (po) equivalence between acyclic MTSs, and show that it enables performing layered transformation within the framework of CCL laws. We also show the preservation of existential (∃) and universal (∀) reachability properties under this transformation.

Keywords: Modal transition system · Layering · Distributed system · Existential reachability · Universal reachability · CCL laws · Partial order equivalence · Refinement

1 Introduction

Modal transition systems (MTSs) [17,20] are labeled transition systems (LTSs) [1,23] equipped with two types of transitions: *may* transitions that any implementation (LTS) may (or may not) have and *must* transitions that any implementation must have. An LTS is an MTS where all the transitions are must transitions. MTSs were originally introduced by Larsen and Thomsen almost 25 years ago [17,20], and have been successfully applied in program analysis [10,29], model checking [5,19], equation solving [21], interface theories [28,31], component-based software development [27] and software product lines [9,18]. The theory of MTS is equipped with parallel and conjunction operators, and allows comparing two MTSs using a refinement relation. A satisfaction relation is used to check whether an LTS is an implementation of a given MTS. MTS specifications are useful for component-oriented design and analysis of distributed

This work is supported by the European Commission SENSATION project.

J.L. Fiadeiro et al. (Eds.): FACS 2013, LNCS 8348, pp. 329–347, 2014.
DOI: 10.1007/978-3-319-07602-7_20, © Springer International Publishing Switzerland 2014

systems. In this setting, a high-level model of the system which abstracts from the implementation details is constructed and used for the verification of interesting properties. A correct implementation can be obtained by applying a series of refinement steps. Model construction involves composing several components in parallel, where each component usually has multiple sub-components that are executed in a sequential manner. Components cooperate through their synchronization over common actions and through their respective action dependencies. Action dependencies between sub-components can be either explicitly stated or derived from the operations performed on data variables that are updated during an action execution (in case of MTS with data [2]). Some example systems that have this structure are distributed algorithms such as the distributed minimum weight spanning tree algorithm [7], the two phase commit protocol [4], Fischer's real-time mutual exclusion protocol, and the randomized mutual exclusion algorithm by Kushilevitz and Rabin [15]. Composing several components using parallel composition naturally leads to the problem of *state-space explosion* [1], where the number of states grows exponentially in the number of parallel components.

In [30], a layered analysis of Kushilevitz and Rabin's randomized mutual exclusion algorithm [15] has been carried out. The underlying model on which layered transformations have been applied is a probabilistic automaton. We modeled and analysed this case study using the PRISM model checker [16]. The obtained results for 3 processes and 5 rounds are summarised in the Table 1. These results clearly indicate that layered reasoning can significantly reduce the state space of system models capturing the behavior of distributed algorithms. In addition, layering has been successfully applied to obtain easier correctness proofs for various distributed systems [11–14]. Motivated by this, we propose a state-space reduction technique for a network of acyclic MTSs based on the notion of layering. The main principle is illustrated in Fig. 1. Here two MTS components $\mathcal{M}$ and $\mathcal{N}$ are composed in parallel (left), where each component consists of n sub-components which are executed in a sequential manner. The system obtained after performing layered transformation is shown in Fig. 1 (right). Note that all the sub-components of $\mathcal{M}$ and $\mathcal{N}$ need to be acyclic, but we do allow outermost level of recursion in $\mathcal{M}$ and $\mathcal{N}$. In other words, every component can have multiple rounds of execution, where a new round is started only when the last sub-component of the previous round has been executed. This is important as deadlock states are usually considered to be undesirable for MTSs modeling distributed algorithms. Roughly speaking, layering exploits the inde-

Table 1. Parallel vs. layered composition

	Parallel	Layered
Build time (s)	898.70	90.39
# States	198063	71619
# Transitions	351432	128920

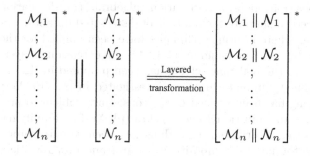

Fig. 1. Layered reduction

pendence between sub-components to transform the system under consideration from a distributed representation to a layered representation. A layered composition operator "•" is used to denote the layered representation of the system. Informally, $\mathcal{M}_1 \bullet \mathcal{M}_2$ allows synchronization on common actions and interleaving on disjoint actions, except when some action a of $\mathcal{M}_2$ depends on one or more actions of $\mathcal{M}_1$; in this case, a can be executed only after all the actions of $\mathcal{M}_1$ on which it depends have been executed. This new composition operator allows formulating *Communication Closed Layer* (CCL) laws [11], which are required to carry out the structural transformations and establish an equivalence between the two systems. Since the sub-components within a component are executed sequentially, a partial order relation is proposed to relate the • and ; (sequential) operator. The reduced system obtained as a result of applying layered transformation can be used for analysis, provided it preserves a rich class of properties of interest. Reachability is one of the most important properties in the area of model checking. Therefore, we focus on proving that the reduced system preserves existential ($\exists$) and universal ($\forall$) reachability properties to reach its set of final states.

Contributions. The main contributions of this paper are as follows:

- We define the notions of *abstract execution* and *realisation*, which are subsequently used to compare the behaviour of acyclic MTSs.
- We define the layered (•) and sequential (;) composition operator, and formulate communication closed layer (CCL) laws for acyclic MTSs.
- We define the partial order (po) equivalence between acyclic MTSs, show that • is po-equivalent to ;, and prove that po-equivalence between • and ; preserves existential ($\exists$) and universal ($\forall$) reachability properties.
- Finally, we show how state space reduction can be achieved by replacing • with ; within the framework of CCL laws.

Related Work

Layering. The decomposition of a distributed program into communication closed layers to simplify its analysis was originally proposed in [6]. In [13], a layered composition operator and various algebraic transformation rules have been introduced to simplify the analysis of distributed database systems. Some other examples where layering techniques have been applied for the analysis of distributed systems can be found in [11,12,14]. An extension of layering operator and CCL laws to the real-time setting has been proposed in [12]. Layered composition for timed automata has been investigated in [25]. In the probabilistic context, layering has been applied to the consensus problem to prove the lower bounds [24]. A probabilistic Kleene Algebra (pKA), for simplifying the reasoning of randomized distributed algorithms has been recently proposed in [22]. Most recently, the layered composition operator and probabilistic counterparts of the CCL laws have been defined for the PA model [30]. The feasibility of this approach has been demonstrated on a randomized mutual exclusion algorithm.

Organisation of the paper. Section 2 briefly recalls the basic concepts of LTSs and MTSs. Section 3 presents the satisfaction and refinement relations for MTSs. Section 4 discusses the composition operators for MTSs, and introduces CCL laws. Section 5 defines po-equivalence between MTSs, and proves that po-equivalence between • and ; preserves existential ($\exists$) and universal ($\forall$) reachability properties. Finally, Sect. 6 concludes the paper. All the proofs are contained in the appendix.

2 Preliminaries

This section recalls the basic concepts of labeled transition systems and modal transition systems with a finite state space.

Definition 1. *A labeled transition system (LTS) is a tuple* $\mathcal{T}=(S, Act, s_0, S_f, V)$ *where:*

- *S is a finite, non-empty set of states,*
- *Act is a finite set of actions,*
- *$s_0 \in S$ is the initial state,*
- *$S_f \subset S$ is the set of final states where $s_0 \notin S_f$,*
- *$V : S \setminus S_f \times Act \times S \to \mathbb{B}_2$ is a two-valued transition function.*

Here $\mathbb{B}_2 = \{\bot, \top\}$, with $\bot < \top$. $V(s, a, s')$ identifies the transition of the transition system: $\top$ indicates its presence and $\bot$ indicates its absence. We write $s \xrightarrow{a} s'$ whenever $V(s, a, s') = \top$. Labeled transition systems are basically directed graphs where nodes represent states, and edges model transitions, i.e., state changes. Transitions specify how the system can evolve from one state to another. In case a state has more than one outgoing transition, the next transition is chosen in a purely non-deterministic fashion. A possible behaviour in an LTS is obtained from the resolution of non-deterministic choices, described in terms of paths. A path π of LTS $\mathcal{T}$ is a (possibly infinite) sequence of the form $\pi = s_0 a_1 s_1 a_2 s_2 a_3 \ldots$ where $\forall n : s_n \xrightarrow{a_{n+1}} s_{n+1}$. Let $last(\pi)$ denote the last state of π (if π is finite). Let $|\pi|$ be the length (number of actions) of a finite path π. For infinite path π and any $i \in \mathbb{N}$, let $\pi[i] = s_i$, the $(i+1)$-st state of π. For finite

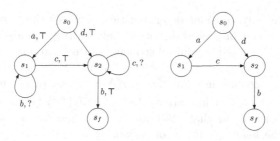

Fig. 2. An MTS $\mathcal{M}$ (left) and an LTS $\mathcal{T}$ (right) that satisfies $\mathcal{M}$

path π of length n, $\pi[i]$ is only defined for $i \leq n$ and defined as for infinite paths. Let $Paths_{fin}(\mathcal{T})$ be the set of all finite paths in LTS $\mathcal{T}$, and $Paths_{inf}(\mathcal{T})$ the set of all infinite paths of $\mathcal{T}$ that start in state s_0. Let $Paths_{fin}^{S_f}(\mathcal{T})$ be the set of all finite paths of $\mathcal{T}$ that start in state s_0 and end in some state $s \in S_f$.

Definition 2. *LTS* $\mathcal{T} = (S, Act, s_0, S_f, V)$ *is deterministic, if* $\forall s \in S.\forall a \in Act.|\{s' \in S \mid V(s, a, s') \neq \bot\}| \leq 1$

Example 1. Consider the LTS $\mathcal{T}$ in Fig. 2 (right), where $S = \{s_0, s_1, s_2, s_f\}$, $Act = \{a, b, c, d\}$, s_0 is the initial state, and $S_f = \{s_f\}$. It is easy to check that $\mathcal{T}$ is deterministic. An example finite path π is $s_0 a s_1 c s_2 b s_f$. We have $|\pi| = 3$, and $\pi[1] = s_1$.

Definition 3. *A modal transition system (MTS) is a tuple* $\mathcal{M} = (S, Act, s_0, S_f, V)$ *where:*

- *S is a finite, non-empty set of states,*
- *Act is a finite set of actions,*
- *$s_0 \in S$ is the initial state,*
- *$S_f \subset S$ is the set of final states where $s_0 \notin S_f$,*
- *$V : S \setminus S_f \times Act \times S \to \mathbb{B}_3$ is a three-valued transition function.*

Here $\mathbb{B}_3 = \{\bot, ?, \top\}$ denotes a complete lattice with the following ordering $\bot < ? < \top$ and meet $\sqcap$ and join $\sqcup$ operators. $V(s, a, s')$ identifies the transition of the automaton: $\top$, ? and $\bot$ indicate a *must*, a *may* and absence of transition respectively. For simplicity we write $s \xrightarrow{a}_\top s'$ instead of $V(s, a, s') = \top$. Similarly, we write $s \xrightarrow{a}_? s'$ instead of $V(s, a, s') = ?$. Let $act(s)$ denote the set of enabled actions from state s, i.e., $act(s) = \{a \in Act \mid \exists s' : V(s, a, s') \neq \bot\}$. By definition, it follows $\forall s \in S_f : act(s) = \varnothing$.

Remark 1. An LTS is an MTS in which every transition is a must-transition. Thus, every LTS is an MTS.

Definition 4. *MTS* $\mathcal{M} = (S, Act, s_0, S_f, V)$ *is deterministic, if* $\forall s \in S.\forall a \in Act.|\{s' \in S \mid V(s, a, s') \neq \bot\}| \leq 1$.

In this paper we only consider deterministic MTSs, as they are sufficient for modeling the behavior of typical distributed algorithms. An abstract execution ρ of an MTS $\mathcal{M}$ is a (possibly infinite) sequence of the form $\rho = s_0 a_1 s_1 a_2 s_2 a_3 \ldots$, where $\forall n : s_n \xrightarrow{a_{n+1}}_\top s_{n+1}$ or $s_n \xrightarrow{a_{n+1}}_? s_{n+1}$. Let $Exec_{fin}(\mathcal{M})$ be the set of all finite abstract executions, and $Exec_{inf}(\mathcal{M})$ the set of all infinite abstract executions of $\mathcal{M}$ that start in state s_0. Let $Exec_{fin}^{S_f}(\mathcal{M})$ be the set of all finite abstract executions of $\mathcal{M}$ that start in state s_0, and end in some state $s \in S_f$. Let $|\rho|$ be the length (number of actions) of a finite abstract execution ρ. For infinite abstract execution ρ and any $i \in \mathbb{N}$, let $\rho[i] = s_i$, the $(i+1)$-st state of ρ. For finite abstract execution ρ of length n, $\rho[i]$ is only defined for $i \leq n$ and defined as for infinite abstract executions. Let $last(\rho)$ denote the last state of ρ (if ρ is finite). Similarly, let $first(\rho)$ denote the first state of ρ.

Example 2. Consider the MTS $\mathcal{M}$ in Fig. 2 (left), where $S = \{s_0, s_1, s_2, s_f\}$, $Act = \{a, b, c, d\}$, s_0 is the initial state, and $S_f = \{s_f\}$. Here, state s_2 has two outgoing transitions: a must b-transition moving to s_f and a may c-transition moving to s_2. Similarly, state s_1 has two outgoing transitions: a must c-transition moving to s_2 and a may b-transition moving to s_1. Note that $\mathcal{M}$ is deterministic. An example finite abstract execution ρ is $s_0 a s_1 c s_2 b s_f$ with $|\rho| = 3$, and $\rho[1] = s_1$.

3 Satisfaction and Refinement

This section presents the notions of *satisfaction* and *refinement* originally introduced in [20]. A satisfaction relation allows to relate an LTS (implementation) with an MTS (specification). A refinement relation is used to compare MTSs w.r.t. their sets of implementations. We also define the notions of realisation, existential ($\exists$) and universal ($\forall$) reachability properties of reaching the set of final states computed over the implementations of MTS $\mathcal{M}$.

Definition 5 (Satisfaction). *Let* $\mathcal{T} = (S, Act, s_0, S_f, V)$ *be an LTS and* $\mathcal{M} = (S', Act, s'_0, S'_f, V')$ *be an MTS.* $R \subseteq S \times S'$ *is a satisfaction relation iff, for any* $(s, s') \in R$, *the following conditions hold:*

- $\forall a \in Act, \forall u' \in S' : V'(s', a, u') = \top \Rightarrow (\exists u \in S : V(s, a, u) = \top \wedge uRu')$,
- $\forall a \in Act, \forall u \in S : V(s, a, u) = \top \Rightarrow (\exists u' \in S' : V'(s', a, u') \neq \bot \wedge uRu')$,
- $s \in S_f \Leftrightarrow s' \in S'_f$.

We say that $\mathcal{T}$ *satisfies* $\mathcal{M}$, *denoted* $\mathcal{T} \models \mathcal{M}$, *iff there exists a satisfaction relation relating* s_0 *and* s'_0. *If* $\mathcal{T} \models \mathcal{M}$, $\mathcal{T}$ *is called an* implementation *of* $\mathcal{M}$.

Intuitively, a state s satisfies state s' iff any must transition of s' is matched by a transition of s, s does not contain any transitions that do not have a corresponding transition (may or must) in s', and the final states of two systems are always related. Let $[\![\mathcal{M}]\!] = \{\mathcal{T} \mid \mathcal{T} \models \mathcal{M}\}$, i.e., $[\![\mathcal{M}]\!]$ is the set of all implementations of MTS $\mathcal{M}$. Let $\mathcal{T} \in [\![\mathcal{M}]\!]$, and $\pi = s_0 a_1 s_1 a_2 s_2 \ldots s_n$ be a finite path of $\mathcal{T}$, i.e., $\pi \in Paths_{fin}(\mathcal{T})$. π is said to be a realisation of $\rho = s_0 a'_1 s_1 a'_2 s_2 \ldots s_n$ where $\rho \in Exec_{fin}(\mathcal{M})$, denoted $\pi \models \rho$, if $\forall i < n : a_{i+1} = a'_{i+1}$.

Example 3. The LTS T in Fig. 2 (right) is an implementation of the MTS $\mathcal{M}$ in Fig. 2 (left). It is easy to check that there exists a satisfaction relation relating the initial states of T and $\mathcal{M}$. Note that in this example, for every implementation T of $\mathcal{M}$, $S_f \neq \varnothing$ (since there exists a finite abstract execution from s_0 to s_f with only must transitions). Finite path $\pi = s_0as_1cs_2bs_f$ of LTS T is a realisation of finite abstract execution $\rho = s_0as_1cs_2bs_f$ of $\mathcal{M}$.

Note that for a deterministic MTS $\mathcal{M}$ and $T \models \mathcal{M}$, if a path $\pi \in Paths_{fin}(T)$ is a realisation of some finite abstract execution $\rho \in Exec_{fin}(\mathcal{M})$, then it cannot be a realisation of another finite abstract execution of $\mathcal{M}$.

Definition 6 (Refinement). *Let* $\mathcal{M} = (S, Act, s_0, S_f, V)$ *and* $\mathcal{M}'=(S', Act, s_0', S_f', V')$ *be MTSs.* $R \subseteq S \times S'$ *is a* strong refinement relation *iff, for all* $(s, s') \in R$, *the following conditions hold:*

- $\forall a \in Act, \forall u' \in S' : V'(s', a, u') = \top \Rightarrow (\exists u \in S : V(s, a, u) = \top \wedge uRu')$,
- $\forall a \in Act, \forall u \in S : V(s, a, u) \neq \perp \Rightarrow (\exists u' \in S' : V'(s', a, u') \neq \perp \wedge uRu')$,
- $s \in S_f \Leftrightarrow s' \in S_f'$.

$\mathcal{M}$ *strongly refines* $\mathcal{M}'$, *denoted* $\mathcal{M} \preceq_S \mathcal{M}'$, *iff there exists a strong refinement relation relating* s_0 *and* s_0'.

Intuitively, a state s strongly refines state s' iff any must transition of s' is matched by a must transition of s, s does not contain any transitions (may or must) that do not have a corresponding transition (may or must) in s', and the final states of two systems are always related.

Remark 2. A satisfaction relation is a special type of refinement relation. In simple words, if T satisfies $\mathcal{M}$, then T also strongly refines $\mathcal{M}$ (since every LTS is an MTS and all the three conditions of refinement are satisfied).

Definition 7 (Refinement equivalence). *We say that* $\mathcal{M}$ *and* $\mathcal{M}'$ *are refinement equivalent, denoted* $\mathcal{M} \equiv \mathcal{M}'$, *iff* $\mathcal{M} \preceq_S \mathcal{M}'$ *and* $\mathcal{M}' \preceq_S \mathcal{M}$.

Since strong refinement implies inclusion of sets of implementations, it follows that refinement equivalent MTSs $\mathcal{M}$ and $\mathcal{M}'$ have the same set of implementations, i.e., $[\![\mathcal{M}]\!] = [\![\mathcal{M}']\!]$.

Assumptions. For the rest of the paper we assume the following:

- Every MTS is acyclic.
- Every MTS has a single final state, i.e., $|S_f| = 1$, and all its states (except the final state) have at least one outgoing transition.
- Dependencies between actions of different components are known in advance.

In this paper we focus on reachability properties, i.e., is it possible to reach the set of final states from the initial state in an LTS T. More formally it is defined as follows:

Definition 8 (LTS reachability). *Let* $T = (S, Act, s_0, S_f, V)$ *be an LTS. Then* T *reaches* S_f, *denoted* $T \models \Diamond S_f$, *iff* $\forall \pi \in Paths_{fin}(T) \exists \pi' \in Paths_{fin}^{S_f}(T)$: π *is a prefix of* π'.

In simple words, all the finite paths starting from the initial state of $\mathcal{T}$ should be extendable s.t. the last state of the new path obtained belongs to S_f.

Example 4. Consider the LTS $\mathcal{T}$ in Fig. 2 (right) where s_0 is the initial state, and s_f is the only final state. Here, $\mathcal{T} \models \Diamond S_f$ since every finite path of $\mathcal{T}$ can be extended s.t. it reaches s_f.

Next, we define two reachability properties of reaching the set of final states determined over the implementations of an MTS $\mathcal{M}$. The first property requires that for an MTS $\mathcal{M}$ there exists at least one implementation $\mathcal{T}$ s.t. $\mathcal{T} \models \Diamond S_f$. The second property requires that all the implementations of $\mathcal{M}$ should be able to reach the set of final states. Formally, these properties are defined as follows:

Definition 9 (Existential reachability). *Let* $\mathcal{M} = (S, Act, s_0, S_f, V)$ *be an MTS. Then* $\mathcal{M}$ *possibly reaches* S_f, *denoted* $\mathcal{M} \models^{\exists} \Diamond S_f$, *iff* $\exists \mathcal{T} \in [\![\mathcal{M}]\!]$: $\mathcal{T} \models \Diamond S_f$.

Definition 10 (Universal reachability). *Let* $\mathcal{M} = (S, Act, s_0, S_f, V)$ *be an MTS. Then* $\mathcal{M}$ *inevitably reaches* S_f, *denoted* $\mathcal{M} \models^{\forall} \Diamond S_f$, *iff* $\forall \mathcal{T} \in [\![\mathcal{M}]\!]$: $\mathcal{T} \models \Diamond S_f$.

Remark 3. The problem of deciding $\mathcal{M} \models^{\exists} \Diamond S_f$ is PSPACE-complete [3]. The same applies to universal reachability.

4   Composition and CCL Laws

In this section we define composition operators for MTSs. We propose sequential, and layered composition operators, and recall parallel composition from [20]. The framework of CCL laws is also formulated, which is required for carrying out the layered transformations.

Definition 11 (Sequential composition). *Given MTSs* $\mathcal{M}_i = (S_i, Act_i, s_{0i}, \{s_{fi}\}, V_i)$, *where* $i \in \{1, 2\}$ *with* $S_1 \cap S_2 = \varnothing$. *The sequential composition of* $\mathcal{M}_1$ *and* $\mathcal{M}_2$, *denoted* $\mathcal{M}_1; \mathcal{M}_2$, *is the MTS* $(S, Act_1 \cup Act_2, s_{01}, \{s_{f2}\}, V)$, *where* $S = S_1 \setminus \{s_{f1}\} \cup S_2$ *and* $V = V_1' \cup V_2$. *Here* $V_1' = V_1[s_{02} \leftarrow s_{f1}]$ *is defined by*

$$V_1'(s, a, s') = V_1(s, a, s') \text{ if } s' \neq s_{f1}, and$$
$$V_1'(s, a, s_{02}) = V_1(s, a, s_{f1}) \text{ otherwise.}$$

Intuitively, sequential composition of two MTSs $\mathcal{M}_1$ and $\mathcal{M}_2$ requires executing the actions of $\mathcal{M}_1$ followed by actions of $\mathcal{M}_2$. Note that all the incoming transitions to state s_{f1} are redirected to s_{02}. Here, s_{01}, s_{f2} are the new initial and final states in the resulting MTS, respectively.

Example 5. The sequential composition of two MTSs $\mathcal{M}_1, \mathcal{M}_2$ (Fig. 3 (left)) is shown in Fig. 3 (right).

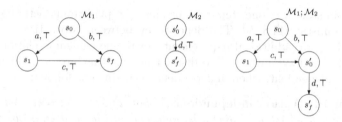

Fig. 3. MTSs $\mathcal{M}_1$ and $\mathcal{M}_2$ (left) and their sequential composition (right)

Definition 12 (Parallel composition). *Given MTSs* $\mathcal{M}_i = (S_i, Act_i, s_{0i}, \{s_{fi}\}, V_i)$, *where* $i \in \{1,2\}$ *with* $S_1 \cap S_2 = \varnothing$. *The parallel composition of* $\mathcal{M}_1$ *and* $\mathcal{M}_2$, *denoted* $\mathcal{M}_1 \| \mathcal{M}_2$, *is the MTS* $(S_1 \times S_2, Act_1 \cup Act_2, (s_{01}, s_{02}), \{(s_{f1}, s_{f2})\}, V)$ *where* V *is defined by:*

- *For all* $(s, s') \in S_1 \times S_2$, $a \in Act_1 \cap Act_2$, *if there exists* $u \in S_1$ *and* $u' \in S_2$, *such that* $V_1(s, a, u) \neq \bot$ *and* $V_2(s', a, u') \neq \bot$, *define* $V((s, s'), a, (u, u')) = V_1(s, a, u) \sqcap V_2(s', a, u')$. *If either* $\forall u \in S_1$, *we have* $V_1(s, a, u) = \bot$, *or* $\forall u' \in S_2$, *we have* $V_2(s', a, u') = \bot$ *then* $\forall (u, u') \in S_1 \times S_2$, $V((s, s'), a, (u, u')) = \bot$.
- *For all* $(s, s'), (u, u') \in S_1 \times S_2$, $a \in Act_1 \setminus Act_2$, *define* $V((s, s'), a, (u, u')) = V_1(s, a, u)$ *if* $s' = u'$, $V((s, s'), a, (u, u')) = \bot$ *otherwise*.
- *For all* $(s, s'), (u, u') \in S_1 \times S_2$, $a \in Act_2 \setminus Act_1$, *define* $V((s, s'), a, (u, u')) = V_2(s', a, u')$ *if* $s = u$, $V((s, s'), a, (u, u')) = \bot$ *otherwise*.

Parallel composition forces synchronization on common actions and interleaving on disjoint actions. Note that the synchronization of two must transitions results in a must transition, and composing may-must, must-may and may-may transitions results in a may transition.

Example 6. The parallel composition of two MTSs $\mathcal{M}_1, \mathcal{M}_2$ (Fig. 3 (left)) is shown in Fig. 4 (left).

Next, we introduce the notion of action independence which is subsequently used to define layered composition. Let $a(s)$ denote the unique state that can be

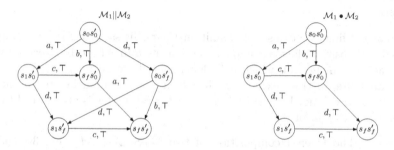

Fig. 4. Parallel composition $\mathcal{M}_1 \| \mathcal{M}_2$ (left) and layered composition $\mathcal{M}_1 \bullet \mathcal{M}_2$ (right) where $a \dagger d$

reached from state s in one step (may or must) by performing action $a \in act(s)$ in a deterministic MTS $\mathcal{M}$. The dependency between two actions a and b is denoted $a \dagger b$. Two additional requirements for the dependency relation are that it is reflexive and symmetric. Two distinct actions that are not dependent are said to be independent, where independence is defined as follows:

Definition 13 (Action independence). *For an MTS $\mathcal{M} = (S, Act, s_0, \{s_f\}, V)$, actions $a, b \in Act$ are said to be independent, denoted by $a \ddagger b$, iff for all states $s \in S$ with $a, b \in act(s)$ we have:*

- *$b \in act(a(s))$, $a \in act(b(s))$, and $a(b(s)) = b(a(s))$.*

The first two conditions assert that a and b should not disable each other. The last condition asserts that the same state should be reached from s by either performing a followed by b, or by performing b followed by a. This notion of action independence originates from the partial-order reduction techniques [8, 26].

Definition 14. *MTSs $\mathcal{M}_1$ and $\mathcal{M}_2$ are independent, denoted $\mathcal{M}_1 \ddagger \mathcal{M}_2$, iff every action of $\mathcal{M}_1$ is independent of every action of $\mathcal{M}_2$ in $\mathcal{M}_1 \| \mathcal{M}_2$.*

Let $s \xrightarrow{*} s'$ denote that state s' is reachable from s through an arbitrary finite sequence of transitions in MTS $\mathcal{M}$. In other words, $s \xrightarrow{*} s'$ means that there exists a finite abstract execution ρ in $\mathcal{M}$ that start in state s s.t. $last(\rho) = s'$.

Definition 15 (Layered composition). *Given MTSs $\mathcal{M}_i = (S_i, Act_i, s_{0i}, \{s_{fi}\}, V_i)$, where $i \in \{1, 2\}$ with $S_1 \cap S_2 = \varnothing$. The layered composition of $\mathcal{M}_1$ and $\mathcal{M}_2$, denoted $\mathcal{M}_1 \bullet \mathcal{M}_2$, is the MTS $(S_1 \times S_2, Act_1 \cup Act_2, (s_{01}, s_{02}), \{(s_{f1}, s_{f2})\}, V)$ where V is defined by:*

- *For all $(s, s') \in S_1 \times S_2$, $a \in Act_1 \cap Act_2$, if there exists $u \in S_1$ and $u' \in S_2$, such that $V_1(s, a, u) \neq \bot$ and $V_2(s', a, u') \neq \bot$, define $V((s, s'), a, (u, u')) = V_1(s, a, u) \sqcap V_2(s', a, u')$. If either $\forall u \in S_1$, we have $V_1(s, a, u) = \bot$, or $\forall u' \in S_2$, we have $V_2(s', a, u') = \bot$ then $\forall (u, u') \in S_1 \times S_2$, $V((s, s'), a, (u, u')) = \bot$.*
- *For all $(s, s'), (u, u') \in S_1 \times S_2$, $a \in Act_1 \setminus Act_2$, define $V((s, s'), a, (u, u')) = V_1(s, a, u)$ if $s' = u'$, $V((s, s'), a, (u, u')) = \bot$ otherwise.*
- *For all $(s, s'), (u, u') \in S_1 \times S_2$, $a \in Act_2 \setminus Act_1$, define $V((s, s'), a, (u, u')) = V_2(s', a, u')$ if $s = u \wedge \forall s^* : s \xrightarrow{*} s^* : act(s^*) \ddagger a$, $V((s, s'), a, (u, u')) = \bot$ otherwise.*

Note that the first two clauses of Definition 15 are the same as for Definition 12. Layered composition does not allow an action say d in $\mathcal{M}_2$ to be executed until all the actions in $\mathcal{M}_1$ (on which it is dependent) have been executed. In other words, all finite abstract executions, in which d is executed before any action say a, s.t. $a \dagger d$ will not be part of $Exec_{fin}(\mathcal{M}_1 \bullet \mathcal{M}_2)$ (this is guaranteed by the last clause of Definition 15).

Example 7. The layered composition of two MTSs $\mathcal{M}_1, \mathcal{M}_2$ (Fig. 3 (left)) is shown in Fig. 4 (right). Note that actions a, d are dependent, and therefore d cannot be executed before a in $\mathcal{M}_1 \bullet \mathcal{M}_2$.

Next, we use the above mentioned composition operators for formulating the communication closed layer (CCL) laws as follows:

Theorem 1 (CCL laws). *For MTSs $\mathcal{N}_1$, $\mathcal{N}_2$, $\mathcal{M}_1$, and $\mathcal{M}_2$, with $\mathcal{N}_1 \ddagger \mathcal{M}_2$ and $\mathcal{M}_1 \ddagger \mathcal{N}_2$, the following communication closed layer (CCL) equivalences hold:*

- $\mathcal{N}_1 \bullet \mathcal{M}_2 \equiv \mathcal{N}_1 \| \mathcal{M}_2$ *(IND)*
- $(\mathcal{N}_1 \bullet \mathcal{N}_2) \| \mathcal{M}_2 \equiv \mathcal{N}_1 \bullet (\mathcal{N}_2 \| \mathcal{M}_2)$ *(CCL-L)*
- $(\mathcal{N}_1 \bullet \mathcal{N}_2) \| \mathcal{M}_1 \equiv (\mathcal{N}_1 \| \mathcal{M}_1) \bullet \mathcal{N}_2$ *(CCL-R)*
- $(\mathcal{N}_1 \bullet \mathcal{N}_2) \| (\mathcal{M}_1 \bullet \mathcal{M}_2) \equiv (\mathcal{N}_1 \| \mathcal{M}_1) \bullet (\mathcal{N}_2 \| \mathcal{M}_2)$ *(CCL)*

5 Partial Order Equivalence and Property Preservation

This section defines the notion of partial order equivalence ($\equiv_{po}^*$) between MTSs which is used to prove that sequential and layered composition of MTSs satisfy the same existential ($\exists$) and universal ($\forall$) reachability properties. For MTSs $\mathcal{M}_1$, and $\mathcal{M}_2$, let $\mathcal{M} = \mathcal{M}_1 \bullet \mathcal{M}_2$. Then we define $\mathcal{M}^{\setminus sync}$ as the MTS obtained from $\mathcal{M}$ s.t. it does not have any synchronized transitions (which are present in $\mathcal{M}$ as a result of synchronization over common actions). Intuitively, this means that abstract executions in $\mathcal{M}$ with synchronized transitions can be rewritten in $\mathcal{M}^{\setminus sync}$ such that for every synchronized transition there is a corresponding sequence of transitions in $\mathcal{M}^{\setminus sync}$ obtained by allowing interleaving on common actions. For example, let $\mathcal{M}$ have a may a-transition which is a result of synchronization of a must a-transition (from $\mathcal{M}_1$), and a may a- transition (from $\mathcal{M}_2$). In this case $\mathcal{M}^{\setminus sync}$ will have a corresponding[1] sequence of transitions, i.e., a must a-transition (from $\mathcal{M}_1$) followed by a may a-transition (from $\mathcal{M}_2$). This transformation is required as we want to establish the result that layered composition is po-equivalent to sequential composition. Note that sequential composition of two MTSs does not have synchronized transitions. This means that for any $\mathcal{M} = \mathcal{M}_1; \mathcal{M}_2$, $\mathcal{M}^{\setminus sync} = \mathcal{M}$.

Example 8. Consider the MTSs $\mathcal{M}_1$ and $\mathcal{M}_2$ shown in Fig. 5 (left). The layered composition of $\mathcal{M}_1$, $\mathcal{M}_2$, i.e., $\mathcal{M}_1 \bullet \mathcal{M}_2$ is shown in the middle, where $\mathcal{M}_1$ and $\mathcal{M}_2$ synchronize on common action a. A may transition is obtained in $\mathcal{M}_1 \bullet \mathcal{M}_2$ (since composing must-may results in a may transition). The MTS $(\mathcal{M}_1 \bullet \mathcal{M}_2)^{\setminus sync}$ without synchronized transitions is shown in Fig. 5 (right). Here the common action of $\mathcal{M}_1$ is executed before the common action of $\mathcal{M}_2$.

Theorem 2. *For MTSs $\mathcal{M}_1$ and $\mathcal{M}_2$, let $\mathcal{M} = \mathcal{M}_1 \bullet \mathcal{M}_2$, and S_f be the set of final states in $\mathcal{M}$. Then the following holds:*

$$\mathcal{M} \models^{\exists} \Diamond S_f \Leftrightarrow \mathcal{M}^{\setminus sync} \models^{\exists} \Diamond S_f$$

$$\mathcal{M} \models^{\forall} \Diamond S_f \Leftrightarrow \mathcal{M}^{\setminus sync} \models^{\forall} \Diamond S_f$$

---

[1] In fact, if $\mathcal{M}$ would not be deterministic, then two corresponding transition sequences making a diamond shape would be obtained in $\mathcal{M}^{\setminus sync}$.

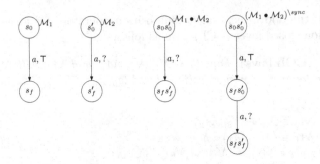

Fig. 5. MTS without synchronized transitions

In simple words this theorem says that reasoning about $\mathcal{M}^{\backslash sync}$ in place of $\mathcal{M}$ is not a restriction, as the behaviour of $\mathcal{M}$ (w.r.t. reachability properties) is mimicked by $\mathcal{M}^{\backslash sync}$. Next, we define the notion of partial order equivalence between two finite abstract executions.

Definition 16 (po-equivalence). *Let $\mathcal{M}_1$ and $\mathcal{M}_2$ be two MTSs with transition functions V_1, and V_2 respectively. Let $\rho_1 \in Exec_{fin}(\mathcal{M}_1^{\backslash sync})$ and $\rho_2 \in Exec_{fin}(\mathcal{M}_2^{\backslash sync})$. Then $\rho_1 \equiv_{po} \rho_2$ iff there exist finite abstract executions ρ', ρ'' and $\exists a_1, b_1$ with $a_1 \neq b_1$ s.t. the following holds:*

- *ρ' represents the same sequence of transitions in ρ_1, ρ_2, and ρ'' represents the same sequence of transitions in ρ_1, ρ_2.*
- *$\rho_1 = \rho' a_1 s b_1 \rho'' \wedge \rho_2 = \rho' b_1 s' a_1 \rho''$, where $a_1 \ddagger b_1$.*
- *$V_1(last(\rho'), a_1, s) = V_2(s', a_1, first(\rho'')) \wedge V_1(s, b_1, first(\rho'')) = V_2(last(\rho'), b_1, s')$.*

Let $\equiv_{po}^{*}$, called po-equivalence, denote the reflexive, transitive closure of $\equiv_{po}$.

Stated in words, if two finite abstract executions ρ_1, ρ_2 are po-equivalent, then ρ_1 can be obtained from ρ_2 by repeated permutation of adjacent independent actions. Note that the first condition of Definition 16 is required to ensure that if for example $\rho' = s_0 c_1 s_1 d_1 s_2$ where c_1 is a must transition and d_1 is a may transition in $\mathcal{M}_1^{\backslash sync}$, then c_1, d_1 are also must and may transitions in $\mathcal{M}_2^{\backslash sync}$.

Definition 17 (Layered normal form). *Let S_f be the set of final states in $(\mathcal{M}_1 \bullet \mathcal{M}_2)^{\backslash sync}$. Then $\rho \in Exec_{fin}^{S_f}((\mathcal{M}_1 \bullet \mathcal{M}_2)^{\backslash sync})$ is in layered normal form (LNF) iff it involves the consecutive execution of actions of $\mathcal{M}_1$, followed by the consecutive execution of actions of $\mathcal{M}_2$.*

Let $Exec_{fin}^{LNF}((\mathcal{M}_1 \bullet \mathcal{M}_2)^{\backslash sync})$ denote the set of all finite abstract executions in $Exec_{fin}^{S_f}((\mathcal{M}_1 \bullet \mathcal{M}_2)^{\backslash sync})$ that are in LNF.

Next we show that for each finite abstract execution of $Exec_{fin}^{S_f}((\mathcal{M}_1 \bullet \mathcal{M}_2)^{\backslash sync})$, a po-equivalent abstract exceution in LNF does exist.

Lemma 1 (LNF existence). *Let $\mathcal{M}_1, \mathcal{M}_2$ be two MTSs. Then we have $\forall \rho \in Exec_{fin}^{S_f}((\mathcal{M}_1 \bullet \mathcal{M}_2)^{\backslash sync}) \exists \rho' \in Exec_{fin}^{LNF}((\mathcal{M}_1 \bullet \mathcal{M}_2)^{\backslash sync})$ s.t. $\rho \equiv_{po}^{*} \rho'$.*

Definition 18 (po-equivalence for MTSs). *Two MTSs $\mathcal{M}_1, \mathcal{M}_2$ are said to be po-equivalent, denoted $\mathcal{M}_1 \equiv_{po}^{*} \mathcal{M}_2$, iff for $i \in \{1,2\}$: $\forall \rho_i \in Exec_{fin}^{S_{fi}}(\mathcal{M}_i^{\backslash sync})$ $\exists \rho_{3-i} \in Exec_{fin}^{S_{f3-i}}(\mathcal{M}_{3-i}^{\backslash sync})$ s.t. $\rho_i \equiv_{po}^{*} \rho_{3-i}$.*

Theorem 3. *For every MTSs $\mathcal{M}_1, \mathcal{M}_2$, we have $\mathcal{M}_1 \bullet \mathcal{M}_2 \equiv_{po}^{*} \mathcal{M}_1 ; \mathcal{M}_2$.*

Example 9. It is easy to check that MTS $\mathcal{M}_1 ; \mathcal{M}_2$ given in Fig. 3 (right) is po-equivalent to MTS $\mathcal{M}_1 \bullet \mathcal{M}_2$ given in Fig. 4 (right).

Theorem 4 (Property preservation). *For MTSs $\mathcal{M}_1, \mathcal{M}_2$, let $\mathcal{M} = \mathcal{M}_1 \bullet \mathcal{M}_2$, $\mathcal{M}' = \mathcal{M}_1 ; \mathcal{M}_2$ with set of final states S_f, and S'_f respectively. If $\mathcal{M} \equiv_{po}^{*} \mathcal{M}'$ then we have:*

$$\mathcal{M} \models^{\exists} \Diamond S_f \; iff \; \mathcal{M}' \models^{\exists} \Diamond S'_f$$

$$\mathcal{M} \models^{\forall} \Diamond S_f \; iff \; \mathcal{M}' \models^{\forall} \Diamond S'_f$$

This theorem asserts that po-equivalence between layered and sequential composition operators satisfies the same reachability properties.

Corollary 1. *Replacing $\bullet$ by ; in the CCL laws yields the po-equivalence which satisfies the same $\exists$ and $\forall$ reachability properties.*

Corollary 1 enable us to replace ; with $\bullet$ and vice versa. This replacement along with CCL laws (Theorem 1) can be used for state space reduction as follows:

State space reduction. Let $\mathcal{N}_1, \mathcal{N}_2$ and $\mathcal{M}_1$ be three MTSs, and $\mathcal{N} = (\mathcal{N}_1 ; \mathcal{N}_2) \| \mathcal{M}_1$. Let us say we want to check whether $\mathcal{N} \models^{\exists} \Diamond S_f$ or $\mathcal{N} \models^{\forall} \Diamond S_f$. Here, S_f is set of final states in $\mathcal{N}$. Assume $\mathcal{M}_1 \ddagger \mathcal{N}_2$, and $\mathcal{N}_1, \mathcal{N}_2, \mathcal{M}_1$ each consist of 20 states. In this case $\mathcal{N}_1 ; \mathcal{N}_2$ has 39 states which combined with the 20 states of $\mathcal{M}_1$ gives 780 states. We can transform $\mathcal{N}$ in the following way:

$$(\mathcal{N}_1 ; \mathcal{N}_2) \| \mathcal{M}_1$$
$$\equiv_{po}^{*} \qquad \text{Corollary 1}$$
$$(\mathcal{N}_1 \bullet \mathcal{N}_2) \| \mathcal{M}_1$$
$$\equiv \qquad \text{CCL-R}$$
$$(\mathcal{N}_1 \| \mathcal{M}_1) \bullet \mathcal{N}_2$$
$$\equiv_{po}^{*} \qquad \text{Corollary 1}$$
$$(\mathcal{N}_1 \| \mathcal{M}_1) ; \mathcal{N}_2$$

Note that the transformed system, i.e., $(\mathcal{N}_1 \| \mathcal{M}_1) ; \mathcal{N}_2$ has 419 states.

·

6   Conclusion

This paper presented a state-space reduction technique for a network of acyclic MTSs, based on the notion of layering. We proposed a layered composition operator, and formulated communication closed layer (CCL) laws. Next, we define the partial order (po) equivalence between acyclic MTSs, show that layered and sequential composition operators are po-equivalent and satisfy the same existential ($\exists$) and universal ($\forall$) reachability properties. As implementations of distributed systems typically are in terms of layers, we believe that enabling transforming system MTS specifications into layered form will substantially ease the proof of correct implementation. The theory of layering proposed in this paper can be extended to acyclic MTSs equipped with data variables. An MTS $\mathcal{M}$ can be extended with data variables such that whenever an action is executed its associated data variables are updated according to an arithmetic expression. These data variables can take values in some finite range D. The definitions of satisfaction, and refinement can be slightly modified by placing an extra condition that ensures that related states have the same valuations. For an MTS with data, two actions are said to be dependent if one of the two writes a variable that is read or written by the other action. More formally, two actions a and b are dependent, denoted $a \dagger b$, if any one of the following holds:

$$Write(b) \cap Read(a) \neq \varnothing,$$
$$Write(a) \cap Read(b) \neq \varnothing,$$
$$Write(a) \cap Write(b) \neq \varnothing.$$

Here, $Write(a)$ denotes the set of data variables written by the action a. Similarly, $Read(a)$ denotes the set of data variables read by the action a. Using this dependency relation, our theory can be applied to MTSs with data. We do not go into details on these matters here, however, refer interested reader to [2,11,30]. Future work includes the application of this technique to practical case studies which involve modeling distributed systems using MTSs.

Acknowledgements. The authors thank Ian Larson for modeling the randomized mutual exclusion algorithm case study in PRISM and conducting the experiments.

Appendix

Proof of Theorem 1

Proof. We provide the proof of the law CCL-L. The proofs of the other CCL laws are similar. Let $\mathcal{T} = (\mathcal{N}_1 \bullet \mathcal{N}_2) \| \mathcal{M}_2$ and $\mathcal{U} = \mathcal{N}_1 \bullet (\mathcal{N}_2 \| \mathcal{M}_2)$. In order to prove that $\mathcal{T} \equiv \mathcal{U}$, we have to show $\mathcal{T} \preceq_S \mathcal{U}$ and $\mathcal{U} \preceq_S \mathcal{T}$. Let $((x,y),z)$ and $(x,(y,z))$ denote states of MTSs $\mathcal{T}$ and $\mathcal{U}$, respectively. Here x, y, z represent the state components of $\mathcal{N}_1, \mathcal{N}_2$ and $\mathcal{M}_2$, respectively. We only prove $\mathcal{T} \preceq_S \mathcal{U}$, the proof of $\mathcal{U} \preceq_S \mathcal{T}$ is very similar. To show $\mathcal{T} \preceq_S \mathcal{U}$, we have to prove that T strongly refines U according to Definition 6. Let S^* and S be the state space of T and U, respectively. Let $R \subseteq S^* \times S$ be a binary relation s.t. $R = \{(((x,y),z),(x,(y,z))),(((x',y),z),(x',(y,z))),(((x,y'),z'),(x,(y',z')))\ldots\}$. Intuitively R relates states of S^* to those states in S that have the same individual state components from N_1, N_2 and M_2. Let us consider a state $s = (x,(y,z))$ from U and $s^* = ((x,y),z)$ from T. From the definition of R, we know that $(s^*,s) \in R$. A transition from s in U or s^* in T can be performed by 1) N_1 individually, or 2) N_2 individually, or 3) M_2 individually, or 4) N_1 and N_2 simultaneously, or 5) N_2 and M_2 simultaneously. We show that for every case[2] the conditions of Definition 6 are satisfied, and thus R is a strong refinement relation between T and U. It is easy to check that condition 3 which requires final states to be related is satisfied. This is because R relates states that have the same individual state components from N_1, N_2 and M_2.

(1) N_1 individually: Let $s \xrightarrow{a}_T s'$ (resp. $s \xrightarrow{a}_? s'$) be a transition of N_1 taken in U, where $s' = (x',(y,z))$. Since N_1 is the left operand of layering in U such a transition is also possible from the related state $s^* = ((x,y),z)$, i.e., $s^* \xrightarrow{a}_T s^{**}$ (resp. $s^* \xrightarrow{a}_? s^{**}$), where $s^{**} = ((x',y),z)$. From the definition of R we know that $(s^{**},s') \in R$. Similarly, it can be shown that for every transition $s^* \xrightarrow{a}_T s^{***}$ (resp. $s^* \xrightarrow{a}_? s^{***}$), there exists a corresponding transition, $s \xrightarrow{a}_T s''$ (resp. $s \xrightarrow{a}_? s''$) s.t. $(s^{***},s'') \in R$.

(2) N_2 individually: Similar to case 1 above.

(3) M_2 individually: Let $s \xrightarrow{a}_T s'$ (resp. $s \xrightarrow{a}_? s'$) be a transition of M_2 taken in U, where $s' = (x,(y,z'))$. Since this transition is possible after layering operator in U, it is also possible in T from the state related to s, i.e., s^* as this action is not waiting for some action of N_1 to be executed, and U induces fewer interleavings due to dominance of layered composition operator. Next, we consider a transition of M_2 taken in T from state s^*. Since $N_1 \ddagger M_2$, a similar transition exists in U from the state related to s^*, i.e., s as putting M_2 after the layering operator is not a problem as it is independent from N_1.

(4) N_1 and N_2 simultaneously: Let $s \xrightarrow{a}_T s'$ (resp. $s \xrightarrow{a}_? s'$) be a transition in U as a result of a synchronization of N_1 and N_2 on action a, where $s' = (x',(y',z))$. Again as U induces fewer interleavings due to dominance of layered operator, a similar transition is possible in T from state related to s, i.e., s^*. Similarly, for any transition in T from s^*, a corresponding transition is enabled in U as $N_2 \| M_2$ will not block it (due to the fact that the synchronizing action is not waiting for an action from M_2 to be executed since parallel composition does not respect dependencies).

(5) N_2 and M_2 simultaneously: Let $s \xrightarrow{a}_T s'$ (resp. $s \xrightarrow{a}_? s'$) be a transition in U as a result of a synchronization of N_2 and M_2 on action a, where $s' = (x,(y',z'))$. As this action is possible in $N_2 \| M_2$, it means that this action is not waiting for the execution of some actions from N_1. It is therefore

---

[2] Note that we do not consider the case where N_1 and M_2 move simultaneously. This is due to the fact that $N_1 \ddagger M_2$, and therefore they cannot have common actions (since the dependency relation is reflexive).

possible to take the same transition in $\mathcal{T}$ from s^* as $\mathcal{N}_1 \bullet \mathcal{N}_2$ will not block it. Similarly, for any transition in $\mathcal{T}$ from s^*, there will be a corresponding transition in $\mathcal{U}$. This is due to the fact this action is not waiting for actions of $\mathcal{N}_1$ to be executed as $\mathcal{N}_1 \ddagger \mathcal{M}_2$. $\square$

Proof of Theorem 2

Proof. ($\exists$ reachability): We provide the proof of $\mathcal{M} \models^\exists \Diamond S_f \Rightarrow \mathcal{M}^{\backslash sync} \models^\exists \Diamond S_f$.
The proof of $\mathcal{M}^{\backslash sync} \models^\exists \Diamond S_f \Rightarrow \mathcal{M} \models^\exists \Diamond S_f$ is similar. Let $\mathcal{T} \in [\![\mathcal{M}]\!]$ be an LTS s.t. $\mathcal{T} \models \Diamond S_f$. We know that every finite path $\pi \in Paths_{fin}^{S_f}(\mathcal{T})$ is a realisation of some finite abstract execution $\rho \in Exec_{fin}^{S_f}(\mathcal{M})$, and no finite path can be a realisation of more than one finite abstract execution in $\mathcal{M}$ (since $\mathcal{M}$ is deterministic). Let η be the set of all such finite abstract executions where $\eta \subseteq Exec_{fin}^{S_f}(\mathcal{M})$. From the definition of $\mathcal{M}^{\backslash sync}$ we know that for each finite abstract execution $\rho \in \eta$ there exists a corresponding finite abstract execution in $Exec_{fin}^{S_f}(\mathcal{M}^{\backslash sync})$ obtained by allowing interleaving on common actions s.t. the common action of $\mathcal{M}_1$ is executed followed by execution of the common action of $\mathcal{M}_2$. Let $\eta' \subseteq Exec_{fin}^{S_f}(\mathcal{M}^{\backslash sync})$ be the set of all such finite abstract executions. Let $\mathcal{T}' \in [\![\mathcal{M}^{\backslash sync}]\!]$ be an LTS s.t. for every finite abstract execution $\rho' \in \eta'$ there exists a finite path π' in $\mathcal{T}'$ that is a realisation of ρ' and $\mathcal{T}'$ does not contain any path $\pi' \in Paths_{fin}^{S_f}(\mathcal{T}')$ which is not a realisation of some finite abstract execution $\rho' \in \eta'$. In other words we have constructed an implementation $\mathcal{T}'$ corresponding to $\mathcal{T}$ s.t. $\mathcal{T}' \models \Diamond S_f$.

($\forall$ reachability): We provide the proof of $\mathcal{M} \models^\forall \Diamond S_f \Rightarrow \mathcal{M}^{\backslash sync} \models^\forall \Diamond S_f$.
The proof of $\mathcal{M}^{\backslash sync} \models^\forall \Diamond S_f \Rightarrow \mathcal{M} \models^\forall \Diamond S_f$ is similar. From the definition of $\forall$ reachability (Definition 10) we know that $\mathcal{M}$ reaches S_f if and only if all the implementations of $\mathcal{M}$ are able to reach S_f. This intuitively means that $\mathcal{M}$ does not have those *may* transitions that block any of its implementations from reaching the final state. Since $\mathcal{M}^{\backslash sync}$ is obtained from $\mathcal{M}$ by allowing interleaving on common actions, such *may* transitions (or equivalent transition sequences) are also absent in $\mathcal{M}^{\backslash sync}$. In other words, every implementation $\mathcal{T}' \in [\![\mathcal{M}^{\backslash sync}]\!]$ reaches S_f, i.e., $\mathcal{T}' \models \Diamond S_f$. $\square$

Proof of Lemma 1

Proof. From the definition of layered normal form (LNF) we know that all finite abstract executions that are in LNF consists of the consecutive execution of actions of $\mathcal{M}_1$, followed by the consecutive execution of actions of $\mathcal{M}_2$. We know that in $((\mathcal{M}_1 \bullet \mathcal{M}_2)^{\backslash sync})$, an action of $\mathcal{M}_2$ occurs only when all the actions in $\mathcal{M}_1$ on which it is dependent have been executed. This intuitively means that all the actions of $\mathcal{M}_2$ that occur in a finite abstract execution before any action of $\mathcal{M}_1$ are independent of this action and thus by repeated permutation of these actions any finite abstract execution $\rho \in Exec_{fin}^{S_f}((\mathcal{M}_1 \bullet \mathcal{M}_2)^{\backslash sync})$ can be converted to a finite abstract execution that is in LNF. $\square$

Proof of Theorem 3

Proof. Let $\mathcal{M}_1, \mathcal{M}_2$ be MTSs. From the definition of LNF (Definition 17), we know that a finite abstract execution in LNF involves the consecutive execution of actions of $\mathcal{M}_1$, followed by the consecutive execution of actions of $\mathcal{M}_2$. This means that for every finite abstract execution $\rho \in Exec_{fin}^{LNF}((\mathcal{M}_1 \bullet \mathcal{M}_2)^{\backslash sync})$ there exists a finite abstract execution ρ' in $((\mathcal{M}_1; \mathcal{M}_2)^{\backslash sync})$ that ends in the final state and where: $\forall n \geq 0 : \rho[n] \approx \rho'[n] \wedge \rho[n] \xrightarrow{a_{n+1}}_{\top} \rho[n+1] \Rightarrow \rho'[n] \xrightarrow{a_{n+1}}_{\top} \rho'[n+1]$ (resp.$\rho[n] \xrightarrow{a_{n+1}}_{?} \rho[n+1] \Rightarrow \rho'[n] \xrightarrow{a_{n+1}}_{?} \rho'[n+1]$). The relation $\approx$ between states of $((\mathcal{M}_1 \bullet \mathcal{M}_2)^{\backslash sync})$ and $((\mathcal{M}_1; \mathcal{M}_2)^{\backslash sync})$ is defined as follows: $S_1 \times S_2$ is the state space of $((\mathcal{M}_1 \bullet \mathcal{M}_2)^{\backslash sync})$ and $(S_1 \setminus \{s_{f1}\} \cup S_2)$ is the state space of $((\mathcal{M}_1; \mathcal{M}_2)^{\backslash sync})$ then $\forall s_1 \in S_1$ where $s_1 \neq s_{f1} : (s_1, s_{02}) \approx s_1$ and $\forall s_2 \in S_2 : (s_{f1}, s_2) \approx s_2$.

In other words we have related every finite abstract execution of $((\mathcal{M}_1 \bullet \mathcal{M}_2)^{\backslash sync})$ that is in LNF to some finite abstract execution in $((\mathcal{M}_1; \mathcal{M}_2)^{\backslash sync})$ that ends in the final state and vice-versa. It is also clear from Lemma 1 that for every finite abstract execution ρ in $((\mathcal{M}_1 \bullet \mathcal{M}_2)^{\backslash sync})$ that ends in the final state, there exists a finite abstract execution ρ' in $((\mathcal{M}_1 \bullet \mathcal{M}_2)^{\backslash sync})$ that is LNF s.t. $\rho \equiv_{po}^* \rho'$. $\qquad\square$

Proof of Theorem 4

Proof. ($\exists$ reachability): We provide the proof of $\mathcal{M} \models^{\exists} \Diamond S_f \Rightarrow \mathcal{M}' \models^{\exists} \Diamond S_f'$. The proof of $\mathcal{M}' \models^{\exists} \Diamond S_f' \Rightarrow \mathcal{M} \models^{\exists} \Diamond S_f$ is similar. Let $\mathcal{T} \in [\![\mathcal{M}^{\backslash sync}]\!]$ be an LTS s.t. $\mathcal{T} \models \Diamond S_f$. We know that every finite path $\pi \in Paths_{fin}^{S_f}(\mathcal{T})$ is a realisation of some finite abstract execution $\rho \in Exec_{fin}^{S_f}(\mathcal{M}^{\backslash sync})$, and no finite path can be a realisation of more than one finite abstract execution in $\mathcal{M}^{\backslash sync}$ (since $\mathcal{M}^{\backslash sync}$ is deterministic). Let η be the set of all such finite abstract executions where $\eta \subseteq Exec_{fin}^{S_f}(\mathcal{M}^{\backslash sync})$. From the definition of po-equivalence for MTSs (Definition 18) we know that for set η there exists a set $\eta' \subseteq Exec_{fin}^{S_f'}(\mathcal{M}'^{\backslash sync})$: $\forall \rho \in \eta \exists \rho' \in \eta' : \rho \equiv_{po}^* \rho'$ and vice versa. Since both $\mathcal{M}^{\backslash sync}$ and $\mathcal{M}'^{\backslash sync}$ are deterministic, this intuitively means that $|\eta| = |\eta'|$. Let $\mathcal{T}' \in [\![\mathcal{M}'^{\backslash sync}]\!]$ be an LTS s.t. for every finite abstract execution $\rho' \in \eta'$ there exists a finite path in $\mathcal{T}'$ that is a realisation of ρ' and $\mathcal{T}'$ does not contain any path $\pi' \in Paths_{fin}^{S_f'}(\mathcal{T}')$ which is not a realisation of some finite abstract execution $\rho' \in \eta'$. In other words we have constructed an implementation $\mathcal{T}'$ corresponding to $\mathcal{T}$ s.t. $\mathcal{T}' \models \Diamond S_f'$.

($\forall$ reachability): We provide the proof of $\mathcal{M} \models^{\forall} \Diamond S_f \Rightarrow \mathcal{M}' \models^{\forall} \Diamond S_f'$. The proof of $\mathcal{M}' \models^{\forall} \Diamond S_f' \Rightarrow \mathcal{M} \models^{\forall} \Diamond S_f$ is similar. From the definition of $\forall$ reachability (Definition 10) we know that $\mathcal{M}$ reaches S_f if and only if all the implementations of $\mathcal{M}$ are able to reach S_f. This intuitively means that $\mathcal{M}^{\backslash sync}$ does not have those *may* transitions that block any of its implementations from reaching the final state. Since $\mathcal{M}'$ is po-equivalent to $\mathcal{M}$ and $\mathcal{M}'$ involves the consecutive execution of actions of $\mathcal{M}_1$, followed by the consecutive execution of actions of

$\mathcal{M}_2$ before reaching S'_f, such *may* transitions are also absent in $\mathcal{M}'^{\backslash sync}$. In other words, every implementation $T' \in [\![\mathcal{M}'^{\backslash sync}]\!]$ reaches S'_f, i.e. $T' \models \Diamond S'_f$. □

References

1. Baier, C., Katoen, J.-P.: Principles of Model Checking. MIT Press, Cambridge (2008)
2. Bauer, S.S., Guldstrand Larsen, K., Legay, A., Nyman, U., Wąsowski, A.: A modal specification theory for components with data. In: Arbab, F., Ölveczky, P.C. (eds.) FACS 2011. LNCS, vol. 7253, pp. 61–78. Springer, Heidelberg (2012)
3. Beneš, N., Černá, I., Křetínský, J.: Modal transition systems: composition and LTL model checking. In: Bultan, T., Hsiung, P.-A. (eds.) ATVA 2011. LNCS, vol. 6996, pp. 228–242. Springer, Heidelberg (2011)
4. Bernstein, P.A., Hadzilacos, V., Goodman, N.: Concurrency Control and Recovery in Database Systems. Addison-Wesley, Boston (1986)
5. Bruns, G.: An industrial application of modal process logic. Sci. Comput. Program. **29**(1–2), 3–22 (1997)
6. Elrad, T., Francez, N.: Decomposition of distributed programs into communication-closed layers. Sci. Comput. Program. **2**(3), 155–173 (1982)
7. Gallager, R.G., Humblet, P.A., Spira, P.M.: A distributed algorithm for minimum-weight spanning trees. ACM Trans. Program. Lang. Syst. **5**(1), 66–77 (1983)
8. Gerth, R., Kuiper, R., Peled, D., Penczek, W.: A partial order approach to branching time logic model checking. In: ISTCS, pp. 130–139 (1995)
9. Gruler, A., Leucker, M., Scheidemann, K.: Modeling and model checking software product lines. In: Barthe, G., de Boer, F.S. (eds.) FMOODS 2008. LNCS, vol. 5051, pp. 113–131. Springer, Heidelberg (2008)
10. Huth, M., Jagadeesan, R., Schmidt, D.A.: Modal transition systems: a foundation for three-valued program analysis. In: Sands, D. (ed.) ESOP 2001. LNCS, vol. 2028, pp. 155–169. Springer, Heidelberg (2001)
11. Janssen, W.: Layered design of parallel systems. Ph.D. dissertation, Universiteit Twente (1994)
12. Janssen, W., Poel, M., Xu, Q., Zwiers, J.: Layering of real-time distributed processes. In: Langmaack, H., de Roever, W.-P., Vytopil, J. (eds.) FTRTFT 1994 and ProCoS 1994. LNCS, vol. 863, pp. 393–417. Springer, Heidelberg (1994)
13. Janssen, W., Poel, M., Zwiers, J.: Action systems and action refinement in the development of parallel systems - an algebraic approach. In: Groote, J.F., Baeten, J.C.M. (eds.) CONCUR 1991. LNCS, vol. 527, pp. 298–316. Springer, Heidelberg (1991)
14. Janssen, W., Zwiers, J.: From sequential layers to distributed processes: Deriving a distributed minimum weight spanning tree algorithm (extended anstract). In: PODC, pp. 215–227. ACM (1992)
15. Kushilevitz, E., Rabin, M.O.: Randomized mutual exclusion algorithms revisited. In : PODC, pp. 275–283 (1992)
16. Kwiatkowska, M., Norman, G., Parker, D.: PRISM 4.0: verification of probabilistic real-time systems. In: Gopalakrishnan, G., Qadeer, S. (eds.) CAV 2011. LNCS, vol. 6806, pp. 585–591. Springer, Heidelberg (2011)
17. Larsen, K.G.: Modal specifications. In: Sifakis, J. (ed.) CAV 1989. LNCS, vol. 407, pp. 232–246. Springer, Heidelberg (1990)

18. Larsen, K.G., Nyman, U., Wąsowski, A.: On modal refinement and consistency. In: Caires, L., Vasconcelos, V.T. (eds.) CONCUR 2007. LNCS, vol. 4703, pp. 105–119. Springer, Heidelberg (2007)
19. Larsen, K.G., Steffen, B., Weise, C.: A constraint oriented proof methodology based on modal transition systems. In: Brinksma, E., Steffen, B., Cleaveland, W.R., Larsen, K.G., Margaria, T. (eds.) TACAS 1995. LNCS, vol. 1019, pp. 17–40. Springer, Heidelberg (1995)
20. Larsen, K.G., Thomsen, B.: A modal process logic. In: LICS, pp. 203–210 (1988)
21. Larsen, K.G., Xinxin, L.: Equation solving using modal transition systems. In: LICS, pp. 108–117 (1990)
22. McIver, A.K., Gonzalia, C., Cohen, E., Morgan, C.C.: Using probabilistic Kleene algebra pKA for protocol verification. J. Log. Algebr. Program. 76(1), 90–111 (2008)
23. Milner, R.: Communication and Concurrency. Prentice-Hall Inc., Upper Saddle River (1989)
24. Moses, Y., Rajsbaum, S.: A layered analysis of consensus. SIAM J. Comput. 31(4), 989–1021 (2002)
25. Olderog, E.-R., Swaminathan, M.: Layered composition for timed automata. In: Chatterjee, K., Henzinger, T.A. (eds.) FORMATS 2010. LNCS, vol. 6246, pp. 228–242. Springer, Heidelberg (2010)
26. Peled, D.: Combining partial order reductions with on-the-fly model-checking. In: Dill, D.L. (ed.) CAV 1994. LNCS, vol. 818, pp. 377–390. Springer, Heidelberg (1994)
27. Raclet, J.-B.: Residual for component specifications. Electr. Notes Theor. Comput. Sci. 215, 93–110 (2008)
28. Raclet, J.-B., Badouel, E., Benveniste, A., Caillaud, B., Passerone, R.: Why are modalities good for interface theories? In: ACSD, pp. 119–127 (2009)
29. Schmidt, D.A.: From trace sets to modal-transition systems by stepwise abstract interpretation. Theoria 33, 53–71 (2001)
30. Swaminathan, M., Katoen, J.-P., Olderog, E.-R.: Layered reasoning for randomized distributed algorithms. Formal Asp. Comput. 24(4–6), 477–496 (2012)
31. Uchitel, S., Chechik, M.: Merging partial behavioural models. In: SIGSOFT FSE, pp. 43–52 (2004)

Define, Verify, Refine: Correct Composition and Transformation of Concurrent System Semantics

Anton Wijs[✉]

Department of Mathematics and Computer Science, Eindhoven University
of Technology, 513, 5600 MB Eindhoven, The Netherlands
A.J.Wijs@tue.nl

Abstract. We present a technique to verify user-defined model transformations, in order to step-wise develop formal models of concurrent systems. The main benefit is that the changes applied to a model can be verified in isolation. In particular, the preservation of safety and liveness properties of such a modification can be determined independent of the input model. This is particularly useful for model-driven development approaches, where systems are designed and created by first developing an abstract model, and iteratively modifying this model until it is concrete enough to automatically generate source code from it. Properties that already hold on the initial model and should remain valid throughout the development in later models can be maintained with our tool REFINER, by which the effort of verifying those properties over and over again can be avoided. This paper generalises our earlier results in various ways, removing several restrictions, improving the focus of the verification method on transformations, and introducing the possibility to add completely new components at any time during the development.

1 Introduction

Concurrent systems tend to be very complex, and therefore very hard to develop correctly, i.e. bug-free. One approach to restrict the potential for introducing errors is by *step-wise* constructing the model of a concurrent system via model transformations. In that way, a model can be made more and more detailed, ultimately describing the system in full detail, which has the potential of allowing automatic source code generation. Such an approach can be made more robust by incorporating efficient verification techniques to determine that each intermediate model is correct, i.e. that desired functional properties are preserved. In [28,29], we presented a new technique to verify that formal definitions of transformations preserve desired functional properties, *independent* of the model they are applied on. Models, in this context, are action-based specifications of concurrent systems. Such specifications can be written in action-based modelling languages, such as process algebras. The definitions of transformations correspond with model transformations, as used in software engineering. The main benefit is that after application of a verified transformation, a model does not need to be rechecked, thereby avoiding state space explosion.

J.L. Fiadeiro et al. (Eds.): FACS 2013, LNCS 8348, pp. 348–368, 2014.
DOI: 10.1007/978-3-319-07602-7_21, © Springer International Publishing Switzerland 2014

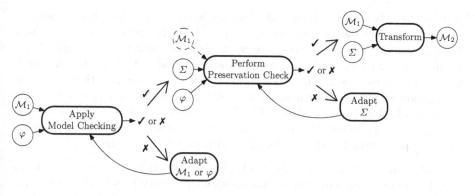

Fig. 1. Schematic depiction of the typical use of REFINER

The new verification technique has been implemented in a prototype tool called REFINER[1], by which a designer can, through a command-line interface, step-wise transform the semantics of processes in concurrent system designs. The designer does this by constructing transformation rule systems, which are formalisations of model transformations that can be analysed efficiently to determine whether they preserve safety or liveness properties *in general*, i.e. independent of the input model. Typically, REFINER is used as in Fig. 1. First, existing action-based model checking toolsets such as CADP [8] and MCRL2 [5] can be applied to verify whether a given property φ, usually written in the modal μ-calculus [17], holds for model $\mathcal{M}_1$. If the property holds, REFINER is used to determine whether the property is preserved by rule system Σ. There are two supported techniques for this: one for determining *model-independent* property preservation, independent of input models, and one for determining property preservation for a particular input model. The latter involves $\mathcal{M}_1$ in the analysis, therefore it is not general, since it does not allow reusing the verification results for transformations of other models. But it may lead to a positive result in cases where the model-independent one does not. The model-independent property preservation check considers all the possibilities for Σ to match on input models. If φ is not preserved, Σ must be adapted and the last step repeated. If φ is preserved, REFINER can be used to transform model $\mathcal{M}_1$ into a model $\mathcal{M}_2$ satisfying φ.

REFINER is primarily a testbed to investigate the possibilities for verifying model transformations that exist, like models, as primary artifacts. This support should be non-intrusive, i.e. verification should be done in the background, hidden from the designer, in order to not burden him or her with the verification task.

Through experimentation, several limitations of the method from [29] have been identified. One is that the approach does not yet support *compositional* development of systems. Existing components can be transformed, but new

---

[1] Available for download at http://www.win.tue.nl/~awijs/refiner.

components cannot be introduced. Another is that a designer can sometimes be confronted by the limitations of the technique; in order for a rule system to be verifiable, it must be complete w.r.t. the behaviour it transforms. If two components can communicate, and one party is modified, then also the other party must be modified. This is not always desired, and requiring this makes the verification intrusive, and threatens scalability, because it may demand a large chain of additional modifications. Finally, we observe that in some cases, rule systems are constructed with particular models in mind. In such cases, checking property preserving for *all* imaginable models may be too restrictive.

Contribution. We build on the results of [29] to address the issues mentioned here. We enrich our transformation formalism with the ability to add new processes, and improve property preservation checking of rule systems. The latter is done by introducing a new construct for transformations, and by defining so-called *non-interface hiding*, which allows analysing the semantics of a subsystem w.r.t. the remainder of the system it is part of. Finally, REFINER exploits multi-core architectures through parallel property preservation checking, and we explain how this is achieved.

Roadmap. Section 2 discusses related work, and Sect. 3 introduces the notions used in this paper. In Sect. 4, property preservation checking from [29] is explained, and this is extended in various ways in Sect. 5. Our implementation and experimental results are shown in Sect. 6, and finally, Sect. 7 contains our conclusions and pointers to future work.

2   Related Work

Property preservation checking of changes applied on a model is most closely related to *incremental model checking* [23,24]. In that work, information about the verification computation is updated to reflect changes applied to the model. Most approaches are limited to checking safety properties, and all of them require at least as much computer memory as straight-forward model checking. Our technique, though, is also suitable for liveness properties and requires far less memory, since no information about the state space is maintained.

In *refinement checking* [1,18], supported by tools such as RODIN [2], FDR2 [2] and CSP-CASL-PROVER [16], it is usually checked that one model refines another. This is very similar to our approach, but refinements are defined in terms of what the new model will be, as opposed to *how* the new model can be obtained from the old one, i.e. model transformations are not represented as artifacts independent of the models they can be applied on. This makes it not directly suitable to investigate the feasibility to verify definitions of model transformations, as opposed to the models they produce.

The BART tool[3] allows automatically refining B components to B0 implementations. Similar to our setting, it treats refinement rules as user-definable

---

[2] http://www.fsel.com/documentation/fdr2/html/index.html
[3] http://www.tools.clearsy.com/tools/bart

artifacts and performs pattern matching to do the refining. Constraints are checked to ensure that the resulting system will be correct. Approaches described in, e.g., [4,9,10,15] prove that a transformation preserves the semantics of any input model, by showing that the transformed model will be bisimilar to the original. Contrary to our work, in all these approaches, no form of automatic hiding of behaviour irrelevant for a desired system property is used, therefore they cannot handle cases where transformations alter the semantics in a way that does not invalidate that property. Others, such as [22,25], perform individual checks for each concrete model.

Finally, incremental system composition, as used by the tools Exp.Open [20] and Bip [3], focusses on incrementally combining processes into a full system, and the latter also provides a fixed number of correct-by-construction model transformations. With Refiner, one can define incremental process adding in terms of transformations, and it can verify transformations provided by the user. It will be interesting to see in how far results on compositional model checking can be reused, to further improve verification of such transformations.

3 Background

In this paper, the semantics of concurrent systems are defined in a compositional, action-based way. This means that the semantics of individual, finite-state processes are captured using *Labelled Transition Systems* (LTSs), and that these can be combined using synchronous composition, to obtain the semantics of a concurrent system as a whole. LTSs are action-based descriptions, indicating how a process can change state by performing particular actions.

An LTS $\mathcal{G}$ is a tuple $\langle \mathcal{S}_\mathcal{G}, \mathcal{A}_\mathcal{G}, \mathcal{T}_\mathcal{G}, \mathcal{I}_\mathcal{G} \rangle$, where $\mathcal{S}_\mathcal{G}$ is a (finite) set of states, $\mathcal{A}_\mathcal{G}$ is a set of actions (including the invisible action τ), $\mathcal{T}_\mathcal{G} \subseteq \mathcal{S}_\mathcal{G} \times \mathcal{A}_\mathcal{G} \times \mathcal{S}_\mathcal{G}$ is a transition relation, and $\mathcal{I}_\mathcal{G} \subseteq \mathcal{S}_\mathcal{G}$ is a set of initial states. Actions in $\mathcal{A}_\mathcal{G}$ are denoted by a, b, c, etc. We use $s_1 \xrightarrow{a}_\mathcal{G} s_2$ to denote $\langle s_1, a, s_2 \rangle \in \mathcal{T}_\mathcal{G}$. If $s_1 \xrightarrow{a}_\mathcal{G} s_2$, this means that in $\mathcal{G}$, an action a can be performed in state s_1, leading to state s_2.

Note that a state s can be interpreted as an LTS $\langle \{s\}, \emptyset, \emptyset, \{s\} \rangle$, and a transition $s_1 \xrightarrow{a} s_2$ as an LTS $\langle \{s_1, s_2\}, \{a\}, s_1 \xrightarrow{a} s_2, \{s_1\} \rangle$. We use underlining of states to indicate which states are initial, so, e.g., $\underline{s_1} \xrightarrow{a} \underline{s_2}$ represents $\langle \{s_1, s_2\}, \{a\}, s_1 \xrightarrow{a} s_2, \{s_1, s_2\} \rangle$.

Network of LTSs. We represent models consisting of a finite number of finite-state concurrent processes by a number of LTSs and a set of *synchronisation laws*, or laws for short, defining how these LTSs interact. Together, these form a *network of LTSs* [20].[4] The process LTSs and laws imply a *system LTS*, representing the state space, which can be obtained by combining the LTSs using the laws. Given an integer $n > 0$, $1..n$ is the set of integers ranging from 1 to n. A vector $\overline{v}$ of size n contains n elements indexed by $1..n$. For $i \in 1..n$, $\overline{v}[i]$ denotes element i in $\overline{v}$.

---

[4] In [20], synchronisation laws are referred to as *rules*, but here, one may confuse these with transformation rules, that are introduced later in this section.

Definition 1 (Network of LTSs). *A network of LTSs $\mathcal{M}$ of size n is a pair $\langle \Pi, \mathcal{V} \rangle$, where*

- Π *is a vector of n (process) LTSs. For each $i \in 1..n$, we write $\Pi[i] = \langle \mathcal{S}_i, \mathcal{A}_i, \mathcal{T}_i, \mathcal{I}_i \rangle$, and $s_1 \xrightarrow{b}_i s_2$ is shorthand for $s_1 \xrightarrow{b}_{\Pi[i]} s_2$;*
- $\mathcal{V}$ *is a finite set of synchronisation laws. A synchronisation law is a tuple $\langle \bar{t}, a \rangle$, where a is an action label, and $\bar{t}$ is a vector of size n called a synchronisation vector, in which for all $i \in 1..n$, $\bar{t}[i] \in \mathcal{A}_i \cup \{\bullet\}$, where $\bullet$ is a special symbol denoting that $\Pi[i]$ performs no action.*

At times, we use a set-notation for synchronisation vectors when the involved actions may appear in any order; e.g., for $n = 2$, $\{a\}$ denotes the set of vectors $\{\langle a, \bullet \rangle, \langle \bullet, a \rangle\}$. Furthermore, for $\langle \bar{t}, a \rangle$, $Ac(\bar{t}) = \{i \mid i \in 1..n \wedge \bar{t}[i] \neq \bullet\}$ refers to the set of processes active for $\langle \bar{t}, a \rangle$, and $A(\bar{t}) = \{\bar{t}[i] \mid i \in 1..n\} \setminus \{\bullet\}$ refers to the set of actions participating in $\langle \bar{t}, a \rangle$.

The synchronous composition of the LTSs in $\mathcal{M}$, i.e. the system LTS LTS($\mathcal{M}$), is the explicit description of the state space of the model. This LTS can be obtained by combining the behaviour of the $\Pi[i]$ according to the laws in $\mathcal{V}$:

- $\mathcal{I} = \{\langle s_1, \ldots, s_n \rangle \mid \forall i \in 1..n.s_i \in \mathcal{I}_i\}$, i.e. vectors of process initial states;
- $\mathcal{A} = \{a \mid \langle \bar{t}, a \rangle \in \mathcal{V}\}$, i.e. all actions that can result from synchronisation;
- $\mathcal{S} = \mathcal{S}_1 \times \ldots \times \mathcal{S}_n$, i.e. all possible combinations of process states;
- $\mathcal{T}$ is the smallest transition relation satisfying:

$$\langle \bar{t}, a \rangle \in \mathcal{V} \wedge (\forall i \in 1..n) \left(\begin{array}{c} (\bar{t}[i] = \bullet \wedge \bar{s}'[i] = \bar{s}[i]) \\ \vee\ (\bar{t}[i] \neq \bullet \wedge \bar{s}[i] \xrightarrow{\bar{t}[i]}_i \bar{s}'[i]) \end{array} \right) \implies \bar{s} \xrightarrow{a} \bar{s}'.$$

Example 1. Consider the two LTSs on the left in Fig. 2, in which the initial states are indicated by incoming arrowheads. We combine these in a network $\mathcal{M} = \langle \Pi, \mathcal{V} \rangle$, with Π containing those LTSs in order of appearance, and $\mathcal{V} = \{(\langle a, a \rangle, a'), (\langle b, b \rangle, b'), (\langle c, \bullet \rangle, c)\}$. The synchronous composition LTS($\mathcal{M}$) is displayed on the right in Fig. 2, where for each state, the ID pair in it indicates which combination of process LTS states it corresponds with. If both process LTS states have an outgoing a-transition, then so will the corresponding state in the synchronous composition. This also holds for b-transitions, but since b has data parameters, this only works if both occurrences have the same parameters d_1, d_2, which is the case here. This demonstrates how data can be used in transition labels, and how synchronisation works with it. Finally, the c-action can be fired independently, meaning that the first process LTS can move from state 2 to 3 without synchronisation.

Divergence-Sensitive Branching Bisimilarity. As equivalence relation between LTSs, we consider divergence-sensitive branching bisimilarity (DSBB) [11,12], which is sensitive to hidden behaviour and the branching structure of an LTS, including τ-cycles. Hence, it supports not only safety, but also liveness property preservation. For liveness properties, the notion of *diverging behaviour* is

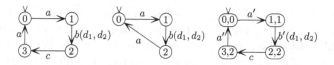

Fig. 2. Two LTSs and their synchronous composition (Example 1)

important. A state s is *diverging* iff an infinite sequence of internal actions can be performed, i.e. there exists an infinite τ-path from s, which for finite LTSs means that a τ-cycle is reachable via τ-transitions. We denote by $\rightarrow^+$ the transitive closure of $\xrightarrow{\tau}$.

Definition 2 (Divergence-Sensitive Branching Bisimulation). *A binary relation B between two sets of states $S_{\mathcal{G}_1}$, $S_{\mathcal{G}_2}$ of LTSs $\mathcal{G}_1$, $\mathcal{G}_2$ is a divergence-sensitive branching bisimulation if B is symmetric and s B t with $s \in S_{\mathcal{G}_1}$, $t \in S_{\mathcal{G}_2}$ implies that*

- *if $s \xrightarrow{a}_{\mathcal{G}_1} s'$ then*
  - *either $a = \tau$ with s' B t;*
  - *or $t \Rightarrow_{\mathcal{G}_2} \hat{t} \xrightarrow{a}_{\mathcal{G}_2} t'$ with s B $\hat{t}$ and s' B t'.*
- *if there is an infinite sequence of states $s_0, s_1, s_2, \ldots \in S_{\mathcal{G}_1}$ such that $s_0 = s$, $s_0 \xrightarrow{\tau}_{\mathcal{G}_1} s_1 \xrightarrow{\tau}_{\mathcal{G}_1} s_2 \xrightarrow{\tau}_{\mathcal{G}_1} \ldots$ and s_i B t for all $i \geq 0$, then there exists a $t' \in S_{\mathcal{G}_2}$ such that $t \rightarrow^+ t'$ and s_k B t' for some $k \geq 0$.*

Two states s and t are divergence-sensitive branching bisimilar, *noted $s \underleftrightarrow{\Delta}_b t$, if there is a divergence-sensitive branching bisimulation B with s B t.*

Two sets of states S, S' are DSBB, i.e. $S \underleftrightarrow{\Delta}_b S'$, iff $\forall s \in S. \exists s' \in S'. s \underleftrightarrow{\Delta}_b s'$ and vice versa. Two LTSs $\mathcal{G}_1, \mathcal{G}_2$ are DSBB, i.e. $\mathcal{G}_1 \underleftrightarrow{\Delta}_b \mathcal{G}_2$, iff $\mathcal{I}_{\mathcal{G}_1} \underleftrightarrow{\Delta}_b \mathcal{I}_{\mathcal{G}_2}$.

In [21], DSBB is related to a fragment of the modal μ-calculus, called L_μ^{dsbr}: if a model $\mathcal{M}_1$ satisfies an L_μ^{dsbr}-property φ, denoted by $\mathcal{M}_1 \models \varphi$, then a second model $\mathcal{M}_2$ satisfies φ iff $\mathcal{M}_1 \underleftrightarrow{\Delta}_b \mathcal{M}_2$. A similar result relates *branching bisimilarity* (BB) [12], i.e. DSBB without the divergence condition in Definition 2, and L_μ^{dsbr} safety properties, in which diverging behaviour is not relevant. In Sect. 4, we use this as follows: if we can determine that a transformation does not alter the system LTS structure, then we can conclude that φ will be preserved.

In [21,29], we actually also involve a hiding mechanism called *maximal hiding*, allowing to move LTSs to the highest possible level of abstraction w.r.t. a L_μ^{dsbr}-property φ. It involves rewriting transition labels not relevant for φ to τ, which roughly corresponds with hiding all labels not mentioned in φ. Incorporating this in property preservation checking makes the technique much more powerful, since it allows altering the semantics of a model through transformation, in ways not relevant for a given property. Given a network $\mathcal{M}_1$, let $H_\varphi(\text{LTS}(\mathcal{M}_1))$ be the maximally hidden synchronous composition of $\mathcal{M}_1$ w.r.t. property φ. Then, first of all, $\text{LTS}(\mathcal{M}_1) \models \varphi$ iff $H_\varphi(\text{LTS}(\mathcal{M}_1)) \models \varphi$, by maximal hiding [21]. Furthermore, by the relation between DSBB and L_μ^{dsbr}, if we can establish that

$H_\varphi(\text{LTS}(\mathcal{M}_1)) \leftrightarrows_b^\Delta H_\varphi(\text{LTS}(\mathcal{M}_2))$, then we can conclude that $H_\varphi(\text{LTS}(\mathcal{M}_2)) \models \varphi$, and hence, that $\text{LTS}(\mathcal{M}_2) \models \varphi$. In other words, it suffices to establish that the maximally hidden synchronous compositions are DSBB. For clarity, we only refer to hiding informally in some of the examples. It suffices to keep in mind that all labels not mentioned in the given property are hidden. For the specifics about L_μ^{dsbr}, the reader is referred to [21].

Transformation. In our setting, changes applied on a concurrent system model are represented by LTS *transformation rules* applied on the semantics of the processes of that model, i.e. on its network of LTSs. To reason about these changes, we define the notions of a rule, and matches of rules on process LTSs.

Definition 3 (Transformation Rule). *A transformation rule* $r = \langle \mathcal{L}^r, \mathcal{R}^r \rangle$ *consists of a left pattern LTS* $\mathcal{L}^r = \langle \mathcal{S}_{\mathcal{L}^r}, \mathcal{A}_{\mathcal{L}^r}, \mathcal{T}_{\mathcal{L}^r}, \mathcal{I}_{\mathcal{L}^r} \rangle$ *and a right pattern LTS* $\mathcal{R}^r = \langle \mathcal{S}_{\mathcal{R}^r}, \mathcal{A}_{\mathcal{R}^r}, \mathcal{T}_{\mathcal{R}^r}, \mathcal{I}_{\mathcal{R}^r} \rangle$, *with* $\mathcal{I}_{\mathcal{L}^r} = \mathcal{I}_{\mathcal{R}^r} = (\mathcal{S}_{\mathcal{L}^r} \cap \mathcal{S}_{\mathcal{R}^r})$.

The states $\mathcal{I}_{\mathcal{L}^r}$ (and $\mathcal{I}_{\mathcal{R}^r}$) are called the *glue-states*, and they are all initial. They form the interface between behaviour subjected to transformation and the other behaviour. Process LTS states matched by glue-states will not be removed, but their incoming and outgoing transitions may be affected.

Definition 4 (Rule Match). *A transformation rule* $r = \langle \mathcal{L}^r, \mathcal{R}^r \rangle$ *has a match* $m_r : \mathcal{S}_{\mathcal{L}^r} \hookrightarrow \mathcal{S}_\mathcal{G}$ *on an LTS* $\mathcal{G} = \langle \mathcal{S}_\mathcal{G}, \mathcal{A}_\mathcal{G}, \mathcal{T}_\mathcal{G}, \mathcal{I}_\mathcal{G} \rangle$ *iff* m_r *is injective and*

1. $\forall s_1 \xrightarrow{a}_{\mathcal{L}^r} s_2.m_r(s_1) \xrightarrow{a}_\mathcal{G} m_r(s_2)$;
2. $\forall s \in \mathcal{S}_{\mathcal{L}^r} \setminus \mathcal{I}_{\mathcal{L}^r}, p \in \mathcal{S}_\mathcal{G}$:
   - $m_r(s) \xrightarrow{a}_\mathcal{G} p \implies \exists s' \in \mathcal{S}_{\mathcal{L}^r}.s \xrightarrow{a} s' \wedge m_r(s') = p$;
   - $p \xrightarrow{a}_\mathcal{G} m_r(s) \implies \exists s' \in \mathcal{S}_{\mathcal{L}^r}.s' \xrightarrow{a} s \wedge m_r(s') = p$;
   - $m_r(s) = p \implies p \notin \mathcal{I}_\mathcal{G}$;

Note the conditions in the second clause of Definition 4. The first two are the *gluing conditions* of the *double-pushout* (DPO) method [14] for graph transformation, preventing conflicts when matching. They prevent so-called *dangling transitions*, which are transitions where only the source or target state will be removed, but not both. The final condition states that no initial state of $\mathcal{G}$ may be removed through transformation, ruling out the possibility of obtaining an LTS without an initial state.

When a left pattern is matched on part of a process LTS, transformation is performed by means of DPO. The result is that each state matched by a glue-state still exists after transformation, each state matched by a non-glue-state is removed, and each non-glue-state in a right pattern has resulted in appropriate representatives for each match of the left pattern.

In Sect. 5, we will introduce a form of *Negative Application Conditions* (NACs) [13]. The NACs of a rule express additional patterns that should *not* be matchable; a match can only be valid if the NAC patterns cannot be matched.

To facilitate explanation, we introduce a simplification without loss of generality. We assume that the $\mathcal{A}_i$ of the $\Pi[i]$ in $\mathcal{M}$ are disjoint. Any network for which this is not the case, e.g. the one given in Fig. 3, can be rewritten to one for which this holds. The simplification implies that for a rule system Σ, each rule $r \in R$ can only be applied on at most one process LTS. We use the convention that rule r_i can only be applied on process LTS $\Pi[i]$.

Sets of rules together make up a *rule system* $\Sigma = \langle R, \hat{\mathcal{V}} \rangle$, with R a set of rules and $\hat{\mathcal{V}}$ a set of new synchronisation laws to be introduced when transforming. Transformation of a network of LTSs $\mathcal{M}$ according to a rule system Σ involves identifying all possible matches for each $r \in R$ on $\mathcal{M}$, and applying transformation on those matches. We say that $I_\Sigma = \{i \mid r_i \in R\}$. It represents the so-called *subsystem under transformation*; all $\Pi[i]$ with $i \in I_\Sigma$ are transformed by Σ.

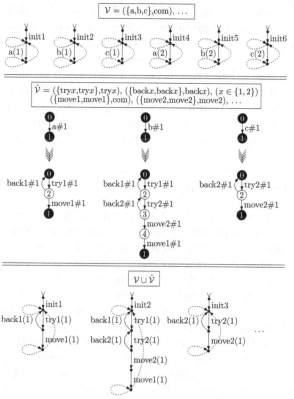

Figure 3 shows an example of applying a rule system on a network of LTSs belonging to a distributed system design consisting of six processes. The behaviour of these processes relevant for our example is displayed at the top of the figure. After an initialisation step, each process can perform internal computations, represented by the unlabelled dashed transitions. At regular intervals, each process must synchronise with two others before commencing its computation. This is defined in the network by a law in $\mathcal{V}$: $(\{a,b,c\},com)$. Actions a, b and c must have the same data parameter values for successful synchronisation, so only the first and the last three processes can potentially synchronise.

Fig. 3. Transforming multi- to two-party communication in a distributed system

In the middle of Fig. 3, the definition of a rule system with three rules is displayed, and the glue-states are coloured black. Each rule is a pair of LTSs: the top one is the left pattern, and the bottom one is the right pattern.

The rule system of Fig. 3 defines how to break down the three-party synchronisation into a series of two-party synchronisations. To make rules more general, we use place-holders $\#1, \#2, \ldots$. A place-holder in a left pattern represents that the parameters of a transition label can have any value, and the presence of the same place-holder in the corresponding right pattern indicates which transition labels should incorporate those values after transformation. In Fig. 3, the use of placeholders allows the rule system to be applicable on both the first three process LTSs and the last three. Additional laws in $\hat{\mathcal{V}}$ define the new synchronisation possibilities. This rule system is very practical if the system should eventually be able to run on hardware that does not support multi-party communication. Finally, part of the transformed network is displayed at the bottom of Fig. 3.

In the context of model transformations, it is crucial that a rule system is *terminating* and *confluent*, i.e. that the transformation is guaranteed to finish, and that it always leads to the same solution, independent of the order in which matches are processed. This is important, since a user defining how a particular model should be transformed typically has a specific resulting model in mind. Therefore, if a rule system is not confluent, it usually means that the user made some mistake. There are techniques to detect confluence, e.g. [19], which we have implemented. Here, we assume that a given rule system is confluent. Termination is achieved by the way in which we define transformation: first, all matches for all rules in the rule system are determined, and then, the rules are applied without looking for new matches. The process LTSs are finite, hence there will always be a finite number of matches.

4   Property Preservation Checking

The main contribution of our approach is the ability to efficiently check whether a rule system preserves desired functional properties, *without* analysing the potential behaviour of the input model. The verification techniques exploit the relations between DSBB and L_μ^{dsbr} properties, and BB and L_μ^{dsbr} safety properties on the one hand, and DSBB, BB, and maximal hiding on the other (see Sect. 3). Our techniques determine whether a rule system is guaranteed to preserve the structure of the synchronous composition of networks w.r.t. a property φ. This involves taking into account how the rule system can possibly be applied on networks, and checking for bisimilarities between combinations of dependent rule patterns, in which the possible synchronisation, and failure to synchronise, between rule patterns before and after transformation is analysed. The potential for synchronisation is derived from the laws and the $r_i \in R$, leading to sets of dependent rules, here referred to as *checks*. In general, a rule system can imply multiple checks. We say that Υ is the set containing all those checks. In order to compute Υ, we need a notion of *direct dependency* between rules. Behaviour in the rule patterns of r_i can directly depend on the behaviour of other rules. This is captured by the set $\delta(r_i)$. It is defined as:

$$\delta(r_i) = \bigcup_{\langle \bar{t}, a \rangle \in \mathcal{V} \cup \hat{\mathcal{V}}} \{ r_j \in R \mid (\bar{t}[i] \in \mathcal{A}_{\mathcal{L}^{r_i}} \wedge \bar{t}[j] \in \mathcal{A}_{\mathcal{L}^{r_j}}) \vee (\bar{t}[i] \in \mathcal{A}_{\mathcal{R}^{r_i}} \wedge \bar{t}[j] \in \mathcal{A}_{\mathcal{R}^{r_j}}) \}$$

Dependency is determined by the actions of the rule patterns, and the old and new laws. The *transitive closure* $\delta^+(r_i)$ contains all the rules on which r_i

depends, directly and indirectly. Essentially, a check consists of a set of dependent rules. Finally, we compute Υ as the set containing the $\delta^+(r_i)$ of all rules $r_i \in \Sigma$.

Example 2. In Fig. 3, let $\Pi[1], \ldots, \Pi[3]$ be the first three process LTSs at the top in order of appearance, and $r_1, \ldots, r_3$ be the rules in the middle in order of appearance. First of all, note that rule r_i is applicable on $\Pi[i]$, for $i \in \{1, 2, 3\}$. The relevant dependencies are $\delta^+(r_1) = \delta^+(r_2) = \delta^+(r_3) = \{r_1, r_2, r_3\}$. The same can be done concerning the other three process LTSs, by which we obtain the same set.

Before we formalise property preservation, we need to discuss one more issue. In order to correctly determine that a rule system preserves a given property, based on bisimilarities between vectors of left and right rule patterns, the rule patterns should be extended for analysis to make explicit which states are glue. For example, consider a rule r that swaps two action labels a and b between two transitions, with $\mathcal{L}^r = \underline{s_0} \xrightarrow{a} \underline{s_1}, \underline{s_0} \xrightarrow{b} \underline{s_2}$, and $\mathcal{R}^r = \underline{s_0} \xrightarrow{b} \underline{s_1}, \underline{s_0} \xrightarrow{a} \underline{s_2}$. The two LTSs are DSBB, but only because s_1 of $\mathcal{L}^r$ (and of $\mathcal{R}^r$) can be related to s_2 of $\mathcal{R}^r$ (and of $\mathcal{L}^r$). However, both these states are glue, and hence can match on states of process LTSs that have in- and/or outgoing transitions that are not present in the patterns, and therefore may not be DSBB. This means that we are actually not interested in *any* DSBB, but a DSBB in which all glue-states in the left pattern are related to themselves in the right pattern. To express this, we add a self-loop with a unique action label to each glue-state in both patterns. Formally, for each glue-state s, we add a transition $s \xrightarrow{\kappa_s} s$, with κ_s the unique label. Since with this extension, each glue-state has at least one outgoing transition that no other state has, it has to be relatable to itself when trying to construct a DSBB. For the aforementioned example, the extended patterns, called $\mathcal{L}^r_\kappa$ and $\mathcal{R}^r_\kappa$, are not DSBB.

Adding κ-*loops* solves the problem of relating glue-states, but in practice, it turns out that it can be too restrictive. We return to this in Sect. 5, and introduce an improved way to extend patterns.

Each set $D \in \Upsilon$ defines two κ-extended vectors of LTSs $\overline{\mathcal{L}}^D_\kappa, \overline{\mathcal{R}}^D_\kappa$, where for $\mathcal{G} \in \{\mathcal{L}, \mathcal{R}\}$ and all $i \in 1..n$, we have $\overline{\mathcal{G}}^D_\kappa[i] = \mathcal{G}^{r_i}_\kappa$ if $r_i \in D$. In case $r_i \notin D$, we use a place-holder state in $\overline{\mathcal{G}}^D_\kappa$ at position i to indicate inactivity of r_i. The pairs $\langle \overline{\mathcal{L}}^D_\kappa, \overline{\mathcal{R}}^D_\kappa \rangle$ are used to check for property preservation. Together with the appropriate laws,[5] these vectors are interpreted as networks of LTSs, which therefore are implicit descriptions of system LTSs in which the synchronisation of process behaviour under transformation is described.

Finally, the property preservation check can be defined as follows.

Definition 5 (Property Preservation). *Given a network of LTSs $\mathcal{M}$, an L^{dsbr}_μ-property φ, and a rule system Σ, let Σ imply a set of rule sets Υ w.r.t. $\mathcal{V}$*

---

[5] Technically, the κ-actions require laws to produce κ-transitions in the synchronous composition of a network. For clarity, we do not include them in the formalisation.

and $\hat{\mathcal{V}}$. *We say that* Σ *is* φ-*preserving* *if for all* $D \in \Upsilon$, $D' \subseteq D$, *we have*

$$H_\varphi(LTS(\langle \overline{\mathcal{L}}_\kappa^{D'}, \mathcal{V} \rangle)) \underset{b}{\leftrightarrow}^{\Delta} H_\varphi(LTS(\langle \overline{\mathcal{R}}_\kappa^{D'}, \mathcal{V} \cup \hat{\mathcal{V}} \rangle))$$

In [6], a correctness proof is provided, i.e. that indeed, Σ is φ-preserving if the DSBB conditions hold.

Note that according to Definition 5, DSBB checks are required for *all subsets* D' of all $D \in \Upsilon$. Strict subsets of D represent situations where some processes are able to synchronise, but others are not. All these situations need to be checked, since they may occur in the system LTS of an input network.

Example 3. Say we want to check the preservation of deadlock freedom for the modification step defined in Fig. 3. In [21], it is explained that this allows to abstract from all transition labels, i.e. all can be rewritten to τ. Therefore, we can restrict checks to the (internal actions) branching structure of the rule patterns.

From Example 2, we know that the only relevant dependency is $\{r_1, r_2, r_3\}$. It implies two κ-extended vectors, containing the corresponding behaviour in the left and right rule patterns, respectively. Placing the vectors in two networks, combined with $\mathcal{V}$ and $\mathcal{V} \cup \hat{\mathcal{V}}$, we can compute two system LTSs. For the first (left patterns) network, we get the system LTS $L_1 = \underline{s_0} \xrightarrow{com\#1} s_1$ (ignoring the κ-loops), and for the second, we get LTS $L_2 = \underline{t_0} \xrightarrow{try1\#1} t_1 \xrightarrow{try2\#1} t_2 \xrightarrow{move2\#1} t_3 \xrightarrow{com\#1} t_4$, $t_1 \xrightarrow{back1\#1} \underline{t_0}$, and $t_2 \xrightarrow{back2\#1} t_1$ (again, ignoring the κ-loops). After hiding all transition labels, we find that $L_1 \not\leftrightarrow_b^{\Delta} L_2$, since L_2 contains τ-cycles and L_1 does not, but they are BB, hence deadlock freedom is preserved.

Definition 5 can be used to efficiently check for the property preservation by a rule system, thereby avoiding verification from scratch of the transformed model. However, a number of conditions regarding the applicability of a rule system were identified in [29].

1. *Universal applicability:* A rule system must be *universally applicable* w.r.t. actions subjected to synchronisation of at least two parties; if such an action a appears in the left pattern of some rule r_i, then *all* occurrences of a in $\Pi[i]$ must be matched on by that rule, i.e. all occurrences will be transformed. Without universal applicability, it is very hard to reason about the ability for the new network to synchronise, since the original and the transformed synchronising behaviour may coexist.
2. *Completeness:* A rule system must be *complete*, i.e. if one synchronising action is transformed, then all actions that it depends on must be transformed.
3. *Synchronisation:* Laws introduced through transformation can only involve new actions that were not present in the input model:

$$\forall \langle \bar{t}, a \rangle \in \hat{\mathcal{V}}, i \in 1..n.\bar{t}[i] \notin \bigcup_{i \in 1..n} \mathcal{A}_i$$

The reason for this is that otherwise, new laws can alter the semantics of a model in a way not expressed by the rules.

One contribution of this paper is a proposal how to remove the completeness condition entirely and relax the synchronisation condition. In addition, we introduce a mechanism to compositionally extend a network through transformation, a new hiding technique called *non-interface hiding*, allowing to focus the analysis on interfaces between subsystems, and the notion of an *exclusive* glue-state, which allows more expressiveness for defining rules.

5   Compositional Reasoning and Exclusivity NACs

Compositional Development. One major limitation of the setup in Sects. 3 and 4 is that it does not support adding new processes. This can be solved by interpreting network vectors as infinite vectors. Each vector can be considered to be infinite, with a finite number of process LTSs and an infinite number of 'place-holder' single states. For this, we define that for all $i > n$, $\Pi[i] = s_i$. Likewise, we interpret synchronisation vectors as being extended with an infinite number of •-elements. Note that interpreting a network vector as being infinite does not affect its system LTS, as the additional processes never change state.

The extension allows the introduction of new process LTSs; a rule $r_i = \langle s, \mathcal{R}^{r_i} \rangle$, with $i > n$, effectively introduces a new process LTS isomorphic to $\mathcal{R}^{r_i}$ at position i in the network vector, since the single-state left pattern is applicable on the place-holder state at position i in the infinite vector. Note that a rule $\langle \mathcal{L}^{r_i}, s \rangle$ can be used to effectively remove a process LTS isomorphic to $\mathcal{L}^{r_i}$.

Removing the Completeness Condition. Another major limitation is the completeness condition of Sect. 4. Consider, for example, an input network with law $(\langle a, b \rangle, c)$, and we wish to transform transitions labelled b to transitions labelled b'. By the completeness condition, we would be forced to define a rule for a-transitions, even if we wish to keep these unchanged. This is not desired, since the verification technique is dictating how we should define a rule system.

Instead, we would like to be able to reason about behaviour subjected to transformation completely independent of behaviour that is not transformed. In the example, we would like to analyse a rule system applicable on b-transitions, without having to address the a-transitions. For this, we need to be able to focus our analysis entirely on the subsystem under transformation, and explicitly involve the potential for synchronisation with processes outside the subsystem, but not involve those processes themselves. Since synchronisation potential is represented by the synchronisation laws, this can be achieved by adding altered versions of laws that define synchronisation between the subsystem and the remainder of the system. The altered versions no longer require the remainder to be involved, thereby we detach the subsystem from the remainder of the system.

Definition 6 (Detaching Laws). *Given a network of LTSs $\mathcal{M} = \langle \Pi, \mathcal{V} \rangle$ and a rule system $\Sigma = \langle R, \hat{\mathcal{V}} \rangle$. We define the set of* detaching laws $\mathcal{V}_{det}$ *as follows:*

$$\mathcal{V}_{det} = \{ \langle \bar{t}', \breve{a} \rangle \mid \langle \bar{t}, a \rangle \in \mathcal{V} \wedge (Ac(\bar{t}) \cap I_\Sigma) \neq \emptyset \wedge (Ac(\bar{t}) \setminus I_\Sigma) \neq \emptyset \},$$

with $\bar{t}'[i] = \bar{t}[i]$ for all $i \in I_\Sigma$, and $\bar{t}'[i] = •$, otherwise, and $\breve{a}$ the action a annotated with the fact that it is the result of a detaching law.

For each law $\langle \bar{t}, a \rangle$ where some of the participating process LTSs $\Pi[i]$ will be transformed, i.e. $i \in Ac(\bar{t}) \cap I_\Sigma$, and some will not be, i.e. $i \in Ac(\bar{t}) \setminus I_\Sigma$, $\mathcal{V}_{det}$ contains a new law based on $\langle \bar{t}, a \rangle$, where behaviour of the latter process LTSs is ignored, and the behaviour of the former is kept. The set $\hat{\mathcal{V}}_{det}$ for the transformed network is defined in a similar way.

It is important to note that the actions resulting from laws in $\mathcal{V}_{det}$ (and $\hat{\mathcal{V}}_{det}$) should be excluded from maximal hiding. For this reason, those actions (the $\check{a}$'s) have been annotated in Definition 6. When analysing the behaviour in the transformation rules, the potential for synchronisation between the subsystem under transformation, and thereby indirectly under analysis, and the remainder of the system, should be taken into account. We refer to this potential as the *interface* of the subsystem. The structure of the interface can be observed by hiding all actions except those that are the result of applying a detaching law. We refer to this as *non-interface hiding*, in which we move an LTS to a level of abstraction where we completely focus on the synchronisation with other LTSs.

Definition 7 (Non-Interface Hiding). *Given an LTS $\mathcal{G}$, the* non-interface hidden *LTS $H^{det}(\mathcal{G})$ is defined as follows:*

- $\mathcal{S}_{H^{det}(\mathcal{G})} = \mathcal{S}_{\mathcal{G}}$;
- $\mathcal{A}_{H^{det}(\mathcal{G})} = \{ \check{a} \mid \langle s, \check{a}, s' \rangle \in \mathcal{T}_{\mathcal{G}} \} \cup \{ \tau \}$;
- $\mathcal{T}_{H^{det}(\mathcal{G})} = \{ \langle s, \check{a}, s' \rangle \mid \langle s, \check{a}, s' \rangle \in \mathcal{T}_{\mathcal{G}} \} \cup \{ \langle s, \tau, s' \rangle \mid \langle s, a, s' \rangle \in \mathcal{T}_{\mathcal{G}} \}$;
- $\mathcal{I}_{H^{det}(\mathcal{G})} = \mathcal{I}_{\mathcal{G}}$.

Maximal hiding based on a property φ and non-interface hiding based on detaching laws can be combined into a general hiding technique that hides all actions except those that are relevant for the interface and/or the property. We denote this hiding by H^{det}_φ. Now, we redefine property preservation, taking the new notions into account.

Definition 8 (Improved Property Preservation). *Given a network of LTSs $\mathcal{M}$, an L^{dsbr}_μ-property φ, and a rule system Σ, let Σ imply a set of rule sets Υ w.r.t. $\mathcal{V}$ and $\hat{\mathcal{V}}$. We say that Σ is φ-preserving if for all $D \in \Upsilon$, $D' \subseteq D$, we have*

$$H^{det}_\varphi(LTS(\langle \overline{\mathcal{L}}^{D'}_\kappa, \mathcal{V} \cup \mathcal{V}_{det} \rangle)) \underset{b}{\overset{\Delta}{\leftrightarrow}} H^{det}_\varphi(LTS(\langle \overline{\mathcal{R}}^{D'}_\kappa, \mathcal{V} \cup \hat{\mathcal{V}} \cup \mathcal{V}_{det} \cup \hat{\mathcal{V}}_{det} \rangle))$$

Compared to Definition 5, the rule networks incorporate $\mathcal{V}_{det}$ and $\hat{\mathcal{V}}_{det}$, which allows for subsystems under transformation to be analysed in isolation.

For this new definition, the completeness condition can be dropped. However, for that to be useful, we need to relax the synchronisation condition. Otherwise, we would not be able to express new laws involving non-transformed behaviour.

The new condition is as follows: for all $\langle \bar{t}, a \rangle \in \hat{\mathcal{V}}$, there must exist a $\langle \bar{t}', a' \rangle \in \mathcal{V}$ such that for all $i \in 1..n \setminus I_\Sigma$, $\bar{t}[i] = \bar{t}'[i]$, and for all $i \in I_\Sigma$, both $\bar{t}'[i] \in \mathcal{A}_{\mathcal{L}^{r_i}} \cup \{ \bullet \}$ and $\bar{t}[i] \in \mathcal{A}_{\mathcal{R}^{r_i}} \cup \{ \bullet \}$. This expresses formally that the remainder of the system involved in the synchronisation was also allowed to synchronise in that setup in the original network, while the subsystem is allowed to be altered.

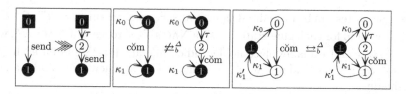

Fig. 4. κ-extension without and with exclusive glue-states

Example 4. Say we have a single rule r_2 with $\mathcal{L}^{r_2} = \underline{s_0} \overset{b}{\rightarrow} \underline{s_1}$, $\mathcal{R}^{r_2} = \underline{s_0} \overset{b'}{\rightarrow} \underline{s_1}$ in a rule system with $\hat{\mathcal{V}} = \{(\langle a, b' \rangle, c)\}$, that we wish to apply on a network $\mathcal{M}$ with $\mathcal{V} = \{(\langle a, b \rangle, c)\}$. By our convention, r_2 matches on $\Pi[2]$. Furthermore, by Definition 6, we have $\mathcal{V}_{det} = \{(\langle \bullet, b \rangle, \check{c})\}$ and $\hat{\mathcal{V}}_{det} = \{(\langle \bullet, b' \rangle, \check{c})\}$. Since there is only one rule, we can only construct check $\{r_2\}$. From this, by Definition 8, we obtain two networks $(\langle s, \mathcal{L}_\kappa^{r_2} \rangle, \{(\langle a, b \rangle, c), (\langle \bullet, b \rangle, \check{c})\})$ and $(\langle s, \mathcal{R}_\kappa^{r_2} \rangle, \{(\langle a, b \rangle, c), (\langle \bullet, b \rangle, \check{c}), (\langle \bullet, b' \rangle, \check{c})\})$, with s a placeholder state. For both networks, the synchronous composition after H_φ^{det}-hiding is the LTS $\underline{s_0} \overset{\check{c}}{\rightarrow} \underline{s_1}$ with κ-loops for s_0 and s_1. The fact that the networks are DSBB indicates that both networks have the same potential for synchronisation with other system parts. This ensures that for a given L_μ^{dsbr}-property φ satisfied by $\mathcal{M}$, the transformed $\mathcal{M}$ satisfies φ as well.

Exclusivity NACs. Consider an LTS $L = \underline{s_0} \xrightarrow{compute} s_1 \xrightarrow{send} s_0$, in which some computation is performed and the result is sent to another process using a law $(\{send, rec\}, com)$. Furthermore, consider that we wish to transform the *send*-transition through a rule system Σ containing a single rule with $\mathcal{L}^r = \underline{0} \xrightarrow{send} \underline{1}$ and $\mathcal{R}^r = \underline{0} \overset{\tau}{\rightarrow} 2 \xrightarrow{send} \underline{1}$. This rule is displayed on the left in Fig. 4. When analysing the rule patterns in isolation, which can be achieved by determining the sets of detaching laws, Σ turns out not to be property preserving for any φ, since added κ-loops prevent that, which is shown in the middle of Fig. 4. In particular, state 2 in the right LTS is not DSBB to state 0 on the left, due to the absence of an outgoing κ_0-transition. However, for our LTS L, the κ-loops do not truly represent the situation, since from state s_1, one can only perform a *send* action, but in the comparison, state 0, directly resulting from the glue-state matched on s_1, has other options, represented by the κ_0-transition.

To remove this limitation, we extend the notion of a rule further with *exclusive out* and *exclusive in/out* glue-states. Exclusive out glue-states are glue-states with the condition that they can only be matched on process LTS states for which all outgoing transitions are matched by the rule left pattern, i.e. they have no outgoing transition with a target state that is not matched. With exclusive out glue-states, a user can express that from particular states, one can only engage in matched behaviour, and not leave the pattern. In addition to this, exclusive in/out glue-states also have a similar condition for incoming transitions.

We extend the definition of a rule r with a set of exclusive out glue-states $\mathcal{E}_{out}^r$, and a set of exclusive in/out glue-states $\mathcal{E}_{in/out}^r$, with $\mathcal{E}_{in/out}^r \subseteq \mathcal{E}_{out}^r \subseteq \mathcal{I}_{\mathcal{L}^r}$ (and therefore, they are also subsets of $\mathcal{I}_{\mathcal{R}^r}$). We define $\mathcal{E}^r = \mathcal{E}_{out}^r \cup \mathcal{E}_{in/out}^r$.

These glue-states can be formalised using NACs. For a given rule $r = \langle \mathcal{L}^r, \mathcal{R}^r, \mathcal{E}^r_{out}, \mathcal{E}^r_{in/out} \rangle$, we add for each glue-state $s \in \mathcal{E}^r$ a NAC $s \not\xrightarrow{*} s'$ to a set of NACs $\mathcal{N}^r$, with s' a new state and $*$ a label place-holder indicating 'any label', and for each glue-state $s \in \mathcal{E}^r_{in/out}$, we add a NAC $s' \not\xrightarrow{*} s$, again with s' a new state and $*$ a label place-holder.

The patterns can be extended, taking exclusive glue-states into account.

Definition 9. *Given rule $r = \langle \mathcal{L}^r, \mathcal{R}^r, \mathcal{E}^r_{out}, \mathcal{E}^r_{in/out} \rangle$, the κ-extended $r_\kappa = \langle \mathcal{L}^r_\kappa, \mathcal{R}^r_\kappa, \mathcal{E}^r_{out,\kappa}, \mathcal{E}^r_{in/out,\kappa} \rangle$ is (re-)defined as follows:*

- *For $\mathcal{G} = \{\mathcal{L}, \mathcal{R}\}$, $\mathcal{G}^r_\kappa = \langle \mathcal{S}_{\mathcal{G}^r_\kappa}, \mathcal{A}_{\mathcal{G}^r_\kappa}, \mathcal{T}_{\mathcal{G}^r_\kappa}, \mathcal{I}_{\mathcal{G}^r_\kappa} \rangle$, where:*
  - $\mathcal{S}_{\mathcal{G}^r_\kappa} = \mathcal{S}_{\mathcal{G}^r} \cup \{\bot\}$
  - $\mathcal{A}_{\mathcal{G}^r_\kappa} = \mathcal{A}_{\mathcal{G}^r} \cup \{\kappa_s \mid s \in \mathcal{I}_{\mathcal{G}^r} \setminus \mathcal{E}^r_{in/out}\} \cup \{\kappa'_s \mid s \in \mathcal{I}_{\mathcal{G}^r} \setminus \mathcal{E}^r\}$
  - $\mathcal{T}_{\mathcal{G}^r_\kappa} = \mathcal{T}_{\mathcal{G}^r} \cup \{\langle \bot, \kappa_s, s \rangle \mid s \in \mathcal{I}_{\mathcal{G}^r} \setminus \mathcal{E}^r_{in/out}\} \cup \{\langle s, \kappa'_s, \bot \rangle \mid s \in \mathcal{I}_{\mathcal{G}^r} \setminus \mathcal{E}^r\}$
  - $\mathcal{I}_{\mathcal{G}^r_\kappa} = \mathcal{E}^r_{in/out} \cup \{\bot\}$
- $\mathcal{E}^r_{out,\kappa} = \mathcal{E}^r_{out}$
- $\mathcal{E}^r_{in/out,\kappa} = \mathcal{E}^r_{in/out}$

with $\bot$ a new initial state.

The new situation for our example is displayed on the right in Fig. 4, given that state 0 in the rule is an exclusive out glue-state (indicated by the fact that it is square in the rule on the left). The new state $\bot$ represents all the states in an LTS outside of a pattern match, and is used to formalise how a match of a pattern can relate to those states.

From $\bot$, the pattern can be entered via glue-states, and exited via non-exclusive glue-states. From state 0, one no longer has an alternative to performing the *cŏm* (or τ)-transition, leading to the two LTSs being DSBB. In the next section, an example of using exclusive in/out glue-states is presented.

Correctness. The extensions presented in this section do not break the correctness of property preservation checking. First of all, exclusive glue-states can be handled in the proof by using the fact that such states do not have unmatched outgoing transitions (and incoming transitions, in the case of exclusive in/out glue-states). Second of all, the extensions concerning the detaching laws and the new synchronisation condition requires a more involved change to the proof.

Essentially, the extensions allow to determine that the LTS described by a subsystem under transformation in isolation is DSBB to the LTS described by the transformed subsystem. Since synchronisation with the remainder of the system can only be done via detaching laws, we know that both the original and the transformed subsystem will interact in the system in bisimilar ways, hence the overall system LTS maintains its structure.

An Example: Developing a Distributed System Finally, we demonstrate the use of the improvements presented in this section as part of our system development technique. We do this by means of an example of a producer-consumer system.

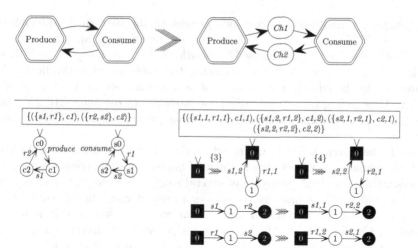

Fig. 5. Introducing channel components in a distributed system

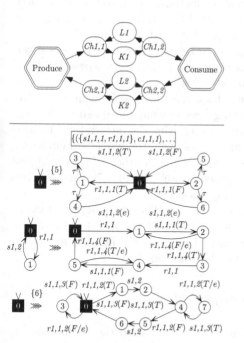

Fig. 6. Introducing ABP

In the left upper corner of Fig. 5, a schematic overview is given of a system in which the first component produces and sends a message, and the second one consumes that and sends a report back. We capture the semantics as displayed below the overview; two LTSs describe the components, in which the initial states are indicated by an incoming arrowhead, and two laws establish their synchronisation (the laws for *produce* and *consume* are not displayed).

In order to capture the use of channels more explicitly, we introduce two new components $Ch1$, $Ch2$ through a rule system Σ_1. The new system is presented schematically to the right of the initial model, and rule system Σ_1 is displayed below that.

The extension to introduce new processes is crucial; the numbers above the transformation arrows indicate the IDs of the newly introduced process LTSs within the new network. Exclusive in/out glue-states are displayed as black, square states with an incoming arrowhead. They can accurately represent the initial states of newly introduced process LTSs, since those states neither have incoming, nor outgoing transitions that are not present in the pattern introducing the process LTS. Say we want to check the preservation of an L_μ^{dsbr}-property $\varphi = [\text{true}^*]\,[produce]\,([(\neg consume)^*]\,\neg\textbf{deadlock} \land [\neg consume]\, \dashv)$, with **deadlock** $= [\text{true}^*][\neg\tau]\textbf{false} \land [\tau]\,\dashv$ expressing the presence of a deadlock. This expresses the inevitable reachability of a *consume* action after a *produce* action. After hiding all actions except for *produce* and *consume* [21], Σ_1 passes the check, i.e. relevant combinations of rule patterns lead to DSBB LTSs w.r.t. φ.

In the final step in Fig. 6, we introduce the Alternating Bit Protocol (ABP) for both channels, to reflect that in the final implementation, these channels will be lossy. Rule system Σ_2 consists of several rules, all of one of the three types that are displayed; the first one introduces a lossy channel, in this case *L1*, but *K1*, *L2*, and *K2* are introduced in a similar way. The second rule is used to transform *Ch1* into *Ch1,1*, which sends messages with an alternating bit to one lossy channel, and receives acknowledgements over the other channel.

Component *Ch2* is transformed similarly to *Ch2,2*. Finally, components *Ch1,2* and *Ch2,1* are introduced, which receive the messages, and, depending on the alternating bit, requests them to be resent, or forwards them to the other party. After hiding w.r.t. φ and detaching laws related to actions *s1,2*, *r1,1*, *s2,2*, and *r2,1*, i.e. the actions of the original channels that need to synchronise with the producer and consumer, Σ_2 does not preserve DSBB, since it introduces divergence, but it preserves BB, hence φ is preserved under the fairness condition that sending a message cannot fail infinitely often.

Note that in the final step, we do not have rules for the Consume and Produce components. Thanks to the detaching laws technique, we can analyse the introduction of ABP in isolation, without incorporating the remainder of the system. Without it, we would have to resort to analysing the whole system again, since all components are (indirectly) dependent on each other. Now, the largest LTS analysed contains 38 states, as opposed to an LTS of 1,720 states when performing the check without the detaching laws.

Finally, the use of exclusive glue-states is crucial. They accurately reflect the possible relation between matches of rule systems and the remaining states of process LTSs in general. This provides us with more potential to define transformations that can be verified in a model-independent way.

6   Implementation and Benchmark Results

REFINER is implemented in PYTHON and can be run from the command-line. It is platform-independent, and allows performing behavioural transformations of networks of LTSs, and checking property preservation. It integrates with the action-based, explicit-state model checking toolsets CADP [8] and MCRL2 [5]. These tools can be used to specify and verify concurrent systems. REFINER uses the MCRL2 tool LTSCOMPARE to perform bisimilarity comparisons.

Definitions 5 and 8 indicate how property preservation checking could be performed in parallel; once the set of rule vectors Υ has been derived, system

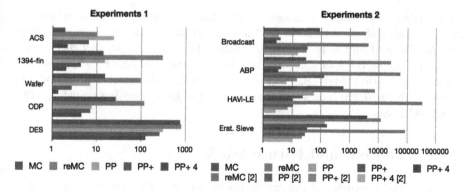

Fig. 7. Runtime comparisons (in seconds) of verification and property preservation checking. *(re)MC* = Model Checking (after transformation). *PP* = prop. pres. *PP+* = improved prop. pres. *PP+ 4* = 4-threaded PP+

LTSs must be constructed and compared for each (non-empty) subset of each $D \in \Upsilon$. The individual comparisons can be done independently of each other. REFINER can launch multiple comparison threads, thereby exploiting multi-core architectures.

We ran REFINER on a machine with a quad-core INTEL XEON E5520 2.27 GHz processor, 1 TB RAM, running FEDORA 12. As test input, we selected nine case studies, two newly created ones, three from the set of MCRL2 models distributed with its toolset, and four from the set of CADP models.[6] Each model was subjected to one or two transformations, of the following types: (1) adding internal computations, (2) adding support for lossy channels by introducing the Alternating Bit Protocol (the ABP case), and (3) breaking down broadcast synchronisations as in Fig. 3 (the broadcast and the HAVi leader election case). To give an indication of the state spaces sizes: the ACS case state space after transformation consists of about 22 thousand states, while after the second transformation, the HAVi-LE state space consists of 3 billion states. Relative to that, the verification runtimes are indicative of the sizes of the other state spaces.

Figure 7 compares runtimes for each model of verifying a property using the CADP 2011-b tools GENERATOR and EVALUATOR (this involves system LTS generation), and checking property preservation of the transformation using REFINER. Note the logarithmic scale. We performed one transformation per model for the experiments on the left, and two for those on the right ('[2]' indicates the runtimes after the second transformation).

The experiments demonstrate that preservation checking with REFINER is several orders of magnitude faster compared to verifying the property again, if the state space is of reasonable size. This is not surprising, as the check only focusses on the applied change, not the resulting state space. Comparing the runtimes with those of other model checkers therefore leads to the same conclusion.

---

[6] The required files are available at http://www.win.tue.nl/~awijs/refiner.

Furthermore, the results demonstrate that the check with the improvements of Sect. 5 is often about 4 times faster than the original check, and linear speedups can be obtained on top of that with parallel checking. The parallel checks were performed using the four cores available on the test machine ($PP+4$), and further parallelisation is trivial. To give an indication of the number of bisimilarity checks performed, the largest number was 315 checks, for the first transformation in the ABP case.

7 Conclusions and Future Work

We presented a number of improvements of our property preservation checking technique for step-wise system development. Now, we are able to compositionally add new components and we have improved the ability to verify rule systems. With the new features, verification is made less intrusive to the designer, and she has more possibilities to step-wise construct her system through verified transformation steps.

As future work, we will continue to determine through experimentation whether there are more limitations in our technique that should be removed. Our final goal is to have a mature theory for verifying rule systems, and based on that, construct a model transformation language suitable for expressing verifiable transformation steps at the level of action-based modelling languages. This theory should also support timed behaviour, either using a timed version of bisimilarity, e.g. [7], or by modelling time in an untimed setting, e.g. [26]. Finally, possible applications of directed search techniques [27,30] will be investigated.

References

1. Abadi, M., Lamport, L.: The existence of refinement mappings. Theor. Comput. Sci. **82**, 253–284 (1991)
2. Abrial, J.-R., Butler, M., Hallerstede, S., Hoang, T.S., Mehta, F., Voisin, L.: RODIN: an open toolset for modelling and reasoning in EVENT-B. STTT **12**(6), 447–466 (2010)
3. Basu, A., Bensalem, S., Bozga, M., Combaz, J., Jaber, M., Nguyen, T.-H., Sifakis, J.: Rigorous component-based system design using the BIP framework. IEEE Softw. **28**(3), 41–48 (2011)
4. Blech, J.O., Glesner, S., Leitner, J.: Formal verification of Java code generation from UML models. In: Fujaba Days 2005, pp. 49–56 (2005)
5. Cranen, S., Groote, J.F., Keiren, J.J.A., Stappers, F.P.M., de Vink, E.P., Wesselink, W., Willemse, T.A.C.: An overview of the mCRL2 toolset and its recent advances. In: Piterman, N., Smolka, S.A. (eds.) TACAS 2013 (ETAPS 2013). LNCS, vol. 7795, pp. 199–213. Springer, Heidelberg (2013)
6. Engelen, L.J.P., Wijs, A.J.: Checking property preservation of refining transformations for model-driven development. CS-Report 12–08, TU Eindhoven (2012)
7. Fokkink, W.J., Pang, J., Wijs, A.J.: Is timed branching bisimilarity an equivalence indeed? In: Pettersson, P., Yi, W. (eds.) FORMATS 2005. LNCS, vol. 3829, pp. 258–272. Springer, Heidelberg (2005)

8. Garavel, H., Lang, F., Mateescu, R., Serwe, W.: CADP 2010: a toolbox for the construction and analysis of distributed processes. In: Abdulla, P.A., Leino, K.R.M. (eds.) TACAS 2011. LNCS, vol. 6605, pp. 372–387. Springer, Heidelberg (2011)
9. Giese, H., Glesner, S., Leitner, J., Schäfer, W., Wagner, R.: Towards verified model transformations. In: 3rd International Workshop on Model Development, Validation and Verification (MoDeVVa 2006), pp. 78–93. IEEE Press, New York (2006)
10. Giese, H., Lambers, L.: Towards automatic verification of behavior preservation for model transformation via invariant checking. In: Ehrig, H., Engels, G., Kreowski, H.-J., Rozenberg, G. (eds.) ICGT 2012. LNCS, vol. 7562, pp. 249–263. Springer, Heidelberg (2012)
11. van Glabbeek, R.J., Luttik, B., Trčka, N.: Branching bisimilarity with explicit divergence. Fundam. Inform. 93(4), 371–392 (2009)
12. van Glabbeek, R.J., Weijland, W.P.: Branching time and abstraction in bisimulation semantics. J. ACM 43(3), 555–600 (1996)
13. Habel, A., Heckel, R., Taentzer, G.: Graph grammars with negative application conditions. Fundam. Inform. 26(3–4), 287–313 (1996)
14. Heckel, R.: Graph transformation in a nutshell. Electron. Notes Theor. Comput. Sci. 148, 187–198 (2006)
15. Hülsbusch, M., König, B., Rensink, A., Semenyak, M., Soltenborn, Ch., Wehrheim, H.: Showing full semantics preservation in model transformation - a comparison of techniques. In: Méry, D., Merz, S. (eds.) IFM 2010. LNCS, vol. 6396, pp. 183–198. Springer, Heidelberg (2010)
16. Kahsai, T., Roggenbach, M.: Property preserving refinement for CSP-CASL. In: Corradini, A., Montanari, U. (eds.) WADT 2008. LNCS, vol. 5486, pp. 206–220. Springer, Heidelberg (2009)
17. Kozen, D.: Results on the propositional μ-calculus. Theoret. Comput. Sci. 27, 333–354 (1983)
18. Kundu, S., Lerner S., Gupta, R.: Automated refinement checking of concurrent systems. In: 26th International Conference on Computer-Aided Design (ICCAD 2007), pp. 318–325. IEEE Press, New York (2007)
19. Lambers, L., Ehrig, H.: Efficient conflict detection in graph transformation systems by essential critical pairs. Electron. Notes Theor. Comput. Sci. 211, 17–26 (2008)
20. Lang, F.: Exp.Open 2.0: a flexible tool integrating partial order, compositional, and on-the-fly verification Methods. In: Romijn, J.M.T., Smith, G.P., van de Pol, J. (eds.) IFM 2005. LNCS, vol. 3771, pp. 70–88. Springer, Heidelberg (2005)
21. Mateescu, R., Wijs, A.: Property-dependent reductions for the modal mu-calculus. In: Groce, A., Musuvathi, M. (eds.) SPIN Workshops 2011. LNCS, vol. 6823, pp. 2–19. Springer, Heidelberg (2011)
22. Narayanan, A., Karsai, G.: Towards verifying model transformations. Electron. Notes Theor. Comput. Sci. 211, 191–200 (2008)
23. Sokolsky, O.V., Smolka, S.A.: Incremental model checking in the modal mu-calculus. In: Dill, D.L. (ed.) CAV 1994. LNCS, vol. 818, pp. 351–363. Springer, Heidelberg (1994)
24. Swamy, G.M.: Incremental methods for formal verification and logic synthesis. Ph.D. thesis, University of California (1996)
25. Varró, D., Pataricza, A.: Automated formal verification of model transformations. In: Critical Systems Development with UML (CSDUML 2003), pp. 63–78 (2003)
26. Wijs, A.J.: Achieving Discrete relative timing with untimed process algebra. In: 12th International Conference on Engineering of Complex Computer Systems (ICECCS 2007), pp. 35–44. IEEE Press, New York (2007)

27. Wijs, A.J.: What to do next?: analysing and optimising system behaviour in time. Ph.D. thesis, VU University, Amsterdam (2007)
28. Wijs, A.J., Engelen, L.J.P.: Incremental formal verification for model refining. In: 9th International Workshop on Model Development, Validation and Verification (MoDeVVa 2012), pp. 29–34. ACM Press, New York (2012)
29. Wijs, A., Engelen, L.: Efficient property preservation checking of model refinements. In: Piterman, N., Smolka, S.A. (eds.) TACAS 2013 (ETAPS 2013). LNCS, vol. 7795, pp. 565–579. Springer, Heidelberg (2013)
30. Wijs, A.J., Lisser, B.: Distributed extended beam search for quantitative model checking. In: Edelkamp, S., Lomuscio, A. (eds.) MoChArt IV. LNCS (LNAI), vol. 4428, pp. 166–184. Springer, Heidelberg (2007)

A Formal Model for Service-Based Behavior Specification Using Stream-Based I/O Tables

Xiuna Zhu[✉]

Institut Für Informatik, Technische Universität München,
Boltzmannstr. 3, 85748 Garching Bei München, Germany
zhux@in.tum.de

Abstract. The increasing complexity of embedded systems makes the formal specification of requirements both more important and more difficult. Services can help provide a foundation for model-driven requirements engineering for multi-functional embedded systems. This paper provides a conceptual framework that applies a novel modeling approach to the development of embedded systems. We suggest tables as pragmatic specification formalism for a both precise and readable specification of systems, their interfaces, and their functional properties. By translating tables into logical formulas, which define precise semantics for them, the structure specification and refinement of system can be contained. The approach is illustrated by a case study – a tabular specification of a SwStore system.

1 Introduction

Over the years, a number of description techniques and models have been proposed to enhance the development process of embedded systems. Tabular notation for state machines may greatly facilitate the specification and analysis of the system in specific domains. Tabular notation seems to be explicitly useful for systems with a large number of transitions between states or rather for those with complex enabling conditions [1]. Using the tabular specification technique for interactive and embedded systems can quickly and smoothly translate the textual requirements to formal specification, which can be easily understood and used by domain experts. Existing approaches using tabular notation in model-driven requirements engineering have been demonstrated by a number of projects (e.g., Darlington Nuclear Power Plants Shutdown System [2]) and tools [3]. Examples of those approaches include Software Cost Reduction (SCR) [4], AND/OR tables in Requirements State Machine Language (RSML) [5], Parnas Tables [6]. Additionally, most of those methods have well-defined semantics [7].

However, because of the high degree of dependency between functional units, effective and pragmatic formal specification of the behavior of components is still a challenge. Furthermore, the structure specification of multi-functional systems is a domain of requirements engineering that is not sufficiently understood so far. In complex embedded systems, such as large-scale heterogeneous embedded

J.L. Fiadeiro et al. (Eds.): FACS 2013, LNCS 8348, pp. 369–383, 2014.
DOI: 10.1007/978-3-319-07602-7_22, © Springer International Publishing Switzerland 2014

ones, software interacts with other systems, devices, sensors, and actuators. Their complexity increases due to the large number of functionalities and components, and due to the dependence relationship between them. Thus, those systems must be decomposed into several smaller components in order to manage complexity and facilitate their implementation and verification.

Behavior model compositionality, therefore, remains a difficult, labor-intensive task. In this paper, we work with the tabular specification method as a description technique for specifying I/O machines, especially stream-based I/O tables [8]. We address the lack of a comprehensive integrated approach to the structured modeling of functional requirements by introducing a tabular specification method based on (de)composition of the tabular behavior specification. We use the FOCUS framework (see [10–12]) as a semantic and methodological basis, which provides an extremely powerful mathematical model for distributed, concurrent, and interactive systems. It furthermore provides a comprehensive class of concepts for the logical specification, refinement, and verification of interactive and reactive systems.

This paper introduces a formal model for system behavior specification and software architectures using stream-based I/O tables. The basic building block of models is a service-based formal representation of the functionality. In order to deal with the complex dependencies and interrelations between system functionalities, we discuss the question of how services can be combined into service-based specifications and composed as component-based architectures. The present work explores an integrated method to specify the behavior formally and generate from these logical formulas specification that allow us to perform logical manipulations and to prove properties of the specified components. The SwStore system using tabular specification is illustrated by this approach.

2   Tabular Specification

2.1   Syntactic Interface

A component can be implemented by many independent services. The overall functionality of an embedded system actually can be structured into a hierarchy of its sub-services. We may decompose each component into a family of sub-services and each of these services again and again into families of their sub-service. Understanding the functionality of a system requires us not only to understand its single service in families of sub-service, but also to figure out the relations between them.

The syntactic interface of a system or component can be defined as follows:

Definition 1 *(Syntactic interface). The syntactic interface of a system or component is denoted by* $(I \blacktriangleright O)$*. Let* I *be a set of typed input channels and* O *be a set of typed output channels, the pair* (I, O) *characterizes the syntactic interface of a system.*   □

Table 1. Schematic form of an stream-based I/O table with input and output channels

preCond	State	I_1	I_2	...	I_n	O_1	O_2	...	O_m	State'	postCond
p_1	s_1	i_1^1	i_2^1	...	i_n^1	o_1^1	o_2^1	...	o_m^1	s_1'	q_1
p_2	s_2	i_1^2	i_2^2	...	i_n^2	o_1^2	o_2^2	...	o_m^2	s_2'	q_2
...	...	...	...	...	...	...	...	...	...	...	...
p_k	s_k	i_1^k	i_2^k	...	i_n^k	o_1^k	o_2^k	...	o_m^k	s_k'	q_k

A component with the syntactic interface $(I \blacktriangleright O)$ is given by the function $F : \overrightarrow{I} \to \wp(\overrightarrow{O})$, which fulfills the timing property only for the input histories with nonempty output set (let $x, z \in \overrightarrow{I}, y \in \overrightarrow{O}, t \in \mathbb{N}$):

$$F.x \neq \varnothing \wedge F.z \neq \varnothing \wedge x{\downarrow}_t = z{\downarrow}_t \Rightarrow \{y{\downarrow}_{t+1} : y \in F(x)\} = \{y{\downarrow}_{t+1} : y \in F(z)\}. \quad (1)$$

The set $Dom(F) = \{x : F(x) \neq \varnothing\}$ is called the *service domain*. The set $Ran(F) = \{y \in F.x : x \in Dom(F)\}$ is called the *service range*. By $F[I \blacktriangleright O]$ we denote the set of all service interfaces with input channels I and output channels O.

Theorem 1 (partial service). *An I/O-function $F : \overrightarrow{I} \to \wp(\overrightarrow{O})$ is called partial if $F(x) = \varnothing$ for some $x \in \overrightarrow{I}$.* $\qquad\qquad\Box$

A component is total, while a service may be partial. For a component there are nonempty sets of behavior for each input. The concept of "service" is close to the idea of a use case in object-oriented analysis. It can be seen as the formalization of this idea. A service provides a partial view of a component, and a service has similar syntactic interface as a component. However, its behavior is "partial" in contrast to the totality of a component interface. Partiality here means that a service is defined only for a subset of its input histories. A service output contrasts to that of a component, in which the causality requirement implies that for a component F either output set $F.x$ are empty for all x or none. A service, instead, may be a partial function.

2.2   Properties of Tabular Specifications

In [1] we have argued that the formal specification of the distributed reactive systems can be written in an easily readable and understandable but still precise manner by tables. In this section we describe how we use the tables in our specifications and which entries we allow in the tables.

The following scheme (Table 1) is provided for the I/O table introduced above. The column blocks are distinguished by this scheme. The I/O table has two blocks of columns with a vertical double line which separates premises (left) from conclusions (right).

The actions of the state transition diagram can be specified as the state transition rules in Table 1. If overlapping conditions trigger different behavior, the specification is *inconsistent* or *nondeterministic*. Nondeterminism can be resolved by transition priorities. Transitions with high priority are preferred to those with low priority. But in our method nondeterminism is considered invalid.

The structure of the tables offers a natural way of checking their soundness. Analyzing the coverage of each header helps to determine if the specification is complete, and analyzing the disjointness of each header helps to determine if the specification is consistent in the sense that there is no unwanted nondeterminism [9]. The safety and causality properties have been discussed in [10]. In this paper we will explain a way to analyze the consistency and completeness properties of specification by analyzing the semantic interpretation of the tables using the following logical formula.

The I/O table can be converted to the formal specification of an abstract I/O table T', as shown below.

$$T' = \begin{array}{|c|} \hline p_1 \\ \hline p_2 \\ \hline \cdots \\ \hline p_k \\ \hline \end{array}$$

Theorem 2 (Domain and range). *Let $F(T)$ be a function that is specified by an I/O table T. Let $dom(F(T))$ and let $range(F(T))$ denote domain and range respectively. Here, $dom(F(T)) \subseteq I_1 \times \cdots \times I_n$ and $range(F(T)) \subseteq O_1 \times \cdots \times O_m$.*   □

Theorem 3 (Consistency and completeness). *Let $x_1, \ldots, x_m$ be a list of all free variables that appear on at least one of the predicates: $p_1, \ldots, p_k$.*

A tuple $(p_1, \ldots, p_k)$ is called consistent if

$$\neg \, (\exists x_1, \ldots, x_m . \vee_{1 \leq i < j \leq k}(p_i \wedge p_j)). \tag{2}$$

A tuple $(p_1, \ldots, p_k)$ is called complete if

$$\forall x_1, \ldots, x_m . p_1 \vee \cdots \vee p_k. \tag{3}$$

□

In order to specify a component, we have to specify possible observations of the behavior of the component from the viewpoint of the environment. Given a component with signature $(I \blacktriangleright O)$, the environment of the component is able to send an input stream I^ω to the component and receive a message O^ω produced by the component. Patterns for multiple input and output ports are just conjunctions of patterns for single ports – that is, predicate expression of the form $p_1 \wedge p_2 \wedge \cdots \wedge p_n$.

2.3 Motivating Example

Our work studies the questions of how to represent a given and specified service by a set of sub-services, how to understand the overall functionality of multi-functional systems, and how to analyze the relationships as well as dependencies between sub-services.

A system called $SwStore$ allows us to store, read and update numbers, with two input channels cx and cz and two output channels cy and cr. The storing and updating service can be switched *off* and *on*. As long as the "mode" is switched *off*, input cz to the system is ignored. The service communicates messages that are listed in the Table 2. Here set(n) is the message for setting the channel cz to $n(n \in \mathbb{N})$. The type of each channel is defined as follows:

$$
\begin{aligned}
type\ Switch &= \{switch\} \\
type\ AccData &= \{read\} \cup \{set(n) : n \in \mathbb{N}\} \\
type\ OnOff &= \{on, off\} \\
type\ Ack &= \{done\} \cup \mathbb{N}
\end{aligned}
\tag{4}
$$

The behavior of the service $SwStore$ is described by the specifications in the FOCUS framework as follows:

$=$ Service:SwStore($constant\ j \in \mathbb{N}$) $=\!=\!=\!=\!=\!=\!=$ timed $=$
in $cx : Switch$; $cz : AccData$
out $cy : OnOff$; $cr : Ack$
loc $m : OnOff$; $v : \mathbb{N}$
init $m = Off$; $v = 0$
$\forall v \in \mathbb{N}, m \in OnOff^* :$ $\quad TiTable_{SwStore}$

In the specification of Service $SwStore$, we define the names and data types of the channels, including each input, output, and local channel, and the initial value of each local channel. As shown in Table 2, the description of the behavior of the service $SwStore$ is specified by a stream-based I/O table named $tiTable_{SwStore}$. In Table 2, m' and v' denote the values of the state attributes after a state transition. By "-" we denote an empty sequence of the message. By "?" we denote an arbitrary value (includes the empty sequences).

3 Tabular Specification of Services

The service-based specification defines the functional viewpoint of the system and structures the user functionality into services without any architectural details. The specification consists of a set of services and a set of dependency

Table 2. Service SwStore as a state transition table

tiTable $Service_{SwStore}$:$\forall\, t, j \in \mathbb{N}$

m	v	cx	cz	m'	v'	cy	cr
off	j	-	?	off	j	-	-
off	j	switch	-	on	j	on	-
off	j	switch	read	on	j	on	j
off	j	switch	set(k)	on	j	on	k
on	j	-	read	on	j	-	j
on	j	-	set(n)	on	n	-	done
on	j	switch	?	off	j	off	-
on	j	-	-	on	j	-	-

relationships between them. A service specifies a partial and non-deterministic relation between certain inputs and outputs of the system, which interact with their environment within a number of scenarios. In other words, a service is a fragmented aspect of the system behavior. Every service obtains inputs from and sends outputs directly to the environment, so the specification does not define the internal data flow of a system. Usually, services describe system reactions of only a certain subset of the inputs. This partial description allows the system functionality to be distributed of over different services while leaving the reaction to certain inputs unspecified.

3.1 Syntactic Interface of Services

A service has a syntactic interface consisting of the sets of typed input and output ports, which represent the system's I/O devices (sensors and actuators) according to [6].

In this paper, the semantics of a service are described by an I/O automaton. In a timed stream $x \in (M^*)^\infty$ we express which messages are transmitted in which time slots. As we have explained, a service is a set of interaction patterns with strong causality. In this section, we show how to specify services and demonstrate them with a set of basic definitions. We start with a formal model of a service, and then present the simple operations of the service and its behavior specification.

Definition 2 *(Port Signature). Let V be a set of local variables and I, O, and H be pairwise disjoint sets of input, output, and hidden or internal ports, respectively. A port signature is a tuple (V, I, O, H).* □

Given a port signature $\Sigma = (V, I, O, H)$, we denote $C = I \cup O \cup H$ as all of the internal or/and external channels in Σ.

3.2   Table-Specified System Model

Definition 3 *(Table-Specified System Model). A table-specified system model M can be described by a tuple: $M = (\mathbb{T}, \mathbb{R}, \Sigma, \Sigma^0)$, where*

- *$\mathbb{T}$ is a finite set of I/O tables which describe the behavior of the service,*
- *$\mathbb{R}$ is a set of relations between the tables ($\mathbb{R} : \mathbb{T} \times \mathbb{T} \to Boolean$),*
- *Σ is a port signature,*
- *and Σ^0 is the initial port signature that defines the initial state of the machine, where $T \in \mathbb{T}$ mainly means I/O tables.*   □

3.3   Refinement of Behaviors

We use refinement to capture the notion of elaboration of a partial description into a more comprehensive one. Refinement can be seen as a 'more defined than' relation between two partial models. Intuitively, a table-specified model N refines M if N preserves all of the required and all of the proscribed behavior of M. Alternatively, and the table-specified model N refines M if N has the required behavior of M, and M can have the possible behavior of N.

Theorem 4 (Refinement). *Let $M_S = (\mathbb{T}_S, \mathbb{R}_S, \Sigma_S, \Sigma_S^0)$ and $M_{S'} = (\mathbb{T}_{S'}, \mathbb{R}_{S'}, \Sigma_{S'}, \Sigma_{S'}^0)$ be two table-specified system models of systems S and S'. Here, S' is a behavioral refinement of S, i.e., $M_{S'} \rightsquigarrow M_S$. Thus, the I/O tabular specification $\mathbb{T}_{S'}$ of the corresponding system models M_S' is a behavioral refinement of tabular specification $\mathbb{T}_S$ of M_S, written $\mathbb{T}_S \preccurlyeq \mathbb{T}_{S'}$.*   □

Here, if there exists a refinement relation between two tabular specification $\mathbb{T}_S$ and $\mathbb{T}_{S'}$, i.e., $\mathbb{T}_S \preccurlyeq \mathbb{T}_{S'}$, such that there must exist a parent/child relation between two signal I/O table, written $(T_S, T_{S'}) \in \preccurlyeq$.

$$\preccurlyeq \subset \mathbb{T} \times \mathbb{T} \to \exists((T_S, T_{S'}) \in \preccurlyeq) \tag{5}$$

3.4   Relations Between Tables

Definition 4 *(Relations). A set of relations between tables can be described by a tuple: $\mathbb{R} = (\preccurlyeq, \sim, =)$.*

- *$\preccurlyeq$ is a parent/child relation, which is a tree-like partial ordering.*
- *$\sim$ is a siblings relation.*
- *$=$ is an equivalence relation.*   □

The parent/child relations between tables depend on the refinement of the behavior of the service.

Here, $T_1 \preccurlyeq T_2$ meaning that T_1 is a descendant of T_2, or T_1 and T_2 are equal in an abstract sense. Tree-like means that $\preccurlyeq$ has the following property:

$$T_1 \preccurlyeq T_2 \wedge T_2 \preccurlyeq T_3 \Rightarrow T_1 \preccurlyeq T_3, \tag{6}$$
$$T_1 \preccurlyeq T_2 \wedge T_2 \preccurlyeq T_1 \Rightarrow T_1 = T_2. \tag{7}$$

If table T_1 is a descendant of T_2, i.e., $T_1 \preccurlyeq T_2$, and there is no T_3 such that $T_1 \preccurlyeq T_3 \preccurlyeq T_2$, we say that the table T_1 is a *subtable* of T_2, i.e., T_1 *subtable* T_2.

Furthermore, we define $\sigma(T_{parent})$ as the set of all children of the table T_{parent}, that is

$$\sigma(T_{parent}) = \{T \mid T, T_{parent} \in \mathbb{T} \wedge T \text{ subtable } T_{parent}\} \tag{8}$$

Here, $\sim$ is a siblings relation to the tables in $\mathbb{T}$. And the following equation holds

$$T_1 \sim T_2 \Rightarrow \exists T \in \mathbb{T} : T_1, T_2 \in \sigma(T) \tag{9}$$

The equivalence relation $\sim$ is used to partition the children of a table into disjoint sets.

3.5 Projection of Behaviors

By the sub-type relation between sets of channels we define the concept of projection of behaviors and projection operation on tables. It is the basis for specifying the sub-service relation.

Definition 5 *(History Projection). Let C and G be two sets of typed channels with Csubtype$G$. We define for history $x \in \vec{G}$ its projection $x \mid_C \in \vec{C}$ to the channels in the set C and to the messages of their types. For channel $c \in C$ with type T specify the projection by the equation:*

$$(x \mid_C)(c) = T \textcircled{c} x(c) \tag{10}$$

where for a stream s and a set M we denote by $M \textcircled{c} s$ the stream derived from s by deleting all messages in the s that are not in set M. $x \mid_C$ is called projection of history x to channel set C. □

To obtain the sub-history of $x \mid_C$ of x by projection, we keep only those channels and types of messages in the history x that belong to the channels and their types in C.

Definition 6 *(Projection of Behaviors). Given syntactic interfaces $(I \blacktriangleright O)$ and $(I' \blacktriangleright O')$ where $(I' \blacktriangleright O')$ **subtype** $(I \blacktriangleright O)$ holds, we define for a behavior function $F \in \mathbb{F}[I \blacktriangleright O]$ its projection $F\dagger(I' \blacktriangleright O') \in \mathbb{F}[I' \blacktriangleright O']$ to the syntactic interface $(I' \blacktriangleright O')$ by the following equation (for all input histories $x' \in \vec{I'}$):*

$$F\dagger(I' \blacktriangleright O')(x) = \{y \mid O' : \exists x \in \vec{I} : x' = x \mid_{I'} \wedge y \in F(x)\}. \tag{11}$$

□

In a projection, we concentrate on the subset of the input and output messages of a system in its syntactic sub-interface $(I' \blacktriangleright O')$. In the projection operation on tables, we delete all input and output columns (channels) that are not part of the syntactic interface $(I' \blacktriangleright O')$ to derive less complex sub-behaviors that allow us to include the properties of the original system.

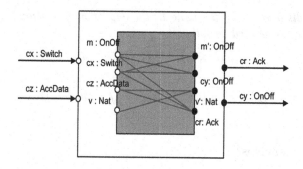

Fig. 1. Dependency graph of system SwStore

4   Service Granularity Refinement

This section clarifies the structural modeling of the functional requirements of embedded systems by introducing a visual and mathematical method based on following steps: *decomposition* disassembles an existing tabular behavior specification into individual or atomic services that can be further recomposed together; *composition* assembles individual and composite elements to form a new service that has the same input channels and is inactively independent; *refinement* assembles individual and composite elements to form a new service that has no dependence relationship or explicit dependence relationship.

4.1   Dependency Graphs

Definition of structured relations between services, refinement of services, refinement multiplexing of services and the structure of related families of services are the main questions which have to be solved. But there are three different dependency relationships concepts which have to be explained at first.

- If a service s_1 outputs a data item with a certain type and service s_2 takes this output as an input, then s_2 depends on s_1.
- If two services s_1 and s_2 both take a typed channel c as an input, then there is a dependency relation between s_1 and s_2.
- Given a service s_1 has output channel o and input channel i, and a service s_2 is a new service generated from service s_1 by deleting input i. If service s_2 is non-deterministic, then there is a dependency relationship between the output channel o and the input channel i, or we can say that output channel o depends on input channel i.

Besides the dependencies between a set of services, here we also consider the dependency graphs to be a description of the dependencies between input/output channels based on the behavior of each service. We capture dependencies between input/output channels of System SwStore in Fig. 1.

Definition 7 (*Dependency Relation between Outputs and Inputs*). *Given table T be a behavior specification of service s with syntactic interfaces ($I \blacktriangleright O$), let*

$P_D(T)$ be the disjointness of the table T, the dependency relation between output o_m and input i_n is defined as follows:

$$\rightarrow_{Dep} (o_m, i_n) = \neg(P_D(T \mid_{C/(o_n \cup i_n)})) \tag{12}$$

where

$$P_D(T) = \neg(\exists x_1, \ldots, x_m. \bigvee_{1 \leq i < j \leq n} (p_i \wedge p_j)). \tag{13}$$

□

4.2   Atomic Services

In this section, (de)composition operations are defined based on the concepts of dependency relationship. For each output channel, we choose the whole set of input channels that have a dependency relationship with this output. These services are called atomic services which can be generated by the projection operation on tables.

Theorem 5 (Projection Operation on Tables). *Projection of behavior* $T = (I, O, H, V)$ *is*

$$T \mid_C = (I \mid_C, O \mid_C, H \mid_C, V \mid_C) \tag{14}$$

where

$$F(T) = \bigvee_{i=1}^{m} (F(T \mid_{o_i})) \tag{15}$$

holds.   □

The following definition characterizes projections that do not introduce additional nondeterminism, since the input deleted by the projection does not influence the output. Let SwStore be the system behavior described above by $T_{SwStore}$. We get the following atomic services a, b, c, d by the faithful projection on $T_{SwStore}$. Since some of the output channels are without influence on the input channels, those columns can be deleted. In so doing, we can get four atomic services a, b, c, d; specified by I/O table T_a, T_b, T_c, T_d, the following holds true:

$$T_{SwStore} = T_a \parallel T_b \parallel T_c \parallel T_d \tag{16}$$

where

$$T_a = T_{SwStore} \mid_{m \cup cx \cup m'}$$
$$T_b = T_{SwStore} \mid_{v \cup cz \cup v'}$$
$$T_c = T_{SwStore} \mid_{cy \cup m \cup cx} \tag{17}$$
$$T_d = T_{SwStore} \mid_{cr \cup m \cup cx \cup cz}$$

We consider the following syntactic interfaces for the four atomic services:

$$IF[\{m : OnOff, cx : Switch\} \blacktriangleright \{m' : OnOff\}]$$
$$IF[\{cz : AccData; v : \mathbb{N}\} \blacktriangleright \{v' : \mathbb{N}\}]$$
$$IF[\{m : OnOff, cx : Switch\} \blacktriangleright \{cy : OnOff\}] \tag{18}$$
$$IF[\{m : OnOff, cx : Switch; cz : AccData\} \blacktriangleright \{cr : Ack\}]$$

Table 3. The tabular specification of service *Access'* and service *Switch'*

(a) I/O Table T_{Switch}

tiTable $Service_{Switch}$:$\forall\, t \in \mathbb{N}$

m	cx	m'	cy
off	-	off	-
off	switch	on	on
on	switch	off	off
on	-	on	-

(b) I/O Table T_{Access}

tiTable $Service_{Access}$:$\forall\, t \in \mathbb{N}$

m	v	cx	cz	v'	cr
off	j	-	?	j	-
off	j	switch	-	j	-
off	j	switch	read	j	j
off	j	switch	set(n)	n	done
on	j	-	read	j	j
on	j	-	set(n)	n	done
on	j	switch	?	j	-
on	j	-	-	j	-

4.3 Composition

In the architectural view, a system is usually described by a network of communicating components. The service composition is similar to those introduced in [17–19]. The internal component communication is not supported by the combination operators. Consequently, we defined the composition operator by services and integrated the architectural view for our framework. The composition permits two services to communicate directly via homonymous input/output port pairs.

Composition is a partial function of the set of all system behaviors and the set of all services. It is defined only if the syntactic interfaces match, which means there are no contradictions or conflicts in their channel types. In our running example, according to atomic services, we consider two sub-interfaces for the system *SwStore*: interface ($\{cx : Switch\}$ ▶ $\{cy : OnOff\}$) for service *Switch* and interface ($\{cz : AccData\}$ ▶ $\{cr : Ack\}$) for service *Access*.

Furthermore, let $\|$, $\otimes$, and ; denote three composition operators for the parallel, alternative, and sequential composition of services.

Fig. 2. $M_{Switch} = M_a \parallel M_c$ **Fig. 3.** $M_{Access} = M_b \parallel M_d$

By parallel composition operation on the atomic services a, b, c, d, we can build service *Switch* and service *Access*, as shown in Figs. 2 and 3.

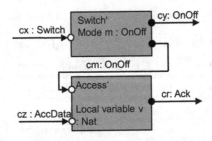

Fig. 4. Alternative composition of services $M_{SwStore} = M'_{Switch} \otimes M'_{Access}$

I/O Table T_{Switch} is the tabular specification of a parallel composition of atomic services a and c, which is presented in Table 3(a). Here, $T_{Switch} = T_{SwStore} \mid_{cx \cup cy \cup m \cup m'}$, $T_a \preccurlyeq T_{Switch}$ and $T_c \preccurlyeq T_{Switch}$ holds.

Similarly, I/O Table T_{Access} is parallel composition of atomic services b and d, which is specified in Table 3(b). Here, $T_{Access} = T_{SwStore} \mid_{cx \cup cz \cup v \cup v' \cup m \cup cr}$, $T_b \preccurlyeq T_{Switch}$ and $T_d \preccurlyeq T_{Switch}$ holds.

4.4   Service Granularity Refinement

The service granularity refinement allows replacing channels by several channels and messages by several messages and vice versa. The main advantage of service granularity refinement arises when we can explicit the relation between the service by composition the atomic services or decomposition into the atomic services.

To describe services of a system in a modular way and to delete the dependency relations between services, we need to capture the dependencies between the inputs that influence the behavior of services. By using *mode channel cm* to transmit message *mode*, we get service *Access'* and service *Switch'* (see Fig. 4).

Modes are a generally useful way to structure service behavior and specify dependencies between services. Modes are used to discriminate different forms of operations for a service. A mode type can be used for attributes of the state space as well as for input or output channels.

As shown in Table 4(a), I/O Table $T_{Access'}$ is the tabular specification of service *Access'*, which is a refinement of service *Access*. Meanwhile, I/O Table $T_{Switch'}$ (see Table 4(b)) is the tabular specification of service *Switch'*, which is a refinement of service *Switch*. Here,

$$M_{SwStore} = M'_{Switch} \otimes M'_{Access} = M_{Switch} \parallel M_{Access} \qquad (19)$$

holds.

In Fig. 5, red dotted line denote the dependence relationship between the services, i.e. they have the same input channel. As shown in Fig. 5, this type of dependency relationship has a transitivity character by the composition operation of the services. For example the dependence between service *Switch* and service *Access*. Service *Switch* is parallel composition of atomic services a and

Table 4. The tabular specification of service *Access'* and service *Switch'*

(a) I/O Table $T_{Access'}$

ti Table $Service_{Access'}$: $\forall t \in \mathbb{N}$

v	cm	cz	v'	cr
j	off	?	j	-
j	on	-	j	-
j	on	read	j	j
j	on	set(n)	n	done

(b) I/O Table $T_{Switch'}$

ti Table $Service_{Switch'}$: $\forall t \in \mathbb{N}$

m	cx	m'	cm	cy
off	-	off	off	-
off	switch	on	on	on
on	switch	off	off	off
on	-	on	on	-

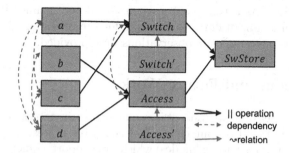

Fig. 5. Dependency relationships between services (Color figure online)

c and service *Access* is parallel composition of atomic services *b* and *d*. By composing the sub-services, the dependence relationships between the sub-services are transitived to the parent-service after composition.

5   Related Work

The work presented in this paper is the extension of the Mode-annotated Service Hierarchy $H = (((K, V), \varphi, D), \psi)$ that was presented in [19]. Prior work to specify a system of textural requirements to formal specification using tabular notation exists in software engineering, but the application of semantic technologies to pragmatically visualize the specification process and combining tabular methodology with diagrams is unique.

Soares and Vrancken propose a model-driven approach to requirements engineering based on SysML requirements and Use Case Diagrams [13]. The main advantages are that user requirements are graphically modeled, and requirements traceability is enhanced using the SysML requirements tables.

As stated in [14], the tabular expression and total function programming approach is able to specify the real-time behavior, which has been successfully implemented in industrial projects although not very often. In contrast to our work, this approach can offer a method to specify single requirements modularly, but neither to refine, nor compose or decompose them, and therefore the method is not able to support the scalability necessary for systems architecture.

The SCR method and tool set [15] can be seen as a variant of the 4-variable model. It proposes to model the system specification as an automaton which reads and writes variables of the four types identified in [6]. The deficits of SCR are its priori discretization and a rather coarse-grained modularity concept: every subsystem has to be completely described by three tables: condition table, event table, and mode transition table. It addresses the time requirements as annotations or as a temporal logic formula, operating in terms of logical system step. A-priori discretization cannot be justified offhand in the early requirements engineering phases. In [16], SCR was extended by the notion of real-time. The system is described as a timed automat in an ad-hoc manner by associating every event with a time stamp. No concepts for the reasoning about durations or non-instantaneous composite observations were provided.

6   Conclusions and Future Work

This method can easily integrate states and modes in tables by taking them as additional input and output channels. Each table represents a finite set of relations between terms (states/modes) which can support a quick understanding of large specifications.

The proposed tabular specification method supports a piece-wise formalization. This can help handle potentially inconsistent requirements. Analyzing and checking the system properties can be obtained by checking the properties of the tables. The relationship between families of the services defined above can help structure the system not only from a theoretical point of view but also from a very practical point of view, for instance the equivalence of services. When comparing multi-functional systems it is a practical question, whether or not two systems offer the same services.

The present work is still in progress. Additional tabular specification patterns as well as the improvement of the existing ones are the next goals for future work. The mathematical and logical style of the syntax of Focus is not always very well-suited for the practical user, however, a CASE tool AutoFOCUS [20], which is a tool based on Focus framework for the model-based development of embedded systems, is provided.

More experienced users may develop their own model patterns using constraints tables. This requires some basic understanding of the data types of the channels and properties of the used services, but no detailed knowledge of the implementation of the involved services. Patterns can be extracted out of existing service compositions or built from scratch by linking together services.

References

1. Broy, M.: Pragmatic and formal specification of system properties by tables. TUM-I9802 (1998)
2. Lawford, M., Froebel, P., Moum, G.: Application of tabular methods to the specification and verification of a nuclear reactor shutdown system. Formal Methods Syst. Des.
3. Bourguiba, I., Janicki, R.: Table-based specification techniques. ICCIE 2009, pp. 1520–1525 (2009)
4. Heitmeyer, C., Bharadwaj, R.: Applying the SCR requirements method to the light control case study. J. Univers. Comput. Sci. **6**, 650–678 (2000)
5. Heimdahl, M.P.E., Leveson, N.G., Reese, J.D.: Experiences from specifying the TCAS II requirements using RSML. 17th Digital Avionics Systems Conference, Nov 1998
6. Parnas, D.L., Madey, J.: Functional documents for computer systems. Sci. Comput. Program. **25**, 41–61 (1995). ISSN: 0167-6423
7. Janicki, R.: On a formal semantics of tabular expressions. Sci. Comput. Program. (1997)
8. Hummel, B., Thyssen, J.: Behavioral specification of reactive systems using stream-based I/O tables. In: Proceedings of the 2009 Seventh IEEE International Conference on Software Engineering and Formal Methods. SEFM '09, pp. 137–146 (2009)
9. Janicki, R., Wassyng, A.: Tabular expressions and their relational semantics. Fundam. Inf. **67**(4), 343–370 (2005)
10. Broy, M., Stølen, K.: Specification and Development of Interactive Systems: Focus on Streams, Interfaces, and Refinement. Springer, New York (2001)
11. Home Page of Focus framework: http://focus.in.tum.de
12. Broy, M., Dederich, F., Dendorfer, C., Fuchs, M., Gritzner, T., Weber, R.: The design of distributed systems - an introduction to FOCUS. TUM-I9202 (1992)
13. dos Santos Soares, M., Vrancken, J.: Model-driven user requirements specification using SysML. J. Softw. **3**, 57–68 (2008). ISSN: 1796-217X
14. Wassyng, A., Lawford, M.: Lessons learned from a successful implementation of formal methods in an industrial project. In: Araki, K., Gnesi, S., Mandrioli, D. (eds.) FME 2003. LNCS, vol. 2805, pp. 133–153. Springer, Heidelberg (2003)
15. Heitmeyer, C., Kirby, J., Labaw, B., Bharadwaj, R.: SCR*: a toolset for specifying and analyzing software requirements. In: Hu, A.J., Vardi, M.Y. (eds.) CAV 1998. LNCS, vol. 1427, pp. 526–531. Springer, Heidelberg (1998)
16. Heitmeyer, C.: Requirements specifications for hybrid systems. Hybrid Systems III, pp. 304–314 (1996)
17. de Alfaro, L., Henzinger, T.A.: Interface automata. ACM SIGSOFT Softw. Eng. Notes **26**, 109–120 (2001)
18. Botaschanjan, J., Harhurin, A.: Integrating functional and architectural views of reactive systems. In: Lewis, G.A., Poernomo, I., Hofmeister, C. (eds.) CBSE 2009. LNCS, vol. 5582, pp. 156–172. Springer, Heidelberg (2009)
19. Broy, M.: Multifunctional software systems: structured modeling and specification of functional requirements. Sci. Comput. Program. **75**, 1193–1214 (2010)
20. Home Page of AUTOFOCUS: http://af3.fortiss.org

Author Index

Printed in the United States
By Bookmasters